# Microsoft® Outlook 2007 Programming
## Jumpstart for Power Users and Administrators

# Microsoft® Outlook 2007 Programming

## Jumpstart for Power Users and Administrators

**Sue Mosher**

ELSEVIER

Amsterdam • Boston • Heidelberg • London • New York • Oxford
Paris • San Diego • San Francisco • Singapore • Sydney • Tokyo
Digital Press is an imprint of Elsevier

Digital
Press

Digital Press is an imprint of Elsevier
30 Corporate Drive, Suite 400, Burlington, MA 01803, USA
Linacre House, Jordan Hill, Oxford OX2 8DP, UK

 Recognizing the importance of preserving what has been written, Elsevier prints its books on acid-free paper whenever possible.

**Library of Congress Cataloging-in-Publication Data**
Application submitted

**British Library Cataloguing-in-Publication Data**
A catalogue record for this book is available from the British Library.

ISBN: 978-1-55558-346-0

For information on all Digital Press publications
visit our Web site at www.books.elsevier.com

Printed in the United States of America

07  08  09  10    10 9 8 7 6 5 4 3 2 1

# *Contents*

# *Introduction*

Microsoft Office Outlook 2007, the sixth version of Microsoft's premier email and collaboration application, has arrived at a fork in the road. On one side are the professional developers who use Visual Studio .NET to produce add-ins that integrate tightly with Outlook. On the other side are the smart end-users and rushed administrators who want to bend Outlook to their will and work (or play) more productively. As the Office 2007 beta was getting under way, K. D. Hallman, Microsoft's General Manager for Visual Studio Tools for Office, estimated that there were 3–4 million professional Office developers and 16 million non-professional Office developers.

I wrote this book for the latter group—mainly for people who don't program Outlook as a full-time job. You are the people who confess in the newsgroups that you've done little programming, but you're willing to try. You are the people who make me smile when you come back a week later and proclaim, "I did it! Hooray!" You will find here all the information you need to get started programming with Outlook VBA and custom forms, or to build upon the skills you already have so that you can take advantage of the many new programming features in Outlook 2007.

Yet, I didn't forget the professional developers. Pro-level books on Outlook development need to explain add-in architectural issues and highlight the essential new programming features in Outlook 2007, such as form regions and the `PropertyAccessor` object. Amid all of this great material, there probably won't be room to review basics such as how to return a particular item or folder, or how to use the `WordEditor` object to manipulate the text and formatting in the body of an Outlook item. Those essential building blocks of Outlook programming form the core of this book, and I invite pro-developers to skip the VBA basics chapters (be kind to the newbies!) and jump straight into Part IV, "Fundamental Outlook Coding Techniques." You will also find in this book the essentials of creating and managing legacy custom Outlook forms if your organization isn't yet ready to migrate its forms applications to form regions.

I have learned a lot from my readers in the four years since *Microsoft Outlook Programming: Jumpstart for Administrators, Power Users, and Developers* was published, and I am very grateful for your input. You've told me what code worked and what you wanted to know more about. You've suggested ways to organize the book better. I hope that I've listened well and that you'll find this update useful. (If you are still using Outlook 2003, the earlier book will be more relevant to you than this book, in which much of the content applies only to Outlook 2007.)

I think it's important to say what this book is not: It is not a complete reference to the Outlook object model, nor is it a guide to building add-ins for installation in the enterprise or for distribution to commercial customers. (Excellent resources area available on both those topics; check my web site at http://www.outlookcode.com for links and downloads of all the code samples in this book.) This book is also not a guide to writing .NET code. All the samples are in VBA or VBScript, which are the languages used by power-users and administrators. Since many professional Outlook developers use VBA for light prototyping, I think that's still the right language for showing Outlook basics to the maximum number of people.

## Conventions used in this book

This book uses different typefaces to differentiate between code and regular text and to help you identify important concepts:

Code statements and the names of programming elements appear in monospace font:

```
Item.BodyFormat = olFormatRichText
```

Placeholders for various expressions appear in *monospace italic* font. You should replace the placeholder with the specific value that your specific application of the code requires.

Text that you type is presented within quotation marks. New terms appear in *italics*.

The Notes, Tips, and Cautions scattered throughout the book try to call attention to information that will help you become a better Outlook programmer. A Note presents interesting information related to the surrounding discussion. A Tip offers advice or teaches an easier way to do something. A Caution advises you of potential problems and helps you to steer clear of disaster.

# *Acknowledgments*

I've already thanked the readers of my previous books for their input. Also crucial to the shaping of this book were the questions and comments from the thousands of other people with whom I've exchanged code ideas in the discussion forums at http://www.outlookcode.com and in Microsoft's newsgroups.

I owe a special debt to all the Outlook MVPs ("Most Valuable Professionals" recognized by Microsoft for great practical knowledge and grace under fire when helping other users). Eric Legault played a pivotal role as tech editor and contributor of code sample and illustration ideas (but if you find any code that won't run, it's my fault). I also need to single out Ken Slovak, Dmitry Streblechenko (developer of Outlook Spy and Redemption), and Michael Bauer. Word MVP Cindy Meister ably updated an earlier Word printing sample to use the new content controls in Word 2007.

At Microsoft, I can't thank Outlook extensibility program manager (and former MVP) Randy Byrne enough for the many questions he fielded and details he provided about Outlook 2007's new capabilities. Randy and his colleagues Peter Allenspach and Ryan Gregg, who taught me all I know about form regions, are largely responsible for making Outlook 2007 the most programmable version ever. I'm also grateful for input from Bill Jacob and especially Angela Wong for the effort she put into Outlook's developer documentation. Among people at other organizations who inspired and instructed were Simon Breeze and Helmut Obertanner.

I must thank Theron Shreve for letting me take my Outlook book ideas and run with them. All the gang at Digital Press contributed their fast-track expertise so that this book could include late-breaking material that didn't come to light until after the official launch of Office 2007. Final production was again in the capable hands of Alan Rose and Lauralee Reinke.

As always, I couldn't have finished this book without the encouragement of my family, Robert and Annie, who endured my frustrations at running beta software and smiled at my little coding triumphs. Annie helped get much of the material from my previous Outlook programming book ready for revision, making it possible to finish this book just a couple of months after Outlook 2007 was released. She also gets an extra nod for the proof-reading and formatting assistance that she provided for my earlier Outlook 2003 book for Digital Press.

Finally, I thank God for the opportunity to share this knowledge and help people connect with each other.

# *What You Can Do with Outlook 2007*

Whether you've been using Microsoft Outlook for just a few days or for several years, you've certainly figured out that it does more than email—much, much more. It's not unusual to find people who have organized their entire lives with Outlook. Companies that develop add-ins for Outlook view the application as a great platform because so many people "live in Outlook."

But if you asked each Outlook user how he or she puts the program to work, you would receive a different answer every time, because people have their own ideas on how to organize the critical information in their lives. Wouldn't it be great if Microsoft could make Outlook so customizable that everyone could use it in his or her own way? It might not be 100 percent possible, but the programming environment included with Outlook 2007 is rich enough to let you make great strides toward bending Outlook to your will, or that of the organization you work for.

This book shows you how to use the programming tools that come with the Outlook application to make it your own. It's OK if you have never programmed before. This book shows you the basics! Progamming Outlook is much easier than you think. For experienced programmers, we cover how to work with Outlook data, how to put its special features to work, and how to work around some of its quirks. Even professional developers can find useful information here on the basic building blocks of Outlook programming. Our focus in this book, though, is on what you can build "out of the box" without Visual Studio or any additional programming tools.

The highlights of this chapter include discussions of the following:

- What kinds of programming projects are possible in Outlook 2007
- What tools you will use
- How to decide which tool to use for a particular project
- How to make an initial sketch of your plans for Outlook programming projects

# 1.1   Why program with Outlook?

Maybe you're an information technology professional managing a network of users and need a way to report on the data visible in Outlook. Or perhaps you're one of those network users and can imagine ways to make your work more productive if only Outlook would do _____ (you fill in the blank). Maybe you even use Outlook at home, as well as at the office, and wish you knew how to extend its capabilities as a personal information manager to organize more of your activities. The good news in this book is that Outlook 2007 makes it easier than ever to customize the application to streamline repetitive tasks, add new capabilities, and integrate with other Office applications.

To help you get excited about the chapters ahead, take a look at this list of things you can do when you learn how to program with Outlook:

- Create your own custom rules to handle incoming messages
- Search and replace data, such as telephone area codes
- Create custom reports by integrating Outlook data into HTML-format messages, Word documents, and Excel worksheets
- Schedule a follow-up call for a meeting
- Create Outlook forms that duplicate the paper phone message, vacation request, and other business forms that you use

# 1.2   Outlook programming tools

Let's start by previewing the primary tools that you will be using:

- Visual Basic for Applications (VBA)
- Outlook forms
- Visual Basic Scripting Edition (VBScript)
- Programming models for other Office applications

## 1.2.1   Visual Basic for Applications

Outlook includes a rich development environment for creating macros, event handlers, and other procedures—Visual Basic for Applications, or VBA for short. Other Office programs also have VBA, but so do AutoCAD and other applications that have licensed VBA as their programming environment.

**Note:** Microsoft has a new application-centric development environment called Visual Studio Tools for Applications (VSTA), built on the .NET Framework, but in Office 2007, only InfoPath supports VSTA. Other Office 2007 applications, including Outlook, still use VBA as their integrated programming environment.

Figure 1.1 shows the VBA programming environment. (Most of the screen shots in this book were taken using Windows Vista. If you use Windows XP or Windows 2003, your screen will look slightly different, but Outlook code should function the same regardless of the operating system version.) The VBA programming environment includes many tools to help you learn how to write VBA code:

- Visual forms designer (to create Windows dialogs in VBA, not custom Outlook forms)

- Intelligent editor with color coding and dropdown lists to avoid code errors

- Detailed index to Outlook programming techniques

- Properties windows and other tools

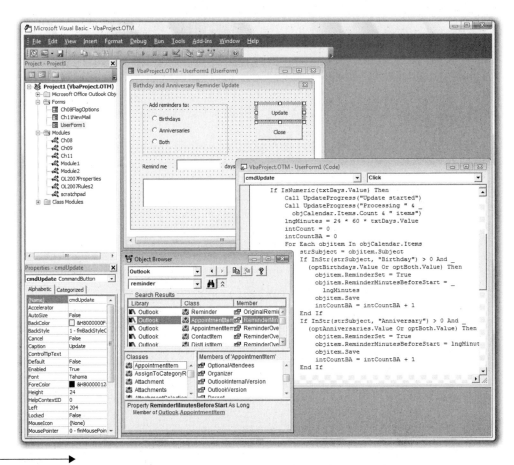

**Figure 1.1**    *VBA includes a rich form and code environment (compare with Figure 1.4).*

VBA code can enhance many of the operations that take place when you work with your Outlook information, such as creating new items or switching from one folder to another. As you'll see, most of those operations have corresponding events in the Outlook programming library that let you respond to such operations automatically.

VBA also gives you the ability to design pop-up dialog boxes to get information from and windows that stay on the screen to provide information to the user. For example, you might build a VBA form to display how many vacation days you have used so far this year or the time that you last received messages in your Inbox.

Furthermore, you can use VBA to create macros that you can add to the Outlook toolbar to launch a telephone message form, search for and replace text, run rules on demand, and expand Outlook's capabilities in many other ways. You can even create VBA procedures that the Outlook Rules Wizard can execute as "run a script" rule actions.

You might have created macros in Word or Excel by turning on a macro recorder that watches your actions and then builds the appropriate code. Outlook does not include a comparable macro recorder, but the examples in this book should give you all the basic building blocks you will need to construct truly useful Outlook macros.

Note that the VBA techniques discussed in this book also apply if you want to move up from Outlook's integrated development environment to building more sophisticated Outlook tools with Microsoft's Visual Studio or other development tools. They also apply to VBA code written in Word, Excel, Access, or other Office applications that need to automate Outlook.

## 1.2.2   Custom Outlook forms

The second stop on the road to Outlook programming proficiency is learning how to customize the basic Outlook forms.

Every item that you open in Outlook—whether it's an email message, a contact, or an appointment—uses a particular form to display its data. (If you have programmed in Microsoft Access, you may already be familiar with using forms as templates to display different data records.) You can customize these forms to show or hide fields or whole pages, respond to user input and actions, and launch other Outlook operations. If you work within an organization that uses Microsoft Exchange as its mail server, you may be able to collaborate with other people by using custom Outlook forms. With a little more effort, it is also possible (although much less common) to use custom forms for collaboration with other Outlook users across the Internet.

In many programming environments, you must start from scratch every time you want to create a new window for the user to interact with. Out-

**Figure 1.2**
*This Contact form
has not been
customized.*

look is different in that it presents you with a group of built-in forms. To build a custom form, you start with one of the built-in forms and then add your own special touches.

For example, people often ask how to show a contact's age, not just record the birthday. Figure 1.2 shows the default Contact form as it normally looks. The Birthday field is on the Details page, and so is not visible. In Figure 1.3, you see the same form, only this time it has been customized with a *form region* to provide a control for entering the birthday from the main page and a box to calculate the age. Form regions are a new feature in Outlook 2007 that allows you add to or replace pages on custom Outlook forms. We'll learn more about them in Chapter 5, "Introducing Form Regions."

**Figure 1.3**
*This Contact form
has been
customized with a
form region to show
the birthday and
age of the contact.*

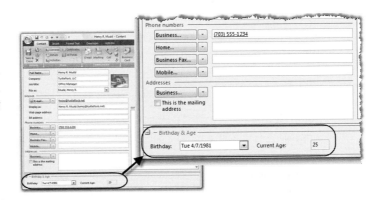

Was any programming code required to do this? Not really. All it took was a formula, not that different from those formulas you might have written for Microsoft Excel worksheets.

Custom form regions are just the newest way to customize Outlook forms. You can also create custom forms by adding controls and custom fields to five or six pages on any of the basic six standard forms that come with Outlook.

Given that no code is required just to add controls and fields, is this truly Outlook programming? Sure it is! Many of the changes you want to make to Outlook might involve nothing more than adding new fields and pages to existing forms to hold that extra data. Without writing any code at all, you can perform simple validation to make sure that the data meets your criteria for correctness and develop formulas such as the one for calculating a person's age.

### 1.2.3   Visual Basic Scripting Edition

A time will come, however, when you want your custom Outlook forms to do more. Maybe you will want to generate a task for a follow-up telephone call from an appointment and have Outlook automatically fill in the contact name for you. Perhaps you want to be able to enter the birth date for a contact's spouse or partner and have Outlook automatically create a new recurring event in your Calendar folder. When you are ready to go beyond entering data and manipulating it in simple ways, you can move up to *VBScript*, the shorthand name for Visual Basic Scripting Edition, the programming language behind Outlook forms.

**Figure 1.4**
*The Outlook form script editor is just a text editor (compare with Figure 1.1).*

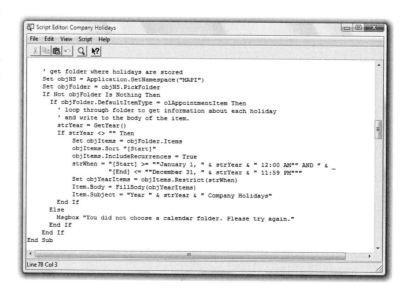

You might have heard of VBScript in the context of Web pages. VBScript is one of several languages that can control what you see when you interact with a Web page. It also works with the Windows Script Host (WSH) scripting environment that Microsoft has included with Windows since Windows 98. With WSH, you can write routines that are stored as simple text files and can be run at a command line.

Scripts don't run as fast as other kinds of programs, but they enjoy the advantage of small size and portability. Having a script associated with an Outlook form hardly increases the size of the form at all.

VBScript is a little scary, though. It's like walking a tightrope without a net, because the built-in editor for building VBScript programs is, well, a text editor. Figure 1.4 shows a sample script for a form to distribute a list of company holidays within an organization. The form script editor has none of the color-coding or automatic syntax checking that you get with VBA.

One sneaky technique that you will learn in this book is to write and test your Outlook form code in the superior VBA code environment, make a few minor adjustments to adapt it to VBScript, and then copy and paste it into the script window of an Outlook form. This method cuts down on programming time immensely.

## 1.2.4  Folder home pages

When you start Outlook for the first time, you see Outlook Today, a summary of your Inbox, Calendar, and Tasks folders. Outlook Today is actually a Web page included with Outlook, a specific example of a *folder home page*. Every folder in Outlook can be set up on its Properties dialog to display a Web page instead of the contents of the folder. The Web page can even include the list of items in the folder, through a special ActiveX control called the Outlook View Control, but it can also show something unrelated to Outlook, such as a SharePoint site or an Intranet help desk page. Folder home pages can also help document for users what kinds of activities they can perform in an Exchange public folder.

Two things make folder home pages interesting to network administrators who want to explore Outlook's configuration scripting support:

- With Group Policy Objects or the Office Customization Tool, you can control which default folders in Outlook show home pages and what pages they show.
- Folder home pages can run VBScript code to access Outlook automation objects and configure such things as rules.

Figure 1.5 shows an example of a folder home page used to deploy Outlook settings. We'll explore such techniques in Chapter 22, "Rules, Views, and Administrator Scripting Tasks."

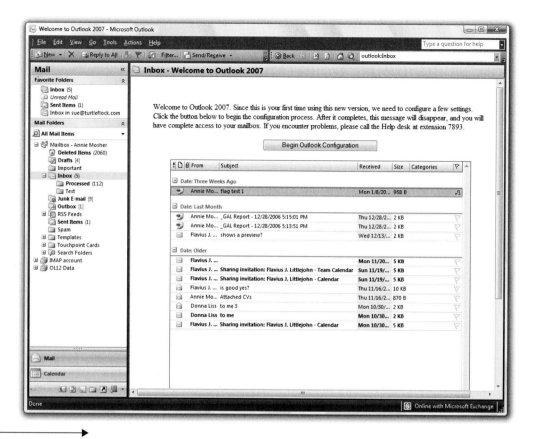

**Figure 1.5**    *Folder home pages can display data from any Outlook folder and run script code like
any other Web page.*

### What happened to CDO?

Previous versions of Outlook relied on a programming interface called
Collaboration Data Objects (CDO) for many programming tasks that
were not possible through the Outlook object model, such as displaying the Address Book dialog or getting the mobile phone number from
a user in the Exchange Global Address List. Outlook 2007's object
model has approximately doubled compared with Outlook 2003, and
it can now handle virtually all the programming tasks that once
required CDO—and do it without triggering security prompts. Therefore, Microsoft is no longer shipping CDO 1.21 with Outlook 2007. It
is, however, available as a Web download for use with legacy applications that require it. This book does not cover programming with
CDO 1.21.

### 1.2.5   Office integration and other object models

Outlook can create Word or Excel documents, and Microsoft Office programs such as Excel and Word can create messages, appointments, and other Outlook items. This integration is possible thanks to something called the *Outlook object model*, a programming library that opens Outlook to automation not just through Outlook VBA but from other applications' code environments as well. Furthermore, all the Office programs and many other Windows components also have object models that reveal what those programs can do, the types of items (or objects) they can work with, and the characteristics of those items. Word objects, for example, are crucial to creating Outlook messages with complex formatting.

## 1.3   How to start

At this point, you might feel that the hardest task in Outlook programming is knowing where to start. Do you use VBScript or VBA? Do you work with a form first and then write the programming code or vice versa?

I would recommend that you start by choosing one or more compelling projects—ideas that will save you time in the long run, make repetitive tasks less burdensome, or perhaps just display information that is hard to extract from the standard Outlook interface. Try to be as specific as possible. Don't decide to build a project to make Outlook work just like GoldMine (a popular sales contact management program). Instead, pick a particular GoldMine feature that you want Outlook to duplicate.

When you choose a project, don't start writing code or moving fields around on a form right away! Instead, take some time to outline what you want the project to accomplish, using what programmers call *pseudo code*.

But wait! You say you don't know how to writing programming code. ("That's why I bought this book!," you protest.) No, I'm not asking you to write a program (not yet), only to lay the groundwork. When you write pseudo code, you're walking through the logic of what you want to happen, without worrying about the exact language required to make it work.

For example, let's say that you want to enhance Outlook's appointment form with a button that would create a new task for a follow-up telephone call to the person you met with. The pseudo code might look something like this:

```
User clicks button
    Show task form
    Copy details of meeting to task body
    Copy contact from meeting to task
    Set task due date for one week from the meeting date
    If task due date falls on a weekend or holiday
        Then adjust the due date to the next business day
    Save the task
```

Nothing in this list looks like programming, but it describes in detail what you want Outlook to do when the user clicks the follow-up call button that you'll add to the form. It won't take much to move from this pseudo code to the programming code that implements those steps.

Once you decide what project to tackle and have an idea of what the finished project should do, how do you decide which tool is appropriate? Table 1.1 provides some recommendations for tools appropriate to particular situations. Don't take these recommendations as hard and fast rules. In many cases, you can approach a project in several ways. As you work through the examples in the chapters that follow, you will develop a better feel for which Outlook tool works best and which approach you feel more comfortable implementing.

Note that Table 1.1 does not include such approaches as add-ins, task panes, custom toolbars, and smart tags. While professional developers include such elements in their Outlook-integrated applications, creating

**Table 1.1**  *Choosing Outlook Tools*

| If you want to . . . | Try this approach . . . |
| --- | --- |
| Show additional information in an individual item window | Modify an Outlook form or design a custom form region |
| Show additional information about an item in the reading pane | Design a custom form region |
| Take some action in response to something that the user does with an Outlook item | Modify an Outlook form with VBScript code |
| Click a button on the Outlook toolbar to make something happen to the current item or items | Write a macro in VBA |
| Make something happen when the user starts Outlook, switches to a different folder, or performs other actions that don't involve a particular Outlook item | Write an event handler in VBA |
| Process an incoming message or meeting request | Write a procedure in VBA that can be invoked from an Outlook rule using a "run a script" action or write a VBA event handler |
| Display status information as the user performs various Outlook tasks | Create a user form in VBA with a routine that keeps the status information up-to-date |
| Show data from multiple Outlook folders in a single view | Use a folder home page with multiple instances of the Outlook View Control |

**Table 1.2** *Key Outlook Development Components*

| Component | Features |
|---|---|
| Microsoft Outlook | .NET Programmability Support |
| | Visual Basic Scripting Support |
| Office Shared Features | Digital Signature for VBA Projects |
| | Visual Basic for Applications |
| Office Tools | Microsoft Forms 2.0 .NET Programmability Support |
| | Microsoft Script Editor (HTML Source Editing)/Web Scripting/Web Debugging (supported on Windows Vista only with Visual Studio 2005) |
| | Smart Tag .NET Programmability Support |

them requires additional development tools such as Microsoft Visual Studio. In this book, we're going to stick to the programming you can do just with Outlook and the other Office programs.

## 1.4 Key Outlook programming components

If you use the default settings to install Office or Outlook, you should have almost all the built-in development tools you need. Table 1.2 lists those components and where you'll find them in the feature installation state lists when you run Setup.exe to install or update Outlook or Office 2007. Note that the Web Debugging component, which is used to debug Outlook custom form VBScript code, is not supported on computers using Windows Vista as the operating system unless you also have Visual Studio 2005 (not Visual Studio 2005 Express) installed. Also, the .NET support components are needed only if you are using Visual Studio. VBA and VBScript code do not need them.

As noted in the "What Happened to CDO?" sidebar, Collaboration Data Objects is no longer a part of an Outlook installation, but is available as a separate download for backward compatibility.

## 1.5 Showing developer commands

Some of the developer features in Outlook don't appear by default. To see developer commands on individual items, follow these steps:

1.  From the main Outlook menu, choose Tools | Options.

2.  Switch to the Mail Format tab.

3.  Click Editor Options.

**Figure 1.6**
*Some Outlook
developer
commands won't be
visible until you
turn on the
Developer tab.*

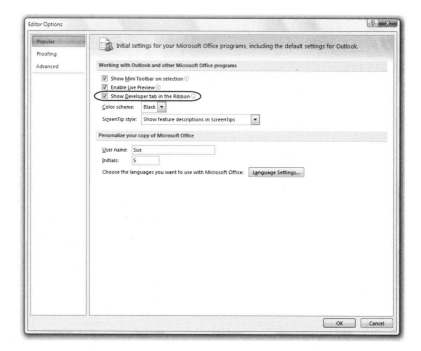

---

**Where's the .NET code?**

You may have noticed that Table 1.2 lists several components that provide .NET program-mability support to Outlook but that none of the approaches in Table 1.1 mentioned .NET. We are not going to cover .NET programming in this book or show any code samples in VB.NET or C#. I know that may sound odd, given that Visual Studio and its .NET languages comprise Microsoft's latest and greatest programming environment. Microsoft even has a special edition of Visual Studio (Visual Studio Tools for Office) for creating add-ins for Outlook. However, the programming tools in the versions of Outlook and Office that you buy at the store or that come preinstalled on a new computer use not .NET, but the older VBA and VBScript programming languages. Future versions of Office may replace VBA with a new .NET programming environment called Visual Studio Tools for Applica-tions that makes its debut in InfoPath 2007, but in Outlook 2007, the customization lan-guages appropriate for administrators and power users (the main audience for this book) are still VBA and VBScript.

That said, the Outlook object model works the same, regardless of what language you use, and so I hope that professional developers working in .NET languages will find some of the material in this book useful to their understanding of how to accomplish the basic pro-gramming tasks in Outlook.

4.    In the Editor Options dialog (see Figure 1.6), check the box for "Show Developer tab in the Ribbon."

The "Ribbon" is Office 2007's new command interface, replacing toolbars and menus on Word documents, Excel worksheets, PowerPoint presentations, and individual Outlook items.

## 1.6    Summary

At first, Microsoft Outlook programming can seem complex because there is more than one tool and no clear indicator of where to start. This book is divided into sections that introduce Outlook skills one at a time, with examples that you can easily try on your own computer. After an introduction in Part I to VBA design, in Part II you will learn about Outlook form design. If you are completely new to writing code, Part III will give you the basics that you'll need to write both VBA and VBScript code. If you already have coding experience, feel free to skip ahead to Part IV, which dives into the specifics of writing code for the Outlook object model, both in VBA and in VBScript behind custom forms. Finally, in Part V, you'll find out how to integrate Outlook with Word and Excel to print reports, work with rules and views, manage forms and some key user settings, and modify the toolbar on Outlook's main menu.

Code samples in this book are available from http://www.outlook-code.com, along with book suggestions for professional developers, more code samples, discussion forums, and other Outlook programming resources.

**2**

# *The VBA Design Environment*

Visual Basic for Applications, or VBA as I'll call it from now on, is the programming environment for writing and testing macros that you can run on demand and procedures that respond to various events that occur when you use Outlook. Because Outlook has no macro recorder (as is found in Word and Excel), you will have to write your Outlook VBA code from scratch.

The highlights of this chapter include discussions of the following:

- How to get started using VBA
- Where to enter program code
- How to use the basic windows in the VBA programming environment
- How to add a new VBA user form
- How to avoid a security message when you start VBA
- How to locate where Outlook saves your VBA code project

## 2.1 VBA: The basics

Here are the absolute basics you need to get started with Outlook VBA.

First, you must change the security level, because Outlook VBA is disabled by default. Follow these steps:

1.    Choose Tools | Macro | Security.

2.    In the Trust Center dialog, under Macro Security, select "Warnings for all macros," and then click OK.

3.    Restart Outlook.

The next step is to start the VBA environment. After Outlook restarts, press Alt+F11 or choose Tools | Macro | Visual Basic Editor. If you see a prompt like that in Figure 2.1, you should choose Enable Macros. (The prompt will not appear if you have not written any VBA code yet.)

**Figure 2.1**
*This message
appears when you
start VBA if your
macro security is set
to "Warnings for
all macros."*

After the VBA editor opens, in the Project Explorer at upper left, click
the + sign to expand the Project1 (VbaProject.OTM) hierarchy, then click
the + sign to expand the Microsoft Office Outlook Objects hierarchy.
Finally, you should see `ThisOutlookSession`, which is a built-in code
module. Double-click the `ThisOutlookSession` module to open it.

**Tip:** Notice that the title of the window changes to "Microsoft Visual Basic
- Project1- [ThisOutlookSession (Code)]." The name of the currently displayed module is part of the VBA editor's caption.

You're now ready to write your first VBA procedure! Type the code in
Listing 2.1 into the `ThisOutlookSession` module.

To run this code, leave the cursor anywhere inside the text that you
typed and do any of the following:

- Press F5.
- From the VBA editor's menu, choose Run | Run Sub/UserForm.
- Click the Run Sub/UserForm button on the VBA editor's toolbar.

You can also run the procedure by closing the VBA editor, and pressing
Alt+F8 while you're in the main Outlook window. Regardless of how you
run the procedure, what you should see is a new Outlook message with a
subject of "Hello World!" and this text in the message body: "How do you
like your first message?" (You may need to minimize or close the VBA editor in order to see the message.)

**Listing 2.1**      *Create your first Outlook Message with VBA code*

```
Sub HelloWorldMessage()
    Dim msg As Outlook.MailItem
    Set msg = Application.CreateItem(olMailItem)
    msg.Subject = "Hello World!"
    msg.Body = "How do you like your first message?"
    msg.Display
    Set msg = Nothing
End Sub
```

To save your work, close Outlook and respond Yes when you see the prompt, "Do you want to save the VBA Project 'ThisOutlookSession'?"

Congratulations! You have created your first VBA procedure. The next few sections will review what you accomplished and give you more details on these basic VBA practices.

### 2.1.1 VBA security

The default VBA security setting does not allow you to run any VBA code. Therefore, before starting VBA for the first time, you should check the security settings by choosing Tools | Macro | Security. Figure 2.2 shows the different options.

With security set to "Warnings for all macros," Outlook will prompt you each time it starts (see Figure 2.1) to confirm that you want to allow your VBA code to run. At the end of this chapter, we'll learn how to sign your project digitally to avoid that prompt and still keep VBA secure.

**Tip:** I usually keep my macro security setting on "Warnings for all macros." Getting the prompt when Outlook starts lets me know for sure that the VBA component has loaded correctly.

**Caution:** If you choose "No warnings and disable all macros" in the dialog shown in Figure 2.2, you can still work on your VBA project, but you will not be able to run any VBA code until you lower the security setting, then exit and restart Outlook.

### 2.1.2 Starting VBA

To start a VBA session, press Alt+F11, or choose Tools | Macro | Visual Basic Editor. The Outlook VBA editor may look terribly complex if you

**Figure 2.2**

*Adjust macro security to "Warnings for all macros" before you first run Outlook VBA.*

have not previously worked with Visual Basic or with VBA in other Office programs. Don't worry! This chapter explains two windows on the left and shows you how to fill out the blank space on the right with a form and a code module, your first two VBA programming components.

---

**Tip:** Working in VBA does not mean that you can't get your email messages. Outlook remains open. To go back to the main Outlook window, just click the View Microsoft Office Outlook button on the far left end of the VBA toolbar or press Alt+F11.

---

### 2.1.3   Saving your work and ending a VBA session

You should save your work in VBA periodically, perhaps after you finish positioning controls on a form or after you finish coding a module. You can do this by clicking the Save button, pressing Ctrl+S, or choosing File | Save in the VBA editor. All the modules and forms are stored in a single project file named VbaProject.OTM.

To end a VBA session, click the close (**x**) button in the upper-right corner of the VBA editor, or choose File | Close and Return to Microsoft Office Outlook. Exiting VBA does not save your VBA programming work. However, when you exit Outlook, if any modules or forms are unsaved, Outlook prompts you to save the VBA project.

## 2.2   **VBA windows**

When you run VBA, the first two windows that appear are the Project Explorer and Properties windows on the left side of the development environment. You can close either of them with the close (**x**) button in the upper-right corner of the window. You will probably want to keep them open though, unless you have limited space on your screen.

---

**Tip:** If the Properties or Project Explorer window is not visible, you can restore either window with the appropriate command on the View menu or the corresponding toolbar button.

---

Besides these two, you will also use module and form windows (the windows that you use to extend Outlook with code and VBA forms) and the Object Browser, which helps you discover what you can do with Outlook and other object models.

**Figure 2.3**
*The VBA environment contains no program code or forms when you first start it.*

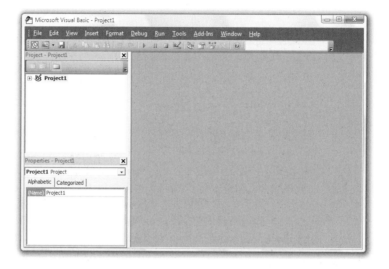

## 2.2.1 Project Explorer

The Project Explorer window lists the currently loaded VBA elements that make up your programming application. For example, compare Figure 2.3 with Figure 2.4. Figure 2.4 shows the Project Explorer after I added a form and a module (more on those shortly). You will also see the `ThisOutlook-Session` module, because Outlook creates it automatically. The `ThisOutlookSession` module is very useful for building code routines that handle Outlook events.

**Figure 2.4**
*Use the Project Explorer as a map or index to the components you are currently working on. The design tools for VBA forms include a toolbox.*

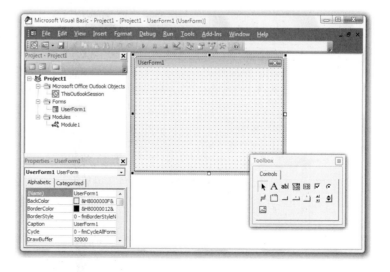

The three buttons at the top of the Project Explorer are (left to right) View Code, View Object, and Toggle Folders. When working with a form, use the View buttons to switch between its code and its layout. The Toggle Folders button flattens the list of elements in the project, hiding the folders and listing all components in alphabetical order.

### 2.2.2    Properties window

The Properties window, which appears below the Project Explorer window, lists all the attributes of any project elements.

In Figure 2.5, you see the properties for a code module (more on such modules shortly) created by choosing Insert | Module and a form created by choosing Insert | UserForm. The only property for the module is its name, `Module1` by default. To change the `Name` property, click next to (Name) in the Properties window and replace `Module1` with a different name.

When you start designing VBA forms, you will see that VBA forms and the controls on them have many, many properties. Some properties you change by typing a new value in the Properties window. Others you pick from a list. Most can also be changed with program code. An example would be turning the text in a control red when the value of the control meets certain criteria.

**Tip:** If you drag the Properties window by its title, you can float it over another part of the VBA environment. Both the Properties window and the Project Explorer (and most other VBA windows) are dockable; you can either park them against one side of the main window or float them anywhere inside the VBA editor. Experiment to discover which arrangement suits you best.

**Figure 2.5**
*Every programming component in VBA has properties.*

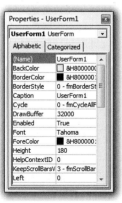

### 2.2.3   **VBA user forms**

To add your first user form to the VBA environment, choose Insert | User-Form. You should see something like the form in Figure 2.4.

VBA forms use controls to display information to the user and gather data. No data resides in the form itself, except during the short time that the form is in use. Most of the VBA forms you will build in Outlook are called *dialog boxes*, because they force the user to carry on a conversation with the program. When a dialog box is displayed, the user can't return to the Outlook application until the conversation ends with the user clicking OK, Cancel, or some other button that closes the dialog box.

### 2.2.4   **Modules**

To add a new code module, choose Insert | Module. A *module* is a collection of programming procedures. You should see something like Figure 2.6, only the module you add will contain no text yet. Notice that a module has only one property in the Properties window (Name).

**Note:** You can also insert another kind of module called a *class module*. The built-in ThisOutlookSession module is an example of a class module. As we'll see in Chapter 11, "Responding to Outlook Events in VBA," class modules allow you to react to the events that occur as users work with Outlook. The code module for a VBA user form is another example of a class module.

VBA code windows use a rather smart text editor with a feature Microsoft calls "intellisense." It checks your code against the VBA programming language, reminds you of the parameters of each function, and colors your text to distinguish different code elements. For example, the text shown at the top of Figure 2.6 appears in VBA in green, because it is a *comment*, text in a program module that is not executed as code. To create a comment statement, start a line of text with an apostrophe ('). You can also insert a comment at the end of a code statement by preceding the comment text with an apostrophe.

To end a code statement and go to the next line, press Enter. If the statement has an obvious syntax error, VBA will color it red until you fix the problem.

In Figure 2.6, notice the pop-up about the MsgBox function explaining what parameters it supports and in what order to use them. (MsgBox is a handy function that pops up a message box on the user's screen.) This information appears as you type the name of a function that VBA recognizes. It

**Figure 2.6**
*Modules contain programming procedures.*

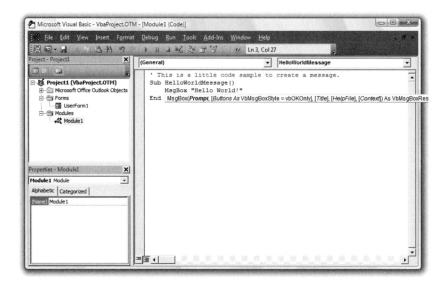

then disappears automatically after you finish typing the current function and its parameters. If you find this distracting, you can turn it off by choosing Tools | Options and clearing the box for Auto Quick Info.

**Tip:** Choose Tools | Options if you want to experiment with the other settings for the code editor.

Did you realize that you already have another place to write programming code for your project? Open UserForm1 from the Project Explorer, and then double-click anywhere on the blank form. A code window like the one in Figure 2.7 appears, ready for you to type in the first procedure that applies directly to the form. (Don't be concerned just yet about what to type; that's coming in the next few chapters.)

**Tip:** You can switch among the forms and modules either with the Project Explorer or by using the Windows menu. Each form or module window has minimize, maximize/restore, and close buttons, just like document windows in programs like Word.

### 2.2.5  **Object Browser**

To complete this initial tour of the VBA editor, you need to look at one more window, the Object Browser. Choose View | Object Browser, click the Object Browser toolbar button, or just press F2. You will probably want to

**Figure 2.7**
*Forms also include programming code, shown in a separate window.*

maximize that window so that it fills whatever space is not occupied by the Project Explorer and Properties windows, as shown in Figure 2.8. In the dropdown list at the top of the Object Browser, switch from <All Libraries> to Outlook.

**Note:** From now on, most figures illustrating work in VBA will show only the particular form or code window, not the entire VBA editor.

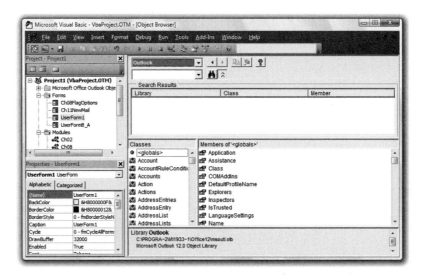

**Figure 2.8**
*The Object Browser describes the various objects you can program with and their properties, methods, and events.*

The Object Browser is your road map and index to the world of Outlook items, folders, and other components for which you can write code. Under Classes, you see each Outlook object. Click on ContactItem, for example, and under Members of 'ContactItem' on the right, you see the characteristics of contacts—what they can do, what you can do to them, and their properties. After you select a class or member, click the question-mark button, press F1, or right-click the member or class and choose Help to read the Help topic about that item. For many topics, you will find a code example you can copy and paste into your application.

**Tip:** The fields you see in the (All Fields) page on an Outlook custom form generally match the object properties for different items, but not always exactly. For example, the `Company` field on a contact form is actually the `CompanyName` property of a `ContactItem` object. In a formula on a form, you would use `[Company]`, but in VBA or VBScript code, you would use `CompanyName`.

## 2.3    Getting help in VBA

In addition to the Object Browser described in the previous section, you can also get help in Outlook VBA by pressing F1 or choosing Help | Microsoft Visual Basic Help. Help topics include:

- Outlook objects, properties, methods, and events
- Key Outlook developer concepts, including many useful how-to articles
- What's new in Outlook 2007 for developers

By default, Help looks first for the content online at Microsoft. This ensures that you access the most recently updated information on any given topic. If you are not connected to the Internet, Outlook will use the Help content stored locally.

Browsing the Concepts section, a new documentation effort by Microsoft, is a particularly good way to acquaint yourself with Outlook's capabilities. Figure 2.9 shows the topics available in under Items, Folders, and Stores.

To locate information about particular Outlook and VBA functions, you can use the Search box at the top of the Help window. Figure 2.10 shows part of the topic for the `MsgBox()` function that you saw in Figure 2.6. The topic includes detailed information on the different parameters for the function, plus code examples.

**Figure 2.9**
*Help topics can guide you through basic Outlook programming concepts.*

**Tip:** You can also get help on VBA functions and Outlook objects, proper-ties, and methods by highlighting a word in your code, then pressing F1.

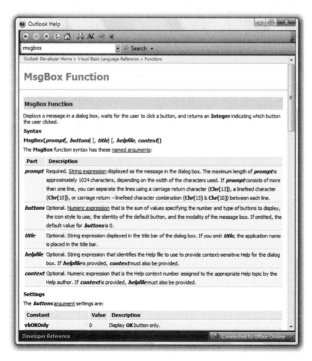

**Figure 2.10**
*Reference topics explain different functions, properties, methods, and Outlook objects.*

## 2.4 Working with VBA projects

Outlook always stores its VBA project in a file named VbaProject.OTM. You can't change the name of the VBA project file or store it in another location. Table 2.1 shows the file's location on the different versions of Windows.

**Note:** Regardless of the operating system, you can display the folder where Outlook keeps the VBA project file by using the path %appdata%\ Microsoft\Outlook in Windows Explorer. %appdata% is an environment variable that acts as a shortcut to the folder containing the user's own application data.

If you have a problem with VBA or want to start with a fresh VbaProject.OTM file for some other reason, shut down Outlook, rename the VbaProject.OTM file, and then restart Outlook. The next time you run VBA, Outlook will create a new, empty VBA project. To return to the original project, repeat the process, renaming the original file back to VbaProject.OTM.

**Note:** Unlike other Office applications, such as Excel and Word, Outlook allows you to work on only one VBA project at a time.

### 2.4.1 Backing up your work

Unlike other Office programs (such as Word and Excel) that allow you to have a VBA project for each document and template, Outlook allows only one VBA project. Because the VbaProject.OTM file contains all your Outlook VBA code, it is a good idea to include it in your regular system backup. Refer back to Table 2.1 for the file's location.

You can also make copies of individual modules and forms, either for backup or for reuse on a different computer. In the Project Explorer, select any form or module, and then choose File | Export File. Outlook exports

**Table 2.1** *Storage Locations for the VbaProject.OTM File*

| Windows Version | VbaProject.OTM Location |
| --- | --- |
| Windows Vista | C:\Users\<user name>\AppData\Roaming\Microsoft\Outlook |
| Windows 2003 Windows XP | C:\Documents and Settings\<user name>\Application Data\Microsoft\Outlook |

modules as .bas files, forms as .frm and .frx files, and the `ThisOutlook-Session` module as a .cls file.

Use the Import File command on the File menu to bring in a module or form that you previously saved. Use the Remove command to remove a module or form that you are no longer using actively; you'll get a prompt asking if you want to export it first. Exporting is a good idea, just in case you want to recover the routines or form later.

### 2.4.2   Signing your project

It is possible to avoid the Enable Macros/Disable Macros prompt (Figure 2.1) when you start VBA and still have a secure VBA environment. The solution is to sign your Outlook VBA project digitally. Office includes a tool called Selfcert.exe that you can use to create a signing certificate. You will find this tool on the Programs menu under Microsoft Office | Microsoft Office Tools | Digital Certificate for VBA Projects. It creates a digital certificate, similar to that which you can get from providers like Verisign, only it's free and doesn't derive from a trusted hierarchy of other certificates. After you run the tool, restart Outlook and switch into the VBA editor. Then choose Tools | Digital Signature, click Choose, select the certificate, and click OK until you return to the VBA editor.

After you sign the project with the certificate, you can adjust your Outlook macro security setting. Switch back to the main Outlook window, choose Tools | Macro | Security, and set security to "Warnings for signed macros; all unsigned macros are disabled." The next time you try to run any VBA code, you will see the slightly ominous prompt in Figure 2.11 in which Outlook asks whether it can trust the "publisher" (that is, you) of the VBA module. You should click on the Show Signature Details link to verify that the certificate name is that of the certificate you created with Selfcert.exe. Once you verify the certificate, you can confidently click "Trust all documents from this publisher" and never see that prompt again for your VBA sessions.

**Figure 2.11**
*Secure your Outlook VBA configuration by digitally signing your VBA project, then trusting the certificate that you used to sign the project.*

### 2.4.3 Distributing VBA code to others

Outlook VBA code is designed for personal use. Microsoft never intended it for distribution to large numbers of users. In document-centric programs like Word and Excel, macros travel with templates and documents. But in Outlook, there is, in fact, no supported way to distribute Outlook macros. If you have prototyped a good solution in VBA, the best approach to distributing that solution throughout your organization is to use your VBA code as a starting point for building an add-in. Creating an add-in requires additional tools and programming skills beyond what this book covers.

Realistically, though, not every organization that wants to make Outlook more functional has the resources to create add-ins. You may also run into situations where just a couple of Outlook VBA macros can cut down on the amount of time that the corporate help desk has to spend with a particular user or make your vice president's assistant work more effectively. In those situations, you can adapt the backup techniques covered earlier—either export and import code or replace the entire VbaProject.OTM file.

Export and import is the least intrusive technique. Give the exported files to other users, and tell them how to reverse the process with File | Import. If you export a form, be sure to distribute both the .frm file and the .frx file.

The advantage of sharing VBA code through export and import is that it preserves any VBA code that the user may have already written. Disadvantages include:

- It's tedious if you have a lot of modules.

- If you export the built-in `ThisOutlookSession` module and then try to import it, the user will get a `ThisOutlookSession1` class module, but code in it won't run automatically as it does in `ThisOutlookSession`. The user will need to cut and paste the procedures from the imported class module into the built-in `ThisOutlookSession` module.

- The user will have to resolve any duplicate procedure names that might raise conflicts between existing modules and those imported.

The brute force approach is to copy the VbaProject.OTM to the user's machine, replacing any existing VbaProject.OTM file. You can do this with whatever technique you normally use in your organization to copy files to users, including walking it around on a disk to each workstation or using a login script.

This method has the advantage of being a relatively simple process of copying a single file. Disadvantages include:

- Any Outlook VBA code the user already has will be lost.

■ The user will need to use Alt+F8 or Alt+F11 manually at least once before any `Application`-level event code will fire.

Note that Microsoft does not provide any support for these VBA code distribution techniques. Also, VBA code has been known simply to disappear without warning because the VbaProject.OTM file has become corrupt. Good backups and patience are essential. Your mileage may vary.

## 2.5  Summary

In the VBA environment, you can create dialog boxes and other user input and display forms. You can also write macros, event handlers, and other procedures in program code modules. In Chapter 7, "Outlook Code Basics," we will start writing VBA macros and learn how to invoke them from toolbar buttons.

In Chapter 3, "Building Your First VBA Form," we will learn how to create forms with VBA. Some of the techniques you'll learn about controls on forms will be transferable to the Outlook custom forms design environment.

# 3

# *Building Your First VBA Form*

Now that you know your way around the VBA editor, your first project is to build a form to add a new feature to Outlook: setting reminders for the birthday and anniversary events that Outlook creates automatically from corresponding dates in contact items. In the process, you will learn the basics of designing VBA user forms.

The highlights of this chapter include discussions of the following:

- How to add controls to a form using the VBA control toolbox
- Which controls can be useful for data entry
- How to add code to a VBA form
- What makes a good dialog box
- When to use option buttons and check box controls
- How to work with list box and combo box controls
- How to manage the way that users move around in a form

## 3.1 Understanding Outlook birthdays and anniversaries

To modify or add to Outlook's functionality, you first should understand what functionality is already built in. Whenever you add a birthday or anniversary on the Details tab of the standard contact form, Outlook automatically creates a matching recurring event in your Calendar folder and adds a shortcut to that event in the contact item. However, these automatically created birthday and anniversary events don't have reminders. Therefore, unless you check the Calendar well in advance, those birthdays could sneak up on you.

> **Note:** If you customize the contact form with your own date/time field, Outlook does not create a matching calendar entry when the user enters a date in that field. If you want Outlook to add a matching calendar item for a custom date/time field, just wait until Chapter 20, "Common Item Techniques," which explains how to create a new event in the Calendar when the user enters a date in a custom property.

You can use VBA to build a tool to globally update all existing birthdays and anniversaries to make sure they have reminders.

## 3.2    Step I: What controls do you need?

The birthday/anniversary reminder tool that you will build in this chapter consists of an Outlook VBA form with code behind it. A key first step in designing any form is to decide what the form will do and what information it needs to complete that task.

We already know the purpose of this form—to add a reminder to all birthdays and anniversaries. To accomplish this, the form requires information from the user on when to set the reminder—a specific number of days, weeks, or months in advance of the event.

> **Note:** Another key decision you will make in designing forms is what kind of feedback to provide the user as the form goes about its work. Chapter 8, "Code Grammar 101," covers this issue.

How many ways could you set the reminder interval? You might consider the following:

- A box where the user types the number of days
- A box where the user types "3 days," "2 wks," or "1m," and so on, as in Outlook's built-in date/time and duration fields
- A spin button control that the user clicks to advance the number of days to the desired interval
- A spin button control to show the number, plus buttons where the user can select days, weeks, or months
- Buttons or a list where the user can select from the most frequently used reminder intervals (as you want to define them)

Which approach is best? There is no right or wrong answer. This is the kind of decision that you must make in every programming project. Few programming projects have one single best solution. "Best" in any scenario is whatever approach allows you to gain the most productivity with the available resources (time, money, and programming skills). It may not be worthwhile to build a beautiful user interface for a program you use only once a year. But for a tool you use every day, you may want to invest extra time to make the user interface easy to use.

In the list above, the first and third approaches are somewhat limited, because they can easily handle only days, not weeks or months. The second approach would take considerable work, because you would need to write code to convert what the user types into the corresponding number of days. (Controls bound to duration and date/time data fields on custom Outlook forms perform this conversion automatically, but VBA controls do not.) The fourth and fifth approaches are a little too complicated for a novice's first project.

---

**Tip:** If you are designing a form for your personal use, don't feel that you must cover every possible option or exception. You would do that, of course, in a program for wider distribution, but for a personal application, you don't need a form with unlimited options for setting reminders.

---

Since this is our first VBA form, we'll keep it simple and use the first approach—a text box where the user enters the number of days before the event, which Outlook will use to calculate when to display the reminder. The form, therefore, will need these controls:

- A text box for the number of days
- At least one label control to give the user some instructions
- A button the user can click to perform the reminder updates on the birthday and anniversary items
- A button the user can click to close the form

## 3.3    Step 2: Create the form

After you have a general plan, the next step is to create the form and set its particular properties. Start the VBA editor by pressing Alt+F11, as discussed in the previous chapter.

To add a form, choose Insert | UserForm. A blank form appears, along with the Toolbox. The Properties window shows the properties for the form. Table 3.1 lists key properties you should set right away.

The value for the (Name) property must follow the naming convention for objects, which allows internal capitalization, but not spaces. You can (and should) include spaces in the Caption property, however.

**Table 3.1**  *VBA Form Properties to Set Immediately*

| Property | Description | Suggested Value |
|---|---|---|
| (Name) | The form name as shown in the Project Explorer and as used in program code | ReminderUpdate |
| Caption | The name shown in the title bar of the form | Birthday and Anniversary Reminder Update |

**Tip:** If you plan to work with the same form for a while, you may want to close the Project Explorer so that you have more room on the screen for other windows. To hide it, choose View | Project Explorer or click the Project Explorer's close (**x**) button. The Properties window will grow taller, making it easier to use. To see the values for properties more easily, make the Properties window wider by dragging its right border toward the right.

**Caution:** Make sure that you set the (Name) property before you start writing program code. If you change the (Name) after you write code for the form, you must use search and replace in your code to update the form name to the new value wherever it appears.

### 3.3.1  Exploring form properties

Click on the Categorized tab of the Properties window to see the properties organized into different groups: Appearance, Behavior, Font, Misc, Picture, Position, and Scrolling. Because the properties in a group are often related, viewing them by category helps to remind you to change those allied properties. For example, if you change the BackColor property, you might also want to change the BorderColor.

**Tip:** If you are not familiar with a particular property, select it, and then click F1 to bring up a Help topic that explains it.

As you explore the form properties, notice that different properties use different methods to enter new values. For some properties, such as Enabled, you click on a dropdown list and select a value. For others, you type in the value; Caption is a good example. In other cases, such as Font and Picture, you click a button with an ellipsis (...) to get a dialog from which you can select the new value.

**Figure 3.1**
*Select colors for the form and its controls from among the System colors for the current Windows color scheme or by using the Palette.*

What about those cryptic values for some of the Appearance properties? What does &H8000000F&, the default value for BackColor mean? The value for each color property is a long integer, a number whose value can range from -2,147,483,648 to 2,147,483,647, but the Properties window shows those values in hexadecimal format, in which numbers are expressed in base 16 notation. (For example, 20 in the decimal notation we normally use is equivalent to 14 in hex, whereas 32 in decimal would be 20 in hex.)

You don't need to know the values for all the colors, nor do you need the ability to convert a decimal number to hexadecimal. The VBA editor makes it easy to select colors with a couple of mouse clicks. For example, click on the BackColor property to select it, and then click the arrow button at the right side of the property's value box. A list of colors appears, as shown in Figure 3.1.

Now, look at the SpecialEffect property shown in Figure 3.2. First, notice that it supports only a few values: 0, 1, 2, 3, and 6. Also, see how each numeric value has a word associated with it. For example, the value 1 also has the word fmSpecialEffectRaised. This is an example of an intrinsic constant, a value built into VBA that doesn't change and has a special word associated with it.

**Figure 3.2**
*Many properties allow only certain values, which have equivalent intrinsic constants.*

You will use intrinsic constants in VBA code to work with the property values for forms, controls, and other objects. Hundreds of intrinsic constants are associated with VBA itself and with various Outlook components. As you might imagine, they make it much easier to read and write program code. For example, for a form named `ReminderUpdate`, this line of code changes the format of the form background from flat to raised:

```
ReminderUpdate.SpecialEffect = 1
```

This line does the same thing, but is much easier to understand, because it contains an intrinsic constant instead of a number:

```
ReminderUpdate.SpecialEffect = fmSpecialEffectRaised
```

You can change many form and control properties with program code while the form is running—or *at runtime*. The Help topic on each property tells you whether or not that is possible.

**Note:** You can use only a limited set of intrinsic constants in VBScript code on Outlook custom forms—only those that VBScript supports, not constants defined in the Outlook object model.

### 3.3.2 Should you use a modal or modeless form?

Another important form property is `ShowModal`, which can have the value `True` (the default) or `False`. While a modal form is on the screen, the user cannot return to the main application window. This is the typical behavior of a dialog box: The dialog opens, the user makes a change, and then the user closes the dialog to return to the application. From a programming standpoint, modal forms are important to controlling program flow. No other code executes until the modal form is either hidden or unloaded.

If a form is modeless, the user can work both with the main application windows and with the form. An example would be a form that provides information to the user, either on demand or according to a schedule.

Because the `ReminderUpdate` form is designed to perform a quick, occasional update, there is no need to make it a modeless form. Because the default for `ShowModal` is `True`, you don't need to make a property change for this form to make it modal.

## 3.4 Step 3: Add user input controls

Ready for the next step? Now that you have a blank form and understand some of its properties, you can add controls to it. The form needs a text box where the user can type the number of days. There are two ways to add a text box to the form:

- To get a standard size text box, drag the TextBox tool from the control toolbox to the form.

- To set a custom size, select the TextBox tool in the Toolbox. Position the mouse pointer over the form where you want one corner of the text box to go. Hold down the left mouse button, and drag the mouse to trace a rectangle with the dimensions you want.

**Note:** The control toolbox should appear automatically when you create a new user form. If you don't see it, choose View | Toolbox on the VBA editor menu or click the View Toolbox button on the toolbar.

Now, use the Label tool (to the left of the TextBox tool in the Toolbox) to add two label controls, one to the left and one to the right of the text box. The form should look like that shown in Figure 3.3. You can always reposition any of the controls, if you need to, by dragging them to a new position on the form.

You should make it a habit to edit the name of each control that holds data, such as the text box you just added. Even though VBA automatically assigns a name to each control, these default names are generic and have no specific meaning in the context of your application. For the text box that will display the number of days, change the name in the Properties window to txtDays. (Isn't that more informative than TextBox1?) You might also want to add a phrase or sentence to the ControlTipText property to pop up information when the user pauses the mouse pointer over the control.

To add your own text to the Label1 control, click the Select Objects tool in the Toolbox (the arrow at upper-left); the mouse pointer will turn into an arrow. Click the Label1 control once to select it; then click a second time. When you see the blinking vertical insertion point inside the control, you can delete the Label1 text and replace it with your own text, relevant to the form, as shown in Figure 3.4.

**Figure 3.3**
*Combine a data entry control with one or more explanatory label controls.*

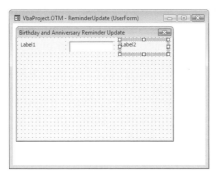

**Figure 3.4**
*Change the text for
a label control by
typing it into the
control or updating
the Caption
property.*

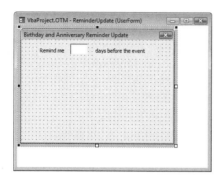

---

**Tip:** That's click once to select the `Label1` control, pause briefly, and then click again to edit its caption. The timing is important. If the clicks are too close together, VBA interprets them as a double-click and opens the form's program code window.

---

You can also enter text for a label control by typing the text as the value for the `Caption` property.

Notice in Figure 3.4 that the controls have been slightly rearranged and resized to make the form look better. To move a control, drag it across the form. To resize a control, drag one of the little white squares, called *drag handles*, which appear when you select a control. You might also want to change the `TextAlign` property of the label on the left from `1 - fmText-AlignLeft` to `3 - fmTextAlignRight`. That will right-align the caption so that it appears closer to the text box. Look in the Format menu for commands to help you size and position VBA form controls.

## 3.5    Step 4: Add command buttons

The form in Figure 3.5 now has a text box and two label controls to give the user an idea of what kind of information to enter. What's missing? There is no way to actually start the process of updating the items in the Calendar folder to add a reminder. The form needs a command button control to run the code you will add to the form. Command buttons are those ubiquitous form controls that make things happen.

You can add two command button controls, one to run the update and the other to close the form. Use the Command Button tool on the Toolbox to drag two standard-size buttons to your form. Set the properties shown in Table 3.2.

**Table 3.2** *Properties for ReminderUpdate Command Buttons*

| Property | CommandButton1 | CommandButton2 |
|---|---|---|
| (Name) | cmdUpdate | cmdClose |
| Accelerator | U | |
| Cancel | False | True |
| Caption | Update | Close |
| Default | True | False |

**Tip:** The form has a close (x) button in the upper-right corner, but putting a command button on the form as well makes it just a little more obvious to the user that the form should be closed when the update finishes. As you will see, you could also include code in the form to close it automatically after the update completes.

The most important of these properties are (Name) and Caption. To see the effect of the other properties in Table 3.2, you must run the form to see what the ReminderUpdate form looks like to a user. Select the form and then click the Run Sub/UserForm button on the toolbar. You can also press F5, or choose Run | Run Sub/UserForm. The form should look like Figure 3.5.

**Tip:** You can select the form or any control on it by picking from the drop-down list at the top of the Properties window.

Until now, you have been working in *design mode*, where you design the appearance of a user form. Figure 3.5 shows the form in *run mode*. The form is running or, in other words, active. If the buttons had program code

**Figure 3.5**
*The ReminderUpdate form is starting to look like a real form, buttons and all.*

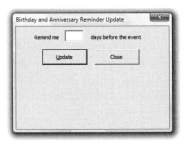

associated with them, that code would run when you clicked them. However, if you click the buttons at this stage, nothing happens, because you have not added code to the form yet.

### 3.5.1 Basic command button properties

Take a closer look at the Update and Close buttons in Figure 3.5 and the properties you set. First, setting the `Accelerator` property for the `cmdUpdate` button to `u` causes the letter `U` in the control's caption to be underlined when the form is in run mode. This means the user can press Alt+U as an alternative to clicking the button. Keyboard accelerators such as this make forms more accessible and friendlier to those who prefer the keyboard to the mouse.

See how the `cmdUpdate` button has a dark border, but the `cmdClose` button doesn't. This is a visual clue that the `cmdUpdate` button is the default button for the form; you set its `Default` property to `True`. Pressing the Enter key on a form is the same thing as clicking the default button. This means that to use your form, the user just needs to type in the number of days, and then press Enter.

Similarly, pressing the Esc key is equivalent to clicking on the `cmdClose` button, because you set the `Cancel` property of that button to `True`. This made `cmdClose` the cancel button.

A form can have only one default button and one cancel button. Neither is required. Setting a command button's `Default` or `Cancel` property to `True` makes it the new default or cancel button.

---

**Caution:** In this example, you made `cmdUpdate` the default button so that you could see what a default button looks like. In reality, though, the default button should never be a button that runs code that can make irreversible changes to many Outlook items. You may even want to consider adding a confirmation message that the user must acknowledge to allow the operation to continue. Chapter 8 shows how to do this with the `MsgBox()` function.

---

Because the `cmdClose` button does not do anything yet when you click it, you cannot use it to close the form. Instead, click the close (**x**) button in the upper-right corner of the `ReminderUpdate` form so that you return to the VBA design environment. Alternatively, switch back to the design environment, and click the Design Mode button.

### 3.5.2 **Adding code**

To make the command buttons do something, we need to add code. You can start with an easy routine to close the form when the user clicks the cmdClose button.

To add code to any command button, double-click the button on the form. A code window appears, such as that in Figure 3.6, where you should see the first and last lines of the subroutine that runs when you click the cmdClose button. VBA automatically creates this subroutine stub when you double-click a command button on a form. The name of the subroutine is cmdClose_Click—the name of the control plus the name of the event that fires, Click, when the user clicks the button. The keyword Private means that this routine runs only in the context of the current form; no other components in your VBA project can use it.

Notice the two dropdown lists at the top of the code window. The one on the left includes the name of every control on the form, as well as User-Form to represent the form itself and a (General) section in which you declare variables and constants (more on that in Chapter 8).

The list on the right includes Click as well as all the other events that can take place on the form or relative to a control. We will learn more about events in Chapter 7. For now, you will work just with the Click event for your two command buttons.

In the space between Private Sub cmdClose_Click() and End Sub, type

```
Unload Me
```

Unload is the command to remove a form from memory and from the computer display. You can use Me instead of the full name of the form, ReminderUpdate, because this code is running behind one of the controls on the form you want to unload. If it were running in another module, you would need to refer to the form by name.

**Figure 3.6**
*A form's code window gives you quick access to all the controls and the events they support.*

**Figure 3.7**
*The two command
buttons now have
code that will run
when the user clicks
each button.*

To add code for the other command button, you do not need to switch back to the form. Instead, at the top of the code window, choose cmdUp-date from the dropdown list of controls. This will add the stub for the cmdUpdate_Click procedure. Inside of that procedure, type:

```
MsgBox "This is the update button."
```

This code pop ups a simple message to the user. The code window should now look like that shown in Figure 3.7.

---

**Tip:** The indenting shown in Figure 3.7 helps make the code more readable, but doesn't affect how it runs. To indent a code line, press the Tab key.

---

Congratulations! You have written your first program code! Click the Run button on the toolbar, press F5, or choose Run | Run Sub/UserForm to see the form in action. First, click the Update button. Your code should generate a message box such as the one in Figure 3.8.

---

**Note:** Message boxes are useful not only for displaying information to the user, but also for forcing the user to make a choice. We will look at message boxes in more detail in Chapter 8.

---

After you click OK to dismiss the message box, click the Close button on the form or press Esc. The cmdClose_Click procedure runs, unloading the form.

**Figure 3.8**
*It's easy to pop up a
simple message box.*

### 3.5.3 **Anatomy of a procedure**

No doubt you're eager to design applications that do more than just open message boxes. To give you some additional practice adding code to a command button, replace the cmdUpdate_Click procedure with the procedure shown in Listing 3.1.

The cmdUpdate_Click procedure contains three sections, separated by blank lines. The first statement in the first section

```
On Error Resume Next
```

allows the procedure to handle errors without prompting the user. The two most likely errors for this procedure are encountering an item in the Calendar folder that isn't really an appointment and having a value in the form's text box that is not a number greater than zero. In Chapter 9, "Handling Errors, Testing, and Debugging," you will learn about the different kinds of errors and how to anticipate and deal with them.

The other lines in the first section begin with Dim and define the variables that the procedure uses. A *variable* gets its name from the fact that it is a placeholder in memory for a value that can <u>vary</u> each time the code runs. The next section, in which each line begins with Set, is a series of assign-

**Listing 3.1**    *Code for the cmdUpdate_Click procedure*

```
Private Sub cmdUpdate_Click()
    On Error Resume Next
    Dim objNS As NameSpace
    Dim objCalendar As Folder
    Dim objItem As AppointmentItem
    Dim strSubject As String
    Dim lngMinutes As Long

    Set objNS = Application.Session
    Set objCalendar = _
      objNS.GetDefaultFolder(olFolderCalendar)

    lngMinutes = 24 * 60 * txtDays.Value
    For Each objItem In objCalendar.Items
        strSubject = objItem.Subject
        If InStr(strSubject, "Birthday") > 0 Or _
          InStr(strSubject, "Anniversary") > 0 Then
            objItem.ReminderSet = True
            objItem.ReminderMinutesBeforeStart = lngMinutes
            objItem.Save
        End If
    Next
    Beep
End Sub
```

ment statements setting up the Outlook object variables. You will learn how to declare variables and work with objects in Chapter 8.

The real work is done by the `lngMinutes = ...` statement and the `For Each ... Next` loop. The statement

```
lngMinutes = 24 * 60 * txtDays.Value
```

calculates the number of minutes (24 hours in a day times 60 minutes in an hour, times the number of days in the text box on the form) and places the result in a variable named `lngMinutes`. The code later uses this value to set the reminder. Note that this is the only statement that gets information directly from the form.

The `For Each ... Next` loop examines each item in the Calendar folder and tests whether the word "Birthday" or "Anniversary" appears in the item's `Subject` property, using the very useful `Instr()` function, which you'll learn more about in Chapter 8. This function returns a number greater than zero if one text string contains another. For each birthday or anniversary, the code sets several properties that tell Outlook to display a reminder a certain number of minutes before the appointment's start time. How many minutes? The number calculated and stored in the `lngMinutes` variable.

---

**Note:** `For Each ... Next` loops, which we cover in Chapter 8, get a real workout in Outlook. You use them extensively to cycle through every sub-folder in a parent folder, every recipient in a message, every attachment to a message, and so on.

---

**Tip:** Did you recognize `olFolderCalendar` as an intrinsic constant from the Outlook object model?

---

Try running the form again, as you did earlier, but with the new code for the `cmdUpdate` button. (Be sure to back up your Calendar folder first, as noted in the next Caution.) Does it operate as you expected, creating reminders in birthday and appointment events?

---

**Caution:** Although Outlook has an Undo command for single actions, you cannot undo bulk changes made by procedures like the one in Listing 3.1. Before you run any procedure that changes all items in a folder, you should back up the contents of that folder. The simplest way is to copy the entire folder, perhaps to a new blank Personal Folders .pst file.

---

# 3.6    Step 5: Plan the next development stage

No development project is ever really finished. You can always think of ways to improve it. Here are some possible ways to enhance the `ReminderUpdate` form:

- Allow the user to update just birthdays, just anniversaries, or both.

- Before running the update routine, validate the entry in the `txtDays` control to make sure that it contains a number greater than zero.

- Don't update any appointment that already has a reminder.

- Speed execution of the update by examining only all-day events, instead of every item in the Calendar folder.

- Add feedback to tell the user how many items were updated.

- Ask the user to confirm each change to a birthday or anniversary.

As you consider possible enhancements, think about not just the functionality, but also the look of the form. Does the layout of the controls make sense to the user? A dialog box should be logical, unambiguous, and consistent. The user should have no doubt about what kind of data to enter in each control. Validation code behind the form should protect the user from "wrong" entries. Controls should be grouped in a clear sequence. They might follow a cycle that mimics the boxes on a paper form, or they might just be grouped in an orderly fashion, either from left to right or top to bottom. (Later in this chapter, we'll look at the `TabStop` and `TabIndex` control properties that control what order the cursor uses to move around the controls as the user presses the Tab key.) The user can scan controls more easily if they are aligned and if controls that do similar things are the same size. If your application uses several dialog boxes, they should have the same color scheme, unless you vary the colors for a particular reason.

# 3.7    More on VBA form controls

The `ReminderUpdate` form is certainly functional, but it is not terribly elegant. To implement some of the enhancements suggested in the previous section, you can add more controls to the form.

## 3.7.1    Check box controls

One enhancement is to allow the user to choose whether to update just birthdays, just anniversaries, or both. This takes a couple of check box controls and a little more code.

To add a check box control to a form, select the CheckBox tool in the Toolbox and then click on the form. Check boxes do not need separate label controls to identify them, because they include their own `Caption` property.

**Figure 3.9**
*Check box controls
give users more
choices.*

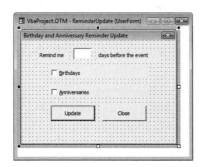

Figure 3.9 shows the ReminderUpdate form with two check boxes added, one for birthdays and one for anniversaries.

The properties for the first check box should be as follows:

```
(Name)          chkBirthdays

Accelerator     B

Caption         Birthdays

Value           True
```

For the second check box, the properties should be as follows:

```
(Name)          chkAnniversaries

Accelerator     A

Caption         Anniversaries

Value           True
```

**Note:** The Accelerator property is case-sensitive if both cases are present in the caption. If you enter a, instead of A, for the accelerator letter for the chkAnniversaries box, the second *a* in the word will be underlined, instead of the initial capital *A*.

Why set the Value for the check boxes to True? Most people probably want reminders for both birthdays and anniversaries. If you set the Value for the check boxes to True, most people won't need to interact at all with the check boxes. They can go straight to the text box and type in the reminder period.

An initial value such as this is called the *default* for the control. Try to set the right defaults so that users need to enter as little information as possible.

You're probably wondering how to change the code from the original reminder update form to use the information in these check boxes. Most check boxes can contain only one of two values, either True or False. If the chkBirthdays box is checked—in other words, if its Value property contains `True`—and the user's Calendar folder includes a birthday event, you want to add a reminder. The same goes for anniversaries.

---

**Note:** The check box control includes a property named `TripleState` that changes a check box to allow the user to set the value to `Null`. In this situation, `Null` means neither `True` nor `False`.

---

Writing out what you want to happen should provide clues to how to code it. Try diagramming each piece of information or action from the description above:

If the `chkBirthdays` box is checked and
  [if] the user's Calendar folder includes a birthday event
    . . . add a reminder

When you want to perform an action if a value is `True` and possibly a different action if the value is `False`, your code needs an `If ... Then` structure. You have already seen an `If ... Then` structure in the code for the `ReminderUpdate` form, where you tested whether an item is a birthday or an anniversary.

To integrate the new check boxes into the procedure, replace the original code for the `Click` event for the `cmdUpdate` button with the new code in Listing 3.2. This code adds `If ... Then` structures to test the values of the check boxes and process the items accordingly.

As we saw earlier in the chapter, you use the `Value` property of a control to get the data the user has entered. For a check box control, the `Value` indicates whether the user has checked the box (`chkBox.Value = True`) or unchecked it (`chkBox.Value = False`).

---

**Note:** You probably noticed that the steps inside the two `If ... End If` code structures are exactly the same. Normally, you wouldn't have such repetition in a routine. In Chapter 8, we will look at ways to streamline such code.

---

## 3.7.2 Option buttons

Check box controls are ideal for obtaining information from the user when the desired answer is Yes or No, True or False, On or Off. If more than two mutually exclusive answers are possible, option button controls work better.

Option button controls are sometimes called *radio buttons* in reference to older radios that had buttons you pushed in to change stations. When you pushed a new button, the last pushed button popped out. The button

**Listing 3.2**    *Use If . . . Then structures to test conditions*

```
Sub cmdUpdate_Click()
    On Error Resume Next
    Dim objNS As NameSpace
    Dim objCalendar As Folder
    Dim objItem As AppointmentItem
    Dim strSubject As String
    Dim lngMinutes As Long
    Set objNS = Application.Session
    Set objCalendar = _
      objNS.GetDefaultFolder(olFolderCalendar)
    lngMinutes = 24 * 60 * txtDays.Value
    If chkBirthdays.Value = True Or _
       chkAnniversaries.Value = True Then
        For Each objItem In objCalendar.Items
            strSubject = objItem.Subject
            If InStr(strSubject, "Birthday") > 0 And _
              chkBirthdays.Value = True Then
                objItem.ReminderSet = True
                objItem.ReminderMinutesBeforeStart = _
                  lngMinutes
                objItem.Save
            End If
            If InStr(strSubject, "Anniversary") > 0 And _
              chkAnniversaries.Value = True Then
                objItem.ReminderSet = True
                objItem.ReminderMinutesBeforeStart = _
                  lngMinutes
                objItem.Save
            End If
        Next
        Beep
    End If
End Sub
```

pressed remained pushed in until you pressed another button for another station. Only one button at a time could be pushed in. Its pushed-in state gave a clear visual indicator as to which station was active.

Option buttons also are useful when you want to force the user to make a choice. If the form opens with one button already selected, the user must either select another button or accept that default option.

Option buttons on forms work the same way: The user can select no more than one option button at a time. In other words, whether it's a choice of five radio stations or four flavors of ice cream or three classes of work orders, you can choose only one. The most common use for option buttons is for such multiple-choice scenarios, but you may also see them when only two choices exist, but those choices don't reduce easily to a True/False description.

To see how option buttons work, try using them instead of check boxes on the `ReminderUpdate` form. Here are the three choices:

- Update birthdays only
- Update anniversaries only
- Update both birthdays and anniversaries.

To replace the check boxes with option buttons, select and delete the check boxes. Next, before you put the buttons on the form, add a frame control to hold them. Select the Frame tool in the Toolbox, and then drag a rectangular shape in the blank area at the top of the form. Set these properties for the frame:

```
(Name)          fraOptions

Caption         Add reminders to:
```

The Properties window will show you that the frame has no `Value` property. The frame itself holds no data. Instead, it lassos the controls you put inside it, organizing them visually and, in the case of option buttons, coordinating their operation.

---

**Tip:** If you have only one set of option buttons on a form, putting a frame around them is optional because the form itself acts as a frame. If you have two sets of option buttons, however, at least one set requires a frame to indicate which buttons work together. Using frames for both sets makes your form more consistent.

---

Add option buttons to the frame by selecting the Option Button tool in the Toolbox and then clicking inside the frame. You might need to rearrange controls to make more room or enlarge the frame by dragging the white size handle boxes that appear at each side and corner of the frame. Give your option buttons these properties:

- Option button 1:

```
(Name)          optBirthdays

Caption         Birthdays

Value           False
```

- Option button 2:

```
(Name)          optAnniversaries

Caption         Anniversaries

Value           False
```

- Option button 3:

```
(Name)          optBoth

Caption         Both

Value           True
```

---

**Note:** From now on, the suggested property settings shown for new controls won't include the `Accelerator` property. You already know how to set it and that it makes forms easier for keyboard users to navigate.

---

Setting the `Value` property on the `optBoth` button to `True` makes it the default choice. Run your form. It should look like that shown in Figure 3.10. Try clicking on each of the three option buttons. Can you select more than one at a time?

To make the `chkUpdate` button use the information from the option buttons, replace the existing `cmdUpdate_Click` procedure code with that in Listing 3.3.

Compare the first `If` statements in Listing 3.3 with the same statement in Listing 3.2. Both check the subject of a Calendar folder item for the text "Birthday" and the value of one or more controls on the `ReminderUpdate` form. Listing 3.2 checks for the value of the `chkBirthday` control with this expression:

```
chkBirthdays.Value = True
```

where Listing 3.3 uses this expression:

```
(optBirthdays.Value Or optBoth.Value)
```

Like check boxes, option buttons on VBA forms can have a value of `True` or `False`. The syntax `optBirthdays.Value` is shorthand for `optBirthdays.Value = True`. The `Or` in the above expression means that the expression returns `True` if the value of either `optBirthdays` or `optBoth` is `True`, that is, if either button is selected.

**Figure 3.10**
*Option buttons
make it easy to
select among three
or more choices.*

**Listing 3.3**  *Use option button values to get the user's choice*

```
Private Sub cmdUpdate_Click()
    On Error Resume Next
    Dim objNS As NameSpace
    Dim objCalendar As MAPIFolder
    Dim objItem As AppointmentItem
    Dim strSubject As String
    Dim lngMinutes As Integer

    Set objNS = Application.Session
    Set objCalendar = _
      objNS.GetDefaultFolder(olFolderCalendar)
    lngMinutes = 24 * 60 * txtDays.Value

    For Each objItem In objCalendar.Items
        strSubject = objItem.Subject
        If InStr(strSubject, "Birthday") > 0 And _
          (optBirthdays.Value Or optBoth.Value) Then
            objItem.ReminderSet = True
            objItem.ReminderMinutesBeforeStart = lngMinutes
            objItem.Save
        End If
        If InStr(strSubject, "Anniversary") > 0 And _
          (optAnniversaries.Value Or optBoth.Value) Then
            objItem.ReminderSet = True
            objItem.ReminderMinutesBeforeStart = lngMinutes
            objItem.Save
        End If
    Next
End Sub
```

### 3.7.3  List box and combo box controls

Check boxes and option buttons make it easy for users to choose among several preferences. However, these can take up a lot of space on a form. Sometimes, you have so many choices that no room would be left for other controls if you used an option button to show each choice.

This is where list box and combo box controls come in handy. These controls, which are very similar to each other, let users select from a potentially large number of choices. List boxes restrict users to the range of choices you provide. Combo boxes can allow users to pick from a list or, optionally, type in a new value. The familiar dropdown boxes that you see in many Windows programs (e.g., the Priority list on any Outlook item) are combo boxes that have been designed not to allow the user to type in a new value. Figure 3.11 shows a variety of list and combo boxes on a VBA user form. The style and behavior of list and combo boxes are controlled by the properties listed in Table 3.3.

**Figure 3.11**
*List and combo boxes come in many varieties to suit many purposes.*

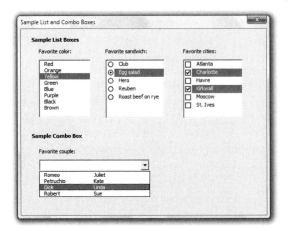

**Note:** If you set the `Multiselect` property to anything other than `0 - Single`, you cannot use the `Value` property to find out what the user has chosen. Instead, you must check the `Selected` property for each row to learn whether it has been marked. The expression `ListBox1.Selected(index)` returns `True` if the `index` number row is selected. Chapter 8 includes an example of how to check the `Selected` property with a `For ... Next` loop.

**Table 3.3**   *Key List and Combo Box Properties*

| Property | List Box | Combo Box | Description |
|---|---|---|---|
| BoundColumn | X | X | In a multicolumn list or combo box, specifies which column is bound to a data field (default = 1) |
| ColumnCount | X | X | Number of columns (default = 1) |
| DropButtonStyle | | X | Sets the symbol on a combo box's button (default = 1 - Arrow) |
| ListRows | | X | Number of rows to display in a combo box's drop-down list |
| ListStyle | X | X | Shows the list with or without a check box or option button for each item. Use 0 - Plain for no check boxes. Use 1 - Option for option buttons on single-selection lists and combo boxes. Also use 1 - Option to display a check box on each row in a multiselect list box. |

**Table 3.3**   *Key List and Combo Box Properties (continued)*

| Property | List Box | Combo Box | Description |
|---|---|---|---|
| MatchEntry | X | X | Controls how the list or combo box tries to match what the user types. Use 0 - First Letter to display the next entry on the list that matches the last character the user typed. Use 1 - Complete to search for an entry matching all user-typed characters and 2 - None to perform no matching. |
| MatchRequired | | X | Determines whether the user's text must match an item on the list (default = False) |
| MultiSelect | X | | Determines whether the user can select more than one item from a list box. Use 0 - Single to restrict the user to one selection, 1 - Multi to allow multiple selection with additional mouse clicks, and 2 - Extended to allow the user to click and then Shift+click to select a range of adjacent entries from within the list. |
| ShowDropButtonWhen | | X | Determines when the user sees a combo box's button. Use 0 - Never to always hide the button, 1 - Focus to show it only when the user is in the control, and 2 - Always to always show it. |
| Style | | X | Determines whether a user can type a new value into a combo box. Use 0 - DropDownCombo to allow both new values and values in the list and 2 - DropDownList to force the user to pick from the list. |
| TextColumn | X | X | In a multicolumn list or combo box, determines which column to use for the Value property of the control. |

You can use the AddItem method to fill a list box, one row at a time. Here is the code used to fill the lstColors list box for Favorite Colors, shown in Figure 3.11.

```
lstColor.AddItem "Red"
lstColor.AddItem "Orange"
lstColor.AddItem "Yellow"
lstColor.AddItem "Green"
lstColor.AddItem "Blue"
lstColor.AddItem "Purple"
lstColor.AddItem "Black"
lstColor.AddItem "Brown"
```

The code to initialize a list box like this usually runs in the UserForm_Initialize event handler of a VBA form.

**Tip:** For multiple column list and combo boxes, such as the "Favorite couple" list in Figure 3.11, you would use a different technique to fill the list box—the `List` method, which fills it from a two-dimensional array of values. Chapter 8 provides an example.

### 3.7.4   Accelerators and tab order

Earlier in this chapter, we saw that the `Accelerator` property of VBA form controls can help keyboard-preferring users get around your form easily. Users who move from control to control by pressing the Tab key appreciate a logical *tab order*. The tab order determines which control gets the focus as the user presses the Tab key to move around the form.

**Tip:** You can direct the focus to a particular control programmatically by calling the `SetFocus` method for the control, for example, `txtDays.SetFocus`.

To see how to set the tab order, return to the `ReminderUpdate` form. Right-click on any empty area of the form, and then choose Tab Order to display the Tab Order dialog. Figure 3.12 shows the tab order after the form has been modified to include the option buttons described earlier. (see Figure 3.12). You can also choose View | Tab Order. Now you see why it's so important to give distinctive names to your controls! If we had left the command buttons as `CommandButton1` and `CommandButton2` instead of renaming them to `cmdUpdate` and `cmdClose`, it would have been much harder to figure out how to adjust the tab order.

**Tip:** Did you notice that the Tab Order dialog itself consists of a label, a list box, and four command buttons?

Use the Move Up and Move Down buttons to rearrange the Tab Order list to match the order in which controls appear on the form itself. The final order should be:

```
fraOptions
txtDays
cmdUpdate
cmdClose
```

Don't worry about the label controls, since the user does not actually interact with them.

What happened to the option buttons? They are actually inside the `fraOptions` frame, which has its own tab order. To set the tab order inside

**Figure 3.12**
*Compare the order of controls listed here with the form shown in Figure 3.11.*

a frame, right-click the frame, then choose Tab Order and make the necessary adjustments.

**Tip:** To exclude a control from the tab order, set its `TabStop` property to `False`. The control will still appear in the Tab Order window but will be bypassed when the user presses Tab to move through the form's controls. You can also use the `TabOrder` property to change the tab order without going through the Tab Order dialog.

After you change the tab order, run the form and press Tab to move through the controls. Does the order seem logical to you?

**Note:** If you choose a right-to-left tab order for one form, don't use a top-to-bottom tab order for another form in the same application. Be consistent, both within a form and within a group of forms that work together.

## 3.8  Summary

If you've followed this walkthrough in the Outlook VBA environment on your own machine, you should be proud of your accomplishment—building your first working application in VBA, one that adds a useful function to Outlook. Among the techniques covered are how to add many types of controls to a VBA form, how to work with a VBA form and control properties, and how to add code to a command button.

The code demonstrated a key Outlook technique that you will use time and time again—looping through a folder to examine each item in the folder. Don't worry if you don't know how to write such code from scratch or don't quite understand how it works yet. Feel free to skip ahead to Chapter 7 if you want to dig deeper into writing code right now.

The next chapter introduces the other kind of forms that Outlook supports: custom forms to display the data from individual items.

# 4

# *Introducing Outlook Forms*

Every Outlook item has an associated form that determines how that item looks when the user opens it. A contact form has special controls for displaying a picture and an electronic business card. A message form includes controls for entering and choosing recipients. In a task or appointment form, you can set a start date and a reminder. Six of the forms—message, contact, appointment, task, journal, and post—are commonly customized to provide additional functionality to Outlook. (The distribution list form is rarely customized. The one type of Outlook item that has no customizable form is the note item, found in the Notes folder.) A custom Outlook form not only can provide a different visual layout, but also can run code to respond to the user's interaction with the form and the item that it displays.

To get you started with Outlook custom forms, this chapter gives a guided tour of the six main standard forms. This should give you an idea of which form might be best for a particular project.

The highlights of this chapter include discussions of the following:

- How Outlook custom forms differ from VBA user forms
- The two types of custom Outlook forms
- How to start and end an Outlook forms design session
- What information each form can store
- Where to save finished forms
- How to get help with Outlook forms design

## 4.1 Understanding the two types of custom forms

Outlook custom forms are very different from the VBA user forms that we learned about in the previous two chapters. While both allow you to position controls to display data and provide opportunities for user interaction, an Outlook custom form, unlike a VBA user form, automatically displays an actual Outlook data item. How does Outlook know which form to use to display an item? Each Outlook item contains a `MessageClass` property, whose value tells Outlook which form to use. For example, almost every e-mail message in your Inbox has a `MessageClass` value of IPM.Note, which tells Outlook to display each message using the standard message form. If you received a message with a message class of IPM.Note.MyForm, Outlook would attempt to locate the custom form for that message class. If no such form exists on your system, Outlook would display the message with the standard IPM.Note form.

**Note:** We'll take a more detailed look at the Outlook forms architecture in Chapter 21, "Deploying and Managing Outlook Forms."

Microsoft provides two different techniques for customizing Outlook forms. The older technique, which we'll refer to as "legacy custom forms," has been available since Outlook 97. The newer technique, form regions, is completely new in Outlook 2007.

Legacy custom forms were intended for use in organizations using Microsoft Exchange as their mail and collaboration server, where custom Outlook forms could be integral to data gathering, workflow, and public folder-based applications. In non-Exchange environments, the older type of custom form was useful mainly for personal productivity applications, such as a custom task form to help coordinate time spent on tasks with time spent in meetings.

Starting with Outlook 2007, Outlook custom forms become an integral part of any application that wants to store and present data within the Outlook interface. What makes this possible is a new way of customizing the standard forms, called *form regions*. With form regions, developers can build a user interface for Outlook items with a set of Windows-themed, Outlook-aware controls, rich enough to almost completely duplicate any built-in form page.

A key difference between form regions and legacy custom forms is that the latter support VBScript code embedded in the form, while with form regions, the layout and the code are totally separate. If a form region needs business logic, an associated Outlook add-in must provide it. Building add-ins is a topic beyond the scope of this book, but form regions have some potential applications that don't involve add-ins. Advantages of form regions over legacy custom forms include:

- Support for a new set of Outlook-specific controls, including an Outlook-aware date/time picker and an info bar control, all supporting Windows themes so that the forms conform to the user's Windows color choices

- Ability to show controls in the reading pane
- Local storage of form regions, avoiding the forms cache problems that can plague traditional custom forms, which must be published to an Outlook forms library
- When used with add-ins, support for control-related events
- Ability to replace or add to the existing tabs on a form
- Support for different icons for read, unread, replied to, and forwarded messages
- Localization features to support the use of a single form region in multiple language environments

Both legacy custom forms and the newer form regions use the same forms designer. In this chapter, we'll see how to use the designer to create traditional custom forms, and then in Chapter 5, we'll move on to form regions.

## 4.2 Starting the forms designer

Every Outlook custom form starts from another Outlook form, rather than from a blank page. This is one of the big differences between Outlook custom forms and VBA user forms. To start designing an Outlook form, choose Tools | Forms | Design a Form from the main Outlook menu. The Design a Form dialog shown in Figure 4.1 appears, listing the forms in the Standard Forms library. This library holds the six basic forms that we'll tour in this chapter, along with other forms that you won't usually customize.

You can't modify the forms in the Standard Forms library. Instead, use them as templates for new custom forms. After you select the form you want to start from, click Open to display the form in the Outlook forms designer. For example, if you select the appointment form, the Outlook

**Figure 4.1**
*Select a form as a template for your form design project.*

forms designer displays a new custom appointment form, not a new version of the appointment form in the Standard Forms library.

**Note:** The Look In list in Figure 4.1 can display other places where Outlook forms may be stored—in the Personal Forms library, in Outlook folders, in the Organizational Forms library on an Exchange server, or in the file system. You can use these forms as templates for creating new forms, in addition to the forms in the Standard Forms library. Later in this chapter we will learn more about where Outlook stores its custom forms.

You can also design a form based on an existing item—for example, a mail message that already contains text that you want the custom form to display. Click on the Developer tab, and then click Design This Form.

**Note:** If you don't see the Developer tab on the ribbon, choose Tools | Options, and then switch to the Mail Format tab and click Editor Options. In the Editor Options dialog, check the box for "Show Developer tab in the Ribbon," and then click OK. The next time you open an Outlook item, you should see a new tab, Developer, on the ribbon. The Developer tab will remain available to all subsequent Outlook sessions, until you turn it off again in the Editor Options dialog.

## 4.3    The six standard Outlook forms

Another big difference between Outlook custom forms and VBA user forms is that custom forms already have a lot of functionality built into them. VBA user forms, on the other hand, have no built-in functionality. If you want a VBA form to perform some task, you must write all the code required to make that happen. Outlook forms already know how to send messages, calculate dates, and perform other operations.

A third difference is that VBA forms have no built-in connection to any kind of data records, while Outlook custom forms are user interface/code templates for working with Outlook's data records. Throughout this book, we try to make a clear distinction between the data record—that is, the *item*—and the *form*—that is, the user interface that displays an item. When you click the Save button on an Outlook form, you are saving an appointment or contact or some other type of item. While it is possible to design an Outlook form that doesn't actually save an item, that's a fairly rare application.

The next few sections introduce all six basic forms to help you understand which form might be best suited for a particular task.

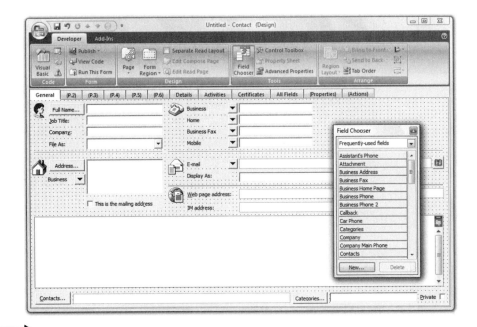

**Figure 4.2**   *The grid of dots indicates that you can customize the General page of a contact form.*

### 4.3.1   The contact form

Let's start with the contact form, opening it with the Tools | Forms | Design a Form command. Figure 4.2 shows a custom contact form open to its main *page*. Each tab that you see in design mode, starting with General and ending with (Actions), represents a page that you can either show to the user or hide. The user sees these pages not as separate tabs, but as separate commands in the Show group on the ribbon, which you see enlarged in Figure 4.3.

---

**Tip:** To toggle a page's visibility to users, in design mode, click on the page's tab, and then click Page | Display This Page.

---

**Figure 4.3**   *Users switch between pages on Outlook forms using the commands in the Show group.*

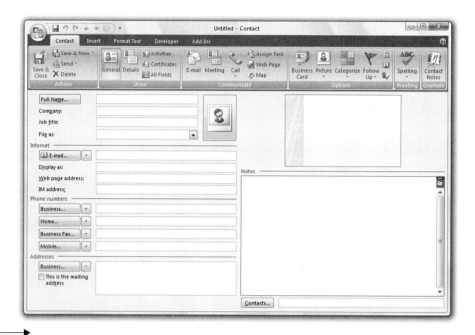

**Figure 4.4**    *The uncustomized General page of a contact form looks quite different from the page you can customize (Figure 4.2).*

What you may find surprising is that the customizable main page of the contact form bears little resemblance to the uncustomized page, which is shown in Figure 4.4. If you make any change at all to the General page, it takes on the layout shown in Figure 4.2. Because the unmodified layout uses several special controls, which are available only to form regions, it is not possible to duplicate the unmodified layout in a legacy custom form. If you want to preserve the look of the built-in page, but just add a few extra fields, then consider using a form region, described in the next chapter, rather than a legacy form. Alternatively, you can put all your customizations on one of the blank pages, such as the P.2 page shown in Figure 4.5. Any page that you customize automatically will appear in the Show group on the ribbon.

Each legacy custom form supports five blank, customizable pages. You cannot add more pages to a legacy form. You can, however, add a multipage control that simulates the appearance of multiple pages by putting a tabbed interface on the form.

The Details page of the contact form, shown in Figure 4.6, is not customizable, because it contains date/time fields. You cannot customize any page that contains a dropdown calendar control, except through custom form regions or by installing an ActiveX date/time control on your system.

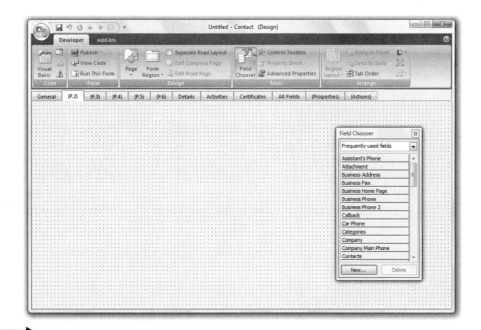

**Figure 4.5**    *Each form contains five blank pages you can customize.*

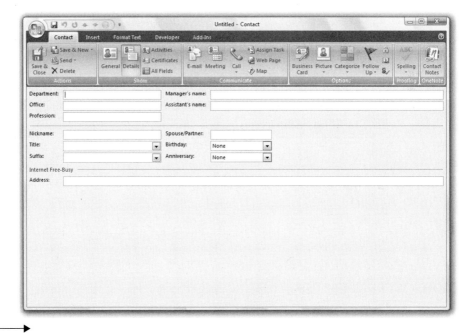

**Figure 4.6**    *The Details page holds additional information about each contact, but is not a customizable page.*

You can, however, hide the built-in pages and use the same fields on your custom pages, only using text boxes instead of date pickers.

One of the distinctive features of the contact form is that it allows you to see other items that are linked to the current contact, either through a direct link or through one of the contact's email addresses. The Activities page of the contact form (see Figure 4.7) searches other Outlook folders to find items related to the current contact. The Show list normally defaults to All Items. If you change it—for example, to Upcoming Tasks/Appointments—Outlook does not save that change with the custom form. The default activities list is a property of the contacts folder, not the contact form. On the contacts folder's Properties dialog, you can change the default activity list and create new activity groups that show data from different folders.

**Note:** An activities group can show multiple folders only in a single Personal Folders .pst file or in an Exchange Server mailbox. It cannot display multiple Exchange public folders or combine items from two different .pst or mailbox stores.

Only contacts have this built-in ability to show related items. That's why you sometimes see a custom contact form used to hold data about items that aren't exactly contacts, but do have related items, such as a project and

**Figure 4.7**   *The Activities page of the contact form tracks related items in other Outlook folders.*

its related tasks, meetings, and contacts. Chapter 20 discusses the Activities page as a key element of linking Outlook items.

The Certificates page shown in Figure 4.8 is unique to the contact form and not customizable. The (All Fields), (Properties), and (Actions) pages are common to all Outlook forms. We will look at them later in the chapter.

The contact form has some limitations. As noted above, if you customize the first page of a contact form, you lose certain features that appear only on the built-in General page:

- The customized General page will have a gray background, rather than the Office theme color that the uncustomized page shows, and won't have themed buttons and other controls.

- The Add Contact Picture control is not available for customized pages.

- The Business Card section won't be visible.

Also you cannot do the following with a custom contact form:

- Add address fields beyond the three that Outlook supports (Business, Home, and Other) or change the display names on the dropdown list for the built-in address fields.

- Add telephone fields to the dropdown list of built-in phone fields or change the display names for the built-in fields.

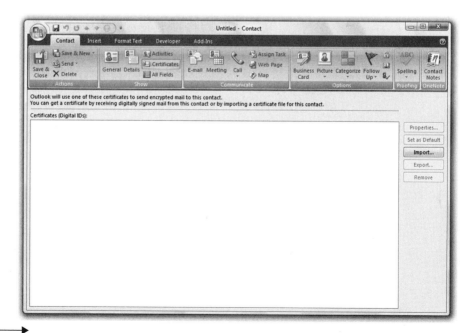

**Figure 4.8**    *The Certificates page of the contact form displays digital security certificate information.*

■ Add more email address fields beyond the three that the form supports or change the display names for the three built-in email address fields. In other words, you can't change "E-mail" to "Work" and "E-mail 2" to "Home."

Finally, contacts created with a custom form will not trigger Outlook's feature that checks for duplicates among existing contacts before saving the current item.

### 4.3.2   The appointment form

Outlook supports three forms that can store date/time information: the appointment, journal, and task forms. What's the difference between them? Each appointment must have a start date and an end date, even for all-day events. On a task, both the start date and the due date are optional. A journal entry has only a start date and measures the time that has passed since that date with a duration field. Both appointments and tasks can display reminders, but journal entries can't. Appointments and tasks also support the concept of recurrence—appointments and tasks that repeat themselves automatically. Because the built-in pages of these forms contain date/time fields, none of those pages are customizable. Instead, use the P.2–P.5 pages or form regions.

Figures 4.9 and 4.10 show the Appointment and Scheduling pages of the appointment form.

**Figure 4.9**
*The appointment form holds information about meetings and events.*

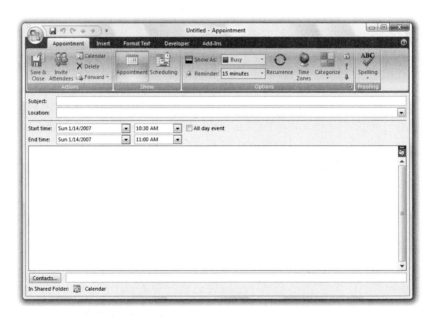

**Figure 4.10**
*The Scheduling page of the appointment form shows the times when people are free for meetings. This view shows the scheduling features available with Exchange 2000 or 2003. Users connecting to Exchange 2007 will see more advanced scheduling options.*

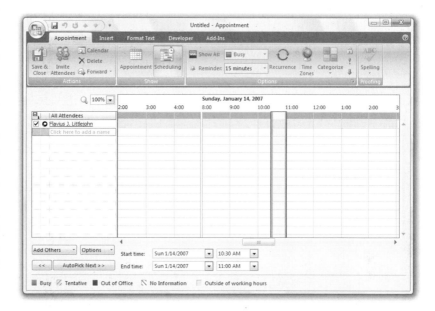

A key built-in feature of appointment forms is the ability to see the meeting availability of other people and to invite other people to meetings. The controls on the Scheduling page depend on what version of Exchange you're connecting to.

### 4.3.3 The task form

The second form that can handle date/time information is the task form. Its two built-in pages, Tasks and Details, neither one customizable, appear in Figures 4.11 and 4.12. Users typically create task items to build a to-do list for themselves or for people they work with.

### 4.3.4 The journal entry form

The journal entry form, shown in Figure 4.13, has just one built-in page, the General page, which you cannot customize. The unique feature of journal entry items is that they display commands to start and stop a timer that keeps track of how much time you spend on a particular activity.

### 4.3.5 The message form

The message form, shown in Figure 4.14, is probably the most familiar of all Outlook forms, because it appears each time you create a new email message. Because the built-in Message page of this form can be customized, you may be tempted to use it for all kinds of Outlook projects, especially those

**Figure 4.11**
*The first page of the
task form holds the
most important
information about
each task.*

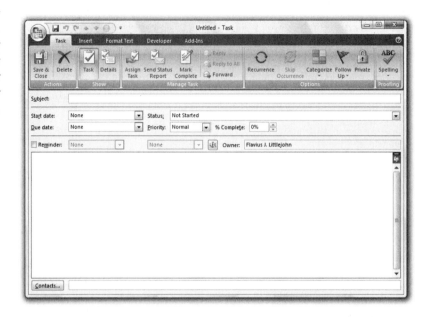

that involve routing information from one person to another. But as we'll
see in Chapter 20, custom message forms work well only in a few limited
scenarios.

One feature that the message form has in common with the post form is
that, by default, it shows different layouts to the sender and the recipient of
the message. Click the Edit Read Page layout button to view the default lay-

**Figure 4.12**
*The Details page of
the task form holds
tracking and other
details.*

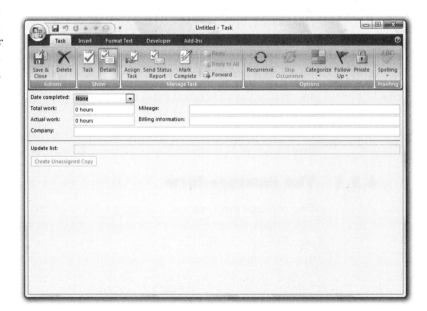

**Figure 4.13**
*The journal entry
form tracks the
time you spend on
different activities.*

out that a recipient would see, as shown in Figure 4.15. Click the Edit
Compose Button to return to the original layout. The presence of two distinct layouts explains why a message you compose looks different from a
message you receive. If you add a control or field to the compose layout,
Outlook does not automatically add it to the read layout for you.

All forms support separate compose and read layouts, as we will see in
Chapter 6, "Extending Form Design with Fields and Controls." However,
only the message and post forms show separate compose and read layouts
by default.

**Figure 4.14**
*You can use the
message form to
create forms that
exchange
information with
other Outlook
users.*

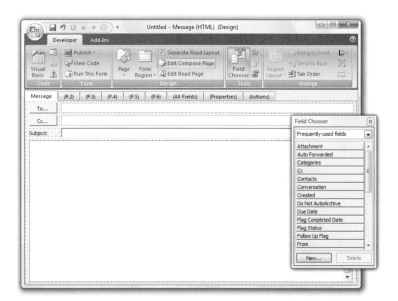

**Figure 4.15**
*Message forms
normally use
distinct layouts for
unsent and sent
layouts. This is the
layout users see by
default when they
read messages.*

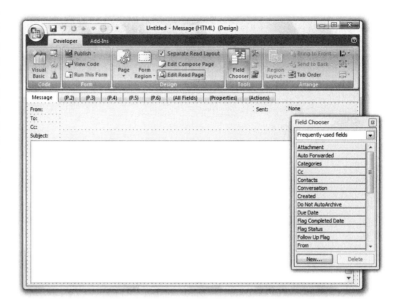

---

**Tip:** Before opening a message form in design mode, turn off your automatic signature in Tools | Forms | Mail Format. Otherwise, your personal signature will become part of the message on your custom form.

---

As with the contact form, customizing the message form has its costs. If you customize the first page, you lose the *infobar* that displays information about the item, such as the last reply or forward. A more serious consequence is that if you create a message using a custom form and include attachments, non-Outlook recipients will not even see those attachments, much less be able to open them. Therefore, message forms have only a limited scope of usefulness, mainly inside organizations where everyone is using Outlook as their email program.

### 4.3.6  The post form

The post form, shown in Figure 4.16, is even simpler than the message form. It is used for posting information directly to a particular folder and, therefore, does not require the To or Cc buttons and boxes associated with the message form.

### 4.3.7  Additional forms

In addition to the six basic forms, the Design Form dialog box (refer to Figure 4.1) also lists Meeting Request <Hidden> and Task Request <Hidden>. These are actually variations on the appointment and task forms that add a

**Figure 4.16**
*You can customize
the post form for
use in any kind of
Outlook folder.*

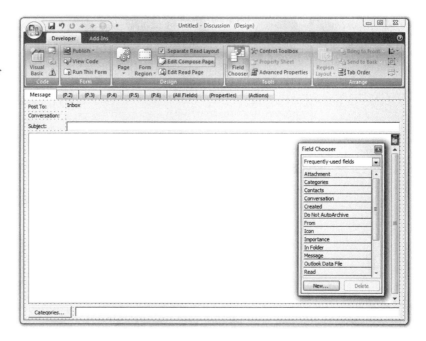

To button and a box for addressing items to meeting attendees or task recipients. When you customize one of these forms, you are actually customizing the appointment or task form. One important quirk to be aware of is that, if you put VBScript code in the Meeting Request form, the code does not run when the user opens the meeting request item or when Exchange 2007 accepts the meeting request automatically. Such code runs only when the user accepts the meeting request manually.

It is also possible, oddly enough, to customize the distribution list form by creating a new list and then using the Design This Form command to open it in design mode. In Chapter 7, we'll see an example of a custom distribution list form that uses VBScript code to keep a running count of the number of recipients in the list.

**Note:** The one type of Outlook item that doesn't support custom forms at all is the "sticky" note in the Notes folder.

### 4.3.8 Common form pages

Every form also includes three other pages: (All Fields), (Properties), and (Actions). The names appear in parentheses because these pages are normally hidden, except on the contact form, which shows the All Fields page by default.

The All Fields page lists the fields available for use in the form, along with their current values. A *field* is a single piece of information related to an Outlook item and stored in that item. Each type of Outlook form uses a distinct set of fields. For example, the contact form has three fields for holding fax numbers, but these do not appear on the task form. A synonym for field is *property*. (Outlook uses "field" in its user interface, but "property" in developer documentation.)

From the Select From list at the top of the All Fields page, you can choose which set of fields to work with. For example, to see all the fields available in a contact form, choose All Contact Fields. You then see the list shown in Figure 4.17. You can also choose Frequently Used Fields or Name Fields, and so on, to see a smaller subset of the many fields available in a Contact item.

---

**Note:** Not all the data stored in an item is exposed through fields visible on the form. Items also contain properties that are hidden from the user interface. As we will learn in Chapter 14, "Using PropertyAccessor and Storage-Item," you can return the value of these properties with Outlook 2007's new `PropertyAccessor` object.

---

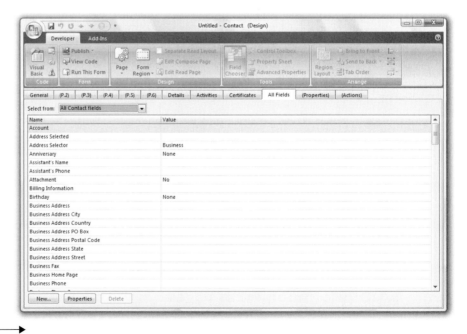

**Figure 4.17**    *The All Fields page shows every field visible in the user interface, but not hidden properties.*

You might also notice the choices for User-Defined Fields in This Item and User-Defined Fields in This Folder, as well as a New button at the bottom of the page. You can create your own fields in Outlook, as described in Chapter 7.

The (Properties) page, shown in Figure 4.18, controls various settings for the form, including the following:

- The icon it displays
- The version number
- An optional category and subcategory to help you track forms if you have many of them
- A contact for the form
- A description

Many of these properties, such as Contact and Description, are especially important if you create forms that other people will use. The version number can assist with troubleshooting. Outlook has no built-in scheme for form versioning. So, devise your own! At the very least, start with 1 and increment the version number each time you change the form. Alternatively, use integers for major versions and a decimal place for minor changes.

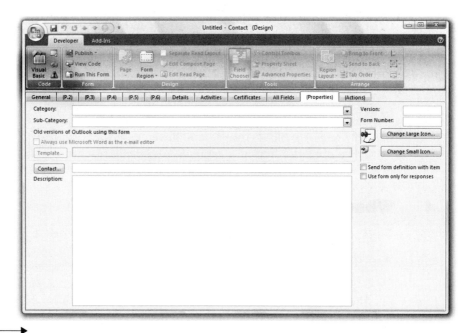

**Figure 4.18**     *The (Properties) page handles information that identifies the form.*

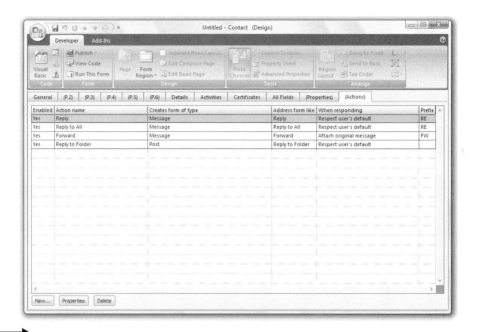

**Figure 4.19**   *The (Actions) page controls commands that appear on the Actions menu.*

---

**Note:** Previous versions of Outlook allowed you to set a form password on the (Properties) page, but it was never secure. Outlook 2007 eliminates form passwords completely.

---

The last page is the (Actions) page, shown in Figure 4.19. It controls what happens when the user performs standard actions, such as Reply, Reply to All, Forward, and Reply to Folder. You can also add custom actions that add new commands to the Actions menu and toolbar, as you will see in Chapter 20.

## 4.4   When to use which form

How do you know which form to use? One approach is to make a pencil-and-paper sketch of the form you have in mind for your project and then find the closest match among the six Outlook forms. You can also look at the (All Fields) page to get a sense of which forms include which fields. You should use the built-in fields as much as possible. It is rarely possible to use a built-in field from one type of item on another type of item. For example, just because the All Contact Fields includes a Business Phone field doesn't mean you can add it to a custom task form and have Outlook automatically insert the phone number for a contact linked to a task.

Fields are just one factor to consider, though. Since you can always customize a form with new fields, most of the time your choice should depend on the functionality you need. For example, if your project involves sending messages back and forth in a kind of workflow, you will probably customize the message form. If the information is gathered in one specific folder, the post form might be appropriate, or—if reminders are needed—either the appointment form or task form.

Don't feel that you must use a particular form only for its original purpose. For example, if you want to keep track of how much time you spend on a project, you can use any of the three forms that include fields to measure time: the appointment, journal entry, and task forms. Since the contact form is the only form with an Activities page, you could use it as the basis for a project form, with all the related components—people, meetings, tasks, and so on—containing a link back to an item using your project form. The parent project would then show on its Activities page all the linked items.

**Note:** The field where users create such links does not display by default. To show it, a user can choose Tools | Options | Contact Options and check the box for "Show Contact Activity information on all forms." Administrators can manage this setting with Group Policy Objects.

As we saw at the beginning of this chapter, the Design Form dialog box (refer to Figure 4.1) has a Look In list from which you can select various locations where forms are stored. Any form you previously modified should appear in one list or another. You can select that modified form and base a new form on it. For example, if you create a new contact form that includes more fields and want to use those same fields in a new project, start with your modified form, rather than going back to the original contact form.

You can also open any Outlook item, make changes to it, and click the Design This Form command on the Developer tab to use that particular item as the starting point for a custom form. Use this approach when you want to include specific default text in the body of an item or if the form you want to customize does not appear on the Standard Forms list. We have already discussed a custom distribution list form as one example of this technique. Another good example is a form with voting buttons. Although you can set the voting options on the (Actions) tab, it's more convenient to set them by creating a new message, switching to the Options tab, then clicking the Use Voting Buttons command. You can then publish the form, as described later in this chapter, to make it easy to reuse. Figure 4.20 shows a custom document transmittal form with voting buttons, as the user would see it. Notice that the main tab on the ribbon is named "Document Trans-

**Figure 4.20**
*Voting buttons
provide an easy
way to create a
custom transmittal
form.*

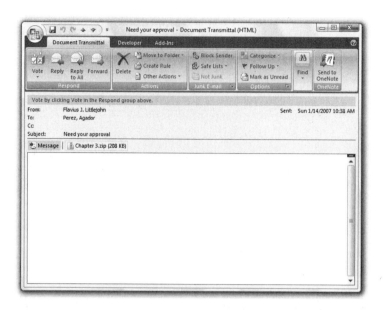

mittal," which is the display name for the published form. That name also
appears on the window caption.

A final word about message forms: Security concerns have reduced the
number of scenarios where a custom message form is effective. In order for
a message form to run code or show custom fields for both the sender and
the recipient, both users need access to the published form definition. This
requirement means that the form must be published to either the Organizational Forms library on Exchange or to each individual user's Personal
Forms library. In many scenarios, neither is possible. While there are still a
few good uses for custom message forms, particularly in generating a structured message from user inputs, you cannot count on being able to use a
message form for surveys, workflow, or other collaborative tasks unless you
can meet these form publishing requirements. Check on the publishing
environment first, before you invest time in a message form design.

## 4.5    Working in the forms designer

Completing this tour of the Outlook forms design environment are three
tools you will use often: Field Chooser, Control Toolbox, and Help. Later
in the chapter, when we walk through the creation of a custom contact
form, we will see two other tools: Property Sheet and Advanced Properties.

### 4.5.1    Controls and the Control Toolbox

The buttons, check boxes, dropdown lists, and boxes for entering text on
the form are all examples of *controls* that make up a custom form's user

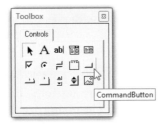

**Figure 4.21**
*Pause the mouse
pointer over any
control in the
Toolbox to see the
name of the
control.*

interface, just as we saw in the previous chapter that controls are the building blocks for a VBA user form's interface. Controls determine how users will enter data, view information, and otherwise interact with the form.

A control can be linked or *bound*, to an Outlook field; if the user changes the data shown in a bound control, the data in the Outlook field also changes, and vice versa. A form also can display *unbound* controls. The data shown in these controls is not tied to Outlook fields. The contents of unbound controls are temporary. When you close the form window, Outlook discards any values from those controls. Thus, in most cases where you want the user to enter data to be saved with an Outlook item, you should use a bound control.

To see the types of controls you can use, click the Control Toolbox button on the ribbon. This will display the Toolbox, shown in Figure 4.21. The easiest way to learn the names of the controls is to place your mouse pointer over a control without clicking. After a moment, the name of the control appears in a screen tip.

**Tip:** Later in this chapter, we'll add screen tip pop-up text to a control on a custom contact form to make it easier for users to understand what the control does.

## 4.5.2   **The Field Chooser**

When you first open a form in design mode and view a customizable page, the Field Chooser appears. As shown in Figure 4.5, it lists the fields you can add to the page. It defaults to Frequently Used Fields, but like the All Fields page, you can click the dropdown arrow at the top of the Field Chooser to either all available fields or a particular subset.

To turn off the Field Chooser, click the close (x) button in its upper-right corner, or click the Field Chooser command in the ribbon to toggle it off.

Dragging a field from the Field Chooser to a page on your form adds a bound control to display the data in that field. In most cases, it also adds a matching label control. Remember that with a bound control, if the user changes the data shown in the control, the data in the Outlook field also changes, and vice versa.

### 4.5.3 Getting forms design help

To get access to Outlook's Help library on form design topics, press F1 while working in form design mode. The main page for Outlook Developer Help will appear. To locate general custom forms topics, click on Concepts, then Forms, then Custom Form Basics. To learn how to write code to work with individual controls on Outlook custom forms, on the main page for Outlook Developer Help, click on Outlook Forms Script Reference.

## 4.6 Saving forms and ending a design session

When you have done enough work on a form for one design session, save the form using one of these two methods:

- Save the form as an Outlook form template .oft file anywhere on your computer.
- Publish the form to a folder or to one of Outlook's special custom forms libraries.

---

**Caution:** You cannot save the form design for reuse by simply closing the form design window and choose Yes to the "Do you want to save changes?" prompt. Instead, you should publish the form in most cases and, to maintain a backup, save it as an .oft form template file.

---

In general, you should do both. Save interim versions as .oft files throughout the design process, so that you always can revert to an earlier version without the latest changes, and make a backup .oft file of the final version. To put a form into actual use, you almost always will need to publish it. You may also want to publish interim versions during the design process as part of your testing.

### 4.6.1 Understanding published forms

*Publishing a form* means saving it to a form library using the Publish Form and Publish Form As commands. Published forms offer several advantages over forms saved as .oft files:

- VBScript code runs only published forms.
- Custom fields that you define in a form are visible only on items created from published forms.

- By default, only published forms can run ActiveX controls that don't ship with Outlook.

- For items created with published forms, the form definition is not normally stored with the item. This means that if you have 5kb worth of data and 200kb worth of form design, items created with your published form are 5kb in size, while items created with the comparable .oft file would be 205kb in size.

To publish a newly customized form based on one of the built-in forms, click the Publish | Publish Form command. When you publish a form, you must tell Outlook what forms library to store it in. Table 4.1 lists the three types of form libraries where you can publish forms. If you don't use Microsoft Exchange as your mail server, you won't see Organizational Forms. Also, some organizations may have Exchange, but not implement an Organizational Forms library, or you may not have permission to publish forms there. Furthermore, you cannot publish new forms to the Standard Forms library; it is reserved for Outlook's built-in forms.

If you publish a form to a folder, the folder's Actions menu will list that form with a "New <name of form>" command. (You will not see this command for any form whose "Use form only for responses" box is checked on the (Properties) dialog.)

If you created your custom form from an existing published form, do not use the Publish | Publish Form command, as that will overwrite the existing published form. Instead, use the Publish | Publish Form As command to publish the form to a different location or with a different name. In the Publish Form As dialog box (see Figure 4.22), use the Look In drop-down list or the Browse button to select a location. Then, give the form a

**Table 4.1**     *Outlook Forms Libraries*

| Library | Description |
| --- | --- |
| Personal forms | The library of forms maintained in your default information store (Exchange Server mailbox or Personal Folders .pst file). |
| Organizational forms | A library of forms stored on the Exchange Server for group use; you need permission from the Exchange administrator to publish to this library. |
| Libraries for individual Outlook folders | Each folder can contain its own library of forms associated with that folder. You must have owner permission to publish to a folder outside your own mailbox and .pst files. |

**Figure 4.22**
*Publishing a
custom contact
form to the
Contacts folder.*

display name and form name, and click Publish. As Figure 4.22 shows, the
display name and form name do not need to be identical.

**Note:** Chapter 21 explains how to remove old forms and convert existing
items to use a new form.

## 4.6.2 Understanding .oft form template files

Saving a form as an .oft template file is a good way to make a backup file. It
is also a good procedure to use if you create a message form with predefined
recipients or text. To save a form as a template file, follow these steps:

1.  Click the Office logo at the upper-left of the form design window,
    and then choose Save As.

2.  In the Save As dialog, under "Save as type," choose Outlook
    Template (.oft). The path under "Save in" list will change to the
    default location for .oft files, which is the %appdata%\
    Microsoft\Templates folder for your Windows login profile. You
    can save .oft files in any other folder on your computer, but if
    you use the Templates folder, you'll be able to find them more
    easily when you use the Tools | Forms | Choose Form or Design
    a Form command.

3.  Give the file a name and click Save.

If the .oft file contains no custom field definitions, you can run it simply
by double-clicking the saved file to open it. If it does contain custom field
definitions, you will need to use the Tools | Forms | Choose Form com-
mand to run the form and the Tools | Forms | Design a Form command to
open it in the forms designer.

Note that a saved .oft file runs no VBScript code. Only published forms can run code.

# 4.7 Creating your first custom contact form

Now that you are acquainted with the Outlook forms design environment, it's time to go to work and create your first custom form—a contact form. In the process, you'll see how to add and modify form pages and the controls that the user interacts with.

Creating a custom form requires a series of steps that should occur in the same order every time:

1. Pick a standard form to start with.

2. Add and modify controls on the pages that can be customized.

3. Test the form.

4. Repeat steps 2 and 3 as necessary to complete the form layout.

5. Set the basic properties of the form.

6. Save a backup copy of the form as an .oft file.

7. Publish the form.

As an example, we're going to build a new page on a custom contact form to learn about some of the frequently used fields that don't appear on the standard General and Details tabs.

## 4.7.1 Adding fields

To begin, use the Tools | Forms | Design a Form command to open a blank contact form in design mode, and then click on the (P.2) page. The Field Chooser should appear with the list of frequently used fields displayed. If it doesn't, click the Field Chooser command in the Design group.

To place a field on the form, drag it from the Field Chooser to the form page. Start with the `Business Home Page` field. Outlook automatically places the field at the top left of the blank page. Next, drag the `Personal Home Page` field to the form. See how Outlook automatically places it directly beneath the first field. Now drag two more fields from the Field Chooser: `Journal` and `Customer ID`. Both are available on the All Contact Fields list in the Field Chooser. Check your form against Figure 4.23.

Also, notice that the name of the page, P.2, is no longer in parentheses. Outlook assumes that if you add fields to a custom page, you want users to see them, so it automatically sets the page to be visible to the user. Both the `Home Page` fields display their data in a control called a *text box* (because the user can normally type text into it). Text boxes are probably the most commonly used form control in Outlook.

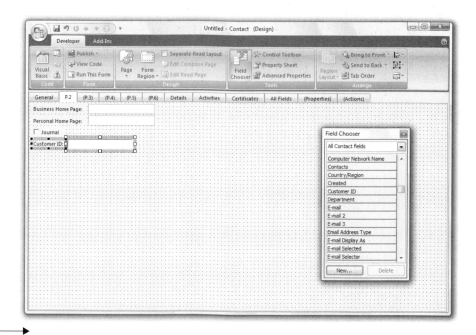

**Figure 4.23**   *This custom page shows four fields dragged from the Field Chooser.*

The text that tells you the name of the field, such as `Business Home Page` for the first field, is called a *label*. Label controls are a key element in making forms easy to understand. Not only do they describe different fields, but you can also use them to provide detailed instructions on the form page.

---

**Tip:** Outlook saves you time by adding a label control for most fields that you drag from the Field Chooser. Some controls, such as check box controls, do not need label controls nearby because they include their own `Caption` property.

---

The `Journal` field uses a *check box* control to allow the user to turn automatic journaling for a contact on and off. This type of control has only two values: on/off, true/false, or yes/no, which are all equivalent.

## 4.7.2   Rearranging controls

When you drag text fields from the Field Chooser, Outlook lines up any accompanying label controls on the left side of the form, then puts the text box controls adjacent to the label controls. Since the label controls have different widths, this can leave the right side looking sloppy. The check box control automatically puts the caption on the right side, so neither the box nor the caption lines up well with any other control. Your next task, therefore, is to make the text box fields and check box align neatly along their left edges.

You could move each control individually. For example, click the Journal field's check box to select it. The box now appears with a gray line around it and eight white boxes called *drag handles* at the corners and sides; you can use these to resize the control. If you move the mouse pointer over one of the sides (but not over a drag handle), the pointer turns into a four-sided arrow. When you see the four-sided arrow, hold down the left mouse button and drag the field to a new location on the form.

There is an easier way to line up those controls, though. You can select a group of controls and then use a layout command to align them.

First, you need to know how to select multiple controls. Earlier, you clicked on one control to select it. To add another control to the selection, hold down the Ctrl key as you click a different control. Continue using Ctrl+click to include the three text boxes and check box in your selection. If you select one of the labels by mistake, use Ctrl+click to deselect it. You can also click anywhere on the background of the form to clear all selections and start over completely.

Did you notice that the drag handles for the last control you clicked are white, whereas those for the controls are black? The control with white drag handles acts as the model for alignment and resizing operations. In this case, you want to line up everything along the left edge of the Business Home Page field's text box, so make sure that you select it last. If one of the other fields was the last selected, use Ctrl+click twice on the Business Home Page text box to make it the last selected. Figure 4.24 shows how the selected controls should look.

**Tip:** You can also select a group of adjacent controls very quickly by holding down the left mouse button and dragging it diagonally across the controls.

With the desired controls selected, click the Align command in the Arrange group, then choose Left. You can also right-click the selected controls and choose Align | Align Left. Repeat the alignment process with the label controls, but choose Align | Align Right for them. After aligning the controls, they should look like Figure 4.25.

**Tip:** If you change the layout of your form and don't like the way it looks, press Ctrl+Z to reverse the last change you made.

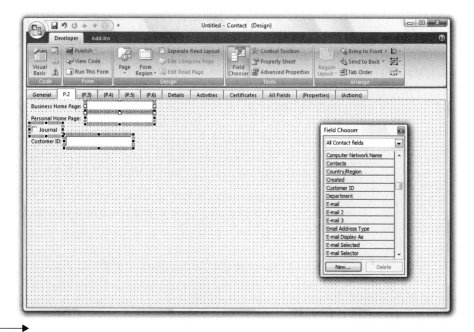

**Figure 4.24**     *When multiple controls are selected, the one with the white drag handles controls any group sizing and alignment operations.*

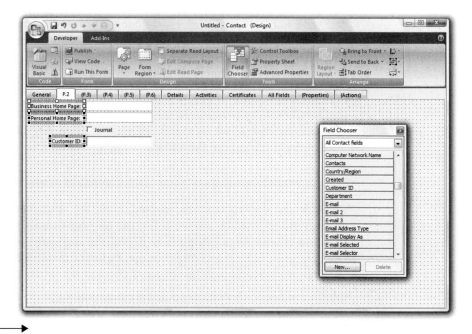

**Figure 4.25**     *Controls that are the same size and aligned along one edge are easier on the user's eye.*

The Arrange group contains other commands, such as Bring to Front and Send to Back, that can help you adjust the layout of your controls. The Tab Order command helps you set the *tab order*, which controls what field gets the focus of the cursor when the user presses Tab or Shift+Tab to move out of a control. We'll come back to the tab order below.

### 4.7.3   Showing, hiding, and renaming pages

Now that your controls are looking neat, you can give that custom page a more descriptive name. To rename a page, in the Design group, choose Page | Rename Page, and type in the new name, for example "Home Pages / Customer ID."

---

**Tip:** Do not use the ampersand (&) character in page names. That character will disappear when you run the form.

---

To hide or show a page, choose Page | Display This Page. A check mark next to the Display This Page command indicates whether the user will see the current page. You can also look at the page name. In design mode, the names of hidden pages are in parentheses.

### 4.7.4   Setting control properties

To finish working with the controls on this, your first custom Outlook form, you need to make some adjustments to their properties. Custom form controls have properties similar to those on the VBA user form controls that we saw in Chapter 3. Outlook divides custom form control properties into two groups: the basic ones you are most likely to want to use and advanced user interface and behavior properties that are less commonly changed.

To work with the basic properties, select a control and then click the Property Sheet command in the Design group (see Figure 4.21) or right-click the control and choose Properties. Figure 4.26 shows the basic properties on the Display tab.

---

**Note:** You will learn about the properties on the Value and Validation tabs in Chapter 6.

---

Every control needs a name to distinguish it from other controls in the tab order and in any programming code you write. Outlook assigns a name automatically. For example, the `Journal` field's check box control, depicted in Figure 4.26, has the default name `CheckBox1`. You should change the name, at least for controls where the user enters data. (Changing the name

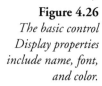

**Figure 4.26**
*The basic control
Display properties
include name, font,
and color.*

of label controls is a less urgent task.) Names should be descriptive, not cryptic; no spaces are allowed. A good descriptive name will help you remember the purpose for the control and make it easier to rearrange the tab order and to write code to work with the controls on the form.

It's important when writing code to know what kind of control you're working with, since different controls have different properties. I recommend using the prefixes in Table 4.2 to help distinguish the different types of controls.

For example, instead of CheckBox1 as the name for the control displaying the Journal field, you could use chkJournal. Similarly, you might change the name of the text box for the Customer ID field to txtCustomerID.

Figure 4.27 shows what the Tab Order dialog looks like after those two controls' names have been changed. It is easy to tell where the chkJournal and txtCustomerID controls appear in the tab order, but you have no way of knowing which fields are associated with the _RecipientControl1 and _RecipientControl2 controls, which still have the names that Outlook automatically assigned to them. (These are the controls for the two Home Page fields. They're not standard text boxes, because they support live

**Figure 4.27**
*Compare the order
of controls listed
here with the
form shown in
Figure 4.25.*

**Table 4.2** *Recommended Outlook Form Control Name Prefixes*

| Control | Prefix |
|---------|--------|
| Label | lbl |
| Text Box | txt |
| Combo Box | cbo |
| List Box | lst |
| Check Box | chk |
| Option Button | opt |
| Toggle Button | tgl |
| Frame | fra |
| Command Button | cmd |
| Tab String | tab |
| Multipage | mlt |
| Scroll Bar | hsb (horizontal) or vsb (vertical) |
| Spin Button | spn |
| Image | img |

hyperlinks.) Use the Move Up and Move Down commands in the Tab Order dialog to change the order.

**Tip:** Controls on a VBA user form also have a tab order that you can adjust in a similar fashion.

Table 4.3 lists Name and the other control properties from the Display tab in the Properties dialog.

Next, click on the Layout tab, shown in Figure 4.28. Here you'll find settings for the control's size and position, as listed in Table 4.4.

The Top, Left, Height, and Width properties also appear on a different Properties dialog box that appears when you right-click any control and then choose Advanced Properties from the pop-up menu. (You can also display it with the Advanced Properties command in the Design group.) You can leave this advanced Properties dialog open as you select controls, even multiple controls.

**Table 4.3**   *Outlook Form Control Display Properties*

| Property | Description |
| --- | --- |
| Name | Unique descriptive name |
| Caption | Text on label, check box, option button, toggle button, frame, or command button |
| Font | Font name, size, style, and color |
| Foreground color | Text color, using the Windows color scheme |
| Background color | Background color, using the Windows color scheme |
| Visible | Can the user see the control? (Yes/No) |
| Enabled | Can the user click on or enter information in the control? (Yes/No) |
| Read only | Can the user change the control's data (Yes/No) |
| Sunken | Add a 3-D look? (Yes/No) |
| Multi-line | Wrap text in a text box, and create a new line when the user presses Enter? (Yes/No) |

**Note:** The two Properties dialog boxes work differently with respect to multiple controls. If you select multiple controls and click Property Sheet, the dialog box controls the properties only for the last control you selected. But if you click Advanced Properties, the dialog box controls the properties for all selected controls. You can use that feature to quickly set the font or width of several controls with one action.

**Figure 4.28**
*Set control size and position on the Layout tab.*

**Table 4.4**   *Outlook Form Control Display Properties*

| Property | Description |
|----------|-------------|
| Top | Position relative to the top edge of the form design surface, in pixels |
| Left | Position relative to the left edge of the form design surface, in pixels |
| Height | Control height, in pixels |
| Width | Control width, in pixels |
| Resize with form | Shrink and enlarge the control when the overall form changes size? (Yes/No) |

Text box controls show a total of 42 properties; other controls have more or fewer, as needed. To change any property, select it in the Properties list and then look at the top of the dialog for either a dropdown list of choices or a text box where you can type in a value. Click the Apply button after you make your choice or type in the new property value.

For example, Figure 4.29 shows the Properties dialog for the Journal check box. Outlook provides this field so you can specify whether you want Outlook to automatically create an entry in the Journal folder whenever you create a new Outlook item related to a particular contact. In case the user is not familiar with this feature, you can change the `ControlTipText` property to add text that pops up when the user pauses the mouse over the check box control. Figure 4.30 shows how a user will see the control tip on the finished form.

### 4.7.5   Testing the form

At any time, you can see how your form will look to a user by choosing Run This Form in the Form group. A new instance of the form appears, as in Figure 4.30, with all the changes you have made to the form so far.

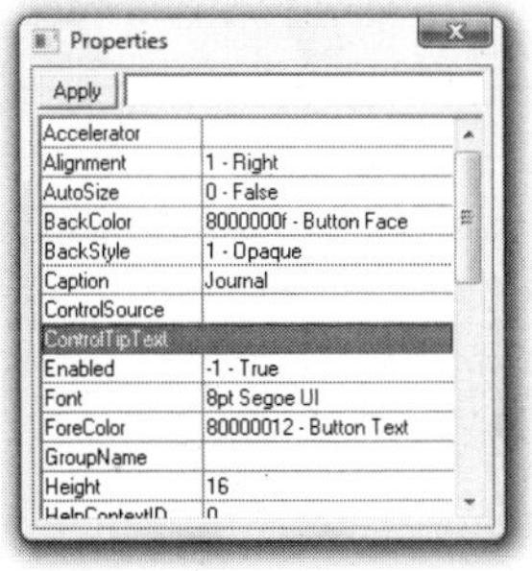

**Figure 4.29**
*Set advanced properties for an Outlook custom form control with this window.*

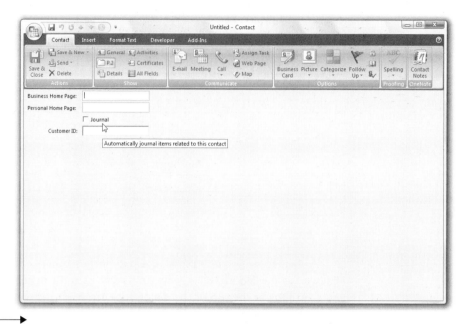

**Figure 4.30**   *The user sees the control tip from the ControlTipText property by pointing the mouse at the control.*

Notice that the page you customized is now listed in the Show group on the ribbon.

You can close the test form with the close (**x**) button at the upper-right corner of the form and return to your working copy of the form, which remains open in design mode. If you get a prompt to save changes, choose No. (This is a prompt to save the item created with the form, not to save the form design.)

## 4.7.6    **Setting form properties**

When you are satisfied with the form's layout and have tested it, it's time to set the operational properties for the form, before you save or publish it. Click on the (Properties) tab to switch to that page, shown in Figure 4.31. This page is normally hidden from users running the form.

---

**Tip:** If the form is too wide for your display monitor and you can't see the (Properties) tab or other tabs on the right side of the form, press Ctrl+Page Down to move through the different form pages one by one.

---

You will almost always want to set the Version, Contact, and Description and also the two icons. Other settings may be optional, depending on the purpose of the form and the environment where you will use it.

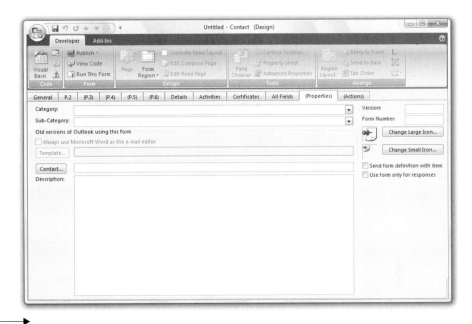

**Figure 4.31**   *Set the form's operational properties on the (Properties) page.*

The version should be a number, increased every time you update the form and publish a new edition. You can use a numbering sequence like 1.0, 1.1, 1.2 and so on, or a sequence as simple as 1, 2, 3, 4, 5. Users can see the version number when they select a form from the Tools | Forms | Choose Form dialog (Figure 4.32).

By default, custom forms always use the same icon as the post form, a yellow slip of paper with a pushpin through it. To change either the large or small icon, click the appropriate button. Then choose an icon from the

**Figure 4.32**
*Information you
enter on the
(Properties) page of
a form's design can
help users select the
right form.*

*.ico files on your system. If Outlook is installed in the default location, you will see many icons in the C:\Program Files\Microsoft Office\ Office12\Forms\1033\ folder. If Outlook is installed somewhere other than C:\Program Files\, look in that other location for the Office12\ Forms\1033\ folder. The folder name 1033 denotes the folder for U.S. English components. Other locales' components will be in other folders. If you want to use the same icon as the standard contact form, choose Contactl.ico for the large icon and Contacts.ico for the small icon. The l and s at the end of the icon file name stand for the large and small versions of the same icon.

---

**Tip:** Use the Search command in Windows to locate more *.ico files on your computer. You can use any icon with Outlook that is exactly $32 \times 32$ pixels in size. The small Outlook icon is $32 \times 32$, just like the large icon, but only the $16 \times 16$ pixels at upper left contain the icon image.

---

The Contact and Description fields should contain information about how the form should be used and whom to contact in case of questions or problems. This information appears when the user chooses Tools | Forms | Choose Form and selects your custom form.

Take a quick look at the less frequently used form properties. Set a Category and optional Subcategory if you use a hierarchy of categories to organize forms, either in your own folders or in the Organizational Forms library. (These categories are not related to the categories you can set on individual Outlook items.) You can add a Form number, in addition to the Version number, to identify your form as part of your organization's classification scheme.

If you are creating forms that users of older versions of Outlook will use, you can require a custom message or post form to use Word as the email editor along with a particular Word template .dot file. This option is available only if your default message format is set to Microsoft Outlook Rich Text in the Tools | Options | Mail Format dialog, and it has no effect on forms used in Outlook 2007.

---

**Note:** Earlier versions of Outlook supported a form password, but this feature provided very little security. Outlook 2007 no longer supports form passwords at all. If you have code behind a form that you want to protect, then you probably should be using a form region and an Outlook add-in, not a traditional custom form.

---

---

**Caution:** Do not check the "Send form definition with item" box. It is an obsolete setting held over from versions of Outlook that did not have as many security features as Outlook 2007. If you check that box, code on the form will not run, even if you publish the form. Items saved or sent with that form will also be much larger, because they will contain both the item data and the form definition (a state known as a *one-off* form).

---

If you want to prevent the user from launching a form directly, check the "Use form only for responses" box. That way, the form works only when launched with a code statement or in conjunction with another form that includes the current form among its custom actions. Custom form actions are covered in Chapter 20.

### 4.7.7   Saving and publishing the form

You have finished your first customized contact form! Make a backup copy by clicking the Office icon at the upper-left and then choosing the Save As command, as described earlier in Section 4.6.2, "Understanding .oft form template files." You should also click the Publish command in the Form group to publish the form either to your Contacts folder or to your Personal Forms library. Remember that when you publish it, you must give it both a display name that will appear on the title bar of new instances of the form and a unique form name that will become part of the form's message class. Often these are the same, but they don't have to be.

### 4.7.8   Using the form

If you like this form so much that you want to use it for every new contact, publish it to your Contacts folder. Then, bring up the Contacts folder's Properties dialog and under "When posting to this folder, use," select the name of your published form, and then click OK or Apply. All new contacts in that folder will use that form. In Chapter 21, we'll see a VBA code procedure to convert all existing items to use a published custom form.

If you published the form to your Contacts folder but did not make it the default form for the folder, switch to the Contacts folder, and then look at the bottom of the Actions menu. You should see a new command there for New <Name of Your Form>. Click that command to create a new contact item using your custom form.

If you published to the Personal Forms library, choose Tools | Forms | Choose Form or File | New | Choose Form. In the Look In list, choose

Personal Forms, then select the form and click Advanced. As Figure 4.32 shows, the properties you entered in the (Properties) dialog provide helpful information to the user about the form.

## 4.8    Summary

This chapter has introduced you to the six standard Outlook forms you can customize and the techniques to start and end a design session and use the Field Chooser and Control Toolbox. You also learned about the different custom form libraries and should have a better idea of when to use which standard form as the basis for a custom form. You also learned that creating a custom form involves adding controls, adjusting their properties and those of the form itself, and publishing the form so you can reuse it easily. How you lay out the form and the properties you set can make the form more pleasing to the eye and easier to use. In Chapter 6, we'll learn how to add custom fields, set validation formulas, and build separate compose and read layouts. But first, we're going to look at another way of customizing Outlook forms that's totally new to Outlook 2007: form regions.

# *Introducing Form Regions*

**5**

Form regions arrive in Outlook 2007 as a new way to change the appearance of Outlook items and give them additional features. Most of the time, professional developers will combine form regions with Outlook add-ins to integrate their applications with the Outlook platform. However, form regions can also add functionality even when an add-in is not involved.

The highlights of this chapter include discussions of the following:

- The difference between adjoining and separate regions
- What new controls Outlook provides for custom form regions
- How to tell Outlook when to use a custom form region
- How to design a custom form region to display a contact's birth date and age in the reading pane

## 5.1 Understanding form regions

A *form region* can add a collapsible pane to an Outlook item's layout (hence the name form "region"), add a new page to a form, or replace all the pages on a form. You design custom form regions in the same Outlook forms designer that you saw in Chapter 4.

Form regions come in two flavors: adjoining and separate. Either can appear when composing a new item, reading an existing item, previewing an existing item, or all of the above, depending on the settings for the region.

An adjoining region appears at the bottom of the item's window or at the bottom of the reading pane. Multiple adjoining regions for the same type of item stack on top of each other. Each one is collapsible. Figure 5.1 shows an example of an adjoining form region to display a contact's age and the date you first made contact with this person. We will see how to build this region later in the chapter.

**Figure 5.1**
*An adjoining form
region displays as a
collapsible pane at
the bottom of an
open or previewed
item.*

A separate form region displays as a stand-alone page when the user opens the item. A separate form region can add a new page, replace the first page of a standard form, or replace all the built-in pages. However, a form region can replace existing pages only for Outlook items whose `Message-Class` property is not one of the default classes—IPM.Note, IPM.Contact, and so on. In other words, you can implement a replacement form region for a custom message class named IPM.Note.MyForm, but for the default message class for mail messages, IPM.Note, Outlook will display only separate form regions that add new pages.

**Note:** Remember that an item's `MessageClass` property determines what form that item will display. Look back at Figure 4.22, which shows the message class of a newly published form at the bottom of the Publish Form As dialog.

Microsoft Exchange 2007 Server, for example, uses replacement form regions to implement its "unified messaging" features that allow Outlook 2007 to listen to voice mail messages and view faxes in Outlook. To support those features, Outlook 2007 registers a form region for IPM.Note.Exchange.Voice and several other IPM.Note.* message classes.

Implementing a custom form region requires three steps:

1.  Design the region in the Outlook forms designer (yes, the same one we saw in Chapter 4). The design process is the same regardless of whether it's a separate region or an adjoining region.

2.  Create an .xml file (i.e., a text file using XML syntax) to tell Outlook where to find the form region and when to display it. This file is known as the *manifest* for the form region.

3.  Add an entry to the Windows registry telling Outlook which message class to apply the region to and where to find the manifest file with the other instructions.

After a review of the new controls that Outlook 2007 provides for form regions, we will walk through the creation of a form region and then see how to save and register it.

## 5.2 Controls for form regions

Outlook 2007 gives form regions a new set of controls that support Windows themes so that they have the same color scheme and other settings as most Windows dialogs. These controls make it possible to almost completely duplicate the look of Outlook's built-in form pages that are not customizable, such as the main page of the appointment form. Also available are Outlook-aware controls such as the "info bar" that displays information about the last time the user replied to or forwarded a message.

Before you can use these controls, you must add them to the Control Toolbox in the form designer. Right-click the Toolbox, and choose Custom Controls. In the Custom Controls dialog (see Figure 5.2), the custom form region controls all have names that begin with "Microsoft Office Outlook." Table 5.1 lists the controls designed specifically for custom form regions and whether they can be bound to an Outlook field.

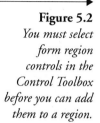

**Figure 5.2**
*You must select form region controls in the Control Toolbox before you can add them to a region.*

*Bound controls* display and set the data stored in the bound field. In other words, when you want to enter data into a control and have that data saved with the Outlook item that the form is displaying, you need to use a bound control. The table also lists the name that each control shows when you hover the mouse over the Control Toolbox to display the control's screen tip. This is also the control's object class name in the Outlook object model. The _DocSiteControl and _RecipientControl objects are hidden; you can see them, though, if you right-click in the VBA Object Browser and choose Show Hidden Members.

Even with this rich set of controls, perfectly duplicating the look and functionality of a page from a standard form may not be possible, but you should be able to come very close.

**Table 5.1**  *Microsoft Office Outlook Controls for Custom Form Regions*

| Control | Screen Tip and Object Name | Description | Can Be Bound? |
|---|---|---|---|
| Microsoft Office Outlook Body Control | _DocSiteControl | Display the message or notes (Body property) | No; already bound to the Body property |
| Microsoft Office Outlook Business Card Control | OlkBusinessCardControl | Display the electronic business card for a contact item | No; already bound to the BusinessCard-LayoutXml property |
| Microsoft Office Outlook Category Control | OlkCategory | Displays the names of the categories that the user selects by clicking the Categorize button | No; already bound to the Categories property |
| Microsoft Office Outlook Check Box Control | OlkCheckBox | Displays a check box and caption | Yes, to any yes/no (Boolean) property |
| Microsoft Office Outlook Combo Box Control | OlkComboBox | Displays a dropdown list of items for the user to choose from | Yes |
| Microsoft Office Outlook Command Button Control | OlkCommandButton | Displays a clickable button | Yes |
| Microsoft Office Outlook Contact Photo Control | OlkContactPhoto | Displays the photo for a contact item | No; used only for the contact photo |
| Microsoft Office Outlook Date Control | OlkDateControl | Displays a dropdown calendar where the user can select a date | Yes, to any date/time property |
| Microsoft Office Outlook Frame Header Control | OlkFrameHeader | Displays the top line and caption of a frame | Yes |

**Table 5.1** *Microsoft Office Outlook Controls for Custom Form Regions (continued)*

| Control | Screen Tip and Object Name | Description | Can Be Bound? |
|---|---|---|---|
| Microsoft Office Outlook Info Bar Control | `OlkInfoBar` | Displays information about the current item in a yellow "info bar" | No |
| Microsoft Office Outlook Label Control | `OlkLabel` | Displays non-editable text | Yes |
| Microsoft Office Outlook List Box Control | `OlkListBox` | Displays a list of items for the user to choose from | Yes |
| Microsoft Office Outlook Option Button Control | `OlkOptionButton` | Used in a set of two or more option buttons to allow the user to make one choice | Yes |
| Microsoft Office Outlook Page Control | `OlkPageControl` | Displays scheduling controls in appointment forms or, in message forms, a tracking grid | No |
| Microsoft Office Outlook Recipient Control | `_RecipientControl` | Displays a list of recipients or linked contacts | Only to fields related to email addresses: Assigned To, Bcc, Cc, Contacts, From, Have Replies Sent To, Optional Attendees, Required Attendees, Resources, and To fields, plus the three email fields on a contact |
| Microsoft Office Outlook Sender Photo Control | `OlkSenderPhoto` | Displays the sender photo in a mail message | No; used only for the sender's photo on messages |
| Microsoft Office Outlook Text Box Control | `OlkTextBox` | Displays editable or non-editable text | Yes |
| Microsoft Office Outlook Time Control | `OlkTimeControl` | Displays a dropdown list for choosing a time | Yes, to any date/time property |
| Microsoft Office Outlook Time Zone Control | `OlkTimeZoneControl` | Displays a dropdown list for choosing a time zone | No |

CHRISTIAN BROTHERS UNIVERSITY

---

**Caution:** Do not attempt to use any of the new `Olk*` controls in a legacy custom form. If you do, the form may become corrupted and lose all the VBScript code behind it.

---

# 5.3   Creating your first form region

To create a custom form region, you use the same form designer as we saw in Chapter 4. Let's look at a practical example. On the Outlook contact form, users must go to the Details page to enter a person's date of birth. In this example, you'll see how to add the `Birthday` field to the first page of the Contact form and to even add a field to calculate and display the person's current age on that page. Then, you'll add a second date/time field—this one with a dropdown calendar—to track the date of your first contact with each person.

Start by using the Tools | Forms | Design a Form command to open a contact form in design mode. Then choose Form Region | New Form Region. You should see a new tab with the name (Form Region) and a plain, blank gray page.

This form region will use the new-style label, text box, and date controls. If you haven't already added these, display the Control Toolbox, right-click it, choose Custom Controls, and add those controls.

Next, we'll put the controls on the region, starting with a text box for entering the birth date.

---

**Tip:** You don't really need a date picker control for the birth date, since you wouldn't normally want to scroll back through a few decades to find the original birth date in the dropdown calendar.

---

Since `Birthday` is an existing Outlook contact property, you can drag it from the Field Chooser to the form page. This adds an old-style text box and label control, not the new controls, but that's OK. When the form region displays at runtime, Outlook will automatically show the newer controls.

Outlook contains no property that automatically calculates a person's age, but you can add one by creating a new field that computes the value of a formula. In the Field Chooser, click New. Give the new field the name "Age," set the Type to Formula, and type in this formula:

```
IIf([Birthday]<>"None",
DateDiff("yyyy",[Birthday],Date())-IIf(DateDiff("d",
CDate(Month([Birthday]) & "/" & Day([Birthday]) & "/" &
Year(Date())),Date())<0,1,0),"")
```

Click OK to save the new field definition. Drag the Age field from the Field Chooser to place it to the right of the controls for the birthday.

**Note:** You'll learn more about formula fields and other kinds of Outlook custom properties in Chapter 6.

**Tip:** When designing an adjoining form region, arrange your controls so that they take up as little vertical space as possible, since an adjoining region stacks at the bottom of the reading pane or item window.

The next step is to create a new date field to hold the date of your first contact with an individual, along with a date picker control for that field. First, add a label control and a date control in line with the controls for the Birthday and Age fields. Change the caption for the label control to "First contact:" using the control's Properties dialog. Use the Align and Size commands to change the height and arrangement of the controls so that the form region looks like Figure 5.3.

The dropdown date picker in Figure 5.3 looks odd doesn't it? It shows a date of 12/30/1899. This is because it has not yet been bound to an Outlook field. We need to create a new field to hold that date and then tell the date picker to display the data from that field. This process is called *binding* the control.

To create the date field, return to the Field Chooser, click New again, and this time create a field with name "First Contact" and the type Date/

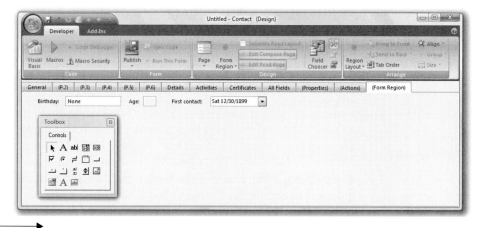

**Figure 5.3**    *Form region controls added to the Toolbox (bottom row) have a different look from the older form controls.*

**Figure 5.4**
*Use a bound
control to display
data from an
Outlook property.*

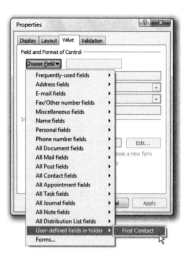

Time. From the Format dropdown list, choose any format that displays just the date, such as "Wed 7/5/06." Click OK.

Right-click the date picker, choose Properties, and switch to the Value tab. Click the Choose Field button, and from the "User-defined fields in folder" list, select First Contact, as shown in Figure 5.4. Also, under Initial Value, check the box for "Set the initial value of this field to" and type Date() into the blank box. Leave selected the default option for "Calculate this formula when I compose a new form." Those Initial Value settings mean that whenever you create a new contact, Outlook will automatically set today's date as the default value for the First Contact field. You will need to change it only if you met the person on some day other than today. Click OK to save the changes to this control. You should see the date displayed in the date picker change from 12/30/1899 to None.

---

**Tip:** The Properties dialog for each form region control includes a Layout tab where you can set the control's automatic alignment and resizing properties.

---

You've finished the form region design! Save your new form region by choosing Form Region | Save Form Region. Make a note of the location that you choose to save the region. Outlook saves form regions with an .ofs file extension. After you save the form region, click the close (**x**) button at upper-left to end the form design session, and choose No when you're asked to save changes.

---

**Tip:** To help organize your form region files, you may want to create a Regions folder on your hard drive and use a different subfolder to store the files for each region.

---

As described earlier, creating the region is just the first of three steps in implementing a custom form region. Before Outlook can use the form region, you must create a special text file to tell Outlook where to find the .ofs file and how to use it, and you must add some information to the Windows registry.

## 5.4 Registering and deploying form regions

After you have designed and saved an .ofs form region file, you next need to create an .xml manifest file with information about your form and also add information to the Windows registry to tell Outlook where to find the .xml file. You can create the file in any text editor, such as Notepad, and save it as a file with an .xml extension. Specialized XML editor tools also exist, but Notepad should be sufficient for the simple .xml files used by form regions. XML is case-sensitive, so if you are not using an XML editor, you need to take special care to use the correct case for any element names.

---

**Note:** *XML* stands for Extensible Markup Language. XML turns up in many places in Office 2007, from the storage of electronic business card details in Outlook to the hidden structure of Word, Excel, and PowerPoint documents. Superficially, it looks a little like the HTML source code for a Web page in that it contains tags enclosed in angle brackets like <this>. However, where HTML code is often concerned with formatting, XML concentrates on structure. It provides an organized way to describe complex structures using plain-text syntax. Because the syntax is in plain text, rather than some proprietary binary format, it is portable and readable both by human eyeballs and by applications like Outlook. Because the syntax is quite strict, it is possible to *validate* an XML document against a standard specification, called a *schema*, to determine whether that document contains "good" XML, as defined for that schema.

---

Let's start with a simple example. Listing 5.1 shows a manifest to display your new form region in the individual windows for new and existing contacts.

**Listing 5.1**    *XML manifest to display an adjoining form region*

```
<?xml version="1.0" encoding="utf-8"?>
<FormRegion xmlns="http://schemas.microsoft.com/office/
outlook/12/formregion.xsd">
  <name>FirstContactRegion</name>
  <title>Key Dates</title>
  <formRegionType>adjoining</formRegionType>
  <layoutFile>firstcontact.ofs</layoutFile>
  <showCompose>true</showCompose>
  <showRead>true</showRead>
  <showPreview>false</showPreview>
  <version>1.0</version>
</FormRegion>
```

**Note:** Individual item windows in Outlook are *Inspector* windows. The windows that display folders are *Explorer* windows.

The first line of the manifest (`<?xml ... ?>`) is a declaration that indicates this is an XML document and that it supports 8-bit Unicode character encoding. The rest of the document consists of *elements* that begin with an open *tag* consisting of the element name in angle brackets (e.g., `<FormRegion ...>`) and end with a matching close tag e.g., (`</FormRegion>`). XML documents typically include nested elements; in this example, you see the elements to describe an adjoining form region nested inside the `<FormRegion>` element. What looks like a Web page URL inside the `<FormRegion ...>` open tag is a reference to the XML schema (available as a reference from Microsoft) that defines form regions. When Outlook tries to load the form region, it validates the information in the manifest against this schema to determine whether all required elements are present, all values are appropriate, and so on. Only if the manifest is valid will Outlook load the form.

The first region element, `<name>`, is required. Outlook add-ins use this name for various standard coding tasks, but if you're loading a form region directly from an .ofs file rather than building an add-in, it doesn't serve any particular purpose.

The `<title>` element determines the title displayed for an adjoining region and the tab caption for a separate region.

**Tip:** Do not use an ampersand (&) character for the `<title>` element of separate form regions. Separate regions appear as separate pages, and Outlook ignores any ampersand in a form page name.

| **Table 5.2** | *Values for the <formRegionType> Element* |
| :--- | :--- |

| Value | Description |
| :--- | :--- |
| adjoining | An adjoining form region appears as a stacked, collapsible pane at the bottom of the reading pane or at the bottom of the main page of an item viewed in an Inspector window. |
| separate | A separate form region appears as a new form tab. (See below for information on the `<displayAfter>` element that determines the tab order.) |
| replace | A replacement form region replaces the first tab on a form. (Does not apply to standard message classes such as IPM.Note.) |
| replaceAll | A replace-all form region replaces the first tab on a form and hides all other standard tabs. (Does not apply to standard message classes such as IPM.Note.) |

Use the `<formRegionType>` element to specify whether the region should load as an adjoining region, a separate page, or a replacement page. This element is required. Table 5.2 lists the supported values.

The `<layoutFile>` element tells Outlook where to find the saved .ofs form region file. It can take three kinds of string values:

- A path relative to the location of the manifest file. If the .ofs file is stored in the same folder as the manifest, specify just the name of the file, as in Listing 5.1.
- A complete file path, such as C:\Data\Form Regions\firstcontact.ofs
- A file path with environment variables, such as %ProgramFiles%\ Microsoft Office\Office12\Addins\firstcontact.ofs

**Note:** An Outlook add-in that provides the storage for a form region would use the `<addin>` element to supply the `ProgID` value for the add-in, instead of using the `<layoutFile>` element to point to a file storage location. Either one or the other of these two elements must be present in the manifest, but not both.

The `<showCompose>`, `<showRead>`, and `<showPreview>` elements determine whether the form region is visible in the window for a new item, the window displaying an existing item, or in the Outlook reading pane, respectively. Each can take the Boolean value `true` or `1` to show the region and `false` or `0` to not show it. All three elements are optional and have a default value of `true`. In other words, if you do not include these elements, the form will appear in all three locations. I find it helpful to include all three even if each value is `true`, to make it absolutely clear in the manifest how Outlook will display the region.

The `<version>` element is an optional element that allows you to provide a string value to indicate the form version. For replacement and replace-all form regions, this version number will appear on the Tools | Forms | Choose Form dialog.

How does Outlook know when to use a form region and which one to use? The third step in deploying a form region is to modify the Windows registry to tell Outlook that the form region is available and where to find its settings. Run the Regedit.exe application and navigate to this registry key:

```
HKEY_CURRENT_USER\Software\Microsoft\Office\Outlook\
FormRegions
```

To deploy the First Contact form region created earlier in this chapter so that it is visible on all Outlook contacts, create a new key named IPM.Contact (the message class for the standard contact form). Under the IPM.Contact key, add a string value that refers to this particular region (e.g., "First Contact") and set its value to the full path to the manifest (e.g., C:\Form Regions\First Contact\firstcontact.xml). Figure 5.5 shows you what the registry should look like.

---

**Note:** The IPM.Note.* regions shown in Figure 5.5 are installed automatically with Outlook to provide support for Exchange 2007 Unified Messaging features.

---

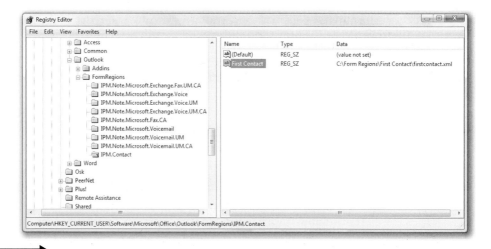

**Figure 5.5**    *A registry value points Outlook to the form region manifest, which in turn contains all the information Outlook needs to load the form.*

**Figure 5.6**
*Adjoining form
regions stack and
can be collapsed.*

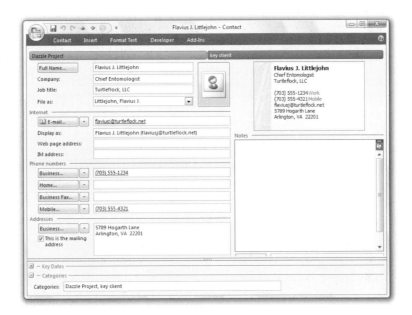

Restart Outlook, then open an existing or new contact to see the form region in action. Since the manifest specifies it as an adjoining region, it appears at the bottom, as shown in Figure 5.1.

**Tip:** To collapse the ribbon and leave more screen room for the contact information, as shown in Figure 5.6, double-click any of the tabs on the ribbon.

Once you register a form region in the registry, if you need to make subsequent changes to the region, you do not need to restart Outlook or make any changes to the manifest file. Just save the changes as a new .ofs file with the same file name, the name referred to in the manifest's `<layoutFile>` element.

## 5.4.1   Other form region manifest settings

In the previous section, you saw some of the settings for the `<FormRegion>` elements that define how Outlook uses a form region. Only four are required: `<name>`, `<title>`, `<formRegionType>`, and either `<layout-File>` or `<addin>`. Listing 5.2 shows another example of a manifest for a form region, this time for a separate form region to replace the first page on a custom task form, but only for Inspector windows, not in the reading pane.

**Listing 5.2**  *XML manifest to display a separate form region*

```
<?xml version="1.0" encoding="utf-8"?>
<FormRegion xmlns="http://schemas.microsoft.com/office/
outlook/12/formregion.xsd">
  <name>TaskWorkRegion</name>
  <title>Task</title>
  <formRegionType>replace</formRegionType>
  <layoutFile>taskwork.ofs</layoutFile>
  <showCompose>true</showCompose>
  <showRead>true</showRead>
  <showPreview>false</showPreview>
  <contact>Sue Mosher (sue@turtleflock.com)</contact>
  <icons>
     <default>taskwork_default.ico</default>
     <window>taskwork_window.ico</window>
  </icons>
  <version>1.0</version>
</FormRegion>
```

An optional element related to form region display is `<hidden>`, which applies only to replacement and replace-all form regions. It controls whether such regions will appear on the Actions menu for the appropriate folders and on the Choose Form dialog for creating a new item. It also takes Boolean values. If you do not include this element, the default value of `false` will apply, which means that the custom form will appear on the Actions menu for all folders of the appropriate item type (e.g., all contact folders) and in the Tools | Forms | Choose Form dialog. Use `true` instead if you do not want the form to appear on the Actions menu or Choose Form dialog.

The optional `<contact>` element provides contact information for the form region.

The optional `<displayAfter>` element contains the internal name of the form region that the current region should follow. Remember that the `<name>` element sets that internal name. This element is relevant for separate and replace-all regions.

The optional `<icons>` element can contain elements for defining the icons associated with various states of the form. As with the `<layoutFile>` element, the paths can be relative or exact and support environment variables. Table 5.3 lists the available icon elements.

Microsoft's official documentation for form region manifests can be found in Help, starting with Help topic HV10204449, "Using the Form Region XML Manifest to Define a Form Region." This topic includes information on other optional elements such as `<customActions>` to add custom actions and `<stringOverride>` to localize the display names of

**Table 5.3** *Form Region Manifest Elements That Control Icons*

| Element Name | Description |
|---|---|
| `<default>` | Default icon |
| `<window>` | Icon used for the window displaying the form region |
| `<page>` | Icon displayed for the region in the ribbon |
| `<unread>` | Icon used when the form's item is unread |
| `<read>` | Icon used when the form's item is read |
| `<replied>` | Icon used when the form's item has been replied to |
| `<forwarded>` | Icon used when the form's item has been forwarded |
| `<unsent>` | Icon used when the form's item is unsent |
| `<signed>` | Icon used when the form's item has been digitally signed |
| `<encrypted>` | Icon used when the form's item has been digitally encrypted |
| `<submitted>` | Icon used when the form's item has been submitted but not sent |
| `<recurring>` | Icon used to identify that the item is recurring |

controls and other strings. The `<formRegionName>` element is used by separate, replacement, and replace-all regions to set the name of the page shown in the Show group on the ribbon; if not present, the `<title>` element is used. The `<loadLegacyForm>` element applies only to replacement and replace-all regions and has a default value of false, which tells Outlook not to look for a legacy custom form of the same message class as the region. If `<loadLegacyForm>` is set to true, Outlook will both load the region and try to locate a legacy form, which could slow down performance.

## 5.4.2 Other considerations for deploying form regions

As you've seen in this section, the components related to a form region consist of .ofs and .xml files and a registry key and values. This simple architecture means that you can create a form region on one machine and deploy it to one or many other machines, using the same tools that you would use to deploy other files and registry changes, such as login scripts or the Office Customization Tool included in the Office 2007 Resource Kit.

The example earlier in this chapter showed deployment of the necessary registry key to the HKEY_CURRENT_USER hive of the registry. Alternatively, you could use the same key, only in the HKEY_LOCAL_MACHINE hive, to deploy a form region to a machine and make it available to all users of that computer.

The keys in the FormRegions key work in an additive fashion, each level inheriting the regions from the lower levels. A form region for the IPM.Contact.Sales.Manager message class would display form regions registered for IPM.Contact and also for IPM.Contact.Sales as well as any regions for IPM.Contact.Sales.Manager.

## 5.5    Limitations of form regions

Custom form regions have two limitations when compared with traditional custom forms:

- They do not support VBScript code behind them. Instead, all business logic is handled with code in an Outlook add-in.
- A form region must be registered on every machine that needs to use it. There is no concept of a centralized registry of form regions analogous to the Organizational Forms library for legacy custom forms.

Creating an Outlook add-in requires an additional developer tool, such as Microsoft Visual Studio Tools for Office, and is not covered in this book.

---

**Caution:** All controls for form regions that display in the reading pane should be set for read-only access. If you leave a control editable, and the user presses the Delete key with the focus in a form region control in the reading pane, Outlook will delete the entire item, instead of deleting text in the control. This means that you may need two versions of a particular region—one with read-only controls deployed with a manifest containing the element `<showPreview>true</showPreview>` and a second version with editable controls and the element `<showPreview>false</showPreview>`.

---

One final limitation; Microsoft does not support designing Outlook form regions in any screen resolution other than 96 dots per inch (dpi). Outlook automatically scales the appearance of text on the screen at runtime if the machine is using a different resolution. But for the scaling to work properly, the form region must be designed at 96 dpi.

## 5.6    Other ideas for form regions

Even with the above limitations, form regions open up some opportunities for building Outlook enhancements. One particularly interesting possibility is consolidating information in the preview pane that formerly required the user to open an item to see it. For example, you could show the tracking tab for messages using the Microsoft Office Outlook Page Control in an adjoining form region. Use the Advanced Properties dialog to change the value of the `Page` property for this control from the default value, `0-Planner`, to the other possible value, `1-Tracker`.

Another kind of enhancement is adding simple data entry. Do you prefer to type in the names of categories, rather than use the Categorize button? If so, you can create an adjoining form region with a text box control bound to the Categories field. Compare Figure 5.6, which shows the Key Dates region collapsed above a second region, Categories, with Figure 5.1.

## 5.7   Summary

The new form regions feature in Outlook 2007 overcomes many past custom form limitations, such as forms cache corruption and no reading pane layout, and provides a rich control environment. The new controls that can help you duplicate the look of almost any standard form page include date and time pickers, an info bar, a control to display tracking information, and controls to show contact pictures and electronic business cards. Although adding business logic to form regions requires building an Outlook add-in, there are still many codeless form region applications that can help you display data in the reading pane and provide the user with new data entry controls.

**6**

# *Extending Form Design with Fields and Controls*

Once you know how to create and save simple customized forms and form regions, you can move on to enhancing forms with more custom fields of different types and more controls. You also can make Outlook forms display different information depending on whether you are composing a new item or viewing an existing item.

The highlights of this chapter include discussions of the following:

- How controls are linked to fields
- How to create custom fields and add them to forms
- Why it's a good idea to use Outlook's built-in fields whenever possible
- How to use formulas to combine information from various fields and prevent users from making data-entry mistakes
- What gives sent messages a different layout from newly composed messages

We'll also review the basic controls available for Outlook forms and offer some tips for using them.

The information in this chapter about creating fields and setting control properties applies not only to custom Outlook forms but also to the new form regions in Outlook 2007. Remember, though, that the new Olk* controls for form regions should not be used on legacy custom forms.

## 6.1    Understanding fields versus controls

The previous two chapters showed how to add built-in fields to an Outlook form or to a form region to make it easier to store and retrieve the information from those fields. This is the key idea behind a field; it stores information permanently as part of an Outlook item's data record. Another word for field is property.

Each control where the user enters data on a form can be *bound* to a particular field. A bound control shows the data in the related field. If you change the data in the control, Outlook updates the information in the field. When you save the Outlook item, the information in the field is stored permanently as part of the item. Outlook displays the saved field value in the bound control the next time you open the item.

Outlook also uses bound controls to display combination fields that combine information from several fields and formula fields that calculate a value using a formula.

*Unbound controls* are also useful. These controls don't have a permanent link to a particular field. Unbound controls store information only temporarily, while an Outlook item is open. The data they hold disappears when the user closes the current item, unless the programmer adds code to the form to save the data in an Outlook property.

Outlook includes a long list of standard, built-in fields for each type of item, plus you can create your own custom fields. Use standard fields as much as possible. One limitation of custom fields is that you cannot import or export them with Outlook's Import and Export Wizard. (You can, of course, write programming code to perform those tasks, as we'll see in Chapter 21.)

---

**Tip:** The Billing Information and Mileage fields are text fields available on any Outlook form. The Contact form includes four extra generic text fields, listed in the Field Chooser as User Field 1, User Field 2, User Field 3, and User Field 4. You can use any of these six fields for storing any kind of information.

---

## 6.2    Creating user-defined fields

To get started with user-defined fields, let's work with the Task form, creating a field and then adding a control to display it on a custom page. Use the Tools | Forms | Design a Form command to open the standard Task form in design mode.

To add a new field, switch to the P.2 page and then click the New button on the Field Chooser. In the New Field dialog box, give the field a name, choose the type, and specify the format. Name the field "Project," and use the Text type and Text format, as shown in Figure 6.1, then click OK.

This process creates a new field in the parent folder for the item displayed in the form. Since you started from a new unmodified task form, the `Project` field is added to the Tasks folder and will appear in the User-defined Fields in Folder list for that folder. To add it to your form, drag the

**Figure 6.1**
*Specify the name,
type, and format
for a user-defined
field.*

`Project` field from the Field Chooser to any customizable page. On a task form, that would be the P.2–P.5 pages. This adds the field to the form. Any items you create with this custom form will contain the `Project` field. To confirm that the field is now defined in both the Tasks folder and your task form, switch to the All Fields tab. It should show the `Project` field under both User-Defined Fields in Folder and User-Defined Fields in This Item.

To design a form for use with a particular folder that is not one of the default folders (such as Contacts or Tasks), use a slightly different procedure to start your form design session. Create a new item in the target folder, then open that item and, on the Developer tab, choose Design This Form. Any fields that you subsequently create in the form's Field Chooser will also be defined in the folder where you created the item, rather than in the usual default folder for that type of item.

**Note:** If a field exists only in a form and not in the folder, you will not be able to display the field in a folder view, search on it in the user interface, or perform searches in code. If you create a form and later want to use it in a different folder, chances are that the folder will not have the necessary field definitions.

### 6.2.1   Field types

Outlook supports several different types of fields. Table 6.1 lists those available in the New Field dialog. Experienced programmers might notice that the field types available in Outlook are a little different from the data types in VBA or other programming environments.

For example, Outlook lists a text type, instead of a string data type. To programmers, string data contains zero or more characters, and those characters can be numbers, letters, or punctuation—any characters at all. Two Outlook field types can contain string data: the text type and the keywords type, which consists of several strings delimited by commas (or another separator, depending on the user's locale setting). The keywords field is difficult to use because the value of a keywords field is not directly accessible by programming code. You can access it only through the value of a bound text box control; the next chapter shows how to do that.

**Table 6.1**  *Custom Property Types (\* = new in Outlook 2007)*

| Field Type | Can Contain |
| --- | --- |
| Text | Any string |
| Number | Any number |
| Percent | Any number, displayed as a percentage |
| Currency | Any number involving money; displayed in the currency format for your locale, as set in the Windows Control Panel under Regional and Language Options |
| Yes/No | Yes (-1)/No (0), True/False, or On/Off |
| Date/Time | Date or time data; stored as a complete date/time value, even if displayed only as date or only as time. A date displayed as "None" is stored as the date 1/1/4501. |
| Duration | Number of minutes |
| Keywords | Multiple strings, separated by commas (or other separator, as set in the Windows Control Panel under Regional and Language Options) |
| Combination | A combination of values from other fields |
| Formula | A calculation based on Outlook fields, literal strings and numbers, and built-in functions |
| *Integer | Any nondecimal number |

Notice the several types for holding numeric data: number, percent, currency, and integer. The yes/no type is actually a special number type that can hold either of just two values, -1 and 0, which stand for Yes, True, or On and No, False, or Off, respectively.

---

**Caution:** Outlook does not allow you to change the name or data type of a user-defined field after you create it. If you change your mind about the data type, you will have to delete the field from both the form and the parent folder and create it again. Make sure you have the type correct before you create any items with the form.

---

Fields using the date/time and duration types allow you to enter data using natural language. For example, if you type "today" into a date/time field, Outlook converts that to the current date. You can type in "next Tues," and it will calculate the date automatically. Try typing "2 wks from Fri," and you will get an idea of just how smart and useful this feature can be. (If you really want a thrill, type in "New Year's Eve.")

Duration fields store time measured in minutes, but allow you to enter a value in days or hours as well. Use the letters "d" for days and "h" for hours. Try typing "2d" into any duration field, and watch it turn into "2 days."

**Tip:** To discover the data type for any built-in Outlook field, select the field on the All Fields page on the form, then click the Properties button. For example, the Categories field uses the keywords type. For some fields, you will see Internal Data Type listed as the type. The values and behaviors of these fields are controlled by Outlook itself, not by the user directly, and they don't fit into any of the types in Table 6.1.

## 6.2.2   Combination fields

As their name implies, combination fields let you combine the values of one or more fields. You can even add text. For example, you can use a combination field to show the first non-empty phone number on a contact. Another combination might show a sentence that uses data from more than one field to describe the status of a task.

To create your first combination field, continue using a task form opened in design mode. On the P.2 page, click New in the Field Chooser, and create a new field named "Long Status" with a type of combination. The New Field dialog will display an Edit button. Click it to display the Combination Formula Field dialog box, and then type in the text shown in Figure 6.2. The [Due Date] and [% Complete] elements shown in brackets are Outlook fields, which the formula combines with the other text to form a complete sentence. You can type in the field names, but you may find it easier—and more accurate—to pick them from a list. To see the list of fields, click the Field button on the dialog. After you complete the formula, click OK twice to save the field definition, then drag it from the Field

**Figure 6.2**
*To create the formula for a combination field, use several fields or combine fields and text.*

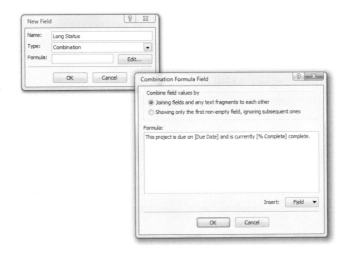

**Figure 6.3**
*The gray
background on the
Long Status field's
text box indicates
that this
combination field
is not editable,
because it is
controlled by a
formula.*

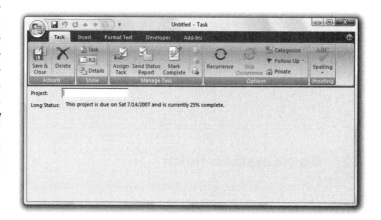

Chooser to the P.2 page. Make the text box for the field wider so that it shows the entire contents of the field.

---

**Note:** Notice in Figure 6.2 that there is a second option for creating a combination field: "Showing only the first non-empty field, ignoring subsequent ones."

---

To test the form, click Run This Form to create a new task, enter a due date, and set some value for the completion percentage. Then, in the Show group on the ribbon, click P.2 to switch to your customized page, which should look something like Figure 6.3. Because the Long Status field is a combination field, its text box appears with a gray background to indicate that it is a read-only field.

### 6.2.3  Formula fields

A combination field is a special case of a formula field that supports only field values and text. Formula fields can invoke simple intrinsic functions and perform calculations to obtain more complex results than a combination field can. Also, in a combination field, you can string text and field names together as you might in a sentence. In a formula field, you need to use the concatenation operator (&) to join text and field values into a single string.

As an example, let's create a formula field that tells you whether a task is overdue. As always, create the field by clicking the New button on the Field Chooser. Name the field "Is Overdue," choose Formula for the type, and then click Edit.

In the Formula Field dialog, you will see not only the Field button that you saw when creating a combination field, but also a Function button.

Functions help you build formulas by performing common calculations. If you have used Microsoft Excel to build formulas, you should recognize many of the functions available to Outlook formula fields. The Outlook formula editor includes conversion, date/time, financial, general, math, and text functions.

To create a formula field, combine field values, functions, literal values, and operators, such as + for addition and / for division. (We will learn more about operators in Chapter 7.) The Is Overdue field uses the built-in Due Date field to determine whether an item is overdue. Type in this formula:

```
([Due Date] <> "None") And ([Due Date] < Date())
```

You can type in the name of the field or choose it from the Field list. You also can type in the Date() function (which returns today's date) or choose it from the Function list. This formula returns True if the task has a due date and that date is earlier than today's date.

---

**Tip:** Most of the time, when the user sees "None" on the screen for a date field, Outlook actually is storing the date January 1, 4501. However, in a formula, you need to test for the literal text "None" not for the literal date #1/1/4501#.

---

Formula fields are not limited to returning True and False values, of course. To return text instead of True if a task is overdue, create another formula field with the name "Is Overdue 2," and enter this formula, which uses the IIf( ) function:

```
IIf( ([Due Date] <> "None") And ([Due Date] < Date() ),
"OVERDUE!!!", "Not due yet")
```

The IIf() function is very useful for Outlook formula fields. To see its basic syntax, add it to the Formula Field dialog by selecting it from the Function | General list of functions. It consists of three parts: expr, truepart, and falsepart:

```
IIf( expr , truepart , falsepart )
```

For the first part, expr, the formula needs an expression that evaluates to True or False. In the Is Overdue 2 field, that expression is ([Due Date] <> "None") And ([Due Date] < Date() ), the same expression used in the Is Overdue field. If expr is True, it returns to the formula field the value found in truepart. In this example, that would be the text "OVERDUE!!!". If expr is False—that is, if there is no due date or if the task is due today or in the future—the formula returns the value of falsepart or "Not due yet".

### 6.2.4   **Working with formula and combination fields**

If you make a mistake in a formula or combination field and want to change it later, after already adding it to a custom form, you must remove the field completely from the form, edit the original formula definition for the field (the definition stored in the folder), and then add the field back to the form.

To update a formula field that you're already using on a form, delete the control that displays the field. Then, switch to the All Fields page and display the "User-defined fields in this item" list. Select the field and delete it. Still on the All Fields page, switch to the "User-defined fields in folder" list, select the field, and then click Edit.

---

**Caution:** Do not try to edit the formula using the Value tab of the control that displays the formula field on the form. If you do that, you will wind up with two different formulas for the same field—one defined at the form/ item level and one at the folder level.

---

After you update the formula, you can drag the field from the Field Chooser onto your custom form page to create a new control to display the updated formula field.

Formula fields have several limitations. Outlook does not allow sorting or grouping on formula fields in a folder view. If you need to be able to sort or group on a field that has a value calculated from other field values, use a regular custom property of the appropriate type (text, number, etc.) instead of a formula field. You can then either set a formula on the control (not the field), as described later in this chapter, or use VBScript code behind the form to perform the calculation.

Also, any formatting must be built into the formula, since a formula field shows the Formula box instead of the Format box. (Compare the New Field dialogs in Figures 6.1 and 6.2.) For example, let's say that you want a formula field to show the date one week from today, but in the format "day month year." Create a new formula field and name it "One Week from Today." In your formula, use the `Format()` function to control the way the date looks to the user:

```
Format(Date() + 7, "dd mmm yyyy")
```

This formula tells Outlook to take today's date—the value returned by the `Date()` function—add seven days, and then apply the `"dd mmm yyyy"` format to the result. `Format()` is a very useful function available in Outlook formulas and VBA, but not in VBScript, that converts an expression into text in a specific format. For details on possible formats it can handle, look it up in Outlook VBA Help.

Finally, a formula field is always read-only. Since the value of the field is determined by the formula, the user can alter the value only by changing the value of one of the fields used in the formula. If you want to use a formula to suggest a value but allow the user to override it, don't use a formula field. Instead, use a regular custom property of the appropriate type and set an initial value on the control that displays the field, as described later in this chapter.

Formula fields do have one advantage over VBScript code that's worth noting: VBScript code runs only on published forms, while Outlook will calculate a formula on any form, including on an .oft form template file.

### 6.2.5   Example: Calculate a contact's age

Let's look at one more example of a custom formula field. Do you remember the form region from Chapter 5 that shows a contact's age? It contains another example of a formula field. See if you can pick out the one field and seven different functions that its formula uses:

```
IIf([Birthday]<>"None",
DateDiff("yyyy",[Birthday],Date())-IIf(DateDiff("d",
DateSerial(Year(Date()), Month([Birthday]),
Day([Birthday])),Date())<0,1,0),"")
```

The one field is `[Birthday]`. The seven functions are `IIf()` and `Date()`, which you already know, plus `DateDiff()`, `DateSerial()`, `Month()`, `Day()`, and `Year()`.

`DateDiff()` compares two dates and returns the number of intervals between them, but this function has a quirk: If you're measuring the interval in years (the `"yyyy"` argument in the formula), `DateDiff()` compares only the year parts of the two dates, which means that if the person's birthday has not taken place yet this year, `DateDiff()` returns an age that's one year too great. That's why the formula uses the following process to calculate the age.

1.  Construct the date of this year's birthday as a text string, using the `Month()`, `Day()`, and `Year()` functions, along with the `DateSerial()` function, which returns a date, taking as its parameters the integer values for the year, month, and day

2.  Use a `DateDiff()` function to determine whether this year's birthday happens after today's date

3.  From an `IIf()` function, return 1 if this year's birthday happens after today and 0 if it happens today or already happened this year

4.  Calculate the difference in years between the date of birth and today's date with another `DateDiff()` function, and subtract the adjustment calculated in Step 3

You'll see these date-related functions again in Chapter 8.

This may be more complex a formula than you'll ever want to write, because it would be very difficult to debug. The only way to debug a formula field is trial-and-error: run the form and eyeball the results. Performing complex calculations is much easier to do in VBScript code, but as noted in the previous section, only published forms run script.

## 6.3   Adding and removing fields on Outlook forms

After you create custom fields in the Field Chooser, you can add them to any custom form page. If you have not already done so, drag the `Project`, `Long Status`, `Is Overdue`, and `Is Overdue 2` fields to P.2 on your custom task form, so that it looks like Figure 6.4. Dragging a field to the form adds it to the "User-defined fields in this item" list on the All Fields tab. Any item created with this form will include that field.

Where did the `Is Overdue` field's value of `0` come from? The formula for `Is Overdue` can return only `True` or `False`, that is, `-1` or `0`. Normally, you should use a check box control to display the value in a yes/no field because few users know that `True` equals `-1` and `False` equals `0`. If you drag a standard yes/no field, such as `Completed`, to a custom form page, Outlook automatically displays the field with a check box control. However, that doesn't happen with `Is Overdue`, because it is a formula field, not a yes/no field. The next section explains how to add a check box to the form and set it to display the `Is Overdue` field's value.

**Figure 6.4**
*Drag user-defined fields from the Field Chooser to the form.*

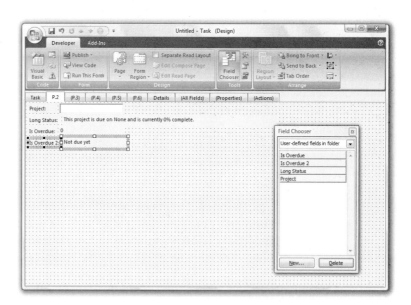

Figure 6.4 demonstrates an alternative to using a check box. The text box displaying the value of the `Is Overdue 2` formula field provides a clear textual explanation of whether the item is due.

To completely remove a field from a form and from the parent folder, delete the control that displays the field. Then, switch to the All Fields page and display the "User-defined fields in this item" list. Select the field and delete it. Then, display the "User-defined fields in folder" list and delete it there, too.

---

**Caution:** Be very careful when removing fields from a form that has been in use for a while. If you remove a field from the form definition, but items using that form have data values in that field, the data remains intact in the individual items, but the form definition may become embedded in the item. This creates a "one-off" form, which, as you'll see in Chapter 21, is something you'll want to avoid.

Also, if you are removing a control, but leaving the field definition on the form, be sure to check the Validation tab of the control's Properties dialog before you remove it. Validation is a property of the field, not the control, so even if the control is no longer present, Outlook will still try to validate the field. More information on validation is coming up later in this chapter.

---

Deleting a field from a form and from a folder does not remove the field from any existing items that already contain that field.

## 6.3.1   Binding a control to a field

If you want to use a check box control to display the `Is Overdue` field, you can't just drag the field from the Field Chooser. Instead, place a check box control on the form, and then bind it to the field. Use this technique any time you want Outlook to display a field in a particular type of control, rather than the default control for that data type. Here's the step-by-step procedure:

1.   Display the Control Toolbox, and drag a check box control to the form.

2.   Right-click the check box and choose Properties to open the basic Properties dialog for the control.

3.   On the Value tab, click the Choose Field button, and select the `Is Overdue` field from the "User-defined fields in folder" list. Outlook fills in the details for the field automatically, as shown in Figure 6.5.

4. Switch to the Display tab, and change the Name of the control to `chkIsOverdue`. You can leave the Caption as "Is Overdue," which Outlook filled in for you, or change it to something more descriptive such as "Task Is Overdue."

5. Click OK to save the changes to the control's properties.

The Value page in Figure 6.5 deserves a bit more explanation. All the controls on the Value and Validation pages are disabled unless the control is bound to an Outlook field. Did you notice the New button? Like the New button on the Field Chooser, this button creates a new user-defined field. If you use the New button on the Value tab to create a new field, Outlook automatically creates it in the parent folder and in the form, all at the same time.

For field types other than formula and combination, you can change the format setting for the field. Each data type has its own format choices. For example, there are 16 formats for date/time fields. The exact formats available depend on your locale, that is, your regional options settings in Control Panel.

## 6.3.2　Initial value

On the Value tab of a bound control's Properties dialog, under Initial Value, you can set the initial value of the field to a formula. To create a formula that sets the default value for a field, select "Calculate this formula when I compose a new form." To create a mandatory formula, one that prevents the user from overriding the default value, select "Calculate this formula automatically."

For example, create a new field named One Week From Today 2 as a date/time field. Drag it to a custom page to add a text box bound to the field. On the text box's Properties dialog, on the Value tab, set the Initial

Value formula to `Date() + 7`, select "Calculate this formula when I compose a new form," and choose the date format that best suits your needs. Run the form and compare the behavior of the new field with the `One Week From Today` field discussed earlier in Section 6.2.4 as a formula field.

Consider what happens if you have an initial value formula on a message form field and the user forwards the message. Because the forwarded message is a new item, the field will contain the value calculated from the initial value, not the value from the field on the original message. If you want the forward message field to contain the original message field's value, you cannot use an initial value formula. Instead, use VBScript code to set the value. We'll return to this scenario in Chapter 20.

### 6.3.3 Simple validation

For fields other than combination and formula fields, you may want to specify that a field must not be left blank or that it can accept only certain values. This technique, called *validation*, is an important method for preventing users (including yourself!) from making mistakes during data entry.

To configure validation, display the Properties dialog for any Outlook form control, and then switch to the Validation page. The simplest option is to check the top box, labeled "A value is required for this field." However, I don't recommend using that approach. If the user leaves the field blank, a message pops up that a value is required for a field, but Outlook doesn't tell you which field!

Instead, I recommend that you set a validation formula by checking the box for "Validate this field before closing the form." Enter a formula that returns `True` or `False` in the "Validation formula" box, and enter text or a formula in the "Display this message if the validation fails" box. Figure 6.6

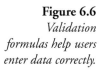

**Figure 6.6**
*Validation formulas help users enter data correctly.*

shows a validation rule for the `Project` field created earlier to make sure the task isn't saved with a blank `Project` field.

Outlook checks the validation formula only when you save or send an item. To validate data entry as you type requires VBScript code, covered in Chapter 12, "Coding Key Form Event Scenarios."

---

**Caution:** Check the Validation tab before removing a control from the form. If you don't plan to remove the validation formula, be sure to include a validation message that specifies which field needs a correct value.

---

## 6.3.4  Validation formulas

The Edit buttons on the Validation tab work just like those to edit the formula for a formula field. Use them when you want to pick fields and functions to build your validation rule or validation message.

A validation formula must return `True` if the data is "good" or `False` if it is incorrect. It should compare the field you're validating with one or more "good" values or compare the field with the value of another field. Table 6.2 shows examples of validation formulas. Notice that the `[Project] <> ""` formula is equivalent to checking the "A value is required for this field" box.

As you can see, validation formulas can use fields and operators just like value formulas. They can also use functions. What you may find surprising is that validation message formulas can, too!

One thing these examples have in common is that the validation formula includes the field you want to validate. It wouldn't make any sense, would it, to have a validation formula that ignored the very value you wanted to test?

The other thing they have in common is that every validation formula evaluates to `True` or `False`. Contrast this with formula fields, where the result of the formula can be any value—`True` or `False`, a number, some text, or a date.

---

**Note:** Did you notice that none of the examples includes an `IIf()` function? That function is redundant in a validation formula, because the first parameter for `IIf()` itself must be an expression that returns `True` or `False`. Thus, a validation formula using `IIf()` would look like `IIf(<some True/False expression>, True, False)` and could be simplified to just `<some True/False expression>`.

---

**Table 6.2**  *Sample Validation Formulas and Validation Messages*

| Validation Formula | Result | Suggested Validation Failure Message Formula |
|---|---|---|
| `[Project] <> ""` | Requires that the `Project` field not be left blank. | `"Please enter a name for the project."` |
| `Len([Project Code]) = 10` | Requires that the `Project Code` field have exactly 10 characters. | `"The project code must be exactly 10 characters long."` |
| `([Due Date] = "None") OR ([Start Date] <> "None")` | If the user has set a due date, the user must also set a start date. | `"Since you have set a due date for this task, you must also set a start date on or before " & [Due Date] & "."` |
| `([Product] <> "Other") OR ([Other Product] <> "")` | If the user has entered `"Other"` as the value for the `Product` field, the `Other Product` field also must have a value. | `"Please enter a value for the Other Project field."` |

The third and fourth examples in Table 6.2 illustrate a very common type of validation formula, where the acceptable value for one field depends on the value in another field. When the formula contains one or more expressions joined by OR, Outlook evaluates each expression and returns True if any expression is true. Therefore, the third validation formula evaluates to True if either there is no due date or if the user has entered some start date. Otherwise, the formula evaluates to False, for example, if the user enters a due date but no start date. Similarly, in the fourth example, the user might select the value for the Product field from a combo box list that includes "Other" as one option. If the user selects "Other" the Other Product field cannot be left blank.

**Tip:** To enter a validation formula for a standard field that appears on a form page that you can't edit, drag the field from the Field Chooser to any blank page on your custom form. You can then set up validation through the properties of the field's control on the custom page. You will want to choose Page | Display This Page to hide the page from users, since it duplicates fields they will see on other pages of the form.

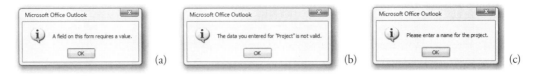

**Figure 6.7**    *Depending on the options you choose, validation messages can range from the cryptic (a) to the specific (c).*

Note that field names for built-in fields are language-specific (although the underlying property names in the Outlook object model, i.e., the names you use in VBScript or VBA code, are not). A validation formula that you create in Outlook set up for U.S. English users might fail for users working with Outlook in French.

### 6.3.5   Validation formula messages

If you use a validation formula, you should also add an expression in the box labeled "Display this message if the validation rule fails." Otherwise, the user gets a cryptic, generic message that the field didn't pass the validation rule. In your validation failure message, don't just tell the user that something is wrong; explain how to fix it. Table 6.2 includes examples of validation failure messages that match the validation rule. Compare the different validation messages in Figure 6.7, all for the same `Product` field.

The validation message in Figure 6.7a results from the "A value is required for the field" option. In Figure 6.7b, you see the message that appears when you provide a validation formula, but no validation message. Figure 6.7c shows the message generated by the settings in Figure 6.6. Which one will do the most to help users fill in the form correctly?

## 6.4   Using form controls

If you have walked through the form design examples in this and the previous chapter, you already have a fair amount of experience working with Outlook form controls. In this section, we'll review the main controls and provide tips to help you use them better, noting which controls can fire a `Click` event when the control is not bound to an Outlook property. That is important information to help prepare you to write code behind a custom form in the next chapter and in Chapter 12.

### 6.4.1   Text boxes

A text box can display just one line of information (the default) or multiple lines. To set a text box for multi-line display, on the Properties dialog, check the Multi-line box.

A multi-line text box does not show a scroll bar to indicate that there is more visible text in the control until the user clicks in the text box. If you want the user to be able to use carriage returns in a multi-line text box, use the Advanced Properties dialog to set the control's `EnterKeyBehavior` property to `True`.

An unbound text box does not trigger a `Click` event.

### 6.4.2 Command buttons

Command buttons on custom forms make it possible for users to perform certain tasks on demand (i.e., at the click of a button). As we will discuss in Chapter 12, to make something happen when the user clicks the button, write code for the `Click` event.

### 6.4.3 Check boxes

Dragging any Yes/No Outlook property, such as the `Complete` property for a task, from the Field Chooser to a custom form page will result in a check box control being placed on the form. Use check boxes whenever you want the user to have an easy way to toggle between the values of `True` and `False` for a property.

You may also find unbound check boxes useful for toggling the appearance of other controls on a form because, like command buttons, unbound check boxes support a `Click` event.

### 6.4.4 Option buttons

As we saw in the VBA birthday and anniversary update form in Chapter 3, option buttons are a good choice of control if the user needs to pick from a small number of mutually exclusive choices. The `Caption` property controls the text that the option button displays.

---

**Tip:** For a Yes/No type of choice, one check box is usually preferable to two options buttons. For a long list of choices, you're better off with a list box or combo box.

---

To use option buttons to set the value of an Outlook property, make two changes to the properties on the Value tab of each button's Properties dialog: At the top of the Value tab, click Choose Field, and bind the button to an Outlook property. Each button in an option button set must be bound to the same Outlook property.

The second property to change is the `Value` property. The value can be text, a number, or even `True` or `False`, but each button must have a different value and the value must be appropriate for the type of property to

**Figure 6.8**
*For a set of option buttons bound to the same Outlook property, assign a different value to each button's Value property.*

which the control is bound. Figure 6.8 shows an option button being set up to handle a custom `Estimated Work Time` property, which was created as a duration property, for a task form.

Figure 6.9 shows three such buttons, along with a text box, all bound to the same `Estimated Work Time` property. The buttons have these properties:

- Option button 1:

  ```
  Caption    One day
  Value      1d
  ```

- Option button 2:

  ```
  Caption    Three days
  Value      3d
  ```

- Option button 3:

  ```
  Caption    One week
  Value      1w
  ```

Normally, you would not also display a text box bound to the same property. The text box in Figure 6.9 is read-only and is present to illustrate how selecting an option button sets the corresponding value for the bound property.

If you have more than one set of option buttons on a form, enclose each set in a frame control. (You can leave one set without a frame; that set will use the form page as a whole as the equivalent of a frame.)

**Tip:** Place the frame control for a set of option buttons on the form, then create the buttons inside the frame. Don't try to move a set of already created option buttons into a new frame control.

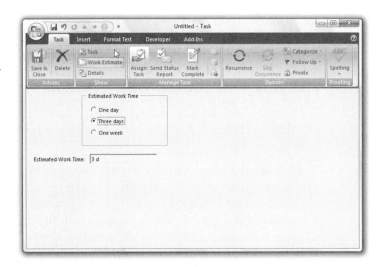

**Figure 6.9**
*Use option buttons
to restrict users to a
small number of
choices.*

If you bind two option buttons to a Yes/No property, on the Value tab for each control, you should set the format to True/False. Set the Value property of one button to `True` and the other to `False`.

If you are using a set of unbound option buttons, the value for each will be either `True` or `False`. You cannot set other values, as you can with buttons bound to Outlook properties. Your form code can either evaluate the values of each button in the set until it finds the one that's `True`, or it can use the `Click` event for each button. A good technique is to use the `Caption` or `Tag` property of the button to store a value that you can then use in the code behind the form to set some value for another control or property on the form. To set the `Tag` property, use the Advanced Properties dialog.

## 6.4.5 Frames

Frame controls have two major uses on Outlook forms:

- to provide grouping for option buttons
- to make it easy to show/hide or enable/disable a group of controls

A good strategy when you want to toggle the display of some controls is to put them all in one frame and use code to set the `Visible` property of the frame, rather than modify the individual controls.

You can also use a frame control to add boxes that logically group different sets of controls, such as one group related to email and another related to calendars. Such groupings can help the user locate the right control more quickly.

To set the tab order for the controls inside a frame, select the frame first, then choose Layout | Tab Order.

Like a label control, a frame fires no events.

## 6.4.6 List box and combo box controls

We learned about list box and combo box controls in the context of VBA user forms in Chapter 3. These controls work much the same way on Outlook custom forms.

One key difference on an Outlook form is that to populate a list or combo box, you can enter a Possible Values list on the Values page of the control, as shown in Figure 6.10. List and combo boxes also support the AddItem method that we saw in Chapter 3 in the context of VBA forms. Chapter 8 contains an example of using a different approach to fill the rows, one especially appropriate for multi-column list or combo boxes: setting the List property to an array.

In a combo box, to require the user to use one of the listed choices, display the Advanced Properties dialog for the control and set the MatchEntry property to -1 - True. If the user does not choose one of the listed choices, Outlook will pop up the message Invalid Property Value. Several properties that work in VBA forms are not supported in Outlook forms, including ColumnHeads, ControlSource, and RowSource.

To make a list box capable of capturing more than one user selection, on the Advanced Properties of the control, set the MultiSelect property to 1 - Multi. A multi-select list should be either unbound or bound to a keywords property. If you bind a multi-select list box to a normal text property, when the user moves the focus to another control, Outlook will no longer display the user's selections in the list box, even though it stores the selections in the text property as a delimited list.

If you decide to use a multi-select list box with a property other than a keywords property, use an unbound list box. You will need to provide code in the Item_Open event handler for the form to set the Selected property for each row in the list that you want to appear selected. The Item_Write event handler for the form will need code to build a delimited list of the user's selections and store it in a specific property of your choosing.

An unbound single-select list box or combo box fires a Click event. A multi-select list box does not.

## 6.4.7 Spin button

A spin button control provides up and down arrows that increment the value of the control as the user clicks them. It's a good choice where you want to provide a limited range of integer values to choose from.

**Figure 6.10**
*You can use the Possible Values property of the control to set up the list of values for a list box or combo box.*

On the Advanced Properties for the spin button, set the Max, Min, and SmallChange properties to control the maximum and minimum values and the amount that the value increments with each click. If you bind the spin button to an Outlook property, you may want to also provide a text box bound to the same property, so the user can see the current value of the property.

An unbound spin button does not support a Click event on Outlook forms.

### 6.4.8 Multi-page control

The multi-page control consists of two or more tabbed pages, each of which can have its own set of controls. The value of the control's Value property controls which page is currently shown. This is a zero-based property, meaning that 0 is the value for the leftmost page. The SelectedItem property of the multi-page control returns a Page object corresponding to the currently displayed page.

No events are fired when the user clicks a tab to switch to a different page. A workaround is to have the user switch pages with command buttons instead.

An individual Page object fires a Click event when the user clicks on the empty body of the page, but that's not terribly useful.

### 6.4.9 Image control

The image control can display many types of picture files. If you don't set its Picture property, you also can use it to enhance a form with simple lines and boxes in different colors.

## 6.4.10  **Outlook View Control**

Outlook includes the Outlook View Control (OVC) to display the data from a folder in an Outlook form, a Web page, or any other programming project that can host an ActiveX control. The OVC can display any named Outlook folder view and can filter the folder to show only items meeting particular conditions. This makes it ideal to use on a custom form to show items that are related to the current item or the current user.

The items displayed in an OVC are fully functional. Users can double-click or right-click them, just as they can in the main Outlook window.

The main limitation of the OVC is that it can show only one folder at a time. It cannot present a consolidated view of several folders, as the Activities page on a contact form can. Also, if you use it outside Outlook—say, on a Web page—its security restrictions prevent the use of the View property to change the display to a different named view.

To add the OVC to the Control Toolbox, right-click the Toolbox, choose Custom Controls, check the box for the Microsoft Office Outlook View Control, and then click OK. To add an instance of the OVC to an Outlook form, select the control in the Toolbox, and then use the mouse to drag out a rectangle the size that you want the control to display. Usually, you'll make it fairly large, so that the user can see as much detail from the folder as possible. By default, the OVC displays the user's Inbox folder. If you want it to display a different folder, you must set the control's Folder property, either through the Advanced Properties dialog or through code behind the form.

To demonstrate the OVC, consider a message form used to request approval of vacation time. To add a custom page to the form that shows all the items in the user's Calendar folder that have "Vacation" as their subject, follow these steps:

1.  Open a message form in design mode.

2.  Display the P.2 page, and use the Page | Rename Page command to rename it to Vacations.

3.  From the Control Toolbox, add an Outlook View Control and resize it to fill the entire page.

4.  Use the Page | Display This Page command to toggle the display off.

At this point the OVC should be showing the user's Inbox and the name of the page should be (Vacations), to show that it's a hidden page. To get the OVC to display the user's Calendar folder, filtered for vacations, we need to add just a little VBScript code to the form. Click the View Code button and type the code in Listing 6.1 to the form's script window.

**Listing 6.1**   *Show the current user's vacations in an Outlook View Control*

```
Function Item_Open()
    If Item.Size = 0 Then
        Set objInsp = Item.GetInspector
        Set objPage = objInsp.ModifiedFormPages("Vacations")
        Set ViewCtl1 = objPage.Controls("ViewCtl1")
        With ViewCtl1
            .Folder = "Calendar"
            .View = "All Appointments"
            .Restriction = "[Subject] = 'Vacation'"
        End With
        objInsp.ShowFormPage "Vacations"
        objInsp.SetCurrentFormPage "Vacations"
    End If
End Function
```

Publish the form to your Personal Forms library, and then run it with the Tools | Forms | Choose Form command.

The code in Listing 6.1 checks to see if the item is a new message (Size = 0), sets some properties of the OVC, and then displays the Vacations page to the user (see Figure 6.11).

**Note:** The syntax for working with a control on an Outlook custom form is more complex than that for a VBA form, because it involves the name of the page as well as the name of the control. In the next chapter, we'll review this syntax in detail.

We'll come back to the Outlook View Control in Chapter 22 to see how it can act as a central component in a folder home page, a Web page associated with an Outlook folder.

### 6.4.11   Some control and field limitations

Outlook users can become spoiled by some elements of the application's user interface, particularly things like the dropdown calendar for picking dates and the list of phone numbers for contacts. The bad news is that you can't duplicate the dropdown calendar on your custom forms (although, as we saw in Chapter 5, you can use the new date and time picker controls on form regions). Nor can you create new phone number fields and have Outlook include them in the dropdown list of phone numbers and format them into international style automatically. Chapter 4 discussed these limitations and others pertaining to specific forms.

The good news is that some fields, such as the Full Name field and the various address fields, do work the same on custom pages as on built-in

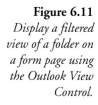

**Figure 6.11**
*Display a filtered
view of a folder on
a form page using
the Outlook View
Control.*

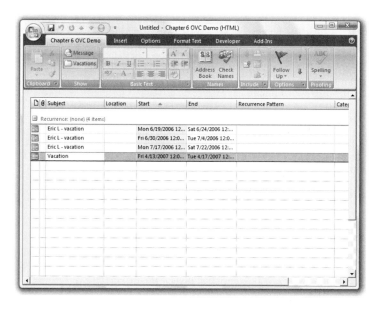

pages. For example, if you type "Alex Smith" into the `Full Name` field on a custom contact form page, Outlook stores "Alex" in the `First Name` field and "Smith" in the `Last Name` field. Also, any user-defined date/time or duration fields support Outlook's shortcuts for entering dates and duration.

To give users the ability to add attachments to an item, you must have a page on your form that displays the `Message` or `Notes` field. The name in the Field Chooser varies, depending on the type of item. On message, post, appointment, and task forms, the Field Chooser lists a `Message` field. For contacts and journal entry, Outlook calls it the `Notes` field.

You can use `Message/Notes` field only once on a form; users will get a warning if you violate that limitation.

**Note:** When you work with the `Message` or `Notes` field in code, it has yet another name, the `Body` property. At least in that context, the property name is the same for every type of Outlook item.

Some Outlook fields do not appear in the fields list for the type of item you're working with. For example, in a shared contacts folder, you might want to know who created each contact item. The All Contacts Fields list contains a `Created` field, but no `Creator` field. It is worth experimenting to see what fields you can use from other types of items. For example, to display a contact's creator, add a text box control to the form and bind it to the `From` field from the All Mail Fields list. Don't be surprised, though, if

Outlook tells you that you cannot use a field from another type of item on your form.

Also, sometimes you'll drag a field from another type of item to your custom form page and get no warning, but it still won't display any data. For example, you can drag the Business Phone field from the All Contact Fields list in the Field Chooser to a custom task form page, but Outlook is not going to automatically copy a contact's phone number to the task. If you want the task to contain that phone number, you'll need to write some code. We'll cover that scenario and some other limitations and techniques related to specific Outlook item types in Chapter 20.

Finally, there is a limit to the number of fields you can add to an Outlook form, but it's not a hard and fast limit. Each item can contain up to 32kb of data, excluding attachments and the data in the Message/Notes field. If you exceed that limit, the form may not display all the data the user has entered or may not calculate formula fields correctly. I start getting a little anxious when a custom form has 150 or so fields and really start worrying when the number of fields passes 200. Be sure to keep good backups of the form as .oft files if you're adding a lot of fields to a form.

## 6.5 Laying out compose and read pages

A common problem that novice Outlook form designers encounter is a received message that doesn't show your custom fields. It happens like this: You create and publish a good-looking mail form, generate a new message from it, send the message to yourself, and then tear out your hair wondering why it looks like the standard message form and not your custom form. Outlook allows you to design two versions of any custom form page, one used when you compose the item, the other when a user reads the saved or sent item. This applies not just to message forms, but to all Outlook forms, but the issue comes up mostly with message forms. Some form designers don't notice that the main Message page uses dual layouts by default or forget to click the Edit Read Page button to create a custom read layout to match the compose layout.

**Note:** Form regions work differently; each region supports a single layout. You can create separate form regions for read, compose, and preview use. The usage for each region is controlled by its manifest.

Open the standard message form in design mode to see how this works. Figure 6.12 shows the compose page for a new message, with the To, Cc, and Subject fields enabled for the user to fill in. Click the Edit Read Page command in the Design Group to see the read page (shown in Figure 6.13) for the same form. This time you see the From and Sent fields, which are

**Figure 6.12**
*The default
Message form
layout includes
separate compose
and read pages.*

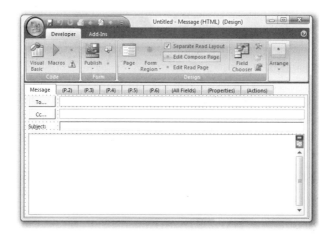

**Figure 6.12**
*The default
Message form
layout includes
separate compose
and read pages.*

not on the read layout, and all the message header fields are displayed in gray to indicate they are disabled.

To convert a page with a single layout to have separate compose and read layouts, check Separate Read Layout in the Design group. Outlook copies all the fields from the original page (making it the compose page) to a new read page. To copy controls manually, select them, and use the right-click Copy and Paste commands. Switch between the two layouts with the Edit Compose Page and Edit Read Page commands. At runtime, the page will show the same name in the Show group on the ribbon, regardless of which layout is active.

To convert a page with dual layouts to a single layout, you must choose which layout to preserve. To keep the compose layout, click Edit Compose Page and then uncheck Separate Read Layout. To keep the read layout,

**Figure 6.13**
*Use the Edit
Compose Page and
Edit Read Page
commands to
switch between
layouts.*

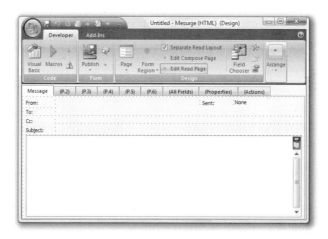

click Edit Read Page and then uncheck Separate Read Layout. In both cases, answer Yes to the prompt that warns you that Outlook is about to discard all changes made to the other layout.

---

**Caution:** Be extremely careful if you decide to uncheck Separate Read Layout and revert to a single page instead of dual layouts. Outlook discards the page that is not currently visible. This change cannot be undone.

---

No single property of an Outlook item can tell you whether it is open to the compose or read layout. In Chapter 12, we'll discuss a `ShowsCompose-Layout()` function that provides this information.

## 6.6    Summary

In this chapter, you learned how to create your own custom fields and add them to Outlook forms. You also worked with validation rules and fields based on formulas to. For additional flexibility, Outlook allows you to maintain separate compose and read layouts for each customized form page. On each page, you can place controls to display and set Outlook field values, display information to the user, and gather information from the user. The biggest difference between an Outlook custom form and a VBA user form is that the controls on an Outlook form connect directly with the fields that store data in Outlook items.

Ensuring that related forms, items, and folders have matching fields can be tricky. Chapter 21 explains how forms and individual items interact and provides code to add field definitions to folders, based on the custom properties present in a custom form.

# 7

# *Outlook Code Basics*

Get ready to dig into coding. This chapter and the others that follow in this part of the book will cover the basics of writing VBA and VBScript programming code in Outlook 2007. The highlights of this chapter include discussions of the following:

- What triggers program code to execute
- When to use a function instead of a subroutine
- How to run an VBA subroutine from a toolbar button
- How to run an VBA subroutine from a rule
- What user interaction can cause code to run on an Outlook custom form
- What syntax to use to refer to Outlook properties and form controls
- How to invoke Outlook objects from other environments, such as VBA in Word

## 7.1    Understanding when VBA code runs

Outlook VBA supports five types of procedures:

- Macros that you can run on demand from the Tools | Macro | Macros dialog or from a toolbar button, such as the `HelloWorldMessage` subroutine that you saw in Listing 2.1
- Subroutines that can be executed on an incoming message or meeting request by a rule
- Procedures that handle events raised on Outlook objects
- Procedures that handle events raised on VBA user forms
- Non-event subroutines and functions that support all the other procedures by performing calculations and automating routine tasks

Of these different types of procedures, *event handlers* are probably the most difficult to understand. Think about the Windows applications you use every day. A money-management program makes a good example. When you start the program, it probably pops up reminders that you have bills to pay or investments to check on. You click a button or maybe a menu command to enter a new transaction. Perhaps when you type "May 15," the program automatically converts your entry to "May 15, 2007" (or whatever the current year might be). Although virtually all of the program runs out of sight, it depends on you, the user, for the key interactions that tell it what to do.

Each time you interact with the program—choosing a menu item, clicking a button, saving an item, and even pressing Tab to move from one control to another—you cause one or more *events* to fire. Each event can have a programming routine associated with it. For example, the `cmdUpdate_Click` procedure in Listing 3.1 is an event handler for the `Click` event that fires every time the user clicks the `cmdUpdate` button on the birthday/anniversary reminder form.

Each type of object (VBA forms, command buttons, text boxes, Outlook folders and items, and so on) has its own set of possible events. Even Outlook itself as an application has events. If you write code for using these events, Outlook can perform certain tasks every time you start Outlook or when a reminder fires. VBScript code behind Outlook forms also uses event handlers associated with the item itself and the controls you add to a custom form.

Not every event will have code related to it. As you build Outlook applications, you must decide which events are important to your application.

## 7.1.1   VBA form events

To build on the example of a VBA form application from Chapter 3, let's take a closer look at the events that VBA user forms support. Add a new form to your VBA project with the Insert | UserForm command. An easy way to see what events are available is to use the View | Code command to display the code window for the form (see Figure 7.1). From the left dropdown list at the top of the form, choose UserForm. (This will place the `Sub` ... `End Sub` stub for a subroutine named `UserForm_Click` in the code window; you can delete or ignore it.) Use the right dropdown list to see all the events for the `UserForm` object, in other words for the current form.

It's important to distinguish between form-level events and control events. For example, the `Click` event for a form fires only when you click on the form background, away from the controls. If you click on a control, the `Click` event for that control fires, not the `Click` event for the form. The form events listed in Table 7.1 are the most useful as you start

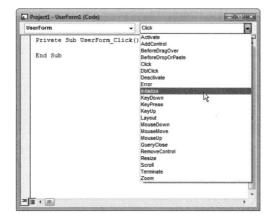

**Figure 7.1**
*The dropdown lists at the top of the VBA code window help you understand what events are available for your form and its controls.*

programming VBA forms. Note that the `Initialize` event fires before the `Activate` event.

---

**Tip:** For most of the forms you create in Outlook VBA, you will be more interested in control events than form events.

---

Controls on forms have their own events. In Chapter 3, we saw an example of code attached to the `Click` event for a command button. Table 7.2 lists `Click` along with other important events for VBA user form controls.

Here are some notes on VBA user form control events:

- The `BeforeUpdate` event is often used to validate the data entered in a control, because it can be cancelled to roll back the control to its previous value.
- Command buttons support only the `Click` event.
- Text boxes do not support the `Click` event.

**Table 7.1**  *Key VBA Form Events*

| Event | Occurs |
| --- | --- |
| Initialize | After the VBA form is loaded, but before it becomes visible |
| Activate | When a VBA form becomes the active, visible window in Outlook |
| Terminate | After the VBA form has been unloaded, but before it is removed completely from memory |

**Table 7.2** *Key VBA Control Events*

| Event | Occurs |
| --- | --- |
| Enter | Just before the focus enters a control |
| Click | When the user clicks on a control |
| BeforeUpdate | Before the user's change to a data entry control takes effect |
| AfterUpdate | After the user's change to a data entry control takes effect |
| Change | When the value in a control changes |
| Exit | When the focus leaves a control |

- For check boxes, the Click event occurs not only when the user clicks in the box, but also when the user changes the value by pressing the spacebar or the accelerator key for the control.
- The Exit event can be cancelled if you want the focus to remain in the control.

**Note:** Controls on Outlook custom forms do not support the Enter, Exit, BeforeUpdate, and AfterUpdate events, only the Click event. Furthermore, on an Outlook custom form, the Click event fires on a data entry control only if the control is not bound to an Outlook property. Some unbound controls on an Outlook custom form, such as text boxes and multiselect list boxes, do not fire a Click event at all.

A good way to become acquainted with the order in which some of these events fire is to create a simple form with one check box, one text box, and one command button. Don't worry about changing the default names of the controls; this is just a test form. To enter code for each event for each control and for the form itself, in the code window, follow these steps:

1. Select the control or form from the left dropdown list.

2. Select the event from the right dropdown list. Do not change the procedure declaration that Outlook VBA creates.

3. Between the Private Sub and End Sub statements of the procedure declaration, enter one statement to pop up a message box with the name of the event. You can use the code in Listing 7.1 as a model.

After you enter the code, run the form by clicking the Run Sub/User-Form button (or pressing F5), and use the mouse and keyboard to move

**Listing 7.1** *Message boxes show the sequence in which control and form events fire*

```
Private Sub CheckBox1_AfterUpdate()
    MsgBox "CheckBox After Update"
End Sub

Private Sub CheckBox1_BeforeUpdate(ByVal Cancel As MSForms.ReturnBoolean)
    MsgBox "CheckBox Before Update"
End Sub

Private Sub CheckBox1_Change()
    MsgBox "CheckBox Change"
End Sub

Private Sub CheckBox1_Click()
    MsgBox "CheckBox Click"
End Sub

Private Sub CheckBox1_Enter()
    MsgBox "CheckBox Enter"
End Sub

Private Sub CheckBox1_Exit(ByVal Cancel As MSForms.ReturnBoolean)
    MsgBox "CheckBox Exit"
End Sub

Private Sub CommandButton1_Click()
    MsgBox "Command Button Click"
End Sub

Private Sub TextBox1_AfterUpdate()
    MsgBox "Text Box After Update"
End Sub

Private Sub TextBox1_BeforeUpdate(ByVal Cancel As MSForms.ReturnBoolean)
    MsgBox "Text Box Before Update"
End Sub

Private Sub TextBox1_Change()
    MsgBox "Text Box Change"
End Sub

Private Sub TextBox1_Enter()
    MsgBox "Text Box Enter"
End Sub

Private Sub TextBox1_Exit(ByVal Cancel As MSForms.ReturnBoolean)
    MsgBox "Text Box Exit"
End Sub

Private Sub UserForm_Activate()
    MsgBox "Form Activate"
End Sub
```

**Listing 7.1**    *Message boxes show the sequence in which control and form events fire (continued)*

```
Private Sub UserForm_Initialize()
    MsgBox "Form Initialize"
End Sub

Private Sub UserForm_Terminate()
    MsgBox "Form Terminate"
End Sub
```

through the various controls, enter data, delete data, and so forth. Each event will pop up a message box to tell you which event is occurring.

### 7.1.2    What is a Sub anyway?

After entering the code in the preceding section, you're probably wondering about the `Private Sub` and `End Sub` statements. These mark the beginning and end of a code procedure called a *subroutine*. The `Private` keyword means that each of these procedures runs only in the context of the particular VBA form. That's appropriate for forms because the event has no meaning without the control or form that it is related to. However, in other code modules you may choose to make a subroutine public so that it can be used elsewhere.

To start a new subroutine, just type "Sub" on a new line in the VBA code editor, followed by the name you want to use for the procedure. Procedure names cannot contain spaces. When you press Enter at the end of the Sub statement, VBA completes the `Sub` statement and adds an `End Sub` statement automatically.

Did you notice that each subroutine name is followed by a pair of parentheses? Inside the parentheses, the procedure declaration defines its *parameters*, that is, the variable names by which inputs are passed to the subroutine. The actual value passed as an input is called an *argument* and can be a constant, a variable, or an expression. Some parameters are optional. In most VBA procedures, the data type of a parameter (for example, Boolean or string) is defined in the procedure declaration.

In most cases, form and control event handlers have no parameters. `BeforeUpdate` and `Exit` are exceptions. They both have `Cancel` as a parameter. To cancel such an event and thus negate the user's action, set the value of the `Cancel` parameter to `True`. If you cancel `BeforeUpdate`, the control returns to the value it had before the user updated it. If you cancel `Exit`, the focus stays on the control and does not move to the next control.

Here is some code you can add to the `ReminderUpdate` form from Chapter 3. It uses the `BeforeUpdate` event for the `txtDays` control to make sure that the user has entered a number that can be used to set the reminder interval.

```
Private Sub txtDays_BeforeUpdate(ByVal Cancel _
  As MSForms.ReturnBoolean)
    If IsNumeric(txtDays.Value) = False Then
        Cancel = True
        MsgBox "Please enter a number."
        txtDays.SelStart = 0
        txtDays.SelLength = Len(txtDays.Value)
    End If
End Sub
```

IsNumeric() is a built-in function that returns True if its argument is a number and False if not. SelStart and SelLength are text box properties that set the start character and length of a text selection in the control.

Also note that this validation procedure runs only when the user actually enters data in the txtDays control. You may also want to add similar validation, using IsNumeric(), in the cmdUpdate_Click event handler to take care of the case where the user clicks the cmdUpdate button without having entered any value in the txtDays text box.

Performing validation with cancelable events can make a form friendlier to the user, because message boxes and other clues can tell the user precisely what to do to correct the problem with their data entry.

### 7.1.3  Outlook VBA application-level events

Application-level events in Outlook VBA can run code to perform actions against outgoing messages, automatically process incoming messages, respond to reminders, modify new or changed items in a folder, and handle many other interesting events related to Outlook folders and items. For example, the ItemAdd event fires when a new item is added to a folder. A practical use for that event would be to update a newly added task with the phone number of a linked contact you want to call. Chapter 20 has an example of such an ItemAdd event handler.

To write code for application-level events, use the dropdown lists at the top of the built-in ThisOutlookSession module to select the event and insert the procedure stub into the module. Listing 7.2 shows a very simple example of an event handler—for the ItemSend event of the Application object—to prevent the user from sending messages with blank subject lines.

Like the BeforeUpdate and Exit events for user form controls, the ItemSend event has a Cancel parameter. If you set Cancel = True, Outlook does not send the item. The item remains visible for the user to work with. The first parameter, Item, is the actual item being sent.

**Listing 7.2**     *ItemSend event handler to avoid sending messages with blank subjects*

```
Private Sub Application_ItemSend(ByVal Item As Object, Cancel As Boolean)
    If Item.Subject = "" Then
        Cancel = True
        MsgBox "You forgot to enter a subject.", _
               vbExclamation + vbSystemModal, "Missing Subject"
        Item.Display
    End If
End Sub
```

Aside from simple events like `ItemSend`, programming responses to application-level events is more complicated than programming VBA forms and simple macros. Therefore, a detailed discussion of this topic is deferred until Chapter 11.

### 7.1.4   Macros to run programs on demand

Outlook users frequently want to know whether they can create toolbar buttons to perform particular tasks, such as launching a custom form or switching to a particular view. With VBA, the answer is yes, you can run macro subroutines from toolbar buttons.

*Macros* are subroutines that are stored in VBA code modules (but not in VBA user form code modules), are public, and have no arguments. If a macro requires some information from the user, you cannot pass that information as an argument to the macro. Instead, the macro must either display a VBA form to get the information from the user or use one of the other input methods discussed in the next chapter.

To run a macro without a toolbar button, press Alt+F8 to open the Macros dialog, or choose Tools | Macro | Macros (see Figure 7.2). The Macros dialog will show all pubic argumentless subroutines (in other words,

**Figure 7.2**
*Run any Outlook macro from the Macros dialog.*

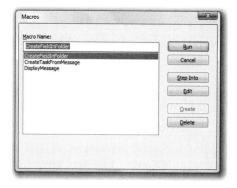

**Figure 7.3**

*Add any macro to
the toolbars in the
main Outlook
window.*

those that do not use the `Private` keyword). You don't have to do anything special to get your subroutines on that list.

Don't look for a macro recorder, such as the ones in Microsoft Word and Excel. As with most Office programs, you must write all Outlook macros from scratch.

To add an Outlook macro to one of the toolbars in the main Outlook window, follow these steps:

1. In the main Outlook window, choose View | Toolbars | Customize.

2. Switch to the Commands tab in the Customize dialog box (see Figure 7.3), and under Categories, select Macros.

3. Drag the desired macro from the Commands list to the location on the toolbar where you want the macro to appear. This will create a button for that macro on the toolbar.

4. With the Customize dialog still open, right-click the new button to pop up a menu of commands for customizing it (see Figure 7.4). You almost certainly will want to change the name to remove the Project1 prefix. You might also want to choose Change Button Image to pick an different icon for your button.

5. When you finish customizing the button, close the Customize dialog box.

You must use a different procedure to add a macro to the Quick Access Toolbar (QAT) that displays at upper-left on an individual item window. Follow these steps:

1. In any open item window, click the dropdown arrow on the right side of the QAT and choose Customize Quick Access Toolbar.

**Figure 7.4**
*Customize the
macro toolbar
button by changing
its name and icon.*

2. From the "Choose commands from" list, select Macros (see Figure 7.5).

3. Select the macro you want to place on the QAT, then click Add.

4. Select the macro command, and use the up and down arrow buttons to position the macro command among the other QAT commands.

5. Click Modify to display the Modify Button dialog (see Figure 7.6), where you can assign a different symbol and change the

**Figure 7.5**
*The only
customizable
toolbar on an
individual item
window is the
Quick Access
Toolbar.*

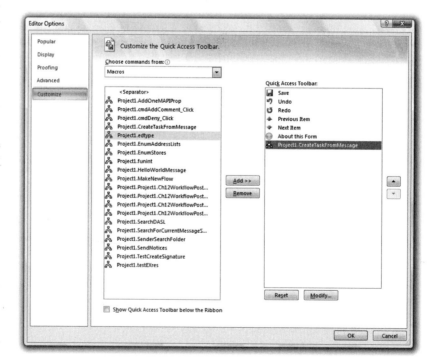

name of the button that appears when you hover the mouse pointer over it. Click OK after you finish making your changes.

6.  Click OK after you finish adding macros to the QAT.

## 7.1.5 "Run a script" rule procedures

The Tools | Rules and Alerts feature in Outlook (also known as the "Rules Wizard") includes a "run a script" rule action along with more familiar rule actions like "move to folder." This action invokes not an external script but a VBA subroutine that contains a single parameter, either a `MailItem` or `MeetingItem`. The item that is passed by that parameter is the item that triggered the rule. The code in the "script" can thus act on that item. Listing 7.3 shows an example of such a rule action procedure that converts an incoming message from HTML or rich-text format to plain text format.

To create a rule that uses the `ConvertToPlain` procedure, follow these steps:

1.  Switch to the Mail navigation pane.

2.  Choose Tools | Rules and Alerts.

3.  Click New Rule.

4.  Under "Start from a blank rule," choose "Check messages when they arrive." Click Next to continue.

**Listing 7.3**  *A "run a script" rule action to convert incoming messages to plain text format*

```
Sub ConvertToPlain(newMsg As MailItem)
    If newMsg.BodyFormat = olFormatHTML Or _
       newMsg.BodyFormat = olFormatRichText Then
        newMsg.BodyFormat = olFormatPlain
        newMsg.Save
    End If
End Sub
```

**Figure 7.7**
*The "run a script"
rule action runs not
an external script
but a specially
constructed
Outlook VBA
subroutine.*

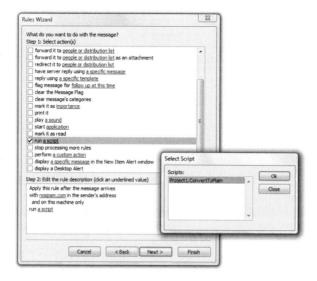

5. Choose one or more conditions to define what messages you want to convert to plain text. For example, you might choose "with specific words in the sender's address" and enter a domain name whose messages you'd rather see in plain text than HTML or rich-text format. Click Next to continue.

6. Check the "run a script" action.

7. Click the underlined "a script" to display the Select Script dialog, where you can select the VBA procedure to run (see Figure 7.7), and then click OK.

8. Click Next and enter any exceptions you want to apply to the rule.

9. Click Next and give the rule a name, then click Finish.

Note that such rules are subject to a limitation that applies to all incoming message rules: if Outlook gets more than 16 new items at once, it may not apply the rule.

## 7.2   Writing VBA code

Now that you understand when VBA code runs, it's time to write some actual code that you can use every day! The next example is a macro to create a new task item with certain fields already filled in—specifically, the due date already assigned to one week from today. This macro can run from a toolbar to create a task that you are due to finish in the next week.

If you don't already have an empty module in the Project Explorer, choose Insert | Module to add one. Then, type "Sub CreateOneWeekTask" into the code window, and press Enter. Sub indicates that this is a subroutine procedure, not a function. "CreateOneWeekTask" is the name of the procedure. Procedure names cannot contain spaces and must be unique within a module. When you press Enter, VBA automatically adds the End Sub statement marking the end of a subroutine and adds parentheses after the procedure name. Because this is going to be a macro run from a toolbar button, no arguments will go inside the parentheses.

**Note:** Starting a procedure in a code module with just Sub is equivalent to a procedure that starts with Public Sub. Public procedures need names that are unique not only within the current module, but also within the entire Outlook VBA code project. Don't worry too much about this. VBA will warn you if you create a public procedure with a duplicate name.

The next step is to initialize an object variable to represent the top-level object in the Outlook programming hierarchy—the Outlook.Application object. Add this statement inside the CreateOneWeekTask procedure:

```
Set objOL = Application
```

The Application object is *intrinsic* to—in other words, built into—Outlook VBA and represents the Outlook.Application object that is always available to programmers while Outlook is running.

Next, add the statement below to create the task:

```
Set objTask = objOL.CreateItem(olTaskItem)
```

Technically, you could simplify this code by combining the above two statements into one:

```
Set objTask = Application.CreateItem(olTaskItem)
```

However, that statement would not work if you were trying to create a task in, say, Microsoft Word's VBA environment. Word VBA has its own intrinsic Application object that represents the running instance of Word. If you want to write Outlook automation code that runs in some environment other than Outlook VBA, Outlook custom form VBScript code, or an Outlook add-in, you must instantiate an Outlook.Application object. Therefore, to make the code in this book as portable as possible to other environments, we'll use a separate object variable for the Outlook.Application object in VBA code.

How do you know that objOL.CreateItem(olTaskItem) creates a task? The key is in the olTaskItem argument. olTaskItem is an example of the intrinsic constants built into Outlook VBA. They are great coding shortcuts because they usually have very descriptive names. For example, it's not difficult to remember that olTaskItem is a constant that you can use with the CreateItem method to create a new task.

**Figure 7.8**    *This procedure to create a new task uses two objects, sets two properties, and runs a method to display a task due one week from today.*

Outlook constants are available only in VBA, though. In VBScript code behind an Outlook form, you must either declare the constant or use its literal value.

## 7.2.1    Variables

Both `objOL` and `objTask` are *variables*. Variables hold values and pointers to the data used in your procedures. Instead of referring to the value or object directly, code procedures refer to the variable name, allowing much more flexibility when you don't know what the value might be in a given scenario. Many statements in programming code manipulate variables and then return new values based on those operations. The next chapter looks in more detail at variables.

Both the statements you've written so far require a `Set` keyword, because they create object variables that represent complex programming constructs, rather than assign the values of variables that hold simple numeric or text data. This is simply a rule of VBA grammar, similar to the rules you have to learn to be proficient in English, Russian, or any other language.

Using `obj` as a prefix for all object variables can help you remember to initialize them with a `Set` statement and release them later with a statement that sets the object to `Nothing` (e.g., `Set objOL = Nothing`). You should always set an object variable to `Nothing` when your code has finished using it, as we've done with the procedure shown in Figure 7.8.

## 7.2.2    Outlook properties and methods

Next, add these two lines to the `CreateOneWeekTask` procedure:

```
objTask.StartDate = Date
objTask.DueDate = Date + 7
```

Both these statements are assignment statements. They assign values to the `StartDate` and `DueDate` properties of the task. `Date` is an intrinsic function, available in VBA and VBScript, returning the current day's date.

The standard syntax for referring to the property of an Outlook item or any other object, such as an Outlook folder, is:

```
object.propertyname
```

For custom properties that you create for Outlook items (see Chapter 6), the syntax is slightly different:

```
item.UserProperties("propertyname")
```

You can also use this syntax for either built-in or custom properties on Outlook items:

```
item.ItemProperties("propertyname")
```

**Note:** Outlook 2007 adds yet another way to access property values: the `PropertyAccessor` object, which we will learn about in Chapter 14. Generally, you will use it to access "hidden" properties that would have required Collaboration Data Objects (CDO) 1.21 in earlier versions of Outlook.

Once you have created the new task, the next step is to show it. To make the new item appear takes just one statement:

```
objTask.Display
```

The `Display` keyword is an example of a *method*. By applying a method to an object, you make the program do something—display an item, send a message, and so on. Earlier you used the `CreateItem` method to create a new task. Notice that a method uses syntax similar to a property: `object.method`.

**Tip:** You may find it helpful to think of objects as the "nouns" in the language of VBA, while properties are the "adjectives" and methods are the "verbs."

This useful macro, shown in its entirety in Figure 7.8, demonstrates how objects, variables, assignment statements, methods, and intrinsic constants comprise key code building blocks. You can now test the macro. From the VBA window, put the cursor inside the macro, and then press F5. Or, return to the main Outlook window, press Alt+F8, select your macro, and run it. Watch your new task appear! If you find this procedure useful, add it to the toolbar, using the technique described in Section 7.1.4, so you can click a button any time to get a new task due one week from today.

## 7.2.3 Subroutines versus functions

Not every procedure you write is a subroutine. You also write *functions*. These are procedures that return data to the program, usually by performing some operations on the inputs that you provide to the function.

**Listing 7.4**　*Quote() function to return a string surrounded by quotation marks*

```
Public Function Quote(data_in) As String
    Quote = Chr(34) & CStr(data_in) & Chr(34)
End Function
```

**Tip:** Think of a function as a magic box with an opening at the top, an opening at the bottom, and a crank on the side. Pour something into the top, turn the crank, and something completely different comes out at the bottom. Your job as a programmer is to supply the magic that makes the box perform its trick. Like any good magic trick, there's a logical technique behind every function.

Listing 7.4 is an example of a very simple, but very useful function. This Quote() function can take anything as its argument (data_in) and returns that data as a *string* (i.e., text) surrounded by quotation marks. Chr() is a built-in function that returns a string consisting of a single character corresponding to a given number. In this case, the number 34 corresponds to a quotation mark. CStr() is another built-in function; it converts the data passed into a string. The ampersand (&) is an operator used to *concatenate* (or join) two bits of text. You'll learn more about operators in the next section.

A function always includes one or more statements that assign the value of the function to some expression. Here, that assignment statement (the Quote = statement) is the only statement in the whole function. Table 7.3 shows the results the Quote() function delivers for various sample arguments. Note that it can even take an object, such as the intrinsic Outlook VBA Application object, as its argument. Most objects have a default property, such as Name, that allows a function, such as Quote(), to return a meaningful result.

Typing the expression Quote("Microsoft Outlook") is easier than typing the equivalent expression Chr(34) & "Microsoft Outlook" & Chr(34). If you haven't already, you should add the Quote() function to

**Table 7.3**　*Sample Results for the Quote() Function*

| Argument | Result |
|---|---|
| Quote("Microsoft Outlook") | "Microsoft Outlook" |
| Quote(2) | "2" |
| Quote(Application) | "Outlook" |

the code module that you're building in Outlook VBA. You will definitely use it later in building message boxes and in searching and filtering for particular Outlook items.

## 7.2.4 Operators

*Operators* are symbols that perform various mathematical and data operations, such as addition, division, joining strings, or comparing two numbers to find out which is greater. Table 7.4 lists those you are most likely to use in Outlook code. Many of them should be familiar from your earliest arithmetic books.

**Tip:** For the complete list of operators or to learn more about any particular operator, open the Outlook VBA window, choose Help | Microsoft Visual Basic Help, and search for "Operator Summary."

## 7.2.5 Referring to VBA forms and controls

We have one more basic VBA coding issue to address: how to refer to VBA forms and controls. It's really simple. Use the value of the Name property of the form or control.

**Table 7.4**  *Commonly Used Operators*

| Operator | Description |
| --- | --- |
| + | Addition |
| − | Subtraction |
| * | Multiplication |
| / | Division |
| & | String concatenation |
| = | Equal to |
| > | Greater than |
| >= | Greater than or equal to |
| < | Less than |
| <= | Less than or equal to |
| <> | Not equal to |
| And | True if both expressions are true; otherwise, False |
| Or | True if either expression is true; otherwise, False |
| Not | True if the expression is false; False if the expression is true |

Look back to Section 3.5.3, to the `cmdUpdate_Click` procedure on the `ReminderUpdate` form, to see an example. In the following statement:

```
lngMinutes = 24 * 60 * txtDays.Value
```

the expression `txtDays.Value` returns the data stored in the `Value` property of the `txtDays` text box on the form. Because the code is running inside the form, attached to the `Click` event for one of the form's command buttons, Outlook knows that the `txtDays` object refers to a control on the form.

If the code is in a separate module or behind a different form, refer to the form and the control on that form with the syntax *formname. controlname*. For example, here is a subroutine that loads the form, disables the `cmdUpdate` button, and then displays the form to the user:

```
Sub RunReminderUpdate()
    Load ReminderUpdate
    ReminderUpdate.cmdUpdate.Enabled = False
    ReminderUpdate.Show
End Sub
```

---

**Tip:** Did you notice that `RunReminderUpdate` is a macro that you can run from a toolbar button or by pressing Alt+F8?

---

Why would you want to disable a control, such as the `cmdUpdate` button? Now that you know how to work with VBA form events, you can write code that watches what the user enters into the `txtDays` box and enables the `cmdUpdate` button only if a valid number is present. To enhance the validation procedure discussed earlier in Section 7.1.2, replace the earlier `txtDays_BeforeUpdate` procedure with this code:

```
Private Sub txtDays_BeforeUpdate(ByVal Cancel _
  As MSForms.ReturnBoolean)
    If IsNumeric(txtDays.Value) = False Then
        Cancel = True
        MsgBox "Please enter a number."
        txtDays.SelStart = 0
        txtDays.SelLength = Len(txtDays.Value)
        cmdUpdate.Enabled = False
    Else
        cmdUpdate.Enabled = True
    End If
End Sub
```

Notice that because the `txtDays.BeforeUpdate` procedure is an event handler on the `ReminderUpdate` form, you do not need to specify the name of the form in the `cmdUpdate.Enabled` expression.

---

**Note:** You will learn about `If ... Then ... Else ... End If` code blocks in Chapter 8.

---

# 7.3 Writing VBScript code for Outlook forms

Outlook custom forms, which we looked at earlier in Chapters 4 and 6, can also run event-driven code. A procedure runs either from an event related to the item, such as `Open` or `Write`, or from the `Click` event on a control. You can add other subroutines and functions, but they must be called from one of the event procedures.

To add code to an Outlook form, open the form in design mode, and then click View Code. You should see right away that the development environment for Outlook form code is very primitive, so basic in fact that Outlook developers jokingly refer to it as "Visual Notepad" (see Figure 7.9). To add code for an item event, in the code window, choose Script | Event Handler, and select from the list in the Insert Event Handler dialog (see Figure 7.10). Outlook adds a `Function ... End Function` or `Sub ... End Sub` stub to the code window, depending on the event. Figure 7.9 shows the stubs for the `Open` and `PropertyChange` events.

---

**Caution:** The Insert Event Handler dialog does not check to see whether a particular event is already present in your form's script. It's possible to add duplicate handlers. If you have more than one procedure with the same name, Outlook will not give you any error message. Instead, it will simply skip any duplicates and run only the last of the duplicate procedures.

---

Like Outlook VBA, custom forms support an intrinsic `Application` object representing the currently running Outlook application. They also support an intrinsic `Item` object that represents the item whose form is running the code. That's why, in Figure 7.9, the event handlers have the name `Item_Open` and `Item_PropertyChange`. The `Open` event fires when the item opens in its own window for viewing or editing. The `Property-Change` event fires when any built-in property of the item changes value.

**Figure 7.9**
*Outlook item event handlers in custom form VBScript code have their own specific syntax, just like VBA application or user form event handlers.*

**Figure 7.10**
*Add Outlook form-level events through this dialog.*

The Name parameter of the PropertyChange event tells you which property changed. As with VBA event handlers, you should not change the procedure declaration that the Event Handler command creates.

## 7.3.1   Declaring constants and variables

Remember this statement earlier in this chapter that creates a new Outlook task:

```
Set objTask = objOL.CreateItem(olTaskItem)
```

VBScript doesn't know that olTaskItem is a constant, much less what value olTaskItem has. You must either declare it as a constant or use its literal value. In either case, you'll need to look up that value. While the form code window does have a mini object browser, accessible through the Script | Object Browser command, it's not very useful. You're better off looking up constant values in the object browser in VBA. Here's how to get the constant you need in order to create a task:

1. In the Outlook VBA environment, press F2 to display the object browser.

2. Change the library selection from <All Libraries> to Outlook.

3. In the search box, type "CreateItem," and then click the Search button (the one with the binoculars icon).

4. When the search results return, CreateItem will be highlighted, as shown in the left window in Figure 7.11, and in the bottom pane you'll see that this method takes a particular value from the OlItemType enumeration of constants.

5. Click OlItemType to browse to that enumeration, as shown in the right window in Figure 7.11, and then select olTaskItem.

6. The bottom pane shows the constant declaration for olTask-Item, which you can copy and paste to your form code window.

Where you declare variables depends on where you plan to use them. If you plan to use a variable in only one code procedure, put its Dim statement in that procedure.

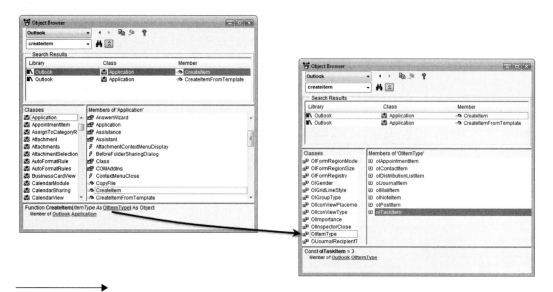

**Figure 7.11** *Use the object browser in VBA to look up Outlook constants so you can copy and paste their declarations into your custom form VBScript code.*

To declare constants so that any procedure can use them, place those `Const` statements before the first procedure. This top area of the code module is called the *declarations section*. I recommend that you also include an `Option Explicit` statement, covered in the next chapter, as the very first statement of the code module. This will help you avoid careless mistakes, because it requires you to include a `Dim` statement for each variable in the module.

Figure 7.12 shows the VBScript code for two form buttons, `CommandButton1` and `CommandButton2`, both of which create tasks when clicked. Compare the VBScript version of the `CreatOneWeekTask` procedure with the VBA version in Figure 7.8.

Don't forget to set object variables to `Nothing` in your VBScript form code after you finish using them, as discussed earlier in Section 7.2.1. If you don't do that, changes that you make to the items might not be immediately visible when you or another user opens the item again.

## 7.3.2 Custom form events

Outlook forms support their own set of events, but they're quite different from the VBA user form events and from the Outlook application-level events you have encountered so far. Table 7.5 lists the 16 item-level events that Outlook forms support and tells you which can be canceled. These events fire not only when the user interacts with the form but also when programming code simulates any of these user actions.

**Figure 7.12**
*If your VBScript code uses an Outlook constant, you muct declare it with a Const statement.*

---

**Note:** The syntax for canceling an event in VBScript form code is different from that in VBA. You will see an example in the next section.

---

**Table 7.5**　*Item Events for Custom Outlook forms (\* = new in Outlook 2007)*

| Event | Occurs | Can Be Canceled |
|---|---|---|
| AttachmentAdd | When an attachment is added to an item | |
| AttachmentRead | When the user opens an attachment | |
| *AttachmentRemove | When an attachment is removed from an item | |
| *BeforeAttachmentAdd | Before an attachment is added to an item | X |
| *BeforeAttachmentPreview | Before an attachment is previewed, either from the reading pane or an open Inspector window | X |
| *BeforeAttachmentRead | Before an attachment is read from an attached file or, in the case of a file link, from the file system | X |
| BeforeAttachmentSave | Just before an attachment is saved into the Outlook item; also occurs when an attachment is updated with changes, just before the parent item is saved | X |

**Table 7.5** *Item Events for Custom Outlook forms (\* = new in Outlook 2007) (continued)*

| Event | Occurs | Can Be Canceled |
|---|---|---|
| \*BeforeAttachmentWriteToTempFile | Before an attached file is written to a temporary file in the file system | X |
| \*BeforeAutoSave | Before Outlook automatically saves the item | X |
| BeforeCheckNames | Before Outlook starts to resolve names in the To, Cc, and Bcc fields on a message (or equivalent fields in other items) against the address book after the user explicitly uses the Check Names command | X |
| BeforeDelete | Before Outlook deletes a displayed item | X |
| Close | When a displayed Outlook item closes | X |
| CustomAction | When a custom action associated with a received message or other saved item occurs; see Chapter 20. | X |
| CustomPropertyChange | When the value of a user-defined property changes | |
| Forward | When the item is forwarded | X |
| Open | Just before Outlook displays an item in its own window | X |
| PropertyChange | When the value of a built-in property changes | |
| Read | When the user displays an item for editing, either in its own window or using in-cell editing in a folder view | |
| Reply | When an item is replied to using Reply | X |
| ReplyAll | When an item is replied to using Reply to All | X |
| Send | When an item is sent | X |
| \*Unload | After the Close event, as the item is being unloaded from memory; item properties and methods are not available | |
| Write | When an item is saved | X |

**Tip:** Listing 22.1 in Chapter 22 shows the `BeforeAttachmentAdd` event being used to allow a form to accept attachments only of a certain file type.

Outlook form controls support just one event, `Click`, which fires only on most (but not all) unbound controls. A control bound to a particular Outlook field never fires a `Click` event. To detect changes in the data stored in bound controls (so that you can perform validation and other code tasks), use the `CustomPropertyChange` and `PropertyChange` events, as explained in Chapter 12. Outlook forms do not support any equivalent for the `BeforeUpdate` event that you find on VBA form controls.

### 7.3.3   Adding VBScript code to an Outlook form

As a practical example of code for an Outlook form, let's look at a common programming task with many uses. Often, you will need to know whether the item displayed in your form is a completely new item that the user just created or an existing item. You may want to initialize certain property values on a new item or change the appearance of certain controls on an existing item.

The first step in writing code is to open a form in design mode. For this example, let's do something a bit out of the ordinary and design a custom distribution list form. The distribution list form does not appear in the list of standard forms when you choose Tools | Forms | Design a Form. Nevertheless, it can be customized. This example will customize it to tell the user how many member addresses the distribution list holds—an important piece of information that you won't find in the Outlook user interface.

Open a distribution list in design mode by choosing File | New | Distribution List, then on the Developer tab, click Design This Form. (If you don't see the Developer tab, click the Office logo at upper-left, then choose Editor Options, and check the box for "Show Developer tab in the Ribbon.") When the distribution list opens in design mode, you'll see that it has custom pages P.2–P.6 and design commands just like other forms.

Click the View Code command to open the code window. The event that fires when the user creates a new item or displays an existing item is the `Open` event. Therefore, choose Script | Event Handler, select Open, then

**Listing 7.5**   *Code to display the number of addresses in a distribution list*

```
Function Item_Open()
    If Item.Size <> 0 Then
        strMsg = "This list has " & _
                    Item.MemberCount & " members."
        MsgBox strMsg, vbInformation, Item.Subject
    End If
End Function
```

click Add. This adds the procedure stub for the Item_Open event handler function to the code window.

There is no point in showing the user the number of addresses in the distribution list if it's a new item. That number is meaningful only for existing items. Therefore, we need a way to tell whether the item is new or existing. The easiest way to do that is to check the value of the Size property. For a new item that has never been saved, Size always equals 0.

---

**Tip:** Another property that distinguishes new items is EntryID. It is always blank if the item has never been saved.

---

Another thing you need to know is what Outlook property can tell you the number of addresses in the distribution list. A quick glance at the object browser's information about the DistListItem object should lead you to the MemberCount property.

The last element needed for this form is a way to get the information to the user. Back in Listing 7.1, you saw the MsgBox method for displaying a pop-up message to the user. It works in VBScript as well as VBA. Put those three elements together—the Open event, the Size property, the Member-Count property, and the MsgBox method—and you get Listing 7.5.

Since this code does nothing on new items (that is, items where Item.Size = 0), to test the form, you can't just use the Run This Form command. Instead, you'll need to publish the form. Click the Publish button and publish it to your Contacts folder with the name "Member Count DL." Leave the form open in design mode so you can make more changes to it later.

To test the form, view your Contacts folder, choose Actions | New Member Count DL, give the distribution list a name, add some members, and then save and close it. Open it again, and you should see a message like that in Figure 7.13. Notice how the message box takes its title from the last parameter in the MsgBox statement, Item.Subject, and gets an icon from

**Figure 7.13**
*The MsgBox method displays a message to the user, with optional title and icon.*

the second parameter, `vbInformation`, a constant supported in VBScript as well as VBA. The next chapter covers `MsgBox` statements and their parameters.

### 7.3.4  Canceling events

Referring back to Table 7.5, you'll see that `Open` is one of several events that can be canceled programmatically. Why would you want to cancel an event? If the user clicks Save but hasn't filled in some property values correctly, you can cancel the `Write` event to prevent the item from saving.

To cancel an Outlook form event, set the return value of the event handler function to `False`. For example, you may want to group all your distribution lists at the top of the Contacts folder (and thus at the top in the Address Book display) by prefixing them with an underscore character. If you want to prevent the user from saving a distribution list that does not start with an underscore, you could add the code in Listing 7.6.

`Left()` is a function with two parameters: a text string and the number of leftmost characters from that string that you want to return, in this case, one character. What Listing 7.6 does is *validate* the data in the item before allowing the user to save it. You can do much more complex validation in VBScript code than you can with the options in the form controls covered in Chapter 6.

### 7.3.5  Referring to Outlook form controls

Sometimes your code will need to work directly with a control, rather than with an Outlook property bound to that control. For example, you might want to show or hide a control or change the color of the text in a text box to red. The syntax to get a control object on a custom form is slightly more complicated than that for VBA user form controls. You always need to know not just the name of the control, but also the name of the page on the Outlook form where it appears. In general, the syntax looks like this:

```
Set objInsp = Item.GetInspector
Set objPage = objInsp.ModifiedFormPages("pagename")
Set objControl = objPage.Controls("controlname")
objControl.property = newvalue
```

**Listing 7.6**   *Canceling an event in VBScript form code*

```
Function Item_Write()
    If Left(Item.Subject, 1) <> "_" Then
        Item_Write = False
        strMsg = "Start the DL name with an underscore."
        MsgBox strMsg, vbExclamation, "Save Canceled"
    End If
End Function
```

where `pagename` is the name of the page, `controlname` is the name of the control, `property` is the control property that you want to change, and `newvalue` is the new value for that property.

To work with the properties of a control inside a frame, you need to go through the frame's own `Controls` property. Here's a code snippet that shows the text inside a text box that is inside a frame. It runs when a command button is clicked:

```
Sub CommandButton1_Click()
    Set insp = Item.GetInspector
    Set Frame1 = _
      insp.ModifiedFormPages("P.2").Controls("Frame1")
    Set TextBox1 = Frame1.Controls("TextBox1")
    MsgBox TextBox1.Text
End Sub
```

In the above example, if you wanted to hide `Frame1` and all the controls contained in `Frame1`, you'd use:

```
Frame1.Enabled = False
```

---

**Tip:** Use the Advanced Properties dialog for a control to see what properties a control supports. For example, most controls support a `Locked` property. Assigning a value of `True` to that property makes the control read-only.

As is so often the case with Outlook, though, there is an exception: The large box that shows the body of an item can be set read-only, even though the Advanced Properties dialog shows no `Locked` property. Instead of `Locked`, the property to use for the item body control is `ReadOnly`.

---

An important control property is `Value`, especially if you are working with unbound controls. The `Value` property returns or sets the data value that the user sees in the control. If the control is bound to an Outlook property, you should work with the property value, not the control value, using the `Item.property` (or `Item.UserProperties("property")`) syntax covered earlier in this chapter and in the next section. But for unbound controls, only the `Value` property of the control is available. This code snippet calculates a value from two unbound controls to set a value in a third control and then changes the color of the text in that control to red if the value is less than zero:

```
Set objInsp = Item.GetInspector
Set objPage = objInsp.ModifiedFormPages("Budget")
Set objIncome = objPage.Controls("Income")
Set objExpenses = objPage.Controls("Expenses")
Set objNet = objPage.Controls("Net")
objNet.Value = objIncome.Value - objExpenses.Value
If objNet.Value < 0 Then
    objNet.Forecolor = vbRed
End If
```

The above snippets use separate expressions to return the `Inspector`, form page, and form controls to enhance readability and ease of debugging, but you can also combine those expressions. This expression, for example, returns the value of the Net control on the Budget page (and is too long to fit all on one line on this page):

```
Item.GetInspector.ModifiedFormPages("Budget").Controls("
Net").Value
```

On a multi-page control, the `Value` property gets or sets the index for the page that is currently displayed. This is a zero-based property, meaning that `0` is the value for the leftmost page. The `SelectedItem` property of the multi-page control returns a `Page` object corresponding to the currently displayed page. Use that `Page` object as you would a page returned from `Inspector.ModifiedFormPages` collection to access the controls on that page of the multi-page control.

In a nutshell, here is what you need to know about Outlook form controls:

- When you want to change the appearance of a control, write code for the control's object and its properties.

- When you want to work with the value displayed in an unbound control, write code for the control's `Value` property.

- When you want to work with the values displayed in bound controls, write code for `Item.property`, `Item.ItemProperties`, or `Item.UserProperties`, as discussed in the next section.

- The syntax for referring to an Outlook form control requires you to know both the page and the control names.

- Any change your code makes to the appearance of a custom form control is not persisted with the data item. The next time the user opens the item, the control will look just the way it did when you originally published the form. If you want it to look different, put code in the `Item_Open` event handler to change the appearance of the control when the user displays the item.

We will return to the last issue—persistence of control appearance—in Chapter 12, when we discuss the concept of the user interface *state* of an Outlook item.

## 7.4    Referring to Outlook item properties

As emphasized in the preceding section, when you want to know the value of an Outlook property, get it directly from the item, not from the control displaying the property. Listings 7.5 and 7.6 showed several examples of reading the value of standard Outlook properties—`Item.Size`, `Item.Subject`, `Item.MemberCount`—from custom form VBScript code. Listing 7.3

→

**Listing 7.7** *Automatically prefix a distribution list name with an underscore character*

```
Function Item_Write()
    If Left(Item.Subject, 1) <> "_" Then
        Item.Subject = "_" & Item.Subject
    End If
End Function
```

showed how to read the `BodyFormat` property of a message in VBA code. All these examples used the same syntax:

```
objItem.property
```

where `objItem` is an Outlook item object and `property` is the name of the property whose value you want to know.

To assign a new value to a property, use the same syntax that you saw in the VBA example in Listing 7.3:

```
objItem.property = NewValue
```

For a custom form VBScript example, instead of asking the user to change the distribution list, as Listing 7.6 does, the code could automatically prefix the subject with an underscore character. The appropriate event for that task would still be the `Write` event. Listing 7.7 uses the same validation expression as Listing 7.6, but instead of canceling the `Write` event, it changes the subject to add the underscore prefix. Since this is VBScript code, we don't need to instantiate an `objItem` object variable to represent the item whose property is to be changed. Instead, the `Item_Write()` event handler uses the intrinsic `Item` object representing the item where the code is running.

Notice that `Item.Subject` appears on both sides of the third statement in Listing 7.7—on the right side to read the property value and on the left side to set the value.

So far in this chapter, we have been working with built-in Outlook properties, such as `Subject`. As we learned in Chapter 6, you can create your own properties, too. Accessing these properties requires a different syntax in your form code and VBA code.

Where you can refer to a built-in property on the current item in VBScript simply with `objItem.property`, the syntax for referring to a custom property involves the `UserProperties` collection of all custom properties:

```
objItem.UserProperties("property")
```

Both these snippets of custom form VBScript code display a message box with the value of the `Project` field that you added to a task form in the previous chapter:

```
MsgBox Item.UserProperties("Project")

Set objProp = Item.UserProperties("Project")
MsgBox objProp.Value
```

Alternatively, you can access both standard and custom properties through the `ItemProperties` collection:

```
MsgBox Item.ItemProperties("Subject")

Set objProp = Item.ItemProperties("Project")
MsgBox objProp.Value
```

Each `ItemProperty` object in the `ItemProperties` collection includes an `IsUserProperty` property that tells you whether it is a built-in or custom property.

### 7.4.1   Working with custom keywords properties

There is one significant exception to the usage of `UserProperties("property")` to get or set a custom property, and that's with a keywords field. A keywords field is a special type of text property that can hold multiple values. To get or set the value of such a property, you must use a custom form and a text box control bound to that property. With that form design, you can access the property through the value of the control.

For example, create a custom form, add a keywords property named `Expertise`, and rename one of the customizable pages to `Info`. On that page, add a text box control named `txtExpertise` and bind it to the `Expertise` property. Also add a command button named `cmdDemoExpertise`. Add this VBScript code to the form to get the current value of the `Expertise` property and append a new value to it:

```
Sub cmdDemoExpertise_Click()
    Set Info = _
      Item.GetInspector.ModifiedFormPages("Info")
    Set txtExpertise = Info.Controls("txtExpertise")
    strExpertise = txtExpertise.Value
    txtExpertise.Value = strExpertise & ", design"
End Sub
```

The chief reason for using a custom keywords property is to be able to group by the property and have each item appear in as many groups as it has keywords, just as the standard By Category view does. If that kind of view is not a necessary component of your Outlook application, a custom text property holding a delimited string may work just as well as a custom keywords property and avoid this cumbersome access problem.

### 7.4.2   Creating custom properties programmatically

Like most other Outlook collections, the `UserProperties` collection supports an `Add` method, used to add a new custom property to an item. If an item is using a custom form, you should never invoke `UserProperties.Add` to add a property to the item. Doing so will cause the form to one-off, that is, to become embedded in the item so that the form never runs code for that item again. Instead, add custom properties to custom forms using the Field Chooser.

There are cases, though, where you may want to add a custom property to an existing item that does not use a custom form. The basic syntax for the `UserProperties.Add` method looks like this:

```
Set objProp = objItem.UserProperties.Add( _
    Name, Type, DisplayFormat, Formula)
```

where `Name` is the name of the property and `Type` is the type of property, using one of the values from the `OlUserPropertyType` enumeration shown in Table 7.6. Both these arguments are required.

---

**Note:** While Outlook will not raise an error if you try to create a `UserProperty` with a `Type` argument of `olCombination` or `olFormula`, assigning a formula to the `UserProperty.Formula` property does not actually set the formula for the property. Therefore, you still need to create combination and formula properties manually, as discussed in the previous chapter. You also cannot create a `UserProperty` with a `Type` value using any of these constants from the `OlUserPropertyType` enumeration: `olEnumeration`, `olOutlookInternal`, `olSmartFrom`.

The optional `AddToFolderFields` parameter controls whether the property is defined in the folder for the item, as well as in the item; the default value is `True`. In order for a property to be visible in a folder view or usable in an `Items.Find` or `Items.Restrict` search, it needs to be defined in the folder. You can also define a property in a folder directly, using this syntax:

```
Folder.UserDefinedProperties.Add(Name, Type, _
    DisplayFormat, Formula)
```

---

The optional `DisplayFormat` argument tells Outlook how to display the value of the property in folder views and on the All Fields page. The Outlook 2007 object model contains several new enumerations that define the formats available for each type of custom property. Table 7.6 lists these, as well as the default `DisplayFormat` value for each `UserProperty.Type`.

## 7.5   **Writing other Outlook automation code**

Outlook features can be automated not just from Outlook VBA and custom form VBScript code but also from just about any other programming environment that can run client-side code. If Outlook is not already running,

**Table 7.6**  *Custom Property Type and DisplayFormat Values*

| Type | Value | DisplayFormat Enumeration | Default DisplayFormat Value |
|------|-------|---------------------------|------------------------------|
| olCurrency | 14 | OlFormatCurrency | olFormatCurrencyDecimal |
| olDateTime | 5 | OlFormatDateTime | olFormatDateTimeShortDayDateTime |
| olDuration | 7 | OlFormatDuration | olFormatDurationShort |
| olInteger | 20 | OlFormatInteger | olFormatIntegerPlain |
| olKeywords | 11 | OlFormatKeywords | olFormatKeywordsText |
| olNumber | 3 | OlFormatNumber | olFormatNumberAllDigits |
| olPercent | 12 | OlFormatPercent | olFormatPercent2Decimal |
| olText | 1 | OlFormatText | olFormatTextText |
| olYesNo | 6 | OlFormatYesNo | olFormatYesNoYesNo |

your code can start Outlook and thus gain access to all the objects, properties, and methods that you'd have available in Outlook VBA.

For example, a common annoyance in Word is that the Send | E-mail command does not generate an email message using your default Outlook mail signature. A good solution is to write a Word 2007 macro to create a new Outlook message and attach the current document, saving the document first if needed. To run the code in Listing 7.8 as a Word macro, follow these steps:

1.   Start Word.

2.   Press Alt+F11 to start the Word VBA environment.

3.   Choose Tools | References and add a reference to the Microsoft Outlook 12.0 Object Library.

4.   In the Project Explorer, select Normal (which points to your Normal.dotm default template for Word documents), and choose Insert | Module.

5.   Type the code in Listing 7.8 into the new module.

You can run the macro from any document by using Alt+F8 to display the list of available macros, or you can add it to the Quick Access Toolbar in Word using the same technique that you saw in Section 7.1.4. When you shut down Word and get a prompt to save changes in the Normal template, respond Yes so this macro will be saved in the template.

One big change in Outlook 2007 is that external applications can automate Outlook without encountering security prompts from the Outlook

**Listing 7.8**    *Word VBA code to attach the current document to an Outlook message*

```
Sub SendMeAsMail()
    ' requires reference to Microsoft Outlook 12.0 library
    Dim objOL As Outlook.Application
    Dim objMail As Outlook.MailItem
    Dim strMsg as String
    Dim ans as Integer
    Dim dlg As Word.Dialog
    On Error Resume Next

    If Not ActiveDocument.Saved Then
        strMsg = "You must save this document " & _
                "before sending it. OK?"
        ans = MsgBox(strMsg, vbYesNo, "Save Document?")
        If ans = vbYes Then
            If ActiveDocument.Path = "" Then
                Set dlg = Application.Dialogs(wdDialogFileSaveAs)
                dlg.Show
            End If
        End If
    End If
    If ActiveDocument.Saved Then
        Set objOL = StartOutlook()
        If Not objOL Is Nothing Then
            Set objMail = objOL.CreateItem(olMailItem)
            objMail.Attachments.Add ActiveDocument.FullName
            objMail.Display
        End If
    End If

    Set objMail = Nothing
    Set objOL = Nothing
End Sub

Function StartOutlook() As Outlook.Application
    Dim objOL As Outlook.Application
    Dim objNS As Outlook.NameSpace
    On Error Resume Next

    Set objOL = GetObject(, "Outlook.Application")
    If objOL Is Nothing Then
        Set objOL = CreateObject("Outlook.Application")
        Set objNS = objOL.GetNamespace("MAPI")
        objNS.Logon
    End If
    Set StartOutlook = objOL

    Set objOL = Nothing
    Set objNS = Nothing
End Function
```

object model. The prerequisite to avoid prompts is that the computer must have an up-to-date anti-virus application running. Chapter 10 contains more information on Outlook security.

## **7.5.1  Starting an Outlook session**

Starting an Outlook session is such a key element of automating Outlook from another program that you probably will want to have a generic function to perform that function for you. The StartOutlook() function in Listing 7.9 uses the GetObject() method to see if a copy of Outlook is already running. If Outlook isn't running, the code uses the CreateObject() method to start Outlook and then performs a logon. Depending on the user's mail profile settings, the Logon statement may prompt the user to select a mail profile or may start Outlook with the user's default mail profile. You can also force Outlook to start with a particular mail profile:

```
objNS.Logon "name of mail profile"
```

or to prompt the user to choose a profile:

```
objNS.Logon "", "", True, True
```

**Listing 7.9**    *Sending a file with a VBScript script*

```
Const olMailItem = 0
On Error Resume Next

Set objOL = StartOutlook()
If Not objOL Is Nothing Then
    Set objMail = objOL.CreateItem(olMailItem)
    objMail.Attachments.Add "C:\Data\MyFile.txt"
    objMail.Display
End If

Set objMail = Nothing
Set objOL = Nothing

Function StartOutlook()
    Dim objOL
    Dim objNS
    On Error Resume Next

    Set objOL = GetObject(, "Outlook.Application")
    If objOL Is Nothing Then
        Set objOL = CreateObject("Outlook.Application")
        Set objNS = objOL.GetNamespace("MAPI")
        objNS.Logon
    End If
    Set StartOutlook = objOL

    Set objOL = Nothing
    Set objNS = Nothing
End Function
```

You can use the `StartOutlook()` function not just in Word, but in Access or Excel or any VBA code environment where you need to start Outlook; just remember to add a reference to the Microsoft Outlook 12.0 Object Library.

The VBScript equivalent of the `StartOutlook()` function is shown in Listing 7.9 as part of a script to create and display a message with a specific file attached. You can create such a script in Notepad, save it as a .vbs file, then double-click the file to run it.

The only real difference between the two versions of the `StartOutlook()` function is that the VBScript version has no data type declarations for the two object variables, `objOL` and `objNS`.

### 7.5.2 **Limitations on Outlook automation**

Just because you can automate Outlook with an external VBA procedure or a stand-alone VBScript script, as demonstrated in Listings 7.8 and 7.9, that doesn't mean you can write Outlook automation code to run in any environment. Any Outlook automation code that is expected to run without user interaction generally won't work. These scenarios in particular are not supported:

■ Code that runs from a Windows scheduler event

■ Server-side code, including database triggers, Web services, and other Web applications

You can write client-side Jscript or VBScript in a Web application to automate Outlook, but even that may run into problems, because Outlook is not a "safe for scripting" component. A call to the `Outlook.Application` object from a Web page script may trigger an ActiveX security prompt, depending on the browser's security settings and the location of the Web page.

Also, some client anti-virus applications block Outlook automation by raising an error on any call to the `Outlook.Application` object. If you want to turn off such a script-blocking feature, you may need to contact technical support for your anti-virus program to find out how to do that.

## 7.6 **Summary**

This chapter has demonstrated the basics of automating Outlook from VBA, from custom form VBScript code, and from external applications. Code modules can include both subroutines and functions, and such procedures can react to events and use object methods to make something happen. For example, by returning an instance of the `Outlook Application` object and using its `CreateItem` method, you can create a new task or a new message. Pay close attention to the difference between the syntax for accessing Outlook item properties and that for accessing custom form control properties.

In Chapter 8, we will continue learning code basics as we explore VBA and VBScript code syntax in more detail, preparing the way in later chapters to learn about the specifics of the Outlook object model.

# 8

# *Code Grammar 101*

So far, your excursion into Outlook programming code has been a lot like beginning language lessons. Most of the initial work in learning a language is oral and repetitive: You work with a teacher or tape, memorizing phrases and repeating them. Sooner or later, though, you must learn more about the structure of a language; you must study grammar. Welcome to "Code Grammar 101," the chapter that reviews the basic syntax of VBA and VBScript, including the most important functions built into VBA and VBScript and many custom functions that are ready to add to your own Outlook project.

Highlights of this chapter include discussions of the following:

- How to write reusable subroutines and functions for both VBScript and VBA
- What built-in functions are available for manipulating text and dates
- How to control the flow of your program and handle repetitive operations
- How to give users feedback and solicit input from them
- How to work with files and other objects from outside the Outlook object model

## 8.1    Option Explicit

I'm going to let you in on a little secret: To create the `CreateOneWeekTask` macro shown in Figure 7.8 and in Listing 8.1 below, you did more typing than you needed to. Outlook can do more of the work for you and at the same time avoid common errors. The key is to set up VBA so that it forces you to declare all your variables.

First, it helps to see what happens when you have a mistake in your code. In the `CreateOneWeekTask` macro, change the `objTask.Display` statement to `objMyTask.Display`, and then run the routine again. You

**Listing 8.1**     *Simple VBA macro to create a task due one week from today*

```
Sub CreateOneWeekTask()
    Set objOL = Application
    Set objTask = objOL.CreateItem(olTaskItem)
    objTask.StartDate = Date
    objTask.DueDate = Date + 7
    objTask.Display
    Set objTask = Nothing
    Set objOL = Nothing
End Sub
```

should receive an "object required" error message, shown in Figure 8.1. Click the Debug button, and VBA takes you directly to the statement with a problem—the one you changed. It's wrong because `objMyTask` isn't the right name for the object variable for the new item; it should be `objTask` instead, because you instantiated the variable with the statement that begins `Set objTask =`.

I want you to notice this error, because it's such a common one—you might change a variable name in the middle of a procedure or just make a typo. A couple of simple changes to the macro code, though, will help you prevent such coding errors.

To stop code execution and get back into design mode to make those changes, click the Reset button on the Toolbar, or choose Run | Reset.

Press Ctrl+Home to move to the top of the module containing the `CreateOneWeekTask` procedure. The dropdown lists at the top of the code window should show (General) and (Declarations). You are now in the *declarations section* of the module, before the first procedure. This is where you place statements that affect the entire module and declare variables and constants that you want to use in more than one procedure.

Make this statement the first line in the declaration section:

`Option Explicit`

The `Option Explicit` statement tells VBA that, within this particular module, all variables must be declared before you use them. This means

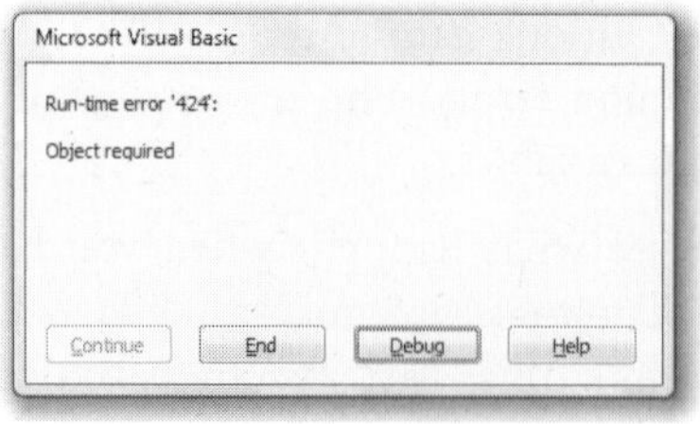

**Figure 8.1**

*Using the wrong variable name can cause an error.*

**Figure 8.2**
*Options for the
VBA code editor
include requiring
all variables to be
explicitly declared.*

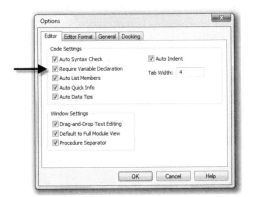

that you can't just throw in a new variable any time you need it. If you do, you'll get a "variable not defined" error when you try to run the code, but that's a good sort of error, one that points out a flaw in the code. To prevent that error, declare each variable, either in the declarations section or inside a procedure. We'll look at variable "scope" a little later in the chapter to help you decide which location is best. Using `Option Explicit` forces VBA to check all variable names when it compiles the code, before running any procedure. Detecting an error early, at the design or compile stage, is better than finding the error only when you run the procedure.

To add `Option Explicit` automatically to the declarations for any new module, choose Tools | Options from the VBA menu. In the Options dialog, shown in Figure 8.2, check Require Variable Declaration. This change affects only new forms and modules. If you want to use `Option Explicit` in an existing VBA module, type it into the module's declarations section.

---

**Tip:** While you're in the Options dialog shown in Figure 8.2, be sure to check out the other options available to customize the appearance and operation of the VBA environment.

---

VBScript also supports `Option Explicit`, and I recommend that you use it in every custom form's code module. Type it as the first line in the module; Outlook can't add it automatically.

## 8.2 Declaring variables and constants

After adding `Option Explicit` to your VBA module, if you now try to run the `CreateOneWeekTask` macro you will receive a "variable not defined" compile error because you didn't declare any variables. That's not a problem! It's a reminder to clean up your code. Use a `Dim` statement to declare each variable at the beginning of the procedure, right after the Sub or Function statement that marks the beginning of the procedure. To declare the variables used in the CreateOneWeekTask macro, add these statements to your code:

```
Dim objOL As Outlook.Application
Dim objTask as Outlook.TaskItem
```

**Tip:** If you write code only inside the Outlook VBA environment, you can omit the Outlook prefix on data type declarations and just use Dim objOL as Application. However, it's a good idea to get into the habit of using a fully qualified declaration in case you later expand your programming efforts to VBA in other Office programs or to other programming environments.

One of the major differences between VBA and VBScript is that the latter does not allow data-typing in variable or procedure declarations. Therefore, a VBScript equivalent to the first declaration above would be simply

```
Dim objOL
```

but even better would be to include the data type as a comment by prefixing it with an apostrophe:

```
Dim objOL ' As Outlook.Application
```

If you forget and include an As data type in a Dim statement in VBScript code behind an Outlook form, you will get an "expected end of statement" error when you try to run the form.

When you type a space after As in a Dim statement, VBA pops up a list of possible ways to complete the statement. This feature, called Auto List Members, is one of the "intellisense" features in VBA that can save you hours of typing and avoid many errors. This is the feature I was referring to earlier in the chapter, when I said that declaring your variables would actually help cut down on the amount of typing you need to do. Intellisense helps you complete a statement or expression by offering a set of appropriate choices. Select an item from the list, and then press Enter to add that text to the current statement. If you press Enter, VBA completes the statement and puts the cursor on the next line. Try pressing Tab or the spacebar instead of Enter. If you press Tab, VBA completes the statement, but leaves the cursor on the same line, immediately after the added text. If you press the spacebar, VBA completes the statement, leaves the cursor on the same line, and adds a space at the end.

When working with object variables, pressing the period (.) key is also useful. For example, if you type "Dim objOL as ou," as shown in Figure 8.3, VBA displays Outlook as the highlighted object. Type a period, and

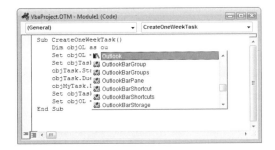

**Figure 8.3**
*The "intellisense" feature in VBA helps you avoid errors by suggesting ways to complete code statements.*

VBA displays a list of Outlook objects. Type "ap," and you'll see Application highlighted. At that point, press Enter, Tab, or the spacebar, and VBA will finish the declaration by completing the word "Application."

---

**Tip:** Another intellisense feature is that it automatically applies the correct capitalization to object, method, operator, and property names. I usually type in all lowercase and let VBA capitalize for me. That way, if parts of the code statement remain lowercase, I know I probably have a typo.

---

### 8.2.1  Variable data types

When you declare a variable in VBA, you normally specify a data type. If you don't, the variable uses the *variant* data type, which is a data type in which the variable can represent any type of data, from an integer to an object. Because variant-type variables support all kinds of operations, VBA cannot optimize the code when it compiles it, as it can if you use explicit data types. Therefore, using explicit data types can make your VBA code run more efficiently. It can also help you avoid certain types of coding errors. For example, if you declare two string variables and then try to multiply them, when VBA compiles the project, you'll see a "type mismatch" error message like that shown in Figure 8.4.

Table 8.1 lists the data types that VBA supports. You should use the variant data type in VBA for variables that hold data from a user form

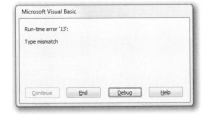

**Figure 8.4**
*A type mismatch error occurs when you try to use an operator, function, or method on the wrong type of variable or object.*

control (where users can type numbers or letters or leave the control blank) and other situations where the exact data type is not known at design time. In VBScript, which does not support data-typing on variable declarations, all variables—including object variables—are considered variant-type variables.

**Note:** In Table 5.1, "E+38" means that you multiply by a factor of "10 to the power of 38," and "E-45" means "10 to the power of -45." This scientific notation, as it's called, is used to simplify the writing of very large and very small numbers.

**Table 8.1**   *VBA Data Types*

| Data Type | Suggested Variable Prefix | Can Contain |
|---|---|---|
| Boolean | `bln` | True (-1) or False (0) |
| Byte | `byt` | Any nondecimal number between 0 and 255 |
| Integer | `int` | Any nondecimal number between –32,768 and 32,767 |
| Long | `lng` | Any nondecimal number between –2,147,483,648 and 2,147,483,647 |
| Single | `sng` | Negative numbers from –3.402823E+38 to –1.40298E-45 and positive numbers from 1.401298E-45 to 3.402823E+38 (single-precision floating point) |
| Double | `dbl` | Negative numbers from –1.79769313486231E+308 to –4.94065645841247E-324 and positive numbers from 4.94065645841247E-324 to 1.79769313486232E+308 (double-precision floating point) |
| Currency | `cur` | Numbers between –922,337,203,685,477.5808 to 922,337,203,685,477.5807 (limit of four decimal places) |
| Decimal | `dec` | Any integer up to +/–79,228,162,514,264,337,593,543,950,335; any decimal number up to +/–7.9228162514264337593543950335 with 28 places to the right of the decimal; smallest nonzero number is +/–0.0000000000000000000000000001 |
| Date | `dte` | Date and time values from January 1, 1000, to December 31, 9999; time values are resolved to the second |
| Object | `obj` | Reference to any object |
| String | `str` | For variable-length strings, from 0 to approximately 2 billion characters; for fixed-length strings, from 1 to 65,400 characters |
| Variant | `var` | Any kind of data, including strings, numbers, and objects |

---

**Caution:** Date/time fields in Outlook do not support the full range of dates that a VBA date variable can hold. Dates on Outlook forms must fall between April 1, 1601, and August 31, 4500, inclusive. Dates that appear in Outlook form fields and folder views as "None" are usually stored as January 1, 4501, although there are some cases where no date is stored in the field.

---

Even though VBA includes an object data type, usually you should declare an object variable as a specific type of object, as you saw in the `Dim` statements earlier in this section, such as:

```
Dim objOL As Outlook.Application
```

Use the object data type when you don't know what type of object you might be dealing with. For example, when accessing items in an Outlook contacts folder, you cannot know in advance whether any given item is an `Outlook.ContactItem` or `Outlook.DistListItem` (distribution list) object. In that case, you'd declare a variable `As Object`:

```
Dim objItem as Object
```

The same is true of the Inbox, which can contain other types of items besides messages—task requests, meeting requests, and nondelivery reports. If you're looping through all the items in the Inbox, use an object variable declared `As Object` for the individual item retrieved in each pass of the loop. (We'll revisit this issue in Chapter 15, "Working with Inspectors and Items.")

### 8.2.2   **Variable naming conventions**

VBA and VBScript variable names must follow certain rules. They must begin with a letter, not a number, and cannot contain a period. Many programmers use a naming convention—a specific pattern for variable names—for a variety of reasons:

- To distinguish variables from constants and intrinsic objects
- To provide a visible reminder of the type of data a variable contains
- To make the code easier to read, especially if someone else might be maintaining it in the future

One simple convention is to think of a name that describes the variable's contents or purpose and then add a prefix (e.g., those in the second column of Table 8.1) that gives the data type. This particular variable naming convention is sometimes known as "Hungarian." For example, if you need a variable to hold the value of the `MessageClass` property of an Outlook item, that property contains text, so a good variable name might be `strMessageClass`.

### 8.2.3  **Understanding scope**

The code examples so far deal with variables only as they occur inside a particular procedure. Sometimes, though, a single variable needs to be available to multiple procedures. For example, in one procedure, you might want to *instantiate* (or create a new instance of) an object variable to represent the current Outlook folder, and then perform some operation on that folder in several other procedures, maybe even procedures in completely different VBA modules. In that case, you would declare and instantiate a global variable in a regular VBA code module (not `ThisOutlookSession`), using code like this:

```
Public g_objMyFolder As Outlook.Folder

Sub SetMyFolder()
    Dim objOL As Outlook.Application
    Dim objExplorer As Outlook.Explorer
    Set objOL = Application
    Set objExplorer = objOL.ActiveExplorer
    Set g_objMyFolder = objExplorer.CurrentFolder
    Set objExplorer = Nothing
    Set objApp = Nothing
End Sub
```

The `ActiveExplorer` object property represents the folder window that the user is currently viewing, while its `CurrentFolder` property returns the actual folder. Therefore, the code above sets a global `Folder` object to the folder currently being displayed in Outlook. Any procedure in that module or any other module would be able to access the properties, such as the number of items in the `Folder` object like this:

```
MsgBox g_objMyFolder.Name & " - " & _
        g_objMyFolder.Items.Count & " items"
```

In VBA, variables have three possible scopes, summarized in Table 8.2. In VBScript code behind an Outlook form, only one module is present, so module-level scope is effectively a global scope.

In the `SetMyFolder` subroutine above, the code sets the `objOL` and `objExplorer` procedure variables to `Nothing` at the end of the procedure. The global `g_objMyFolder` variable is not set to `Nothing` because it will be used in other procedures. Outlook VBA will release global- and module-scope variables when Outlook shuts down.

**Tip:** You can use either `Dim` or `Private` to declare module-level variables, but `Private` makes your intent perfectly clear.

Scope also affects your choice of variable names. In the `SetMyFolder` subroutine, the "g_" prefix for `g_objMyFolder` provides a reminder that it's a global variable. (You can use an "m_" prefix for module-scope variables.)

**Table 8.2**  *Variable and Constant Scope Definitions*

| Scope | Description |
|---|---|
| Procedure | The variable or constant is available only within the current procedure. Declare with a `Dim` statement at the beginning of the procedure. |
| Module | The variable or constant is available only to procedures within the current module. Declare with a `Dim` or `Private` statement in the declarations section of the module. |
| Global | The variable or constant to any procedure in any module. Declare with a `Public` statement in the declarations section of any regular module (not a class module, such as `ThisOutlookSession` or a userform's code module). |

You should not have a module-level variable `strMsg` and also use a procedure variable with the same name. (VBA will use the local procedure variable, not the module-level variable, but the overlapping names have the potential to cause confusion, if not outright errors.) Repeated variable names are OK, as long as they are local to the procedures in which they are used. For example, you can use variable names such as `intAns` and `strAns` (`Ans` being short for "Answer") across many procedures to hold the results from `MsgBox()` and `InputBox()` functions in multiple procedures. This won't be a problem if you declare the variable as a local variable inside each procedure.

Why care about scope at all? For two main reasons: to make code run more efficiently and to keep two procedures from inadvertently changing the same variable value.

The efficiency issue involves memory. The broader the scope, the longer the variable remains in memory. A variable is removed from memory when it goes out of scope—in other words, when all the code in the procedure or module has run and the variable is no longer needed or, in the case of an object variable, when it is specifically released with a `Set objVar = Nothing` statement. In general, you should use the tightest scope possible. Because you can use arguments to pass variable values or references from one procedure to another (as you will see shortly), global and module variables should be the exception, not the rule.

We'll return to the issue of scope a little later in the chapter, when we look at it in the context of procedure declarations.

## 8.2.4 Declaring constants

Everything you've just learned about variable declarations also applies to constants. You can make constants available only to a single procedure's code, have other constants that work anywhere in the current module, and—in VBA—declare still others that are global in scope. The `Const`, `Private`, and `Public` statements used to declare a constant and assign its value are analogous to the `Dim`, `Private`, and `Public` statements used to declare variables. One key difference is that the value of the constant is set in its declaration to some literal data value (not an expression) and never changes after that.

Names for constants follow the same constraints and patterns as variable names. Some programmers use all caps for constants, to easily distinguish them from variables.

For procedure-level constants, place the `Const` statement at the beginning of a procedure, along with any `Dim` statements to declare variables. For module-level constants, place the `Const` statement in the declarations section of the module; optionally, add the `Private` keyword to define the scope. For global constants in VBA, place a constant assignment statement that begins with the `Public` keyword in the declarations section of the module. These are examples of constant declaration statements for VBA:

```
Const ATTEMPTS = 5 As Integer

Private Const M_COMPANYNAME = "Turtleflock, LLC" _
  As String

Public Const G_VACATIONDAYS = 10 As Integer
```

To declare the same constants in VBScript behind an Outlook form, omit the `As` expressions. You can also omit the `Public` or `Private` keyword for constant declarations at the module level, since VBScript has only one module:

```
Const ATTEMPTS = 5

Const M_COMPANYNAME = "Turtleflock, LLC"

Const G_VACATIONDAYS = 10

Const olFolderTasks = 13
```

Notice that constants can hold any kind of data; they're not limited to numbers. The last constant is an example of a technique you should use often in VBScript code—providing a constant declaration for an intrinsic Outlook constant. You don't need to declare such constants in VBA, but you do in VBScript. You can use the VBA object browser to look up Outlook constants, as shown in Figure 8.5, select the constant declaration at the bottom of the object browser, and then right-click and choose Copy to get text that you can paste into your VBScript code, for example:

```
Const olMailItem = 0
```

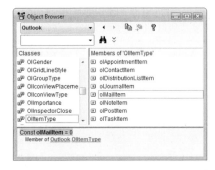

**Figure 8.5**
*Look up Outlook constant declarations in the VBA object browser.*

Both VBA and VBScript support many intrinsic constants whose names begin with vb. You do not need to declare these constants in either VBA or VBScript. Table 8.3 lists many that you are likely to use. We will see others later in the chapter, in the section on message boxes.

**Table 8.3** *Key Intrinsic Constants for VBA and VBScript*

| Constant | Value | Description |
|---|---|---|
| *Color Constants* | | |
| vbBlack | &h00 | Black |
| vbRed | &hFF | Red |
| vbGreen | &hFF00 | Green |
| vbYellow | &hFFFF | Yellow |
| vbBlue | &hFF0000 | Blue |
| vbMagenta | &hFF00FF | Magenta |
| vbCyan | &hFFFF00 | Cyan |
| vbWhite | &hFFFFFF | White |
| *Date Constants* | | |
| vbSunday | 1 | Sunday |
| vbMonday | 2 | Monday |
| vbTuesday | 3 | Tuesday |
| vbWednesday | 4 | Wednesday |
| vbThursday | 5 | Thursday |
| vbFriday | 6 | Friday |
| vbSaturday | 7 | Saturday |

**Table 8.3**    *Key Intrinsic Constants for VBA and VBScript (continued)*

| Constant | Value | Description |
|---|---|---|
| *Date Format Constants* | | |
| vbGeneralDate | 0 | Displays a date and/or time format-ted according to your system settings |
| vbLongDate | 1 | Displays a date using your com-puter's long date format |
| vbShortDate | 2 | Displays a date using your com-puter's short date format |
| vbLongTime | 3 | Displays a time using your com-puter's long time format |
| vbShortTime | 4 | Displays a time using your com-puter's short time format |
| *String Constants* | | |
| vbCr | Chr(13) | Carriage return |
| vbCrLf | Chr(13) & Chr(10) | Carriage return + linefeed |
| vbLf | Chr(10) | Linefeed |
| vbTab | Chr(9) | Horizontal tab |

**Note:** Color constant values listed in Table 8.3 with &h prefixes are long integers written in hexadecimal format. The Chr() function returns a character with a particular ASCII value. For example, 9 is the ASCII value for the character placed in a message when you press the Tab key, so Chr(9) returns the tab character.

## 8.3    Writing procedures

Now that you've learned how to declare variables and constants, let's look at the techniques involved in writing the main building blocks of your Outlook applications: subroutines and functions. You have already written several procedures—a VBA macro and some VBA and Outlook form event handlers. Recall that each procedure begins with a Sub or Function declaration and ends with an End Sub or End Function statement.

At the beginning of the chapter, I promised that you could cut down on the amount of typing you do in the VBA code window if you declare all your variables. As you use any declared object variable, the intellisense feature in VBA displays a list of *members* of that object class. Members include the events, methods, and properties—in other words, everything you might be able to do with or find out about an object.

You saw a small demonstration of this feature when you added Dim statements earlier; VBA helped you pick the right data or object type. It gets even better when you start using those object variables. To see how this feature works, create a new VBA procedure named TestAutoListMembers, and add the following code:

```
Dim objOL as Outlook.Application
Dim objAppt as Outlook.AppointmentItem
Set objOL = Application
```

On a new line, type "set objappt = objol." (with a period at the end) and then pause briefly. After you type the period, you will see a list of all the methods and properties for the Outlook.Application object (see Figure 8.6).

Type "cr" and watch the members' list jump to CreateItem, which is the method you want for this example. Press Tab to paste "CreateItem" into the text of the statement. Then type an open parenthesis. As soon as you type that character, VBA again pops up a list—this time one of appropriate intrinsic constants—as well as information on the CreateItem method and its parameters (see Figure 8.7).

---

**Tip:** To see the syntax for any method on demand, highlight it in the VBA code editor, then press Ctrl+I.

---

To finish the statement, press the down arrow key to select olAppointmentItem, press Tab to add it to the code window, and type a closing parenthesis. The code statement you entered looks like this:

```
Set objAppt = objOL.CreateItem(olAppointmentItem)
```

**Figure 8.6**
*The Auto List Members feature helps automatically complete your VBA code statements.*

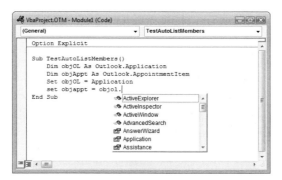

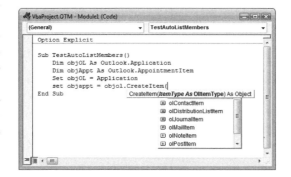

**Figure 8.7**
*The Auto Quick Info feature provides the syntax for functions, methods, and their parameters as you type in the code window.*

but what you actually typed was

```
Set objAppt = objOL.cr( [Tab] [Down])
```

That's 27 keystrokes using the intellisense Auto List Members feature (as it's called) versus 50 keystrokes to type the entire statement by hand. See, it really will save you lots of typing and prevent many mistakes! Now, try it again, to see how few keystrokes it takes to add an `objAppt.Display` statement to show the new appointment to the user.

But what about VBScript? An Outlook form's code window has no intellisense features. Don't let that stop you! Many Outlook programmers prototype their form code in the VBA environment, then convert it to VBScript code by adding Outlook constant declarations and commenting out data type `As` statements. Here's what the code you typed above would look like in VBScript behind an Outlook form:

```
Sub TestAutoListMembers()
    Dim objOL    ' as Outlook.Application
    Dim objAppt ' as Outlook.AppointmentItem
    Const olAppointmentItem = 1
    Set objOL = Application
    Set objAppt = objOL.CreateItem(olAppointmentItem)
    objAppt.Display
End Sub
```

See if you can spot these key changes:

- An Outlook constant declaration
- Two data type `As` expressions that have been commented out

We'll look at the process of converting VBA code to VBScript in more detail in the next chapter.

## 8.3.1   Calling procedures

Some computer applications boast of thousands or millions of lines of code. All that code is not contained in just one subroutine. Applications typically break down into many chunks, each of which performs a certain role in the larger application. The event handlers that we saw in the previous chapter are one kind of procedure, but they in turn are likely to transfer control to other procedures to perform specific processing tasks or return values to variables in the event handler. To transfer control from one procedure to another, a procedure *calls* another procedure. Most functions and many subroutines have one or more *parameters* that pass a value—a constant, a literal value, a variable, or an expression—from one procedure to another.

To call a function, assign a variable to the value returned by the function; pass any parameters as arguments in parentheses after the function name. For example, this statement

```
strToday = FormatDateTime(Date, vbLongDate)
```

assigns a string variable named `strToday` by using the built-in `FormatDateTime()` function to return today's date. The date is formatted to show the computer's long date format (which normally includes the day of the week).

Subroutines can be called with the subroutine name, followed by arguments separated by commas, or with the `Call` keyword and the arguments in parentheses. Both these statements call the same subroutine:

```
MyProc arg1, arg2, arg3

Call MyProc(arg1, arg2, arg3)
```

Using the `Call` type of statement is less ambiguous and makes it easier to spot the points in your code where you branch to a different subroutine.

When you call a subroutine, the code in the called procedure executes. When it finishes, program control returns to the next line of the calling procedure. For example, consider these two VBA procedures:

```
Sub ProcOne()
    Dim intA As Integer
    intA = 10
    Call ProcTwo()
    intA = 10 * 10
End Sub

Sub ProcTwo()
    Dim intB as Integer
    intB = 20
    intB = 20 * 20
End Sub
```

First, the value of `intA` is set to 10. Then `ProcTwo` executes and sets the value of `intB`. Finally, execution returns to `ProcOne` to change the value of `intA` once more.

## 8.3.2    Passing arguments

For procedures with arguments, the default in both VBA and VBScript is to pass the variable by reference, which means that the value of the original variable changes as a result of the statements inside the called procedure. The alternative is to pass variables by value, which means the original variable remains unaltered, no matter what happens in the procedure to which it is passed.

Most of the time, you don't need to worry about whether a variable is passed by value or by reference, but since passing a variable the wrong way can cause your code to behave in an unexpected fashion, it's worth looking at an example. This is definitely a concept that's easier to see in action than to read about. Listing 8.2 contains a demonstration you can add to a VBA module and run to see what happens.

The code sets the value of two variables, R and V, each to 10, and then calls the ByRefSub procedure, passing R by reference (the default) to the X argument and V by value to the Y argument. Because V is passed to the Y variable by value, the statement Y = Y + 20 has no effect on the value of V in the first procedure. However, the statement X = X + 20 not only changes X in the ByRefSub procedure, but also changes the value of R in the calling procedure to 30 because R was passed to the X variable by reference. V, however, does not change from its original value of 10, because it was passed by value.

---

**Tip:** Did you notice how Listing 8.2 declared two variables in one statement in the ByValDemo procedure?

---

**Tip:** Debug.Print is a convenient method for seeing the result of VBA code. It shows the data in columns in the Immediate window, which you can view by pressing Ctrl+G or choosing View | Immediate Window. Make sure, though, that you take any Debug.Print statements out of your final code, because they can slow down the program.

---

To test the same concept in an Outlook custom form, create a new form, drag a command button from the Control Toolbox to any custom page, add the code in Listing 8.3, then run the form and click the button. The message box should show the same results for R and V—30 and 10, respectively—as in the VBA example.

You could use a ByRef keyword with the argument for X in the Sub ByRefSub declaration to make it perfectly clear that you're passing R by

**Listing 8.2** *ByVal makes a difference in how code runs in VBA*

```
Sub ByValDemo()
    Dim R As Integer, V As Integer
    R = 10
    V = 10
    Call ByRefSub(R, V)
    Debug.Print R, V
End Sub

Sub ByRefSub(X, ByVal Y)
    X = X + 20
    Y = Y + 20
End Sub
```

reference. However, because passing variables by reference is the default, that keyword is optional.

Using ByVal in the procedure declaration, as in the two examples above, is one way to pass an argument by value. Another approach is to put parentheses around the argument. For example, if you declare and call a procedure like this

```
Sub ByRefSub(X, Y)
Call ByRefSub(R, (V))
```

the second variable, Y, is passed by value because it is enclosed in parentheses:

That approach is less transparent—in other words, results in less readable code—than explicitly using ByVal in the procedure declaration,

**Listing 8.3** *ByVal also makes a difference in VBScript*

```
Sub CommandButton1_Click()
    Call ByValDemo()
End Sub

Sub ByValDemo()
    Dim R, V
    R = 10
    V = 10
    Call ByRefSub(R, V)
    MsgBox R & vbTab & V
End Sub

Sub ByRefSub(X, ByVal Y)
    X = X + 20
    Y = Y + 20
End Sub
```

though. We won't be using it in any examples in this book, but now you'll know it when you see it in someone else's code.

### 8.3.3 Adding data types to parameters and functions

In VBA, you can improve the efficiency and consistency of your code by declaring the data type not just for variables in procedures, but also for the functions you create and for the parameters for both subroutines and functions. Use the same `As` data type syntax as you learned for `Dim` statements. For example, it's obvious from the data type declarations in this `Mail-Addr()` function that you need to supply an Outlook contact and an integer as arguments and that it will return a text string:

```
Function MailAddr _
             (objContact As Outlook.ContactItem, _
              intX As Integer) As String
    Dim strAddress As String
    Dim strPropName As String
    If intX >= 1 And intX <= 3 Then
        strPropName = _
           "Email" & CStr(intX) & "Address"
        strAddress = _
           objContact.ItemProperties(strPropName)
    Else
         strAddress = ""
    End If
    MailAddr = strAddress
End Function
```

The `MailAddr()` function always returns a string value corresponding to the first, second, or third email address in the contact (if there is one) or a blank string if you use a number other than 1, 2, or 3 for the `intX` parameter.

### 8.3.4 Making code reusable

Typos are one of the biggest sources of code errors. Therefore, one way to avoid errors is to avoid typing. In this chapter, we've already seen how the intellisense features in Outlook VBA allow you to pick from a list of properties or allowable arguments to avoid making mistakes when working with Outlook objects. Another approach is to design your code so that it's reusable. If half of a project can be built with code you already have, that means you only have to type half as much code to finish the job.

A key technique in making code reusable is using variables or procedure parameters instead of literal (in other words, "hard coded") values. We can examine this concept in a context that has great practical applications for Outlook.

Outlook provides a `Selection` object that represents the items that the user has selected in an Outlook folder window. (For more information

**Listing 8.4** *Procedure to process up to fifty selected items*

```
Sub ReusableSelectionExample()
    Dim objOL As Outlook.Application
    Dim objItem As Object
    Dim objSel As Outlook.Selection
    Dim intMaxItems As Integer
    Dim blnDoProcess As Boolean
    ' *** Use next line to set maximum number ***
    ' *** of items this routine is allowed to ***
    ' *** process.                           ***
    intMaxItems = 50
    blnDoProcess = False
    Set objOL = Application
    Set objSel = objOL.ActiveExplorer.Selection
    Select Case objSel.count
        Case 0
            MsgBox "No items were selected"
        Case Is > intMaxItems
            MsgBox "Too many items were selected"
        Case Else
            blnDoProcess = True
    End Select
    If blnDoProcess = True Then
        ' process the items here
        For Each objItem In objSel
            Debug.Print objItem.Subject
        Next
    End If
    Set objItem = Nothing
    Set objSel = Nothing
    Set objOL = Nothing
End Sub
```

about the `Selection` object, see Chapter 15.) Let's say, though, that you don't want to process a selection of more than fifty items. Listing 8.4 is a VBA subroutine for working with a maximum number of selected items. The number of items is specified by the assignment statement for the `int-MaxItems` variable. This example copies the subject of each selected item to the VBA Immediate window; you could put your own processing code in the section marked with the comment "process the items here."

`Select Case ... End Select` is a structure that allows code to consider multiple possible values of a given variable or expression, in this case the number of items selected. In the second `Case` statement, you could specify the literal value for the maximum number of items you want to process, rather than using the `intMaxItems` variable. However, if you wanted to copy that code and adapt it to another scenario, you would have to dig down to that `Case` statement to change the maximum number of items. Assigning the number to `intMaxItems` near the beginning of the procedure makes it much easier to reuse this code in other modules that need to process `Selection`, especially since it has a prominent comment calling your attention to the `intMaxItems` = statement.

Another alternative approach is to pass the maximum number of items as a parameter. Omitting the `Dim` and `Set obj = Nothing` statements, the revised VBA procedure would look like this:

```
Sub ReusableSelectionExample(intMaxItems As Integer)
    blnDoProcess = False
    Set objOL = Application
    Set objSel = objOL.ActiveExplorer.Selection
    Select Case objSel.count
        Case 0
            MsgBox "No items were selected"
        Case Is > intMaxItems
            MsgBox "Too many items were selected"
        Case Else
            blnDoProcess = True
    End Select
    If blnDoProcess = True Then
        ' process the items here
        For Each objItem In objSel
            Debug.Print objItem.Subject
        Next
    End If
End Sub
```

The VBScript version would be identical, except that you'd omit the `As Integer` parameter data type, along with the `As type` portion of the `Dim` statements.

## 8.3.5  Documenting your procedures

To document your application, add comments to your program code. A *comment* is any text preceded by an apostrophe ('). VBScript and VBA both support comments, but only VBA shows comment text in green.

---

**Tip:** You can add commands to the VBA toolbar to make it easy to comment and uncomment large blocks of text. Choose View | Toolbars | Customize. On the Commands tab, under Categories, select Edit. From the Edit commands list, drag the Comment Block and Uncomment Block commands to the toolbar.

---

Comments can introduce a section of your code and explain what each section does and also provide remarks on variables as you declare them, as shown in Listing 8.4 in the previous section. In complex modules, you may want to provide the author, purpose, history, arguments, and other information about each procedure. The following VBA code provides an example of each of these types of comments:

```
'
'*********************************************************
' Name:     CommentTextExample
' Author:   Sue Mosher
' History:  Version 1.1, 27 Jul 2006
' Purpose:  Demonstrate placement of different
'           types of comments
' Args:     None
' Returns:  Nothing
'
'*********************************************************
Sub CommentTextExample()
    Dim strStart As String          ' start date from form
    Dim strEnd As String            ' end date from form
    'get dates from modal form
    frmReminderUpdate.Show
    strStart = frmReminderUpdate.txtStartDate
    strEnd = frmReminderUpdate.txtEndDate
    Unload frmReminderUpdate
End Sub
```

You don't need to comment everything in every procedure, but try to provide enough information so that you (or another developer) will be able to follow the code logic at any time in the future.

## 8.3.6 More code style tips

Most programmers follow two style conventions that tend to make code easier to read:

- Keeping statements together in blocks indented the same amount of space.

- Using an underscore (_) character as a continuation character at the end of a line when the statement would otherwise run off the screen, as shown in the code sample in section 8.3.3.

In VBA, press Tab every time you want to indent the default four characters. To change the indentation of a group of statements at one time, select the statements, then press Tab to increase the indent, or Shift+Tab to decrease the indent. You can change the indent size in Tools | Options in the VBA editor.

In the VBScript code window for a custom form, the indent that results from pressing Tab is six characters and cannot be changed.

The order in which procedures occur in a module doesn't really matter to VBA or VBScript, but it does matter to someone (you!) who is trying to understand the code. The dropdown list on the upper-right corner of the code window in VBA keeps track of procedures in alphabetical order. (VBScript has no equivalent.) Within a code module, you might want to keep procedures in order of importance: main procedure first and then subsidiary subroutines and functions.

Here's one more concept that will make your code more readable when you work with object variables in either VBA or VBScript. You can use a `With ... End With` code block to set properties and invoke methods on a single object, without specifying the object variable in each statement. For example, if you have a `ContactItem` object variable named `objContact` (in other words, an Outlook contact item), you can set the name and other properties and then save the item with a block of statements like this:

```
With objContact
    .FullName = "Sue Mosher"
    .Company = "Turfleflock, LLC"
    .BusinessAddressStreet = _
        "1234 Something Place"
    .BusinessAddressCity = "Arlington"
    .Save
End With
```

The above code snippet sets four properties and then invokes the `Save` method. Did you notice the indentation that sets off the statements inside the `With ... End With` block and the underscore character that allows the `.BusinessAddressStreet =` statement to span two lines?

## 8.4    Working with expressions and functions

Much of the work of programming involves performing calculations and updating variables with new values. The key code components for this work are expressions and built-in functions, and functions you create yourself. You've seen examples of all of these as we've looked at other code components. In this section, you'll encounter most of the basic VBA and VBScript functions that help you manipulate dates, parse text, and do math. Many of those functions also work in value and validation formulas. We can't cover all of Outlook's functions in one chapter, of course, only those most commonly used.

### 8.4.1    Elements of an expression

Many code statements include a variable on the left side of an equals sign and terms on the right side that assign a value to the variable. Those terms comprise an *expression*. The expression may be a combination of string values or numbers or dates, but the key concept is that it can be reduced to some finite value. A statement like

```
strPhone = "+1 (" & strAreaCode & ") " & strNumber
```

means "set the value of the `strPhone` variable equal to the result of the expression on the right side of the equals sign." The expression itself consists of four terms—two literals, two variables—joined by the ampersand (&) operator for string concatenation:

```
"+1 ("              string literal

strAreaCode         string variable

") "                string literal

strNumber           string variable
```

---

**Tip:** A phone number is a string, not a numeric value, because it contains spaces and punctuation as well as numbers

---

**Note:** Not all code statements set a variable equal to an expression, of course. Some statements control program flow, instantiate object variables, or execute object methods.

---

A literal value is a specific value that doesn't change, but is expressed in code statements as the value itself, not as a constant. You must enclose string literals in quotation marks and date literals (including time values) in number or hash signs (#). Here are more examples of literals that code might use:

```
"tomorrow"
#March 2, 2007#
#3/2/2007#
#10:00 a.m.#
3298
```

The last item is a literal, too—a numeric literal. You do not need to enclose numbers with special characters when you use their literal values.

---

**Tip:** The #3/2/2007# literal always means March 2, 2007, even if your system is set to use a day/month/year short date format. We look at this issue later in Section 8.6.4, "Time zones and international dates."

---

If you use the naming conventions described earlier in this chapter, you should have no problem distinguishing literals from variables, constants, and functions. Variable names should follow the naming rules with prefixes that indicate their scope and content. Constants should either be in all caps or, for Outlook constants in VBScript code, use the same ol-prefix names as the intrinsic constants in VBA. String and date literals have their surrounding quotation marks and number or hash signs, and number literals are, well, just numbers. You can combine functions, literals, variables, and constants into expressions.

### 8.4.2   Using mathematical expressions

We encountered the principle mathematical operators earlier, in Chapter 7. You actually do less math in Outlook programming than in some other applications. More often, you are manipulating Outlook items and working with text and dates.

When working with mathematical expressions, remember that they are evaluated from left to right. Also, if an expression contains more than one operator, the terms involving operators are evaluated in a particular sequence, according to the operator precedence order, which you can look up in Help. Rather than worry about operator precedence, though, you should control the order yourself by using parentheses to group related terms.

Text boxes on VBA forms and the variant-type variables in VBScript code can hold different kinds of data. You can't always be sure what type of data you're working with. Even if you give a variable a name that indicates it should contain numeric data, there could be something wrong with your code or the variable could contain a value of Null—in other words, it might contain no data. To avoid an error with code that assumes a numeric value, you can perform a test first, using the built-in IsNumeric() function, which works in both VBA and VBScript. It returns True or False, depending on whether the argument can be evaluated to a number. You've already seen this function in the VBA birthday/reminder form that we enhanced in Chapter 7:

```
If IsNumeric(txtDays.Value) = False Then
    Cancel = True
    MsgBox "Please enter a number."
End If
```

**Note:** The expression IsNumeric(txtDays.Value) = False can also be expressed as Not  IsNumeric(txtDays.Value). Similarly, if expr is an expression that evaluates to True or False (that is, a Boolean expression), then the expressions expr and expr = True are equivalent.

The presence of Null in any mathematical expression causes the entire expression to resolve to Null. For example, Null + 2 is not the same as 0 + 2. The expression Null + 2 resolves to Null, not 2.

## 8.5   Working with strings

A great deal of Outlook programming code is devoted to manipulating text—or more precisely, manipulating string variables and text property values—by breaking them into parts and putting them back together again using techniques to *parse* text. For example, if you have a variable named `strPhone` that contains a number using the standard pattern +xx (yyy) zzz-zzzz or (yyy) zzz-zzzz, this code extracts the area or city code from within the parentheses and assigns it to a new variable, `strAreaCode`:

```
intLeftPar = InStr(strPhone, "(")
intRightPar = InStr(intLeftPar, strPhone, ")")
strAreaCode = Mid(strPhone, intLeftPar + 1, _
    intRightPar - intLeftPar -1)
```

The code finds the positions of the two parentheses, and then extracts the text between them. Did you notice the string literals for the parenthesis characters?

The next few sections will teach you about the `Instr()` and `Mid()` string parsing functions and others that work in both VBA and VBScript.

### 8.5.1 Extracting string parts

The code in the preceding section uses two important string functions: `Instr()` and `Mid()`. The `Instr()` function finds the position of a string within another string, while `Mid()` returns text from inside a string, starting at a particular position and (optionally) continuing for a specific number of characters. Table 8.4 lists `Mid()` and two other essential string-parsing functions, `Left()` and `Right()`. The examples assume that `strPhone = "+1 (203) 555-7890"`.

Notice that you can use `Mid()` with or without a length parameter. If you omit the length parameter, `Mid()` returns all the text from the starting point to the end of the string.

### 8.5.2 Comparing strings

Often you will want to know whether one string is the same as another or contains specific text as a substring. Table 8.5 lists three essential functions for comparing strings.

**Table 8.4**  *Functions to Extract String Parts*

| Function | Example Where strPhone = "+1 (203) 555-7890" | Evaluates to |
|---|---|---|
| Left(*String*, *Length*) | Left(strPhone, 3) | "+1" |
| Right(*String*, *Length*) | Right(strPhone, 8) | "555-7890" |
| Mid(*String*, *Start*, *Length*) | Mid(strPhone, 5, 3) | "203" |
| Mid(*String*, *Start*) | Mid(strPhone, 4) | "(203) 555-7980" |

**Table 8.5**  *Functions for Comparing Strings*

| Function | Example | Evaluates to |
|---|---|---|
| InStr(*Start*, *String1*, *String2*, *Compare*) | InStr(3, "repeated", "e") | 4 |
| InStrRev(*String1*, *String2*, *Start*, *Compare*) | InStrRev("repeated", "e") | 7 |
| StrComp(*String1*, *String2*, *Compare*) | StrComp("ABCDE", "abcde", vbTextCompare) | 0 |

The *Start* parameter in the InStr() and InStrRev() functions is optional, unless you are also using the *Compare* parameter; the default value is 1.

The *Compare* parameter in all three functions is optional. String comparisons are case-sensitive by default. To make string comparisons ignore upper and lower case, set the optional Compare parameter to the intrinsic constant vbTextCompare, as shown in the example for the StrComp() function in Table 8.5.

**Tip:** You can use the intrinsic constants vbTextCompare (= 1) and vb-BinaryCompare (= 0) in any functions that take a *Compare* argument.

In VBA, you can set an entire module to use case-insensitive string comparison by adding an Option Compare Text statement to the declarations section of the module. If no Option Compare statement is present, binary (case-sensitive) comparison is used. VBScript does not support Option Compare.

**Note:** Using text comparison, rather than binary comparison, may flatten the difference between letters in the standard English alphabet and letters from other languages that use diacritical (accent) marks. However, the result will depend on your Windows language settings, so you may need to experiment.

The InStrRev() function works like the InStr() function, which you saw a little earlier, only it starts the comparison from the end of *String1*, not the beginning. Its arguments are in a slightly different order, too. A common practical use of InStrRev() is to determine the extension of a file:

```
strFile = "filename.doc"
intRes = InStrRev(strFile, ".")
```

**Table 8.6**  *Possible Return Values for StrComp()*

| Comparison | Return Value |
|---|---|
| *String1* is less than *String2* | -1 |
| *String1* is equal to *String2* | 0 |
| *String1* is greater than *String2* | 1 |
| *String1* or *String2* is Null | Null |

```
strExt = Mid(strFile, intRes + 1)
If LCase(strExt) = "doc" Then
    MsgBox "It's a Word document!"
End If
```

Where the InStr() and InStrRev() functions tell you exactly where in a string a substring occurs, the StrComp() function performs a more general comparison. It returns one of the values shown in Table 8.6.

### 8.5.3  Replacing parts of a string

There are two basic ways to replace one part of a string with another that work in both VBA and VBScript:

- Break the string into substrings, change one or more substrings, and then join the substrings back together using the ampersand (&) concatenation operator.

- Use the Replace() function to create a new string that replaces part of the original string with another.

Let's go back to telephone numbers for some examples. Consider a scenario in which your local area code, say 717, is being split into 717 and 570. The fact that telephone numbers use a standard format with area/city and country code—for example, +1 (717) 555-1234—makes it easy to parse the different parts of the number and replace 717 with 570. For a variable named strPhone, the three statements below return the updated number to a variable named strNewPhone by breaking out two characters on the left (the country code) and the eight characters on the right (the local number, including the dash), and then concatenating them with the new area code in the middle:

```
strCountryCode = Left(strPhone, 2)
strNumber = Right(strPhone, 8)
strNewPhone = strCountryCode & " (507) " & strNumber
```

The same operation performed with the Replace() function takes just one code statement:

```
strNewPhone = Replace(strPhone, "(717)", "(570)")
```

`Replace()` also supports optional *Start*, *Count*, and *Compare* parameters to return only the portion of the string beginning at *Start*, make a specific *Count* of replacements, and, as with the `InStr()` function, set the comparison type. Here is the full syntax for `Replace()`:

```
strText = Replace(Expression, Find, Replace, _
                  Start, Count, Compare)
```

Another practical application of `Replace()` is adding text to an HTML-format mail message. The property of a `MailItem` object that contains the HTML content is `HTMLBody`, but you can't just append text to that property, because any appended text would be placed after the `</body>` tag that signifies the end of the HTML content of the message. Thus, you need to insert the text just before the `</body>` tag. This code snippet inserts a new paragraph of text at the end of the message represented by `objMail`:

```
strText = "<p>This is a new paragraph.</p></body>"
strHTML = Replace(objMail.HTMLBody, "</body>", _
                  strText, , , vbTextCompare)
```

The commas with spaces between them are placeholders for the optional *Start* and *Count* parameters. You must write the `Replace()` statement that way for VBScript, although it's not much fun to count commas in order to figure out how many to insert before the last parameter, *Compare*. Many functions in VBA, however, support the concept of *named parameters*. See how much more understandable the `Replace()` statement becomes if you use named parameters:

```
strHTML = Replace(Expression:=objMail.HTMLBody, _
                  Find:="</body>", _
                  Replace:=strText, _
                  Compare:=vbTextCompare)
```

When using named parameters, use `:=` to assign a value to the parameter. To see the names of all the parameters, highlight the function name in the VBA code window and press Ctrl+I.

### 8.5.4  **Other useful string functions**

There is more to manipulating strings than extracting, comparing, or combining text. Table 8.7 lists functions to fill a string with a particular character, return the length of a string, remove leading or trailing spaces, and change a string to upper or lower case.

### 8.5.5  **Example: Parsing text from a structured text block**

A common Outlook VBA programming task involves extracting data from the body of a message, such as the results mailed from data that a visitor to

**Table 8.7** *Other Useful String Functions*

| Function | Example | Evaluates to |
|---|---|---|
| String(*Number*, *Character*) | String(4, "+") | "++++" |
| Space(*Number*) | Space(10) | "          " |
| Len(*String*) | Len("Microsoft Outlook") | 17 |
| Trim(*String*) | Trim("    sloppy text    ") | "sloppy text" |
| LTrim(*String*) | LTrim("    sloppy text    ") | "sloppy text    " |
| RTrim(*String*) | RTrim("    sloppy text    ") | "    sloppy text" |
| UCase(*String*) | UCase("Microsoft Outlook") | "MICROSOFT OUTLOOK" |
| LCase(*String*) | LCase("Microsoft Outlook") | "microsoft outlook" |

your Web site entered on a form there. Such a message might have multiple lines each with a different Label: Data pair. Listing 8.5 is a very practical example of using basic string functions—InStr(), Len(), Mid(), and Trim()—to return specific text from a larger text string.

**Listing 8.5** *VBA function to parse text from a structured text block*

```
Function ParseTextLinePair(strSource As String, _
                           strLabel As String)
    Dim intLocLabel As Integer
    Dim intLocCRLF As Integer
    Dim intLenLabel As Integer
    Dim strText As String

    ' locate the label in the source text
    intLocLabel = InStr(strSource, strLabel)
    intLenLabel = Len(strLabel)
        If intLocLabel > 0 Then
        intLocCRLF = InStr(intLocLabel, strSource, vbCrLf)
        If intLocCRLF > 0 Then
            intLocLabel = intLocLabel + intLenLabel
            strText = Mid(strSource, _
                          intLocLabel, _
                          intLocCRLF - intLocLabel)
        Else
            strText = Mid(strSource, _
                          intLocLabel + intLenLabel)
        End If
    End If
    ParseTextLinePair = Trim(strText)
End Function
```

The `ParseTextLinePair()` function takes two parameters—the text to be parsed and the "label" that marks what text you're looking for. Let's consider, for example, that you get a message that contains text like this:

```
Date Needed:  4-17-07
Type of Request: site visit
Requestor Name:  Jane Doe
Requestor Phone #:  123 456 1234
Requestor Email:  Jane_Doe@domainname.com
```

Each of the lines above can be parsed into a "label" that ends in a colon (:) and data that follows the label. To return the data for a specific label, the code follows this sequence of operations:

1.    Locate the label in the text.

2.    Locate the first carriage return/linefeed that follows the label.

3.    Return the text between the end of the label and the carriage return/linefeed.

4.    Trim off any extraneous spaces.

One application would be to forward such an incoming message to someone who could handle the request, copying in the original requestor. This snippet processes the item currently selected in the folder view:

```
Set objItem = Application.ActiveExplorer.Selection(1)
strAddress = ParseTextLinePair(objItem.Body, _
                               "Requestor Email:")
strName = ParseTextLinePair(objItem.Body, _
                            "Requestor Name:")
strRequest = ParseTextLinePair(objItem.Body, _
                               "Type of Request:")
If strRequest <> "" Then
    Set objForward = objItem.Forward
    With objForward
        .To = "fixer@domainame.com"
        .CC = strAddress
        .Subject = UCase(strRequest) & _
                   " request from " & strName
    End With
    objForward.Send
End If
```

As you can see, the `ParseTextLinePair()` function is a practical demonstration of the power of simple text parsing functions. You can extend its technique—the basic sequence of operations described above—to virtually any situation where you know the start point and end point of a piece of text that you're interested in.

## 8.6    Working with dates and times

Date manipulation skills are critical to Outlook programming because virtually every Outlook item has one or more important dates associated with it—the date an email message was received, the due date for a task, a friend's birthday, the time of your appointment tomorrow, and so on. In this section, you learn how to extract components from dates and perform date arithmetic. We also briefly visit issues related to time zones and international dates.

---

**Tip:** You may find yourself building your own date-related functions to supplement those built into VBA and VBScript. For example, Listing 16.1 in Chapter 16, "Searching for Outlook Items," is a `GetMonthStart()` function that returns the first day of a month, given two parameters—a starting date and the number of months offset from that date.

---

Remember that standard and custom Outlook date fields may contain date values only between April 1, 1601, and August 31, 4500, inclusive. Dates that appear in Outlook form fields and folder views as "None" usually are stored as January 1, 4501.

### 8.6.1   Basic date-related functions

What is a date? In the context of Outlook, a date is any built-in or custom property designed to handle dates <u>or</u> times. In addition to working with such properties, Outlook code often needs to get dates from users through controls on a VBA user form or an Outlook custom form. Value and validation formulas on custom forms and form regions may also use dates.

How can you tell whether the user has entered a valid date in a text box control on a custom form that isn't bound to a date/time field? Both VBA and VBScript support the `IsDate()` function to test for a valid date. `IsDate()` takes any expression as its argument and returns `True` if the expression represents a valid date between January 1, 1000, and December 31, 9999. `IsDate()` is smart about detecting dates from a variety of formats. Any of the following expression returns `True`:

```
IsDate("3/31/07")
IsDate("31/3/2007")
IsDate("10:00")
IsDate("31 Mar 2007")
```

You might wonder why `IsDate("10:00")` returns `True`. Remember that a time always has a date component (and a date always has a time component) even if Outlook displays only the date.

The examples above use the slash (/) as a date separator character; `IsDate()` allows that separator in dates regardless of the regional settings for Windows. If the local date separator is some other character, a date string using that localized separator will also be valid. For example,

`IsDate("3.31.2007")` returns `True` in countries that use a period as a date separator character.

`CDate()` is one of several available functions to convert values from one data type to another, in this case to a date value. Normally, you would use it with `IsDate()` because you will get an error if you try to convert a non-date value to a date. As an example, this `MakeDate()` function for VBA returns today's date if the `somedate` parameter does not contain a valid date:

```
Function MakeDate(somedate) As Date
    If IsDate(somedate) Then
        MakeDate = CDate(somedate)
    Else
        MakeDate = Date
    End If
```

The `Date` function above is one of three functions that return the current date/time values. The other two are `Time` and `Now`.

Finally, the `FormatDateTime()` function returns any date or time as text, using the user's Windows preferences for formatting dates. Its basic syntax is:

```
FormatDateTime(Date, NamedFormat)
```

The `NamedFormat` parameter is optional; if it is not present, `vbGeneralDate` is the default format.

You can use `FormatDateTime()` in both VBA and VBScript. Table 8.8 shows the constants allowed in VBA and VBScript for available options for the `NamedFormat` parameter and gives examples using the default Windows settings for U.S. users.

---

**Tip:** Experimenting with `FormatDateTime()` and different date expressions can help you gain a deeper understanding of how Outlook handles dates. For example, it might surprise you to find out that while the strings `"3/31/2007"` and `"31/3/2007"` are both interpreted as March 31, 2007, the string `"31/3/07"` is interpreted as March 7, 1931.

---

The `Format()` function offers even more flexibility than `FormatDateTime()` in arranging date elements in a string, but VBScript does not support `Format()`. You can read about the date (and other) formats that `Format()` supports in Help.

## 8.6.2   Date extraction functions

Being able to extract components from dates means that you can find out whether Valentine's Day falls on a weekend or what journal entries you made on Monday. Table 8.9 lists functions you can use to get just the date

**Table 8.8** *NamedFormat Arguments for FormatDateTime()*

| Constant | Value | Example |
|---|---|---|
| `vbGeneralDate` (default) | 0 | `12/31/2007 6:30:00 PM` |
| `vbLongDate` | 1 | `Tuesday, December 31, 2007` |
| `vbShortDate` | 2 | `12/31/2007` |
| `vbLongTime` | 3 | `6:30:00 PM` |
| `vbShortTime` | 4 | `18:30` |

or just the time portion of a date or extract any particular date component. Parameters shown in brackets are optional.

Let's look at a few examples. This expression returns the day of the week that the next New Year's Day will fall on:

```
WeekdayName(Weekday("1/1/" & CStr(Year(Date) + 1)))
```

`CStr()` is a function that converts any value to a string. Can you identify the four date-related functions that the expression uses?

**Table 8.9** *Functions to Extract Date Parts*

| Function | Returns |
|---|---|
| `Date` | Current system date |
| `DatePart(Interval, Date [ , Firstday [, Firstweek]])` | Part specified by the *interval* string:<br>`"yyyy"` Year<br>`"q"` Quarter<br>`"m"` Month<br>`"y"` Day of the year<br>`"d"` Day<br>`"w"` Day of the week<br>`"ww"` Week of the year<br>`"h"` Hour<br>`"n"` Minute<br>`"s"` Second |
| `DateValue(Date)` | Date component without any time value |
| `Day(Date)` | Day of the month, from 1 to 31 |
| `FormatDateTime(Date [, NamedFormat])` | Date/time formatted as text with optional *NamedFormat* (see Table 8.8) |
| `Hour(Time)` | Hour of the day, from 0 to 23 |

**Table 8.9**    *Functions to Extract Date Parts (continued)*

| Function | Returns |
| --- | --- |
| Minute(*Time*) | Minute of the hour, from 0 to 59 |
| Month(*Date*) | Month of the year, from 1 to 12 |
| MonthName(*Month* [, *Abbreviate*) | Name of the month, given the month number |
| Now | Current system date and time |
| Second(*Time*) | Second of the minute, from 0 to 59 |
| Time | Current system time |
| Timer | Number of seconds since midnight |
| TimeValue(*Time*) | Time component without any date value |
| Weekday(*Date* [, *Firstdayofweek*]) | Number from 1 to 7 representing the day of the week, counting from *Firstdayofweek* |
| WeekdayName(*Weekday* [, *Abbreviate* [, *Firstday* ]]) | Name of the day, given its number |
| Year(*Date*) | Number representing the year |

In Listing 8.6, the Weekday() function plays a role in building an IsWeekend() function to check whether a particular date falls on a Saturday or Sunday.

Remember vbMonday is a VBA and VBScript constant that you saw in Table 8.3.

If your weekend falls on Friday and Saturday instead of Saturday and Sunday, and you want an IsWeekend() function that works in VBScript, you can use the version that appears in Listing 8.7.

Both versions of the IsWeekend() function use the optional firstday parameter of the Weekday() function to designate the first day of the week—Monday in Listing 8.6 and Sunday in Listing 8.7—so that the weekend days (Saturday and Sunday in Listing 8.6 and Friday and Saturday in Listing 8.7) fall on the sixth and seventh days of the week. That makes it

**Listing 8.6**    *VBA function to indicate whether a date falls on a Saturday or Sunday*

```
Function IsWeekend(dteDate As Date) As Boolean
    Dim intWeekday As Integer
    intWeekday = Weekday(dteDate, vbMonday)
    IsWeekend = (intWeekday >= 6)
End Function
```

**Listing 8.7** *VBScript function to indicate whether a date falls on a Friday or Saturday*

```
Function IsWeekend(dteDate)
    Dim intWeekday ' As Integer
    intWeekday = Weekday(dteDate, vbSunday)
    IsWeekend = (intWeekday >= 6)
End Function
```

easy to test for Saturday or Sunday with the `(intWeekday >= 6)` expression, which evaluates to `True` or `False`. To adjust either `IsWeekday()` function to handle a different pair of consecutive weekend days, just adjust the `firstday` argument.

### 8.6.3 Performing date arithmetic

Date arithmetic involves calculating the time elapsed between two dates (or times) or adding or subtracting time to or from a particular date to get a new date. It can also involve merging the date part from one date/time value with the time part from another value. Possible uses include:

- Figuring the number of weeks since your last vacation day
- Calculating how long since you had any interaction with a contact
- Projecting the next day you should call a contact
- Combining the data entered in separate date and time controls

Outlook stores dates in the same format as double-type numbers—the integer portion representing the date and the decimal portion representing the time. This means that for the simplest sort of date arithmetic, you can simply add or subtract a number of days. For example, `Date() + 3` returns the date three days from today.

For more complicated calculations—such as the number of weeks between two dates or a date 13 months in the future—use the `DateAdd()` and `DateDiff()` functions:

```
DateAdd(Interval, Number, Date)
DateDiff(Interval, Date1, Date2, Firstday, Firstweek)
```

The *Firstday* and *Firstweek* parameters in `DateDiff()` are optional.

The *Interval* parameter takes the same values as in the `DatePart()` function in Table 8.9.

In the `DateAdd()` function, the *Number* parameter is the number of interval periods you want to add. To get a date in the future, add a positive number. To get a date in the past, add a negative number.

The `NextBusinessDay()` function in Listing 8.8 calculates the next business day that occurs `intAhead` days from `dteDate`, adding one or two

**Listing 8.8**    *VBA function to calculate the next business day*

```
Function NextBusinessDay(dteDate As Date, _
                          intAhead As Integer) As Date
    Dim dteNextDate As Date
    Dim intWeekDay As Integer
    dteNextDate = DateAdd("d", intAhead, dteDate)
    intWeekDay = Weekday(dteNextDate, vbMonday)
    If intWeekDay >= 6 Then
        dteNextDate = DateAdd("d", 8 - intWeekDay, dteNextDate)
    End If
    NextBusinessDay = dteNextDate
End Function
```

days if the date falls on a Saturday or Sunday. It makes use of the `Weekday()` and `DateAdd()` functions.

The VBScript version of `NextBusinessDay()` in Listing 8.9 takes a different approach. Instead of using `DateAdd()`, it simply adds the number of days directly. Note that it also ensures that `intAhead` is an integer value by first checking whether it is a number and, if it is, converting it to an integer with the `CInt()` function. You don't need to perform those operations in the VBA version, because the procedure declaration guarantees that the `intAhead` argument will be an integer.

**Note:** As with the `IsWeekend()` functions in Listings 8.5 and 8.6, you could adjust the `NextBusinessDay()` functions to handle weekends other than Saturday or Sunday by changing the second argument of the `Weekday()` function to the appropriate first day of the work week.

`DateDiff()` returns a negative number if `date1` is later than `date2`. For example, if `objTask` is an object variable representing an Outlook task, then `DateDiff("d", Date, objTask.DueDate)` returns either a positive number representing the number of days until the task is due or a negative number representing how many days it is overdue.

In Chapter 5, a complex application of `DateDiff()` was used to calculate a person's age in a formula. Remember that `DateDiff()` can't perform that calculation by itself because it rounds up to the nearest year if you compare two dates where the day and month of the earlier date fall after the day and month of the later date. To avoid the rounding and get an accurate count, you can use the `YearsDiff()` function in Listing 8.10 (which is written without data-typing so you can use it in either VBScript or VBA).

As our final date arithmetic example, consider the case of a custom form with separate controls for entering the date and time—data that you want

*Listing 8.9*  *VBScript function to calculate the next business day*

```
Function NextBusinessDay(dteDate, intAhead)
    Dim dteNextDate     ' As Date
    Dim intWeekDay      ' As Integer
    If IsNumeric(intAhead) Then
        intAhead = CInt(intAhead)
        dteNextDate = dteDate + intAhead
        intWeekDay = Weekday(dteNextDate, vbMonday)
        If intWeekDay >= 6 Then
            dteNextDate = dteNextDate + (8 - intWeekDay)
        End If
    End If
    NextBusinessDay = dteNextDate
End Function
```

to combine into a single Outlook field. You can't just bind both controls to the same field, because changing the time in one also changes the date to today's date, while selecting a new date changes the time to 12:00 AM. The solution is a formula that uses the DateValue() and TimeValue() functions to get values from each control that can be combined.

To demonstrate this, create a new custom form—the item type doesn't matter—and, in the Field Chooser, create four new date/time fields—Date1, Date2, Date2d, and Date2t. Display the P.2 page, and drag the Date1 field from the Field Chooser to the left side of the form three times, to create three text box controls bound to Date1. Bring up the Properties dialog for each control in turn, and on the Value tab, under Format, set one control to display only the date, one to display only the time, and one to display both date and time. Run the form and watch what happens when you enter a date (or type "tomorrow") in the control that displays only the date. Try typing a time in the control that displays only a time. The control formatted to show the full date and time never displays the date from the date-only control combined with the time from the time-only control. It always adds today's date value to the time you enter and a default time value to whatever date you enter. After you see how this works, close the item and return to the form designer.

Now, on the right side of the page, place the other three controls. Format the control for Date2d to show only a date, Date2t to show only a time, and Date2 to show both. For the Date2 control, enter this formula:

```
IIf( [Date2d] <> "None", DateValue( [Date2d] ) + IIf (
[Date2t] <> "None", TimeValue( [Date2t] ) , Null ) , Null)
```

and set that control to "Calculate this formula automatically." Run the form again, and this time, enter dates in the Date2d control and times in the Date2t control. The Date2 control should always show the correct date + time, combining values from the two controls. The secret is the formula,

Listing 8.10  *Calculating the number of years between two dates*

```
Function YearsDiff(dteDate1, dteDate2)
    Dim dteEarly
    Dim dteLate
    Dim dteEarlyMonDayLateYear
    Dim blnReverse ' flag for dates in reverse order
    Dim intYears
    On Error Resume Next

    ' get dates into chronological order
    If dteDate1 > dteDate2 Then
        dteLate = dteDate1
        dteEarly = dteDate2
        blnReverse = True
    Else
        dteLate = dteDate2
        dteEarly = dteDate1
    End If

    ' combine month and day from earlier date
    ' with year from later date
    dteEarlyMonDayLateYear = _
        CDate(Month(dteEarly) & "/" & _
            Day(dteEarly) & "/" & _
            Year(dteLate))

    ' calculate the years
    If dteEarlyMonDayLateYear <= dteLate Then
        intYears = DateDiff("yyyy", dteEarly, dteLate)
    Else
        intYears = DateDiff("yyyy", dteEarly, dteLate) - 1
    End If
    If blnReverse Then
        intYears = intYears * (-1)
    End If

    YearsDiff = intYears
End Function
```

which extracts the date from `Date2d` and the time from `Date2t` and combines them to update the value for `Date2`.

One of the exciting aspects of the new form region feature in Outlook 2007 is that its date and time controls do not require you to use a complicated formula like this. If you bind a date and a time control to the same field, each control updates only its part of the underlying field.

### 8.6.4  Time zones and international dates

If you need to deal with people in multiple time zones or in different countries, Outlook presents some challenges. For one thing, Outlook has no concept of an all-day event that is time-zone independent. For example, if you work in New York and create an all-day event for New Year's Day in an Exchange Server public folder that holds company holidays, your office in London will see it not as an all-day event, but as an appointment running from 5 AM January 1 to 5 AM January 2.

There are no easy solutions to this issue within the scope of this book. Outlook 2007 appointments do have a new Time Zones command to display an extra set of controls where the user can enter the Start and End dates using a non-local time zone. These correspond to new `Appointment-Item` properties—`StartTimeZone` and `EndTimeZone`, and `StartIn-StartTimeZone` and `EndInEndTimeZone` properties.

The `Application` object exposes information about time zones in a new `TimeZones` collection. You can, for example, return the name of the current time zone with this expression:

```
Application.TimeZones.CurrentTimeZone.Name
```

Time zone conversions are also possible with a new `ConvertTime` method:

```
Application.TimeZones.ConvertTime _
    (SourceDateTime, SourceTimeZone, DestinationTimeZone)
```

**Note:** We will return to the issue of time zones in Chapter 14, when we discuss the use of the new `PropertyAccessor` object to set and return property values. Any dates that `PropertyAccessor` returns are in UTC (Universal Coordinated Time) not local time, so you'll usually need to perform a conversion.

While American users are accustomed to entering dates in month/day/year format, many people in other countries instead use day/month/year (or even day.month.year). In general, Outlook VBA and VBScript code will correctly interpret whatever the user types into a date/time field as the correct date that the user intended, according to the user's Windows regional settings. However, for dates that your application displays as strings, you may want to use an unambiguous format. For example, you might want to display the fourth day of March as "04 Mar 2007" instead of "3/4/2007," which could mean March 4 or April 3, depending on the country. The `FormatDateTime()` function listed in Table 6.5 is available in both VBA and VBScript for use on Outlook forms. It can turn any date or time into text formatted with the user's own Windows regional preferences. The format settings on the Properties dialog for form controls are related to the user's local settings, but should display an appropriate format even if someone from another country runs the custom form.

## 8.7 Using arrays, dictionaries, and the Split() and Join() functions

I'd like to finish up this review of key VBA and VBScript functions with two more string functions, `Split()` and `Join()`, to help introduce the topic of *arrays* and *dictionaries*, which are a special application of arrays. These two functions can help you parse text, fill the rows of a combo box or list box, or manage the contents of the built-in `Categories` and `Companies` fields.

The `Split()` and `Join()` functions are designed to make it easy to handle a delimited list and its component substrings. The full syntax for the `Split()` function is

```
Split(Expression, Delimiter, Limit, Compare)
```

where the parameters—all optional except `Expression`—represent the following:

| | |
|---|---|
| *Expression* | a delimited string expression |
| *Delimiter* | one or more characters operating as a delimiter; the default is the space character |
| *Limit* | number of substrings to be returned; the default value is `-1`, which means return all |
| *Compare* | comparison option, same as for `Instr()`; useful if *Delimiter* contains alphabetic characters and not just spaces, punctuation, or numbers |

Both `Categories` and `Companies` fields are keyword fields, consisting of multiple string values. When you view either property in a text box on an Outlook form, you'll see the individual categories separated by a delimiter character. On most computers in the U.S., a comma functions as the delimiter, but depending on the user's Windows regional settings, the delimiter also could be a semicolon or some other character.

If a comma is the delimiter, the statement such as

```
arr = Split(objItem.Categories, ", ")
```

returns to the `arr` variable an array of the categories for an Outlook item represented by the object variable `objItem`. An *array* holds one or more values as separate elements. Refer to the elements of an array by subscript, starting with 0 for the first element (e.g., `arr(0)`). The lowest subscript is called the *lower bound* of the array. The largest subscript is the *upper bound*.

**Note:** VBA allows you to create arrays that use 1 as the lowest subscript, but VBScript doesn't support that type of array, so we'll stay away from it.

Join() is the opposite of Split() and uses this syntax

Join(*Array, Delimiter*)

to return a string consisting of the items in an array, separated by the Delimiter character(s). The code below processes the currently open Outlook item. Split() parses the value of the Categories field into an array, then Join() reassembles the array elements into a single text string with each pair of individual categories separated by a carriage return/linefeed:

```
Sub CategoryMsg()
    Dim objItem As Object
    Dim arr() As String
    On Error Resume Next
    Set objItem = Application.ActiveInspector.CurrentItem
    arr = Split(objItem.Categories, ", ")
    MsgBox Join(arr, vbCrLf)
    Set objItem = Nothing
End Sub
```

**Note:** Did you recognize that Replace() can accomplish the same thing as Split() followed by Join()? For example, using the same objItem object as in the CategoryMsg procedure, you could use MsgBox Replace(objItem.Categories, ", ", vbCrLf).

If the Option Explicit statement is present in your code module, you must declare any arrays, just as you would need to declare any variables. If you are creating an array with Split(), use the simple Dim arr() As String syntax in VBA or Dim arr() in VBScript. The parentheses indicate that arr is an array.

Use this syntax in VBA to declare an array named arr with a fixed number of elements, all of a specific data type:

Dim arr(*upper_bound*) As *data_type*

Here are some VBA examples:

```
Dim integerArray(3) As Integer
Dim stringArray(4) As String
```

In VBScript, you would omit the As Integer and As String expressions. Note that the number is the *upper bound*—that is, the highest subscript in the array—not the number of elements. Since the array's lower bound is 0, the upper bound is the number of elements minus one. For example, if an array has 4 elements, its lower bound is 0, and its upper bound is 3. To assign values to the array elements individually, use this syntax:

arr(*subscript*) = *value*

For example, you can assign values to the `integerArray` array declared above with this code snippet:

```
integerArray(0) = 1
integerArray(1) = 2
integerArray(2) = 3
```

If you later need to change the size of the array, use `Redim arr(upper_bound)`. Include the Preserve keyword if you want to keep the existing data in the array, for example:

```
Redim Preserve arr(12)
```

If you omit the `Preserve` keyword, changing the size of an array with a `Redim` statement causes the array to be reinitialized and all existing data lost.

As you can imagine, writing code to populate an array with many elements could get to be quite tedious. Fortunately, there are a number of different ways to streamline the process. You've already seen how to use the `Split()` function to populate an array from a delimited string. You also can use the `Array()` function to create an array from a series of values. For example, here is an alternative way to declare and fill an integer array:

```
Dim integerArray()
integerArray = Array(1, 2, 3, 4)
```

Note that, if you are using `Array()` to fill an array, your `Dim` statement should not specify a data type.

### 8.7.1   Working with multidimensional arrays

So far, we have been working with one-dimensional arrays, which are analogous to a single list of words or a single column of numbers. `Split()`, `Join()`, and `Array()` are handy functions for working with this type of array. However, arrays with more dimensions have a place in Outlook, too, particularly for filling the rows of list and combo boxes that have more than one column. For example, here is the code used to initialize the `cboCouples` combo box ("Favorite couple") that you saw in Figure 3.11.

```
Dim arrCouples(4, 1) As String
arrCouples(0, 0) = "Romeo"
arrCouples(0, 1) = "Juliet"
arrCouples(1, 0) = "Edward"
arrCouples(1, 1) = "Wallis"
arrCouples(2, 0) = "Dick"
arrCouples(2, 1) = "Linda"
arrCouples(3, 0) = "Robert"
arrCouples(3, 1) = "Sue"
cboCouples.ColumnCount = 2
cboCouples.List = arrCouples
```

This technique takes advantage of a combo or list box's `List` property, which can be assigned to an array. The second parameter in the `Dim` statement corresponds to the number of columns in the combo or list box. (Remember that arrays are zero-based.) The first statement puts the text "Romeo" in the first element of the first dimension of the array, which corresponds to the first row, first column of the combo box. Because the `Dim` statement defines the array as having five elements in its first dimension, but the code fills only the first four, the last element is blank, so the combo box gains a blank line at the bottom of the row list, making it easy for the user to clear the contents of the control.

## 8.7.2 Building and using dictionaries

A *dictionary* is an object that gives your code the ability to look up a piece of information based on a *key*. It is often called a "super array." Instead of entries being indexed by position, the `Dictionary` object indexes them according to key values. You can then use those values to perform lookups and return an item associated with a particular key. This object is a feature of VBScript, but you can also use it in VBA. To be able to declare a `Dictionary` object in VBA, you will need to choose Tools | References and add a reference to the Microsoft Scripting Runtime library.

Using a `Dictionary` object can help you streamline code that might otherwise require a complicated set of `If` statements or a `Select Case` block (both of which we'll learn more about later in this chapter). For example, let's say that you're using a custom Outlook contact form and need the user to fill in a custom `County` property, but you expect most of the entries to come from the same few postal codes. You could make data entry easier and more accurate by automatically filling in the county based on the postal code, pulling the data from a `Dictionary` object created when the form opens. Listing 8.11 shows the code for an Outlook custom contact form that performs such a lookup.

The code in Listing 8.11 assumes that you've modified a contact form to add a property named `County`. Some notes on the code:

- `CreateObject()` is a method you can use to instantiate an object from the many different programming libraries available to VBA and VBScript. We saw an example earlier in the `StartOutlook()` function in Listing 7.7, which instantiated an `Outlook.Application` object for use in Word VBA code.

- The `PropertyChange` event fires when a built-in property value changes on an Outlook item. It passes the name of the property that changed as its parameter. (You'll learn more about `PropertyChange` and the corresponding event for user-defined properties, `CustomPropertyChange`, in Chapter 12.)

- The `Dictionary.Add` method takes two arguments—a key and a value.

**Listing 8.11**     *Using a dictionary for Zip code lookups*

```
Dim objDict

Function Item_Open()
    Set objDict = CreateObject("Scripting.Dictionary")
    objDict.Add "22041", "Fairfax"
    objDict.Add "22042", "Fairfax"
    objDict.Add "22043", "Fairfax"
    objDict.Add "22044", "Fairfax"
    objDict.Add "22047", "Fairfax"
    objDict.Add "22040", "Falls Church City"
    objDict.Add "22046", "Falls Church City"
End Function

Sub Item_PropertyChange(ByVal Name)
    Dim strZip
    If Name = "MailingAddressPostalCode" Then
        strZip = Left(Item.MailingAddressPostalCode, 5)
        If objDict.Exists(strZip) Then
            Item.UserProperties("County") = _
                objDict.Item(strZip)
        End If
    End If
End Sub
```

- The `Dictionary.Exists` method returns `True` if the key passed as the argument for `Exists` is present in the dictionary.

- The `Dictionary.Item` method returns the item corresponding to a key.

Other useful `Dictionary` properties and events include `Count` to return the number of entries, `Remove` to remove a single entry, `RemoveAll` to remove all entries, `Keys` to return an array of all the keys, and `Items` to return an array of all the items entered into the dictionary.

**Note:** The examples in this chapter demonstrate `Dictionary` objects where both the key and the item were strings. However, the keys can be any kind of individual values (not an array), and the items can also be any kind of data, including objects.

More examples of the `Dictionary` object appear toward the end of the book. The `GetFolderCatArray()` function in Listing 22.5 returns an array of all the unique categories applied to items in a given folder—in just a few seconds. In Listing 24.11, we build an invoice report from data in an Outlook contact and its related journal entries, and the `Dictionary` provides a look-up feature for the Word 2007 content controls that comprise the data entry areas for the report.

### 8.7.3 Example: Parsing structured text with an array and a dictionary

Let's consider the issue of parsing structured text again. The ParseText-LinePair() function in Listing 8.5 operates by searching the text for a key value and then parsing the rest of the line where that key text appears. Another approach, shown in Listing 8.12, would be to parse the entire body of text into a Dictionary object and then look up the text corresponding to

**Listing 8.12** *VBA function to create a dictionary from a structured text block*

```
Function TextDict(strSource)
    Dim objDict As Scripting.Dictionary
    Dim arrLines() As String
    Dim strLine As String
    Dim arrEntry() As String
    Dim i As Integer

    Set objDict = CreateObject("Scripting.Dictionary")
    arrLines = Split(strSource, vbCrLf)
    For i = 0 To UBound(arrLines)
        strLine = arrLines(i)
        arrEntry = Split(strLine, ":", 2)
        If UBound(arrEntry) > 0 Then
            objDict.Add Trim(arrEntry(0)), Trim(arrEntry(1))
        End If
    Next
    Set TextDict = objDict
End Function

Sub ForwardRequestWithDict()
    Dim objItem As Object
    Dim objDict As Scripting.Dictionary
    Dim strAddress As String
    Dim strName As String
    Dim strRequest As String
    Dim objForward As Outlook.MailItem
    Set objItem = Application.ActiveExplorer.Selection(1)
    Set objDict = TextDict(objItem.Body)
    strAddress = objDict.Item("Requestor Email")
    strName = objDict.Item("Requestor Name")
    strRequest = objDict.Item("Type of Request")
    If strRequest <> "" Then
        Set objForward = objItem.Forward
        With objForward
            .To = "fixer@domainame.com"
            .CC = strAddress
            .Subject = UCase(strRequest) & _
                       " request from " & strName
        End With
        objForward.Send
    End If
    Set objForward = Nothing
    Set objItem = Nothing
    Set objDict = Nothing
End Sub
```

any key value. Remember the sample text used this structure with a colon as the character that signifies the end of the label and the beginning of the data:

```
Date Needed:  4-17-07
Type of Request: site visit
Requestor Name:  Jane Doe
Requestor Phone #:  123 456 1234
Requestor Email:  Jane_Doe@domainname.com
```

The code uses `Split()` once to parse the text into lines, then a second time to break out the text on each line into two parts. The part before the colon becomes the dictionary key, while the part after the colon becomes the dictionary item. After building the dictionary with the `TextDict()` function, you can perform a lookup for any key value with no further text parsing. The `ForwardRequestWithDict()` subroutine functions like the code snippet in Section 8.5.5, parsing the text of the currently selected item in order to forward it with the correct `Subject` and `Cc` values.

The third parameter in the expression `Split(strLine, ":", 2)` directs the `Split()` function to return a maximum of two elements to the array, even if more than one colon appears in `strLine`.

## 8.8    Controlling program flow

It's hard to write code without running into issues of program flow. How do you get the code to perform a certain action in one situation and a different action under other conditions? How do you process all the items in an Outlook folder, examining each in turn? You've already seen how to pass parameters from one subroutine to another—that's one way to control the flow of a program. You will learn several more techniques in the sections that follow, including `If ... Then ... ElseIf ... End If` blocks to create program branches, `For ... Next` loops to process multiple items, `Select Case` blocks instrumental in handling some specific Outlook events, and `GoTo` statements that can open the door to useful error handling.

### 8.8.1    If . . . Then statements

We have already seen several examples of `If ... Then` statements in earlier chapters. The basic syntax is simple:

```
If expression Then
    code to perform actions
End If
```

The *expression* in the first part of the `If ... Then` statement must evaluate to `True` or `False`. These are examples of such expressions that you might find in Outlook code:

```
IsNumeric(txtDays.Value)
Instr(strSubject, "Birthday") > 0
strAddress <> ""
intDoIt = vbYes
```

**Tip:** The intrinsic constant vbYes is used with the MsgBox function for getting user feedback with a message box, which we'll see later in this chapter.

Typically, the If ... Then expression will be either a function that returns True or False or an expression using one of the comparison operators we encountered in Chapter 7. You can also use a more complex expression involving more than one condition linked with the comparison operators And, Or, or Not, such as this one from the ReminderUpdate form in Chapter 3:

```
If InStr(strSubject, "Birthday") > 0 And _
    chkBirthdays.Value = True Then
```

The expression to be evaluated could also have been written as

```
InStr(strSubject, "Birthday") > 0 And chkBirthdays.Value
```

Why? Because chkBirthdays is a check box control and thus has one of two values, True or False. Thus, the expression chkBirthdays.Value is equivalent to chkBirthdays.Value = True. Similarly, an equivalent expression for chkBirthdays.Value = False would be Not chkBirthdays.Value, because the Not operator returns a value of False if the expression is True and vice versa.

After the If ... Then statement, you must supply the statements that you want the program to run if the expression is True. If you have only one statement to run, you can include it with the If ... Then statement on a single line, for example:

```
If D > 10 Then D = D * 1.20
```

Notice that you leave out the End If statement when you write an If ... Then statement on a single line.

The single-line format works for only the simplest of If ... Then statements. Most of the time, you will have more than one code statement to execute and, therefore, must place each statement on a separate line after the If ... Then statement and before the End If statement. This example of an If ... End If block tests whether a given Outlook item is a contact and, if it is, tests whether the contact has a business phone number, and if so, displays that number in a message box:

```
If objItem.Class = olContact Then
    strNum = objItem.BusinessTelephoneNumber
    If strNum <> "" Then
        MsgBox strNum, , "Business Phone"
    End If
End If
```

**Tip:** Since Outlook folders can contain more than one type of item, you usually should test whether an item is of the expected type before you try to use any properties or methods specific to that type of item. If you wanted to use the above code in VBScript, you'd declare `olContact` as a constant (`Const olContact = 40`) or substitute its literal value, 40.

As you saw above, you can nest `If ... Then` statements inside each other. Here's another example, to manage the foreground and background colors for a text box control named `txtOldCategory`:

```
If txtOldCategory.ForeColor = vbRed Then
    If txtOldCategory.BackColor = vbRed Then
        txtOldCategory.BackColor = vbBlack
    End If
End If
```

**Tip:** Remember that you saw in Table 8.3 that VBA and VBScript provide constants for eight commonly used colors.

Too many levels of nesting can make `If ... End If` blocks very difficult to read and debug, especially when you start nesting them with other kinds of program control statements. All it takes is one extra or one missing `End If` to make your procedure stop dead in its tracks. When you use nested `If ... End If` blocks, take extra care to indent all the statements within each block consistently. This will also make it easier to see that each block has the correct starting and ending statement.

A common variation on `If ... End If` blocks adds an `Else` block. In this structure, the code performs one set of actions if the test expression is `True` and a second set if the expression is `False`. Expanding on the earlier code to manage the foreground and background colors in a `txtOldCategory` text box control, you might have:

```
If txtOldCategory.ForeColor = vbRed Then
    If txtOldCategory.BackColor = vbRed Then
        txtOldCategory.BackColor = vbBlack
    End If
Else
    txtOldCategory.BackColor = vbYellow
End If
```

A less common variation uses `ElseIf` to test for another condition. In fact, you can add several `ElseIf` statements, as this example shows.

```
If txtOldCategory.ForeColor = vbRed Then
    If txtOldCategory.BackColor = vbRed Then
        txtOldCategory.BackColor = vbBlack
    End If
```

```
ElseIf txtOldCategory.ForeColor = vbWhite Then
    txtOldCategory.BackColor = vbBlack
ElseIf txtOldCategory.ForeColor = vbBlue Then
    txtOldCategory.BackColor = vbWhite
End If
```

The logic in `If ... Then ... ElseIf` statements can be difficult to follow. A more readable way to accomplish the same result is to use a `Select Case` block, which is covered in the next section.

A look at the structure of multiple `If ... End If` blocks can sometimes offer clues as to where your code can be simplified. Take, for example, this code from Listing 3.2:

```
If InStr(strSubject, "Birthday") > 0 And _
  chkBirthdays.Value = True Then
    objItem.ReminderSet = True
    objItem.ReminderMinutesBeforeStart = lngMinutes
    objItem.Save
End If
If InStr(strSubject, "Anniversary") > 0 And _
  chkAnniversaries.Value = True Then
    objItem.ReminderSet = True
    objItem.ReminderMinutesBeforeStart = lngMinutes
    objItem.Save
End If
```

Each `If ... End If` block contains the same three `objItem` statements. You can simplify the code by using the original `If ... End If` blocks to assign a value to a Boolean variable, `blnUpdate`, that indicates whether to proceed with the update and add a third `If ... End If` block to perform the actual update only if `blnUpdate` is `True`:

```
If InStr(strSubject, "Birthday") > 0 And _
  chkBirthdays.Value = True Then
    blnUpdate = True
End If
If InStr(strSubject, "Anniversary") > 0 And _
  chkAnniversaries.Value = True Then
    blnUpdate = True
End If
If blnUpdate Then
    With objItem
        .ReminderSet = True
        .ReminderMinutesBeforeStart = lngMinutes
        .Save
    End With
End If
```

This version is about the same length as the preceding code, but much easier to maintain. If you later decide to change how the reminder is set, you will need to make changes in only one location, in the `If blnUpdate Then` block.

---

**Tip:** Did you notice that we also streamlined the new version by adding a `With ... End With` block?

---

## 8.8.2  Select Case statements

The next program flow control tool is the `Select Case` block. Use this construct when you want to test a particular variable or property that could have several values, not just `True` or `False`. The syntax of `Select Case` looks like this:

```
Select Case expression
    Case value1
        code to perform actions
    Case value2
        code to perform actions
    Case value3, value 4
        code to perform actions
    Case Else
        code to perform actions
End Select
```

---

**Note:** On Outlook forms, the `Select Case` statement is essential to handling the `PropertyChange` and `CustomPropertyChange` events. Chapter 12 covers these events.

---

The *expression* in a `Select Case` statement can be a variable, an object property, or a more complex expression. Each `Case` statement handles one or more values that the expression can take on. You can even include more than one value in the same statement, as shown in the `Case value3, value4` statement above. Because you can't always anticipate every possible value, the optional `Case Else` statement provides a way to handle exceptions to the known values. If you don't include `Case Else` and the expression does not match any of the given `Case` values, the program control moves directly to the statement following `End Select`.

The previous section showed an example of a code snippet with a couple of `ElseIf` statements. It wasn't very easy to read, was it? See if this version using a `Select Case` block is easier to follow:

```
Select Case txtOldCategory.ForeColor
    Case vbRed
        If txtOldCategory.BackColor = vbRed Then
            txtOldCategory.BackColor = vbBlack
        End If
    Case vbWhite
        txtOldCategory.BackColor = vbBlack
```

```
        Case vbBlue
            txtOldCategory.BackColor = vbWhite
    End Select
```

Notice that you can nest `If ... End If` blocks inside `Case` blocks. The reverse is also true: you can nest a `Select Case` block inside an `If ... End If` block. Be careful, though, to get the ending statements in the correct order. The following code snippet would trigger a compile error because the `End Select` statement appears before the `End If` statement of the nested `If ... End If` block:

```
Select Case expression1
    Case value1
        your code goes here
    Case value2
        If expression2 Then
            your code goes here
End Select
End If
```

---

**Note:** VBA supports a couple of refinements to `Case` statements, such as `Case expression1 to expression2` to specify a range of values and the `Case Is comparisonoperator value1` expression to allow the use of comparison operators in `Case` statements. These are not available in VBScript.

---

### 8.8.3 Do loops

The next program flow tool is the venerable `Do` loop. The basic principle of a `Do` loop is that it continues to run a series of statements until a certain condition is satisfied. Here are several variations:

```
Do Until expression1
    code block 1
Loop

Do While expression2
    code block 2
Loop

Do
    code block 3
Loop While expression3

Do
    code block 4
Loop Until expression4
```

The first example repeats the statements in `code block 1` until `expression1` turns `True`. The second example repeats the statements in `code block 2` as long as `expression2` remains `True`. The third example always runs at least once, but repeats only if *expression3* is still `True`. Similarly, the fourth example runs at least once and keeps looping until *expression4* returns `True`.

Use a `Do` loop when you don't know how many times a block of statements should run. If you want the loop to run at least once, consider using the syntax in the third and fourth examples above. If you can't be sure whether the loop will need to run at least once, the first or second version might be more appropriate. Somewhere inside the loop, you'll need one or more statements to change the value of the test expression. Otherwise, there may be no way for the code to exit the loop. In the example below, code inside the loop changes the value of both x and y:

```
x = 12
y = 1
Do Until y > x
    x = x - 2
    y = y + 1
    lngReps = lngReps + 1
Loop
```

Execution of the loop stops after four repetitions, when x reaches a value of 4 and y is 5. The `lngReps = lngReps + 1` statement counts the number of repetitions (a bit of functionality common to many `Do` loops).

---

**Caution:** Think through the logic of your `Do` loops carefully, and make sure that they include a way for the procedure to exit the loop. Otherwise, the routine might find itself in an infinite loop. If you run VBA code that you suspect is trapped in an infinite loop, press Ctrl+Break to break out of the routine.

---

In addition to the `Until` or `While` keywords that control when looping stops, you might want to provide an additional test that causes the routine to exit the loop if it takes too much time. You can use the `Timer()` function, which returns a value representing the number of seconds elapsed since midnight. (In VBA, `Timer()` returns a numeric value using the single data type.) This code stops a `Do` loop after 60 seconds pass:

```
sngStart = Timer()
x = 12
y = 1
Do Until y > x
    x = x - 1
    y = y - 1
    lngReps = lngReps + 1
    If Timer - sngStart > 60 Then
        Exit Do
    End If
Loop
```

**Caution:** Because the `Timer()` function's value resets to 0 each day at midnight, if a procedure using `Timer()` runs just before midnight and then again right after midnight, the results may not be what you expect. Listing 11.27 in Chapter 11 includes a `TimeToQuit()` function to work around this midnight timing problem.

## 8.8.4    For . . . Next loops

Another type of loop is the `For ... Next` loop. These loops cycle through either a known quantity of items or all the items in a collection of objects, such as all the items in an Outlook folder.

One type of `For ... Next` loop continues until a particular number of iterations has occurred. Its syntax looks like this:

```
For i = intStart to intEnd
    your code runs here
Next
```

This type of `For` statement requires three elements:

- A numeric variable to hold the current value of the iteration; `i` is a customary choice.
- A numeric expression, `intStart`, that evaluates to an integer and represents the starting value for `i`
- A numeric expression, `intEnd`, that evaluates to an integer and represents the ending value for `i`

Both `intStart` and `intEnd` can be literal integers, or you can substitute any variable or expression that evaluates to an integer. For example, if you want to fill a message box (which we'll learn more about later in this chapter) with the contents of an array, you can use the lower and upper bounds of the array as the start and end points for the loop, as in this example:

```
arr = Array("red", "blue", "green")
For i = 0 To UBound(arr)
    strList = strList & vbCrLf & arr(i)
Next
MsgBox Mid(strList, 3)
```

Instead of counting up—for example, from 0 to `UBound(arr)` as in the above example—you can count down by specifying a `Step` parameter with a negative value. For example, Listing 8.13 illustrates how to use this technique with a `Step` parameter value of -1 to delete all the attachments in any Outlook item.

To use the code in Listing 8.13 in VBScript behind an Outlook form, all you need to do is remove the `As Object`, `As Outlook.Attachment`, and `As Integer` data type descriptions.

**Listing 8.13**　*Delete all attachments in an Outlook item using a For . . . Next loop*

```
Sub DeleteAttachments(objItem As Object)
    On Error Resume Next
    Dim objAtt As Outlook.Attachment
    Dim intCount As Integer
    Dim i As Integer
    intCount = objItem.Attachments.Count
    If intCount > 0 Then
        For i = intCount To 1 Step -1
            Set objAtt = objItem.Attachments.Item(i)
            objAtt.Delete
        Next
        objItem.Save
    End If
    Set objAtt = Nothing
End Sub
```

**Note:** If the code in Listing 8.13 counted up instead of down, it would remove only half the attachments from the item, because each time an attachment was deleted, Outlook would recalculate the Index property used to return the next attachment with `objItem.Attachments.Item(Index)`. If you delete the attachment with an `Index` property value of 1, the attachment whose `Index` was originally 2 now has an `Index` of 1, and the attachment whose `Index` was 3 now has an `Index` of 2. With a loop that counts up, when the `Next` statement increments the value of i from 1 to 2, the original second attachment is skipped, and the code deletes the original third attachment, the one whose `Index` is now 2.

Code to move Outlook items to another folder would run into similar problems, because moving items involves deleting them. Thus, you would want to also use a countdown loop for bulk moves.

Another important technique is the `Exit For` statement, which you can use to end the iteration of a `For ... Next` loop when you don't want to process any additional items. When processing the items in array, for example, you might want to stop processing once you find that a particular value is present, for example:

```
arr = Array("red", "blue", "green")
For i = 0 To UBound(arr)
    If arr(i) = "blue" Then
        MsgBox "We found blue!"
        Exit For
    End If
Next
```

### 8.8.5 **Example: Handling multiselect list boxes**

The code inside a `For ... Next` loop typically does something with the counter value. In Listing 8.11, the expression `objItem.Attachments.Item(i)` returns the *i*th attachment in the Outlook item.

Another practical example occurs if you have a multi-select list box either on a VBA user form or on an Outlook custom form. (Refer back to Section 7.3.4 if you need a refresher on the syntax for working with Outlook form controls.) On list boxes where only one selection is allowed, you can use the `Value` or `ListIndex` property of the control to determine which row the user has selected. With a list box that allows multiple selections, that approach doesn't work. Instead, you must check the `Selected` property of each item in the list to learn whether the user has chosen it. To return each item in the list, use the list box's `List` property, passing the row index as the argument. This code builds a list of the items selected in a list box and then displays that list in a message box:

```
For i = 0 To (lstBox.ListCount - 1)
    If lstBox.Selected(i) = True Then
        txtItems = txtItems & vbCrLf & lstBox.List(i)
    End If
Next
MsgBox "You selected:" & vbCrLf & txtItems
```

The `For` loop starts with 0 because that's the row index of the first item in the list. The number of items in the list is `ListCount`. Since the row index for the first item in the list is 0, the index for the last item is `ListCount - 1`. The syntax for getting a particular item from a single-column list box is `lstBox.List(index)`.

---

**Tip:** `List` returns or sets an array of variant values. If your list box has more than one column, you need to specify which column's value you want, by including value for the column index. For example, `lstBox.List(i, 0)` would return the *i*th value from the first column, while `lstBox.List(i, 2)` would return the *i*th value from the third column.

---

### 8.8.6 **For Each . . . Next loops for collections**

The other type of `For ... Next` loop works with collections. A *collection* is an object that comprises a set of other objects of a particular type. For example, each Outlook `Folder` object (formerly `MAPIFolder` in earlier versions) has an `Items` collection that includes all the items in the folder and a `Folders` collection that includes all the subfolders of the folder. Listing 8.13 illustrates another collection—the `Attachments` collection on an individual Outlook item.

Collections typically have a `Count` property, just as list boxes do, so you could work with them using the same type of `For ... Next` loop that you saw in the previous two sections. However, you also can work with them by using this type of `For ... Next` loop:

```
For Each object in collection
    your code to work with object runs here
Next
```

If, for example, you want to change one or more properties for all items in a folder, you can use a `For Each ... Next` loop to get each item in turn, alter the property, and then save the item. Listing 8.14 is a generic VBA routine for working with the standard properties of items in the currently displayed Outlook folder. You could use it, for example, to update the `MessageClass` property of items to point to a new published custom form's message class.

The `WorkWithCurrentFolderItems` procedure performs this sequence of operations:

1.   Get the currently displayed folder (`ActiveExplorer.Current-Folder`).

2.   Get the first item in the folder.

3.   Change some built-in properties of the item.

4.   Save the item.

5.   Repeat with the next item in the folder until all items have been processed.

**Listing 8.14**   *Use this generic code to work with items in the current Outlook folder*

```
Sub WorkWithCurrentFolderItems()
    Dim objApp As Outlook.Application
    Dim objFolder As Outlook.Folder
    Dim objItem As Object
    On Error Resume Next
    Set objApp = Application
    Set objFolder = objApp.ActiveExplorer.CurrentFolder
    For Each objItem In objFolder.Items
        With objItem
            .property1 = newvalue1
            .property2 = newvalue2
            ' more property changes
            .Save
        End With
    Next
    Set objItem = Nothing
    Set objFolder = Nothing
    Set objApp = Nothing
End Sub
```

**Tip:** Don't forget to save any item whose properties you change or whose attachments you remove. Not including a `Save` statement is a common Outlook coding error.

At the end of a `For Each ... Next` loop, you might want to report back to the user on the operations performed on the items in the collection. One way is to increment a variable each time an operation occurs, as you saw earlier in the section on `Do` loops.

**Note:** Bulk processing of items in a Microsoft Exchange Server folder, either in a mailbox or in the Public Folders hierarchy, can present a problem, because only 255 open remote procedure (RPC) calls to the server are allowed, unless the administrator changes a setting on the server. Generally, this is not a problem in VBA and VBScript environments, which release objects quickly, but if you later convert the application to a .NET add-in, you can run into out-of-memory and other errors. One workaround would be to process large numbers of items in batches, say only 200 or so items at a time.

### 8.8.7  GoTo statements

The last program flow technique discussed in this chapter is the `GoTo` statement, which applies only to VBA not VBScript, and is used primarily for error handing. A `GoTo` statement works in conjunction with labels that set off subsections in your procedures. Here's an example:

```
Sub GoToDemo()
    Dim intAns As Integer
    On Error GoTo Err_Handler
    intAns = MsgBox("Do you want to simulate an error?", _
                    vbYesNo)
    If intAns = vbYes Then Err.Raise 1
    MsgBox "No error occurred."
    Exit Sub
Err_Handler:
    MsgBox "Error Number " & Err.Number & " occurred."
End Sub
```

The statement `On Error GoTo Err_Handler` tells the procedure to branch to the section labeled `Err_Handler:` whenever it encounters an error. Program flow continues with the statements in the `Err_Handler:` section until the end of the procedure. An `Exit Sub` statement is placed before the `Err_Handler:` label so that if no error has occurred, the code exits the procedure before running the statements in the `Err_Handler:` section.

**Note:** You can use the `Err.Raise` method to simulate an error so that you can find out what your program will do when an error occurs. You can also use it to raise an error specific to certain conditions in your application. Error handling and debugging are covered in the next chapter.

You could also use `GoTo` statements by themselves to branch from one portion of a procedure to another section. However, the other program flow techniques that we've studied in this chapter produce much clearer code. The `GoTo` statement, therefore, is largely relegated just to error handling in VBA.

# 8.9    Providing feedback

VBA provides two main methods for providing feedback to the user: message boxes triggered by `MsgBox` statements and VBA user forms. `MsgBox` statements also work in VBScript.

**Tip:** A third and very simple VBA technique is to use a `Beep` statement to get a user's attention with an audible alert when a long operation finishes or an error occurs.

## 8.9.1    Feedback with message boxes

In several procedures, you have seen `MsgBox` statements displaying pop-up messages to the user. The basic syntax for this type of statement is:

```
MsgBox Prompt, Buttons, Title
```

The arguments for the `MsgBox()` function include

- *Prompt*—String expression for the text that you want the user to see in the message box; can contain special characters like carriage returns, linefeeds, and tabs, but no text formatting

- *Buttons*—Optional numeric expression that determines the number of command buttons, the default button, and other characteristics of the message box; see Table 8.10

- *Title*—Optional string expression for the title of the message box

If you omit the `Title` parameter, the title for the message box defaults to "Microsoft Outlook" in VBA and "VBScript" in VBScript code behind Outlook forms.

You can use the `Buttons` parameter to call attention to a message with a warning icon. The easiest way to get the value for the `Buttons` parameter for a feedback message box is to pick an icon constant and a modality constant from Table 8.10 and add them together:

*icon* + *modality*

All the MsgBox constants work in both VBA and VBScript.

If you omit the Buttons parameter, but still want to include a title, leave the comma delimiter for the *buttons* parameter in place. All these are valid MsgBox() expressions in both VBA and VBScript:

```
MsgBox "Have a great day!"
MsgBox "Have a great day!", , "Take a Day Off"
MsgBox "Have a great day!", 36, "Take a Day Off"
MsgBox "Have a great day!", _
        vbExclamation + vbYesNo, "Take a Day Off")
```

**Table 8.10**   *MsgBox Constants*

| Constant | Value | Description |
|---|---|---|
| *Button Type Constants* | | |
| vbOKOnly | 0 | Display OK button only (default) |
| vbOKCancel | 1 | Display OK and Cancel buttons |
| vbAbortRetryIgnore | 2 | Display Abort, Retry, and Ignore buttons |
| vbyesNoCancel | 3 | Display Yes, No, and Cancel buttons |
| vbYesNo | 4 | Display Yes and No buttons |
| vbRetryCancel | 5 | Display Retry and Cancel buttons |
| *Icon Constants* | | |
| vbCritical | 16 | Display Critical Message icon (refer to Figure 8.8) |
| vbQuestion | 32 | Display Warning Query icon |
| vbExclamation | 48 | Display Warning Message icon |
| vbInformation | 64 | Display Information Message icon |
| *Default Button Constants* | | |
| vbDefaultButton1 | 0 | First button is default (default) |
| vbDefaultButton2 | 256 | Second button is default |
| vbDefaultButton3 | 512 | Third button is default |
| *Modality Constants* | | |
| vbApplicationModal | 0 | Application modal—the user can't use Outlook without first responding to the message box (default). |
| vbSystemModal | 4096 | System modal—the user can't use any other application without first responding to the message box. |

**Figure 8.8**  *From left to right, the Critical Message, Warning Query, Warning Message, and Information Message icons.*

However, this statement

```
MsgBox "Have a great day!", "Take a Day Off")
```

would not be valid, because it omits the comma that occurs after the optional `buttons` parameter. In VBA (but not in VBScript), you could omit the buttons parameter and its comma by using named arguments, like this:

```
MsgBox Prompt:="Have a great day!", _
       Title:="Take a Day Off"
```

Message boxes have several disadvantages as a feedback mechanism:

- Execution of your code halts while the message box is on the screen. It restarts only when the user clicks OK.

- You cannot control the look of the message box, only change the text. There is no way, for example, to show the text in red to call attention to a problem.

- A message box can show only one piece of information at a time. If you want to provide feedback on two different operations, you would need to combine that information into one string and use that string to set the `MsgBox prompt` parameter.

Still, message boxes are extremely simple to code. You'll probably find yourself using them often. They are particularly handy for troubleshooting VBScript code, displaying variable and object property values and other messages as an alternative to stepping through code in the script debugger.

### 8.9.2  **Feedback with VBA forms**

Providing feedback with a VBA form avoids the limitation of message boxes. Of course, it has the disadvantage that you can use a VBA form for feedback only when you are running VBA code, not VBScript code behind an Outlook form.

In a VBA form, you can use multiple controls to provide information on different operations. Controls can change color or font size to call attention to critical feedback. You can even use graphics on the form to provide a different kind of visual feedback. In the next section, you'll see how to add feedback to the birthday/anniversary reminder form we built in Chapter 3.

One basic technique is to update the text in a text box as a procedure runs. As shown in Chapter 3, the syntax for getting or setting the data in almost any control is *control*.Value, where *control* is the name of the control. If you want to change the text in a text box named `txtProgress` to show when an update procedure started running, you could put the following statement in the procedure. This syntax assumes that the procedure updating the form is running from code behind the form:

```
txtProgress.Value = "Update started at " & _
    FormatDateTime(Now, vbShortTime)
```

An advantage of a VBA feedback form is that it can be a non-modal form. A procedure running from another module can display the form and update it as long as the user leaves the form on the screen. In that case, the code would use a slightly different syntax, specifying the name of the form. If the form were named `MyForm`, the code would set `MyForm.txtProgress.Value` instead of `txtProgress.Value`.

One variation is to use a text box where the `Multiline` property is set to `True` and add a line to that control every time something happens in your procedure that you want to notify the user about. Use the `vbCrLf` constant to put each new addition on its own line at the top of the text box, so the user sees the most recent progress report at the top:

```
MyForm.txtProgress.Value = "Update started at " & _
    FormatDateTime(Now, vbShortTime)
DoEvents
MyForm.Repaint
' some code here to perform a lengthy operation
MyForm.txtProgress.Value = "Finished at " & _
    FormatDateTime(Now, vbShortTime) & _
    vbCrLf & vbCrLf & MyForm.txtProgress.Value
DoEvents
MyForm.Repaint
```

After you update the control value, you need to give Windows an opportunity to update the screen display with these statements:

```
DoEvents
formname.Repaint
```

where `formname` is the name of the form. The `Repaint` method redisplays the form on the screen. `DoEvents` is a method that yields processing time to the operating system. If you don't include these statements, users will never see the feedback until the main procedure finishes.

Obviously, updating the form control adds extra processing time, but in many cases it's worth it. If you don't provide feedback, especially for lengthy operations, you run the risk of the user deciding that Outlook is hung. The user might then shut down Outlook or even the entire computer.

### 8.9.3 Example: Adding feedback to the birthday/anniversary reminder form

Let's see how you might add feedback to a familiar form—the birthday/anniversary reminder form created and customized in Chapter 3.

Figure 8.9 shows the form modified to add a new text box at the bottom and to rearrange the command buttons. The new text box should have these properties:

```
(Name)         txtProgress

BackColor      Button Face (&H800000F&)

Locked         True

Multiline      True
```

The `Locked` and `BackColor` properties ensure that the text box is both read-only and has a gray background so that the user doesn't automatically assume that it's a text box for data entry.

We need to make a few changes in the code for the `cmdUpdate_Click` event hander from Listing 3.3 and add a new procedure, `UpdateProgress`. Listing 8.15 shows the entire updated code for the form.

The `UpdateProgress` subroutine adds a timestamp to the text for the update, posts it to the text box, and then updates the screen. Using a separate procedure to perform the details of the feedback update simplifies the main code procedure immensely. In the `cmdUpdate_Click` event handler, all you need is a single call for each update to the `UpdateProgress` procedure.

You can see the results in Figure 8.9—a line corresponding to each time `UpdateProgress` was called. Notice that the lines for number of items increment in tens. This code snippet shows why:

```
If intCount Mod 10 = 0 Then
    Call UpdateProgress _
        (intCount & " items processed")
End If
```

**Figure 8.9**
*Even though this update finished in less than a minute, the feedback about its progress is reassuring to the user.*

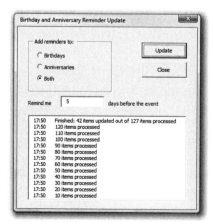

---

**Listing 8.15** *The birthday/anniversary reminder form, updated to include feedback*

```
Private Sub cmdUpdate_Click()
    On Error Resume Next
    Dim objOL As Outlook.Application
    Dim objNS As Outlook.NameSpace
    Dim objCalendar As Outlook.Folder
    Dim objItem As Outlook.AppointmentItem
    Dim strSubject As String
    Dim lngMinutes As Long
    Dim intCount As Integer
    Dim intCountBA As Integer
    Set objOL = Application
    Set objNS = objOL.Session
    Set objCalendar = objNS.GetDefaultFolder _
                    (olFolderCalendar)
    If IsNumeric(txtDays.Value) Then
        Call UpdateProgress("Update started")
        Call UpdateProgress("Processing " & _
          objCalendar.Items.Count & " items")
        lngMinutes = 24 * 60 * txtDays.Value
        intCount = 0
        intCountBA = 0
        For Each objItem In objCalendar.Items
            strSubject = objItem.Subject
            If InStr(strSubject, "Birthday") > 0 And _
              (optBirthdays.Value Or optBoth.Value) Then
                objItem.ReminderSet = True
                objItem.ReminderMinutesBeforeStart = _
                  lngMinutes
                objItem.Save
                intCountBA = intCountBA + 1
            End If
            If InStr(strSubject, "Anniversary") > 0 And _
              (optAnniversaries.Value Or optBoth.Value) Then
                objItem.ReminderSet = True
                objItem.ReminderMinutesBeforeStart = lngMinutes
                objItem.Save
                intCountBA = intCountBA + 1
            End If
            intCount = intCount + 1
            If intCount Mod 10 = 0 Then
                Call UpdateProgress _
                    (intCount & " items processed")
            End If
        Next
        Call UpdateProgress _
          ("Finished: " & intCountBA & _
          " items updated out of " & _
          intCount & " items processed")
    Else
        Call UpdateProgress("Value for days is not numeric.")
    End If
    Beep
```

**Listing 8.15**   *The birthday/anniversary reminder form, updated to include feedback (continued)*

```
    Set objItem = Nothing
    Set objCalendar = Nothing
    Set objNS = Nothing
    Set objOL = Nothing
End Sub

Private Sub UpdateProgress(strUpdate As String)
    txtProgress.Value = _
        FormatDateTime(Now, vbShortTime) & vbTab & _
        strUpdate & vbCrLf & txtProgress.Value
    Me.Repaint
    DoEvents
End Sub

Private Sub cmdClose_Click()
    Unload Me
End Sub
```

Mod is a special operator that returns just the remainder from a division operation, so it will equal 0 only when intCount is an even multiple of 10. Change the number from 10 to 100, and you'll see a progress update for only every 100 items processed. You can use this technique to provide periodic updates when processing large numbers of items without overburdening the user with information.

# 8.10   Getting user input

Earlier you learned how to use a MsgBox statement to pop up a simple message to the user. You can also use a message box to get a response back from the user that your code can use to decide what it should do next. Other methods for getting user input include input boxes and integrating a VBA user form into a calling procedure.

## 8.10.1   Using message boxes

Getting feedback from a MsgBox requires a slight variation from the syntax you saw earlier in the chapter, because you need to return a value to a variable:

```
    intAns = MsgBox(Prompt, Buttons, Title)
```

**Note:** The MsgBox() function also supports two other optional arguments that supply the name of a Windows Help file and the context number for the help topic you want to display. The creation of Help files is not covered in this book, however, so we'll ignore those arguments.

A typical series of statements requesting a simple Yes or No answer with a `MsgBox()` function looks like this:

```
intAns = MsgBox(prompt, vbYesNo, title)
If intAns = vbYes Then
    your code runs here
Else
    alternative code runs here
End If
```

As with MsgBox statements used to provide feedback, you can set the value for the *Buttons* parameter by constants from the groups listed in Table 8.10, up to four different constants.

```
buttontype + icon + defaultbutton + modality
```

Use only one constant from each of the four groups to create your *Buttons* argument. This message box asks users to give a Yes or No answer to a question about whether they really want to proceed:

```
intAns = MsgBox("Do you really want to do this?", _
        vbYesNo + vbQuestion + vbDefaultButton2, _
        "Dangerous operation")
```

It sets the default button to the second button, No, so that the user must actively decide to proceed by clicking the Yes button.

If the prompt for the message is lengthy or is itself an expression, use a separate string variable to build it. (This will make it easier to debug if the message box text doesn't look right.) In Listing 8.4, you encountered the `Selection` object that represents the items that a user has highlighted in an Outlook folder view. Instead of just telling users that they have selected too many items for processing, you could give them more specific information and ask if they want to proceed. This code snippet assumes that you have already set an `objSelection` variable representing `Active-Explorer.Selection`. It builds a `strMsg` string from two bits of text and the number of items selected (`objSelection.Count`):

```
strMsg = "This selection includes " & _
        objSelection.Count & " items. " & _
        "Do you want to continue?"
intAns = MsgBox(strMsg, _
            vbYesNo + vbQuestion + vbDefaultButton2, _
            "Process Selection")
```

Figure 8.10 shows what the user sees—the actual number of items selected and an option to proceed.

The `intAns` variable in all the message box examples is the key to getting the user's response. The `MsgBox()` function returns one of the integers in Table 8.11, all of which have Visual Basic intrinsic constant equivalents (so you don't need to memorize the numbers).

**Figure 8.10**    *When you ask users to make a choice, provide enough information for them to make an informed decision; in this case, give the size of the selection.*

Always ask for confirmation for risky operations, especially those with the potential for data loss. Removing attachments from items is an example. Listing 8.16 provides an updated version of the DeleteAttachments subroutine that you saw earlier in Listing 8.13. It asks for input in three places:

- If the item contains only one attachment, the first MsgBox() function asks whether the user really wants to delete it.

- For items with multiple attachments, the second MsgBox() function asks whether the user wants to be prompted to remove each attachment. The prompt includes the number of attachments.

- If the user does choose to be prompted, the code uses the name of the file to build the prompt message for the third MsgBox() function.

## 8.10.2    Using input boxes

The MsgBox() function provides a limited number of possible responses—basically, Yes, No, Cancel, and variations on those themes. If you want some other kind of input from the user, you must use another method. The

**Table 8.11**    *Return Values for the MsgBox() Function*

| When the User Presses | MsgBox() Returns | Constant |
|---|---|---|
| OK | 1 | vbOK |
| Cancel | 2 | vbCancel |
| Abort | 3 | vbAbort |
| Retry | 4 | vbRetry |
| Ignore | 5 | vbIgnore |
| Yes | 6 | vbYes |
| No | 7 | vbNo |

**Listing 8.16**   *Adding user input to the DeleteAttachments() subroutine*

```
Sub DeleteAttachments2(objItem As Object)
    Dim objAtt As Outlook.Attachment
    Dim intCount As Integer
    Dim i As Integer
    Dim strMsg As String
    Dim intResAsk As Integer
    Dim intResDel As Integer
    On Error Resume Next
    intCount = objItem.Attachments.count
    If intCount = 1 Then
        strMsg = "Do you really want to remove " & _
                "the attachment from this item?"
        intResDel = MsgBox(strMsg, _
          vbQuestion + vbYesNo + vbDefaultButton2, _
          "Remove Attachment")
        If intResDel = vbYes Then
            objItem.Attachments(1).Delete
        End If
    ElseIf intCount > 1 Then
        strMsg = "This item has " & intCount & _
                " attachments. Do you want to be " & _
                "prompted to remove each one?"
        intResAsk = MsgBox(strMsg, _
          vbQuestion + vbYesNo + vbDefaultButton2, _
          "Remove Attachments")
        For i = intCount To 1 Step -1
            Set objAtt = objItem.Attachments(i)
            If intResAsk = vbYes Then
                strMsg = "Do you really want to " & _
                    "delete this file:" & _
                    vbCrLf & vbCrLf & objAtt.FileName
                intResDel = MsgBox(strMsg, _
                  vbQuestion + vbYesNo + vbDefaultButton2, _
                  "Remove Attachment")
            Else
                intResDel = vbYes
            End If
            If intResDel = vbYes Then
                objItem.Attachments(i).Delete
            End If
        Next
    End If
    If objItem.Attachments.count < intCount Then
        objItem.Save
    End If
    Set objAtt = Nothing
End Sub
```

**Figure 8.11**
*An input box asks
the user for one
piece of
information.*

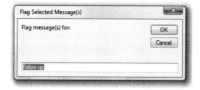

InputBox() function provides an easy way to get a single number, string, or date from the user, as shown in Figure 8.11.

**Note:** Try not to beleaguer the user with a series of input and message boxes. If you need more input or confirmation than one or two Input-Box() or MsgBox() functions can provide, use a VBA form instead, as described in the next section.

The basic InputBox() syntax looks like this:

```
InputBox(Prompt, Title, Default, Xpos, Ypos)
```

All parameters except *Prompt* are optional. The *Prompt* and *Title* parameters work just like they do in the MsgBox() function. The *Default* parameter is an optional string expression for the text you want to display in the input box as the default response in case the user types nothing in.

The *Xpos* and *Ypos* parameters are optional numeric expressions that set the screen location of the input box. They use the distance from the left and top of the screen, respectively, measured in twips; there are 1,440 twips to an inch. If you omit these arguments, Outlook centers the input box horizontally, about one-third of the way down the screen.

**Note:** Like the MsgBox() function, the InputBox() function also supports additional optional parameters to call a Windows Help file.

An input box returns a string consisting of whatever the user types into the box. Here is the VBA code snippet that created the input box in Figure 8.11:

```
Dim strAns as String
strAns = InputBox("Flag message(s) for:", _
            "Flag Selected Message(s)", _
            "Follow up")
```

In VBScript, the InputBox() statement would be exactly the same. The only difference is that you'd use Dim strAns without the data type declaration.

---

**Tip:** A statement using InputBox() is often followed by one or more statements that test the value returned by the function to make sure that it's more than an empty string or that it's a valid number or date. Remember the IsNumeric() and IsDate() functions encountered earlier in this chapter?

---

The code in Listing 8.17 uses an InputBox() to prompt the user, then sets a flag on all the messages the user has selected so that the item appears in the To Do Bar and also has a reminder.

Here are a few notes on the code in Listing 8.17:

- The If Trim(strFlag) <> "" ... End If block ensures that the code updates the items only if the user doesn't leave the follow-up input box blank.

- Checking the Class property ensures that the code only acts on messages.

**Listing 8.17** *Using an InputBox() to prompt the user*

```
Sub FlagSelectedItems()
    Dim objApp As Outlook.Application
    Dim objSelItem As Object
    Dim objSelection As Outlook.Selection
    Dim strFlag As String
    On Error Resume Next
    Set objApp = Application
    Set objSelection = objApp.ActiveExplorer.Selection
    strFlag = InputBox("Flag message(s) for:", _
            "Flag Selected Message(s)", "Follow up")
    If Trim(strFlag) <> "" Then
        For Each objSelItem In objSelection
            With objSelItem
                If .Class = olMail Then
                    .MarkAsTask olMarkThisWeek
                    .TaskDueDate = Date + 7
                    .TaskSubject = strFlag & " - " & _
                        objSelItem.ConversationTopic
                    .FlagRequest = strFlag
                    .ReminderSet = True
                    .ReminderTime = Date + 7
                    .Save
                End If
            End With
        Next
    End If
    Set objSelItem = Nothing
    Set objSelection = Nothing
    Set objApp = Nothing
End Sub
```

- MarkAsTask is a new MailItem method in Outlook 2007 that creates a task in the To Do Bar task list. Invoking MarkAsTask sets default values for the TaskDueDate and TaskSubject properties, but you can modify these values, as Listing 8.17 does.

- ReminderSet and ReminderTime set a reminder alarm for the message.

## 8.10.3 Using VBA forms

What if you wanted the user to provide both a message flag and a due date in the FlagSelectedItems routine in Listing 8.17? Can you do that with an InputBox() function? No, each input box returns only one piece of information, and popping up one input box after another is not considered good application design. The solution is to display a VBA form to gather multiple pieces of information from a single dialog.

We've already seen one VBA form: the birthday/anniversary reminder form from Chapter 3. That form contained its own code to process Outlook items. You can also have VBA forms whose purpose is solely to gather input for use in another VBA procedure, not to run any Outlook-specific code.

A VBA form for such user input should be modal and contain controls where the user enters data or makes selections, as well as an OK button to signal that the user's entries are ready to be processed. The code behind a form should set a global variable that the calling subroutine uses to determine whether the user clicked OK or canceled the form dialog. To make use of the form's data, the calling subroutine should follow these steps:

1. Use the Show method to display the form.

2. After the user interacts with the form, check the global variable to see whether the user clicked OK.

3. If the user did click OK, get data from the (now hidden) form's controls.

4. After obtaining all the necessary data from the form, unload the form.

In many cases, you can largely duplicate the look of Outlook's own dialog boxes with VBA forms of your own. In this example, you will create a macro to set a message flag on selected items, after prompting the user for the flag text and due date. Here's what you need to do:

1. Create a new VBA user form named Ch08FlagOptions with the caption "Flag for Follow Up."

2. Add a text box named txtFlagTo and a matching label with the caption "Flag to:".

3. Add a text box named `txtStartDate` and a matching label with the caption "Start on:".

4. Add a text box named `txtDueBy` and a matching label with the caption "Due by:".

5. Add a command button named `cmdOK` with the caption "OK," and set its `Default` property to `True`.

6. Add a command button named `cmdCancel` with the caption "Cancel," and set its `Cancel` property to `True`.

**Listing 8.18** *Code for a VBA form for user input with validation*

```
Dim blnUserChose As Boolean

Private Sub cmdCancel_Click()
    g_blnCancel = True
    blnUserChose = True
    Unload Me
End Sub

Private Sub cmdOK_Click
    If IsDate(txtDueDate.Value) And _
        IsDate(txtStartDate.Value) Then
        If CDate(txtDueDate.Value) >= _
            CDate(txtStartDate.Value) Then
            g_blnCancel = False
            blnUserChose = True
            Me.Hide
        Else
            MsgBox "Due date can't occur before start date."
        End If
    ElseIf Trim(txtDueDate.Value) = "" And _
            Trim(txtStartDate.Value) = "" Then
        g_blnCancel = False
        blnUserChose = True
        Me.Hide
    Else
        MsgBox "Please enter both dates or leave blank."
    End If
End Sub

Private Sub UserForm_Initialize()
    txtFlagTo.SelStart = 0
    txtFlagTo.SelLength = Len(txtFlagTo.Text)
    txtStartDate.Value = FormatDateTime(Date, vbShortDate)
    txtDueDate.Value = FormatDateTime(Date + 7, vbShortDate)
End Sub

Private Sub UserForm_Terminate()
    If blnUserChose = False Then
        g_blnCancel = True
    End If
End Sub
```

**Listing 8.19**   *Processing user input from a modal VBA form*

```
Public g_blnCancel As Boolean

Sub FlagSelectedItems2()
    Dim objApp As Outlook.Application
    Dim objSelItem As Object
    Dim objSelection As Outlook.Selection
    Dim strFlag As String
    Dim dteDue As Date
    Dim dteStart As Date
    Dim blnBlankDates As Boolean
    On Error Resume Next
    Set objApp = Application
    Set objSelection = objApp.ActiveExplorer.Selection
    Ch08FlagOptions.Show
    If Not g_blnCancel Then
        strFlag = Ch08FlagOptions.txtFlagTo.Value
        If Trim(strFlag) <> "" Then
            If Trim(Ch08FlagOptions.txtDueDate.Value) <> "" Then
                dteDue = CDate(Ch08FlagOptions.txtDueDate.Value)
                dteStart = _
                    CDate(Ch08FlagOptions.txtStartDate.Value)
            Else
                blnBlankDates = True
            End If
            For Each objSelItem In objSelection
                With objSelItem
                    If .Class = olMail Then
                        .MarkAsTask olMarkNoDate
                        .TaskSubject = strFlag & " - " & _
                            objSelItem.ConversationTopic
                        .FlagRequest = strFlag
                        If Not blnBlankDates Then
                            .TaskStartDate = dteStart
                            .TaskDueDate = dteDue
                            .ReminderSet = True
                            .ReminderTime = Date + 7
                        End If
                        .Save
                    End If
                End With
            Next
        End If
    End If
    Unload Ch08FlagOptions
    Set objSelItem = Nothing
    Set objSelection = Nothing
    Set objApp = Nothing
End Sub
```

**Figure 8.12**
*A VBA dialog can gather user input just like one of Outlook's built-in dialog boxes.*

7. In the form's code window, add the code in Listing 8.18. When clicked, the command buttons set the value of a global variable (g_blnCancel) and then hide or unload the form. The UserForm_Initialize event handler sets default values for the user input controls. The UserForm_Terminate event handler subroutine is necessary to make sure that the global variable is set, even if the user clicks the form's close (**x**) button. Validation takes place in the cmdOK_Click event handler to ensure that the user has entered valid or blank date values.

8. Add the code in Listing 8.19 to a regular VBA module. It contains the FlagSelectedItems2 macro that displays the form and updates the selected items with the data the user enters.

Here's how it works: The Ch08FlagOptions.Show statement in Listing 8.19 displays the Flag for Follow Up form shown in Figure 8.12. Because the form's ShowModal property is set to True (the default), execution of the FlagSelectedItems2 procedure halts until the user interacts with the form by pressing one of the buttons or closing the form.

If the user clicks the OK button, the g_blnCancel variable is set to False. If the user clicks the Cancel button or clicks the close (**x**) button (which triggers the UserForm_Terminate procedure), g_blnCancel is set to True. After the user completes the form and clicks one of those three buttons, control returns to the FlagSelectedItems2 procedure. If g_blnCancel = False (in other words, if the user clicked the OK button and the data entered was valid), the procedure gets the values from the text boxes on the form (which was only hidden, not unloaded), and uses those values to flag each selected item. (Compare that section of Listing 8.19 with the code in Listing 8.17.) Finally, the Unload Ch08FlagOptions statement terminates the user form and releases its memory.

## 8.11 **Working with files and other objects**

The previous chapter covered the syntax for Outlook object properties and methods. A similar syntax applies to objects exposed by other Office applications such as Word and Excel and even by Windows itself. Once you know what objects are available and how to instantiate variables for them, you can work with their properties and methods the same way you do with Outlook objects. In VBA, the first step often is to add a reference to a new programming library; this step is not necessary (or even supported) in VBScript. Later, Chapter 24, "Generating Reports on Outlook Data," will demonstrate a number of examples that use the Word and Excel programming libraries. In this chapter, we highlight two libraries that provide access to many basic Windows operations, such as checking for the existence of a file or folder—Scripting Runtime and Windows Script Host.

---

**Tip:** Another useful programming library is that from Internet Explorer. In Chapter 12 shows an example of launching a Web page from the `Click` event of a control on a custom Outlook form.

---

## 8.11.1   Adding programming library references in VBA

The object browser window in the VBA programming environment, discussed in Chapter 2, displays information about not only Outlook objects, but also other objects you can use in VBA. It even lists any modules or forms you have created in VBA under the `Project1` library.

Outlook VBA loads at least four standard programming libraries by default, including the core library for Office. To see the libraries currently installed and add more, choose Tools | References. In the References dialog box, shown in Figure 8.13, the items at the top, marked with check marks, are already installed and part of your VBA environment. (The Microsoft Forms library will be present only if you have created one or more VBA user forms.) Feel free to explore these libraries' capabilities using the object browser. For example, you can use this syntax from the VBA library to delete a file on your hard drive, given its path:

```
Kill "C:\my test file.txt"
```

To add another reference, scroll down the alphabetical list of unchecked items until you find the library you want to use. Then, click the desired library's check box. You can also install new references by clicking the Browse button and finding the appropriate reference file on your system. Reference files can include the following:

- Outlook VBA files (.otm)
- Object type libraries (.olb, .tlb, .dll)
- Executable files (.exe)
- ActiveX controls (.ocx)

After you add a reference, its object, properties, methods, and events will become visible in the object browser.

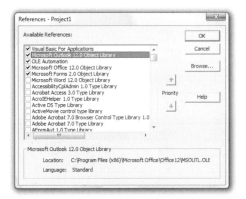

**Figure 8.13**
*These libraries are installed in Outlook VBA by default.*

---

**Tip:** To more easily locate a library in the object browser, add references one at a time, checking the object browser after each addition. Not all library names in Tools | References match their object browser names.

---

To remove a reference if you're no longer using its objects in your project, clear its check box in the Tools | References dialog.

Two libraries may contain objects with the same name. To avoid conflicts, use a fully qualified declaration for each object. For example, `Selection` could be a Word, Excel, or Outlook object. In VBA code, you should declare it as `Outlook.Selection`, `Word.Selection`, or `Excel.Selection`. If you do not use a fully qualified declaration, VBA will use the library nearest the top of the reference list that has a matching member.

## 8.11.2  Using the Scripting Runtime library

While the VBA library has a `FileSystem` object for working with files and folders, you will probably find it more convenient to use the Scripting Runtime library for file and folder operations because it is a bit easier to use and is also available to custom form VBScript code. The Scripting Runtime library's `FileSystemObject` is the starting point for such drive, file, and folder tasks as:

- Checking whether a particular file exists
- Getting the user's Temp or other special folder
- Reading data from a text file
- Transferring attachments from one Outlook item to another

To use the `FileSystemObject` in your VBA code, use the Tools | References command to add a reference to the Microsoft Scripting Runtime library (scrrun.dll). The library list in the object browser will then show

Scripting as an available library. To instantiate a `FileSystemObject` in VBA, use this code:

```
Dim fso as Scripting.FileSystemObject
Set fso = CreateObject("Scripting.FileSystemObject")
```

In VBScript, the declaration would be simply `Dim fso`, without the `As` clause.

---

**Note:** Some anti-virus applications may block programmatic access to the Scripting Runtime library.

---

The `FileSystemObject` offers a variety of methods for working with drives, files, and folders, including those that return a particular `Folder` or `File` object from a path. A special object is the `TextStream`, which represents a text file that has been opened for reading, writing new data, or appending to existing data. Tables 8.12 through 8.14 list the `FileSystem-Object` methods you are most likely to use in Outlook programming.

**Table 8.12**    *Key FileSystemObject Methods*

| Method | Returns | Outlook Usage and Notes |
|--------|---------|-------------------------|
| `BuildPath(Path, Name)` | `String` with full path and file name combined | Build a full path from a folder path, especially a special system folder, and a file name. |
| `CreateFolder(Path)` | `Scripting.Folder` | Create a new folder for storing attachments, logs, saved messages, etc. |
| `CreateTextFile(FileName, Overwrite, Unicode)` | `Scripting.TextStream` | Create a new file for storing logs, etc. and open it for reading and writing. The *Overwrite* and *Unicode* parameters are optional. |
| `DeleteFile(FileSpec, Force)` | n/a | Delete a file. Set the optional *Force* parameter to `True` to delete a read-only file. |
| `FileExists(FileSpec)` | `True` or `False` | Check whether a file with the same name already exists before saving a message or attachment as a file. |
| `GetExtensionName(FileSpec)` | `String` with name of the file extension | Use `GetBaseName` and `GetExtensionName` together to break a file name into its name and extension parts. |
| `GetFile(FilePath)` | `Scripting.File` | Return a `File` object you can examine for version number, created or modified date, or other file properties. |

**Table 8.12** *Key FileSystemObject Methods (continued)*

| Method | Returns | Outlook Usage and Notes |
|---|---|---|
| GetBaseName(*FileSpec*) | String with the name of last component in a *FileSpec*, without any file extension | Use GetBaseName and GetExtensionName together to break a file name into its name and extension parts |
| GetSpecialFolder(*SpecialFolder*) | Scripting.Folder | Get the user's temporary folder for saving files for short-term use. See Table 8.14 for possible values for *SpecialFolder*. |
| GetTempName() | String with name of the file | Get an automatically generated name for a temporary file. |
| OpenTextFile(*FileName*, *IOMode*, *Create*, *Format*) | Scripting.TextStream | Open a text file for reading or writing. See Table 8.13 for possible values for the optional *IOMode*, *Create*, and *Format* parameters. |

**Table 8.13** *Parameter Values for OpenTextFile*

| Parameter | Description | Constant | Literal Value |
|---|---|---|---|
| IOMode | Add text at the end of the file | ForAppending | 8 |
| | Read the file | ForReading | 1 |
| | Write data to the file | ForWriting | 2 |
| Create | Create a new file if it doesn't already exist | True | |
| | Don't create a new file | False (default) | |
| Format | Open the file as Unicode | TristateTrue | -1 |
| | Open the file as ASCII | TristateFalse (default) | 0 |
| | Open the file using the system default | TristateUseDefault | -2 |

**Table 8.14** *Values for the SpecialFolder Parameter for GetSpecialFolder*

| Folder | Constant | Literal Value |
|---|---|---|
| Temporary folder | TemporaryFolder | 2 |
| System folder (e.g., C:\Windows\System) | SystemFolder | 1 |
| Windows folder | WindowsFolder | 0 |

To demonstrate how you might use some of the methods in Table 8.12, Listings 8.20 for VBA and 8.21 for VBScript show how to create a new ASCII text file and open it for writing data to it. Both routines allow for the possibility that a file with the desired name might already exist; they try to create a file by appending a number up to 99 to the filename. A typical usage of the `OpenNewFileToWrite()` function would look like this:

```
Set objStream = OpenNewFileToWrite("C:\", "mydata.txt")
If Not objStream Is Nothing Then
    objStream.Write "some data " & Now
    objStream.Close
End If
```

**Listing 8.20**   *Create and open a new text file for writing (VBA)*

```
Function OpenNewFileToWrite _
  (folderPath As String, fileName As String) As TextStream
    Dim objFSO As Scripting.FileSystemObject
    Dim objStream As Scripting.TextStream
    Dim strFilePath As String
    Dim strFileName As String
    Dim strFileExt As String
    Dim i As Integer
    Set objFSO = CreateObject("Scripting.FileSystemObject")
    strFilePath = objFSO.BuildPath(folderPath, fileName)
    If Not objFSO.FileExists(strFilePath) Then
        Set OpenNewFileToWrite = _
          objFSO.OpenTextFile (strFilePath, ForWriting, True)
    Else
        i = 0
        strFileName = objFSO.GetBaseName(strFilePath)
        strFileExt = objFSO.GetExtensionName(strFilePath)
        Do While objFSO.FileExists(strFilePath)
            If i < 99 Then
                i = i + 1
            Else
                Exit Do
            End If
            strFilePath = _
              objFSO.BuildPath(folderPath, _
                strFileName & CStr(i) & "." & strFileExt)
        Loop
        If Not objFSO.FileExists(strFilePath) Then
            Set OpenNewFileToWrite = _
              objFSO.OpenTextFile(strFilePath, ForWriting, True)
        Else
            Set OpenNewFileToWrite = Nothing
        End If
    End If
    Set objFSO = Nothing
End Function
```

Table 8.15 shows `Write` and other key methods for the `TextStream` object.

Another common use for `TextStream` is to import data from a comma- or tab-delimited file. Listing 8.22 assumes that you have a text file with names and addresses in a tab-delimited format (as they would be if you saved an existing distribution list as a text file and edited it to remove the header information at the top); it creates and displays a new distribution list based on the file data.

**Listing 8.21**   *Create and open a new text file for writing (VBScript)*

```
Function OpenNewFileToWrite(folderPath, fileName)
    Dim objFSO
    Dim objStream
    Dim strFilePath
    Dim strFileName
    Dim strFileExt
    Dim i As Integer
    Const ForWriting = 2
    Set objFSO = CreateObject("Scripting.FileSystemObject")
    strFilePath = objFSO.BuildPath(folderPath, fileName)
    If Not objFSO.FileExists(strFilePath) Then
        Set OpenNewFileToWrite = _
          objFSO.OpenTextFile(strFilePath, ForWriting, True)
    Else
        i = 0
        strFileName = objFSO.GetBaseName(strFilePath)
        strFileExt = objFSO.GetExtensionName(strFilePath)
        Do While objFSO.FileExists(strFilePath)
            If i < 99 Then
                i = i + 1
            Else
                Exit Do
            End If
            strFilePath = _
              objFSO.BuildPath(folderPath, _
                strFileName & CStr(i) & "." & strFileExt)
        Loop
        If Not objFSO.FileExists(strFilePath) Then
            Set OpenNewFileToWrite = _
              objFSO.OpenTextFile(strFilePath, ForWriting, True)
        Else
            Set OpenNewFileToWrite = Nothing
        End If
    End If
    Set objFSO = Nothing
End Function
```

**Table 8.15**    *Key Methods for the TextStream Object*

| Method | Description |
| --- | --- |
| `Close` | Close the `TextStream`, saving any new data written to it |
| `Read(Chars)` | Read a specified number of characters from the text file |
| `ReadAll` | Read all data from the text file |
| `ReadLine` | Read one line from the stream. Repeat `ReadLine` to read each line in succession. |
| `Write(Text)` | Write a string of text to the stream |
| `WriteBlankLinks(Lines)` | Write a number of blank lines to the stream |
| `WriteLine(Text)` | Write a string of text, plus an end of line character, to the stream |

> **Note:** The File | Import and Export wizard in Outlook is not programmable in any way. To perform import and export operations, you'll need to write your own code using the Outlook object model and the programming library appropriate for the source or destination file.

The `ImportTextToDL` procedure in Listing 8.22 checks to see whether a file exists and, if it does, opens it for reading. Each line is read and split into an array, using the tab character (`vbTab`) as the delimiter. A dummy message item is used to build a list of recipients from the addresses in the second column of the array. (The names in the first column are ignored.) The `AtEndOfStream` property of the `TextStream` object enables the `Do` loop to know when all lines from the text file have been processed.

## 8.11.3    Using Windows Script Host techniques

The Windows Script Host library provides methods for launching programs, reading the Windows registry, and performing other Windows-related tasks. Since this library is used extensively for applications other than Outlook, you will find a wealth of material on the Internet to help you explore it further.

To launch any application or run any file in its native application, you can use code like this:

```
Set objWSH = CreateObject("WScript.Shell")
objWSH.Run """C:\my document.doc"""
```

The `Run` method can take as its argument any program file, document file, or URL that you can successfully launch with the Start | Run command

**Listing 8.22**  *Import a distribution list from a text file*

```
Sub ImportTextToDL(fileSpec As String)
    Dim objOL As Outlook.Application
    Dim objDL As Outlook.DistListItem
    Dim objMsg As Outlook.MailItem
    Dim objRecip As Outlook.Recipient
    Dim objFSO As Scripting.FileSystemObject
    Dim objStream As Scripting.TextStream
    Dim strLine As String
    Dim arr() As String
    Set objFSO = CreateObject("Scripting.FileSystemObject")
    If objFSO.FileExists(fileSpec) Then
        Set objStream = objFSO.OpenTextFile(fileSpec, ForReading)
        Set objOL = Application
        Set objNS = objOL.Session
        Set objDL = objOL.CreateItem(olDistributionListItem)
        With objDL
            .Subject = objFSO.GetBaseName(fileSpec)
            Set objMsg = objOL.CreateItem(olMailItem)
            Do While Not objStream.AtEndOfStream
                strLine = objStream.ReadLine
                If strLine <> "" Then
                    arr = Split(strLine, vbTab)
                    Set objRecip = objMsg.Recipients.Add(arr(1))
                End If
            Loop
            .AddMembers objMsg.Recipients
            .Display
        End With
        objStream.Close
    End If
    Set objOL = Nothing
    Set objDL = Nothing
    Set objMsg = Nothing
    Set objFSO = Nothing
    Set objStream = Nothing
End Sub
```

in Windows. In most cases, you will need to specify a full file path, not just the file name.

You can declare `objWSH` as `Object` in VBA or add a reference to the WSH Object Model (wshom.ocx) to your Outlook VBA project and declare `objWSH` as `IWshRuntimeLibrary.IWshShell`.

The Windows registry contains a huge amount of information about user and computer settings that can come in handy. You can read the registry with the WSH `RegRead` method. The `WSHListSep()` function in Listing 8.23 is a practical application—reading the character that Windows uses to separate items in a list, such as entries in the `Categories` property

**Listing 8.23**   *Use Windows Script Host to get the user's list separator*

```
Function WSHListSep()      ' As String
    Dim objWSHShell        ' As Object
    Dim strReg             ' As String
    strReg = "HKCU\Control Panel\International\sList"
    Set objWSHShell = CreateObject("WScript.Shell")
    WSHListSep = objWSHShell.RegRead(strReg)
    Set objWSHShell = Nothing
End Function
```

of an Outlook item. If you are writing code for use by people in different countries, you'll need to know the separator character.

**Note:** The `IWshShell` object also includes `RegWrite` and `RegDelete` methods for modifying the Windows registry. However, those techniques (and the even more powerful registry scripting techniques available from Windows Management Instrumentation library) are beyond the scope of this book. Changing the registry should always be approached with caution. Furthermore, while many Outlook options are maintained as registry settings, changing the registry value does not affect the currently running Outlook session, because the registry values are not read by Outlook until the next time it starts.

## 8.12  Summary

This long chapter has provided a good grounding in the basic techniques of writing VBA and VBScript code. You should refer back to it often as you apply those techniques to your Outlook programming projects. In addition to using basic techniques, you have also seen how to combine them to perform tasks that can be very useful in Outlook, such as parsing text from a structured text block (Listings 8.5 and 8.12), determining whether a date falls on a weekend (Listings 8.6 and 8.7), calculating the next business day (Listing 8.9), and calculating the number of years between two dates (Listing 8.10).

Also in this chapter were code samples for a number of key Outlook operations:

- Create a task due one week from today (Listing 8.1)
- Process items in a selection (Listing 8.4) or all the items in folder (Listing 8.14)
- Delete attachments (Listings 8.13 and 8.16)
- Flag selected messages to add them to the To Do Bar (Listing 8.17)

We enhanced the birthday/anniversary reminder VBA form from Chapter 3 with a control to provide feedback to the user (Listing 8.15).

Through the use of the Scripting Runtime (`FileSystemObject`) and Windows Script Host libraries, you have learned how to work with files and folders, read text from a file, write text to a file, run any application or file, and perform simple registry read operations.

Finally, you have seen some of the most common errors you're likely to encounter when writing Outlook code—including the "object required" error (Figure 8.1) and the "type mismatch" error (Figure 8.4). In the next chapter, we'll learn more about detecting and handling errors and debugging your code.

# *Handling Errors, Testing, and Debugging*

This chapter gives you a break from writing code procedures as it explores what might go wrong with your Outlook VBA or VBScript code and how to fix it. Outlook includes many tools to assist you in tracking down such problems, especially in VBA.

For VBScript, your options are more limited. There is no script debugging support for Outlook 2007 running on Windows Vista, unless Visual Studio is also installed on the machine. Therefore, we will look at some alternatives, including testing custom form code in Outlook VBA.

Highlights of this chapter include discussions of the following:

- What types of errors you are likely to encounter
- What debugging techniques Outlook VBA supports
- How to handle errors you can't avoid
- How to use the script debugger on systems where it is available
- How to convert VBA code to VBScript for use in custom forms

## 9.1 Understanding errors

Many types of errors can occur in the course of designing and running a code procedure. We have already seen many examples of typical Outlook coding errors, especially in the previous chapter. An error is not necessarily bad! Some errors can give you essential information on the status of your application.

We will consider these five varieties of errors:

- Simple syntax errors
- Compile errors
- Runtime errors
- Logic errors
- Outlook application bugs

Outlook's VBScript code editor for writing procedures for custom forms has no features for finding errors during the code writing process. The only time you'll find out about VBScript errors is when the code behind the form runs. VBA, on the other hand, has several features to help you find code errors before you run a procedure.

### 9.1.1  Simple syntax errors

The first kind of error that the VBA programming environment can detect is simple syntax errors, those that occur as you type code statements in VBA. For example, you might type this statement:

```
Set objOL + Application
```

when what you meant to type was:

```
Set objOL = Application
```

When you press the Enter key at the end of the statement, VBA pops up a message such as that in Figure 9.1, colors the problem statement in red, and highlights the portion of the statement that appears to be in error.

This kind of error checking is analogous to the spelling and grammar checker in Microsoft Word. Like Word's spell check, you can turn off VBA's syntax checker if you find it intrusive. With the VBA environment open, choose Tools | Options, and then clear the box for Auto Syntax Check. I recommend keeping it active, though, since it can help you prevent many mistakes.

If you make the same simple syntax mistake in the VBScript code behind an Outlook form—not using a equals sign (=) with a Set statement—you won't see any error until you run the form. At that time, Outlook will display an error like that in Figure 9.2 and give you the exact line number of the problem statement. In the form's script editor, use the Edit | Go To command or press Ctrl+G to go to that line and make your correction.

**Figure 9.1**
*VBA tries to help you correct simple syntax errors as you type.*

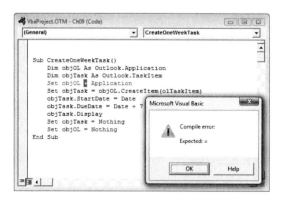

**Figure 9.2**
*For simple
VBScript code
syntax errors,
Outlook gives you
the line number to
fix.*

### 9.1.2 **Compile errors**

The Auto Syntax Check feature in VBA can detect errors only in single statements. It doesn't alert you to missing `End If` statements or undeclared variables in modules that contain an `Option Explicit` declaration. You won't be prompted about those types of errors until you *compile* your VBA code, a process that converts the typed code statements into lower-level programming instructions. A VBA procedure must be compiled before it can run. VBA automatically compiles procedures when you run them, but you can also manually compile the entire Outlook VBA project, including all modules, by choosing Debug | Compile.

Some compile errors are easy to fix. Others are not. One easy-to-fix example is the "variable not defined" error that occurs when the code module contains an `Option Explicit` declaration but not all variables are declared with `Dim`, `Public`, or `Private` statements. Such errors are easy to correct by adding the necessary variable declarations.

For an example of a tougher compile error, take a look at Figure 9.3. The error message indicates that something is wrong with the `If ... End If` block. However, you can see clearly that you do have both an `If` statement and an `End If` statement. So what's the problem? In a case like this, examine the statements immediately above the highlighted statement. That's where the error is likely to be. In the code in Figure 9.3, the problem is a missing `End Select` statement for the `Select Case` block nested inside the `If ... End If` block.

---

**Tip:** Imagine how much harder it would have been to discover the error in Figure 9.3 if the nested `If ... End If` block and `Select Case ... End Select` blocks were not so consistently indented!

---

When you compile, VBA highlights only one error at a time. After you correct the first error, compile again to see whether additional errors are present. Keep compiling until you receive no further compile error messages.

**Figure 9.3**
*Some errors, such
as a missing End
Select statement,
are detected only
when you compile
the code.*

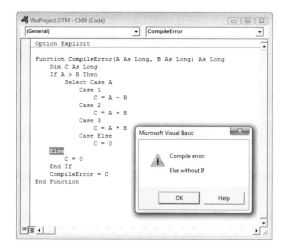

VBScript code behind Outlook forms can also have compile errors, but the error messages won't appear until you run the form, and they may be somewhat cryptic. If you copy the code in Figure 9.3 as-is into a custom form's code editor, then run the form, you'll get the error message shown in Figure 9.4. The problem is with the very first statement:

```
Function CompileError(A As Long, B As Long) As Long
```

The error message about the expected closing parenthesis doesn't tell you that the real problem is that this statement contains data type declarations (As Long) for the parameters and procedure declaration, and such data type declaration are not supported in VBScript. To fix the problem, you'd need to change the function declaration to:

```
Function CompileError(A, B)
```

### 9.1.3   Runtime errors

The third type of error, a runtime error, comes to light only when a procedure runs and a statement with an error executes—making this type of error potentially difficult to find. Both VBA and VBScript code are subject to

**Figure 9.4**
*While VBScript
will tell you where
a compile error
occurred, it won't
necessarily give you
a clue as to how to
fix it.*

runtime errors. The following VBA procedure contains one of the most common runtime errors you are likely to see in Outlook programming. Can you find it?

```
Sub NoObjectError()
    Dim objApp As Outlook.Application
    Dim objFolder As Outlook.Folder
    Dim objMsg As Outlook.MailItem
    Set objApp = Application
    Set objFolder = _
       objApp.Session.GetDefaultFolder(olFolderDrafts)
    objMsg = objFolder.Items.Add("IPM.Note.Sales")
    objMsg.Display
    Set objApp = Nothing
    Set objFolder = Nothing
    Set objMsg = Nothing
End Sub
```

The error is in the statement

```
objMsg = objFolder.Items.Add("IPM.Note.Sales")
```

Because `objMsg` is an object variable, you cannot assign it with a simple = statement, as you would with a string or numeric variable. Instead, you need to use the `Set` keyword, as in the statements for the `objApp` and `obj-Folder` variables.

If you run the `NoObjectError` subroutine, when the program gets to that problem statement, it cannot continue and pops up the error message shown in Figure 9.5. The runtime error dialog box gives you several choices. The Continue button is usually disabled because most runtime errors are so bad that the program cannot continue to run until you correct the problem.

If you choose End, program execution halts. After you correct the problem, you can run the procedure again.

If you choose Debug, VBA pauses program execution, switching to what's called *break mode*. (Notice the word "[break]" in the title bar in Figure 9.6.) The next statement to be executed is highlighted in yellow and marked with an arrow to the left. This is the statement you must fix before

**Figure 9.5**
*Runtime errors halt execution of your procedure.*

**Figure 9.6**
*In break mode, VBA highlights the next statement to be executed.*

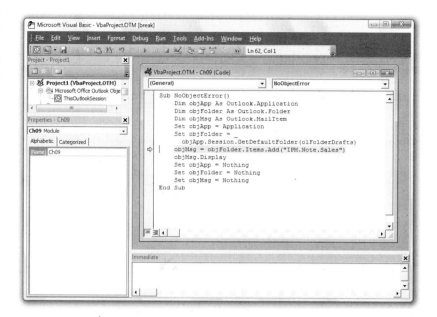

**Figure 9.7**
*Click Help on a runtime error message dialog in VBA to see more information on the problem.*

the program can continue. After you correct it, click the Continue button on the toolbar, or choose Run | Continue to pick up execution with the highlighted statement.

Certain edits will cause program execution to halt completely. VBA will warn you if you're about to make such an edit. After making that kind of correction, you'll need to restart the procedure from the beginning, not from the problem statement.

If you are unsure about the meaning of a runtime error, click the Help button on the message box about the error (refer to Figure 9.5). In most cases, a Help topic (see Figure 9.7) appears, explaining why the error may have occurred and how you might correct it. In this example, you can correct the error by prefixing the statement with the Set keyword:

```
Set objMsg = objFolder.Items.Add("IPM.Note.Sales")
```

When a similar runtime error occurs in VBScript code behind an Outlook form, you get a different error message. Here is the comparable code for a published custom form that contains a command button control named CommandButton1:

```
Sub CommandButton1_Click()
    Call NoObjectError()
End Sub

Sub NoObjectError()
    Dim objApp          'As Outlook.Application
    Dim objFolder       'As Outlook.Folder
    Dim objMsg          'As Outlook.MailItem
    Const olFolderDrafts = 16
    Set objApp = Application
    Set objFolder = _
      objApp.Session.GetDefaultFolder(olFolderDrafts)
    objMsg = objFolder.Items.Add("IPM.Note.Sales")
    objMsg.Display
    Set objApp = Nothing
    Set objFolder = Nothing
    Set objMsg = Nothing
End Sub
```

**Figure 9.8**  *A runtime error for VBScript code behind a custom form code may tell you which variable is causing the problem.*

Click the button and you'll see the error message shown in Figure 9.8. VBScript tells you exactly which object variable is causing the problem. If you are running Outlook 2007 on Windows Vista and don't have Visual Studio installed, that's all the information you'll get. If you are using Windows XP and have installed the script debugger, as described in Chapter 1, you will be able to invoke the script debugger using a Break command similar to that in VBA. Once you're in the debugger, the problem statement will be highlighted. You cannot, however, edit the script for your form in the script debugger. You can only read the script. We'll look more in depth at the VBScript debugger a little later in this chapter.

**Note:** Some runtime errors are unavoidable and need to be anticipated by your code. One example of error handing appeared in Section 8.8.7 on GoTo statements, and you'll see other examples later in this chapter.

### 9.1.4   Logic errors

The next type of error is the logic error, or as many programmers call it, the idiotic mistake. You can't blame the program for this kind of problem, because it is caused by flaws in your own logic.

For example, let's say you have a VBA user form with two text box controls, txtStart and txtEnd, where the user enters start and end dates. Before processing Outlook items in that date range, your code uses a function named DatesOK() to make sure that both entries are dates and that the end date is later than the start date. At least that's what you think your code does. However, when you run the form and enter what seem to be valid dates, DatesOK() often returns a value of False even when the dates seem correct to the eye. Take a look at the code for DatesOK() and see whether you can pick out the logic error:

```
Function DatesOK() As Boolean
    If IsDate(txtStart.Value) And IsDate(txtEnd.Value) Then
        If txtEnd.Value >= txtStart.Value Then
            DatesOK = True
        Else
            DatesOK = False
        End If
    End If
End Function
```

Did you find it? The problem is with the expression txtEnd.Value >= txtStart.Value. The Value property for each text box control is not date/time data; it's a variant, like the values returned by all form controls. This means that when you apply a comparison operator such as >=, the two terms are compared as if they are string values, a fatal flaw when you're trying to compare dates! For example, 4/10/07 may be a later date than 4/4/ 07, but the expression `"4/10/07" >= "4/3/07"` returns a value of `False`.

To fix this logic error, you must make sure that you are actually comparing date values. The `CDate()` date conversion function, which we saw in the previous chapter, does the trick. Change the problem expression to:

```
CDate(txtEnd.Value) >= CDate(txtStart.Value)
```

As you can see, logic errors can be tough to track down. These defensive strategies can help you prevent them:

- Sketch out your procedures well with pseudo code before writing real code statements.
- Use properly declared and typed variables in VBA. In VBScript, use conversion functions to make sure you have dates when you need dates and numbers when you need numbers.
- Test with lots of different data.

### 9.1.5   Outlook bugs

The final type of error can be the most frustrating—bugs built into the Outlook application itself. No matter how much testing takes place before the product is released, some problems known to Microsoft always remain. Others may come to light only after thousands of developers begin putting all the new features to use. When you encounter a suspected program bug, you don't have to suffer alone in silence. The resources at http://www.outlookcode.com can help you confirm whether you've run up against a program limitation and whether a patch or workaround is available.

## 9.2   Testing and debugging in VBA

All code needs to be tested and run against real-world data. Often, your tests will turn up errors. *Debugging* is the process of tracking down errors—mainly logic and runtime errors—by following the sequence in which code statements execute and monitoring the resulting changes in the values of your variables. VBA includes several tools that allow you to set the location where you want to start debugging and follow the variable values. These include:

- Breakpoints
- The Immediate window
- The Watch window and Quick Watch feature
- The Locals window
- The Call Stack

These tools are found on the Debug and View menus in VBA.

### 9.2.1   **Using breakpoints**

The idea of a *breakpoint* is to pause program execution so that you can take a look at the code and the variable values and make any necessary changes before continuing with the next statements. You can set manual breakpoints or have VBA switch to break mode automatically under conditions that you set.

---

**Note:** As you saw in the earlier section on runtime errors, you can switch to break mode by clicking Debug if a runtime error message appears. You can also get into break mode by pressing Ctrl+Break while the program is executing. However, pressing Ctrl+Break provides no control over which procedure will be interrupted.

---

To set a breakpoint, click in the gray left margin of the module window next to the line of code where you want to stop code execution. After the break occurs, this statement will not run until you continue code execution. You can also click in the code line and then press F9 to set the breakpoint, or choose Debug | Toggle Breakpoint. Follow the same steps to remove a breakpoint. To remove all breakpoints in the project, choose Debug | Clear All Breakpoints.

To have VBA switch to break mode automatically under a certain condition, you can set a *watch* for a particular variable or expression. The easiest way is to select the variable or expression you want to use in your VBA code window, then right-click and choose Add Watch. The Add Watch dialog (see Figure 9.9) appears. Check to make sure that you picked the right variable (or expression) and the right context, and then set the Watch Type at the bottom. You can have VBA go into break mode either when the value in the Expression box returns True or whenever the value changes.

Watches are shown in the Watches window (see Figure 9.10). You can toggle this window on and off with the View | Watch Window command.

**Figure 9.9**
*Watch expressions can switch VBA to break mode automatically while your code is executing.*

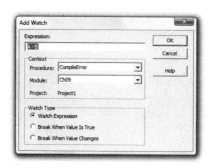

**Figure 9.10**
*The Watches
window shows each
expression for
which you have set
a watch, along
with its current
value if VBA is in
break mode.*

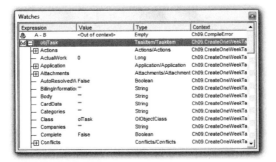

To change or remove a watch, right-click it in the Watches window; then
choose Edit Watch or Delete Watch. When VBA is in break mode, you can
use the Watches window to examine the values of the watch expressions.
For object variables, you will see a + sign to the left of the expression. Click
it to expand the information about the object to show all its properties and
their values.

**Tip:** If you just want to add a watch without setting it to break, select a
variable or expression, and then choose Debug | Quick Watch.

### 9.2.2 Working in break mode

What can you do when you're in break mode in VBA? Here are some of the
techniques that programmers use in break mode to work out the problems
in their code:

- Check the sequence of procedures that have already run
- Edit code to correct problems
- Examine and change the values of variables
- Restart the procedure from the breakpoint or from another statement
- Step through the code, statement by statement or procedure by procedure

To check what procedures ran before the break occurred, choose View |
Call Stack. The Call Stack window shows the sequence of procedures, with
the most recent at the top of the list.

While in break mode, you can edit your program code. Some changes
may cause a message to appear that the project will reset. This means that
program execution will halt and VBA will return to design mode, where
you can restart your procedure from the beginning.

**Figure 9.11**
*Screen tips pop up
with the current
variable or object
property values.*

As you saw in Figure 9.10, the Watches window shows the current values of any variables or expressions for which you set a watch. Another way to see the value of any variable or object variable property is to pause the mouse pointer over the variable where it appears in your code. After a second or two, a screen tip will appear, giving the current value (see Figure 9.11).

To see more variable and object property values, choose View | Locals. The Locals window (see Figure 9.12) works much like the Watches window, except that it shows all variables, not just those for which watches were set.

### 9.2.3   Using the Immediate window

Another VBA tool for examining variables is the Immediate window, which you can display by choosing View | Immediate Window. In the Immediate window, not only can you check the value of any variable, but you can also change values and even evaluate functions or run code statements.

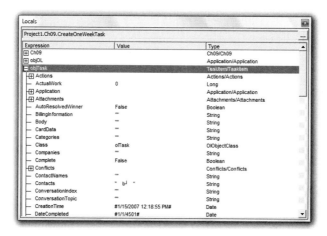

**Figure 9.12**
*The Locals window
displays all variable
and object property
values.*

To check the value of any variable or expression, in the Immediate window, type ? or Print, followed by the variable or expression, and then press Enter. The value appears on the next line in the Immediate window.

**Note:** One advantage of the Immediate window over the Watches or Locals window is that it's easier to see the value of string variables containing long blocks of text—even multiple lines of text.

You can also add a Debug.Print statement to your VBA program code and have it "print" information to the Immediate window as the code executes. In Listing 9.1, also shown in Figure 9.13, we've taken the Delete-Attachments subroutine from Listing 8.13, added code to run it for every

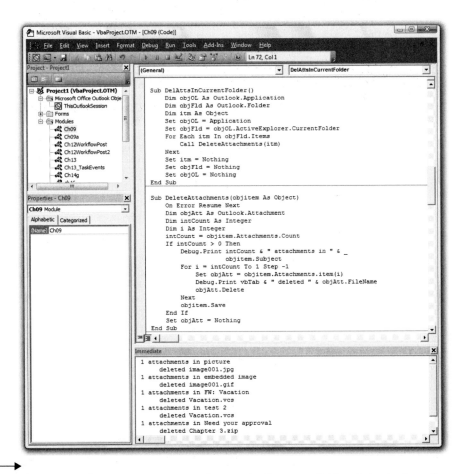

**Figure 9.13**  *Use a Debug.Print statement to show results from your VBA code in the Immediate window.*

**Listing 9.1**     *Delete all attachments from items in the current folder*

```
Sub DelAttsInCurrentFolder()
    Dim objOL As Outlook.Application
    Dim objFld As Outlook.Folder
    Dim itm As Object
    Set objOL = Application
    Set objFld = objOL.ActiveExplorer.CurrentFolder
    For Each itm In objFld.Items
        Call DeleteAttachments(itm)
    Next
    Set itm = Nothing
    Set objFld = Nothing
    Set objOL = Nothing
End Sub

Sub DeleteAttachments(objItem As Object)
    On Error Resume Next
    Dim objAtt As Outlook.Attachment
    Dim intCount As Integer
    Dim i As Integer
    intCount = objItem.Attachments.Count
    If intCount > 0 Then
        Debug.Print intCount & " attachments in " & _
                    objItem.Subject
        For i = intCount To 1 Step -1
            Set objAtt = objItem.Attachments.Item(i)
            Debug.Print vbTab & " deleted " & objAtt.FileName
            objAtt.Delete
        Next
        objItem.Save
    End If
    Set objAtt = Nothing
End Sub
```

item in the currently displayed folder, and added a `Debug.Print` statement inside the `Attachments` loop, so that the procedure can report on its actions.

While in break mode, you can change the value of any variable or set an object property value by typing the appropriate variable assignment statement in the Immediate window and pressing Enter. When you continue with code execution, the code runs with the new value of the variable or property.

### 9.2.4  Continuing program execution

After you make changes to your code in break mode, check variable values, and execute statements in the Immediate window, you may want to continue running the procedure. To continue from the breakpoint, click the Continue button or choose Run | Continue.

To continue from a statement other than the breakpoint, select the statement you want to start from. Choose Debug | Set Next Statement, and then click the Continue button or choose Run | Continue. You can also right-click the desired statement and choose Set Next Statement.

To restart from the beginning, click the Reset button or choose Run | Reset. You can then restart the current procedure or any other procedure with the Run button.

These methods continue program execution until the end of the current procedure (or its calling procedure) or the next breakpoint. You can also step through the code, statement by statement, to get a feeling for exactly what happens when each statement executes. To continue program execution in this fashion, press F8 or choose Debug | Step Into.

---

**Tip:** If you want to step through a procedure without setting a breakpoint or watch first, choose Debug | Step Into instead of Run to begin execution of the procedure in step mode. The Debug menu includes several other commands to help you step through your code in various ways: Step Over, Step Out, and Run to Cursor.

---

### 9.2.5 Adding VBA error handlers

The runtime error that you saw in Figure 9.5 doesn't tell an end user what went wrong or how to fix it. To provide a friendlier message with some detail about the error, you can add general error handling to any VBA procedure. The following procedure is a slightly more involved version of the type of error handler that we saw in Section 8.8.7 in the previous chapter:

```
Sub ErrorHandlerDemo()
    Dim strMsg As String
    On Error GoTo ErrorHandlerDemo_Err
    your program code goes here
    GoTo ErrorHandlerDemo_Exit

ErrorHandlerDemo_Err:
    strMsg = "Error number " & Err.Number & _
            vbCrLf & vbCrLf & Err.Description
    MsgBox strMsg, vbExclamation, "Error in
ErrorHandlerDemo"

ErrorHandlerDemo_Exit:
    ' release any object variables and
    ' perform other cleanup
End Sub
```

The `On Error GoTo` *linelabel* statement specifies that, if an error occurs, program execution continues with the section named *linelabel*. In general, labels for sections appear at the end of a procedure, with a labeled section to release any object variables and perform other cleanup last. If no such cleanup is needed, you could replace the `GoTo ErrorHandlerDemo_Exit` statement with an `Exit Sub` statement. Either one will prevent the code in the `ErrorHandlerDemo_Err` section from executing unless an error has occurred.

The `MsgBox` statement, which we learned about in the previous chapter, uses two properties of the intrinsic `Err` object representing the error that has occurred: `Number` and `Description`. Compare Figure 9.14 with Figure 9.5.

---

**Note:** `Err.Number` and `Err` by itself can be used interchangeably because `Number` is the default property of the `Err` object. If you have an error, the value for `Err.Number` will be non-zero. If `Err = 0`, you know that no error has occurred.

---

You are not limited just to displaying message boxes in response to errors, of course. If you want to trap particular known errors, you can expand the error-handling block with a `Select ... End Select` block such as this one. You would replace `err1` and `err2` with the specific error numbers that you want to address:

```
Select Case Err.Number
    Case err1
        error-handling code goes here
    Case err2
        error-handling code goes here
    additional Case statements
    Case Else
        catchall error-handling code goes here
End Select
```

In such an error-handling block, a useful statement is `Resume Next`. This causes program execution to continue with the statement immediately following the one in which the error occurred. Using `Resume` by itself will continue program execution with the statement that raised the error; use it if your error-handling code corrects the problem that caused the error.

**Figure 9.14**
*Your application can display its own message boxes in response to errors.*

---

**Tip:** To test how your code responds to a particular error, add an `Err.Raise` *errnum* statement to your code, in which *errnum* is the specific number for the error, for example, 91 in the case of the error shown in Figure 9.14. The statement `Err.Clear` clears the current `Err` object so that `Err.Number` once again returns 0.

---

## 9.3 Debugging Outlook form VBScript code

Compared with VBA's debugging features, the tools available to debug VBScript code range from primitive to almost non-existent, depending on what operating system you're using. On Windows Vista, no Outlook form script debugging is possible unless you also have Microsoft Visual Studio, a separate programming application for professional developers, installed.

Even without a script debugger, though, you should build some basic error handling into the VBScript code behind your Outlook forms. Otherwise, if the script encounters a runtime error, it will not be able to recover and complete the code in the procedure that encountered an error.

---

**Tip:** If you don't want a form's code to run when you open the form, hold down the Shift key until the form opens completely.

---

### 9.3.1 Error handling in VBScript

The `Err` object is intrinsic to VBScript, and its properties work the same as in VBA. However, VBScript code does not support `On Error GoTo` statements or labeled sections within a procedure. Therefore, basic standard error handling in form script code consists of:

- An `On Error Resume Next` statement to prevent the procedure from halting when an error occurs; this also prevents users from seeing error messages that they might not understand.

- Occasional checks to see if an error has occurred; get the value of `Err.Number` whenever it is important to your application to know whether there was an error.

While usually you will want to avoid errors, there are cases where letting an error occur and handling it gracefully can actually simplify your code! For example, if you want to create an item in another user's Exchange mailbox folder, you could first check to see whether you have permission to create an item in that folder (as we'll see in Chapter 13, "Working with Stores,

Explorers, and Folders"). Or you could take a more direct approach: Try to create the item and handle the error that will occur if you don't have permission to do so. Listing 9.2 is code intended to run when the user clicks a button named `CommandButton1`. It attempts to create a new task in the mailbox for a user in the same Exchange organization with the alias "donnal."

Notice that Listing 9.2 checks the value of `Err.Number` not once but twice: first, after the attempt to access the other user's folder with the `GetSharedDefaultFolder()` method, and then again after the attempt to create the task. This reflects the fact that the current user might have permission to view the other person's Tasks folder, but might not be able to create a task there. But, if the user can't access the folder at all, there's no point in trying to create an item in it.

**Listing 9.2**   *VBScript code to add a task to another user's Exchange mailbox*

```
Sub CommandButton1_Click()
    Dim objFld      ' As Outlook.Folder
    Dim objTask     ' As Outlook.TaskItem
    Dim objRecip    ' As Outlook.Recipient
    Dim strMsg      ' As String
    Const olFolderTasks = 13
    On Error Resume Next
    Set objRecip = Application.Session.CreateRecipient("donnal")
    Set objFld = Application.Session.GetSharedDefaultFolder _
                (objRecip, olFolderTasks)
    If Err.Number = 0 Then
        Set objTask = objFld.Items.Add
        With objTask
            .Subject = "Test of folder permission " & Now
            .Save
            If Err.Number <> 0 Then
                strMsg = "Could not create item in " & _
                        "other user's Tasks folder"
                MsgBox strMsg, vbCritical, "Error"
            Else
                .Display
            End If
        End With
    Else
        strMsg = "Could not access other user's Tasks folder"
        MsgBox strMsg, vbCritical, "Error"
    End If
    Set objTask = Nothing
    Set objRecip = Nothing
    Set objFld = Nothing
End Sub
```

### 9.3.2 **Using the script debugger**

As noted earlier, script debugging is available if:

- You are running Outlook 2007 on Windows XP and you installed the Web Debugging component for Office 2007, as described in Chapter 1; or

- You are running Outlook 2007 on Windows Vista, and you have installed Microsoft Visual Studio.

The script debugger is available only when you are running an Outlook form and does not allow you to edit the actual form script code.

Here is a simple test to determine whether the script debugger is available. Create a new custom form of any type and add this code to it:

```
Function Item_Open()
    MsgBox "Item is opening"
    Stop
    MsgBox "Item is still open"
End Function
```

Publish the form, and then create a new item using that form. The Item_Open event handler code will run when the item opens, and when it reaches the Stop statement, Outlook will try to call the debugger. If the debugger is not available, Outlook will ignore the Stop statement and show you both message boxes. If the debugger is present, you will see a dialog similar to that in Figure 9.15. Choose New Instance of Microsoft Script Editor and then click Yes. The debugger should then open (see Figure 9.16) with the Stop statement highlighted. Click the Step Into button or press F11 to step through the code.

**Figure 9.15**
*Your computer may have more than one script debugger available.*

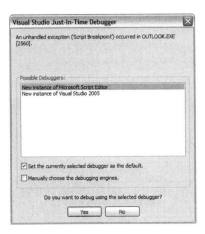

**Figure 9.16**

*The Microsoft
Script Editor
includes most of the
same debugging
commands as the
Outlook VBA
editor.*

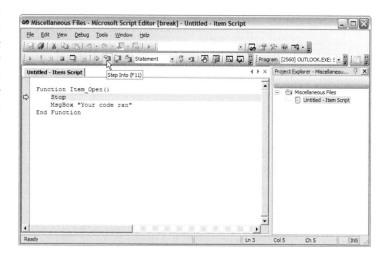

**Tip:** As Figure 9.15 suggests, your computer may have more than one script debugger available. Feel free to test multiple debuggers to see which works best for you.

This method invokes the debugger when the item opens. You will also have situations where you want the debugger to start after the form is already open. To do that, run the form from design mode (or create an item or open an existing item using the published form) and on the Developer tab, in the Code group, choose Script Debugger. You'll see the dialog in Figure 9.15 again, but when the debugger opens, no statement will be highlighted. Set a breakpoint in any procedure using the F9 key, and the debugger will stop code execution at that statement, whenever that event happens to fire.

Compared with the debugging environment in VBA, the chief limitation of the script debugger is that there is no way to go from the error message directly into the script to make a correction. You must figure out the problem by stepping through the code in the debugger, then switch to the Outlook form's code window to make the necessary changes.

Here are some strategies that can help you locate problems in your form code using the script debugger:

- Use the Locals window to track the value of key parameters. Figure 9.17 shows the debugger running with a breakpoint in the PropertyChange event handler, with the Locals window showing the value of Name, the parameter for that event that indicates which property changed.

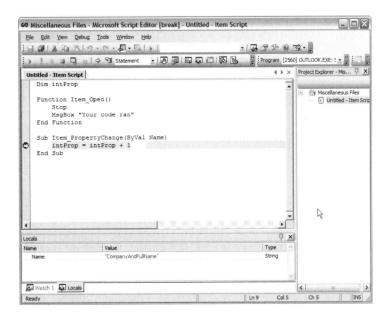

**Figure 9.17**
*Use breakpoints in the script debugger to watch what happens when your form code executes.*

- Right-click an expression in your code, and then choose Add Watch to add a watch for that expression.
- If you determine that a particular section of your code is causing a problem, you can bypass it. Right-click a later statement, and then choose Set Next Code Statement.

---

**Tip:** On machines where the script debugger is not available, a good tactic for troubleshooting problems in a form's VBScript code is to use Msg-Box statements to display the values of different variables at key points in the code. Such statements can tell you a lot about the sequence in which your code statements execute and the state of key variables and object properties.

---

## 9.3.3    Using VBA to prototype VBScript code

So far in this book, the VBScript code you've seen has been quite simple. Some Outlook forms, however, have complex code modules running into hundreds of lines. Writing that much code in the form code window, without the features you're accustomed to in VBA, makes it likely that you will make a lot of simple mistakes—and probably some gigantic ones, too. Therefore I (and many other Outlook developers) recommend that you write as much of your form code as possible in VBA and perform initial testing in VBA. You can then make a few changes to make it compatible with VBScript syntax and copy it into the form code window for final testing on the actual form.

The idea, in other words, is to use VBA as a code prototyping tool for VBScript.

Before you get started with that technique, let's review the key differences between VBScript and VBA code, which you should remember from earlier in the book:

- VBScript does not support the Outlook intrinsic constants (the ones that start with `ol`), only the Visual Basic constants. In VBScript code, you must either declare those constants that your form code needs or use their literal values. Listing 9.2, for example, includes a declaration for the `olFolderTasks` constant. You can get both the constant declarations and the literal values from the object browser. (See Section 8.2.4.)

- The `Item` object intrinsic to VBScript form code, representing the current item where the code is running, is not supported in VBA. You must instantiate an object variable to represent the Outlook item whose methods and properties you want to invoke. (See Section 7.3.)

- VBScript variables support only the variant data type, which can represent any type of data. You do not use typed variable declarations, such as `Dim strMsg As String` in VBScript, only `Dim strMsg`.

- A few VBA functions, such as `Format()`, have no VBScript equivalent.

Figure 9.18 shows the `CommandButton_Click` procedure in Listing 9.2 being prototyped in VBA before being converted to VBScript after successful VBA testing. If you compare the two, you'll see that the only changes necessary to make it compatible with VBScript were to comment out the data types for the variable declarations and to uncomment the constant declaration.

---

**Note:** Even though the `CommandButton1_Click()` procedure in Figure 9.18 is designed to be an event handler for an Outlook form command button, you can run it on demand in VBA just as you would any other macro.

---

Listing 9.2 and Figure 9.18 constitute simple examples of this kind of prototyping, because they don't make any reference to `Item`, the item where the code would be running if it were VBScript code. If you want to prototype form code that refers to the form's item, things get a bit more complicated. We need to look at two types of procedures—those that refer to `Item` properties and methods and those that provide handlers for `Item` events.

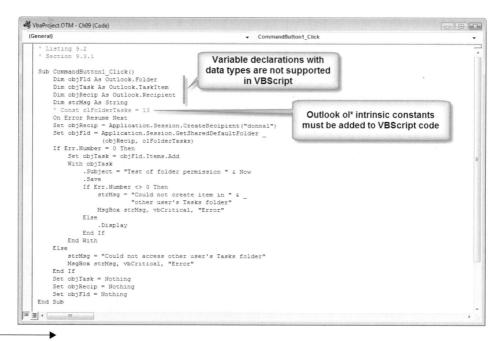

**Figure 9.18**   *Much of your VBScript code for custom forms can be prototyped in VBA first to save time and avoid errors.*

As an example of a procedure that refers to `Item` properties and methods, let's modify the code shown in Figure 9.18 so that instead of creating a new task, it copies the current item (assume this is a task form) to the other user's folder. Listing 9.3 shows the VBA prototype.

To test the code, open a task, and then run the macro in Listing 9.3. The key changes that make this VBA code work with the currently open item are the addition of these three statements to declare, instantiate, and release an object representing the currently open item:

```
Dim Item As Outlook.TaskItem

Set Item = Application.ActiveInspector.CurrentItem

Set Item = Nothing
```

The expression `Application.ActiveInspector.CurrentItem` returns the item that is currently open in its own window. Thus, Listing 9.3 now has an `Item` object to work with!

Converting the code in Listing 9.3 to work behind an Outlook form involves taking out those three added statements and making the same two changes that were used to create Listing 9.2: comment out variable data types and declare the necessary Outlook constant. You see the result in Listing 9.4.

**Listing 9.3**    *VBA prototype to copy the current task to another user's mailbox*

```
Sub CommandButton2_Click()
    Dim objFld As Outlook.Folder
    Dim Item As Outlook.TaskItem
    Dim objTask As Outlook.TaskItem
    Dim objRecip As Outlook.Recipient
    Dim strMsg As String
    ' Const olFolderTasks = 13
    On Error Resume Next
    Set objRecip = Application.Session.CreateRecipient("donnal")
    Set objFld = Application.Session.GetSharedDefaultFolder _
                (objRecip, olFolderTasks)
    If Err.Number = 0 Then
        Set Item = Application.ActiveInspector.CurrentItem
        Set objTask = Item.Copy
        objTask.Subject = "Copy of " & objTask.Subject & _
                        " from " & Time
        objTask.Move objFld
        If Err.Number <> 0 Then
            strMsg = "Could not create item in " & _
                    "other user's Tasks folder"
            MsgBox strMsg, vbCritical, "Error"
        Else
            strMsg = "Copied current item to " & _
                    "other user's Tasks folder"
            MsgBox strMsg, vbOKOnly, "No Error"
        End If
    Else
        strMsg = "Could not access other user's Tasks folder"
        MsgBox strMsg, vbCritical, "Error"
    End If
    Set Item = Nothing
    Set objTask = Nothing
    Set objRecip = Nothing
    Set objFld = Nothing
End Sub
```

It takes just a few code statements to copy an item to another folder. (Note that you make a copy first, and then move the copy.) More often your form code will need to perform an extended operation on an item. In that case, you may prefer to put the bulk of the code in a separate VBA procedure and call it from the VBA macro, passing the currently open item as an argument. If you're working on a task form, that structure would look like this:

```
Sub CommandButton3_Click()
    Dim Item as Outlook.TaskItem
    Set Item = Application.ActiveInspector.CurrentItem
    Call MyProc(Item)
    Set Item = Nothing
End Sub
```

```
Sub MyProc(ByVal objItem as Outlook.TaskItem)
    ' code to process objItem goes here
End Sub
```

Converted to VBScript, that code would look like this:

```
Sub CommandButton3_Click()
    Call MyProc(Item)
End Sub

Sub MyProc(ByVal objItem)
    ' code to process objItem goes here
End Sub
```

The last type of prototyping involves testing Outlook item-level event handlers in VBA. As examples, we'll use the Write and Open events that you first saw in Section 7.3.2. Add the code in Listing 9.5 to the built-in This-OutlookSession module in VBA, and then run the StartItemTests subroutine. Now, you can test the Open and Write event handlers by opening

**Listing 9.4** *VBScript code to copy the current task to another user's mailbox*

```
Sub CommandButton2_Click()
    Dim objFld            ' As Outlook.Folder
    Dim objTask           ' As Outlook.TaskItem
    Dim objRecip          ' As Outlook.Recipient
    Dim strMsg            ' As String
    Const olFolderTasks = 13
    On Error Resume Next
    Set objRecip = Application.Session.CreateRecipient("donnal")
    Set objFld = Application.Session.GetSharedDefaultFolder _
                    (objRecip, olFolderTasks)
    If Err.Number = 0 Then
        Set objTask = Item.Copy
        objTask.Subject = "Copy of " & objTask.Subject & _
                        " from " & Time
        objTask.Move objFld
        If Err.Number <> 0 Then
            strMsg = "Could not create item in " & _
                    "other user's Tasks folder"
            MsgBox strMsg, vbCritical, "Error"
        Else
            strMsg = "Copied current item to " & _
                    "other user's Tasks folder"
            MsgBox strMsg, vbOKOnly, "No Error"
        End If
    Else
        strMsg = "Could not access other user's Tasks folder"
        MsgBox strMsg, vbCritical, "Error"
    End If
    Set objTask = Nothing
    Set objRecip = Nothing
    Set objFld = Nothing
End Sub
```

**Listing 9.5**  *Event handlers to test item-level events in VBA*

```
Dim WithEvents Item As Outlook.TaskItem
Dim WithEvents allInsp As Outlook.Inspectors

Private Sub Item_Open(Cancel As Boolean)
    MsgBox "The Open event fired on " & Item.Subject
End Sub

Private Sub Item_Write(Cancel As Boolean)
    MsgBox "The Write event fired on " & Item.Subject
End Sub

' run this to get things started
Sub StartItemTests()
    Set allInsp = Application.Inspectors
End Sub

Private Sub allInsp_NewInspector _
  (ByVal Inspector As Inspector)
    Set Item = Inspector.CurrentItem
End Sub
```

any single task, making changes, and saving the item. You should see a message box when the item opens and another message box when it saves.

Here's how Listing 9.5 works: Running the StartItemTests procedure instantiates an Inspectors variable declared WithEvents, which sets up Outlook to handle the events for Inspectors. The one event we're interested in is NewInspector, which fires whenever the user opens an item in its own window. The sole parameter for NewInspector is Inspector, representing that window, and Inspector has a property, CurrentItem, that returns the item that was opened. We use Inspector.CurrentItem to instantiate an Item object that was declared WithEvents, thus setting up Outlook to handle the events for Item, including Open and Write.

We'll look at VBA event handlers in more detail in Chapter 11 and form-level events in Chapter 12. However, I hope this brief excursion into testing item-level events gets you excited about the possibility of rapidly prototyping event handlers for your forms in VBA.

## 9.3.4  A recipe for VBA to VBScript code conversion

Here is a general list of steps to follow if you have a subroutine or function that works in VBA and you want to use it in an Outlook item's VBScript code:

1.   Copy the VBA procedure code and paste it into an Outlook form's script window.

2.　Comment the As *data_type* portion of any Dim or Const declaration, and remove the data type from any procedure arguments.

3.　For each Outlook constant, add a Const statement at the beginning of the script.

---

**Tip:** Here's another way to get the constant values: In the VBA code editor, right-click the constant and then choose Quick Info from the pop-up menu.

---

4.　If the VBA procedure is a macro (in other words, an argumentless subroutine), when you transfer it to the VBScript environment, it will need to be called from some event handler in VBScript, such as the Click event for a command button.

5.　If the VBA procedure is an item-level event handler, in the form's code editor use the Script | Event Handler command to insert the corresponding event handler for VBScript. Copy only the body of the VBA procedure to the VBScript editor, not the procedure declaration. For cancelable events, replace any Cancel = True statement with an event_handler = False statement, where event_handler is the name of the event-handling function, for example, Item_Write = False.

The reason for that last point is that the declarations for item-level events are slightly different between VBA and VBScript form code. The easiest way to get the correct version for the form is to use the Script | Event Handler command.

## 9.4　Summary

Producing reliable applications means testing your code and fixing problems as you go along. Outlook provides many debugging tools in the VBA environment. Error handling helps make your code more professional and more likely to deliver the results you want. While the Outlook form code scripting environment is nowhere near as rich as the VBA environment, it too supports a certain level of error-handling. If you write your form code in the VBA environment and then transfer it to the form's script, you probably will make fewer coding mistakes that require troubleshooting.

With the set of good coding practices that we've developed in the past few chapters, we're now ready to dive into the specifics of Outlook programming, starting with the next chapter on the object model, Outlook security, and basic object and collection techniques.

# 10

# *Outlook Programming Basics*

We have been sneaking up for several chapters on "real" Outlook programming. Many of the examples that illustrated basic VBA and VBScript coding concepts were actually also useful examples of key Outlook programming concepts. In the course of learning about those examples, you've probably seen the word *object* several times without the need to really understand what it means. In this chapter, we'll learn about objects in general and the Outlook object model—that is, the Outlook programming model—in particular. We also examine an issue that will apply to almost all the coding you do in Outlook: security.

Highlights of this chapter include discussions of the following:

- How to use the object browser to discover what you can accomplish with Outlook

- Why a collection is a special kind of object

- How to programmatically create a message with voting buttons

- What security features in Outlook protect it from becoming a conduit for virus distribution

- How Outlook's security affects your code and other Outlook extensibility features

- How to create and send a message from VBA in another Office application

## 10.1 Introducing the Outlook object model

Most of the code you have seen so far has worked with three basic kinds of data:

- Static data, either literal values or constants

- Simple text, numeric, Boolean, and date/time variables

- Object variables, such as a variable to represent an Outlook item or folder

An object variable differs from a simple text or numeric variable because it contains not just one but many pieces of information. An object variable representing an Outlook contact, for example, has properties that return the name, addresses, and phone numbers for that contact. You can also assign new values to those properties.

Not only do objects often contain more than one piece of information in the form of multiple properties, they also support specific events and methods that determine how that data behaves and what you can do with it programmatically. Those properties, events, and methods together define the object *class*. The methods, events, and properties are called *members* of the class. Together, all the objects in a particular programming library are called an *object model*. In this book, we are chiefly concerned with the Outlook object model, although in later chapters, you will also see how other object models, such as those for Word and Excel, can be useful to your Outlook programming projects.

When you use a Set statement to assign an object variable to a particular object, you *instantiate* the variable or create a new *instance* of the class. For example, this Outlook VBA or custom form VBScript statement creates a new MailItem (Outlook message) and points an object variable to that new item:

```
Set objMail = Application.CreateItem(0)
```

Not all Set statements create a new object, though. Some statements create a new object while others point the object variable to an existing object. This example sets an object variable to an existing object, the currently viewed folder:

```
Set objFolder = Application.ActiveExplorer.CurrentFolder
```

Objects of different classes may act much the same. For example, Outlook has a different type of object for each type of item—ContactItem, MailItem, TaskItem, and so on—but all those item objects share certain properties, events, and methods.

Objects often exist in parent-child relationships. An Outlook JournalItem object, for example, has a parent Folder object that represents the folder that stores that journal entry.

Trying to understand the concept of objects, properties, methods, and events might seem like a lot of trouble when what you really want to do is write Outlook applications, but the effort pays off in the end. Grasping the core of the Outlook object model helps you know what you can do in Outlook, and which objects, properties, methods, and events you can use to accomplish your goals.

### 10.1.1    Launching the VBA Object Browser

The Outlook 2007 object model includes sixty-seven new classes, roughly doubling the size of the object model. We don't have room to cover all those classes in this book, only those that you're most likely to use. Therefore, you need to know how to research the other classes on your own.

The main tool for exploring the Outlook object model and other object models is the object browser window in VBA. Chapter 2 provided a brief introduction to the object browser, but it's time to take a more detailed look at it.

To display the object browser, press Alt+F11 to enter the VBA programming environment, and then press F2 or choose View | Object Browser. When the Object Browser window appears, you may want to maximize it to be able to see more information on the screen.

When you launch the object browser, the default display lists all the objects in all the programming libraries available to you. To focus on Outlook objects, select Outlook from the dropdown list at the top of the object browser (the list that defaults to <All Libraries>). To view the members of any object class, click on that object. Figure 10.1 shows the `JournalItem` class.

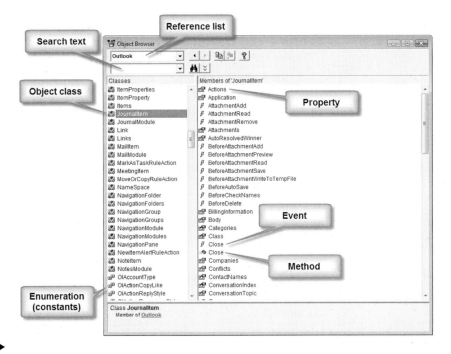

**Figure 10.1**    *Use the object browser to explore Outlook's objects and their properties, methods, and events.*

**Note:** You can add more programming libraries to VBA by using the Tools | References dialog. Chapters 8 and 24 cover other libraries you may find useful in Outlook programming projects.

Pay close attention to the icons that help distinguish the different types of object classes and their members. For example, the `JournalItem` object includes both a `Close` event and a `Close` method. It's easy to tell them apart by the icon. The event icon is a lightning bolt, while the method icon is a green box in motion.

**Tip:** If you prefer to see all the properties together, followed by methods and then events, right-click the list of members and choose Group Members.

## 10.1.2    Searching for objects and getting help

You can search the object browser for classes and members related to particular topics. Type a word in the second dropdown list box, the one marked Search Text in Figure 10.1, and then press Enter or click the Search button. Figure 10.2 shows the results of a search of the Outlook library for the word "folder." It turns up a long list of objects, methods, events, properties, and constants whose names contain "folder."

To close the search results pane, click the Hide Search Results button next to the Search Text button. You can view the search results again by clicking the same button (now with the screen tip Show Search Results).

If you have been browsing through objects for a while and want to retrace your steps, use the right and left arrow buttons at the top of the Object Browser window, above the search controls.

The object browser functions as an index to the Help topics on the Outlook object model. Select any class or member, then click the Help button or press F1 to get help on that topic, including related properties, methods, and events, often with sample code.

**Note:** Not all libraries shown in the object browser have help files associated with them. Sometimes, you may need to refer to a separate help file or other documentation.

Figure 10.3 shows the help topic for the `Folder.GetCalendar-Exporter` method, a new method added to Outlook 2007 to facilitate

**Figure 10.2**
*Search in the object browser for classes and members containing particular text.*

**Figure 10.3**
*Help topics tell you how to use Outlook objects, properties, methods, and events.*

calendar sharing using the iCalendar specification for calendar data exchange across the Internet. Notice the links at the top for the parent `Folder` object and the `CalendarSharing` object that `GetCalendarExporter` returns. The How To article link provides a detailed code sample and other tips on using this method.

The links at the very top of the help window in Figure 10.3 can help you locate related information, such as other methods for the `Folder` object. Click the link for Outlook Object Model Reference to see a list of all Outlook object classes (see Figure 10.4).

The bottom right of the help window in Figure 10.3 shows the connection status as Connected to Office Online. By default, help uses content from the Office Web site. This allows Microsoft to provide programmers with the very latest help topics without the need to update the installation on the local machine. When you are not connected to the Internet, the connection status will display as Offline. To see what the offline help looks like, click on the connection status in the status bar and choose "Show content only from this computer."

Another advantage of working with the online help content is that you can provide feedback. Each online topic has buttons under "Was this information helpful?" where you can click "Yes," "No," or "I don't know" and

**Figure 10.4**
*Click any Outlook object in this help topic to learn more about it.*

provide a short description of how to make the help topic better. Microsoft uses this feedback to improve developer help.

---

**Caution:** Always closely examine and test any code that you copy from a help topic. Some code samples may not be quite right for the Outlook VBA or VBScript code environments. For example, some topics use the expression `New Outlook.Application` to instantiate an `Outlook.Application` object. However, that is never the correct usage in Outlook VBA or form code VBScript, both of which support an intrinsic `Application` object.

---

## 10.2    Outlook object and collection code techniques

Programming with objects requires some special code techniques. We've already covered four object techniques for VBA and VBScript:

- Use a `Set  obj  =  expression` statement to instantiate an object variable
- Use a `Set  obj  = Nothing` statement to dereference and release an object variable
- Use a `With  ...  End` block to work with the properties and methods of a particular object
- Use the syntax `obj.property` to return or set the value of text, numeric, and other simple object properties.

In addition to simple properties, many Outlook objects have properties that are themselves objects. For example, the expression `Application.ActiveExplorer` returns an `Explorer` object representing the current folder window, and `Application.ActiveExplorer.CurrentFolder` returns a `Folder` object representing the folder that `Explorer` displays. Use the `Set` keyword to instantiate an object variable to point to such object properties:

```
Set objExpl = Application.ActiveExplorer
Set objFolder = objExpl.CurrentFolder
MsgBox objFolder.Name
```

In addition to objects like `JournalItem`, `Explorer`, and `Folder`, the Outlook object model also contains many *collection* objects. Each collection itself is an object, but it also is a set of objects, usually of the same class, that can be accessed through the properties and methods of the collection. Examples from earlier chapters include the `Items` collection representing all the items in a folder and the `Attachments` collection of all attachments on an Outlook item. (See Listing 9.1.)

How can you use the object browser to determine if an object is a collection? One telltale sign is that most if not all collections have a `Count`

**Table 10.1**     *Standard Object and Collection Properties*

| Property | Returns |
|----------|---------|
| Application | Parent `Outlook.Application` object |
| Class | Constant for the object class, from the `OlObjectClass` enumeration |
| Parent | Parent object of the object or collection |
| Session | `Namespace` object for the current Outlook session |

property that returns the number of items in the collection. This property is read-only, because the only way to change the count is to remove an item from the collection or add an item to the collection.

**Tip:** Another way to explore collections is to search the Outlook Object Model Reference in help for "collection."

Every object, including every collection, has four standard properties, listed in Table 10.1. All these properties are also read-only.

**Note:** An *enumeration* is a list of constants defined in the object model and visible in the object browser.

Some newcomers to Outlook programming are bewildered to see that every collection is listed in the object browser as read-only. What this means is that you cannot directly access the information held in the collection as you would a property of, say, the `MailItem` object. Instead, you must use specific collection methods to change the contents of the collection or to retrieve any particular item in the collection. Most Outlook collections include these three methods:

- `Add` to add a new object to the collection
- `Item` to refer to a specific object in the collection
- `Remove` to delete an object from the collection

Some collections, such as `AddressLists`, do not support the `Add` or `Remove` method, only the `Item` method.

## 10.2.1   Item method

To use the `Item` method to return a specific object from a collection, you must know either the index for the object or the value of its default property. The index is the position of the object in the collection, starting with 1 and going up to a number equal to the value of the collection's `Count` property. For example, the following VBA code uses the syntax `obj-Folder.Items.Item(1)` to open and display the first item in the Inbox:

```
Set objFolder = _
   Application.Session.GetDefaultFolder(olFolderInbox)
Set objItem = objFolder.Items.Item(1)
objItem.Display
```

**Note:** A folder has both an `Items` collection and a `Folders` collection. The collection of all items in a folder is *folder*.`Items`, not *folder*, so the `Item` method syntax is *folder*.`Items`.`Item(`*index*`)`, even though that might look redundant.

A potential problem with using `Item` with an index is that you cannot know exactly what object you may get. The "first" item in the `Items` collection for the Inbox folder is not necessarily the one you see at the top of the Inbox display in the user interface. More than likely, it will be the oldest item in the Inbox.

**Note:** Chapter 15 covers how to sort a folder's `Items` collection to return items in a specific order.

The other way to use the `Item` method is look up an item using the value of the item's default property. This property varies from object to object. For Outlook messages, contacts, and other data items, the default property is the `Subject` property. For a `Folder` object, it is the `Name` property. Here is another VBA code snippet, this time to display a particular contact by first prompting the user for the contact's name:

```
strName = InputBox("Name of contact to open", _
        "Open First Matching Contact")
If strName <> "" Then
    Set objNS = Application.Session
    Set objFolder = _
      objNS.GetDefaultFolder(olFolderContacts)
    Set objItem = objFolder.Items.Item(strName)
    If Not objItem Is Nothing Then
      objItem.Display
    End If
End If
```

See how it uses `strName` as the argument for the `Item` method instead of an index number.

This version of the `Item` syntax has its limitations, too. It requires an exact match for the text used as an argument for `Item`, and if there is more than one matching object, only the first match is returned. Chapter 14 explains many additional techniques for finding a particular item.

Item is the default member for a collection, which means that, strictly speaking, you do not need to use the Item method in VBA and VBScript code. These two expressions, for example, are equivalent:

```
objFolder.Folders.Item("My First Subfolder")
objFolder.Folders("My First Subfolder")
```

Note that folder Name values are always unique within a given Folders collection, while an Items collection may have multiple items with the same value for the Subject property.

## 10.2.2    Add method

The Add method creates a new object in a collection and returns that new object to an object variable. The syntax looks like this:

```
Set obj = collection.Add(param1, param2, param3)
```

with the number of parameters varying with the collection. Not all collections use parameters with the Add method. As you will see in Section 10.2.4, in some cases, the code must create the object with the Add method first and then set properties on that object separately.

One key Outlook collection is the Explorers collection of open Outlook folder windows. Listing 10.1 illustrates the Add method by adding a new Explorer object to open a new Outlook window with the default

**Listing 10.1**    *Display a folder in a new window*

```
Sub ShowCalendar()
    Dim objApp As Outlook.Application
    Dim colExplorers As Outlook.Explorers
    Dim objFolder As Outlook.Folder
    Dim objExpl As Outlook.Explorer

    Set objApp = Application
    Set colExplorers = objApp.Explorers
    Set objFolder = _
      objApp.Session.GetDefaultFolder(olFolderCalendar)
    Set objExpl = colExplorers.Add(objFolder, _
                            olFolderDisplayNoNavigation)
    objExpl.Activate
    objExpl.WindowState = olMaximized

    Set objExpl = Nothing
    Set objFolder = Nothing
    Set colExplorers = Nothing
    Set objApp = Nothing
End Sub
```

Calendar folder displayed. The `Explorers.Add` method requires one argument—the `Folder` object representing the folder to be displayed. You can also include an optional `Displaymode` argument that specifies whether the view should include the navigation pane.

If you want to see another example of the `Add` method, jump ahead to Section 10.2.4.

## 10.2.3 Remove method

The `Remove` method, as you might expect, is the opposite of `Add`. It deletes an object from the collection, using this syntax:

```
collection.Remove index
```

Normally, however, you don't know the position of any particular item in the collection, so you don't know the *index* value that the `Remove` method requires. To remove a particular object from the collection, it's usually easier to return the object with some other method and then use the `Delete` method on the object to remove it from the collection.

Where `Remove` comes in handy is for bulk deletion operations, such as removing all attachments from a message. In Listing 9.2, you saw how to remove attachments with the `Delete` method. Listing 10.2 is a VBA procedure that replaces the `For ... Next` loop from the earlier listing with a `Do ... Loop` block that on each pass deletes the attachment with an index value of 1. This works because the index is reset after each deletion, so a different attachment has an index value of 1 on each pass, until no attachments remain.

**Listing 10.2**    *Remove all attachments from an item*

```
Sub RemoveAttachments(objItem As Object)
    On Error Resume Next
    Dim objAtt As Outlook.Attachment
    Dim colAtts As Outlook.Attachments
    Dim intCount As Integer
    Set colAtts = objItem.Attachments
    intCount = colAtts.count
    If intCount > 0 Then
        Debug.Print intCount & " attachments in " & _
                    objItem.Subject
        Do While colAtts.count > 0
            colAtts.Remove 1
        Loop
        objItem.Save
    End If
    Set objAtt = Nothing
End Sub
```

---

**Tip:** You may find it useful to prefix your collection object variables with `col`, as we've done with the `Explorers` and `Attachments` collections in Listings 10.1 and 10.2, to make them stand out from objects and other variables.

---

## 10.2.4  Example: Creating a voting button message

Outlook includes a useful feature for creating *voting button messages* that allow users to ask recipients to vote on a finite list of choices such as Accept and Reject. A `MailItem` object (in other words, a message) maintains that list of choices in its `Actions` collection. If you have a favorite set of voting button responses other than one of the defaults on the Options tab, you can use the `Add` method in a little bit of VBA code to create several new `Action` items in the `Actions` collection.

In most cases, the `Add` method requires one or more arguments, as you saw in the code for adding and displaying an `Explorer` object. In a few cases, such as creating an `Action`, you use the `Add` method with no argument and then work with the returned object's properties. The Outlook VBA sample in Listing 10.3 illustrates the use of the `Actions` collection to create a message and add voting buttons. The names for the buttons come from text that the user types into an input box.

---

**Tip:** To see the voting buttons on an unsent message, click on the Options tab, and then click Use Voting Buttons.

---

Notice this syntax for the Add method:

```
Set objAction = objMsg.Actions.Add
```

This is equivalent to these two statements:

```
Set colActions = objMsg.Actions
Set objAction = colActions.Add
```

In other words, you do not always need to declare an explicit object variable to represent a collection in VBA or VBScript. Instead, you can use its parent object with the syntax *parent.collection*.Add.

The statements in the `With ... End With` block assign property values that correspond to the default values that Outlook uses for voting buttons when you create them manually in the user interface. Also notice that the procedure performs some validation to make sure that the user enters at least two voting button names. If the user enters only one, the procedure offers the user a choice with a `MsgBox()` function and calls itself if the user wants to try again.

Listing 10.3    *Add action objects to create a voting button message*

```
Sub CreateVoteMessage()
    Dim objOL As Outlook.Application
    Dim strMsg As String
    Dim strActions As String
    Dim arrActions() As String
    Dim i As Integer
    Dim objMsg As Outlook.MailItem
    Dim objAction As Outlook.Action
    Dim intRes As Integer
    Dim strActionName As String
    strMsg = "Enter voting button titles, " _
            & "separated by commas."
    strActions = Trim(InputBox(strMsg, "Create Voting Button Message"))
    If strActions <> "" Then
        If Right(strActions, 1) = "," Then
            strActions = Left(strActions, Len(strActions) - 1)
        End If
        arrActions = Split(strActions, ",")
        If UBound(arrActions) > 0 Then
            Set objOL = Application
            Set objMsg = objOL.CreateItem(olMailItem)
            For i = 0 To UBound(arrActions)
                strActionName = Trim(arrActions(i))
                If strActionName <> "" Then
                    Set objAction = objMsg.Actions.Add
                    With objAction
                        .CopyLike = olRespond
                        .Enabled = True
                        .Name = Trim(arrActions(i))
                        .Prefix = ""
                        .ReplyStyle = olOmitOriginalText
                        .ResponseStyle = olPrompt
                        .ShowOn = olMenuAndToolbar
                    End With
                End If
            Next
            objMsg.Display
        Else
            strMsg = "You entered only one voting button " & _
                    "name. A voting button message " & _
                    "needs at least two choices. Do you " & _
                    "want to try again?"
            intRes = MsgBox(strMsg, vbYesNo, "Create Voting Button Message")
            If intRes = vbYes Then
                Call CreateVoteMessage
            End If
        End If
    End If
    Set objAction = Nothing
    Set objMsg = Nothing
    Set objOL = Nothing
End Sub
```

**Tip:** Chapter 20 provides more information about working with voting buttons and the `Actions` collection.

### 10.2.5   Releasing objects

If you pay attention to scope when writing your procedures and declare variables with the narrowest scope possible, you shouldn't have any problem with procedure-level object and collection variables staying in memory and using system resources after you need them. However, it still is a good practice to release them explicitly as part of the end of each procedure, using a `Set object = Nothing` statement. `Nothing` is a special keyword that disassociates the variable from the object to which it refers.

**Tip:** Use the statement `If Not object Is Nothing Then` to test whether a previous `Set object` assignment statement was successful before you try to use any of the properties or methods of `object`. Otherwise, as described in the previous chapter, you may get an "object required" runtime error.

Always use a `Set object = Nothing` statement to release any module or global object variables when your code no longer needs them. The one exception is objects declared `WithEvents` in `ThisOutlookSession` or another class module. Objects declared `WithEvents` are those that support event handlers. If you release them, the event handlers will no longer run. Outlook VBA will automatically release those variables when Outlook shuts down.

**Caution:** If you advance from VBA to writing add-ins for Outlook, your add-ins will need to release all Outlook object variables, including those involved in event handlers. Otherwise, Outlook may not shut down completely.

## 10.3   Understanding Outlook security

Outlook's VBA and form VBScript environments represent a balance between security and useful functionality. Early versions of Outlook allowed external programs to freely automate Outlook, with disastrous results. Viruses propagated inside email messages were able to harvest more email addresses from Outlook data on infected machines and then send out more messages to infect more Outlook users. Subsequent versions eliminated that vulnerability, but at what many users found to be a high cost: interruption by security prompts when external programs—and even some Outlook VBA or VBScript code—tried to automate Outlook.

Outlook 2007 is secure enough to block virus propagation by email messages, but (when running on Windows XP or Vista) flexible enough not to get in the way of legitimate programs that do need to automate Outlook. (This flexibility does not apply to Windows Server 2003 installations.)

Security features in Outlook 2007 that affect programmability include:

- An "object model guard" that displays user confirmation dialogs for code operations that could be used to harvest addresses or send messages, unless the machine is adequately protected against viruses

- Disabling of scripts and some other functionality on unpublished Outlook forms and items using custom forms in shared mailbox folders

- Blocking of potentially dangerous attachments that could be used to propagate viruses

- HTML message rendering that blocks scripts and other elements with potential security implications

- A new restriction on folder home pages that blocks their implementation for non-default information stores

The sections that follow examine each of these security features in detail and their implications for your Outlook programming projects.

## 10.3.1   Automation security

Outlook's object model guard feature can block access to properties and methods that malicious programming code could use to harvest addresses or send messages. Blocked properties include the contents of the bodies of messages and other items. Restricted methods include SaveAs, which saves a copy of an Outlook item as a file (which could be read by an external program).

By default, all Outlook VBA code and custom form VBScript code "trusts" the intrinsic Application object with regard to the object model guard. As a result, VBA and VBScript code that derives all its Outlook objects from the intrinsic Application object will not trigger security prompts. What that means is that, if your Outlook VBA code uses Application.CreateItem(olMailItem) to create a new message, when the code executes the Send method on that message, Outlook won't display a security prompt to the user. The same is true for VBScript code running behind an Outlook form.

---

**Note:** This is the same default VBA and custom form VBScript automation security model that Outlook 2003 uses. If code on your machine acts differently and you're working on a networked computer, you can ask your network administrator if settings are being applied to your machine to override Outlook's default behavior.

---

What's radically new in Outlook 2007 is that, on stand-alone machines with adequate anti-virus protection, the object model guard also allows any <u>external</u> program, including other Microsoft Office programs like Word or Excel, to automate Outlook. In that scenario, the key question becomes, what is "adequate" anti-virus protection? In order for Outlook to turn off the object model guard prompts, these requirements must be met:

- The operating system must be Windows XP or Vista. (Windows Server 2003 doesn't count, because it does not have a built-in Windows Security Center that monitors the anti-virus protection state.)

- The anti-virus application's state—whether it is enabled and whether its virus signatures are up to date—must be detectable by the Security Center. You can check your anti-virus protection state in the Security Center applet in Control Panel.

Many anti-virus tools for Windows XP and Vista can meet those requirements, but you should make sure they are set to download updates automatically. Otherwise, the anti-virus tool might not be up to date, and external applications automating Outlook could start triggering security prompts.

---

**Note:** Even if your system has adequate anti-virus protection, external automation of Outlook may be blocked by that anti-virus application. Some anti-virus programs have "script blocker" features that suppress any attempt to start an Outlook automation session with statements like `New Outlook.Application`, `CreateObject("Outlook.Application")`, or `GetObject(,"Outlook.Application")`. Consult your anti-virus program's documentation for details.

---

If your computer meets the Windows requirements for valid anti-virus protection, you should see that confirmed in the Tools | Trust Center | Programmatic Access dialog in Outlook and see the options that Figure 10.5 shows for configuring programmatic access.

Notice that the default setting for programmatic access is "Warn me about suspicious activity when my anti-virus software is inactive or out of date," which means that you won't see prompts if the anti-virus software is running and up to date.

**Figure 10.5**
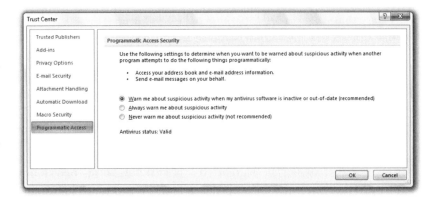
*Machines with up-to-date anti-virus programs by default will not display security prompts for programmatic access to Outlook, even by external programs.*

---

**Note:** For Outlook running on Windows Vista, the user must run Outlook as an administrator in order to gain access to change the option on the Programmatic Access dialog from the default setting.

---

The situation may be different on machines running on a network, because the network administrator can control the programmatic access for external programs with centralized settings. For more information, see the article "Customize programmatic settings in Outlook 2007" in the 2007 Office Resource Kit at http://www.microsoft.com.

How does Outlook automation security affect your Outlook code? In other words, when should you build into your code the ability to handle cases where the security prompts occur? To review, in the default configuration:

- Outlook VBA code deriving Outlook objects from the intrinsic `Application` object will not raise security prompts.

- Custom form VBScript code deriving Outlook objects from the intrinsic `Application` object will not raise security prompts.

- If an anti-virus application is installed, active, and up to date, external programs that automate Outlook will not raise security prompts.

Any Outlook code that you write for your own personal use—in Outlook VBA, a custom form, an external script, or another application like Word—should not trigger security prompts if your anti-virus status is valid.

Therefore, you probably will be concerned about security prompts only when you are writing code that someone else will run. This could include VBA code in a Microsoft Access database that someone else uses or code on a custom Outlook form published in a Microsoft Exchange environment.

Figure 10.6
*Attempts to access
address-related
properties and
methods may raise
this prompt.*

Whenever someone else may be running your code, you should handle the case where the user gets a security prompt and does not confirm the operation. Figures 10.6 and 10.7 show the two security prompts users may see: one for programmatic access to address information, the other for code that tries to send an item.

As an example, Listing 10.4 is a VBA macro written for Word (or Excel or Access) VBA that creates and sends an Outlook message. Its one special feature is that it attempts to insert text into the body of the message while retaining the user's default signature. To test this code in Word VBA, use the Tools | References command to add a reference to the Microsoft Outlook 12.0 Library.

Creating a message that includes the user's default signature requires you to display the message and then prefix your own text to the text already present in the message after it has been displayed. This statement may raise a security prompt:

```
strBody = .Body
```

The `Body` property is considered a blocked property because message bodies often contain email addresses in the message signatures. Note that these two statements do not trigger security prompts:

```
.To = "sue@turtleflock.com"

.Body = "This message created on " & Now()
```

Assigning a value to an address-related property never triggers a security prompt. Only reading a value from such a property can trigger a prompt.

Figure 10.7
*Users seeing this
prompt for sending
a message must
wait five seconds
before they can
click Approve.*

**Listing 10.4**   *Create and send an Outlook message from VBA in another Office application*

```
Sub SendOutlookMessage()
    Dim objOL As Outlook.Application
    Dim objNS As Outlook.NameSpace
    Dim objMail As Outlook.MailItem
    Dim blnWeOpenedOutlook As Boolean
    Dim strBody As String
    Dim strMsg As String
    Dim intRes As Integer

    On Error Resume Next
    ' start an Outlook session
    Set objOL = GetObject(, "Outlook.Application")
    If objOL Is Nothing Then
        Set objOL = CreateObject("Outlook.Application")
        Set objNS = objOL.GetNamespace("MAPI")
        objNS.Logon
        blnWeOpenedOutlook = True
    End If

    ' create and send the message
    Set objMail = objOL.CreateItem(olMailItem)
    With objMail
        .BodyFormat = olFormatPlain
        ' display message in order to use signature
        .Display
        .GetInspector.WindowState = olMinimized
        .Subject = "Test at " & Time()
        .To = "someone@nowhere.com"
        ' handle possible error from reading Body
        strBody = .Body
        If Err.Number = 0 Then
            .Body = "This message created on " & Now() & _
                vbCrLf & strBody
        Else
            .Body = "This message created on " & Now()
            Err.Clear
        End If
        ' handle possible error from calling Send
        .Send
        If Err.Number <> 0 Then
            strMsg = "Outlook cannot send the message " & _
                "unless you click Allow on the " & _
                "security prompt. Do you want to " & _
                "try again?"
            intRes = MsgBox(strMsg, vbQuestion + vbYesNo, _
                "SendOutlookMessage")
            If intRes = vbYes Then
                Err.Clear
                .Send
            End If
        End If
    End With
```

**Listing 10.4**   *Create and send an Outlook message from VBA in another Office application (continued)*

```
        ' if no send error, perform a Send/Receive
        If Err.Number = 0 Then
            objNS.SendAndReceive False
        End If
        ' leave Outlook the way we found it
        If blnWeOpenedOutlook Then
            objOL.Quit
        End If

        Set objMail = Nothing
        Set objNS = Nothing
        Set objOL = Nothing
    End Sub
```

If the user sees the security prompt in Figure 10.6 and clicks Deny or closes the dialog, an error occurs. Therefore, the code uses the expression `Err.Number = 0` to check for an error and assigns a different value to `Body` depending on whether there was an error, in other words, whether the original `Body` could be read. It then uses `Err.Clear` to reset the error handler for the next possible error.

A different technique is used for the error that can occur if the user sees the prompt in Figure 10.7 and chooses Deny or closes the dialog. In that case, the code uses a `MsgBox` statement to offer another opportunity to attempt to send.

If sending the message occurs without error, the code then uses the `SendAndReceive` method—which is new to Outlook 2007—to perform the same operation as clicking the Send/Receive All command.

**Note:** Besides the code for creating and sending a message, Listing 10.4 demonstrates another useful general Outlook technique: starting an Outlook session with the `GetObject()` or `CreateObject()` method and then returning Outlook to its original state.

## 10.3.2   Form security

As with the restrictions on Outlook automation, several security controls in Outlook prevent custom forms from being used as a vehicle for malicious code. Security features that affect custom form code include:

- Code runs only on published forms.
- Code does not run, by default, for items stored in a shared Exchange mailbox folder.

- Unpublished forms that include custom properties will not display their custom layouts if launched from a file or, in the case of a message, if viewed by a recipient.

- On unpublished forms, ActiveX controls other than those included with Outlook are blocked by default.

Chapter 4 explained the importance of published forms. Unpublished forms include both forms stored as .oft file templates and items where the form definition has become embedded in the item, a (fortunately) rare condition called a *one-off form*. In general, if you follow the recommendations on creating and publishing forms in this book, your VBScript form code should always run on items in your own Exchange mailbox, Exchange public folders, and Personal Folders .pst files.

Code will not run by default, though, on items stored in another Exchange user's mailbox. The default behavior can be changed either by the application of a group policy setting by the network administrator or, in the absence of a policy setting, with the Tools | Trust Center | E-mail Security dialog shown in Figure 10.8. Note that there is also an option related to form code script in Public Folders; form code in Public Folders is allowed by default.

The other two form security issues affect only unpublished forms. (By now, you should be getting the message loud and clear that unpublished forms are something to avoid.)

The presence of custom properties on an unpublished form raises security issues. If those properties are not already defined in the default folder for that type of item, Outlook will suppress the display of the custom form layout when the user opens either an .oft file directly or an existing item

**Figure 10.8**
*Custom form code for items in other Exchange users' mailboxes does not run by default.*

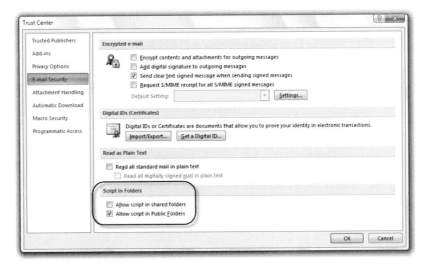

with an embedded one-off form. In the case of an .oft file, the workaround for the user is to launch the form with the Tools | Forms | Choose Form command.

The practical impact of this issue is that it is all but impossible to use an Outlook custom message form to gather responses—such as those from a survey—over the Internet. The only scenario in which a survey form can work is inside an Exchange organization, where the custom form can be published either to the Organizational Forms library or to each user's Personal Forms library.

---

**Note:** The tool in Office 2007 best suited to creating survey forms is Microsoft InfoPath 2007. Microsoft Access 2007 also has a useful feature for gathering external data through email messages processed through an Outlook add-in that Office installs automatically.

---

The final unpublished form issue is that such forms display an error message if they contain any ActiveX control other than those distributed with Outlook. Administrators can change this behavior by deploying a policy setting.

## 10.3.3   Attachment security

By default, users with Outlook 2007 cannot open or save certain file attachments that Microsoft considers dangerous, such as .exe files, because they could potentially be used to transmit viruses. This block extends to programmatic access to the `Attachments` collection; a blocked attachment will not be accessible in code.

---

**Note:** If you need to write code to access blocked attachments, a good option is to use the Redemption library from http://www.dimastr.com/redemption/.

---

Users will see a warning if they try to send a message that contains a blocked file attachment. However, many users misinterpret the warning message. Outlook does not actually strip the outgoing attachment. It just warns that recipients may not be able to access it.

On the other hand, if the user (or your code) tries to forward a message containing a blocked file, Outlook strips the attachment from the forwarded copy.

Stand-alone users can add a registry value to reduce the security on certain file types so that they can be opened from email messages:

Key: `HKEY_CURRENT_USER\Software\Microsoft\Office\12.0\`
`Outlook\Security`
Value name: `Level1Remove`
Value type: `REG_SZ` (string)
Value data: semicolon-delimited list of extensions to unblock (e.g., `url;lnk`)

After changing the value of Level1Remove, the user should restart Outlook.

Network administrators have additional options for managing attachment block settings with a Group Policy Object; see the article "Customize attachment settings in Outlook 2007" in the 2007 Office Resource Kit at http://www.microsoft.com.

### 10.3.4   HTML message security

Outlook has no editor for modifying the source code for HTML-format messages directly. However, you can create HTML-format messages programmatically by setting the value of the `MailItem.HTMLBody` property to the fully tagged HTML content that you want to appear in the message; for example:

```
strHTML = "<html><body><p>This text is " & _
          "<strong>bold</strong>.</p></body></html>"
Set objMsg = Application.CreateItem(olMailItem)
objMsg.HTMLBody = strHTML
objMsg.Display
```

However, certain HTML elements common on Web pages are not supported in Outlook messages for security reasons—chief among them `<script>`, `<iframe>`, and `<form>`. A complete guide to what is and is not supported is available on Microsoft's Web site, along with an HTML code validation tool. For more information, see the Microsoft Developer Network article "Word 2007 HTML and CSS Rendering Capabilities in Outlook 2007" at http://msdn.microsoft.com.

### 10.3.5   Folder home page security

As explained in Chapter 1, a folder home page is a Web page that Outlook displays instead of the contents of the folder. Outlook 2007 makes a significant security change to allow folder home pages to display <u>only</u> for folders in the user's default information store and, for Exchange users, in Public Folders. Users cannot assign folder home pages for other folders, and attempts to do so programmatically with the `Folder.WebViewURL` and `.WebViewOn` properties will fail. Also, if an earlier version of Outlook sets a home page for a folder in a non-default store, Outlook 2007 will ignore that setting and will not display the folder.

If a folder home page in some other location is essential to an organization, an administrator can change this behavior by deploying a policy setting.

## 10.4  Summary

Outlook has a rich object model that you can explore on your own through the object browser and by writing your own code in VBA to see the results of different properties and methods. Collections are an important part of the Outlook object model, storing information about folders, items, attachments, recipients, and other key Outlook data. Access to collection data is somewhat indirect, through Item and other collection methods.

Compared with earlier versions, Outlook 2007 strikes the best balance yet between security and programmability. Security changes in Outlook 2007 mean fewer security prompts, but reduced access to folder home pages and certain HTML message features.

# *Responding to Outlook Events in VBA*

One of the features that makes Outlook 2007 a rich programming environment is the many events in the object model that respond to the user's interaction with Outlook. In addition, events are available to process what happens behind the scenes when, for example, a reminder fires or a new item is saved in a folder. Here are just a few of the events for which you can write code:

- Starting Outlook
- Sending a message
- Receiving new mail
- Creating or modifying items or folders
- Switching to a different folder or to a different view
- Right-clicking on an item or folder

Although not every possible event is included in the Outlook object model, the range of available events is enough to keep any programmer busy for a long, long time. Highlights of this chapter include discussions of the following:

- What event code to place in the `ThisOutlookSession` module in VBA
- How to set up folders to watch for new and changed items
- How to automatically add reminders for birthdays and anniversaries
- Five events that can help you process new messages
- How to run code according to a schedule
- How to set a better reminder for new all-day events
- How to avoid sending messages with blank subjects and missing attachments

If you jumped ahead to this chapter, you might want to make sure you understand the material in Part III, "Writing VBA and VBScript Code," because this chapter requires a good understanding of basic coding techniques.

# 11.1   Application object events

The `Application` object stands at the top of the Outlook object model hierarchy and offers a number of events useful to VBA programmers, plus one (`OptionPagesAdd`) of interest mainly to developers building Outlook add-ins (a subject that is beyond the scope of this book).

In addition to the events in Table 11.1, the `Application` object also supports six events that fire when the user right-clicks on different parts of the Outlook user interface. We'll cover these context menu events in Chapter 23, "Menus, Toolbars, and the Navigation Pane." It also supports two events—`AdvancedSearchComplete` and `AdvancedSearchStopped`—that are used with the `AdvancedSearch` method, which we'll examine in Chapter 15. There also is an `Application.Quit` event, but it has little utility in VBA, since all Outlook objects are already released (and thus unavailable) when `Quit` fires.

---

**Tip:** In the object browser (F2 in VBA), you can see the events for the various Outlook objects more easily if you right-click in the Members pane on the right and choose Group Members.

---

You can build VBA code for any `Application` event in the `ThisOutlookSession` module found in the Project Explorer under Project1 and then Microsoft Outlook Objects, as shown in Figure 11.1. Double-click `ThisOutlookSession` to open it in a module window. This is a special kind of module, called a *class module*, that can respond to events.

Since Outlook created the `ThisOutlookSession` module automatically, it does not include an `Option Explicit` statement to force you to declare variables. You should add that statement to the module's declaration section, as shown in Figure 11.1.

To add an `Application` event handler, select Application from the list at the top left of the module window. Then, from the list on the right, select the event for which you want to write code. VBA places a stub for the event handler procedure in the module window with the correct syntax. Figure 11.1 shows the procedure stubs for the `ItemSend` and `Startup` events.

**Table 11.1** *Key Application Object Events (\* = new in Outlook 2007)*

| Application Event | Description | Argument |
|---|---|---|
| StartUp | Occurs when Outlook starts, after all add-ins have loaded. | None |
| MAPILogonComplete | Occurs after the Startup event fires, when Outlook has logged on to all services and accounts. | None |
| *ItemLoad | Occurs when Outlook begins to load an item into memory, either to display it in an Inspector window or to display it in the reading pane. | The item being loaded, but exposing only the item's Class and MessageClass properties |
| ItemSend | Occurs when you send an item. Can be canceled. | The item being sent |
| NewMail | Occurs when new mail arrives, even if a Rules Wizard rule moves the item out of the Inbox. Fires at intervals, not necessarily for every new message. | None |
| NewMailEx | Occurs when new mail arrives, even if a Rules Wizard rule moves the item out of the Inbox. Fires at intervals, not necessarily for every new message. | An array of EntryID values for the incoming messages |
| Reminder | Occurs when a reminder is triggered by an appointment or task item or a flagged message or contact. If the option to display reminders is turned on, the Reminder event occurs just before the reminder is displayed. | The item that triggered the reminder |

**Figure 11.1**
*Get started with Application-level events in the ThisOutlookSession module.*

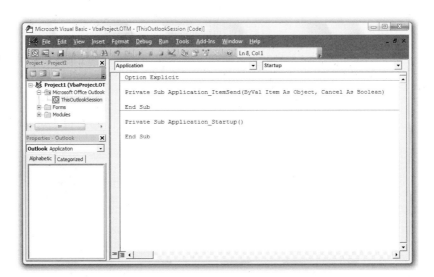

### 11.1.1  Using the Startup, MAPILogonComplete, and Quit events

A common use for the Startup event is to instantiate global variables, including object variables and classes that you want to handle other events. For example, if you want to keep track of the time that Outlook started and use that date/time value in other code procedures, use the Insert | Module command to add a regular code module (not a class module) and add this variable declaration:

```
Public g_dteStartup as Date
```

Then put this code in the ThisOutlookSession module (not the regular code module you just created) to initialize that variable:

```
Private Sub Application_Startup()
    g_dteStartup = Now
End Sub
```

When Outlook starts, it will set the value of the g_dteStartup variable, which will be available to any other VBA procedure since it is a public variable. This ShowOutlookWorkTime procedure, which you can place in the regular code module you created, uses the value of that variable:

```
Sub ShowOutlookWorkTime()
    Dim intMinutes As Integer
    intMinutes = DateDiff("n", g_dteStartup, Now)
    MsgBox "Outlook has been running for " & _
            Round(intMinutes / 60, 2) & " hours.", _
            vbInformation, "Show Outlook Work Time"
End Sub
```

Perhaps the most important use of the Startup procedure is to instantiate other Outlook objects for which you plan to write event handlers, as we will see later in the chapter. You can also do that in the MAPILogonComplete event handler.

The MAPILogonComplete event handler is the ideal place to place code that processes Outlook items or folders at the beginning of an Outlook session. For example, let's say that you are an assistant with two bosses' schedules to manage, and you like to keep each schedule open in its own window in Outlook. You can use the code in Listing 11.1 to open each person's Calendar folder in its own minimized window. Put both procedures in the ThisOutlookSession module.

Did you notice that the LaunchSharedFolder() procedure is declared as a Public subroutine? That means you could also call it from a subroutine in another code module besides ThisOutlookSession. The syntax to call the procedure from a regular code module would like this:

```
Call ThisOutlookSession.LaunchSharedFolder("Donna Liss")
```

**Listing 11.1**   *Load other user's Calendar folders when Outlook starts*

```
Private Sub Application_MAPILogonComplete()
    Dim objExpl As Outlook.Explorer
    Set objExpl = Application.ActiveExplorer
    Call LaunchSharedFolder("Henry Mudd")
    Call LaunchSharedFolder("Donna Liss")
    objExpl.Activate
    Set objExpl = Nothing
End Sub

Public Sub LaunchSharedFolder(strUser As String)
    Dim objNS As Outlook.NameSpace
    Dim objRecip As Outlook.Recipient
    Dim objFolder As Outlook.Folder
    Dim objExpl As Outlook.Explorer
    On Error Resume Next
    Set objNS = Application.Session
    Set objRecip = objNS.CreateRecipient(strUser)
    If objRecip.Resolve Then
        Set objFolder = _
          objNS.GetSharedDefaultFolder _
           (objRecip, olFolderCalendar)
        objFolder.Display
        Set objExpl = objFolder.GetExplorer
        objExpl.WindowState = olMinimized
    End If
    Set objNS = Nothing
    Set objRecip = Nothing
    Set objFolder = Nothing
    Set objExpl = Nothing
End Sub
```

The Quit event is not very useful in VBA, because all Outlook windows have already closed by the time the Quit event fires as you exit Outlook, and you no longer have access to Outlook items and folders. Also, by the time Quit fires, Outlook has already released any global variables. This means that you cannot use the Quit event to ask the user if she really wants to quit Outlook (and no other means is available in Outlook VBA to add such functionality).

## 11.1.2   Using NewMail and NewMailEx to handle incoming mail

Outlook offers several built-in options for notifying the user that new mail has arrived, but perhaps you want something more customized. Or perhaps you frequently need to step out of your office and want to know whether you received any new messages while you were gone. The NewMail event can help provide a solution, because it fires whenever Outlook receives one

**Figure 11.2**
*This VBA form
displays whenever
the NewMail event
fires.*

or more new messages. It only fires once for each batch of new messages, though, so it's not suitable for processing individual incoming messages. (We'll look at the NewMailEx event and some other approaches for that.)

Take a look at Figure 11.2, which shows a small VBA user form in action. This form has with two label controls and a command button. Name the command button cmdHide and set its Cancel property to True. Name the label, which will show the date and time information, lblReceived. Name the form Ch11NewMail, and set the form's Caption property to "You Have New Mail." Set the form's ShowModal property to False. Add this code to the command button's event handler:

```
Private Sub cmdHide_Click()
    Me.Hide
End Sub
```

To make the form display the most recent mail delivery time, add the following code to the Application_NewMail event handler in the ThisOutlookSession module:

```
Private Sub Application_NewMail()
    Ch11NewMail.Show
    With Ch11NewMail
        .lblReceived.Caption = Now
        .Repaint
    End With
End Sub
```

Because you set the ShowModal property to False, the form can stay on the screen while you do other work. Click the Hide button to make the form disappear until the next batch of new mail arrives.

The NewMailEx event differs from NewMail in that it supplies an argument that consists of a comma-delimited string of EntryID values for one or more new messages that have arrived since the last time that NewMailEx fired. (EntryID is a property common to all Outlook items; it consists of an ID string that is unique, at least within the information store that holds that item.) Depending on the type of email accounts in the current mail profile and how fast messages arrive, NewMailEx may fire once for each message, once for a number of messages, or not at all. As a general rule of thumb, if a mail account pops up notification messages from the system tray, it will also fire NewMailEx when new items arrive.

**Listing 11.2** *Use NewMailEx to work with the EntryID values of incoming items*

```
Private Sub Application_NewMailEx _
  (ByVal EntryIDCollection As String)
    Dim objItem As Object
    Dim objNS As NameSpace
    Dim arr() As String
    Dim i As Integer
    Dim strList As String
    On Error Resume Next
    Set objNS = Application.Session
    arr = Split(EntryIDCollection, ",")
    For i = 0 To UBound(arr)
        Set objItem = objNS.GetItemFromID(arr(i))
        strList = objItem.Subject & vbCrLf & strList
    Next
    MsgBox strList, , "NewMailEx event"
    Set objNS = Nothing
    Set objItem = Nothing
End Sub
```

NewMailEx fires before any Outlook rules operate on the incoming message(s). Even if a rule moves the item, the EntryID property value should remain the same, as long as no rule moves the item to a different information store. The code in Listing 11.2 assumes that the incoming items remain in the user's default information store (i.e., the one where the default Inbox is located). It processes all the items and pops up a message box with a list of their subjects. Add this code to the ThisOutlookSession module.

The Namespace.GetItemFromID method in Listing 11.2 returns an item from the default information store, using an EntryID value passed as an argument. As we'll see in Chapter 14, it can also return items from other stores, if you know the other store's StoreID property value.

Later in this chapter, when we cover new mail processing, you'll see a more complex example of using NewMailEx to process mail not just in the default information store but also for accounts that don't deliver to the default Inbox, such as IMAP accounts.

### 11.1.3    Using the ItemSend event

When the user clicks Send to transmit a message, Outlook fires the Application.ItemSend event. At that point, Outlook has not yet sent the item, so it is not too late to change it. Typical applications include checking the item to make sure that it meets certain conditions or forcing the item to be sent with a different mail account. You can cancel the sending of the message by setting the Cancel parameter of the event handler to True. For example, Listing 11.3 aborts the send process and prompts the user if the subject is blank or if the message contains the word "attached" but no attachments. Put all the code in the ThisOutlookSession module.

Notice that the CancelBlankOrNoAttachments procedure—the subroutine that actually checks the text in the Subject and Body properties of the message—is a separate procedure returning a Boolean value. Breaking it out as a separate procedure makes make it easy to add more such "rules" to the ItemSend event handler to deal with other scenarios where you might not want to send a message or might want to alter it before it goes out.

For example, in Listing 11.4, we've enhanced the Application_Item-Send procedure from Listing 11.3 to call another procedure that checks the sending account. This scenario assumes that the user has an Exchange account plus a POP3 or IMAP4 account and wants all messages sent to

**Listing 11.3**   *Check the contents of outgoing messages with ItemSend*

```
Private Sub Application_ItemSend _
  (ByVal Item As Object, Cancel As Boolean)
    Dim objMail As Outlook.MailItem
    If Item.Class = olMail Then
        Set objMail = Item
        If CancelBlankOrNoAttachments(objMail) = True Then
            Cancel = True
        End If
    End If
    Set objMail = Nothing
End Sub

Function CancelBlankOrNoAttachments _
  (myMail As Outlook.MailItem) As Boolean
    Dim strMsg As String
    Dim intPos As Integer
    Dim intRes As Integer
    If Trim(myMail.Subject) = "" Then
        CancelBlankOrNoAttachments = True
        strMsg = "Please enter a subject before sending."
        MsgBox strMsg, vbExclamation, "ItemSend Event"
    ElseIf myMail.Attachments.Count = 0 Then
        intPos = InStr(1, myMail.Body, _
                       "attached", vbTextCompare)
        If intPos > 0 Then
            strMsg = "Did you mean to add an attachment?"
            intRes = MsgBox(strMsg, _
              vbYesNo + vbDefaultButton1 + vbQuestion, _
              "ItemSend Event")
            If intRes = vbYes Then
                CancelBlankOrNoAttachments = True
            End If
        End If
    End If
End Function
```

people marked with the category "Family" to be transmitted with the Internet mail account, not the Exchange account. Again, place all the code in the `ThisOutlookSession` module. Replace the earlier `ItemSend` event handler with this new version.

Listing 11.4 makes use of several new features in the Outlook 2007 object model:

- A `SendUsingAccount` property to read or set the account used to send a message or other item
- A `Namespace.Accounts` collection of all the user's mail accounts
- An `Account` object whose `AccountType` property tells you what type of mail account it is (Exchange, IMAP, and so on)
- An `AddressEntryUserType` property for the `AddressEntry` object that tells you what type of address it is, even distinguishing among users, public folders, and distribution lists when working with Exchange addresses
- An `AddressEntry.GetContact` method to return the Outlook `ContactItem` associated with a given recipient (`AddressEntry` also has new `GetExchangeUser` and `GetExchangeDistributionList` methods)

**Listing 11.4**   *Add an account test to outgoing messages*

```
Private Sub Application_ItemSend(ByVal Item As Object, _
                                 Cancel As Boolean)
    Dim objMail As Outlook.MailItem
    If Item.Class = olMail Then
        Set objMail = Item
        ' CancelBlankOrNoAttachments from Listing 11.3
        If CancelBlankOrNoAttachments(objMail) = True Then
            Cancel = True
        ElseIf CheckSendAccount(objMail) = True Then
            Cancel = True
        End If
    End If
    Set objMail = Nothing
End Sub

Function CheckSendAccount(myMail As Outlook.MailItem) As Boolean
    Dim objRecip As Outlook.Recipient
    Dim objAE As Outlook.AddressEntry
    Dim objContact As Outlook.ContactItem
    Dim strCats As String
    Dim arrCats() As String
    Dim blnToFamily As Boolean
    Dim i As Integer
    Dim strMsg As String
    Dim objNS As Outlook.NameSpace
```

**Listing 11.4**    *Add an account test to outgoing messages (continued)*

```vba
Dim objExAcct As Outlook.Account
Dim objInetAcct As Outlook.Account
Dim intRes As Integer
On Error Resume Next
For Each objRecip In myMail.Recipients
    If blnToFamily = False Then
        Set objAE = objRecip.AddressEntry
        If objAE.AddressEntryUserType = _
          olOutlookContactAddressEntry Or _
          objAE.AddressEntryUserType = _
          olSmtpAddressEntry Then
            Set objContact = objRecip.AddressEntry.GetContact
            If Not objContact Is Nothing Then
                strCats = objContact.Categories
                If IsInCategories("Family", strCats) Then
                    blnToFamily = True
                End If
            End If
        End If
    End If
Next
If blnToFamily = True Then
    Set objExAcct = GetExchangeAccount()
    If Not objExAcct Is Nothing Then
        If myMail.SendUsingAccount = objExAcct Then
            strMsg = "You have at least one Family " & _
                     "category recipient in this " & _
                     "message. Do you still want " & _
                     "to use your Exchange account " & _
                     "to send the message?" & vbCrLf & _
                     vbCrLf & "Click Yes to send " & _
                     "the message, No to send " & _
                     "with your other account, " & _
                     "or Cancel to see the message " & _
                     "again."
            intRes = MsgBox(strMsg, _
                    vbQuestion + vbYesNoCancel, _
                    "CheckSendAccount")
            Select Case intRes
                Case vbNo
                    Set objInetAcct = _
                      GetFirstNonExchangeAccount()
                    If Not objInetAcct Is Nothing Then
                        myMail.SendUsingAccount = _
                            objInetAcct
                        CheckSendAccount = False
                    Else
                        CheckSendAccount = True
                    End If
                Case vbCancel
                    CheckSendAccount = True
```

**Listing 11.4**   *Add an account test to outgoing messages (continued)*

```
                         Case Else
                             CheckSendAccount = False
                     End Select
                 End If
             End If
         End If
         Set objNS = Nothing
         Set objExAcct = Nothing
         Set objInetAcct = Nothing
End Function

Function IsInCategories(strCatName, strCatList)
    Dim arrCats() As String
    Dim i As Integer
    If strCatList <> "" Then
        arrCats = Split(strCatList, ",")
        For i = 0 To UBound(arrCats)
            If UCase(arrCats(i)) = UCase(strCatName) Then
                IsInCategories = True
                Exit For
            End If
        Next
    End If
End Function

Function GetExchangeAccount() As Outlook.Account
    Dim objAccount As Outlook.Account
    Dim objNS As Outlook.NameSpace
    Set objNS = Application.Session
    For Each objAccount In objNS.Accounts
        If objAccount.AccountType = olExchange Then
            Set GetExchangeAccount = objAccount
            Exit For
        End If
    Next
    Set objNS = Nothing
End Function

Function GetFirstNonExchangeAccount() As Outlook.Account
    Dim objNS As Outlook.NameSpace
    Dim objAccount As Outlook.Account
    Set objNS = Application.Session
    For Each objAccount In objNS.Accounts
        If objAccount.AccountType <> olExchange Then
            Set GetFirstNonExchangeAccount = objAccount
            Exit For
        End If
    Next
    Set objNS = Nothing
End Function
```

Let's walk through some of the key concepts in Listing 11.4, starting with the `Application_ItemSend` event handler itself. First, notice the difference between Listing 11.3, which had this code to check the outgoing item:

```
If CancelBlankOrNoAttachments(objMail) = True Then
    Cancel = True
End If
```

and Listing 11.4 which uses this code:

```
If CancelBlankOrNoAttachments(objMail) = True Then
    Cancel = True
ElseIf CheckSendAccount(objMail) = True Then
    Cancel = True
End If
```

If you wanted to perform a third check on the outgoing item, and cancel the send process if the item doesn't meet certain conditions, you would create another function that returns `True` if the send should be canceled and `False` if the send should proceed and then call that function using another `ElseIf` statement:

```
If CancelBlankOrNoAttachments(objMail) = True Then
    Cancel = True
ElseIf CheckSendAccount(objMail) = True Then
    Cancel = True
ElseIf AnotherFunction(objMail) = True Then
    Cancel = True
End If
```

**Tip:** Jump ahead to Listing 18.3 if you want to see a third "rule" added to the `ItemSend` event handler—one that asks the user to confirm Cc and Bcc recipients.

When you program each set of conditions as a separate function, it becomes easy to call those functions in sequence inside the `ItemSend` event handler.

The `CheckSendAccount()` function loops through the outgoing message's `Recipients` collection with a `For Each ... Next` loop, checking each `Recipient.AddressEntry` object to locate items where the `AddressEntryUserType` indicates that the recipient is either an Outlook contact or a raw SMTP address. For such addresses, it uses the new `AddressEntry.GetContact` method to try to return a `ContactItem` related to the recipient. If that operation succeeds, it uses the `IsInCategories()` helper function to see if "Family" is one of the categories for the related contact.

Notice that the `IsInCategories()` function cannot simply use `Instr()` to check whether "Family" appears in the text of the `Contact-`

`Item.Categories` property, because the contact could also have a category named "Family & Friends" or even "Not Family." If you want to check the `Categories` property for an exact match of a category name, you must process the `Categories` string as an array of values, which is what `IsIn-Categories()` does.

Two other helper functions, `GetExchangeAccount()` and `GetFirst-NonExchangeAccount()`, return the user's Exchange account and the first non-Exchange account found in the `Namespace.Accounts` collection. (Remember that, for the scenario handled by Listing 11.4, we assumed that the user had only two mail accounts: one Exchange and one non-Exchange.)

---

### Why doesn't ItemSend always work?

The `ItemSend` event does not fire when the user creates and sends a message using the right-click Send To | Mail Recipient command in Windows Explorer or the File | Send commands in Internet Explorer, Word, Excel, or other Office applications. The reason is that those commands do not use Outlook to create and send the message. Instead, they use a more basic interface called Simple MAPI that bypasses Outlook's functionality.

It is possible in Windows XP, though, to get Windows Explorer and the Office applications to fire Outlook's `ItemSend` event, by adding new commands. In Windows Explorer, navigate to the %userprofile%\SendTo folder.

---

**Note:** %userprofile% is an environment variable that Windows evaluates to take you to the current user's folders holding Windows profile data and settings. Depending on your Windows configuration, you may not have permission to add new shortcuts to the SendTo folder.

---

Once you are in the SendTo folder, create a new shortcut there with this path:

```
"C:\Program Files\Microsoft Office\Office12\OUTLOOK.EXE" /a
```

(Note that this path is the default for Office 2007; earlier versions will use a different path, as will users who do not install Office in the default location.) The /a switch tells Outlook to create a new message with an attachment. Name the shortcut "Outlook." When you want to create a message with a file attachment, right-click the file, and choose Send To | Outlook to invoke your new shortcut.

For Office applications, you can create a macro that saves the current document and sends it as a mail message. In the Word VBA environment, for example, choose Tools | References and add a reference to the Microsoft Outlook 12.0 Object Library. If the Normal project doesn't have an existing code module, add one using the Insert | Module command. Then, add the code in Listing 11.5.

Be sure to save changes to the Normal.dotm template when you close Word 2007, so that the macro will be saved, too. To add the `SendToOutlook` macro to the Quick Access Toolbar (QAT) in Word, follow these steps:

1. Click the Customize Quick Access Toolbar command arrow (to the right of the QAT) and choose More Commands.

2. Under "Choose commands from," select Macros.

3. Select the `SendToOutlook` macro, and then click Add.

4. Select the `SendToOutlook` macro, and then click Modify.

5. In the Modify Button dialog, shorten the display name (which will appear in the button's screen tip) to just "SendToOutlook" and, if you like, change the symbol.

6. Click OK twice to save your changes.

The code for sending an Excel workbook as an attachment would be almost identical, except that it would use `ActiveWorkbook` instead of `ActiveDocument`.

If the code determines that the message is going to a contact within the "Family" category, it uses the expression `myMail.SendUsingAccount = objExAcct` to determine whether the message is being sent with the Exchange account. If so, then the user gets a choice. The message can be

**Listing 11.5**    *Attach the current Word document to an Outlook message*

```
Sub SendToOutlook()
    Dim strMsg As String
    Dim objOL As New Outlook.Application
    Dim objMail As Outlook.MailItem
    On Error Resume Next
    If ActiveDocument.Saved = False Then
        ActiveDocument.Save
    End If
    If ActiveDocument.Saved = True Then
        Set objMail = objOL.CreateItem(olMailItem)
        objMail.Attachments.Add _
          ActiveDocument.Path & "\" & ActiveDocument.Name, _
          olByValue
        objMail.Subject = ActiveDocument.Name
        objMail.Display
    Else
        strMsg = "This document must be saved before " & _
                 "you can send it as an Outlook attachment."
        MsgBox strMsg, vbExclamation, "SendToOutlook"
    End If
    Set objMail = Nothing
    Set objOL = Nothing
End Sub
```

allowed to go as-is, or the code can change the account to the Internet account using this statement:

```
myMail.SendUsingAccount = objInetAcct
```

Or, the code can cancel the send operation completely, by returning `True` as the value of `CheckSendAccount()` function.

No doubt you can imagine many other useful scenarios that involve checking the content of an outgoing message and canceling the send operation or forcing the item to send with a different mail account. Chapter 20 demonstrates how to determine the user's default mail account and set each outgoing item to use it.

## 11.1.4  Using the ItemLoad event

A key new event is Outlook 2007 is the `Application.ItemLoad` event, which fires when the user opens an item or selects an item for viewing in the reading pane. While the `ItemSend` event provides what is known as a *strong reference* to the item being sent, with all its properties, the `ItemLoad` event provides only a *weak reference* to the item being loaded, exposing only two properties, `Class` and (in most cases, but not all) `MessageClass`. These properties allow you to know what type of item it is, which is all you need to know to be able to instantiate another object of the correct class—a `MailItem` for a message, for example—whose events, properties, and methods are fully exposed. Listing 11.6 demonstrates how this works.

After entering the code in Listing 11.6 in the `ThisOutlookSession` module, test it by spending some time opening items and previewing them in the reading pane. Then, display the Immediate window in VBA. You should see a line for each item opened and each item read, that line produced by the appropriate `Debug.Print` statement for that item type. Notice that the `Unload` event, which fires after the `Close` event, gives you an opportunity to release the object.

---

**Note:** The `ItemLoad` event, new to Outlook 2007, makes it somewhat easier for professional developers to build add-ins that handle individual item events such as `Open` and `Read` for multiple open items. However, that technique involves a complex class module solution that puts it beyond the scope of this book. We will deal with events for individual Outlook items mainly in the context of the `NewInspector` event, covered a little later in this chapter, and within VBScript code behind Outlook forms, starting with the next chapter, Chapter 12.

---

The next section goes into more detail on the technique of writing event handlers like this for objects other than `Application`.

**Listing 11.6**    *Use ItemLoad to instantiate other event-enabled objects*

```
Dim WithEvents m_objAppt As Outlook.AppointmentItem
Dim WithEvents m_objCont As Outlook.ContactItem
Dim WithEvents m_objJour As Outlook.JournalItem
Dim WithEvents m_objMail As Outlook.MailItem
Dim WithEvents m_objTask As Outlook.TaskItem

Private Sub Application_ItemLoad(ByVal Item As Object)
    On Error Resume Next
    Dim strClass As String
    Select Case Item.Class
        Case olMail
            Set m_objMail = Item
        Case olTask
            Set m_objTask = Item
        Case olAppointment
            Set m_objAppt = Item
        Case olContact
            Set m_objCont = Item
        Case olJournal
            Set m_objJour = Item
        Case Else
            strClass = CStr(Item.Class)
            strClass = strClass & " - " & Item.MessageClass
            Debug.Print strClass, Time()
    End Select
End Sub

Private Sub m_objAppt_Open(Cancel As Boolean)
    Debug.Print "open", m_objAppt.Subject
End Sub

Private Sub m_objAppt_Read()
    Debug.Print "read", m_objAppt.Subject
End Sub

Private Sub m_objAppt_Unload()
    Set m_objAppt = Nothing
End Sub

Private Sub m_objCont_Open(Cancel As Boolean)
    Debug.Print "open", m_objCont.Subject
End Sub

Private Sub m_objCont_Read()
    Debug.Print "read", m_objCont.Subject
End Sub

Private Sub m_objCont_Unload()
    Set m_objCont = Nothing
End Sub
```

**Listing 11.6**    *Use ItemLoad to instantiate other event-enabled objects  (continued)*

```
Private Sub m_objJour_Open(Cancel As Boolean)
    Debug.Print "open", m_objJour.Subject
End Sub

Private Sub m_objJour_Read()
    Debug.Print "read", m_objJour.Subject
End Sub

Private Sub m_objJour_Unload()
    Set m_objJour = Nothing
End Sub

Private Sub m_objMail_Open(Cancel As Boolean)
    Debug.Print "open", m_objMail.Subject
End Sub

Private Sub m_objMail_Read()
    Debug.Print "read", m_objMail.Subject
End Sub

Private Sub m_objMail_Unload()
    Set m_objMail = Nothing
End Sub

Private Sub m_objTask_Open(Cancel As Boolean)
    Debug.Print "open", m_objTask.Subject
End Sub

Private Sub m_objTask_Read()
    Debug.Print "read", m_objTask.Subject
End Sub

Private Sub m_objTask_Unload()
    Set m_objTask = Nothing
End Sub
```

# 11.2  Writing handlers for other object events

As you saw in the previous section with its item-level `Open` and `Read` events, VBA handling of Outlook events is not limited to events associated with the `Application` object. You can write event handlers for other objects, too. Setting up such an event handler requires two extra steps that you didn't need to take for `Application` events:

- In a class module, declare an object variable with a `Dim WithEvents` or `Private WithEvents` statement
- Instantiate that object variable

WithEvents declarations work only in *class modules*—special code modules that establish and work with object classes and their methods, events, and properties. The built-in ThisOutlookSession module itself is a class module. You can create your own class modules to help you better organize your event-handling code.

Once you have an object variable declared WithEvents in a class module, you can choose that object from the dropdown list at the top of the module and then select one of its events to have VBA insert the correct event handler procedure definition.

---

**Tip:** The code behind a VBA user form is also a type of class module. That's why it can fire events for command buttons and other controls on the form.

---

### 11.2.1   Handling events in ThisOutlookSession

Take a look back at Listing 11.6. It illustrates the basic concepts involved in setting up event handlers in the built-in ThisOutlookSession module. For example, this statement makes it possible to write procedures to handle the events fired by the m_objAppt object:

```
Dim WithEvents m_objAppt As Outlook.AppointmentItem
```

The m_objAppt object is instantiated by this statement in the Application_ItemLoad procedure:

```
Set m_objAppt = Item
```

Listing 11.6 contains three event handlers for the m_objAppt object:

```
Private Sub m_objAppt_Read()
    Debug.Print "read", m_objAppt.Subject
End Sub

Private Sub m_objAppt_Open(Cancel As Boolean)
    Debug.Print "open", m_objCont.Subject
End Sub

Private Sub m_objAppt_Unload()
    Set m_objAppt = Nothing
End Sub
```

Look through Listing 11.6 to match up each of the objects declared WithEvents with the statement that instantiates it and with its event handlers.

When you set up event handlers in the ThisOutlookSession module, the event-enabled objects (that is, those declared WithEvents) should be instantiated by code in one of the Application events or in the event handler for some other object that itself was instantiated by code in an Application event. Often, Application_Startup is the event handler used to instantiate other event-enabled objects, but you can also use `Application_MAPILogonComplete`.

## 11.2.2   Handling events in class modules

As an alternative to putting all your event handlers in the `ThisOutlookSession` module, you can also write separate class modules to hold your event handlers, especially handlers for objects other than `Application`. One advantage of using a separate class module for each type of object is that you can export and import such a class module using the File | Import File and Export File commands in VBA, making it easier to backup and share them with others. Coding separate class modules for different objects' events also helps you organize your code better. You may find it easier to locate, say, all the events related to `Explorers` and `Explorer` objects if you keep them in a single class module that handles only `Explorers` and `Explorer` events.

For an event handler in a class module, you follow the same two steps discussed in the previous section—declare an object `WithEvents` and instantiate that object. The difference is that those steps take place in the class module's code, not in the `ThisOutlookSession` module. Plus, you must add a third step: creating an instance of the class itself.

As an example to show you how all those steps fit together, let's assume that you want each new `Explorer` window (remember that `Explorer` windows show the items in Outlook folders) to display the Folder List navigation pane. The `Application` object has an `Explorers` collection and that collection supports a `NewExplorer` event. To display the Folder List navigation pane in each new `Explorer` window that the user opens, you could put the code in Listing 11.7 all in the `ThisOutlookSession` module.

The `Application_Startup` event handler in Listing 11.7 instantiates an `Explorers` object, which has been declared `WithEvents`. The `NewExplorer` event fires when the user displays a new `Explorer` window and runs code to display the Folder List in the navigation pane. The `Explorer.NavigationPane` object and `GetNavigationModule` methods are new to Outlook 2007.

Now, let's look at the alternative approach—a separate class module to handle the `NewExplorer` event—and see how it differs from the `ThisOutlookSession` version in Listing 11.7. Use the Insert | Class Module command in Outlook VBA to create the new module. In the Properties pane of the VBA environment, name the new module `Ch11ExplorerEvents`. Then put the code in Listing 11.8 in the new class module.

Notice that the module-level declaration and the `m_colExplorers_NewExplorer` event handler in Listing 11.8 are identical to the same code elements in Listing 11.7. What's different in Listing 11.8 is the `Class_`

**Listing 11.7**   *ThisOutlookSession code to display the Folder List navigation pane in each new Explorer window (compare with Listing 11.8)*

```
Dim WithEvents m_colExplorers As Outlook.Explorers

Private Sub m_colExplorers_NewExplorer _
  (ByVal Explorer As Explorer)
    Dim objModule As Outlook.NavigationModule
    Set objModule = _
      Explorer.NavigationPane.Modules.GetNavigationModule _
      (olModuleFolderList)
    If Not objModule Is Nothing Then
        Set Explorer.NavigationPane.CurrentModule = _
          objModule
    End If
    Set objModule = Nothing
End Sub

Private Sub Application_Startup()
    Set m_colExplorers = Outlook.Explorers
End Sub
```

`Initialize` procedure, which runs when an instance of the class is created. In Listing 11.7, the `Application_Startup` procedure instantiates the `m_colExplorers` object. In Listing 11.8, that job falls to the `Class_Initialize` procedure.

So, you should be wondering, where is the code that makes the `Class_Initialize` procedure run? What we need is a code statement to create a

**Listing 11.8**   *Class module code to display the Folder List navigation pane in each new Explorer window (compare with Listing 11.7)*

```
Dim WithEvents m_colExplorers As Outlook.Explorers

Private Sub m_colExplorers_NewExplorer _
  (ByVal Explorer As Explorer)
    Dim objModule As Outlook.NavigationModule
    Set objModule = _
      Explorer.NavigationPane.Modules.GetNavigationModule _
      (olModuleFolderList)
    If Not objModule Is Nothing Then
        Set Explorer.NavigationPane.CurrentModule =
objModule
    End If
    Set objModule = Nothing
End Sub

Private Sub Class_Initialize()
    Set m_colExplorers = Application.Explorers
End Sub
```

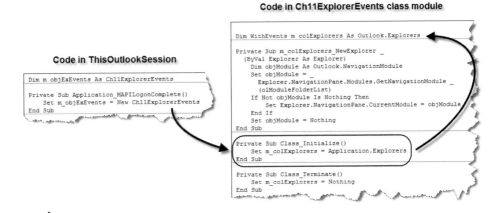

**Figure 11.3**  *Code in the Application_MAPILogonComplete event handler can instantiate a new class, which has its own event handlers.*

new instance of this class. That code needs to go into the `ThisOutlook-Session` module and run from the `Startup` or `MAPILogonComplete` event handler:

```
Dim m_objExEvents As Ch11ExplorerEvents

Private Sub Application_MAPILogonComplete()
    Set m_objExEvents = New Ch11ExplorerEvents
End Sub
```

Recall that `Ch11ExplorerEvents` is the new class module that you created. Figure 11.3 illustrates how the code execution transfers from the `ThisOutlookSession` module to the `Ch11ExplorerEvents` module. The `Dim m_objExEvents` statement is necessary to make sure that the class instance stays active ("in scope") while Outlook is running, so that it can continue to fire events as long as Outlook is running.

Listing 11.8 introduces a new declaration technique: the `New` keyword. When you use the `New` keyword in a declaration, you are creating a new instance of a class, in this case the class module named `Ch11-ExplorerEvents`. Once you have an instance of the class, your code can call any of the class' public methods, that is, its subroutines and functions.

We'll continue looking at the `Explorer` object in the next section.

## 11.3  Explorers and Explorer events

Each window that displays an Outlook folder is represented by an `Explorer` object in the `Explorers` collection. As you saw in the previous section, the `Explorers` collection has a single event, `NewExplorer`, which fires when the user displays a new folder window.

Events related to the `Explorer` object fire when the user changes views; selects, copies, cuts, or pastes items; resizes the window; or switches to a new folder or view. Table 11.2 summarizes the `Explorer` events. Note that all the events whose name begins with `Before` can be canceled.

To detect when a user has opened a new window (for example, so that you can then change the appearance of that window), `SelectionChange` is the best event to use. By the time it fires, the full user interface is available. `SelectionChange` also fires when the user opens a second calendar side-by-side with another calendar folder.

**Table 11.2**    *Explorers and Explorer Events*

| Explorers Event | Description |
| --- | --- |
| NewExplorer | Occurs when the user or an application displays a new folder window; includes the new `Explorer` as an argument |

| Explorer Events | Description |
| --- | --- |
| Activate | Occurs when the user switches to the `Explorer` |
| BeforeFolderSwitch | Occurs before the `Explorer` displays a new folder; includes the new folder as an argument; cancelable |
| BeforeItemCopy | Occurs when the user copies an item; cancelable |
| BeforeItemCut | Occurs when the user cuts an item; cancelable |
| BeforeItemPaste | Occurs when the user pastes an item; cancelable |
| BeforeMaximize | Occurs when the user maximizes the window; cancelable |
| BeforeMinimize | Occurs when the user minimizes the window; cancelable |
| BeforeMove | Occurs when the user repositions the window; cancelable |
| BeforeSize | Occurs when the user resizes the window; cancelable |
| BeforeViewSwitch | Occurs before the `Explorer` displays a new view; includes the new view as an argument; cancelable |
| Close | Occurs when the `Explorer` closes (in VBA, when the last `Explorer` closes, Outlook begins to shut down, and no further work can be done with Outlook objects) |
| Deactivate | Occurs before the focus switches from the `Explorer` to another window |
| FolderSwitch | Occurs after the `Explorer` displays a new folder |
| SelectionChange | Occurs when the user selects different items or a different date/time range on a day/week/month view |
| ViewSwitch | Occurs after the `Explorer` displays a new view |

The `BeforeFolderSwitch`, `BeforeViewSwitch`, `FolderSwitch`, and `ViewSwitch` events can be triggered either by the user changing the folder, by the user switching to a different view, or by code that assigns a new value to the `CurrentFolder` or `CurrentView` property of the `Explorer`.

To make use of `Explorer` events, you must declare appropriate object variables in the `ThisOutlookSession` module or another class module and initialize those variables with code in the `Application_Startup` event handler in `ThisOutlookSession`.

**Note:** The techniques discussed in this book show how to gain access to the `Explorer` events for the current `Explorer` window. Handling all events for multiple open `Explorer` windows requires a "wrapper" class module, which is beyond the scope of this book, but is covered in more advanced Outlook programming books.

Here are some ideas for practical applications for `Explorer` events:

- Controlling the state, size, and position of new folder windows
- Controlling the view shown for a folder
- Turning on a custom toolbar or button when you switch to a particular folder and turning it off again when you switch to a different folder

The next two sections provide sample code for the first two ideas. We'll discuss toolbar programming in Chapter 23.

### 11.3.1   Example: Controlling the state of new folder windows

One peculiarity of Outlook is that it always displays new folder windows in a normal window, even if the main Outlook window is maximized. If you prefer for all Outlook windows to open maximized, you can place the code in Listing 11.9 in the built-in `ThisOutlookSession` module.

**Listing 11.9**   *Show all new Explorer windows in a maximized state*

```
Dim WithEvents colExpl As Outlook.Explorers

Private Sub Application_Startup()
    Set colExpl = Application.Explorers
End Sub

Private Sub colExpl_NewExplorer(ByVal Explorer As Explorer)
    Explorer.WindowState = olMaximized
End Sub
```

Either restart Outlook or run the `Application_Startup` procedure so that the `colExpl` collection is instantiated and can fire the `NewExplorer` event.

The `Explorer` object supports size and position properties, so if you wanted to show the window in its normal state but control its size and position on the screen, you could use this alternative code for the `NewExplorer` event handler:

```
Private Sub colExpl_NewExplorer_
  (ByVal Explorer As Explorer)
    Explorer.Height = 700
    Explorer.Width = 900
    Explorer.Top = 30
    Explorer.Left = 100
End Sub
```

## 11.3.2   Example: Setting a default folder view

If you're like me and have several thousand items in your Sent Items folder, viewing just the last few days' worth makes the folder seem to display faster. Outlook includes a Last Seven Days view that filters out all but the last week's worth of items.

---

**Tip:** Instead of using the Last Seven Days view, you may want to create a custom view (name it "Sent in Last Seven Days") to show different fields. Use the View | Current View | Define Views command to create the new view, remove the Received and From fields, and add instead the Sent and To fields. Replace "Last Seven Days" in Listing 11.10 with "Sent in Last Seven Days" or whatever you call your new custom view.

---

To make Outlook automatically turn on the Last Seven Days view, you must create an event handler for the `FolderSwitch` event. Since the previous example was designed to run in `ThisOutlookSession`, let's build this one in a class module.

First, in the `ThisOutlookSession` module, add this code:

```
Dim m_objExEvents As Ch11ExplorerEvents2

Private Sub Application_MAPILogonComplete()
    Set m_objExEvents = New Ch11ExplorerEvents2
End Sub
```

We're using the `MAPILogonComplete` event instead of the `Startup` event, just in case the user has Sent Items set as the initial folder for Outlook to display. We want to make sure the code to change the view runs only after Outlook's folders are fully initialized.

Since the `Dim` statement refers to a `Ch11ExplorerEvents2` class, that's the next task. Use the Insert | Class Module command to add a new class module and change its name to `Ch11ExplorerEvents2`.

Now, put the code in Listing 11.10 in the `Ch11ExplorerEvents2` class module.

**Listing 11.10**   *Class module code to display the Last Seven Days view on the Sent Items folder*

```
Dim WithEvents m_objExpl As Outlook.Explorer
Dim blnStartup As Boolean
Dim m_objOL as Outlook.Application

Private Sub Class_Initialize()
    Set m_objOL = Application
    If m_objOL.Explorers.Count > 0 Then
        Set m_objExpl = m_objOL.ActiveExplorer
    End If
    blnStartup = True
End Sub

Private Sub m_objExpl_SelectionChange()
    If blnStartup Then
        Call ShowLastSevenDays
        blnStartup = False
    End If
End Sub

Private Sub m_objExpl_FolderSwitch()
    Call ShowLastSevenDays
End Sub

Private Sub m_objExpl_Close()
    If m_objOL.Explorers.Count > 0 Then
        Set m_objExpl = m_objOL.ActiveExplorer
    End If
End Sub

Private Sub ShowLastSevenDays()
    Dim objNS As Outlook.NameSpace
    Dim objSentItems As Outlook.Folder
    Set objNS = m_objOL.Session
    Set objSentItems = _
      objNS.GetDefaultFolder(olFolderSentMail)
    If m_objExpl.CurrentFolder = objSentItems Then
        m_objExpl.CurrentView = "Last Seven Days"
    End If
    Set objNS = Nothing
    Set objSentItems = Nothing
End Sub
```

In Listing 11.10, the `ShowLastSevenDays` procedure does most of the work—checking to see whether the `Explorer.CurrentFolder` object points to the default Sent Items folder and, if so, changing the view to Last Seven Days. What's interesting is that `ShowLastSevenDays` is called by two different event handlers—`FolderSwitch` and `SelectionChange`. The purpose of the `FolderSwitch` event should be obvious because of its name: It fires when the user changes the display in the `Explorer` window from one folder to another.

The use of `SelectionChange` is less obvious. It's needed to handle the case, albeit unlikely, that the user has set the Sent Items folder as the startup folder for Outlook. In that scenario, no `Explorer.FolderSwitch` event occurs when Outlook starts, so you need to use some other event. As it turns out, `Explorer.SelectionChange` is the right event, because whenever a new `Explorer` displays, it fires the `SelectionChange` event as the last event after the folder display has been completely initialized. Since we need to use `SelectionChange` only if Outlook displays the Sent Items folder on startup, a module-level Boolean variable, `blnStartup`, tracks Outlook's state so that the code doesn't call `ShowLastSevenDays` every time the user changes the selection in the folder display.

To test this code, restart Outlook or manually run the `Application_MAPILogonComplete` procedure to activate the new event handlers. Then switch to the Sent Items folder. Check the view by looking at the View | Current View menu to see which view is currently selected.

## 11.4  Inspectors and Inspector events

Just as Outlook has an `Explorers` collection with each `Explorer` object representing a folder window, it also has an `Inspectors` collection, where each `Inspector` object represents an individual Outlook item window. The `Inspectors` collection has one event, `NewInspector`, which fires whenever a new `Inspector` window opens. You first saw the `NewInspector` event back in Listing 9.5, which demonstrated how to prototype with individual item event handlers in VBA. The `NewInspector` event also fires if a user is viewing an item window and then clicks the Next or Previous button on the Quick Access Toolbar.

Unfortunately, the `NewInspector` event does not fire in all cases when the user sees a new message. As with the `Application.ItemSend` event discussed earlier in the sidebar "Why doesn't ItemSend always work?" you will get no `NewInspector` event when you invoke a Send or Send To command from Windows Explorer, Internet Explorer, or other Office applications. (The new window will, however, be present in the `Application.ActiveInspectors` collection, along with any other item windows.)

Just as `NewExplorer` provides access to the most recently opened `Explorer` window, the `NewInspector` event provides access to the most recently opened `Inspector`. That makes it useful for handling initialization tasks when the user displays an item.

---

**Note:** To handle other events for all open Outlook `Inspector` windows would require a wrapper class module, which is beyond the scope of this book, but covered in more advanced Outlook programming books.

---

An individual `Inspector` object has the events shown in Table 11.3. You can see that many are very similar to those for the `Explorer` object in Table 11.2.

One peculiarity of `NewInspector` is that the `Inspector` object that it passes as an argument may not be fully initialized when `NewInspector` fires. To get the caption of the window, for example, you need to use the `Inspector.Activate` event. Listing 11.11 shows the basic syntax for setting up a `NewInspector` event handler in `ThisOutlookSession` and using it to instantiate an `Inspector` object whose `Activate` event you can write

**Table 11.3** *Inspectors and Inspector Events (* = new in Outlook 2007)*

| Inspectors Event | Description |
| --- | --- |
| NewInspector | Occurs when the user or an application displays an item in its own window or if a user is viewing an item window and then clicks the Next or Previous button on the Quick Access Toolbar; includes the NewInspector as an argument |

| Inspector Events | Description |
| --- | --- |
| Activate | Occurs when the user switches to the Inspector window or when the Next or Previous button is used to view another item in the current Inspector |
| BeforeMaximize | Occurs when the user maximizes the window; cancelable |
| BeforeMinimize | Occurs when the user minimizes the window; cancelable |
| BeforeMove | Occurs when the user moves the window; cancelable |
| BeforeSize | Occurs when the user resizes the window; cancelable |
| Close | Occurs when the Inspector closes |
| Deactivate | Occurs just before the focus switches from the Inspector to another window or when the Next or Previous button is used to view another item |
| *PageChange | Occurs when the active form page changes, either because the user switched pages or because code changed the page; includes the active form page as an argument |

**Listing 11.11**    *Basic structure for Inspectors.NewInspector and Inspector.Activate events*

```
Dim WithEvents colInsp As Outlook.Inspectors
Dim WithEvents objInsp As Outlook.Inspector

Private Sub Application_Startup()
    Set colInsp = Application.Inspectors
End Sub

Private Sub colInsp_NewInspector(_
  ByVal Inspector As Inspector)
    Set objInsp = Inspector
End Sub

Private Sub objInsp_Activate()
    Debug.Print objInsp.Caption
End Sub
```

code for (in this case, a `Debug.Print` statement to show the caption of the window).

Remember that you cannot have two procedures with the same name in the same module. If you already have an `Application_Startup` event handler that looks like this:

```
Private Sub Application_Startup()
    Set colExpl = Application.Explorers
End Sub
```

add support for `Inspectors` by inserting a `Set colInsp` statement so that the procedure looks like this:

```
Private Sub Application_Startup()
    Set colExpl = Application.Explorers
    Set colInsp = Application.Inspectors
End Sub
```

Perhaps the most practical use of the `NewInspector` event is to perform initialization tasks—changing the window's size or position or making a change to the item displayed in the `Inspector` window. In the next two sections, we look at two practical examples:

- Automatically starting the journal timer
- Setting a new default reminder on all-day events

## 11.4.1    Example: Start the journal timer automatically

Consider a user who makes heavy use of Outlook's Journal feature to track the work done during the day. In Outlook 2003, this user learned to use Ctrl+Shift+J as a keyboard shortcut to create a new journal entry and Alt+M to start and pause the timer. However, in Outlook 2007, Alt+M doesn't function as a shortcut to start the timer.

**Listing 11.12**  *Start the timer automatically on a new journal entry*

```
Private Sub objInsp_Activate()
    Dim objJournal As Outlook.JournalItem
    If objInsp.CurrentItem.Class = olJournal Then
        Set objJournal = objInsp.CurrentItem
        If objJournal.Size = 0 Then
            objJournal.StartTimer
        End If
    End If
    Set objJournal = Nothing
End Sub
```

**Tip:** The new keyboard shortcut to start the timer in Outlook 2007 is Alt+H, T; and to pause, Alt+H, P.

You can help this user out with a small VBA routine using `NewInspector` to detect when a new window opens, then check to see whether it's a new journal entry and, if so, start its timer with the `JournalItem.StartTimer` method. Add the code in Listing 11.11 to your `ThisOutlookSession` module, replacing the `objInsp_Activate` event handler with the version in Listing 11.12.

Several interesting things are going on in the `Activate` event handler that you should take note of, since you'll see them in other Outlook code samples:

- `Inspector.CurrentItem` returns a reference to the item that the `Inspector` is displaying.

- The item's `Class` property tells you what type of Outlook item it is.

- If the `Size` of the item is 0, then you know it's a new, unsaved item.

## 11.4.2  Example: Set a reminder on new all-day events

A common complaint about Outlook is that there is no option to set a default reminder interval for all-day events. Even though you can set a default reminder interval for regular appointments in Tools | Options | Calendar Options, the reminder interval for all-day events is fixed at 18 hours, which many people don't find useful. In this next example, we'll use `Inspectors.NewInspector` and `Inspector.Activate` to determine whether an item is an `AppointmentItem` (using the `Class` property, remember?) and specifically, whether it's a new all-day appointment. If so, we'll set the reminder interval to three days.

Let's build on the example in the previous section, so you can see how to handle different types of items that the user will be opening in `Inspector`

**Listing 11.13**     *Set an all-day event reminder (and start the journal timer)*

```
Private Sub objInsp_Activate()
    Dim objJournal As Outlook.JournalItem
    Dim objAppt As Outlook.AppointmentItem
    Select Case objInsp.CurrentItem.Class
        Case olAppointment
            Set objAppt = objInsp.CurrentItem
            If objAppt.Size = 0 Then
                If objAppt.AllDayEvent Then
                    If objAppt.ReminderSet Then
                        objAppt.ReminderMinutesBeforeStart = _
                            3 * 24 * 60
                    End If
                End If
            End If
        Case olJournal
            Set objJournal = objInsp.CurrentItem
            If objJournal.Size = 0 Then
                objJournal.StartTimer
            End If
    End Select
    Set objJournal = Nothing
    Set objAppt = Nothing
End Sub
```

windows. If you haven't already done so, add the code in Listing 11.11 to the `ThisOutlookSession` module, but replace the `objInsp_Activate` event handler with the code in Listing 11.13. Notice that it includes the journal timer routine from Listing 11.12.

To test this code, restart Outlook or run the `Application_Startup` procedure. Display your Calendar folder in the week or day view, and double-click in the shaded area at the top of any day to create a new all-day event. When the new event opens, the code in Listing 11.13 will change the reminder from the default 18 hours to three days.

Did you notice that the code in Listing 11.13 uses a `Select Case` block statement to check the `Class` property of `objInsp.CurrentItem`, instead of an `If ... Then` block? This makes it easy to add processing for other kinds of Outlook items; just add a new `Case` statement for the different `Class` values from the `Outlook.OlObjectType` enumeration (which you can look up in the object browser if you're curious).

Again, `Size = 0` tells us whether it is a new appointment. If it is, the code checks the value of the `AppointmentItem.ReminderSet` property to find out if the user has reminders turned on by default. If there is an existing reminder, the code does the math to set the value of the `ReminderMinutesBeforeStart` property to three days—or 3 days times 24 hours in a day times 60 minutes in an hour (`3 * 24 * 60`). You can, of course, change that expression to apply a reminder interval of any number of minutes.

## 11.5 Folders, Folder, and Items events

Another major category of events is those that affect the `Folders` and `Items` collections and the `Folder` object—in other words, Outlook folders, subfolders, and the items they contain. With these events, Outlook reacts to the creation of a new folder or item, a change to an existing folder or item, or the deletion of a folder or item. Table 11.4 summarizes these events.

Two new events added in Outlook 2007—`Folder.BeforeFolderMove` and `Folder.BeforeItemMove`—give Outlook developers something they've wanted for years—the ability to know what item or folder is being moved or deleted and to cancel that move or deletion. Many applications need the ability to do some processing on items before they're deleted or to prevent certain items from being deleted, but the `Folders.FolderRemove` and `Items.ItemRemove` events provide no information on which folder or item was removed. Thus, these new events are a welcome addition.

As an example of how to use `BeforeFolderMove`, let's say that you have a top-level folder (that is, at the same level as your Inbox) named Critical

**Table 11.4**  *Folders and Items Events (\* = new in Outlook 2007)*

| Folders Events | Description |
| --- | --- |
| FolderAdd | Occurs when a new subfolder is created; includes the new `Folder` as an argument |
| FolderChange | Occurs when the properties of a folder are modified or when an item is added to or removed from a folder; includes the modified `Folder` as an argument |
| FolderRemove | Occurs after a subfolder has been deleted |
| **Folder Events** | **Description** |
| \*BeforeFolderMove | Occurs when a subfolder is about to be moved or permanently deleted; includes the destination `Folder` (or, in the case of a permanent deletion, `Nothing`) as an argument; can be canceled |
| \*BeforeItemMove | Occurs when an item is about to be moved or permanently deleted; includes the destination `Folder` (or, in the case of a permanent deletion, `Nothing`) and the moved item as arguments; can be canceled |
| **Items Events** | **Description** |
| ItemAdd | Occurs when a new item is saved either by the user or programmatically; includes the new item as an argument |
| ItemChange | Occurs when an item is modified; includes the modified item as an argument |
| ItemRemove | Occurs after an item has been deleted |

**Listing 11.14**    *Prevent the user from deleting a folder*

```
Dim WithEvents objCritFolder As Outlook.Folder

Private Sub Application_Startup()
    Dim objRootFolder As Outlook.Folder
    Set objRootFolder = _
      Application.Session.DefaultStore.GetRootFolder
    Set objCritFolder = objRootFolder.Folders("Critical")
    Set objInbox = Nothing
    Set objRootFolder = Nothing
End Sub

Private Sub objCritFolder_BeforeFolderMove _
  (ByVal MoveTo As MAPIFolder, Cancel As Boolean)
    Dim strMsg As String
    Cancel = True
    strMsg = "You can't delete the Critical folder."
    MsgBox strMsg, vbCritical, "Folder Move Not Allowed"
End Sub
```

and you need to make sure this folder is never deleted. Listing 11.14 shows code for the ThisOutlookSession module to prevent the user from deleting or moving that folder.

Listing 11.14 shows how to return a specific folder in the default information store by name. We'll review this and other techniques for getting folders in Chapter 13.

For an example of the Folders.FolderAdd method, let's add some functionality to Outlook's Search Folders feature. Users often create search folders to locate certain Outlook items faster (such as a folder for today's unread items) but don't always remember to put them in the Favorite Folders list at the top of the Mail navigation pane so that they are easily accessible. The code in Listing 11.15, written for the ThisOutlookSession module, watches for the creation of new search folders in the default information store and asks the user about adding them to the Favorite Folders list.

The ability to add, remove, and enumerate entries in the different navigation pane modules using the NavigationPane object is another new programming capability in Outlook 2007. We'll look at it in more detail in Chapter 23.

## 11.5.1    Limitations of Items events

The FolderAdd, FolderChange, and FolderRemove events are fairly straightforward, because the user can create, change, or delete only one folder at a time. When it comes to items, though, that is not the case. The user can induce a bulk property change on multiple items with a drag-and-drop operation within a folder, and can delete hundreds of individual items

**Listing 11.15**        *Add new search folders to the Favorite Folders list*

```
Dim WithEvents colSearchFolders As Outlook.Folders

Private Sub Application_Startup()
    Dim objStore As Outlook.Store
    Set objStore = Application.Session.DefaultStore
    Set colSearchFolders = objStore.GetSearchFolders
    Set objStore = Nothing
End Sub

Private Sub colSearchFolders_FolderAdd _
 (ByVal folder As MAPIFolder)
    Dim strMsg As String
    Dim intRes As Integer
    strMsg = "Do you want to add your new " & Chr(34) & _
            folder.Name & Chr(34) & " search folder " & _
            "to the Favorite Folders list?"
    intRes = MsgBox(strMsg, vbYesNo + vbQuestion, _
            "New Search Folder")
    If intRes = vbYes Then
        Call AddToMailFavs(folder)
    End If
End Sub

Public Sub AddToMailFavs(ByVal mailFolder As Outlook.Folder)
    Dim objExpl As Outlook.Explorer
    Dim objNavPane As Outlook.NavigationPane
    Dim objNavMod As Outlook.MailModule
    Dim objNavGroup As Outlook.NavigationGroup
    On Error Resume Next
    Set objExpl = Application.ActiveExplorer
    Se objNavPane = objExpl.NavigationPane
    Set objNavMod = _
       objNavPane.Modules.GetNavigationModule(olModuleMail)
    Set objNavGroup = _
       objNavMod.NavigationGroups.GetDefaultNavigationGroup _
       (olFavoriteFoldersGroup)
    objNavGroup.NavigationFolders.Add mailFolder
    Set objExpl = Nothing
    Set objNavPane = Nothing
    Set objNavMod = Nothing
    Set objNavGroup = Nothing
End Sub
```

at a time. Furthermore, the user can drag multiple items between folders, and a send/receive session can deliver many items to an Inbox at one time.

It's important to know, therefore, that when it comes to the ItemAdd, ItemChange, and ItemRemove events, Outlook has limits: It may not fire those events if more than sixteen items are being added, changed, or removed at one time.

What does that mean for your Outlook code? If you have scenarios that need to be able to do bulk processing, you may need to use more than `ItemAdd` and `ItemChange` to know which items to process. Later in this chapter, we'll see how to schedule a periodic pass through a folder to handle items that have not yet been processed.

## 11.5.2   Example: Adding birthday and anniversary reminders

Your first VBA project in this book was a user form to update existing birthday and anniversary entries in the Calendar folder to add a reminder. Wouldn't it be nice if you could automatically have a reminder added whenever Outlook creates a new birthday or anniversary event? That's a good task for the `Items.ItemAdd` event. Add the code in Listing 11.16 to the `ThisOutlookSession` module, and then either restart Outlook or run the

**Listing 11.16**   *Add reminders automatically to birthday and anniversary events*

```
Dim WithEvents colCalItems As Outlook.Items

Private Sub Application_Startup()
    Dim objCalFolder As Outlook.folder
    Set objCalFolder = _
      Application.Session.GetDefaultFolder_
      (olFolderCalendar)
    Set colCalItems = objCalFolder.Items
    Set objCalFolder = Nothing
End Sub

Private Sub colCalItems_ItemAdd(ByVal Item As Object)
    Dim objAppt As Outlook.AppointmentItem
    If Item.Class = olAppointment Then
        Set objAppt = Item
        If InStr(objAppt.Subject, "'s Birthday") > 0 Then
            Call B_and_A_Update(objAppt)
        ElseIf _
          InStr(objAppt.Subject, "'s Anniversary") > 0 Then
            Call B_and_A_Update(objAppt)
        End If
    End If
    Set objAppt = Nothing
End Sub

Public Sub B_and_A_Update(myAppt As Outlook.AppointmentItem)
    With myAppt
        .ReminderSet = True
        .ReminderMinutesBeforeStart = 7 * 24 * 60
        .Save
    End With
End Sub
```

`Application_Startup` procedure. Edit a contact to add a new birthday or anniversary, then look at that new event in your Calendar folder to confirm that it is showing a one-week reminder.

You can, of course, change the reminder interval by changing the 7 in the expression `7 * 24 * 60` to, for example, 14 to get reminders two weeks in advance.

If you're one of those people who doesn't like Outlook's built-in behavior of creating birthday and anniversary events, you can use a similar technique to get rid of them. The `B_and_A_Update` subroutine is a separate procedure for two reasons—one, so that we don't have a lot duplicate code in the `ItemAdd` event handler to process both birthdays and anniversaries, but also so that it's easy to change how those events are processed. Substitute the version below for the one in Listing 11.16, and VBA will automatically delete the birthday and anniversary events that Outlook creates when you add a birthday or anniversary date to a contact:

```
Public Sub B_and_A_Update _
  (myAppt As Outlook.AppointmentItem)
    myAppt.Delete
End Sub
```

**Note:** Listing 11.16 assumes that you're using an English-language version of Outlook. If you're using Outlook in another language, you'll need to adjust the `Instr()` expression to look for the equivalent text that Outlook uses for the subject of birthdays and anniversaries in that language.

## 11.6 Processing incoming mail

Just as you might use the `ItemAdd` event for the Calendar folder's `Items` collection to watch for new birthdays or anniversaries, you can also monitor the Inbox (or multiple folders) for new incoming mail messages and thus build your own alternative to the Outlook rules wizard. `ItemAdd` is just one approach, though. We'll look at it and others so that you can have a complete picture of what Outlook VBA can do to help you handle incoming mail.

One thing that all these methods have in common is that they act only on items that are passed by Outlook's junk mail filter. Junk mail processing occurs before any other processing, either Outlook rules or VBA code.

It is not possible to know whether a rule or a VBA event handler will act on a given message first. Therefore, you generally should not use both rules and VBA event handlers to try to process the same message. If you want to combine rules and VBA code, use the "run a script" action in a rule to run the VBA code.

**Table 11.5**   *Techniques for Processing Incoming Mail*

| Technique | Advantage | Disadvantages |
|---|---|---|
| Invoke a VBA procedure in a "run a script" rule action | Easy to write; the procedure passes a reference to the item that triggered the rule. | Rules may not fire if too many items are received at one time. |
| Use the `Application.NewMailEx` event | Easy if you have only one mail account. Provides an array of `EntryID` values you can use to return all items that arrived. | Code becomes complex if you need to handle multiple IMAP accounts, since `NewMailEx` doesn't tell you where the incoming message is stored. Also, `NewMailEx` may not fire if too many items are received at one time. |
| Use the `Items.ItemAdd` event | Easy to write; the event handler definition passes a reference to the new item. | If you need to monitor multiple Inbox folders (as in multiple IMAP accounts), you must set up an event handler for each one. Also, `ItemAdd` may not fire if too many items are added at the same time. |
| Use the `Application.NewMail` event | Most useful if you are interested primarily in knowing when new mail arrives, not in processing the actual items. | Tells you only that mail has arrived, not which items or where those messages might be found. |
| Schedule processing at regular intervals using a reminder | Can be very useful to clean up items skipped when a rule, `ItemAdd`, or `NewMailEx` procedure didn't fire because too many items arrived at once. Also can be used as the sole way to process items in a folder. | Adds complexity to the application. |

Table 11.5 lists the available methods for processing new mail, roughly ranked from easiest to most difficult to implement.

The next three sections look at the "run a script" rule action, `Application.NewMailEx`, and `Items.ItemAdd` methods in detail. We already covered `NewMail` earlier in the chapter.

While there are a number of different ways to build a procedure based on a timer (including using the timer available from Windows itself), the technique most appropriate for Outlook VBA is to use a task that has a reminder set for it. We'll cover reminder-related events in the last section of this chapter and show how to apply them to two different new mail processing scenarios.

## 11.6.1    Using a "run a script" rule

Outlook's Rules Wizard can run VBA code as part of a rule, specifically a rule that has a "run a script" action. That action is misnamed because it runs not an external script but a public VBA procedure that has a `Mail-Item` or `MeetingItem` as its sole parameter.

The one tricky aspect of writing such a procedure is that you need to make sure that the message or meeting request that your code acts on is derived from the intrinsic `Application` object. If you don't do that, your code may trigger Outlook security prompts. Listing 11.17 shows the basic syntax for both kinds of "run a script" rule procedures. Such procedures should be created either in the built-in `ThisOutlookSession` module or in a code module that you add with the Insert | Module command.

The `Debug.Print` statements in Listing 11.17 are there to demonstrate that the code won't trigger security prompts. Your own rules would, of course, replace those statements with code to process the message or meeting item. Let's look next at a practical example.

**Listing 11.17**    *Basic syntax for "run a script" rule action procedures*

```
Sub ProcessMessage(myMail As Outlook.MailItem)
    Dim strID As String
    Dim objNS As Outlook.NameSpace
    Dim objMsg As Outlook.MailItem

    strID = myMail.EntryID
    Set objNS = Application.GetNamespace("MAPI")
    Set objMsg = objNS.GetItemFromID(strID)
    Debug.Print objMsg.SenderName

    Set objMsg = Nothing
    Set objNS = Nothing
End Sub

Sub ProcessMeeting(myMtg As Outlook.MeetingItem)
    Dim strID As String
    Dim objNS As Outlook.NameSpace
    Dim objMtg As Outlook.MeetingItem

    strID = myMtg.EntryID
    Set objNS = Application.GetNamespace("MAPI")
    Set objMtg = objNS.GetItemFromID(strID)
    Debug.Print objMtg.SenderName

    Set objMtg = Nothing
    Set objNS = Nothing

End Sub
```

A feature that Outlook users have long requested is the ability to mark an incoming message with the same categories that the sender's record has in the user's Contacts folder. In other words, if you have a contact marked with the category "Key Contact," you'd want any messages from that person also to be marked with the category "Key Contact."

Listing 11.18 provides a "run a script" rule to accomplish that, using the new `AddressEntry.GetContact` method in Outlook 2007 to look up the matching contact. You should recognize it and the `IsInCategories` procedure; you saw them earlier in Listing 11.4. Put the `MarkWithContactCategories` and `IsInCategories` procedures in a regular code module created with the Insert | Module command.

**Listing 11.18**    *"Run a script" rule procedure to mark a message with the sender's categories*

```
Sub MarkWithContactCategories(myMail As Outlook.MailItem)
    Dim strID As String
    Dim objNS As Outlook.NameSpace
    Dim objMsg As Outlook.MailItem
    Dim objRecip As Outlook.Recipient
    Dim objAE As Outlook.AddressEntry
    Dim objContact As Outlook.ContactItem
    Dim strCats As String
    Dim strMsgCats As String
    Dim arrCats() As String
    Dim i As Integer
    On Error Resume Next
    strID = myMail.EntryID
    Set objNS = Application.Session
    Set objMsg = objNS.GetItemFromID(strID)
    Set objRecip = _
      objNS.CreateRecipient(objMsg.SenderEmailAddress)
    If objRecip.Resolve Then
        Set objAE = objRecip.AddressEntry
        Set objContact = objAE.GetContact
        If Not objContact Is Nothing Then
            strCats = objContact.Categories
            strMsgCats = objMsg.Categories
            If strCats <> "" Then
                arrCats = Split(strCats, ",")
                For i = 0 To UBound(arrCats)
                    If Not IsInCategories _
                      (arrCats(i), strMsgCats) Then
                        objMsg.Categories = _
                          objMsg.Categories & _
                          "," & arrCats(i)
                    End If
                Next
                objMsg.Save
            End If
        End If
    End If
End If
```

**Listing 11.18** *"Run a script" rule procedure to mark a message with the sender's categories (continued)*

```
        Set objMsg = Nothing
        Set objNS = Nothing
        Set objAE = Nothing
        Set objRecip = Nothing
        Set objContact = Nothing
End Sub

Function IsInCategories(strCatName, strCatList)
    Dim arrCats() As String
    Dim i As Integer
    If strCatList <> "" Then
        arrCats = Split(strCatList, ",")
        For i = 0 To UBound(arrCats)
            If UCase(arrCats(i)) = UCase(strCatName) Then
                IsInCategories = True
                Exit For
            End If
        Next
    End If
End Function
```

Once you've added the `MarkWithContactCategories` procedure, follow these steps to create a rule to run it:

1. Choose Tools | Rules and Alerts.

2. In the Rules and Alerts dialog, click New Rule.

3. In the first screen of the Rules Wizard, under "Start from a blank rule," select "Check messages as they arrive," and then click Next.

4. Because categories are available only for people you've saved as Outlook contacts, select the "Sender is in specified Address Book" condition, and then click on the underlined text and select your Contacts folder.

5. Select any other conditions you want to apply, and set their parameters. Selecting conditions means that you want the rule to apply only to messages that meet all the conditions. (Alternatively, you can select no conditions if you want the rule to apply to all messages.) Click Next to continue.

6. Select the "run a script" action, which appears near the bottom of the list of actions.

7. Click the underlined text, and select the `Project1.MarkWith-ContactCategories` procedure.

8. Select any other actions you want to apply. Include the "stop processing more rules" action if this is the only rule you want to apply to items matching your conditions. Click Next to continue.

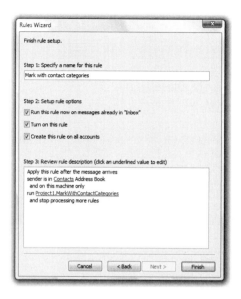

**Figure 11.4**
*A "run a script" rule to mark new messages with categories from the sender's contact record.*

9.    Select any exceptions you want to apply. Exceptions ensure that the rule does not run on items matching the exception conditions that you choose. Click Next to continue.

10.   Give the rule a descriptive name, such as "Mark with Contact Category." You can also select options to apply the rule to all mail accounts and to run it immediately. The rule settings should look like Figure 11.4.

11.   Click Finish and the rule will automatically become active and ready to process new messages.

## 11.6.2    Using Application.NewMailEx

Earlier in this chapter, we discussed that the `Application.NewMailEx` event is similar to the `NewMail` event in that it fires each time new mail is received, but different in that it passes information that can be used to determine <u>which</u> new items arrived. Specifically, `NewMailEx` passes a comma-delimited list of `EntryID` values, each corresponding to a different incoming item.

The chief challenge of using `NewMailEx` is that the `EntryID` may not be enough to retrieve the item. If you have IMAP accounts, for example, to retrieve a message, you need to know both the `EntryID` and the `StoreID` value for the item's parent folder—in other words, the ID for the information store that holds the item. Listing 11.19 shows how to accomplish this by maintaining an array of information store IDs for use with `GetItemFromID`. Note that it uses the same technique as the previous section to process the

**Listing 11.19** *Using NewMailEx to process incoming items from multiple accounts*

```
Private m_arrStoreIDs() As String

Private Sub Application_Startup()
    m_arrStoreIDs = GetStoreIDArray()
End Sub

Private Sub Application_NewMailEx _
  (ByVal EntryIDCollection As String)
    Dim objItem As Object
    Dim objMsg As Outlook.MailItem
    Dim arr() As String
    Dim i As Integer
    On Error Resume Next
    Debug.Print "new mail at " & Time
    arr = Split(EntryIDCollection, ",")
    For i = 0 To UBound(arr)
        Set objItem = GetItemNoStoreID(EntryIDCollection)
        If Not objItem Is Nothing Then
            If objItem.Class = olMail Then
                Set objMsg = objItem
                If objMsg.DownloadState = olFullItem Then
                    ' MarkWithSenderCategories from Listing 11.18
                    Call MarkWithSenderCategories(objMsg)
                End If
            End If
        End If
    Next
    Set objItem = Nothing
    Set objMsg = Nothing
End Sub

Private Function GetItemNoStoreID(itemID As String) As Object
    Dim objNS As Outlook.NameSpace
    Dim i As Integer
    Dim objItem As Object
    On Error Resume Next
    Set objNS = Application.Session
    Set objItem = objNS.GetItemFromID(itemID)
    If objItem Is Nothing Then
        For i = 0 To UBound(m_arrStoreIDs)
            Set objItem = _
              objNS.GetItemFromID(itemID, m_arrStoreIDs(i))
            If Not objItem Is Nothing Then
                Exit For
            End If
        Next
    End If
    Set GetItemNoStoreID = objItem
    Set objNS = Nothing
    Set objItem = Nothing
End Function
```

**Listing 11.19**     *Using NewMailEx to process incoming items from multiple accounts (continued)*

```
Private Function GetStoreIDArray()
    Dim strStoreIDs As String
    Dim strDefaultStoreID As String
    Dim objNS As Outlook.NameSpace
    Dim objStore As Outlook.Store
    Dim objRoot As Outlook.Folder
    Dim objInbox As Outlook.Folder
    Dim arr() As String
    On Error Resume Next
    Set objNS = Application.Session
    strDefaultStoreID = objNS.DefaultStore.StoreID
    For Each objStore In objNS.Stores
        Set objRoot = objStore.GetRootFolder
        Set objInbox = objRoot.Folders("Inbox")
        If Not objInbox Is Nothing Then
            If objStore.StoreID <> strDefaultStoreID Then
                strStoreIDs = _
                    strStoreIDs & "," & objStore.StoreID
            End If
        End If
    Next
    strStoreIDs = Mid(strStoreIDs, 2)
    arr = Split(strStoreIDs, ",")
    GetStoreIDArray = arr()
    Set objNS = Nothing
    Set objStore = Nothing
    Set objRoot = Nothing
End Function
```

message and add the sender's categories, calling the separate subroutine from Listing 11.18, `MarkWithSenderCategories`, which you should already have in a regular code module (not in `ThisOutlookSession`) if you walked through the previous example.

Processing messages this way with `NewMailEx` involves several specific activities:

- Returning the item based on its `EntryID`, here handled by the `GetItemNoStoreID()` function

- Getting an array of information store IDs for the `GetItemNoStoreID()` function to use; in this sample, the `Application_Startup` event hander calls the `GetStoreIDArray()` to set a module-level array variable that `GetItemNoStoreID()` can use at any time, without having to iterate all the stores every time new mail arrives.

- Performing the actual item processing; the `Application_NewMailEx` procedure in Listing 11.19 hands off the processing to `MarkWithSenderCategories`, after it confirms that the new item is really a fully downloaded mail message. (Most properties are not available if the item has not been completely downloaded.)

**Tip:** Since the store IDs are gathered only when Outlook starts, if you add a new account during the current Outlook session, you'll want to restart Outlook or run `Application_Startup` to refresh the ID array.

If you wanted to perform other processing on the message, you could write and call other procedures besides `MarkWithSenderCategories` from within the `NewMailEx` event handler.

### 11.6.3   Using Items.ItemAdd

Another message processing technique is the `Folder.Items.ItemAdd` event. You encountered it earlier in Listing 11.16, which was the example about adding reminders to new birthday and anniversary events. `Items.ItemAdd` is different from `NewMailEx` in that it fires on only one folder, not all incoming mail accounts. Like `NewMailEx`, it provides information about the new item, but only for one item at a time.

As you'll recall, to use the `ItemAdd` event, you must declare an `Items` object `WithEvents`, instantiate that object, and write an event handler. The code in Listing 11.20, which was written for the `ThisOutlookSession`

**Listing 11.20**   *Set categories on new Inbox items with Items.ItemAdd*

```
Dim WithEvents m_colInbox As Outlook.Items

Private Sub Application_Startup()
    Dim objNS As Outlook.NameSpace
    Dim objInbox As Outlook.Folder
    Set objNS = Application.Session
    Set objInbox = objNS.GetDefaultFolder(olFolderInbox)
    Set m_colInbox = objInbox.Items
    Set objNS = Nothing
    Set objInbox = Nothing
End Sub

Private Sub m_colInbox_ItemAdd(ByVal Item As Object)
    Dim objMsg As Outlook.MailItem
    On Error Resume Next
    If Item.Class = olMail Then
        Set objMsg = Item
        ' Uses the MarkWithSenderCategories
        ' subroutine from Listing 11.18
        Call MarkWithSenderCategories(objMsg)
    End If
    Set objMsg = Nothing
End Sub
```

module, does all that. Note that it calls the same `MarkWithSenderCatego-ries` procedure from Listing 11.18; make sure you have added that subroutine to a regular code module.

If you wanted to handle new items not just in your default Inbox, but in other folders, you'd need to follow the same process for each folder—declare another `Items` object `WithEvents`, instantiate that object, and provide an event handler for it. In Chapter 13, we will see several techniques besides `Namespace.GetDefaultFolder` that will allow you to return a `Folder` object for any folder you might want to monitor for new items.

As with the earlier `NewMailEx` sample, you could call other procedures besides `MarkWithSenderCategories` to perform other processing on the newly received items.

As a final example of processing incoming mail, we'll build an application that depends on an Outlook task that has a reminder set. But first, we need to look at reminders and reminder events in general.

## 11.7   Using the Application.Reminder and Reminders events

Any Outlook message, appointment, contact, or task can trigger a reminder. One significant change in Outlook 2007 is that reminders will fire from items in any folder in the user's default information store, not just from the Calendar, Contacts, Inbox, and Tasks folders.

As discussed earlier in the chapter, the `Application` object itself has a `Reminder` event, which fires whenever any Outlook item triggers a reminder. The `Application` object also has a `Reminders` collection, which adds more events to provide greater flexibility in handling reminders. Table 11.6 summarizes these events.

You probably noticed that three different events—`Application.Re-minder`, `Reminder.BeforeReminderShow`, and `Reminder.Reminder-Fire`—all fire when an item triggers a reminder. They occur in this order:

- `Reminder`
- `ReminderFire`
- `BeforeReminderShow`

Generally, you will want to use the `Reminders` events, rather than the `Application.Reminder` event, because they provide more flexibility. To work with `Reminders` events, you must declare a `Reminders` object `With-Events` and instantiate it, just as you did with the `Explorers`, `Folders`, and `Items` collections earlier in the chapter.

Let's look at some examples of `Reminders` events in a class module. Use the Insert | Class Module command to create a new class module and

**Table 11.6**   *Events Related to Reminders*

| Application Event | Description |
| --- | --- |
| Reminder | Occurs when a reminder is triggered by an appointment or task or by a flagged message or contact; includes the item that triggered the reminder as an argument |

| Reminders Event | Description |
| --- | --- |
| BeforeReminderShow | Occurs before Outlook displays the Reminders window; cancelable |
| ReminderAdd | Occurs after a new reminder has been created; includes the item that has the reminder as an argument |
| ReminderChange | Occurs after a reminder has been changed; includes the item that fired the reminder as an argument |
| ReminderFire | Occurs just before a reminder fires; includes the item that triggered the reminder as an argument |
| ReminderRemove | Occurs when a user dismisses a reminder, deletes an item that contains a reminder, or turns off the reminder for an item; also occurs when a reminder is dismissed programmatically with the `Reminder.Dismiss` method or removed from the `Reminders` collection |
| Snooze | Occurs when the user clicks the Snooze button on the `Reminders` dialog or when a reminder is snoozed programmatically with the `Reminder.Snooze` method; includes the item that triggered the reminder as an argument |

change its `Name` property to `Ch11ReminderEvents`. Add this code to the `ThisOutlookSession` module to instantiate the class:

```
Dim m_ReminderEvents As Ch11ReminderEvents

Private Sub Application_MAPILogonComplete()
    Set m_ReminderEvents = New Ch11ReminderEvents
End Sub
```

Then add the code in Listing 11.21 to the `Ch11ReminderEvents` class. To test the code, either restart Outlook or run the `Application_MAPI-LogonComplete` procedure.

The code in Listing 11.21 initializes the class by instantiating a `Reminders` object and a module-level integer variable to keep track of whether the user is busy. When the class initializes, Outlook asks the user whether this is a busy day. If it is, the `BeforeReminderShow` event handler sets `Cancel = True` so that the reminder window does not show.

Let's suppose as an alternative that you want the Reminders window to display, but only for important reminders, which we can define as reminders for items that you have marked as highly important. Since the `Before-ReminderShow` event provides no information about which items will appear in the Reminders window, we need to use a different event—

**Listing 11.21**     *Class module to handle Reminder events*

```
Dim WithEvents m_colReminders As Outlook.Reminders
Dim m_intBusyStatus As Integer

Private Sub Class_Initialize()
    Dim strMsg As String
    Set m_colReminders = Application.Reminders
    strMsg = "Are you really busy today?"
    m_intBusyStatus = MsgBox(strMsg, _
      vbYesNo + vbDefaultButton2 + vbQuestion, _
      "Busy Day?")
End Sub

Private Sub m_colReminders_BeforeReminderShow _
                          (Cancel As Boolean)
    Dim strMsg As String
    Const ME_BUSY = vbYes
    If m_intBusyStatus = ME_BUSY Then
        Cancel = True
    End If
End Sub
```

`ReminderFire`. Listing 11.22 provides a `ReminderFire` event handler that you can add to the `Ch11ReminderEvents` class module to show the user only reminders for important items. (Be sure to comment out the `Before-ReminderShow` event handler in Listing 11.21 if you added it to the module, since it blocks the display of the Reminders window if the user is busy.)

This statement

```
ReminderObject.Snooze 60
```

tells Outlook to snooze the reminder and not try to show it again for another hour. You can change the number to any other integer to apply a different number of minutes for the snooze interval.

**Listing 11.22**     *Use the ReminderFire event to show only important reminders*

```
Private Sub m_colReminders_ReminderFire _
        (ByVal ReminderObject As Reminder)
    Const ME_BUSY = vbYes
    On Error Resume Next
    Dim objItem As Object
    If m_intBusyStatus = ME_BUSY Then
        Set objItem = ReminderObject.Item
        If objItem.Importance <> olImportanceHigh Then
            ReminderObject.Snooze 60
        End If
    End If
    Set objItem = Nothing
End Sub
```

> **Tip:** If you call `Snooze` during the `ReminderFire` event handler, Outlook will not display the reminder in the Reminders window. This is the big advantage of using `Reminders.ReminderFire` over `Application.Reminder`.

Let's look at another example that involves reminder snoozing before we get back to the issue of processing incoming messages.

### 11.7.1   Example: Don't snooze important reminders

Let's say you want to see all your reminders, but you don't want it to be too easy to snooze the ones for important items. In that scenario, you would replace the `BeforeReminderFire` and `ReminderFire` event handlers with a `Snooze` event handler. If you already have a `Ch11ReminderEvents` class module, rename it and create a new `Ch11ReminderEvents` class module, then add the code in Listing 11.23 to it.

As in the earlier examples, you'll need code in the `ThisOutlookSession` module to instantiate the class:

```
Dim m_ReminderEvents As Ch11ReminderEvents

Private Sub Application_MAPILogonComplete()
    Set m_ReminderEvents = New Ch11ReminderEvents
End Sub
```

To test the code, either restart Outlook or run the `Application_MAPILogonComplete` procedure. Then, create some items with reminders and varying degrees of importance and see what happens when you try to snooze those reminders.

### 11.7.2   Example: Processing messages and running other code on a schedule

The final two examples in this chapter return to the issue of how to get VBA code to run at specific intervals or on a schedule. We'll look specifically at scenarios involving the processing of new messages, but the techniques are applicable to many other situations.

First, let's review some key facts you already know about reminders:

- In Outlook 2007, reminders fire for items in any folder in the default information store.
- If you snooze a reminder in the `ReminderFire` event, the user won't see it in the reminder window.
- When you snooze a reminder, you have the option of setting the number of minutes before the reminder fires again. (The default, if you don't set a snooze interval, is five minutes.)

**Listing 11.23**    *Make it hard to snooze important reminders*

```
Dim WithEvents m_colReminders As Outlook.Reminders

Private Sub Class_Initialize()
    Set m_colReminders = Application.Reminders
End Sub

Private Sub m_colReminders_Snooze _
                      (ByVal ReminderObject As Reminder)
    Dim objItem As Object
    Dim strMsg As String
    Dim dteNextReminder As Date
    Dim intRes As Integer
    On Error Resume Next
    Set objItem = ReminderObject.Item
    If objItem.Importance = olImportanceHigh Then
        dteNextReminder = ReminderObject.NextReminderDate
        strMsg = Replace(TypeName(objItem), "Item", "")
        strMsg = "You just snoozed the reminder for " & _
                vbCrLf & vbCrLf & _
                vbTab & strMsg & ": " & objItem.Subject & _
                vbCrLf & vbCrLf & _
                "It was originally due " & _
                FormatDateTime(dteNextReminder) & "." & _
                vbCrLf & vbCrLf & _
                "Did you really want to do that? " & _
                "If not, click No to edit the item " & _
                "and change the reminder."
        intRes = MsgBox(strMsg, _
                vbYesNo + vbDefaultButton2 + vbExclamation, _
                "You Snoozed an Important Reminder !!!")
        If intRes = vbNo Then
            objItem.Display
        End If
    End If
    Set objItem = Nothing
End Sub
```

The goal for these examples is to invoke the same MarkWithSender-Categories subroutine from Listing 11.18 that you saw the ItemAdd and NewMailEx events call, but do it at scheduled intervals, rather than directly in response to new mail arriving. First, we'll consider a scheduling routine running on its own, with no other new mail processing under way. Then, we'll combine a NewMailEx event handler with a scheduled cleanup routine to process the messages that NewMailEx might have skipped because too much mail arrived at once.

First, if you already have a class module named Ch11ReminderEvents, rename it. Then create a new class module, name it Ch11ReminderEvents, and add this code to the ThisOutlookSession module to instantiate it.

```
                        Dim m_ReminderEvents As Ch11ReminderEvents

                        Private Sub Application_MAPILogonComplete()
                            Set m_ReminderEvents = New Ch11ReminderEvents
                        End Sub
```

Next, place the code in Listing 11.24 in the new `Ch11ReminderEvents` class module.

**Listing 11.24**   *Processing new messages at regular intervals*

```
Private WithEvents m_colReminders As Outlook.Reminders
Private m_dteLastInboxProcessTime As Date
Private m_objNS As Outlook.NameSpace
Private m_objSystemTasksFolder As Outlook.Folder

Private Sub Class_Initialize()
    Set m_colReminders = Application.Reminders
    m_dteLastInboxProcessTime = Now
    Set m_objNS = Application.Session
    Call InitializeInboxTask
End Sub

Private Sub m_colReminders_ReminderFire _
                        (ByVal ReminderObject As Reminder)
    Dim objTask As Outlook.TaskItem
    On Error Resume Next
    If ReminderObject.Item.Class = olTask Then
        Set objTask = ReminderObject.Item
    End If
    If Not objTask Is Nothing Then
        If objTask.Parent = m_objSystemTasksFolder Then
            Select Case objTask.Subject
                Case "Process Inbox"
                        ReminderObject.Snooze 2
                        Call ProcessInbox
            End Select
        End If
    End If
    Set objTask = Nothing
End Sub

Private Sub InitializeInboxTask()
    Dim objTask As Outlook.TaskItem
    Dim strFind As String
    On Error Resume Next
    Set m_objSystemTasksFolder = GetSystemTasksFolder()
    If Not m_objSystemTasksFolder Is Nothing Then
        strFind = "[Subject] = " & Quote("Process Inbox")
        Set objTask = _
            m_objSystemTasksFolder.Items.Find(strFind)
        If objTask Is Nothing Then
            Set objTask = m_objSystemTasksFolder.Items.Add
            objTask.Subject = "Process Inbox"
        End If
```

**Listing 11.24**     *Processing new messages at regular intervals (continued)*

```
            If Not objTask Is Nothing Then
                With objTask
                    .ReminderSet = True
                    .ReminderTime = DateAdd("n", 1, Now)
                    .ReminderPlaySound = False
                    .Save
                End With
            End If
        End If
        Set objTask = Nothing
    End Sub

    Private Function GetSystemTasksFolder() As Outlook.Folder
        Dim objFolderTasks As Outlook.Folder
        Dim objFolderSysTasks As Outlook.Folder
        On Error Resume Next
        Set objFolderTasks = _
          m_objNS.GetDefaultFolder(olFolderTasks)
        Set objFolderSysTasks = _
          objFolderTasks.Folders("Outlook System Tasks")
        If objFolderSysTasks Is Nothing Then
            Set objFolderSysTasks = _
              objFolderTasks.Folders.Add("Outlook System Tasks")
        End If
        Set GetSystemTasksFolder = objFolderSysTasks
        Set objFolderTasks = Nothing
        Set objFolderSysTasks = Nothing
    End Function

    Private Sub ProcessInbox()
        Dim objInbox As Outlook.Folder
        Dim objitem As Object
        Dim objMail As Outlook.MailItem
        Dim strFind As String
        Dim colItems As Outlook.Items
        On Error Resume Next
        strFind = Format(m_dteLastInboxProcessTime, _
                     "dd mmm yyyy hh:mm")
        strFind = "[CreationTime] >= " & Quote(strFind)
        Set objInbox = m_objNS.GetDefaultFolder(olFolderInbox)
        Set colItems = objInbox.Items.Restrict(strFind)
        For Each objitem In colItems
            If objitem.Class = olMail Then
                Set objMail = objitem
                ' MarkWithSenderCategories from Listing 11.18
                Call MarkWithSenderCategories(objMail)
            End If
        Next
        m_dteLastInboxProcessTime = Now
        Set objInbox = Nothing
    End Sub

    Private Function Quote(myInput) As String
        Quote = Chr(34) & CStr(myInput) & Chr(34)
    End Function
```

**Figure 11.5**

*Class initialization code creates a special folder and task, if needed, and instantiates module-level variables.*

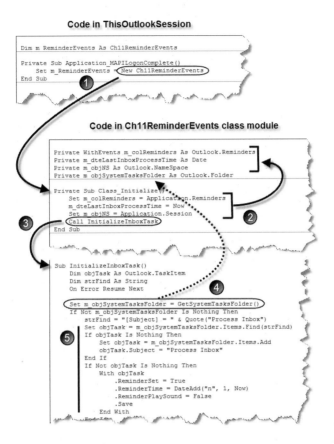

This is the most complex example yet in the book, so let's take some time to understand it. Roughly half the code helps set up the application, while the other half does the actual message processing. Figure 11.5 diagrams the flow of the setup operations that instantiate the class and different objects in these five steps:

1. The `Application_MAPILogonComplete` procedure creates a new instance of the `Ch11ReminderEvents` class.

2. The `Class_Initialize` procedure instantiates three module-level variables: a `Reminders` object to fire events, a date variable to track the last time the Inbox was processed, and an `Outlook.Namespace` object that several events in other procedures will use.

3. The `Class_Initialize` procedure then calls another procedure, `InitializeInboxTask`, that does the bulk of the setup work.

4. `InitializeInboxTask` calls a procedure, `GetSystemTasks-Folder` (not shown in the diagram), that returns a subfolder of

the default Tasks folder. That subfolder is named "Outlook System Tasks," and the code creates it if it does not already exist.

5.     `InitializeInboxTask` also checks the Outlook System Tasks folder for a task named "Process Inbox" and creates that task if it does not already exist, setting a reminder for the task to fire one minute from the moment the setup code runs.

What drives the actual Inbox processing is the reminder for that Process Inbox task:

1.     When the time for the task's reminder arrives, the `ReminderFire` event fires.

2.     The `m_colReminders_ReminderFire` event handler checks to see if the item that fired the reminder is a task named Process Inbox from the Outlook System Tasks folder and, if it is, calls the `ProcessInbox` procedure. It also snoozes the task's reminder for two minutes.

3.     The `ProcessInbox` procedure searches the Inbox for items created since the last processing time (stored as `m_dteLastInbox-ProcessTime`) and sends any recent messages that it finds to the `MarkWithSenderCategories` procedure for processing.

4.     You already know the `MarkWithSenderCategories` from Listing 11.18 and saw it used with a "run a script" rule and also in the `New-MailEx` example in Listing 11.19. Yes, `ProcessInbox` and `Application_NewMailEx` can both call the same public procedure.

5.     After all the items have been processed, `ProcessInbox` updates the `m_dteLastInboxProcessTime` date, for use during the next processing session.

---

**Note:** The initialization and the Inbox processing routines in Listing 11.24 and Listing 11.25 use various techniques to return folders and search for items. We'll study these in detail in subsequent chapters.

---

What Listing 11.24 creates is the framework for a potentially much larger scheme of "system" tasks that don't trigger visible reminders but instead fire off background processing tasks. Take a closer look at this section of the `m_colReminders_ReminderFire` event handler:

```
If objTask.Parent = m_objSystemTasksFolder Then
    Select Case objTask.Subject
        Case "Process Inbox"
            ReminderObject.Snooze 2
            Call ProcessInbox
    End Select
End If
```

This code essentially says, "If the task that fired the reminder is from the Outlook System Tasks folder, check its subject, and run the procedure associated with that task. And, while you're at it, snooze the reminder so the whole process can start again in a couple of minutes." The use of a `Select Case` block makes it very easy to plug in other procedures for other tasks that you might create in the Outlook System Tasks folder. All you would need to do is add another `Case` block, something like this:

```
If objTask.Parent = m_objSystemTasksFolder Then
    Select Case objTask.Subject
        Case "Process Inbox"
            ReminderObject.Snooze 2
            Call ProcessInbox
        Case "Another System Task"
            ReminderObject.Snooze 60
            Call AnotherSystemTaskProcedure
    End Select
End If
```

where `AnotherSystemTaskProcedure` is the subroutine associated with the task named "Another System Task," perhaps a task that needs to run only every hour (= 60 minutes).

As mentioned before, Listing 11.24 processes all the items in the Inbox, starting a new processing routine every couple of minutes. You can also combine that kind of interval-based processing with `NewMailEx` to get a thorough and efficient mail processing system. The idea is to let `NewMailEx` do the bulk of the work, then sweep up any unprocessed messages with the reminder-based code. On an adequately powerful machine, `NewMailEx` should be able to handle all the messages coming in, even if the volume is as high as a message every second. If it gets overwhelmed, though, you won't get any warning or runtime errors. `NewMailEx` simply will ignore a few messages as it catches up. You can ensure those messages eventually do get processed by running <u>both</u> `NewMailEx` and a reminder-based processing arrangement like the one you saw in Listing 11.24. The key to making that system work efficiently is for `NewMailEx` to mark each message it processes, so that the `ProcessInbox` routine can come along later and process only those skipped by `NewMailEx`.

This means that we need to make two major changes in the code you've seen so far. The `NewMailEx` event handler needs to mark the messages, and the code called by the `ReminderFire` event handler needs to search for unmarked messages, rather than for recent messages. Listing 11.25 has the new version of `Application_NewMailEx`. It adds these two statements to mark the processed messages:

```
objMsg.BillingInformation = "Processed"
objMsg.Save
```

The `BillingInformation` property is common to all Outlook items and is a good place to store "state" information like this.

**Listing 11.25**    *Mark incoming messages as processed, so you can clean up stragglers later with a reminder-based approach*

```
Private Sub Application_NewMailEx _
   (ByVal EntryIDCollection As String)
      Dim objitem As Object
      Dim objMsg As Outlook.MailItem
      Dim arr() As String
      Dim i As Integer
      On Error Resume Next
      Debug.Print "new mail at " & Time
      arr = Split(EntryIDCollection, ",")
      For i = 0 To UBound(arr)
          Set objitem = GetItemNoStoreID(EntryIDCollection)
          If Not objitem Is Nothing Then
              If objitem.Class = olMail Then
                  Set objMsg = objitem
                  If objMsg.DownloadState = olFullItem Then
                      Call MarkWithSenderCategories(objMsg)
                      objMsg.BillingInformation = "Processed"
                      objMsg.Save
                  End If
              End If
          End If
      Next
      Set objitem = Nothing
      Set objMsg = Nothing
End Sub
```

You'll need to make quite a few more changes in the reminder-based routines. I suggest that you create a new class module and name it `Ch11ReminderEvents2`. Use this code in `ThisOutlookSession` to instantiate it:

```
Dim m_ReminderEvents As Ch11ReminderEvents2

Private Sub Application_MAPILogonComplete()
    Set m_ReminderEvents = New Ch11ReminderEvents2
End Sub
```

In the `Ch11ReminderEvents2` module, place the code in Listing 11.26, plus the `InitializeInboxTask`, `GetSystemTasksFolder`, and `Quote` procedures from Listing 11.24, which require no changes. (Maybe now you're starting to see why breaking your code into procedures that perform discrete functions is a good idea: it lets you try out new techniques more easily.)

One thing you should notice is that Listing 11.26 has an integer variable (`m_intReminderSnoozeMinutes`) representing the number of snooze minutes, rather than a date variable representing the last time items were processed. You may need to experiment to find the perfect snooze interval for the Process Inbox task's reminder, based on the volume of mail you receive

**Listing 11.26**   *Use this code to initialize the reminder-based scheme for processing messages that New-MailEx overlooks*

```
Dim WithEvents m_colReminders As Outlook.Reminders
Dim m_objOL As Outlook.Application
Dim m_objNS As Outlook.NameSpace
Dim m_objSystemTasksFolder As Outlook.Folder
Dim m_intReminderSnoozeMinutes As Integer

Private Sub Class_Initialize()
    Set m_objOL = Application
    Set m_objNS = m_objOL.Session
    ' Use the InitializeInboxTask and GetSystemTasksFolder
    ' procedures from Listing 11.24
    Call IntializeInboxTask
    m_intReminderSnoozeMinutes = 2
    Set m_colReminders = m_objOL.Reminders
End Sub
```

and the frequency of send/receive sessions. Assigning the value to a variable in the `Class_Initialize` procedure puts the information at the top of the module, where it's easy to change, without the need to hunt through the depths of your code.

The rest of the code that you need to add to the `Ch11ReminderEvents2` module is in Listing 11.27.

The only change in the `m_colReminders_ReminderFire` event handler is that the `Snooze` statement now uses the module-level variable that holds the number of minutes to snooze the reminder until the next processing session:

```
ReminderObject.Snooze m_intReminderSnoozeMinutes
```

In the `ProcessInbox` procedure, you should notice quite a few changes:

- Instead of searching for items created since the last processing session, it searches for items with no value in the `BillingInformation` property. The method used is `Application.AdvancedSearch`. We'll defer a detailed discussion of it until Chapter 16. For now, the main thing you need to know is that it doesn't return results immediately. That's the reason for the `Do` loop that waits until either there are some results from the search or a minute passes. (You don't want to get stuck inside a `Do` loop with no way to get out of it.)

- The `TimeToQuit()` helper function returns `True` if more than a minute has elapsed. It takes into account the fact that the built-in `Timer` function in VBA returns the number of seconds since midnight.

- The `DoEvents` statement allows other actions to take place in Outlook while the loops are processing items.

**Listing 11.27**    *Use this code to process the messages that NewMailEx leaves untouched*

```
Private Sub m_colReminders_ReminderFire _
        (ByVal ReminderObject As Reminder)
    Dim objTask As Outlook.TaskItem
    On Error Resume Next
    If ReminderObject.Item.Class = olTask Then
        Set objTask = ReminderObject.Item
    End If
    If Not objTask Is Nothing Then
        If objTask.Parent = m_objSystemTasksFolder Then
            Select Case objTask.Subject
                Case "Process Inbox"
                    ReminderObject.Snooze _
                        m_intReminderSnoozeMinutes
                    Call ProcessInbox
            End Select
        End If
    End If

    Set objTask = Nothing
End Sub

Sub ProcessInbox()
    Dim strFind As String
    Dim objSearch As Outlook.Search
    Dim objitem As Object
    Dim objMail As Outlook.MailItem
    Dim sngTimeStart As Single
    On Error Resume Next
    strFind = _
      Quote("urn:schemas:contacts:billinginformation") & _
      " IS NULL"
    Set objSearch = _
      m_objOL.AdvancedSearch("Inbox", strFind)
    sngTimeStart = Timer
    Do While objSearch.Results Is Nothing
        If TimeToQuit(sngTimeStart, 60) Then Exit Do
        DoEvents
    Loop
    sngTimeStart = Timer
    For Each objitem In objSearch.Results
        If objitem.Class = olMail Then
            Set objMail = objitem
            Call MarkWithSenderCategories(objMail)
            objMail.BillingInformation = "Reminder processed"
            objMail.Save
        End If
        If TimeToQuit(sngTimeStart, 60) Then Exit For
        DoEvents
    Next
    Set objSearch = Nothing
    Set objitem = Nothing
    Set objMail = Nothing
End Sub
```

**Listing 11.27** *Use this code to process the messages that NewMailEx leaves untouched (continued)*

```
Function TimeToQuit _
        (startMark As Single, maxSeconds As Integer) _
        As Boolean
    If Timer > startMark Then
        If Timer - startMark > maxSeconds Then
            TimeToQuit = True
        End If
    ElseIf (Timer + (CLng(24 * 60) * 60)) > maxSeconds Then
        TimeToQuit = True
    Else
        TimeToQuit = False
    End If
End Function
```

- The `For Each ... Next` loop that actually processes items also is limited to only a minute of operation, to avoid bogging down the system.

- Items processed by `ProcessInbox` get stamped with a value in `BillingInformation`, so they won't be processed again.

To test this code, restart Outlook, or run the `Application_MAPILogonComplete()` procedure.

## 11.8 Summary

This chapter has provided a thorough grounding in the essential events for much of your Outlook VBA code that will go beyond simple macros. You now know how to create event handlers both in `ThisOutlookSession` and in separate class modules and have quite a few practical event samples that can help you start dealing with some of Outlook's little annoyances on your own. We will defer discussion of events related to context menus and searches until later chapters. In the next chapter, we will take up the subject of item-related events in the context of custom form VBScript code.

In addition, this chapter has provided a comprehensive look at the different techniques available to process incoming messages, from a simple "run a script" rule action to a combination of the `Application.NewMailEx` and `Reminders.ReminderFire` events. You can start with a simple approach for new message processing and, as your confidence in your Outlook programming skills increases, expand the techniques in this chapter to add more processing tasks. Our consistent example has involved marking incoming items with the categories related to the sender's contact record, but I'm sure you can think of many other actions you might want to take on incoming messages.

# 12

# *Coding Key Custom Form Scenarios*

VBScript code behind Outlook custom forms is event-driven. Code behind a form runs when the user's interaction with a form causes item and control events to fire. Writing code to respond to such user interaction is a large part of the job of an Outlook form designer. Just as important is being able to use form event code to validate the data that the user enters into the form. Another basic custom form coding task is to determine whether the form is displaying a new item or an existing item, or whether the form is displaying the read layout or the compose layout, or whether a new message is completely new or is a reply or forward.

The highlights of this chapter include discussions of the following:

- What events fire in which order when the user creates, edits, and saves items

- How to respond to a user's interaction with a form

- How to perform validation when the user enters data or saves or sends an item

- How to recognize a new item or an item displaying the read layout

- How to prevent the user from making changes to custom form items from a table view

- What custom properties can help you create workflow items with a custom form

## 12.1  Working with Outlook item events

To add code to an Outlook form, as explained in Chapter 7, open the form in design mode and then click View Code. To add code for an item event, choose Script | Event Handler, and select from the list in the Insert Event Handler dialog. Outlook adds a `Function ... End Function` or `Sub ... End Sub` wrapper to the code window, depending on the event.

Table 7.5 lists the 16 item-level events that custom forms support. In addition, some form controls support a `Click` event.

## 12.1.1   Understanding item event order

By investigating the order in which related events fire, you can gain better control over the behavior of Outlook forms. For example, you can prevent users from making changes to items in table views that have in-cell editing turned on. To understand what events fire when a user creates an event in a table view, create a new tasks folder and open a task form in design mode. Add the code in Listing 12.1 to the task form, and then publish that form to the new tasks folder. On the Properties dialog for the folder, make the new form the default for the folder.

After you publish the form, launch it from the Actions menu for the folder where you published it, and create a new item with it. Also experiment with creating new items using the new item row, opening existing items, and editing items in the table view with in-cell editing turned on. You should see a message box pop up each time one of the five events in Listing 12.1 fires. Make sure that you try different methods of saving and closing the item. See if you can duplicate the results in Table 12.1.

---

**Tip:** To access the setting for in-cell editing and the new item row, choose View | Current View | Customize Current View | Other Settings.

---

**Listing 12.1**    *Investigate the order in which key form events fire*

```
Function Item_Open()
    MsgBox "Open fired"
End Function

Function Item_Read()
    MsgBox "Read fired"
End Function

Function Item_Write()
    MsgBox "Write fired"
End Function

Function Item_Close()
    MsgBox "Close fired"
End Function

Function Item_Send()
    MsgBox "Send fired"
End Function
```

**Table 12.1**   *Event Firing Order for Opening and Closing Items*

| User Action | Event Order |
|---|---|
| Display a new item with the Actions or Choose Form command | Open |
| Open an existing item | Read |
|  | Open |
| If the custom form is the default for the folder, create a new item in the new item row of a table view with in-cell editing turned on | Write |
| Make changes in an existing item using in-cell editing | Read |
|  | Write |
| Make changes in an open item, then close it with the close (x) button in the upper-right corner or the Esc key | Close |
|  | Write (if the user answers Yes to the Do You Want to Save Changes? prompt |
| Make changes in an open item, then close it with the Save and Close command | Write |
|  | Close |
| Make changes in an open item, then save it with the Save command | Write |
| Send a message | Send |
|  | Write |
|  | Close |

Did you notice that the `Write` and `Close` events can occur in different orders, depending on how the user closes the item? If the user clicks Save and Close, `Write` fires first, then `Close`. However, if the user presses the Esc key or clicks the close (x) button in the upper-right corner of the form's window, `Close` fires first. The `Write` event fires later—if at all!—only <u>after</u> the user answers Yes to the "Do You Want to Save Changes?" prompt.

**Caution:** You cannot close, move, or delete an item within its own `Close` event handler. Code that attempts to do so will raise an error. Furthermore, calling `Item.Close` from other events may cause the initial release of Outlook 2007 to crash. Hopefully, Microsoft will fix the crash problem with an update.

When a user clicks Send on a message form, the `Send` event fires first, followed by `Write`, then `Close`. Any operations that you want to perform on an outgoing message should be coded into the `Item_Send` event handler.

**Note:** Sending a message places it in the Outbox. Only when the item has actually been delivered by the appropriate mail account to that account's outgoing server does it move to the Sent Items folder and acquire a time stamp indicating when it was sent.

## 12.1.2   Preventing the user from making changes in a folder view

Many Outlook folder views allow users to make changes to an item without opening it first. For example, you might drag an appointment to a new date. Or, you might drag an item between groups in a By Category view to add a new category to the item. Some table views, such as the default Tasks folder view, have in-cell editing turned on, so you can edit properties or even create new items by typing in the folder view. Also, a user can click in

**Listing 12.2**   *Force the user to make changes only if the item is displayed in a form*

```
Dim mblnIsOpen
Dim mblnIsClosing

Function Item_Open()
    mblnIsOpen = True
    mblnIsClosing = False
End Function

Function Item_Write()
    Dim strMsg
    If Not mblnIsOpen Then
        Item_Write = False
        strMsg = "You cannot save an item without " & _
                 "opening it first." & vbCrLf & vbCrLf & _
                 "If you were editing this item using " & _
                 "in-cell editing, press Esc to cancel " & _
                 "the edits."
        MsgBox strMsg, , "Can't Save Unopened Item"
    End If
    If mblnIsClosing Then
        mblnIsClosing = False
    End If
End Function

Function Item_Close()
    mblnIsClosing = True
    If Item.Saved Then
        mblnIsOpen = False
    End If
End Function
```

the Calendar folder's Day/Week/Month view and just start typing to create a new appointment.

All these folder-based item creation and editing methods bypass the layout of any custom form. If you provide a lot of feedback to users with your custom form, you'll want the user always to enter data using only the controls in that form. The code in Listing 12.2 uses the events discussed in the previous section to prevent the user from saving changes to an item that has not been opened in its own window.

When the `Close` event fires before `Write`, the value of `Item.Saved`, as in the `Item_Close` event handler in Listing 12.2, tells you whether the user will be prompted to save the item.

### 12.1.3   Locking an item for changes

In an Exchange environment, you may be using custom forms for items in a public folder or in a shared mailbox folder and want a way to avoid having two people change the item at the same time. One approach to that situation is to check a property value when each user opens an item. A certain value for that property could indicate that it is OK to edit the item. Another value could indicate the item is not OK to edit because another user already has it open.

---

**Note:** Outlook normally blocks code from running behind forms used for items in another user's Exchange mailbox, but that option can be changed. Chapter 10 explains this form security setting in more detail.

---

To try this technique, open an appointment form in design mode and add a label control to the P.2 page. Set the label's caption to "Item is locked." Rename that page to Locked. Hide all the Appointment and Scheduling pages. Finally, add the code in Listing 12.3 to the form. To test the form, create a new calendar folder in the Public Folders hierarchy and publish the form to that folder. On the Properties dialog for the folder, make the new published form the default and grant permission to a colleague to create and edit items in the folder. Now, get that colleague to help you create and edit items, each of you working from your own machine.

Listing 12.3 uses the standard `BillingInformation` property to hold the "lock state" information. (You could also use a `UserProperty` or a hidden property created with the `PropertyAccessor` object that we'll see in the next chapter.) If the item is safe to edit, the `Item_Open` code shows the Scheduling and Appointment pages and hides the Locked page. It invokes the `ShowFormPage` and `HideFormPage` methods of the `Inspector` object for the current item, which is returned by `Item.GetInspector`. If another

**Listing 12.3**    *Lock an item against changes by another user*

```
Dim mblnIsOpen
Dim mblnIsClosing
Dim mblnIsUnlocking

Function Item_Open()
    Dim objInsp
    Dim strMsg
    If Item.BillingInformation <> "Locked" Then
        Set objInsp = Item.GetInspector
        objInsp.ShowFormPage "Appointment"
        objInsp.ShowFormPage "Scheduling"
        objInsp.HideFormPage "Locked"
        mblnIsOpen = True
        Item.BillingInformation = "Locked"
        Item.Save
    End If
    mblnIsClosing = False
    mblnIsUnlocking = False
End Function

Function Item_Write()
    Dim strMsg
    If Not mblnIsOpen Then
        Item_Write = False
        strMsg = "You cannot save changes to this item."
        MsgBox strMsg, , "Item Is Locked"
    End If
    If mblnIsClosing Then
        If Not mblnIsUnlocking Then
            mblnIsUnlocking = True
            Item.BillingInformation = ""
            Item.Save
            mblnIsUnLocking = False
        End If
        mblnIsOpen = False
        mblnIsClosing = False
    End If
End Function

Function Item_Close()
    mblnIsClosing = True
    If mblnIsOpen and Item.Saved Then
        mblnIsUnLocking = True
        Item.BillingInformation = ""
        Item.Save
        mblnIsOpen = False
    End If
End Function
```

user has the item open, the second user trying to open the item sees only the Locked page. The `Item_Close` and `Item_Write` procedures handle the unlocking of the item.

Listing 12.3 should look similar to Listing 12.2 in structure. It builds on the same technique as the earlier listing and blocks drag-and-drop and in-cell editing.

If you want the second user to be able to view but not edit data in the item, you have two choices, both of which would be implemented in the `Item_Open` event handler:

- Populate the Locked page (or other custom pages) with read-only controls for the fields you want the second user to be able to see. In the `Item_Open` event handler, hide those pages when a user opens the item and it is safe for editing.

- For customizable pages, such as the main page of the contact and post forms and any P.# pages, iterate all the controls on the page and set the `Locked` property of each control to `True` to make the control read-only. Refer back to Chapter 7 if you need a refresher on custom form control syntax.

Finally, note that this technique performs locking only for users working online against the Exchange server. Users configured for Cached Exchange mode can work offline with shared folders by default and, depending on the configuration, possibly also with certain public folders. They will probably see conflicts occasionally and should be shown how to resolve them by choosing which item to keep.

## 12.2 Responding to user input on forms

Chapter 8 discussed how to gather responses from users with the `Msg-Box()` and `InputBox()` functions. Each of these functions can gather only one response at a time. While they're quite direct and easy for the programmer to use, a series of prompts would discourage the user. In most cases, it's better to allow the user to interact with a form and provide information in whatever sequence the user prefers, with code behind the form responding to the user's interaction. In earlier chapters, we saw that VBA forms have no shortage of control events that fire when the user changes the value in a control or interacts in other ways with the form. Outlook custom forms are far more limited in the control events they support: You must build all your user-interaction code into three events—the `PropertyChange` and `CustomPropertyChange` events that fire when the value of a standard or custom property changes, and the `Click` event that fires for changes to some (but not all!) controls that are *not* bound to Outlook properties.

**Table 12.2**      *Events That Fire for User Interaction with Custom Forms*

| Bound/Unbound State of Control | Resulting Event Handler |
|---|---|
| Bound to a standard Outlook property | `Item_PropertyChange` |
| Bound to a custom property | `Item_CustomPropertyChange` |
| Not bound to any property | `control_Click` |

Whether a control is bound to an Outlook property determines what event will fire when the user interacts with that control. Table 12.2 lists the event handlers for the three available scenarios.

As we'll see a little later in this chapter, not all unbound controls fire a `Click` event. Three that definitely do not fire a `Click` event are an unbound text box, an unbound combo box with the style set to `Drop-DownCombo (0)`, and an unbound multi-select list box.

Another reason that it's important to be aware of whether a control is bound or unbound is that Outlook saves the value displayed in a control only for bound controls. The fact that the control is bound to an Outlook property tells Outlook where to save that data, in other words, what property to store it in.

Outlook does not automatically save data entered into unbound controls, nor does it save any information about changes that you might have made in the appearance of any controls. Any unbound control values or user interface changes are discarded when the form closes. It is possible, however, to write code in a form's `Item_Write` event handler to read such information from the control's properties and store it in Outlook custom properties, to be restored when the `Item_Open` event handler runs. We'll see how to do that in the last portion of this chapter.

The next few sections provide examples of user interaction code using the events in Table 12.1. What you won't see is any code to determine which control currently has the user's focus or what form page the user is currently viewing. Outlook provides no Item-level events for those scenarios, although Outlook 2007 does introduce a `PageChange` event for the `Inspector` object that you can use in VBA code.

**Tip:** Another way that the user interacts with an item is by adding attachments. In Listing 22.1, the `BeforeAttachmentAdd` event is used to permit a form to accept attachments only of a certain file type.

## 12.2.1   Using the PropertyChange and CustomPropertyChange events

When the value of an Outlook property changes, the `PropertyChange` or `CustomPropertyChange` event fires. It doesn't matter whether the user or programming code changed the property value.

Both the `PropertyChange` and `CustomPropertyChange` events pass the name of the changed property as their sole parameter. The script for any given form should contain only one `PropertyChange` event handler and only one `CustomPropertyChange` event handler. These two event handler procedures together handle <u>all</u> the changes to <u>all</u> property values. A useful way to get acquainted with them is to add this code to your form:

```
Sub Item_PropertyChange(ByVal Name)
    MsgBox Name, , "PropertyChange"
End Sub

Sub Item_CustomPropertyChange(ByVal Name)
    MsgBox Name, , "CustomPropertyChange"
End Sub
```

Try adding that code to a task form. Also add a few custom properties using the Field Chooser and drag them to a custom page. Click the Run This Form command to run the form, and enter data for both the built-in and custom properties. You should see a message box not only for the properties you change directly, but also for related properties. For example, if you use the dropdown Status list to change the value from Not Started to Completed, these properties will all change. Each change will fire a `PropertyChange` event:

```
ReminderSet
DateCompleted
PercentComplete
Complete
Status
```

Let's expand the code snippet above to show the values of the properties as they change:

```
Sub Item_PropertyChange(ByVal Name)
    On Error Resume Next
    val = CStr(Item.ItemProperties(Name))
    If Err <> 0 Then
        val = "Error: Could not get property value"
        Err.Clear
    End If
    MsgBox Name & ": " & val, , "PropertyChange"
End Sub

Sub Item_CustomPropertyChange(ByVal Name)
    val = CStr(Item.UserProperties(Name))
```

```
    If Err <> 0 Then
        val = "Error: Could not get property value"
        Err.Clear
    End If
    MsgBox Name & ": " & val, , "CustomPropertyChange"
End Sub
```

Replace the earlier code with the above enhanced version, and run the form again to create a new task and see what else you can discover about these two events. Several interesting things should become apparent:

- A `PropertyChange` event fires when a new item opens, because Outlook sets the value of the `ConversationIndex` property even before the user has a chance to interact with the item.

- A `PropertyChange` or `CustomPropertyChange` event fires only after the user moves out of the control displaying that property. The property value is not stored until the user moves the control focus or saves the item.

- The value that Outlook stores in one of its standard properties may not be the same as what the user sees on the screen. If you change the value in the Status dropdown to Completed, the code above shows that the value Outlook actually stores is 2. This corresponds to a value in the `OlTaskStatus` enumeration. Use the object browser in Outlook VBA to look up that enumeration and see the constants (and their literal values) that Outlook uses to store task status information.

- Some standard properties can't be accessed through the `Item.Item-Properties` collection, for example, any property involving recipients, such as the `StatusUpdateRecipients` and `StatusOnCompletion-Recipients` collections that are related to assigned tasks.

- Not all standard properties support the `PropertyChange` event. When you type in the large notes/message body on an Outlook form, you are changing the `Body` property. However, the code above won't pop up a message box after you make changes to the task body.

---

**Note:** You might be tempted to work around the `Body` property issue by creating a formula field to display the contents of the body property (listed as `[Notes]` or `[Message]` in the formula editor's field list, depending on what type of form it is). Sure you can do that, but it's not very useful, because a single change in the `Body` property may result in `CustomProper-tyChange` firing up to nine times!

---

An Outlook item can have dozens of properties, but for any given form project, probably only a few are significant and useful to watch with an event handler. As we learned in Chapter 8, there are two primary code constructions for testing the possible values of expressions—`If ... Then ...`

Else blocks and Select ... End Select blocks. To monitor changes in just one property, you can use an If ... Then ... Else block. This code nags the user for trying to plan a task more than three weeks in advance:

```
Sub Item_PropertyChange(ByVal Name)
    If Name = "DueDate" Then
        If DateDiff("w", Date, Item.DueDate) > 3 Then
            MsgBox "You shouldn't plan more than " & _
                        "3 weeks ahead", , "Long Range Task"
        End If
    End If
End Sub
```

Compare the procedure declarations for the PropertyChange event handlers that you've seen so far. All of them use the same declaration:

```
Sub Item_PropertyChange(ByVal Name)
```

Don't be tempted to change Name to DueDate because you're watching for changes in the DueDate property. The parameter passed by Property-Change and CustomPropertyChange is <u>always</u> the name of the property that changed. It's up to your code inside the procedure to look at the value of the Name parameter and determine whether it's a property that you're interested in. In other words, code for the PropertyChange and Custom-PropertyChange events generally requires three operations, in sequence:

1.    Find out what property changed by checking the value of the Name parameter passed by the procedure.

2.    Determine the value of the property that changed. (Refer back to Chapter 7 if you need a refresher on how to return the value of a standard or custom property.)

3.    Execute code based on the value you learned from Step 2.

To watch for value changes in more than one property, a Select Case ... End Select block is the best way to structure that code. This Prop-ertyChange event handler watches for changes in two standard task properties:

```
Sub Item_PropertyChange(ByVal Name)
    Select Case Name
        Case "DueDate"
            If DateDiff("w", Date, Item.DueDate) > 3 Then
                MsgBox "You shouldn't plan more than " & _
                        "3 weeks ahead", , "Long Range Task"
            End If
        Case "Complete"
            If Item.Complete = True Then
                MsgBox "Congratulations! " & _
                        "you finished this task!", , _
                        Item.Subject & ": Done!"
            End If
    End Select
End Sub
```

To handle three properties instead of two, you would simply add another `Case "`*`property name`*`"` block.

---

**Note:** As you compared the procedures in this section, did you notice that you can get the property value either with the `Item.`*`property_name`* syntax or with `Item.ItemProperties("`*`property name`*`").Item.`*`property_name`* is more efficient, and many people find it more readable.

---

An event handler for the `CustomPropertyChange` event can use the same `Select Case` structure. Use the `Item.UserProperties("`*`property_name`*`")` syntax to return the value of any custom property:

```
Sub Item_CustomPropertyChange(ByVal Name)
    Select Case Name
        Case "Prop1"
            If Item.UserProperties("Prop1") = value1 Then
                ' perform some action regarding Prop1
            Else
                ' perform some other action
            End If
        Case "Prop2"
            If Item.UserProperties("Prop2") = value2 Then
                ' perform some action regarding Prop2
            Else
                ' perform some other action
            End If
        Case "Prop3"
            If Item.UserProperties("Prop3") = value3 Then
                ' perform some action regarding Prop3
            Else
                ' perform some other action
            End If
    End Select
End Sub
```

This structure should help you see the relationship between the `Name` value in each `Case` statement and the code inside the `Case` block to process the change in that property's value. Obviously, you will have scenarios where you have more or fewer than three properties to process, and you won't always need an `If ... Else ... End If` block to check property values.

You may want to ignore any `PropertyChange` or `CustomProperty-Change` events that occur while your form is loading, since Outlook itself may set some properties at that time or your own code may be setting property values. The solution is to set the value of a module-level Boolean variable (`mblnIsLoaded`) in the `Item_Open` event handler and check that variable's value in the property event handler(s). In this example, you won't see a message box when the code in the `Item_Open` event sets the `Billing-Information` property value:

```
Dim mblnIsLoading

Function Item_Open()
    mblnIsLoading = True
    ' your code to initialize form controls
    ' and item properties goes here
    Item.BillingInformation = _
      "Item last opened at " & Now
    Item.Save
    mblnIsLoading = False
End Function

Sub Item_PropertyChange(ByVal Name)
    If Not mblnIsLoading Then
        MsgBox Name, , "PropertyChange"
    End If
End Sub

Sub Item_CustomPropertyChange(ByVal Name)
    If Not mblnIsLoading Then
        MsgBox Name, , "CustomPropertyChange"
    End If
End Sub
```

We'll return to these events a little later in this chapter to examine an important practical application: performing validation on the user's data entry.

## 12.2.2   Handling Click events from unbound controls

As discussed in Chapter 7, Outlook uses a more complicated syntax to return a control and its value and other properties than VBA does. Specifically, you can access only controls on customized pages, and you need to know which page of the form the control resides on. Another peculiarity of Outlook forms, compared with VBA user forms, is that the only event supported by controls on an Outlook custom form is the Click event. For example, you can use Click to track when a user selects a new value from an unbound combo box (cboCompanies) set up as a dropdown list:

```
Sub cboCompanies_Click()
    Set objPage = _
      Item.GetInspector.ModifiedFormPages("My Page")
    Set cboCompanies = objPage.Controls("cboCompanies")
    MsgBox "The value in the " & cboCompanies.Name & _
      " control has changed to " & cboCompanies.Value & "."
End Sub
```

However, not all unbound controls support the Click event. The Click event fires on a dropdown list combo box (the default for a combo box), but not if the user types a value into a combo box with the Style property set to DropDownCombo (0). It fires for unbound label, check box, option button, and command button controls, but not for text box or spin button controls. For list boxes, an unbound list must be single-select, not

**Listing 12.4**    *Click event for a check box to show or hide a frame control*

```
Sub chkNeedCheck_Click()
    Set objPage = _
      Item.GetInspector.ModifiedFormPages("General")
    objPage.Controls("fraCheckData").Visible = _
      objPage.Controls("chkNeedCheck").Value
End Sub
```

multi-select, and the user must click on a list item, not in a blank area in the list box, in order for the `Click` event to fire.

A common application of the `Click` event is to use a combo box, list box, check box, or option buttons to change the appearance of another control. For example, you might want to change the items displayed in a list box or combo box or display a group of controls that were previously hidden. In Listing 12.4, for example, `chkNeedCheck` is an unbound check box and `fraCheckData` is a frame control on the General page containing bound controls where the user can enter additional information.

Clicking on the `chkNeedCheck` check box toggles the value of the `Visible` property of the frame, so that the frame and its controls are visible when the check box is checked and hidden when it is unchecked. Using a frame control is the most efficient way to show and hide a group of controls.

Besides the `Click` event, you can use the `Item`-level `Write`, `Close` or `Send` events to process information in unbound controls, returning the `Value` property from each control of interest. Note, however, that if the user changes only the data in an unbound control—and never changes any data in a bound control—the `Write` event will not fire, even if the user clicks Save. Also remember that Outlook saves no data from unbound controls, nor does it keep a record of changes to any control properties, such as the value of the `Visible` property for a frame. Any such control changes are considered user interface (UI) changes and are discarded when the item closes. Later in this chapter, we'll see how to store that UI information so that you can restore a form's UI to the state that it was in when the user closed the item.

## 12.2.3    Example: Using option buttons to change a caption color

Consider a form with a custom page named `Color` and three option buttons inside a frame named `fraColor`. These buttons will demonstrate how to change the color of the caption for the frame based on the user's selection. The `Caption` and `Tag` properties of each button reflect the color. One holds the name of the color, while the other holds the literal value of the vbRed, vbBlack, or vbBlue constant:

- Option button 1:

  | Name | optColor1 |
  |------|-----------|
  | Caption | Red |
  | Tag | 255 |

- Option button 2:

  | Name | optColor2 |
  |------|-----------|
  | Caption | Black |
  | Tag | 0 |

- Option button 3:

  | Name | optColor3 |
  |------|-----------|
  | Caption | Blue |
  | Tag | 16711680 |

To set the Tag property for each control, use the Advanced Properties dialog.

**Listing 12.5**   *Use option buttons to change the appearance of another control*

```
Dim m_objControls

Function Item_Open()
    Dim objPage
    Set objPage = _
      Item.GetInspector.ModifiedFormPages("Color")
    Set m_objControls = objPage.Controls
    Set objPage = Nothing
End Function

Function Item_Close()
    Set m_objControls = Nothing
End Function

Sub optColor1_Click()
    m_objControls("fraColor").ForeColor = _
      m_objControls("optColor1").Tag
End Sub

Sub optColor2_Click()
    m_objControls("fraColor").ForeColor = _
      m_objControls("optColor2").Tag
End Sub

Sub optColor3_Click()
    m_objControls("fraColor").ForeColor = _
      m_objControls("optColor3").Tag
End Sub
```

In Listing 12.5, each option button has its own `Click` event handler to change the color of the frame caption to the value in the `Tag` property of the clicked button. The `Open` and `Close` event handlers set and dereference a module-level variable, `m_objControls`, to make it easy to work with the Color page's `Controls` collection in the `Click` event handlers.

When the user selects one of the option buttons, the frame's caption changes to the matching color.

## 12.2.4   Example: Creating a hyperlink on an Outlook form

A very practical use for the `Click` event is to create a control that launches a Web page in a browser. While the `ContactItem` object has several properties with built-in hyperlink capability (`BusinessHomePage`, `FTPSite`, `PersonalHomePage`, `WebPage`), other Outlook items do not have properties with hyperlink functionality. A good workaround is to put the text for a hyperlink in the `Caption` property of a label control and use code like that in Listing 12.6 to launch the link in Internet Explorer when the user clicks the label named `lblWebPage`.

You may want to format the label control to show the link as blue and underlined, using the `Font` and `Forecolor` properties on the Advanced Properties dialog

Since Outlook has Web browser capability, you can also use the code in Listing 12.7 to display a Web page using Outlook's built-in browser capability.

We will see more examples of using `CommandBars` techniques to execute toolbar and menu commands in Chapter 23.

## 12.2.5   Performing validation in Outlook form code

Validation is an important concept in form design. As much as possible, you should provide feedback when the user enters inappropriate data values. Chapter 6 covered how to associate validation formulas with fields displayed in bound controls. When your validation needs grow beyond a

---

**Listing 12.6**    *Click event for a label control to launch a Web page in Internet Explorer*

```
Sub lblWebPage_Click()
    Set objPage = _
      Item.GetInspector.ModifiedFormPages("General")
    Set objWeb = _
      CreateObject("InternetExplorer.Application")
    objWeb.Navigate objPage.Controls("lblWebPage").Caption
    objWeb.Visible = True
End Sub
```

**Listing 12.7** *Click Event for a label control to launch a Web page in Outlook*

```
Sub lblWebPage_Click()
    Set objPage = _
      Item.GetInspector.ModifiedFormPages("General")
    Set objCB = Application.ActiveExplorer.CommandBars
    set objWebButton = objCB.FindControl(26, 1740)
    objWebButton.Text = _
      objPage.Controls("lblWebPage").Caption
End Sub
```

simple formula, it's time to consider performing validation in the VBScript code behind the form.

An event handler for `PropertyChange` or `CustomPropertyChange` provides one way to validate data entry on an Outlook form, because those events fire immediately after the user makes a change to a property. Another validation method is to include code in the `Item_Write` or `Item_Send` event handler to check property values and use the statement `Item_Write = False` or `Item_Send = False` to cancel the write or send operation and allow the user to correct the data entry error.

Which event is best depends on two factors—whether you want the user to get immediate feedback and whether valid property values are interdependent. If you can't know if the value for `PropertyA` is valid until the user fills in the value for `PropertyB`, then you should put validation code in the `Item_Send` event handler for messages and in `Item_Write` for other forms. If all property values are independent, `Item_CustomPropertyChange` and `Item_PropertyChange` should work well to provide immediate feedback, but you will still need code in `Item_Write` or `Item_Send`. Remember that the `PropertyChange` and `CustomPropertyChange` events fire only after the user presses Tab or Enter or otherwise moves the focus to another control. If the user changes the value of a property and then immediately saves the item without moving the focus, the `PropertyChange` or `CustomPropertyChange` event does not fire. Therefore, if you are using those events to perform validation, you should also run that same validation code from the `Item_Write` or `Item_Send` event handler.

If the property whose value doesn't pass validation appears on a customized form page, you can use the `SetFocus` method to direct the user's attention to the control that needs action. Changing the control's text or the background color (or both) is also a good attention-getter. Listing 12.8 reminds the user to fill in the `Job Title` field on a customized General page for a contact form.

You can use `SetFocus` to set the focus only to a control on the customized form page that is currently displayed. Use the `Inspector.SetCurrentFormPage` method to show the desired page.

**Listing 12.8**    *Write an event handler to remind the user to fill in a property value*

```
Function Item_Write()
    If Item.CompanyName <> "" Then
        If Item.JobTitle = "" Then
            Item_Write = False
            strMsg = "If you fill in the Company, " & _
                     "you need to fill in Job Title, too."
            MsgBox strMsg, vbExclamation, "Missing Job Title"
            Set objPage = _
              Item.GetInspector.ModifiedFormPages("General")
            Set objJobTitle = objPage.Controls("JobTitle")
            Item.GetInspector.SetCurrentFormPage "General"
            With objJobTitle
                .SetFocus
                .BackColor = vbYellow
            End With
        End If
    End If
End Function
```

### 12.2.6   Example: A custom contact form with required categories

Outlook allows users to build a personal list of frequently used categories, which Outlook 2007 stores as a hidden item in the user's Calendar folder. (Earlier Outlook versions store the user's master category list in the Windows registry.) In a public folder on an Exchange server, a common form requirement is to make the user categorize each item from a limited set of category choices. One solution is to write validation code for the form to block the item from being saved until the user chooses one of the required categories.

This example uses a contact form with one custom page, named Categories, shown in Figure 12.1. It contains an unbound label control (lbl-Categories) and a list box (lstCategories) bound to the Categories property. The third control comes from the Field Chooser. From the All Contact Fields list, drag the field named Categories ... to the Categories page. Outlook will create a button that launches the Categories dialog. We've edited the caption of the button so that it reads "More Categories ...".

The code behind this form, shown in Listing 12.9, wraps up many of the concepts in this chapter: It uses the Open event to initialize the appearance of two controls and applies validation using the Write event.

The HasRequiredCategory() function provides a good example of comparing the contents of two arrays: the user's category choice(s) and the list of required categories from the mstrRequiredCats variable. (Change

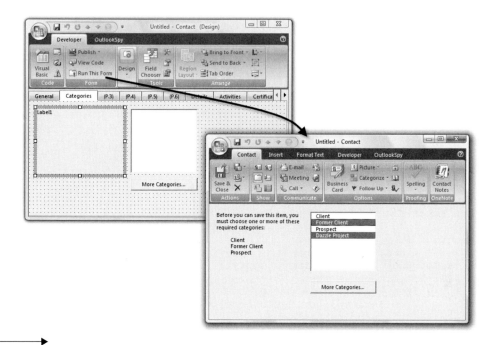

**Figure 12.1** *Using validation code, you can force users to select from a limited list of categories before saving an item.*

the value of this variable under ### USER OPTIONS ### to adapt it to your own scenario.) The code also uses the WSHListSep() function to return the list separator character for the current user's locale, a function we first saw in Chapter 8.

**Listing 12.9** *Force the user to select from a list of categories*

```
Option Explicit
Dim mstrRequiredCats
Dim lstCategories
Dim lblCategories

Function Item_Open()
    Dim objPage
    Dim arrRCats
    Dim strLabel
    Dim i
    ' ### USER OPTION ###
    ' list of categories in the order you want them to appear
    mstrRequiredCats = "Client;Former Client;Prospect"
    Set objPage = _
       Item.GetInspector.ModifiedFormPages("Categories")
    Set lstCategories = objPage.Controls("lstCategories")
    Set lblCategories = objPage.Controls("lblCategories")
```

**Listing 12.9**    *Force the user to select from a list of categories (continued)*

```
    strLabel = "Before you can save this item, you " & _
               "must choose one or more of these " & _
               "required categories:" & vbCrLf
    arrRCats = Split(mstrRequiredCats, ";")
    lstCategories.List = arrRCats
    For i = 0 To UBound(arrRCats)
        strLabel = strLabel & _
                    vbCrLf & Space(10) & Trim(arrRCats(i))
    Next
    lblCategories.Caption = strLabel
    mstrRequiredCats = UCase(mstrRequiredCats)
    Set objPage = Nothing
End Function

Function Item_Write()
    Dim blnGotCat
    blnGotCat = HasRequiredCategory()
    If Not blnGotCat Then
        Item_Write = False
        Item.GetInspector.SetCurrentFormPage "Categories"
        lstCategories.SetFocus
        lblCategories.ForeColor = vbRed
    End If
End Function

Function HasRequiredCategory()
    Dim arrCats
    Dim arrRCats
    Dim strListSep
    Dim blnMatch
    Dim i, j
    blnMatch = False
    strListSep = WSHListSep()
    If mstrRequiredCats <> "" Then
        arrCats = Split(UCase(Item.Categories), strListSep)
        arrRCats = Split(mstrRequiredCats, ";")
        For i = 0 To UBound(arrCats)
            For j = 0 To UBound(arrRCats)
                If Trim(arrCats(i)) = _
                   Trim(arrRCats(j)) Then
                    blnMatch = True
                    Exit For
                End If
            Next
            If blnMatch = True Then
                Exit For
            End If
        Next
    Else
        blnMatch = True
    End If
    HasRequiredCategory = blnMatch
End Function
```

**Listing 12.9** *Force the user to select from a list of categories (continued)*

```
Function WSHListSep()
    Dim objWSHShell
    Dim strReg
    strReg = "HKCU\Control Panel\International\sList"
    Set objWSHShell = CreateObject("WScript.Shell")
    WSHListSep = objWSHShell.RegRead(strReg)
    Set objWSHShell = Nothing
End Function
```

## 12.3 Handling form and control state issues

Two examples from the first part of this chapter introduced a key programming concept with some specific applications to Outlook form programming—the concept of *state*. In Listing 12.2, you saw how information on the "open" state of an item could be held in the blnIsOpen variable. Listing 12.3 also used an blnIsOpen variable to track not only whether an item was open, but also its "locked" state. In addition, it used the Billing-Information property to store information about an item's "locked" state that other users could read.

The concept of state has many different applications in Outlook custom form coding. These are common examples:

- Whether an item is a new message, a reply, or a forward
- Where the item is in the stages of a workflow
- Whether an item shows the compose or read layout of a custom form
- Whether the user has completed data entry for an item

The last example is one we've already seen in this chapter—*validation*, the process of making sure data entry is complete and accurate. This section covers other key issues related to item state in form programming, including what state information is available from standard properties and how to store custom state information in an item.

### 12.3.1 Checking item state in the Open event

A lot of information about the state of an item is available from standard Outlook properties. You can determine whether an item is displaying the compose or read layout of a custom form (assuming the form has dual layouts) and whether a message is a new item, a reply, a forward, or a received message.

A new unsaved item has a blank EntryID property and a Size property value of 0. Thus, you can use code like this to perform actions on new items that you don't need to perform on existing items:

```
Function Item_Open
    If Item.Size = 0 Then
        ' run code for a new item
    End If
End Function
```

Some of your forms may have separate compose and read layouts, but not all saved items will show the read layout. Specifically, an unsent message will continue to show the read layout. Thus, `Size = 0` is not sufficient to determine whether the compose or read layout is showing. In the case of messages, you also need to check the `Sent` property, which is a Boolean value. Listing 12.10 implements this technique with a reusable `ShowsComposeLayout()` function and shows how to call it from the `Item_Open` event handler.

It takes a bit more effort to determine whether a message is a new message, reply, forward, or received message. `Size` matters, again, as does `Sent`. A reply or forward has a non-blank `ConversationIndex`, but a reply always has at least one recipient. Received messages can be distinguished from sent messages by the `ReceivedByName` property representing the name of the recipient. Using all these properties, the `GetMessageState()` function in Listing 12.11 returns a string to the calling procedure to indicate what state the message is in.

For example, this code gives the user a reminder about this being a draft:

```
Function Item_Open()
    If GetMessageState(Item) = "DRAFT" Then
        MsgBox "Don't forget to send this draft!"
    End If
End Function
```

You should call `GetMessageState()` only from the `Item_Open` event handler, because some of the properties that the function checks might change while the user is working on the item.

For maximum reuse, the `GetMessageState()` is written with a single parameter representing the message whose state you want to check. You can use this procedure in VBA as well as in VBScript. In VBA, comment out the `Const` statement.

## 12.3.2   Storing and restoring control state

One of the most troublesome concepts for new Outlook form developers is that, if your code changes the look of an Outlook form based on the user's interaction with it, those user interface (UI) changes don't save with the item. Outlook saves only the values entered into its standard and custom properties. Put those two ideas together: If Outlook saves only property values, the solution to saving the UI changes is to store information about them in some property value.

**Listing 12.10**   *Determine whether a form shows the compose or read layout*

```
Function Item_Open
    If ShowsComposeLayout() Then
        ' run code to update the look of the
        ' compose layout
    Else
        ' run code to update the look of the
        ' read layout
    End If
End Function

Function ShowsComposeLayout()
    Const olMail = 43
    If Item.Class = olMail Then
        If Not Item.Sent Then
            ShowsComposeLayout = True
        End If
    ElseIf Item.Size = 0 Then
        ShowsComposeLayout = True
    Else
        ShowsComposeLayout = False
    End If
End Function
```

**Listing 12.11**   *Return the state of a message—new, reply, forward, or received*

```
Function GetMessageState(msg)     ' As String
    Const olMail = 43             ' remove for use in VBA
    On Error Resume Next
    If msg.Class = olMail Then
        If msg.Size = 0 Then
            If msg.ConversationIndex = "" Then
                GetMessageState = "NEW"
            ElseIf msg.Recipients.Count > 0 Then
                GetMessageState = "REPLY"
            Else
                GetMessageState = "FORWARD"
            End If
        ElseIf msg.Sent = False Then
            GetMessageState = "DRAFT"
        Else
            If msg.ReceivedByName = "" Then
                GetMessageState = "SENT"
            Else
                GetMessageState = "RECEIVED"
            End If
        End If
    Else
        GetMessageState = "NOT MAIL"
    End If
    Set objPA = Nothing
End Function
```

As an example, look back at Listing 12.4, which toggled the `Visible` property of a frame control based on data in a check box. What if you want the frame to be visible or hidden depending on the state it had when the item was saved or sent? In that case, you must save sufficient information to restore that state when the user opens the item again. Specifically, you can save the value of the frame's `Visible` property in a custom property and then read that value when the user opens the item to reset the frame's appearance.

One approach would be to bind the check box to a new custom yes/no property. That way, the state of both the check box and the frame are automatically stored. That approach would require a change to the form's code. Instead of toggling the frame's `Visible` property in the check box control's `Click` event handler, you would need to toggle `Visible` in the `Item_CustomPropertyChange` event handler and also in the `Item_Open` event handler.

If you want to keep the check box unbound so you can keep its `Click` event handler, then you need to add a new property to the form to store the check box and frame state. Use the form's Field Chooser to add a yes/no property named `CheckDataState`, and drag that property from the Field Chooser to the General page where the check box resides. (That ensures that the property is defined in the form, not just in the folder.) You can then delete the control for `CheckDataState` property from the General page. Listing 12.12 shows the code to set the value of `CheckDataState`. It also includes an `Item_Open` event handler to read the property value and reset the check box and frame states.

**Listing 12.12**  *Saving and restoring the state of an unbound control*

```
Sub chkNeedCheck_Click()
    On Error Resume Next
    Set objPage = _
       Item.GetInspector.ModifiedFormPages("General")
    objPage.Controls("fraCheckData").Visible = _
       objPage.Controls("chkNeedCheck").Value
    Set objProp = Item.UserProperties("CheckDataState")
    objProp.Value = objPage.Controls("chkNeedCheck").Value
End Sub

Function Item_Open()
    On Error Resume Next
    If Item.Size > 0 Then
        Set objPage = _
           Item.GetInspector.ModifiedFormPages("General")
        objPage.Controls("chkNeedCheck").Value = _
           Item.UserProperties("CheckDataState")
    End If
End Function
```

Notice that the `Item_Open` event handler doesn't need to set the frame's `Visible` property directly. All it has to do is set the check box's `Value`. The `Click` event for the check box fires when you set its value in code, not just when the user clicks in the check box.

In the case of a form that uses a separate read layout where the frame is visible but not the check box, you would not set the check box's value, but instead would need to read the saved value and set the frame's `Visible` property:

```
objPage.Controls("fraCheckData").Value = _
    Item.UserProperties("CheckDataState")
```

### 12.3.3   Handling state in a folder-based workflow

The last concept of state that we need to cover is related to *workflow*, the process of performing multiple operations in sequence. In some workflows, such as the steps needed to take a real estate listing to closing, one person might perform and track all the steps. In other cases, different people might be involved. For example, a vacation request might need approval by the employee's immediate manager and also by a department head before it can be entered on a master calendar of all the department's vacation weeks. Such a request might have five different states:

1.   In the process of composition

2.   Pending manager approval

3.   Pending department head approval

4.   Pending entry on master calendar

5.   Processing complete

Of course, if the manager or department head denies the vacation request, the item will never reach the later states.

To manage a workflow, a custom Outlook form requires three key components:

- A property to store the current state of the workflow item
- Code to change the state property (and thus move the item to the next phase of the workflow) when the user takes an action
- Code to alter the appearance of the item so that the user can easily see the current state of the workflow item and the appropriate action(s)

To illustrate these components, let's look at a generic workflow technique. A workflow form with its basic set of controls is shown in Figure 12.2. This particular form is a post form, but you could use the same technique on an appointment, contact, or task form. In the Design group, clear the check box for Separate Read Layout. Also, use the Page | Rename Page command to change the name of the page from Message to Workflow.

**Figure 12.2**
*Basic controls for managing folder-based workflow.*

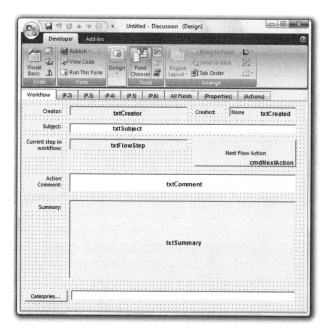

The form needs the controls described in Table 12.3, five of which are bound to user-defined properties that you need to create in the form's Field Chooser.

As Figure 12.2 shows, the form also contains the standard controls for the Subject and Categories properties. You can add other controls and properties to meet the requirements of your application.

The controls and properties in Table 12.2 are those essential to managing the workflow, but three of the properties in Table 12.2 are not displayed on the form. Create the FlowState, WorkflowActions and WorkFlow-Steps using the Field Chooser, and then drag them to a separate custom page. That will ensure that these fields are defined in the form. You can then hide that page.

After you create the form, publish it to the folder that will hold the workflow items and on the folder's Properties dialog, make it the default form for that folder.

The values for WorkflowActions and WorkflowSteps control how many steps the workflow contains and the names of the steps and actions that the user will see in the controls on the form. The number of actions must equal the number of steps. You can set the value of these properties in several different ways:

- By typing them into the All Fields page before publishing the form
- By adding code to the form's Item_Open event handler

- By creating a new workflow item programmatically and then setting the property values

As an example of the latter method, this code snippet assumes that you have already returned an `objFolder` object representing the workflow items folder and that the `MessageClass` for the published form is IPM.Post.MyWorkflow form:

```
Set objItem = objFolder.Items.Add("IPM.Post.MyWorkflow")
objItem.Subject = "Workflow to start a new day"
objItem.UserProperties("WorkflowSteps") = _
  "Settling in,Checking to-do list,Reading email"
objItem.UserProperties("WorkflowActions") = _
  "Start Outlook,Confirm to-do list checked," & _
  "Confirm email read"
objItem.Display
```

**Table 12.3**   *Controls and Properties to Manage Workflow*

| Control Name | Bound to Property (* = custom) | Property Data Type | Description |
|---|---|---|---|
| txtCreator | Creator (*) | Text | Name of the person who created the workflow item |
| txtCreated | Created | Date/time | Date/time that the workflow was created |
| | FlowState (*) | Integer | Stage of the workflow, starting with 0 for a newly created workflow item |
| txtSummary | Summary (*) | Text | Running summary of action steps completed in the workflow, with comments; turn on the multi-line option for the control |
| | WorkflowActions (*) | Text | Comma-delimited text of actions to be taken; used to set the caption on the cmdNextAction command button |
| | WorkflowSteps (*) | Text | Comma-delimited list of workflow steps; used to set the text in the txtFlowStep control |
| txtFlowStep | Unbound | | Name of the current step in the workflow, derived from the FlowState and WorkflowSteps properties |
| txtComment | Unbound | | Comment related to the current workflow step |
| cmdNextAction | n/a | | Command button to execute the action appropriate to the current workflow step; Caption property value derived from the FlowState and WorkflowActions properties |

---

**Note:** We'll see many different techniques for returning an object variable for a folder in the next chapter.

---

As you can see in Figure 12.2, only the `cmdNextAction` button and the controls for entering the Subject, Action Comment, and Categories are enabled. To keep workflow item information in the folder where the items are posted, on the (Actions) page of the form, you should bring up the Properties for each of the three standard actions and disable each one.

The code for the form is shown in Listing 12.13. When the user creates a new workflow item or opens an existing item, the code in the `Item_Open` event handler reads the information from the `WorkflowSteps` and `WorkflowAction` properties into arrays using the `Split()` function and then uses the value of the `FlowState` property to look up the current step and next action from those arrays, putting the text for the current step in the controls. When the user clicks the `cmdNextAction` button, the code updates the `Summary` property with information about the completed action, including any comment in the `txtComment` box, and saves the item. Finally, the code disables the controls that were previously enabled. The user will need to close and open the item again to complete another step in the workflow. (Another way to handle the workflow would be to leave the controls enabled and call `InitControls` again to update the display values to reflect the new workflow state.)

---

**Tip:** Did you notice that the `Item_Open` and `cmdNextAction_Click` procedures both use `Application.Session.CurrentUser` to return the name of the current Outlook user?

---

You probably noticed that this example doesn't actually do much besides track the current state of the workflow item and record when the user completes the action associated with that state. To provide additional functionality, such as sending notification messages or creating other new Outlook items, create a procedure for each action related to each state and call those procedures from a `Select Case` block inside the `cmdNextAction_Click` event handler. Such a block might look like this:

```
Select Case intState
    Case 0
        Call ProcedureForState0
    Case 1
        Call ProcedureForState1
    Case 2
        Call ProcedureForState2
End Select
```

**Listing 12.13**  *Code for generic folder-based workflow manager*

```
Dim intState
Dim arrSteps
Dim arrActions
Dim objPage
Dim cmdNextAction
Dim txtFlowStep
Dim txtComment

Function Item_Open()
    If Item.Size = 0 Then
        Item.UserProperties("FlowState") = 0
        Item.UserProperties("Creator") = _
          Application.Session.CurrentUser
    End If
    Call InitControls
End Function

Function Item_Close()
    Set objPage = Nothing
    Set cmdNextAction = Nothing
    Set txtFlowStep = Nothing
    Set txtComment = Nothing
End Function

Sub InitControls()
    Dim objInsp
    Dim arrActions
    intState = Item.UserProperties("FlowState")
    arrSteps = Split(Item.UserProperties("WorkflowSteps"), ",")
    arrActions = _
      Split(Item.UserProperties("WorkflowActions"), ",")
    Set objInsp = Item.GetInspector
    Set objPage = objInsp.ModifiedFormPages("Workflow")
    Set cmdNextAction = objPage.Controls("cmdNextAction")
    Set txtFlowStep = objPage.Controls("txtFlowStep")
    Set txtComment = objPage.Controls("txtComment")
    If UBound(arrSteps) > 0 Then
        If intState <= UBound(arrSteps) Then
            cmdNextAction.Caption = arrActions(intState)
            txtFlowStep.Value = arrSteps(intState)
            If intState > 0 Then
                Set txtSubject = objPage.Controls("txtSubject")
                txtSubject.Enabled = False
            End If
        Else
            cmdNextAction.Caption = "Workflow Already Complete"
            cmdNextAction.Enabled = False
            txtComment.Enabled = False
            txtFlowStep.Text = "WORKFLOW COMPLETE"
        End If
```

**Listing 12.13**   *Code for generic folder-based workflow manager (continued)*

```
    Else
        cmdNextAction.Caption = "No Workflow Steps Defined"
        cmdNextAction.Enabled = False
        txtComment.Enabled = False
        txtFlowStep.Text = "None"
    End If
    Set objInsp = Nothing
End Sub

Sub cmdNextAction_Click()
    Dim strAction
    strAction = cmdNextAction.Caption & " - Completed " & _
                Now & " by " & _
                Application.Session.CurrentUser & vbCrLf & _
                txtComment.Value & vbCrLf & vbCrLf
    Item.UserProperties("Summary") = strAction & _
      Item.UserProperties("Summary")
    Item.UserProperties("FlowState") = intState + 1
    If intState = 0 Then
        Set txtSubject = objPage.Controls("txtSubject")
        txtSubject.Enabled = False
    ElseIf intState >= UBound(arrSteps) Then
        Item.UserProperties("Summary") = _
          "*** WORKFLOW COMPLETE ***" & vbCrLf & vbCrLf & _
          Item.UserProperties("Summary")
    End If
    Item.Save
    cmdNextAction.Enabled = False
    txtComment.Enabled = False
    txtFlowStep.Value = txtFlowStep.Value & " - DONE !"
End Sub
```

This `Select Case` block handles three distinct workflow states. If you needed to handle more, you would simply add another `Case` block and one or more additional procedures to be called from that `Case` block.

## 12.4   Summary

This chapter has demonstrated many techniques for dealing with common Outlook custom form scenarios—initializing controls, preventing users from editing items in a folder view, responding to user interaction, validating user input, persisting unbound control values, and managing state in a workflow. Whenever you design a new custom form, you may want to look back in this chapter to see which of these basic procedures might be appropriate to your form.

In the next few chapters, we will learn the most essential techniques for working with Outlook folders, items, address lists, and attachments—techniques that you will certainly use to write code behind Outlook forms.

# 13

# *Working with Stores, Explorers, and Folders*

Beginning in this chapter, you'll have the opportunity to learn about the Outlook objects that programmers use most often and see the most important basic how-to techniques. This chapter is devoted to techniques for working with Outlook information stores and folders—creating them, exploring their properties, and accessing folders, regardless of where they appear in the folder hierarchy. It also looks at the `Explorer` object that represents a window which displays a folder.

Highlights of this chapter include discussions of the following:

- Where Outlook stores information and which information stores users are likely to see
- How to access the default information store
- When you might want to use a new `Explorer` object to display a different folder
- How to access a folder, regardless of where it is located in the folder hierarchy
- How to create, copy, move, and delete folders
- How to share an Exchange mailbox folder
- How to subscribe to an RSS feed, WebCal calendar, or SharePoint list

## 13.1  Information store concepts

Outlook stores messages and other items in folders. Each folder resides in what is known as an *information store*. Every Outlook session has at least one information store. Not all users see the same types of stores, however. Some may work only with an Exchange Server mailbox and public folders, while others use a mixture of Personal Folders files, IMAP folders, and folders for HTTP mail services like Office Live.

**Note:** The only HTTP accounts that are compatible with Outlook 2007 are paid MSN and Office Live accounts. Free Hotmail and Office Live accounts cannot be added to an Outlook 2007 mail profile.

If the user has multiple information stores, one will be designated as the default. Within the default store, you can always find the default Outlook folders, such as Inbox and Calendar. The Outlook object model provides the `Namespace.GetDefaultFolder` method to access these folders; we've already seen it at work in several code samples in earlier chapters.

For a user connected to Microsoft Exchange Server, the basic store is the Exchange mailbox. For other users, the basic store is a Personal Folders .pst file. (PST stands for *personal store*.) An Exchange user may also have one or more .pst files. For users with IMAP accounts or SharePoint lists, Outlook synchronizes the server data with local .pst files, but those .pst files cannot act as the user's primary information store. Users with HTTP accounts may have a synchronized .pst file, as with an IMAP account, or can use the Microsoft Office Outlook Connector to create an information store (using an .ost file) that can hold appointments, contacts, and tasks, as well as e-mail messages. An Outlook Connector .ost file can act as a default information store. In addition, third-party providers offer information store components that can display database tables as Outlook folders or help Outlook connect to other mail servers.

Users with Exchange accounts may also have access to *public folders*, a hierarchy of folders for shared access. Exchange users may also be able to access other users' mailbox folders. For example, an executive assistant may have access to the boss' folders.

**Caution:** When writing code for Exchange folders other than those in the user's own mailbox, you must allow for the possibility that the user will not have full access to a folder. A user might be able to see a folder in the hierarchy, but might not be able to work with the items within the folder because of permission restrictions.

Regardless of whether the default store is an Exchange mailbox, a Personal Folders .pst file, or a Microsoft Office Outlook Connector store, any user may have several .pst files open in Outlook. For instance, I have a .pst file holding materials related to this book, as well as several .pst files filled with archived items.

## 13.2 **Information store techniques**

In the Outlook object model, all work involving stores—including adding and removing a .pst file from the current Outlook session—takes place through the `Namespace` object, which has a `DefaultStore` object and a `Stores` collection containing individual `Store` objects. The code in Listing 13.1 enumerates all the available stores in the current Outlook session and lists them in the VBA Immediate window. It uses five important new properties— `Store.ExchangeStoreType`, `Store.IsDataFileStore`, `Store.FilePath`, `Namespace.DefaultStore`, and `Folder.IsSharePointFolder`—to distinguish among the different types of stores and to return the file path for most (but not all) .pst files. Where `Store.FilePath` does not return a string, the `EnumStores` procedure attempts to extract the file path from the `Store.StoreID` property, along with the name of the provider .dll that Outlook uses for that store. To do this, Listing 13.1 contains the helper functions `Hex4ToString()` and `Hex2ToString()`, which convert the hexadecimal values from the `StoreID` into readable text.

**Listing 13.1**   *Enumerate all stores in the current Outlook session*

```
Sub EnumStores()
    Dim objOL as Outlook.Application
    Dim objStore As Outlook.Store
    Dim strInfo As String
    Dim strPath As String
    Set objOL = Application
    For Each objStore In objOL.Session.Stores
        Select Case objStore.ExchangeStoreType
            Case olPrimaryExchangeMailbox
                strInfo = vbTab & "Primary Exchange mailbox"
            Case olExchangeMailbox
                strInfo = vbTab & "Secondary Exchange mailbox"
            Case olExchangePublicFolder
                strInfo = vbTab & "Exchange Public Folders"
            Case olNotExchange
                If objStore.IsDataFileStore Then
                    If objStore.DisplayName = _
                      "SharePoint Folders" Then
                        If IsSPStore(objStore) Then
                            strInfo = vbTab & _
                              "SharePoint cache" & vbCrLf & _
                              vbTab & objStore.FilePath
                        Else
                            strInfo = vbTab & "PST File" & _
                              vbCrLf & vbTab & objStore.FilePath
                        End If
```

**Listing 13.1**    *Enumerate all stores in the current Outlook session (continued)*

```vb
                Else
                    strInfo = vbTab & "PST File" & _
                        vbCrLf & vbTab & objStore.FilePath
                End If
            Else
                strInfo = _
                    GetStoreProvider(objStore.StoreID)
                Select Case strInfo
                    Case "pstprx.dll"
                        strPath = GetStorePath( _
                            objStore.StoreID, "pstprx.dll")
                        strInfo = vbTab & _
                            "HTTP or IMAP account cache" & _
                            vbCrLf & vbTab & strPath
                    Case "msncon.dll"
                        strPath = GetStorePath( _
                            objStore.StoreID, "msncon.dll")
                        strInfo = vbTab & _
                            "Outlook Connector cache" & _
                            vbCrLf & vbTab & strPath
                    Case Else
                        strInfo = vbTab & strInfo & _
                            " - Unknown provider type"
                End Select
            End If
        End Select
        If objStore = objOL.Session.DefaultStore Then
            Debug.Print objStore.DisplayName & " - *** DEFAULT STORE ***"
        Else
            Debug.Print objStore.DisplayName
        End If
        Debug.Print strInfo
    Next
    Set objOL = Nothing
    Set objStore = Nothing
End Sub

Function GetStoreProvider(strStoreID As String)
    Dim intStart As Integer
    Dim intEnd As Integer
    Dim strProviderRaw As String
    intStart = InStr(9, strStoreID, "0000") + 4
    intEnd = InStr(intStart, strStoreID, "00")
    strProviderRaw = _
        Mid(strStoreID, intStart, intEnd - intStart)
    GetStoreProvider = Hex2ToString(strProviderRaw)
End Function

Function GetStorePath(strStoreID As String, strProvider)
    Dim intStart As Integer
    Dim intEnd As Integer
    Dim strPathRaw As String
```

Listing 13.1    *Enumerate all stores in the current Outlook session (continued)*

```
Select Case strProvider
    Case "pstprx.dll"
        intStart = InStrRev(strStoreID, "00000000") + 8
        strPathRaw = Mid(strStoreID, intStart)
        GetStorePath = Trim(Hex4ToString(strPathRaw))
    Case "msncon.dll"
        intStart = InStrRev(strStoreID, _
                            "00", Len(strStoreID) - 2) + 2
        strPathRaw = Mid(strStoreID, intStart)
        GetStorePath = Trim(Hex2ToString(strPathRaw))
    Case Else
        GetStorePath = "Unknown store path"
    End Select
End Function

Public Function IsSPStore(st As Outlook.Store) As Boolean
    Dim objFolder As Outlook.Folder
    Dim blnIsSharePoint As Boolean
    For Each objFolder In st.GetRootFolder.Folders
        If objFolder.Name <> "Deleted Items" Then
            If objFolder.IsSharePointFolder = True Then
                blnIsSharePoint = True
                Exit For
            End If
        End If
    Next
    IsSPStore = blnIsSharePoint
End Function

Public Function Hex4ToString(Data As String) As String
    Dim strTemp As String
    Dim strAll As String
    Dim i As Integer
    For i = 1 To Len(Data) Step 4
        strTemp = Mid(Data, i, 4)
        strTemp = "&H" & Right(strTemp, 2) & Left(strTemp, 2)
        strAll = strAll & ChrW(CDec(strTemp))
    Next
    Hex4ToString = strAll
End Function

Public Function Hex2ToString(Data As String) As String
    Dim strTemp As String
    Dim strAll As String
    Dim i As Integer
    For i = 1 To Len(Data) Step 2
        strTemp = "&H" & Mid(Data, i, 2)
        strAll = strAll & ChrW(CDec(strTemp))
    Next
    Hex2ToString = strAll
End Function
```

To access the folders in a store, you can use the `Store.GetRootFolder` method to return the store's root `Folder` object. Each `Folder` in turn has a `Folders` collection containing all its subfolders, an `Items` collection containing all its items, and a `Store` object pointing to its parent information store.

Sometimes it is important to know whether a particular folder is located in the default store. To determine that, you can compare the `StoreID` for the folder with the `StoreID` for the default store:

```
If objfolder.Store.StoreID = _
   objfolder.Session.DefaultStore.StoreID Then
     MsgBox objfolder.Name & " is in the default store"
End If
```

Every Outlook folder and item in a particular information store has the same value for its `StoreID` property. Once an item has been saved, the `StoreID` can be obtained from the item's parent `Folder` object, that is, from *item*.`Parent.StoreID`. Thus, to discover whether a particular Outlook item is in the default store, compare the value of the `StoreID` property of the item's `Parent` folder with the `StoreID` for the default store.

Here's another use for the `StoreID` property: You can use the `Namespace.GetStoreFromID` method to return any information store, given the value of its `StoreID`.

## 13.2.1  Adding a Personal Folders .pst file store

The only type of store that you can add to Outlook programmatically using the Outlook object model is a Personal Folders .pst file. To create a new .pst file or open an existing .pst file in the current Outlook session, use the `Namespace.AddStore` method, which is compatible with older versions of Outlook, or the `AddStoreEx` method, which is new to Outlook 2007. Both require a file path string as an argument, but the `AddStoreEx` requires a second parameter designating the type of PST file as one of the constants from the `OlStoreType` enumeration:

| | |
|---|---|
| `olStoreANSI` | 3 |
| `olStoreDefault` | 1 |
| `olStoreUnicode` | 2 |

The basic syntax for both methods in Outlook VBA is similar:

```
Set objOL = Application
Set objNS = objNS.Session
objNS.AddStore "C:\Outlook Data\mynewfile.pst"
objNS.AddStoreEx "C:\Outlook Data\mynewfile2.pst", _
                 olStoreDefault
```

If the specified .pst file name already exists, Outlook opens the existing file, adds it to the `Namespace.Stores` collection, and displays it in the folder list. If it doesn't exist, Outlook creates it.

> **Caution:** If you provide only a file name to `AddStore` or `AddStoreEx` and not a full path, Outlook will create the new .pst file in the Program Files\ Microsoft Office\Office12 folder. Surprisingly, it ignores Outlook's normal default location for new .pst files.

The key difference between the two methods is that `AddStoreEx` requires you to specify what format the new.pst file will use—the legacy ANSI format that is compatible with Outlook 97–2002 or the Unicode format introduced in Outlook 2003, which is more stable and supports much larger .pst files. For example, if you want to create an ANSI .pst file to ensure compatibility with earlier versions, you can use this statement in VBA:

```
objNS.AddStoreEx _
    "C:\Outlook Data\mynewfile.pst", olStoreANSI
```

> **Note:** What about adding stores other than .pst files? Microsoft provides at least three techniques to work with them, but none of those methods are accessible through Outlook VBA. The Office Customization Tool can generate text files with a .prf extension and a highly structured format to provide information that enables Outlook to create or modify a mail profile and to add or change accounts and the stores associated with them. A very low-level programming interface is Extended MAPI, while the Account Management API provides access to account information. Neither of those interfaces can be used with VBA or VBScript.

## 13.2.2  Removing a .pst store

Just as you can add only a .pst store, you can remove only a .pst store. Other stores are tightly bound to accounts, RSS feeds, SharePoint lists, and so on. The `Namespace.RemoveStore` method takes a `Folder` object, not a `Store` object as its parameter. This keeps it backward compatible with the `RemoveStore` method from earlier Outlook versions. It's easy to get a store's root folder with the `Store.GetRootFolder` method, as in this VBA code snippet to remove a store (`myStore`):

```
Set objOL = Application
Set objNS = Application.Session
objNS.RemoveStore myStore.GetRootFolder
```

You'll see another example of `RemoveStore` in the next section.

Note that you should always be prepared to handle the error that will occur if the store you're removing is not a .pst file or if there is some problem with the profile configuration that prevents the store from being removed.

### 13.2.3    Renaming a .pst store

One limitation of the `AddStore` and `AddStoreEx` methods is that neither
allows you to give a new .pst store a display name at the time that Outlook
creates it. The name for a new .pst store is always Personal Folders (or the
localized equivalent). The `Store` object does have a `DisplayName` property,
but it is read-only. The key to renaming a .pst store is to rename its root
`Folder` object, but the real challenge is to determine which store is the one
that was just added. The procedure in Listing 13.2 adds a new Unicode .pst
file store, performs a before-and-after comparison of the `StoreID` values of
active stores to determine which is the new store, and then changes that
new store's display name. It also returns the new store as a `Store` object, so
that other code can start working with it immediately. This is an example of
the syntax used to call `AddNewPST`:

```
Set objStore = _
   AddNewPST("C:\Outlook Data\My PST.pst", "New PST")
```

The `AddNewPST()` function loops through `objNS.Stores` and calls
`StoreIsInArray()` twice. That's because to make the store's new display
name visible in the user interface, it is necessary to remove the store and add
it again.

Listing 13.2    *Add a new .pst store with a specific display name*

```
Function AddNewPST _
  (strFileName As String, strDisplayName As String) _
  As Outlook.Store
    Dim objOL As Outlook.Application
    Dim objNS As Outlook.NameSpace
    Dim objStore As Outlook.Store
    Dim objNewStore As Outlook.Store
    Dim arr() As String
    Dim i As Integer
    Dim blnStoreIsNew As Boolean
    Dim objFolder As Outlook.Folder
    On Error Resume Next
    Set objOL = Application
    Set objNS = objOL.Session
    ReDim arr(objNS.Stores.Count - 1)
    i = 0
    For Each objStore In objNS.Stores
        If objStore.IsDataFileStore Then
            arr(i) = objStore.StoreID
            i = i + 1
        End If
    Next
    Set objStore = Nothing
    objNS.AddStoreEx strFileName, olStoreUnicode
    For i = objNS.Stores.Count To 1 Step -1
        If objNS.Stores(i).IsDataFileStore Then
```

Listing 13.2   *Add a new .pst store with a specific display name (continued)*

```
                Set objNewStore = objNS.Stores(i)
                If Not StoreIsInArray(objNewStore, arr()) Then
                    blnStoreIsNew = True
                    Exit For
                End If
            End If
        Next
        If blnStoreIsNew Then
            Set objFolder = objNewStore.GetRootFolder
            objFolder.Name = strDisplayName
            ' remove the store to refresh the folder name
            objNS.RemoveStore objFolder
            Set objFolder = Nothing
            Set objNewStore = Nothing
            ' then add the store again
            objNS.AddStore strFileName
            blnStoreIsNew = False
            For i = objNS.Stores.Count To 1 Step -1
                If objNS.Stores(i).IsDataFileStore Then
                    Set objNewStore = objNS.Stores(i)
                    If Not StoreIsInArray( _
                            objNewStore, arr()) Then
                        blnStoreIsNew = True
                        Exit For
                    End If
                End If
            Next
        End If
        If blnStoreIsNew Then
            Set AddNewPST = objNewStore
        Else
            Set AddNewPST = Nothing
        End If
        Set objOL = Nothing
        Set objNS = Nothing
        Set objNewStore = Nothing
        Set objStore = Nothing
        Set objFolder = Nothing
    End Function

    Function StoreIsInArray _
      (st As Outlook.Store, arr() As String) As Boolean
        On Error Resume Next
        Dim blnInArray As Boolean
        Dim i As Integer
        blnInArray = False
        For i = 0 To UBound(arr)
            If st.StoreID = arr(i) Then
                blnInArray = True
                Exit For
            End If
        Next
        StoreIsInArray = blnInArray
    End Function
```

## 13.3  **Working with Explorers**

The `Explorers` collection is an object property of the `Application` object and represents all the windows currently displaying folders in Outlook. The `Application.ActiveExplorer` object is the folder window that the user is currently looking at or most recently looked at.

Table 13.1 lists the most useful methods and properties for the `Explorer` object. Note that an `Explorer` object has both `Activate` and `Close` methods and `Activate` and `Close` events, listed in Table 11.2.

The `ShowCalendar` procedure in Listing 10.1 demonstrated how to display a folder in a new `Explorer` window. If you want to see another example, jump ahead to Listing 13.8.

**Table 13.1**   *Useful Explorer Methods and Properties (* = new in Outlook 2007)*

| Method | Description |
|---|---|
| Activate | Bring the window to the foreground and give it the focus |
| *ClearSearch | If the window is showing the results of an instant search, clear the search results |
| Close | Close the window |
| Display | Display the window |
| IsPaneVisible(*Pane*) | Return `True` or `False` depending on whether the *Pane* pane is visible in the window; *Pane* values can be: <br><br> olFolderList      2 <br> olNavigationPane      4 <br> olOutlookBar      1 <br> olPreview      3 <br> olToDoBar      5 <br><br> If `IsPaneVisible(olFolderList)` or `IsPaneVisible(olOutlookBar)` returns `True`, then `IsPaneVisible(olNavigationPane)` will also return `True`, because the Folder List and the Shortcuts pane (current incarnation of the Outlook Bar) are part of the navigation pane. |
| *Search *Query*, *SearchScope* | Perform a search using the specified `Query` and one of these two `olSearchScope` values: <br><br> olSearchScopeAllFolders      1 <br> olSearchScopeCurrentFolder      0 |
| ShowPane *Pane*, *Visible* | Show or hide the *Pane*, using the same *Pane* values as `IsPaneVisible`. *Visible* can be `True` or `False`. |

→

**Table 13.1** *Useful Explorer Methods and Properties (\* = new in Outlook 2007) (continued)*

| Property | Description |
|---|---|
| Caption | Title displayed on the window (read-only) |
| CommandBars | Collection of toolbars and menus for the current window |
| CurrentFolder | Folder object representing the folder displayed in the window |
| CurrentView | View object for the view applied to the window |
| Height | Height of the window, in pixels |
| HTMLDocument | If CurrentFolder.WebViewOn = True, returns an MSHTML.HTML-Document for the currently displayed Web page |
| Left | Left position of the window, in pixels |
| NavigationPane | Returns a read-only NavigationPane object |
| Panes | Returns a Panes collection |
| Selection | Returns a Selection collection containing the items the user has selected in the folder |
| Top | Top position of the window, in pixels |
| Width | Width of the window, in pixels |
| WindowState | Display state of the window, one of these constants:<br>olMaximized    0<br>olMinimized    1<br>olNormalWindow  2 |

To close a folder window, use the Explorer.Close method. However, if you close all Explorer objects, the user may no longer have any Outlook windows open and Outlook may thus begin shutting down.

We'll look at the Explorer.Search method—new in Outlook 2007—in Chapter 15, as one of several ways to gain access to a selected set of Outlook items.

In Chapter 23, we'll look at techniques for working with components of the Explorer window. The new NavigationPane object provides some useful capabilities, although Outlook 2007 does not allow developers to add their own modules to the navigation pane.

## 13.3.1 Basic view techniques for Explorer windows

To change the view of the folder to a different view that already exists, use the Explorer.CurrentView property:

```
Application.ActiveExplorer.CurrentView = "Day/Week/Month"
```

If the current view is a calendar view, the `View.GoToDate` method displays the calendar for the desired date:

```
Application.ActiveExplorer.CurrentView.GoToDate #8/21/2007#
```

**Note:** The `CalendarView` object, which is new to Outlook 2007, includes a `DisplayedDates` property, intended to return a list of what dates a calendar view is showing. However, it does not work in the initial released version of Outlook 2007. The `CalendarViewMode` and `DayWeekTimeScale` properties apparently are also broken.

Techniques for creating and modifying views are covered in Chapter 24. In the next chapter, though, you'll see how to remove one-off copies of views that Outlook saves whenever the user modifies the view in a folder.

### 13.3.2    Setting the currently displayed folder

Each `Explorer` has a `CurrentFolder` property that returns a `Folder` object representing the displayed folder. To display a particular folder in an existing window, set the `Explorer.CurrentFolder` property to a `Folder` object representing the desired folder. This statement for Outlook VBA updates the currently displayed folder window to show the user's Sent Items folder:

```
Set Application.ActiveExplorer.CurrentFolder = _
    Application.Session.GetDefaultFolder(olFolderSentMail)
```

**Caution:** If you omit the `Set` keyword in a VBA or VBScript statement that attempts to assign a new value to `ActiveExplorer.CurrentFolder`, the currently displayed folder may be renamed.

## 13.4   Accessing folders

The `Folder` object is one of the basic building blocks of almost any Outlook application. Each information store has a root folder, returned by the `Store.GetRootFolder` method. Those root folders also comprise the `Namespace.Folders` collection. Each store root folder itself has a `Folders` collection of the top-level folders from that store. Each of those folders also has a `Folders` collection containing all its subfolders, and so on all the way down the folder hierarchy. Similarly, every folder has a `Parent` object which, except for a store root folder, points to a parent `Folder` object. The `Parent` of a store root folder is the `Namespace` object.

**Tip:** For the best view of the complete folder hierarchy, display the Folder List navigation pane.

**Note:** The basic folder object in Outlook 2007 is `Folder`, but in previous versions, it was `MAPIFolder`. Any legacy code you have that uses `MAPIFolder` will also work fine in Outlook 2007.

Previous chapters have presented several different techniques for accessing folders, including the `Namespace.GetDefaultFolder` method to return one of Outlook's default folders. Outlook 2007 includes many new

**Table 13.2** *Key Methods That Return a Folder Object (\* = new in Outlook 2007)*

| Method | Returns |
| --- | --- |
| *`AddressList.GetContactsFolder` | Contacts folder associated with an address list in the address book |
| `Application.ActiveExplorer.CurrentFolder` | Folder that the user most recently viewed |
| *`CalendarSharing.Folder` | Folder associated with a `CalendarSharing` item created with the `Folder.GetCalendarExporter` method |
| `Explorer.CurrentFolder` | Folder displayed in an `Explorer` window |
| `Folders.Item(index)` | Subfolder of a `Folder` |
| `Namespace.GetDefaultFolder(FolderType)` | Any of the default Outlook folders |
| `Namespace.GetFolderFromID(EntryIDFolder, EntryIDStore)` | Any folder from any information store |
| `Namespace.GetSharedDefaultFolder(Recipient, FolderType)` | Default folder from another user's Exchange mailbox |
| *`Namespace.OpenSharedFolder(Path, Name, DownloadAttachments, UseTTL)` | Folder storing data from an RSS feed, SharePoint list, Web calendar, or multi-item iCalendar .ics file |
| `Namespace.PickFolder` | Folder chosen by the user from the folder hierarchy |
| *`NavigationFolder.Folder` | Folder associated with an entry in the navigation pane |
| *`Store.GetSearchFolders.Item("FolderName")` | Search folder, given its name |
| *`Store.GetRootFolder` | Root folder of an information store |
| *`Store.GetSpecialFolder(FolderType)` | All Tasks or Reminders search folder for a store |

methods to return a folder as part of its expanded support for collaboration and new information sources, such as RSS feeds and Web calendars. Table 13.2 summarizes the most important Outlook 2007 methods that return a Folder object.

Notice that no method is available to return a folder given only its name, except in the case of search folders. Even though a folder name is unique within a given Folders collection (in other words, within a group of subfolders of a single folder), a folder name can be reused many, many times within different Folders collections and different information stores. Therefore, to return a specific folder that is not one of your own default folders, you need one of the following combinations of information:

- For a default folder in another user's mailbox, the user's alias or email address to create a Recipient object as a parameter for the Namespace.GetSharedDefaultFolder method

- The EntryID for the folder and, if it's outside the default store, the StoreID for the information store that contains the folder, for use with Namespace.GetFolderFromID

- The complete path to the folder through the folder hierarchy (analogous to the path to a folder on your hard drive), starting with the name of the information store

In the next few sections, you'll see examples of the most common techniques for accessing Outlook folders.

## 13.4.1  Getting a default folder

The following twelve default folders are always present in Outlook's default information store:

- Calendar
- Contacts
- Deleted Items
- Drafts
- Inbox
- Journal
- Junk E-mail
- Notes
- Outbox
- RSS Feeds
- Sent Items
- Tasks

Exchange users may have other default folders. The folder list will also show a Search Folders folder, but this is not an actual folder where you can store items. Instead it is a visual container for search folders, covered in Section13.4.6.

To return any default folder, use the `Namespace.GetDefaultFolder` method. The single argument for `GetDefaultFolder` is an intrinsic Outlook constant; possible values appear in Table 13.3. Here's how to set a variable named `objCal` to the user's default Calendar folder in VBA:

```
Set objOL = Application
Set objNS = objOL.Session ' or objOL.GetNamespace("MAPI")
Set objCal = objNS.GetDefaultFolder(olFolderCalendar)
```

**Table 13.3** *OlDefaultFolders Enumeration Constants for GetDefaultFolder (\* = also for GetSharedDefaultFolder)*

| Folder | Constant | Value |
|---|---|---|
| *Calendar | olFolderCalendar | 9 |
| *Contacts | olFolderContacts | 10 |
| Deleted Items | olFolderDeletedItems | 3 |
| *Drafts | olFolderDrafts | 16 |
| *Inbox | olFolderInbox | 6 |
| *Journal | olFolderJournal | 11 |
| Organizational Folders (Exchange 2007 only) | olFolderManagedEmail | 29 |
| *Notes | olFolderNotes | 12 |
| Outbox | olFolderOutbox | 4 |
| Public Folders\All Public Folders (Exchange only) | olPublicFoldersAllPublicFolders | 18 |
| RSS Feeds | olFolderRssFeeds | 25 |
| Sent Items | olFolderSentMail | 5 |
| Sync Issues\Conflicts (Exchange only) | olFolderConflicts | 19 |
| Sync Issues (Exchange only) | olFolderLocalFailures | 20 |
| Sync Issues\Local Failures (Exchange only) | olFolderLocalFailures | 21 |
| Sync Issues\Server Failures (Exchange only) | olFolderServerFailures | 22 |
| *Tasks | olFolderTasks | 13 |
| To-Do List | olFolderToDo | 28 |

In VBScript, you either declare a constant for `olFolderCalendar`:

```
Const olFolderCalendar = 9
Set objCal = _
   Application.Session.GetDefaultFolder(olFolderCalendar)
```

or use the constant's literal value:

```
Set objCal = Application.Session.GetDefaultFolder(9)
```

Refer back to Listing 10.1 to see another example of `GetDefault-Folder`.

---

**Tip:** The `Namespace` object itself represents the current Outlook session, but you don't have to worry about exactly what it means. Just learn to use its properties and methods. In Outlook VBA and custom form VBScript code, you can return the `Namespace` with `Application.Session`. As we saw in Chapter 7, if you are programming Outlook from an external application, you should use `Application.GetNamespace("MAPI")` to return a `Namespace` object and then call the `Namespace.Logon` method.

---

### 13.4.2   Getting the current folder

As discussed earlier in the chapter, the `Application` object includes an `ActiveExplorer` object that represents the folder window that the user is currently viewing or the last folder window that the user viewed. To return the folder which that window displays, use `ActiveExplorer.Current-Folder`, using this syntax in VBA or VBScript:

```
Set objFolder = Application.ActiveExplorer.CurrentFolder
```

---

**Caution:** Don't assume that `ActiveExplorer` will always return an actual window displaying a folder. There are scenarios in which the user might have only an individual item window open, and no folder windows.

---

Remember that the user can switch folders at any time unless a modal dialog box is active. This means that you should use `ActiveExplorer` in a timely manner. For example, if, in the code behind an Outlook form, you want to know what folder the user was viewing when the item was opened, invoke the `ActiveExplorer.CurrentFolder` object in the form's `Item_Open` event handler. Don't wait and try to get it in a later procedure; the user might have switched folders by then.

### 13.4.3   Letting the user choose a folder

We've seen how to get any Outlook default folder or the currently displayed folder. You can also allow the user to choose from any folder in the Outlook

**Figure 13.1**    *Use the Namespace.PickFolder method to pop up this dialog.*

hierarchy by using the `Namespace.PickFolder` method. A typical application looks like this in both VBA and VBScript:

```
On Error Resume Next
Set objOL = Application
Set objNS = objOL.Session
Set objFolder = objNS.PickFolder
If Not objFolder Is Nothing Then
    MsgBox objFolder.FolderPath
Else
    MsgBox "You did not pick a folder."
End If
```

When this code runs, Outlook pops up the Select Folder dialog, shown in Figure 13.1, in which the user can create a new folder or select an existing folder. Select Folder is a modal dialog, which means that execution of your code stops until the user clicks OK or Cancel.

Because the user can click Cancel in the Select Folder dialog, code using the `PickFolder` method must handle the possibility that the user may choose no folder at all. The expression `Not objFolder Is Nothing` returns `True` if a folder was selected or `False` if the user clicked Cancel.

**Note:** It is not possible to programmatically set the folder that appears selected when the Select Folder dialog first displays.

### 13.4.4    Example: Setting the save folder for a message

Users migrating from Lotus Notes or Domino often ask if Outlook can prompt them for the location to save each outgoing message. In Listing 13.3, code for the `Application.ItemSend` event prompts the user to select a folder and, if the chosen folder is appropriate, sets the `SaveSent-MessageFolder` property for the message to the selected folder. If the selected folder is not a mail folder or if it is in another user's Exchange mailbox or in the Public Folders hierarchy, the code presents the user with the choice of saving to the default Sent Items folder, not saving the message at all, or canceling the current send operation so that the user can send again and get a new opportunity to select a folder. Place the code for Listing 13.3 in the built-in ThisOutlookSession module in Outlook VBA.

**Listing 13.3**     *Setting the save folder for an outgoing message*

```
Private Sub Application_ItemSend(ByVal Item As Object, _
                                 Cancel As Boolean)
    Dim objNS As Outlook.NameSpace
    Dim objFolder As Outlook.Folder
    Dim strMsg As String
    Dim intRes As Integer
    Dim blnIsGoodFolder As Boolean
    On Error Resume Next
    If Item.Class = olMail Then
        Set objNS = Application.Session
        Set objFolder = objNS.PickFolder
        If Not objFolder Is Nothing Then
            Select Case objFolder.Store.ExchangeStoreType
                Case olNotExchange, olPrimaryExchangeMailbox
                    If objFolder.DefaultItemType = _
                        olmailitem Then
                            blnIsGoodFolder = True
                    Else
                            blnIsGoodFolder = False
                    End If
                Case olExchangePublicFolder, _
                    olExchangeMailbox
                    blnIsGoodFolder = False
            End Select
            If blnIsGoodFolder = True Then
                Set Item.SaveSentMessageFolder = objFolder
            Else
                strMsg = "The selected folder -- " & _
                    objFolder.FolderPath & _
                    " -- cannot be used to save this" & _
                    " outgoing item. Do you want to" & _
                    " save it to your default Sent" & _
                    " Items folder instead? " & vbCrLf & _
                    vbCrLf & "Click Yes to save to " & _
                    "Sent Items." & vbCrLf & "Click " & _
                    "No not to save the message." & _
                    vbCrLf & "Click Cancel to return " & _
                    "to the message without sending it."
                intRes = MsgBox(strMsg, _
                    vbQuestion + vbYesNoCancel, _
                    "Save Outgoing Message")
                Select Case intRes
                    Case vbYes
                        Set Item.SaveSentMessageFolder = _
                            objNS.GetDefaultFolder _
                            (olFolderSentMail)
```

Listing 13.3    *Setting the save folder for an outgoing message (continued)*

```
                    Case vbNo
                            Item.DeleteAfterSubmit = True
                    Case vbCancel
                            Cancel = True
                            Item.GetInspector.Activate
                End Select
            End If
        End If
    End If
    Set objFolder = Nothing
    Set objNS = Nothing
End Sub
```

Notice that Listing 13.3 uses three of the techniques we've seen in this chapter:

- Allowing the user to pick a folder with `Namespace.PickFolder`
- Checking the type of store
- Returning one of the user's default folders with `Namespace.GetDefaultFolder`

Another concept worth noting is that `SaveSentMessageFolder` takes a `Folder` object as its value. This means that it is an *object property*. Thus, code to assign a value to `SaveSentMessageFolder` requires the `Set` keyword, just as a statement to instantiate an object variable would. The `Explorer.CurrentFolder` property discussed in Section 13.3.2 is another example of an object property that requires a `Set` keyword to assign a new folder to the property.

## 13.4.5  Getting a default folder from another Exchange mailbox

To get a default Outlook folder from another Exchange mailbox, the `Namespace.GetSharedDefaultFolder` method requires a folder constant from Table 13.3 and a `Recipient` object representing the other user. We'll look at recipients in detail later in Chapter 18, "Working with Recipients and Address Lists." For now, what you need to know is that the easiest way to make this technique work is to use the other user's SMTP address, which you can see in the Address Book. That address is always guaranteed to be unique, which means it will always resolve to a valid `Recipient` object and thus be usable to open the other user's folder. Listing 13.4 shows a practical VBA application of this technique to return another user's Contacts folder, given only the user's email address. Listing 13.5 is the VBScript version.

It's important to understand that there is every possibility that you won't get a valid recipient or that you won't be able to return or work with the

---

**Listing 13.4**     *Getting another Exchange user's Contacts folder (VBA version)*

```
Function GetOtherUserContacts(strUserSMTP As String) As Folder
    Dim objOL As Outlook.Application
    Dim objNS As Outlook.NameSpace
    Dim objFolder As Outlook.Folder
    Dim objRecip As Outlook.Recipient
    On Error Resume Next
    Set objOL = Application
    Set objNS = objOL.Session
    Set objRecip = objNS.CreateRecipient(strUserSMTP)
    Set objFolder = _
      objNS.GetSharedDefaultFolder(objRecip, olFolderContacts)
    If objFolder Is Nothing Then
        MsgBox "Could not find Contacts for """ & _
                strUserSMTP & """", vbExclamation, _
                "User not found"
    End If
    Set GetOtherUserContacts = objFolder
    Set objFolder = Nothing
    Set objRecip = Nothing
    Set objNS = Nothing
    Set objOL = Nothing
End Function
```

---

**Listing 13.5**     *Getting another Exchange user's Contacts folder (VBScript version)*

```
Function GetOtherUserContacts(strUserSMTP)
    Dim objOL
    Dim objNS
    Dim objFolder
    Dim objRecip
    Const olFolderContacts = 10
    On Error Resume Next
    Set objOL = Application
    Set objNS = objOL.Session
    Set objRecip = objNS.CreateRecipient(strUserSMTP)
    Set objFolder = _
      objNS.GetSharedDefaultFolder(objRecip, olFolderContacts)
    If objFolder Is Nothing Then
        MsgBox "Could not find Contacts for """ & _
                strUserSMTP & """", vbExclamation, _
                "User not found"
    End If
    Set GetOtherUserContacts = objFolder
    Set objFolder = Nothing
    Set objRecip = Nothing
    Set objNS = Nothing
    Set objOL = Nothing
End Function
```

---

folder, perhaps because of connectivity or permissions issues. Therefore, as with the `PickFolder` method, your code to call `GetOtherUserContacts` needs to handle possible errors and test for the actual availability of the folder—and its contents—before proceeding. This would be typical VBA or VBScript code to call `GetOtherUserContacts`:

```
On Error Resume Next
Set objContacts = _
  GetOtherUserContacts("flaviusj@turtleflock.com")
If Not objContacts Is Nothing Then
    Err.Clear
    strCount = CStr(objContacts.Items.Count)
    If Err = 0 Then
        MsgBox "Number of items in folder = " & strCount
    Else
        MsgBox "Problem getting items from folder"
    End
    Err.Clear
End If
```

---

**Note:** In many cases, you can use the other user's mailbox alias, which is also shown in the Address Book entry, with `CreateRecipient`, but the alias is not guaranteed to be unique. You could have one alias "smitha" and another "smithab." The SMTP address, however, will always be unique.

---

You can return only seven default folders from other users' mailboxes, not the entire list from Table 13.3. If you need to return a folder other than one of those defaults, the mailbox must be visible in the Folder List, and as with other folders in the Folder List, you can walk down the folder hierarchy to reach the desired folder, as explained later in the chapter. Alternatively, if a shared folder is listed in the navigation pane, you can return that folder from the new `NavigationFolder` object that Outlook 2007 introduces. Both these techniques are discussed later in the chapter.

### 13.4.6 Getting a search folder

*Search folders*, introduced in Outlook 2003, are "virtual" folders. They themselves do not contain any items or subfolders, but when displayed by the user, they show all the items that meet particular search criteria. When accessed programmatically, a search folder returns a `Folder` object with an `Items` collection of items found by the search. It does not, however, support a `Folders` collection.

A search folder cannot search across information stores. Therefore, each store may have its own set of search folders for searching the items in that store. Search folder names are unique. That makes it possible to return any search folder by name, using the `Store.GetSearchFolders` method to return a collection of all active search folders for a given store, ignoring any search folders the user has never used or has not used recently. This VBA or VBScript code snippet returns the user's Unread Mail search folder from the default store as a `Folder` object named `objUnread`:

```
Set objOL = Application
Set objNS = objOL.Session
Set objDefStore = objNS.DefaultStore
Set objUnread = _
    objDefStore.GetSearchFolders.Item("Unread Mail")
```

**Tip:** We will see how to create a search folder programmatically in Chapter 16.

## 13.4.7   Walking the folder tree to get any folder

What if you need to return a folder that isn't the currently displayed folder, isn't in the navigation pane, and isn't a search folder? If you know the `EntryID` and `StoreID` values for the folder, you can use the `Namespace.GetFolderFromID` method, listed in Table 13.2. However, more likely than knowing the ID values is that you will know where the folder stands in relationship to the overall folder hierarchy. In that scenario, your code can start with a known folder and navigate up or down the folder hierarchy until you locate the desired folder. To go up the hierarchy, use the `Parent` property of any Outlook item or folder. To go down the hierarchy, use the `Folders` property of a `Folder` object, which returns a collection of that folder's subfolders. What known folders can you start from? You already know how to return any default folder and the root folder of any information store, so those are available starting points. You can also use the `Namespace.Folders` collection, which contains all the store root folders. Figure 13.2 shows a portion of the folder hierarchy in an Exchange mailbox and illustrates how the `Parent` and `Folders` properties can help you move up or down the hierarchy, along with other key methods for returning folders.

Let's start with a couple of simple examples, first a folder named Subscriptions that is a subfolder of the Inbox. Return the Inbox using the `Namespace.GetDefaultFolder` method, and then use the Inbox's `Folders` collection. This code snippet would work in VBScript behind an Outlook form:

```
Const olFolderInbox = 6
Set objOL = Application
Set objNS = objOL.Session
Set objInbox = objNS.GetDefaultFolder(olFolderInbox)
Set objSubsFolder = _
    objInbox.Folders.Item("Subscriptions")
```

To make the same code work in VBA, simply omit the constant declaration.

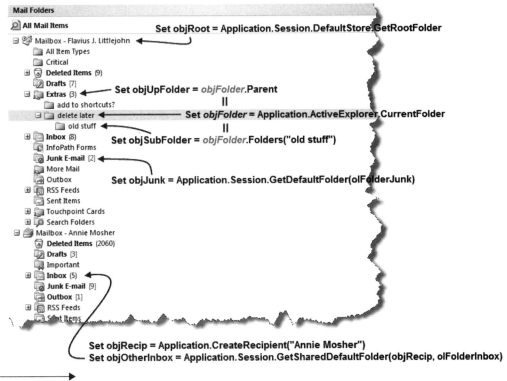

**Figure 13.2** *The Outlook object model has many methods to help you return any available folder as a Folder object.*

---

**Note:** Although a folder has an `Items` collection as well as a `Folders` collection, `Item` in the previous code snippet does not refer to an individual Outlook item. Instead, it refers to the `Item` method used with collections to return a specific item from the collection.

---

For a second example, consider a folder named Important Stuff that is at the same level as the Inbox. The easiest way to return it is as a subfolder of the default store's root folder:

```
Set objOL = Application
Set objNS = objOL.Session
Set objRoot = objNS.DefaultStore.GetRootFolder
Set objImportant = _
  objRoot.Folders.Item("Important Stuff")
```

Here's a more complicated example. Consider a top-level folder named Sales Department in the Public Folders hierarchy on an Exchange server that has a subfolder named Sales Contacts. You could return that folder with code like this:

```
Set objOL = Outlook.Application
Set objNS = objOL.Session
Set objFolder = objNS.Folders.Item("Public Folders"). _
                Folders.Item("All Public Folders"). _
                Folders.Item("Sales Department"). _
                Folders.Item("Sales Contacts")
```

The `Set objFolder` statement takes up four whole lines! Not only is it hard to type, but it also would be very difficult to debug if there was a typo on one of the folder names or the user didn't have permission to view the Sales Department folder. And what if the folder you wanted was a subfolder of the Sales Contacts folder? The `Set objFolder` statement would be even more complex.

---

**Tip:** For easier debugging, never return more than one new object in any code statement. Instead, break up a complex statement into multiple statements that each returns just one object.

---

Rather than type out a long `Set objFolder` statement or multiple statements to walk each level of the folder hierarchy, I recommend that you use a generic function that can return any folder once you know the path through the folder hierarchy to that folder. How can you get the folder path? One way is to eyeball it by writing down the name of each folder that leads to the desired folder, starting with the root folder of the information store.

But there are easier ways! For example, select the folder in the Folder List navigation pane, type this expression into the Immediate window in VBA, and then press Enter:

```
? Application.ActiveExplorer.CurrentFolder.FolderPath
```

On the next line in the immediate window, VBA will display the value of the `FolderPath` property of the currently displayed folder. In the case of our example, that would be "\\Public Folders\All Public Folders\Sales Department\Sales Contacts." Another method is to use the View | Toolbars | Web command to display the Web toolbar, which shows the URL for the currently displayed Outlook folder or Web page. An Outlook folder's URL is its path, preceded by `Outlook:`. With either of these methods, you can quickly copy and paste the folder path for any folder into your code.

Once you have the path, you can use it as the argument for the `Get-Folder()` function shown in VBA and custom form VBScript versions in Listings 13.6 and 13.7 respectively. Don't forget that the path needs to include the display name of the information store that contains the folder.

Do you recognize the `Split(strFPath, "\")` expression from Chapter 8? That expression breaks the path into an array of strings, each string

**Listing 13.6**   *Walk the folder hierarchy by parsing the folder path (VBA version)*

```
Function GetFolder(strFPath As String)
    Dim objOL As Outlook.Application
    Dim objNS As Outlook.NameSpace
    Dim colFolders As Outlook.Folders
    Dim objFolder As Outlook.Folder
    Dim arrFolders() As String
    Dim i As Long
    On Error Resume Next
    ' parse path string into array
    strFPath = Replace(strFPath, "/", "\")
    If Left(strFPath, 2) = "\\" Then
        strFPath = Mid(strFPath, 3)
    End If
    arrFolders = Split(strFPath, "\")
    ' walk folder tree
    Set objOL = Application
    Set objNS = objOL.Session
    Set colFolders = objNS.Folders
    For i = 0 To UBound(arrFolders)
        Set objFolder = Nothing
        Set objFolder = colFolders.Item(arrFolders(i))
        If objFolder Is Nothing Then
            Exit For
        Else
            Set colFolders = objFolder.Folders
        End If
    Next
    Set GetFolder = objFolder
    Set objOL = Nothing
    Set objNS = Nothing
    Set colFolders = Nothing
    Set objFolder = Nothing
End Function
```

being the name of a folder. With each iteration of the For ... Next loop, the code works its way down the path, attempting to get the corresponding folder by name from the colFolders collection of subfolders of the last folder reached. If there is no matching folder at any level, the function exits the loop and returns Nothing.

The path string parsing in the GetFolder() function is designed to be flexible enough to work with several different formats, so you don't have to remember which way the slashes slant. All these path string formats would return the same folder:

```
\\Personal Folders\Important Stuff\My Stuff
Personal Folders\Important Stuff\My Stuff
Personal Folders/Important Stuff/My Stuff
```

If a desired folder is in another user's Exchange mailbox, you can use the GetFolder() function to return that folder only if the folder is visible in

**Listing 13.7**     *Walk the folder hierarchy by parsing the folder path (VBScript version)*

```
Function GetFolder(strFPath)
    Dim objNS
    Dim colFolders
    Dim objFolder
    Dim arrFolders
    Dim i
    On Error Resume Next
    strFPath = Replace(strFPath, "/", "\")
    If Left(strFPath, 2) = "\\" Then
        strFPath = Mid(strFPath, 3)
    End If
    arrFolders = Split(strFPath, "\")
    Set objNS = Application.Session
    Set colFolders = objNS.Folders
    For i = 0 To UBound(arrFolders)
        Set objFolder = Nothing
        Set objFolder = colFolders.Item(arrFolders(i))
        If objFolder Is Nothing Then
            Exit For
        Else
            Set colFolders = objFolder.Folders
        End If
    Next
    Set GetFolder = objFolder
    Set objOL = Nothing
    Set objNS = Nothing
    Set colFolders = Nothing
    Set objFolder = Nothing
End Function
```

the Folder List navigation pane. The folder path would start with the display name for the other user's mailbox root, for example:

```
strPth = "\\Mailbox - Mosher, Sue\Contacts\Team Contacts"
Set objFolder = GetFolder(strPth)
```

As with other uses of `GetFolder()`, using it with folders in other users' mailboxes requires you to obtain the exact path to the folder. Later in the chapter, we'll see how to use the navigation pane to return a previously viewed folder shared from another user's mailbox. That technique works even if the other user's mailbox is not visible in the Folder List navigation pane.

## 13.4.8   Returning an Exchange public folder

Getting a folder from the Public Folders hierarchy on Exchange presents two challenges that `GetFolder()` can't quite handle. One is that the \\Public Folders\All Public Folders or \\Public Folders\Favorites part of the folder path might be localized in a language other than English. Another is that the user might be working offline. In that case, the All Public Folders hierarchy would not be accessible, but the user still might have the folder in the \\Public Folders\Favorites.

To address these issues, you can use the GetPublicFolder() function shown in Listing 13.8 as a VBScript version that will also work in VBA if you comment out the Const statements. (For VBA, you can also uncomment the As  datatype portion of the Dim statements.) This function requires a shortened version of the folder path, omitting "\\Public Folders\ All Public Folders" or "\\Public Folders\Favorites." Thus building on the earlier example, you could call GetPublicFolder() with this statement:

```
Set objSalesCont = GetPublicFolder _
    ("Sales Department\Sales Contacts\NE Contacts")
```

Several factors make Listing 13.8 rather complex. To keep the technique suitable in both English and non-English environments, it uses a

**Listing 13.8** *Return a folder from the Exchange Public Folders hierarchy*

```
Function GetPublicFolder(strPFPath)
    ' example: "Sales Department\Sales Contacts\NE Contacts"
    Dim objOL        ' As Outlook.Application
    Dim objNS        ' As Outlook.NameSpace
    Dim colFolders   ' As Outlook.Folders
    Dim objFolder    ' As Outlook.Folder
    Dim objFavRoot   ' As Outlook.Folder
    Dim arrFolders   ' As String - VBA should use arrFolders()
    Dim i            ' As Integer
    Dim j            ' As Integer
    Const olPublicFoldersAllPublicFolders = 18
    On Error Resume Next
    strPFPath = Replace(strPFPath, "/", "\")
    arrFolders = Split(strPFPath, "\")
    ' check Exchange online/offline status
    Set objOL = Application
    Set objNS = objOL.Session
    If Not objNS.Offline Then
        ' look in Public Folders\All Public Folders
        Set objFolder = objNS.GetDefaultFolder _
                    (olPublicFoldersAllPublicFolders)
        Set colFolders = objFolder.Folders
        For i = 0 To UBound(arrFolders)
            Set objFolder = Nothing
            Set objFolder = colFolders.Item(arrFolders(i))
            If Not objFolder Is Nothing Then
                Set colFolders = objFolder.Folders
            Else
                Exit For
            End If
        Next
    Else
        ' look in Public Folders\Favorites
```

**Listing 13.8**   *Return a folder from the Exchange Public Folders hierarchy (continued)*

```
    Set objFavRoot = GetPFFavs()
    Set colFolders = objFavRoot.Folders
    ' look for folder using full path
    For i = 0 To UBound(arrFolders)
        Set objFolder = Nothing
        Set objFolder = colFolders.Item(arrFolders(i))
        If Not objFolder Is Nothing Then
            Set colFolders = objFolder.Folders
        Else
            Exit For
        End If
    Next
    ' look for folder using partial path
    If objFolder Is Nothing Then
        For i = UBound(arrFolders) To 0 Step -1
            Set colFolders = objFavRoot.Folders
            Set objFolder = Nothing
            Set objFolder = colFolders.Item(arrFolders(i))
            If Not objFolder Is Nothing Then
                If i = UBound(arrFolders) Then
                    Exit For
                Else
                    j = i
                    Do While j <= UBound(arrFolders)
                        j = j + 1
                        Set colFolders = objFolder.Folders
                        Set objFolder = Nothing
                        Set objFolder = _
                          colFolders.Item(arrFolders(j))
                        If Not objFolder Is Nothing Then
                            If j = UBound(arrFolders) Then
                                Exit Do
                            End If
                        Else
                            Exit Do
                        End If
                    Loop
                    If Not objFolder Is Nothing Then
                        Exit For
                    End If
                End If
            End If
        Next
    End If
    End If
    Set GetPublicFolder = objFolder
    Set objOL = Nothing
    Set objNS = Nothing
    Set colFolders = Nothing
    Set objFolder = Nothing
End Function
```

**Listing 13.8**  *Return a folder from the Exchange Public Folders hierarchy (continued)*

```
Function GetPFFavs()
    ' returns localized Public Folders\Favorites
    Dim objOL       ' As Outlook.Application
    Dim objNS       ' As Outlook.NameSpace
    Dim colFolders  ' As Outlook.Folders
    Dim objFolder   ' As Outlook.Folder
    Dim objAllPF    ' As Outlook.Folder
    Dim objStore    ' As Outlook.Store
    Dim blnPFFound  ' As Boolean
    Const olExchangePublicFolder = 2
    Const olPublicFoldersAllPublicFolders = 18
    On Error Resume Next
    Set objOL = Application
    Set objNS = objOL.Session
    For Each objStore In objNS.Stores
        If objStore.ExchangeStoreType = _
          olExchangePublicFolder Then
            blnPFFound = True
            Exit For
        End If
    Next
    If blnPFFound Then
        Set objFolder = objStore.GetRootFolder
        If objFolder.Folders.Count = 1 Then
            Set GetPFFavs = objFolder.Folders.Item(1)
        Else
            Set objAllPF = objNS.GetDefaultFolder _
                            (olPublicFoldersAllPublicFolders)
            If objAllPF Is Nothing Then
                Set objFolder = objFolder.Folders.Item(1)
                If objFolder Is Nothing Then
                    Set objFolder = objFolder.Folders.Item(1)
                End If
                Set GetPFFavs = objFolder
            Else
                If objFolder.Folders.Item(1).EntryID = _
                  objAllPF.EntryID Then
                    Set GetPFFavs = objFolder.Folders.Item(2)
                Else
                    Set GetPFFavs = objFolder.Folders.Item(1)
                End If
            End If
        End If
    End If
    Set objOL = Nothing
    Set objNS = Nothing
    Set colFolders = Nothing
    Set objFolder = Nothing
    Set objAllPF = Nothing
    Set objStore = Nothing
End Function
```

`GetPFFavs()` function to return the Public Folders\Favorites folder without referring to the literal names of either of those folders.

Also, where a folder appears in the Public Folders\Favorites hierarchy depends on how the user added the folder to Favorites. Our example folder resides on the Exchange server as Public Folders\All Public Folders\Sales Department\Sales Contacts\NE Contacts. However, the replica in Public Folders\Favorites could use any of these three paths:

- Sales Department\Sales Contacts\NE Contacts
- Sales Contacts\NE Contacts
- NE Contacts

The `GetPublicFolder()` function initially tries to return the folder with the full path, that is, the first path listed above. If that returns `Nothing`, it then tries to locate the folder by its name alone, as in the last path shown above. Finally, if that also returns `Nothing`, it parses the path string working up the hierarchy (rather than down, as in `GetFolder()`) to take care of partial paths like the second one listed above.

## 13.4.9  Returning shared folders using the navigation pane

When you open a calendar from another user, either from a sharing invitation sent by that user or with the File | Open | Other User's Folder command, Outlook places a link to that folder in a group in the navigation named People's Calendars, People's Contacts, and so on. While most people will probably want to work with those calendars side-by-side, an assistant who manages other people's calendars might want to have each calendar from the People's Calendars group open in its own window. The code in Listing 13.9 opens each of the folders listed under People's Calendars in its own window, using the same `Explorers.Add` method you saw in Listing 10.1, this time called from the `Application_Startup` event handler in the built-in `ThisOutlookSession` module in Outlook VBA.

What makes the technique in Listing 13.9 possible are the new objects in Outlook 2007 related to the navigation pane. We'll look at them more closely in Chapter 23. For now, what is most relevant to this chapter is the fact that each `NavigationFolder` object—in other words, each link displayed in a navigation pane group—has a `Folder` object property that you can use to return the folder related to that link.

If you have turned on the Hide When Minimized option for the Outlook icon in the Windows system tray, you should comment out this statement in Listing 13.8:

```
objExpl.WindowState = olMinimized
```

Listing 13.9    *Display all folders from the People's Calendars group*

```
Private Sub Application_Startup()
    Call ShowOtherUserCalFolders
End Sub

Sub ShowOtherUserCalFolders()
    Dim objOL As Outlook.Application
    Dim objNS As Outlook.NameSpace
    Dim objExpCal As Outlook.Explorer
    Dim objNavMod As Outlook.CalendarModule
    Dim objNavGroup As Outlook.NavigationGroup
    Dim objNavFolder As Outlook.NavigationFolder
    Dim objFolder As Outlook.Folder
    Dim colExpl As Outlook.Explorers
    Dim objExpl As Outlook.Explorer
    Set objOL = Application
    Set objNS = objOL.Session
    Set colExpl = objOL.Explorers
    Set objExpCal = _
      objNS.GetDefaultFolder(olFolderCalendar).GetExplorer
    Set objNavMod = objExpCal.NavigationPane.Modules. _
      GetNavigationModule(olModuleCalendar)
    Set objNavGroup = objNavMod.NavigationGroups. _
      GetDefaultNavigationGroup(olPeopleFoldersGroup)
    For Each objNavFolder In objNavGroup.NavigationFolders
        Set objFolder = objNavFolder.Folder
        Set objExpl = _
          colExpl.Add(objFolder, olFolderDisplayNormal)
        objExpl.Activate
        objExpl.WindowState = olMaximized
        objExpl.WindowState = olMinimized
    Next
    Set objOL = Nothing
    Set objNS = Nothing
    Set objNavMod = Nothing
    Set objNavGroup = Nothing
    Set objNavFolder = Nothing
    Set objFolder = Nothing
    Set colExpl = Nothing
    Set objExpl = Nothing
End Sub
```

You can also show the windows non-maximized by setting Window-State to olNormalWindow instead of olMaximized.

## 13.4.10  Recursing folders

Another common Outlook programming technique is to process not just a single folder but also that folder's subfolders (and each subfolder's subfolders) all the way down the folder hierarchy. As you'll recall, a Folder object

**Listing 13.10**   *Basic folder recursion with item iteration (VBScript)*

```
Sub ProcessFolder(StartFolder)
    Dim objFolder
    Dim objItem
    ' process all the subfolders of this folder
    For Each objFolder In StartFolder.Folders
        Call ProcessFolder(objFolder)
    Next
    ' process all the items in this folder
    For Each objItem In StartFolder.Items
        Call ProcessItem(objItem)
    Next
    Set objFolder = Nothing
End Sub
```

has both a `Folders` collection containing all its subfolders and an `Items` collection of all the items (messages, contacts, and so on) in the folder. The procedure in Listing 13.10 provides a basic folder and item iteration framework for VBScript behind an Outlook form.

If you wanted to process items as well as folders with `ProcessFolder`, your script would also need to include a `ProcessItem` subroutine with a single parameter—the item to be processed. `ProcessItem` could do whatever you want with the item—remove attachments, mark it unread, and so on.

This is an example of how to start the processing by passing a specific starting folder to `ProcessFolder`:

```
Set objFolder = Application.ActiveExplorer.CurrentFolder
Call ProcessFolder(objFolder)
```

Listing 13.11 uses the same folder recursion technique, only this time as a VBA macro, to loop through all the folders in the current Outlook session. It builds and displays a new email message that lists the folder path and number of items in each folder. It also totals running sums of the number of folders and items.

Note the use of three module-level variables to allow both `ListAllFolders` and `ProcessFolder` to write to and/or read from the two running sums and the list of folders.

The `ProcessFolder` subroutines in Listings 13.10 and 13.11 are known as *recursive* procedures, because the `ProcessFolder` procedure calls itself. Recursion is a key programming technique where an object contains a collection of objects of the same class as the original object, as here a `Folder` contains a `Folders` collection of other `Folder` objects.

Listing 13.11 *List the folders and number of items in the current Outlook session (VBA)*

```
Dim mlngItemCount As Long
Dim mlngFolderCount As Long
Dim mstrList As String

Sub ListAllFolders()
    Dim objOL As Outlook.Application
    Dim objNS As Outlook.NameSpace
    Dim objFolder As Outlook.Folder
    Dim objMsg As Outlook.MailItem
    mlngItemCount = 0
    mlngFolderCount = 0
    mstrList = ""
    Set objOL = Application
    Set objNS = objOL.Session
    For Each objFolder In objNS.Folders
        Call ProcessFolder(objFolder)
        mstrList = mstrList & vbCrLf
    Next
    Set objMsg = objOL.CreateItem(olMailItem)
    mstrList = mstrList & vbCrLf & _
            "Total folders in Outlook = " & _
            Format(mlngFolderCount, "###,###") & _
            vbCrLf & "Total items in Outlook = " & _
            Format(mlngItemCount, "###,###")
    objMsg.Body = mstrList
    objMsg.Display
    Set objOL = Nothing
    Set objNS = Nothing
    Set objFolder = Nothing
End Sub

Sub ProcessFolder(startFolder As Outlook.Folder)
    Dim objFolder As Outlook.Folder
    On Error Resume Next
    mstrList = mstrList & vbCrLf & startFolder.FolderPath & _
            vbTab & startFolder.Items.Count
    mlngItemCount = mlngItemCount + startFolder.Items.Count
    mlngFolderCount = mlngFolderCount + 1
    For Each objFolder In startFolder.Folders
        Call ProcessFolder(objFolder)
    Next
    Set objFolder = Nothing
End Sub
```

**Tip:** If you want to peek ahead at another example of folder recursion, Listing 14.6 in the next chapter shows how to process all folders to remove cached copies of the Messages view so that the settings in the master copy of the Messages view will apply to all folders.

# 13.5   Working with folders

Many useful techniques for working with Outlook folders are based on the collection methods discussed in Chapter 8. Each `Folder` object (except for a `Store` root folder) is a member of the `Folders` collection of its `Parent` object. Therefore, you can use the `Add` or `Remove` method on that `Folders` collection to create or delete a folder.

As you saw in Listings 13.6 and 13.7, you can use the `Item` method to retrieve a folder by name. You can also use an index number with `Item`. The `Folders` collection also includes `GetFirst`, `GetLast`, `GetNext`, and `GetPrevious` methods for moving through the collection, each one returning either the appropriate folder or `Nothing` if there are no more folders to be returned.

For an individual Outlook folder, which is represented by the `Folder` object, Table 13.4 lists available methods.

**Table 13.4**   *Folder Object Methods (\* = new in Outlook 2007)*

| Method | Description | Returns |
|---|---|---|
| AddToPFFavorites | Adds the folder to the Public Folders\Favorites folder so that it can be cached locally and used offline; applies only to folders in the Public Folders hierarchy on an Exchange server | n/a |
| CopyTo(*DestinationFolder*) | Copies the entire folder and its contents, including any hidden items | A `Folder` object representing the new copy of the folder |
| Delete | Deletes the folder | n/a |
| Display | Shows the folder in a new `Explorer` window | n/a |
| *GetCalendarExporter | Allows the user to export the contents of a calendar folder using an iCalendar .ics file | A `CalendarSharing` object that can be used to send the contents of the folder to another user as an iCalendar .ics file |
| GetExplorer(*DisplayMode*) | Instantiates an `Explorer` object for the folder | The `Explorer` object for the folder; use the `Activate` method to show it |
| *GetStorage(*StorageIdentifier*, *StorageIdentifierType*) | Obtains a hidden item containing information about the folder, creating it if it does not already exist | A `StorageItem` object containing private data either for built-in Outlook functionality or for your custom solution |

**Table 13.4**  *Folder Object Methods (* = new in Outlook 2007) (continued)*

| Method | Description | Returns |
|---|---|---|
| *GetTable(*Filter, TableContents*) | Allows the program to work with a read-only table of either hidden or visible items in the folder | A Table object containing all or a filtered set of items from the folder |
| MoveTo(*DestinationFolder*) | Moves the entire folder | A Folder object representing the moved folder in its new location |

The `Folder.GetStorage` method is covered in the next chapter, while the `Folder.GetTable` method is covered in Chapter 15.

### 13.5.1  Working with folder properties

An Outlook folder has three different kinds of settings:

- Standard `Folder` object properties listed in the Outlook object model, such as `Name` and `CurrentView`, accessed with the `Folder.property_name` syntax
- Other properties not listed in the Outlook object model, often known as *MAPI property tags*
- Hidden items that store information about the folder

Chapter 14 explains how to access the last two types of settings using two key new objects in Outlook 2007. Table 13.5 lists the most commonly used Outlook object model properties of the `Folder` object. In general, only an owner of a folder can make changes to the folder's properties. A user has sufficient rights to change properties on any of their own Exchange mailbox folders and on all folders in any open Personal Folders .pst file.

**Table 13.5**  *Useful Folder properties (* = read-only property)*

| Property | Description |
|---|---|
| AddressBookName | Display name used if `ShowAddressBook = True` |
| CurrentView | `View` object representing the currently displayed view of the folder |
| CustomViewsOnly | Show only views created for the folder, not standard views; default is `False` |
| *DefaultItemType | Identifies the type of folder; can be one of these six values: |
| | olAppointmentItem    1         olMailItem    0 |
| | olContactItem    2         olNoteItem    5 |
| | olJournalItem    4         olTaskItem    3 |

**Table 13.5**  *Useful Folder properties (\* = read-only property) (continued)*

| Property | Description |
|---|---|
| *DefaultMessageClass | Another way to identify the type of folder, from the message class for the default type of item (e.g., IPM.Contact for a folder with DefaultItemType = olContactItem) |
| Description | Text describing the folder, as shown on the General tab of the folder's Properties dialog |
| *EntryID | Folder ID unique within the information store |
| *FolderPath | Complete path string to the folder from its parent store's root folder |
| Folders | Collection of the folder's subfolders |
| IsSharePointFolder* | Returns True if the folder is in a local replica of a SharePoint folder; default is False |
| Items | Collection of the items the folder contains; use Items.Count to return the total number of items in the folder |
| Name | Name of the folder; must be unique among folders in the same parent folder |
| Parent | For store root folders, returns the Namespace object; for other folders, returns the parent Folder |
| *PropertyAccessor | Object used to access hidden properties (new in Outlook 2007) |
| ShowAsOutlookAB | For contacts folders, if True, Outlook displays the folder in the Outlook Address Book with the display name set in AddressBookName; default is False; always False for non-contact folders |
| ShowItemCount | Determines what type of item count the folder displays in the navigation pane; can be one of these values from the OlShowItemCount enumeration:<br><br>olNoItemCount     0<br>olShowTotalItemCount     2<br>olShowUnreadItemCount     1 |
| Store | Store object representing the information store containing the folder |
| StoreID | Unique ID related to Store |
| UnReadItemCount | Number of unread items in the folder |
| UserDefinedProperties | Collection of UserDefinedProperty custom properties defined for use by items stored in the folder (new in Outlook 2007) |
| Views | Collection of View objects representing the views that can be applied to the folder |
| WebViewOn | If True, display the Web page whose URL is listed in WebViewURL instead of the items in the folder; default is False |

**Table 13.5** *Useful Folder properties (\* = read-only property) (continued)*

| Property | Description |
|---|---|
| WebViewURL | URL for Web page that will be displayed instead of the items in the folder if WebViewURL = True; default is blank, except for the root of the default information store, which uses the URL for the Outlook Today page that comes with Outlook |

We'll look at views and folder home pages, which are Web pages that Outlook displays instead of the items in a folder, in Chapter 22.

## 13.5.2 Creating and deleting folders

To create a folder, use the Add method on the parent folder where you want to create the new folder. The Add method takes two parameters: the name of the new folder and an optional Type constant that defines what kind of items the folder can hold. Table 13.6 lists the possible values for Type.

If you omit the second argument, the folder Type, the new folder inherits its Type setting from the parent folder. If the parent folder is the root folder of an information store and you omit the Type, the new folder will contain message items.

To see an example of creating a folder, look back at Listing 11.24, which created a folder named Outlook System Tasks as a subfolder of the Tasks folder. In this VBA code snippet, m_objNS is a Namespace object:

```
Set objFolderTasks = _
  m_objNS.GetDefaultFolder(olFolderTasks)
Set objFolderSysTasks = _
  objFolderTasks.Folders("Outlook System Tasks")
If objFolderSysTasks Is Nothing Then
    Set objFolderSysTasks = _
      objFolderTasks.Folders.Add("Outlook System Tasks")
End If
```

You will get a runtime error if you try to add a new folder with the same name as an existing folder in the same Folders collection. Since a folder name must be unique in the Folders collection, you should always check for the existence of a folder before trying to create a new folder with that name.

Besides Folders.Add, the other method available to create a new folder is Search.Save, which creates a new search folder from the filter criteria that create a Search object. We'll look at that technique in Chapter 16.

To remove a folder, use the Delete method, for example, objFolderSysTasks.Delete. You can also use the Remove method on its parent Folders collection.

**Table 13.6**   *Add Folder Types (from OlDefaultFolders enumeration)*

| Folder Contains | Type Constant | Value |
| --- | --- | --- |
| Appointment items | `olFolderCalendar` | 9 |
| Contact items | `olFolderContacts` | 10 |
| Journal items | `olFolderJournal` | 11 |
| Message items | `olFolderInbox` or `olFolderDrafts` | 6, 16 |
| Note items | `olFolderNotes` | 12 |
| Task items | `olFolderTasks` | 13 |

### 13.5.3   Moving and copying folders

You can copy or move entire folders, with all their items, to a new location in the folder hierarchy. Folders often contain more than visible items. They may also contain hidden items including custom Outlook forms published to the folder and custom views on the folder. Copying or moving the entire folder ensures that those hidden items are also copied or moved, along with the visible items.

To copy or move a folder, you need two `Folder` object variables, one for the folder being moved or copied and a second for the destination parent folder. The syntax for these two methods is similar. Each returns the copied or moved folder as a new `Folder` object:

```
Set objCopiedFolder = objFolder.CopyTo(objDestFolder)
Set objMovedFolder = objFolder.MoveTo(objDestFolder)
```

Moving a folder to the Deleted Items folder is equivalent to executing the `Folder.Delete` method.

### 13.5.4   Sharing a folder

Outlook 2007 includes two ways in which a user can share the data in a folder programmatically, both new to the Outlook object model—one for Exchange, and one for all Outlook configurations but only for calendar folders. The calendar sharing method is particularly good for distributing company events, such as holidays and conferences, to users.

In an Exchange environment only, use the `Namespace.CreateSharingItem` method to make the folder available to another user in the same Exchange organization. This VBA code snippet sends a sharing invitation for the current user's Calendar folder:

```
Set objOL = Application
Set objNS = objOL.Session
```

```
Set objCal = objNS.GetDefaultFolder(olFolderCalendar)
Set objShItem = _
  objNS.CreateSharingItem(objCal, olProviderExchange)
With objShItem
    .To = "flaviusj@turtleflock.net"
    .Type = olSharingMsgTypeInvite
    .Send
End With
```

The first parameter for the `CreateSharingItem` is the folder you want to share. If the folder is not in the user's Exchange mailbox, a runtime error will occur. For a default folder, such as Calendar or Contacts, the `Type` property can have one of these three values from the `OlSharingMsgType` enumeration:

| | | |
|---|---|---|
| `olSharingMsgTypeInvite` | 2 | Invite the other person to share the current user's folder |
| `olSharingMsgTypeInviteAndRequest` | 3 | Invite the other person to share the current user's folder and request a reciprocal share |
| `olSharingMsgTypeRequest` | 1 | Request access to the other user's folder |

For a non-default folder, the only valid `Type` is `olSharingMsgType-Invite`.

Sharing a default folder causes Outlook to grant Reviewer access to the other person. If you share a non-default folder, you can set the value of the `SharingItem.AllowWriteAccess` property to `True` and thus grant the other person Editor access.

---

**Tip:** The `CreateSharingItem` method can also generate sharing messages for other types of information besides Outlook folders, such as RSS feeds, SharePoint lists, and Web calendars. In those scenarios, the first parameter is a string—the URL for the information—and the second parameter uses the appropriate provider value from the `OlSharingProvider` enumeration, which you can look up in the object browser.

---

You can process sharing invitations that you receive with these three `SharingItem` methods:

| | |
|---|---|
| `Allow` | Grant the sender's request for Reviewer access to a default folder |

Deny                              Deny the sender's request for access to a default folder

OpenSharedFolder                  Display the shared folder and add it to the appropriate navigation pane

The permissions on the folder determine whether the recipient of the sharing invitation can only view items or can also create new items. Listing 14.1 in the next chapter provides code to determine whether a user has write permission on a given folder.

For calendar folders only (both Exchange and non-Exchange), use the Folder.GetCalendarExporter method to create a message that attaches the appointments as a multi-item iCalendar .ics file. (The recipient of the message needs Outlook 2007 or another application that can handle such files.) This is a one-way sharing method. The recipient of the .ics file cannot make any changes to the original user's calendar folder. Listing 13.12 exports a Tech Conferences subfolder of the Calendar folder, both saving it as a local .ics file and sending it to another user in a mail message. The With objCalExp ... End With block demonstrates the many different options available for this type of export.

If you set IncludeWholeCalendar to True, Outlook ignores any values for StartDate and EndDate and sends the entire contents of the folder.

The ForwardAsICal method returns a mail message with the .ics file as an attachment and a highly formatted message body with information about the calendar appointments. This method's required parameter has two possible values: olCalendarMailFormatEventList to format the message as a list of events, and olCalendarMailFormatDailySchedule to format the message with each day's free/busy information. If you wanted to generate just an email message with your availability during working hours, you could use ForwardAsICal and delete the .ics attachment. This variation on the code in Listing 13.12 transmits a day-by-day listing of the current user's availability as an email message only, with no attachment:

```
Set objCal = objNS.GetDefaultFolder(olFolderCalendar)
Set objCalExp = objCal.GetCalendarExporter
With objCalExp
    .IncludeWholeCalendar = False
    .StartDate = Date
    .EndDate = DateAdd("m", 1, Date)
    .CalendarDetail = olFreeBusyOnly
    .IncludePrivateDetails = False
    .RestrictToWorkingHours = True
    Set objMail = _
      .ForwardAsICal(olCalendarMailFormatDailySchedule)
    With objMail
        .To = "flaviusj@turtleflock.net"
```

```
                            .Attachments.Remove 1
                            .Send
                    End With
            End With
```

Note that the `Folder.GetCalendarExporter` method will raise a runtime error if you attempt to use it on a non-calendar folder.

For more examples of the `CreateSharingItem` and `GetCalendarExporter` methods, check out these articles in Outlook developer Help:

- How to: Export a Calendar Using Payload Sharing (HV10045353)
- How to: Send a Sharing Invitation for a Calendar (HV10045361)
- How to: Send a Sharing Invitation for an RSS Feed (HV10045374)

**Listing 13.12**    *Using iCalendar to send a Calendar folder to another user*

```
Sub ExportTechCal()
    Dim objOL As Outlook.Application
    Dim objNS As Outlook.NameSpace
    Dim objCal As Outlook.Folder
    Dim objCalExp As Outlook.CalendarSharing
    Dim objMail As Outlook.MailItem
    On Error Resume Next
    Set objOL = Application
    Set objNS = objOL.Session
    Set objCal = objNS.GetDefaultFolder(olFolderCalendar)
    Set objCal = objCal.Folders("Tech Conferences")
    If Not objCal Is Nothing Then
        Set objCalExp = objCal.GetCalendarExporter
        With objCalExp
            .IncludeWholeCalendar = False
            .StartDate = Date
            .EndDate = DateAdd("yyyy", 1, Date)
            .CalendarDetail = olFullDetails
            .IncludeAttachments = True
            .IncludePrivateDetails = False
            .RestrictToWorkingHours = False
            .SaveAsICal "C:\TechConferences.ics"
            Set objMail = _
              .ForwardAsICal(olCalendarMailFormatEventList)
            With objMail
                .To = "flaviusj@turtleflock.net"
                .Send
            End With
        End With
    End If
    Set objOL = Nothing
    Set objNS = Nothing
    Set objCal = Nothing
    Set objCalExp = Nothing
    Set objMail = Nothing
End Sub
```

The numbers in parentheses are topic IDs you can search for in Help to find the articles faster.

### 13.5.5  Adding an RSS feed, Web calendar, or SharePoint list

`OpenSharedFolder` is a method not just of the `SharingItem` object covered in the previous section, but also of the `Namespace` object. The syntax to subscribe to a blog or other Web site that has an RSS (really simple syndication feed), to a WebCal calendar, or to a SharePoint list looks like this:

```
Set objNS = Application.Session
Set objFolder = objNS.OpenSharedFolder( _
  Path, Name, DownloadAttachments, UseTTL)
```

where *Path* is the URL for the RSS feed, calendar, or SharePoint list. *Path* is the only required parameter. If you omit *Name*, Outlook will use the feed, calendar, or list name.

Use `True` for the *DownloadAttachments* parameter if you want the subscription to download enclosures for an RSS feed or attachments for a calendar. The default is `False`.

Use `False` for the *UseTTL* parameter if you do not want the feed or calendar to use the publisher's recommendation for the update frequency (contained in the site's time-to-live setting). The default is `True`.

For example, to subscribe to a popular feed of Outlook tips and display the latest tips, use this code snippet:

```
Set objOL = Application
Set objNS = objOL.Session
strFeed = "feed://outlook-tips.net/cs/" & _
          "blogs/outlooktips/rss.aspx"
Set objFolder = objNS.OpenSharedFolder(strFeed)
objFolder.Display
```

Note the use of the prefix `feed://` for an RSS feed. For a WebCal calendar, the URL prefix would be `webcal://` and for a SharePoint list, `stssync://`. Users manage all three types of subscriptions in the Tools | Account Settings dialog.

## 13.6  Summary

After working through the examples in this chapter, you should have a good understanding of the various information stores you might encounter and the relationship between `Explorer` objects and the `Folder` objects they display. You have begun to build a toolkit of useful Outlook techniques, including accessing, creating, deleting, moving, and sharing folders. The useful code techniques in this chapter have included routines to set the default form for a folder, loop through all the folders in the current Outlook session, and return any folder for which you know its path in the Outlook folder hierarchy.

This is not the end of our excursion into stores, `Explorer` windows, and folders. Chapter 16 will demonstrate how to create a new search folder, and we'll look at more folder views in Chapter 22.

Folders continue to be in the spotlight in the next chapter, where we'll learn about the important new `PropertyAccessor` and `StorageItem` objects that provide access to data and settings that the Outlook object model does not expose in any of its standard properties or objects.

# 14

# *Using PropertyAccessor and StorageItem*

One of Microsoft's design goals for Outlook 2007 was to eliminate the need for lower-level programming interfaces such as Collaboration Data Objects, Outlook Redemption, or Extended MAPI to retrieve and set property values that are not exposed in the Outlook object model, the so-called *hidden* or *MAPI properties*. To address this need, Microsoft added two key new objects to the Outlook object model. The `PropertyAccessor` object provides access to hidden properties of items, folders, attachments, address entries, and certain other objects. The `StorageItem` object provides access to hidden items that contain settings such as folder archive options. Much of your work with `StorageItem` objects will involve using `Property-Accessor` to access a hidden item's properties.

Developers can also create their own properties and, in certain folders, their own storage items to hold information specific to their applications. Because such information stays with the items and folders, it is ideal for applications designed for Exchange environments, where, for example, a shared folder might need to expose information about the application to all users who connect to that folder.

Highlights of this chapter include discussions of the following:

- What resources can help you find your way through the maze of schema property names
- Where to look for information on what properties are already available and what storage items are already present
- When to use the `PropertyAccessor` object instead of the `User-Properties` or `ItemProperties` collection
- What limitations prevent `PropertyAccessor` and `StorageItem` from completely replacing older techniques like the CDO `Fields` and `HiddenMessages` collections

We'll walk through a number of practical applications of `Property-Accessor` and `StorageItem` to generate a spam report with message headers and the complete original message, to set the default form for a folder, and to remove cached copies of views so that the master view's settings can be applied to a folder.

# 14.1   Using the PropertyAccessor object

Let's look first at the new `PropertyAccessor` object. You can use `PropertyAccessor` to access many (but not all) properties of folders, stores, individual items, address entries, recipients, address lists, Exchange users and distribution lists, and attachments:

- Most standard properties from the Outlook object model

- For individual items, any custom property from the `UserProperties` collection

- Most hidden properties, also known as MAPI property tags, that the object model does not expose

The `PropertyAccessor` object has some significant limitations. You cannot use it to access object properties, such as the `Recipients` collection of a message or the contents of an individual attachment, nor can it access the item body or binary properties containing more than 4kb of data. You also cannot use it to delete MAPI properties. These limitations and techniques for trapping related errors are discussed in more detail later in the chapter.

Using `PropertyAccessor` is more complicated than the methods we learned in Chapter 7 for referring to standard and user-defined item properties. The basic technique is to get a `PropertyAccessor` object, then use the appropriate method to read, write, or delete the desired property or properties. Table 14.1 lists the key `PropertyAccessor` methods. Note that the `PropertyAccessor.SetProperty` and `SetProperties` methods simplify the operation of setting property values by creating any properties that do not already exist. You do not need to create the property and then set its value in two separate code statements.

---

**Tip:** Not only is the `PropertyAccessor` technique more complex, but it's also more costly in terms of runtime code efficiency. Therefore, you should continue to use the `object.property_name` syntax for standard properties and `item.UserProperties("property_name")` for user-defined properties wherever possible. Of course, `item.ItemProperties("property_name")` is also an option as well.

---

The code in Listing 14.1 shows how to use `PropertyAccessor` to return the value of a folder property that contains information about the

**Table 14.1**   *PropertyAccessor Methods for Deleting, Reading, Creating, and Modifying Property Values*

| Method | Description | Returns |
| --- | --- | --- |
| DeleteProperties(*SchemaNames*) | Deletes the properties in the *SchemaNames* array | `Nothing` or an array of `Err` objects, one for each property |
| DeleteProperty(*SchemaName*) | Deletes the *SchemaName* property | n/a |
| GetProperties(*SchemaNames*) | Gets the values of the properties in the *SchemaNames* array | Variant array of property or `Err` values |
| GetProperty(*SchemaName*) | Gets the value of the *SchemaName* property | Property value |
| SetProperties(*SchemaNames,  Values*) | Sets the value of the properties in the *SchemaNames* array, creating any properties that do not already exist | `Nothing` or an array of `Err` objects, one for each property |
| SetProperty(*SchemaName,  Value*) | Sets the value of the *SchemaName* property, creating it if it does not already exist | n/a |

**Listing 14.1**   *Find out if a user can create items in a folder*

```
Function HasWriteAccess(fld) ' As Boolean
    Dim objPA                ' As Outlook.PropertyAccessor
    Dim intAccessRights      ' As Integer
    Dim intRightsTest        ' As Integer
    On Error Resume Next
    Const PR_ACCESS = _
      "http://schemas.microsoft.com/mapi/proptag/0x0FF40003"
    Const MAPI_ACCESS_CREATE_CONTENTS = 16
    Set objPA = fld.PropertyAccessor
    intAccessRights = objPA.GetProperty(PR_ACCESS)
    If Err = 0 Then
        intRightsTest = _
          intAccessRights And MAPI_ACCESS_CREATE_CONTENTS
        If intRightsTest = MAPI_ACCESS_CREATE_CONTENTS Then
            HasWriteAccess = True
        Else
            HasWriteAccess = False
        End If
    Else
        HasWriteAccess = False
    End If
    Set objPA = Nothing
End Function
```

access rights the current user has on the folder. These statements return the property value using the two-stage process outlined above:

```
Const PR_ACCESS = _
    "http://schemas.microsoft.com/mapi/proptag/0x0FF40003"
Set objPA = fld.PropertyAccessor
intAccessRights = objPA.GetProperty(PR_ACCESS)
```

The `HasWriteAccess()` function is written for VBScript, but would also work in VBA, and meets a common need in custom form design. The user may be able to display a new item using a custom form published to the folder, but may not have permission to actually save that item in a folder. By using the `HasWriteAccess()` function, you can warn the user or show or hide certain pages of the form. For example, you might call it from the `Item_Open` event handler for a form published to an Exchange public folder:

```
Function Item_Open()
    If Item.Size = 0 Then
        If Not HasWriteAccess _
            (Application.ActiveExplorer.CurrentFolder) Then
            MsgBox "You don't have permission " & _
                    "to save an item in this folder."
        End If
    End If
End Function
```

The `HasWriteAccess()` function uses `PropertyAccessor.GetProperty` to read the value of a property. Later, you will see an example of setting folder properties with `PropertyAccessor.SetProperties`.

---

**Note:** The property value retrieved by the `HasWriteAccess()` function potentially contains more information about the user's access rights on the folder than we actually used. Each bit in the binary representation of the value is a "flag" for a different folder access right. Such values are called *bitmasks*, and you can use bitwise operator `And` to test for the presence of any given flag. In this example, the expression `intAccessRights And MAPI_ACCESS_CREATE_CONTENTS` returns `MAPI_ACCESS_CREATE_CONTENTS` if the flag for write access is turned on.

---

### 14.1.1   Example: Send a spam report

Some mail providers encourage their users to submit examples of junk mail messages so that the provider can fine-tune its spam filter. The RFC 822 headers for a mail message are accessible as a hidden property on a message received from the Internet. Therefore, you can use `PropertyAccessor` to obtain those headers and include them in a mail message. The code in Listing 14.2 gets the headers from the item currently selected in a folder

---

→

**Listing 14.2**   *Get Internet headers and send a spam report*

```
Sub SendSpamReport()
    Dim objOL As Outlook.Application
    Dim objItem As Object
    Dim objPA As Outlook.PropertyAccessor
    Dim objMsg As Outlook.MailItem
    Dim strHeader As String
    Const PR_TRANSPORT_MESSAGE_HEADERS = _
        "http://schemas.microsoft.com/mapi/proptag/0x007D001E"
    Set objOL = Application
    Set objItem = objOL.ActiveExplorer.Selection(1)
    If Not objItem Is Nothing Then
        If objItem.Class = olMail Then
            Set objPA = objItem.PropertyAccessor
            strHeader = _
              objPA.GetProperty(PR_TRANSPORT_MESSAGE_HEADERS)
            If strHeader <> "" Then
                Set objMsg = objOL.CreateItem(olMailItem)
                With objMsg
                    .BodyFormat = olFormatPlain
                    .Subject = "Spam Report"
                    .To = "spam@yourisp.com"
                    .Body = "Below are the headers from " & _
                            "the attached message:" & _
                            vbCrLf & vbCrLf & "----------" & _
                            vbCrLf & vbCrLf & strHeader
                    .Attachments.Add objItem, olEmbeddeditem
                    .Display
                End With
            End If
        End If
    End If
    Set objOL = Nothing
    Set objItem = Nothing
    Set objPA = Nothing
    Set objMsg = Nothing
End Sub
```

---

(`ActiveExplorer.Selection(1)`) and then creates a new mail message containing the headers and an attachment of the original item.

Just as in Listing 14.1, the work done by the `PropertyAccessor` object in Listing 14.2 takes place in three statements, one to set a constant, a second to get a `PropertyAccessor` object, and the third to get the property value:

```
Const PR_TRANSPORT_MESSAGE_HEADERS = _
    "http://schemas.microsoft.com/mapi/proptag/0x007D001E"
Set objPA = objItem.PropertyAccessor
strHeader = objPA.GetProperty(PR_TRANSPORT_MESSAGE_HEADERS)
```

If you want to use the `SendSpamReport` procedure to generate spam reports to your own mail provider, don't forget to replace the spam@your-isp.com address with the correct address for your mail host.

## 14.1.2  Where to find property schema names

All the `PropertyAccessor` methods in Table 14.1 take a `SchemaName` or `SchemaNames` parameter. Now that you have seen a couple of examples of `GetProperty`, you are probably wondering about those unusual values for the `SchemaName` parameter. They are like nothing you've yet seen in Outlook:

- `http://schemas.microsoft.com/mapi/proptag/0x0FF40003`
- `http://schemas.microsoft.com/mapi/proptag/0x007D001E`

Such property names are the most complicated aspect of using the `PropertyAccessor` method. The Outlook developer Help topic "Referencing Properties by Namespace" explains in detail what different formats you can expect for property names. The ones in Listings 14.1 and 14.2 come from the MAPI namespace (which is why you'll see them called *MAPI properties*).

---

**Note:** The Outlook documentation on properties often talks about referring to properties through a "namespace." This bears no relation to the `Namespace` object in the Outlook object model, but to the broader concept of a *namespace* as an abstraction containing items all of which have names that are unique within that namespace. *Schema* is a synonym for namespace in this context, as evidenced in the `SchemaName` parameter in the `Property-Accessor` methods.

---

Even though it starts with "http://," the property name `http://schemas.microsoft.com/mapi/proptag/0x0FF40003` has nothing to do with the Internet! For MAPI properties, the `http://schemas.microsoft.com/mapi/proptag/` portion of the property name refers to the MAPI proptag namespace, while the individual property is represented by a hexadecimal number such as `0x0FF40003` or `0x007D001E`.

I recommend that you try two tools if you're going to do any amount of work with `PropertyAccessor`. The Outlook Spy utility from http://www.dimastr.com//outspy/ helps developers browse folders, items, and other objects and see not just the property values but also the schema names that you need for `PropertyAccessor` and several other Outlook methods and properties. Figure 14.1 shows Outlook Spy's window on the Tasks folder with a custom default form that was added with the `SetFolder-DefaultClass` procedure you'll see in Listing 14.3.

**Figure 14.1**
*Outlook Spy makes
it easy to examine
Outlook objects'
properties and
hidden folder
items.*

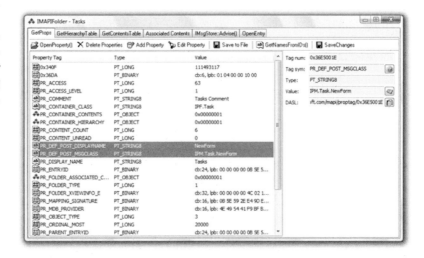

**Listing 14.3**   *Set the default message class on a folder*

```
Sub SetFolderDefaultForm(fld As Outlook.Folder, _
                         msgClass As String)
    Dim objPA As Outlook.PropertyAccessor
    Dim strBaseType As String
    Dim strMsg As String
    Dim intLoc As Integer
    Dim blnBadForm As Boolean
    Dim arrSchema()
    Dim arrValues()
    Dim arrErrors()
    Dim i As Integer
    Const PR_DEF_POST_MSGCLASS = _
      "http://schemas.microsoft.com/mapi/proptag/0x36E5001E"
    Const PR_DEF_POST_DISPLAYNAME = _
      "http://schemas.microsoft.com/mapi/proptag/0x36E6001E"
    On Error Resume Next
    Select Case Left(UCase(msgClass), 8)
        Case "IPM.NOTE" ' cannot be default for any folder
            blnBadForm = True
        Case "IPM.POST" ' default only for mail/post folders
            If StrComp(fld.DefaultMessageClass, _
                    "IPM.NOTE", vbTextCompare) <> 0 Then
                blnBadForm = True
            End If
        Case Else
            If InStr(1, msgClass, fld.DefaultMessageClass, _
                    vbTextCompare) <> 1 Then
                blnBadForm = True
            End If
    End Select
```

**Listing 14.3**    *Set the default message class on a folder (continued)*

```
If Not blnBadForm Then
    intLoc = InStrRev(msgClass, ".")
    arrSchema = Array _
      (PR_DEF_POST_MSGCLASS, PR_DEF_POST_DISPLAYNAME)
    arrValues = _
      Array(msgClass, CStr(Mid(msgClass, intLoc + 1)))
    Err.Clear
    Set objPA = fld.PropertyAccessor
    arrErrors = objPA.SetProperties(arrSchema, arrValues)
    If Err <> 0 Then
        strMsg = "Error " & Err.Number & ": " & _
        Err.Description
    End If
    If Not (IsEmpty(arrErrors)) Then
        For i = 0 To UBound(arrErrors)
            If IsError(arrErrors(i)) Then
                strMsg = strMsg & vbCrLf & _
                        arrSchema(i) & vbCrLf & _
                        CStr(arrErrors(i)) & " - " & _
                        Error(Mid(CStr(arrErrors(i)), 7))
            End If
        Next
    End If
Else
    strMsg = msgClass & " cannot be used as the " & _
            "default form for the """ & fld.Name & _
            """ folder."
End If
If strMsg <> "" Then
    MsgBox strMsg, vbExclamation, _
            "Problem Processing Form Class"
End If
Set objPA = Nothing
End Sub
```

Outlook Spy also displays the hidden items that you can access with the `StorageItem` object, so you can see what properties they contain, most of which you'll use `PropertyAccessor` to access.

Microsoft provides a free tool named MFCMAPI.exe with property and hidden item viewing capability similar to that in Outlook Spy, but the latter is much easier to use. Also, the version of MFCMAPI available when Outlook 2007 was released did not provide any listing of namespace schema names for properties, although plans were in the works to add that feature.

Other Outlook operations that require schema names are the search techniques that you'll learn about in Chapter 16 and the view techniques covered in Chapter 22. To locate the schema names for standard and user-defined properties to use in a search or in a view filter, you don't need a special tool. Instead, you can use a view's Filter dialog. For example, let's say you need the schema name for the `TaskItem.Importance` property. Follow these steps:

1.    Display the Tasks folder.

2.    Choose View | Current View | Customize Current View | Filter

3.    On the Advanced tab, click Field and from the "Frequently-used fields" list, select Priority. Set the Condition to "equals" and select any of the three values offered. Then click Add to List.

4.    Switch to the SQL tab, and check the "Edit these criteria directly" box so you can read the SQL statement more clearly. If you chose Low for the Priority value, you should see this SQL statement:

```
"urn:schemas:httpmail:importance" = 0
```

5.    Once you get the information you need from the Filter dialog, you can click Cancel to close it.

This process tells you that `urn:schemas:httpmail:importance` is the schema name for the field that appears in the Task folder user interface as `Priority`, which is actually the `TaskItem.Importance` property. The namespace for this property is `urn:schemas:httpmail`—a major namespace for properties common to email messages, including some like `Importance` that also apply to other types of Outlook items.

---

**Tip:** To try to eliminate some of the confusion over Outlook object model property names that use different field names in the user interface, the Outlook developer Help contains an article called "Outlook Fields and Equivalent Properties." This is where you'll find out that the `Priority` field for a task is really the `Importance` property in the object model and that the `Company` field in the user interface can either be the `Companies` property or the `CompanyName` property, depending on the type of item you're working with.

---

The `Importance` property can also be represented by the `http://schemas.microsoft.com/mapi/proptag/0x00170003` property from the MAPI proptag namespace. Microsoft recommends using the MAPI proptag namespace schema name for standard Outlook properties.

## 14.1.3    Example: Set the default message class on a folder

Now, let's look at an example of setting property values with `PropertyAccessor`. In the Outlook object model, the `Folder.DefaultMessageClass` property returns the message class for the default type of item that the folder contains and is read-only. It does not tell you if the folder has a custom form as its default form for the folder, and you cannot use it to set a published form as the default form for the folder.

You can set the default form, though, by using the `PropertyAccessor` object. The `SetFolderDefaultForm` procedure in Listing 14.3, for Outlook VBA, uses `PropertyAccessor` to set not one but two specific properties related to the folder's default form.

Here is an example of how to call `SetFolderDefaultClass` in VBA with a `Folder` object and a string for the message class of a custom form (legacy form or form region):

```
Set objFolder = _
  Application.Session.GetDefaultFolder(olFolderTasks)
  Call SetFolderDefaultClass(objFolder, "IPM.Task.NewForm")
```

The `SetFolderDefaultClass` procedure first checks to make sure that the form message class is appropriate for the folder by comparing the published form's message class with the folder's base class from the value of `Folder.DefaultMessageClass`. If the form class is appropriate, the code uses a `PropertyAccessor` object to set the form class and form display name properties on the folder. As you saw in Table 14.1, this object has both `SetProperty` and `SetProperties` methods. We used `SetProperties`, passing it an array of property names and an array of values. `PropertyAccessor.SetProperties` returns either `Nothing` or an array of errors corresponding to each entry in the property name array. We'll look at error handling a little later in the chapter.

## 14.1.4   Understanding PropertyAccessor versus UserProperties

As noted earlier in the chapter, when working with Outlook items, the `PropertyAccessor` technique is more costly in terms of runtime code efficiency than the *object.property_name* syntax for standard properties and `item.UserProperties("property_name")` for user-defined properties. But what about Outlook item properties that your code creates to store information for your application? Should those be created with `UserProperties.Add` or with `PropertyAccessor.SetProperty`?  Understanding two distinct differences should help you decide:

A custom property created with the `UserProperties.Add` method is visible to Outlook users. A property created with `PropertyAccessor.SetProperty` is hidden from users.

If you use `UserProperties.Add` to add a property to a mail message, when the user sends or forwards that message, the presence of a `UserProperty` will force the message to be sent with a TNEF (transport neutral encapsulation format) wrapped in a Winmail.dat attachment. Any files attached to the message will be stored in Winmail.dat and thus inaccessible to any non-Outlook recipient. A property added with `PropertyAccessor.SetProperty` does not cause a Winmail.dat file to be sent with the message. However, such a property does not transmit with the message.

Therefore, if you want to create a hidden property or don't want to risk sending Winmail.dat, the best method to use is `PropertyAccessor.SetProperty`. If you want to create a visible property or need to send a custom property in a message to other Outlook recipients, use `UserProperties.Add`.

One final issue related to creating properties with `PropertyAccessor.SetProperty` is what namespace to use. Microsoft recommends using the MAPI string namespace, which uses this syntax for the property name:

```
http://schemas.microsoft.com/mapi/string/{HHHHHHHH-HHHH-
HHHH-HHHH-HHHHHHHHHHHH}/name
```

where `{HHHHHHHH-HHHH-HHHH-HHHH-HHHHHHHHHHHH}` is a GUID (globally unique ID) and `name` is the property name itself. Developers of Outlook add-ins should use the GUID for their application as the GUID for the property. Users writing code in VBA or VBScript for a custom form can use the same GUID that Outlook uses for properties in the `UserProperties` collection, `{00020329-0000-0000-C000-000000000046}`. The code in Listing 14.4 creates a new task and adds a hidden `ProjectID` property to it.

Did you notice that when you create a property in the MAPI string namespace, you don't specify the data type? The data type for the property can change, depending on what type of data you store in it with the `SetProperty` method. This gives hidden properties a slight flexibility edge over properties in the `UserProperties` collection.

## 14.1.5    PropertyAccessor limitations and errors

Be prepared for errors with `PropertyAccessor`, which has a number of limitations:

- It doesn't support object-type properties like a message's recipients.

- For binary properties, only those whose values are under 4,088 bytes in size can be set or retrieved. Attempts to use larger values will raise an out-of-memory error.

- For string properties, the size limit depends on the information store. For Personal Folders .pst files and Exchange offline folders .ost files, the limit is 4,088 bytes. For direct online access to Exchange mailbox or Public Folders hierarchy, the limit is 16,372 bytes.

- The body of an Outlook message, contact, or other item is not accessible at all through `PropertyAccessor`. Nor is the content of an attachment.

**Listing 14.4**    *Create a task with a hidden property*

```
Sub CreateTaskWithHiddenProperty()
    Dim objOL As Outlook.Application
    Dim objTask As Outlook.TaskItem
    Dim objPA As Outlook.PropertyAccessor
    Dim strProp As String
    On Error Resume Next
    Set objOL = Application
    Set objTask = objOL.CreateItem(olTaskItem)
    objTask.Subject = "A New Task"
    Set objPA = objTask.PropertyAccessor
    strProp = "http://schemas.microsoft.com/mapi/string/" & _
              "{00020329-0000-0000-C000-000000000046}/" & _
              "ProjectID"
    Err.Clear
    objPA.SetProperty strProp, "ID001"
    If Err = 0 Then
        objTask.Save
    Else
        MsgBox "Error " & Err.Number & " - " & Err.Description
    End If
    Set objOL = Nothing
    Set objTask = Nothing
    Set objPA = Nothing
End Sub
```

- Date/time values are always handled as Coordinated Universal Time (UTC). The `PropertyAccessor.LocalTimeToUTC` and `.UTCTo-LocalTime` methods can assist in converting such date/time values from or to the user's local time zone.

- The time converter methods for both `PropertyAccessor` and `Row` round the result to the nearest minute, ignoring any seconds part of the date/time value.

**Tip:** Besides `LocalTimeToUTC`, and `UTCToLocalTime`, the `PropertyAccessor` object also supports two other helper methods—`BinaryToString` and `StringToBinary`—to assist with data conversions. You can use these four methods with any data, not just with property values obtained with `PropertyAccessor`.

Given the many limitations, error handling can play an important role in code that uses `PropertyAccessor`. An error can occur for many reasons, other than the limitations above, including the following:

- For `SetProperties`, the arrays for properties and values might not have the same number of elements.

- For `SetProperty` and `SetProperties`, you might not have permission to create a new property if the property doesn't already exist or there might be a mismatch between the property and the type of value it can accept.

- For `DeleteProperty` and `DeleteProperties`, you might be trying to delete a read-only property.

- For `GetProperty` and `GetProperties`, the property might not be present on the item.

If you want to handle `PropertyAccessor` errors, rather than ignore them, use a two-pronged approach: Check both the value of `Err` after invoking a `PropertyAccessor` method and the value that the method returns. This code snippet checks the result returned by `Property-Accessor.GetProperty` and, if it is `Empty`, checks whether an error occurred:

```
On Error Resume Next
Err.Clear
res = objPA.GetProperty(strProp)
If IsEmpty(res) Then
    If Err <> 0 Then
        MsgBox "Error " & Err.Number & " - " & _
            Err.Description
    End If
Else
    MsgBox res
End If
```

When using the three `PropertyAccessor` methods that use arrays, check `Err` before checking the method's result:

```
On Error Resume Next
Err.Clear
res = objPA.SetProperties(arrProps, arrValues)
' or try one of these statements
' res = objPA.GetProperties(arrProps)
' res = objPA.DeleteProperties(arrProps)
If Err = 0 Then
    For i = 0 To UBound(res)
        If IsError(res(i)) Then
            strMsg = strMsg & vbCrLf & _
                    CStr(res(i)) & " - " & _
                    Error(Mid(CStr(res(i)), 7))
        Else
            strMsg = strMsg & vbCrLf & CStr(res(i))
        End If
    Next
Else
    strMsg = "Error " & Err.Number & "  - " & _
            Err.Description
End If
MsgBox strMsg, , "PropertyAccessor Results"
```

Of course, your application may want to present any error information more elegantly than with a `MsgBox` statement.

## 14.2   Using the StorageItem object

We saw in the last chapter how to work with standard folder properties. Then earlier in this chapter, you saw an example of hidden folder properties that you can manage with `PropertyAccessor`, specifically those related to the default form for a folder. A third type of folder settings involves a concept new to the Outlook 2007 object model: *solution storage*. When Outlook needs to maintain folder- or store-specific information that is larger or more complex than a simple folder property, it keeps that information in an item that the user can't see. Views, custom form definitions, archive settings, and many other configuration options are maintained in such hidden items. Not only can `StorageItem` code retrieve and modify hidden items that Outlook itself creates, but you can also create new hidden items to maintain data for your own solutions in mail/post folders.

To return an existing or new `StorageItem`, use the `Folder.GetStorage` method which takes two parameters:

```
Set objStI = objFolder.GetStorage _
  (StorageIdentifier, StorageIdentifierType)
```

The *StorageIdentifer* parameter is a string containing one of the following pieces of information:

- The `EntryID` for the exact `StorageItem` you want to retrieve
- A `MessageClass` value if you want to return a `StorageItem` with that class if one exists and create one if it doesn't
- A `Subject` value if you want to return a `StorageItem` with that subject if one exists and create one if it doesn't

The *StorageIdentifierType* parameter uses one of the values from the `OlStorageIdentifierType` enumeration, shown in Table 14.2, specifically the value appropriate for the type of information contained in *StorageIdentifier*.

If you use `GetStorage` to retrieve a `StorageItem` by `MessageClass` or `Subject` and no such item exists in the folder, Outlook creates a new `StorageItem`, assuming the user has owner rights on the folder. (However, as noted in the next section, this technique works only in mail/post folders in the initial release of Outlook 2007.) If more than one matching item exists, Outlook returns the one most recently modified.

Once you return a `StorageItem` object, you can work with its limited number of standard properties and use `PropertyAccessor` to read, write, create, and delete its other properties. The `StorageItem` object itself has very few properties, compared with normal Outlook items. It does support

**Table 14.2**    *OlStorageIdentifierType Values for Use with Folder.GetStorage*

| OlStorageIdentifierType | Value |
|---|---|
| olIdentifyByEntryID | 1 |
| olIdentifyByMessageClass | 2 |
| olIdentifyBySubject | 0 |

`Body`, `Subject`, and `UserProperties`, along with a `Creator` property that can hold information specific to the application that created the `Storage-Item`. For most other properties, you need to use `PropertyAccessor`.

Section 14.2.2 demonstrates a practical use of `StorageItem`—to clean up one-off copies of standard views. For another example of `StorageItem` in action, read the Help article "How to: Save Auto-Archive Properties of a Folder in Solution Storage" (HV10045893), which shows how to create a new set of archive options or change the existing archive options for a folder.

### 14.2.1  StorageItem limitations

Three issues limit the usefulness of the `StorageItem` object, at least in the initial release of Outlook, two related to new items, and one related to existing items.

A severe constraint affects the creation of new `StorageItem` objects. If in a non-mail folder, you use the `GetStorage` method to try to create a new `StorageItem` object, Outlook does not create a `StorageItem` in that folder. Instead, it creates a visible item in the user's Inbox. Therefore, custom storage using `StorageItem` is possible only in mail/post folders. Let's hope that Microsoft releases an update for Outlook 2007 that fixes this problem.

It is also not possible to create new storage items in folders in the Exchange Public Folders hierarchy. This means that you cannot, for example, use a storage item to store lists that might be used to populate controls on a custom form used in a public contacts folder.

Regarding existing storage items, the `GetStorage` method raises an error if you try to return a hidden item from an Exchange public folder or from an Exchange system folder, such as the Organizational Forms library. This means that you cannot use `GetStorage` to help with such maintenance chores as deleting obsolete custom forms published to a public folder or to Organizational Forms.

Since `StorageItem` objects expose a small number of properties to the Outlook object model, most code needs to use the `PropertyAccessor` object to access StorageItem properties. Therefore, all the Property-Accessor limitations discussed in Section 14.1.5 also are relevant to work with StorageItem.

## 14.2.2   Example: Clean up one-off folder views

Consider a common issue related to folder views. Outlook comes with a set of standard views, such as the Messages view that applies to all mail folders and the Day/Week/Month view for calendar folders. Whenever a user changes the settings for one of those standard views while viewing a folder, Outlook caches a folder-specific copy of the view as a StorageItem in that folder. While that behavior allows a user to return to a previously used folder and see the same view as the folder had the last time the user looked at it, it can also give rise to a potential problem. If, for example, the user modifies the view settings while using the Messages view, any subsequent changes to the master copy of the Messages view won't be reflected in any folder that has a cached copy of the Messages view. Also, more rarely, a cached view will become corrupted and give the user error messages. Out of the box, Outlook has only a brute force solution for both these situations—start Outlook with the /cleanviews command-line switch, which will clear not only all folder-specific cached copies of views, but also all of the user's saved custom views. That's not a great solution if all you want to do is clean up one cached view on one folder.

As an alternative, you can write your own solution that targets one specific view in one specific folder. The CleanView procedure in Listing 14.5 removes the StorageItem for a specific named view from a folder. That view might be either a cached copy of a standard view or a custom view that the user (or programming code) has created. (It is not possible to remove

**Listing 14.5**   *Remove a cached or custom view from a folder*

```
Sub CleanView(fld As Outlook.Folder, strView As String)
    Dim objStI As Outlook.StorageItem
    Dim objPA As Outlook.PropertyAccessor
    Dim strClass As String
    Const PR_MESSAGE_CLASS = _
        "http://schemas.microsoft.com/mapi/proptag/0x001A001E"
    On Error Resume Next
    Set objStI = fld.GetStorage(strView, olIdentifyBySubject)
    Set objPA = objStI.PropertyAccessor
    strClass = objPA.GetProperty(PR_MESSAGE_CLASS)
    If strClass = "IPM.Microsoft.FolderDesign.NamedView" Then
        objStI.Delete
    End If
    Set objStI = Nothing
    Set objPA = Nothing
End Sub
```

the master copy of a standard view, nor is it possible to modify the master view programmatically.) Call `CleanView` with a statement like this, where `objFolder` is the folder whose view you want to remove:

```
Call CleanView(objFolder, "Messages")
```

The `CleanView` example uses the `Subject` property value to locate the `StorageItem`. We have no way of knowing its `EntryID` value, and there could be other cached views in the folder, all with the same `MessageClass`. Therefore, the `Subject` property is the best way to identify a specific cached view.

Notice, though, that `CleanView` does use `PropertyAccessor` to confirm that the returned `StorageItem` has a particular `MessageClass` value. In this example, the value `"IPM.Microsoft.FolderDesign.NamedView"` confirms that `objStI` is a `StorageItem` for a view.

If you want to clear all cached copies of a standard view, you can use the basic folder recursion technique that you saw in Listing 13.9 to call `Clean-View` for each folder in the hierarchy. In Listing 14.6, the `CleanMessages-ViewAllFolders` procedure iterates the information store root folders and calls `ProcessFolder` for each one. The `ProcessFolder` procedure in turn

**Listing 14.6**    *Remove cached copies of the messages view from all folders*

```
Sub CleanMessagesViewAllFolders()
    Dim objOL As Outlook.Application
    Dim objNS As Outlook.NameSpace
    Dim objFolder As Outlook.Folder
    Set objOL = Application
    Set objNS = objOL.Session
    For Each objFolder In objNS.Folders
        Call ProcessFolder(objFolder)
    Next
    Set objOL = Nothing
    Set objNS = Nothing
    Set objFolder = Nothing
End Sub

Sub ProcessFolder(startFolder As Outlook.Folder)
    Dim objFolder As Outlook.Folder
    On Error Resume Next
    For Each objFolder In startFolder.Folders
        If objFolder.DefaultItemType = olMailItem Then
            ' CleanView procedure from Listing 14.5
            Call CleanView(objFolder, "Messages")
        End If
        Call ProcessFolder(objFolder)
    Next
    Set objFolder = Nothing
End Sub
```

calls the `CleanView` procedure from Listing 14.5 for each mail folder and performs recursion by calling itself.

After you remove all cached copies of the Messages view, any settings in the master copy of the Messages view will apply when the user displays the Messages view for a folder.

## 14.3  Summary

The new `PropertyAccessor` and `StorageItem` objects are very powerful tools that give Outlook 2007 the ability to work with hidden properties and settings. You can use these in almost any scenario that previously required the `Fields` and `HiddenMessages` collections from the Collaboration Data Objects object model, although there are some limitations. Accessing properties with `PropertyAccessor` requires an understanding of schema names for properties, but online resources and other tools and techniques are available to help you find the property names you need.

This chapter is full of practical examples, including sending a spam report, setting the default form for a folder, and cleaning up cached copies of views.

The `PropertyAccessor` object is also very useful for getting and setting the values of hidden properties on individual items, and it is to those items that we turn in the next four chapters.

# 15

# *Working with Inspectors and Items*

In Chapter 13, we discussed Outlook folders and the `Explorer` windows that display them. This chapter explores individual Outlook items and their `Inspector` windows, including how to create a new item, return existing items, and work with those items' methods. Chapters 7 and 14 covered how to access items' properties.

One significant change in Outlook 2007 is that it uses only one editor for all items, except "sticky note" items, and that editor is Word 2007—or more precisely, a component derived from Word. Another big change is the addition of a `Table` object for rapid, read-only access to Outlook items.

Highlights of this chapter include discussions of the following:

- How to work with the `Inspector` windows that display Outlook items
- How to create new Outlook items from scratch and from vCard .vcf and iCalendar .ics files
- How to process all the items in a folder or all the items the user has selected in a folder view
- What methods of the `Items` collection can help you sort and iterate items
- How to use the new `Table` object to return data quickly from a large number of items
- How to create, move, copy, delete, and perform other common item operations

This is actually the first of four chapters on working with items. Chapter 16 explores the many different ways to search for items; Chapter 17 examines techniques for working with the bodies of messages and other items; and Chapter 20 reviews item-specific issues and techniques, such as sending a message with a particular account, and suggests ways to build links between items.

# 15.1  Working with Inspectors

The Inspectors collection is a member of the Application object and represents all the windows that are currently open to display individual Outlook items. You have seen the ActiveInspector object in several previous chapters where it was used to create macros that operate on the currently displayed item. This VBA code snippet sets an objItem variable to the current item:

```
Dim objItem as Object
On Error Resume Next
Set objInsp = Application.ActiveInspector
If Not objInsp Is Nothing Then
    Set objItem = objInsp.CurrentItem
End If
```

It is important to test whether ActiveInspector returns Nothing, to handle the case where the user has no item windows open.

You never need to use Application.ActiveInspector.CurrentItem in an Outlook form's VBScript code, because the current item is always Item, the intrinsic object representing the item where the code is running. From that Item object, you can return an Inspector object with the GetInspector method. As we saw in Chapters 7 and 12, Item.GetInspector is an essential statement in any code that works with the customized pages and controls on a custom form.

If an Inspector showing the desired item already is available, you can use the Activate method to switch the focus of the Outlook application to that Inspector:

```
objInsp.Activate
```

Use the Close method to close any Inspector, using this syntax:

```
objInsp.Close SaveMode
```

Unlike the Close method for the Explorer object, for the Inspector.Close method, you must supply a value for the SaveMode parameter. Table 15.1 lists the possible values from the OlInspectorClose enumeration.

**Table 15.1**  *OlInspectorClose Values for the SaveMode Parameter of the Inspector.Close Method*

| Option | SaveMode | Value |
|---|---|---|
| Close without saving changes | olDiscard | 1 |
| If the item was changed, prompt the user to save changes (no prompt occurs if no changes were made) | olPromptForSave | 2 |
| Save changes without prompting (no save occurs if no changes were made) | olSave | 0 |

To close the windows for all items except the one currently being viewed, you can close all `Inspector` windows, and then redisplay the last item that the user viewed. The code in Listing 15.1 gets a reference to the current item (`ActiveInspector.CurrentItem`), closes all `Inspector` windows, uses the `GetInspector` method on the item most recently viewed, and finally applies the `Activate` method to display that `Inspector`.

---

**Note:** Notice the use of a `Do` loop to close all the `Inspector` windows in Listing 15.1. An alternative would have been a `For ... Next` countdown loop. A `For Each ... Next` loop would not have been suitable because you're removing items from the `Inspectors` collection as they're closed.

---

You do not actually need to invoke an `Inspector` to show a particular item, because all Outlook items support a `Display` method. In the code in Listing 15.1, you could replace these two statements:

```
Set objInsp = objItemKeep.GetInspector
objInsp.Activate
```

with this single statement:

```
objItemKeep.Display
```

Table 15.2 lists useful the most useful methods and properties for the `Inspector` object. Chapter 17, "Working with Item Bodies," dives deeply

**Listing 15.1**  *Close all but the current Inspector window*

```
Sub CloseAllButCurrentInspector()
    Dim objOL As Outlook.Application
    Dim colInsp As Outlook.Inspectors
    Dim objInsp As Outlook.Inspector
    Dim objItemKeep As Object
    Set objOL = Application
    Set colInsp = objOL.Inspectors
    If colInsp.Count > 0 Then
        Set objItemKeep = objOL.ActiveInspector.CurrentItem
        Do Until colInsp.Count = 0
            colInsp.Item(1).Close olPromptForSave
        Loop
        Set objInsp = objItemKeep.GetInspector
        objInsp.Activate
    End If
    Set objOL = Nothing
    Set colInsp = Nothing
    Set objInsp = Nothing
    Set objItemKeep = Nothing
End Sub
```

**Table 15.2**  *Useful Inspector Methods and Properties*

| Method | Description |
|---|---|
| Activate | Bring the window to the foreground and give it the focus |
| Close *SaveMode* | Close the window |
| HideFormPage *PageName* | Hide the *PageName* page of the form displayed in the window |
| SetCurrentFormPage *PageName* | Switch to the *PageName* page of the form displayed in the window; raises an error if the page is not visible |
| ShowFormPage *PageName* | Unhide the *PageName* page of the form displayed in the window |

| Property | Description |
|---|---|
| Caption | Title displayed on the window (read-only) |
| CommandBars | Collection of toolbar and menu commands that can be executed for the current window |
| CurrentItem | Returns the item displayed in the window |
| Height | Height of the window, in pixels |
| Left | Left position of the window, in pixels |
| ModifiedFormPages | Returns a collection of customized pages |
| Top | Top position of the window, in pixels |
| Width | Width of the window, in pixels |
| WindowState | Display state of the window, using one of these constants from the OlWindowState enumeration: <br> olMaximized    0 <br> olMinimized    1 <br> olNormalWindow  2 |
| WordEditor | For appointment, contact, journal entry, message, post, and task items, returns a Word.Document object for the body of the item displayed in the window |

into the message and item body techniques available with the WordEditor object.

In Outlook VBA, the Inspector.CommandBars collection remains useful for executing item-related commands, such as displaying the Insert File dialog, but it cannot be used to customize the user interface. The Inspector window uses the new ribbon interface, which cannot be customized with Outlook VBA code.

## 15.2  Creating items

Outlook 2007 has four main methods for creating new items (one more than previous versions), plus an additional technique that you can use from Word or Excel to create an email message. Which one should you use? It depends on what type of item you want to create:

- A new standard item
- A new item based on a published custom form
- A new item based on a form saved as an .oft file template
- A new item imported from a vCard (.vcf), iCalendar (.ics), vCalendar (.vcs), or Outlook message format (.msg) file (new in Outlook 2007)
- A new email message based on the content of a Word document or an Excel worksheet

The next few sections cover each of these scenarios. We'll see other methods that return a new item—those related to copying, moving, replying to, and forwarding items—a little later in the chapter. Plus, as we will see in Chapter 20, voting buttons and other custom actions on Outlook forms can also create new items.

Two general notes regarding newly created Outlook items:

- Outlook does not store a new item permanently until it is saved or sent, either by the user or by your code. After creating a new item, you may want to use code to set certain properties before you display the item to the user or save it.
- If you create an Outlook item using code on a VBA form, make sure that either the VBA form is modeless or that you unload or hide it before you display the new Outlook item. Otherwise, the user will see a Dialog Box Is Open error.

### 15.2.1  Creating a new standard item

To create a new standard item in one of the user's default folders, use the `Application.CreateItem` method to return an object reference for the new item. You can then set the item's properties, and display, save, or send it. The `CreateItem` method requires one of the constants listed in Table 15.3 from the `OlItemType` enumeration.

A common application of `CreateItem` in code behind a custom form is to create a notification message or a new Outlook item as part of a workflow. This VBScript code snippet for a custom form creates and displays an email message for the user to address:

```
Const olMailItem = 0
Set objMsg = Application.CreateItem(olMailItem)
With objMsg
    .Subject = "Update on " & Item.Subject
```

```
        .Body = "Here is the latest information:"
        .Display
End With
```

Notice that the code sets the new message's `Subject` property using text from the original item's `Subject`.

For items other than email messages, the `CreateItem` method always creates items in the default Outlook folders such as Calendar and Tasks. Newly created unsent messages always save in the Drafts folder.

To create a non-message item in a non-default folder, use the `Add` method on the target folder's `Items` collection. You should recall that every `Folder` object has both a `Folders` collection representing its subfolders and an `Items` collection representing the items in the folder. Chapter 13 gave you many techniques for returning a specific folder. Once you have an object representing the folder where you want to create the new standard item, use this syntax to return the new item. This example assumes that `objFolder` is a task folder:

```
Set objTask = objFolder.Items.Add
```

When invoked with no parameters, the `Items.Add` method creates a new item of the default type for the target folder, for example a new `Task-Item` in a folder that holds tasks. If the folder holds contacts and you want to create a new distribution list in it, you will need to specify the type of item using either the constant from Table 15.3 or the correct message class string:

```
Set objDL = objFolder.Items.Add(olDistributionListItem)
Set objDL = objFolder.Items.Add("IPM.DistList")
```

**Table 15.3**   *OlItemType Constants for Use with the CreateItem Method*

| Outlook Item | ItemType Constant | Value |
|---|---|---|
| Message | olMailItem | 0 |
| Appointment | olAppointmentItem | 1 |
| Contact | olContactItem | 2 |
| Task | olTaskItem | 3 |
| Journal entry | olJournalItem | 4 |
| Note | olNoteItem | 5 |
| Post | olPostItem | 6 |
| Distribution list | olDistributionList | 7 |

For another example of `Folder.Items.Add`, look back at Listing 9.2, which creates a new item in the Tasks folder in another Exchange user's mailbox.

You cannot use the `Folder.Items.Add` method to create a new message in a specific folder. As noted earlier, a new, unsent message saves in the Drafts folder regardless of whether you create it with `Items.Add` or `CreateItem`. If you want to store the unsent message in a different folder, you will need to save it and then move it with the `Move` method discussed later in the chapter.

### 15.2.2 Creating a new item from a custom form

Guess what? You already know how to create a new item from a published custom form, because it's the same technique as in the last code statement in the previous section: Use the `Add` method on the target folder's `Items` collection, passing the message class string as the sole parameter:

```
Set objContact = _
    objFolder.Items.Add("IPM.Contact.Custom")
```

The message class can be that of a published custom form or a form region whose `formRegionType` is `replace` or `replaceAll`.

### 15.2.3 Creating a new item from an .oft template

Although you can create an Outlook template .oft file from any Outlook item—from an empty standard task to a highly customized contact form with default property values—such files actually are useful only in two very specific cases:

- Standard items containing preset values for standard properties, such as an appointment with a specific category
- Messages containing boilerplate text and specific formatting

Users can simply double-click these types of .oft files to create new items based on those templates.

Why are other types of .oft files less useful? A template can't run VBScript code like a published custom form can. Also, a template designed with custom properties will not display its custom layout if the user opens it by double-clicking the .oft file. Instead, it will display the standard layout for that type of item. To see the custom layout, the user would need to launch the template with the Tools | Forms | Choose Form command or with the `CreateItemFromTemplate` method.

**Tip:** Despite their limitations, .oft files are still quite useful as backups for published custom forms.

Therefore, in this book, we will assume that if you're working with an .oft template file, it is within one of the two scenarios described above.

To create a new item based on an .oft file, use the `Application.CreateItemFromTemplate` method, passing the path to the file as a parameter. This statement creates a new message from a saved file:

```
Set objMsg = Application.CreateItemFromTemplate _
   ("C:\Data\My Message Template.oft")
```

In Chapter 17, we will look again at `CreateItemFromTemplate` in the context of modifying the body of a template-generated message to fill in some recipient-specific information.

### 15.2.4 Creating a new item from a vCard, iCalendar, or .msg file

One of the more versatile new programming features in Outlook 2007 is the ability to import from common file types used to exchange contact and appointment information over the Internet—.vcf vCard files and .ics iCalendar appointment files. The `NameSpace.OpenSharedItem` method takes the path to the file as its sole parameter and returns a `ContactItem` or `AppointmentItem` as appropriate. To store the imported item in the default folder for that type of item, use the `Save` method. You can also use the `Move` method, covered later in this chapter, to move it to another folder.

This example opens a vCard file and saves it to the Contacts folder:

```
Set objNS = Application.Session
On Error Resume Next
strPath = "C:\Donna Liss.vcf"
Set objContact = objNS.OpenSharedItem(strPath)
If Not objContact Is Nothing Then
    objContact.Save
End If
```

The `On Error Resume Next` statement is crucial to handling the scenario where the file named in the argument does not exist.

---

**Note:** Use `Namespace.OpenSharedItem` to open an .ics file that contains a single appointment. To process an .ics file that contains multiple appointments, use the `Namespace.OpenSharedFolder` method, which we saw in Chapter 13.

---

The `OpenSharedItem` method can also open any Outlook item that has been saved as an .msg file. In that case, you cannot know in advance what type of object the method will return; it depends on the type of item. For example, if you use `OpenSharedItem` to open a task that was saved as an .msg file, it will return a `TaskItem`. For a code sample that saves embedded

Outlook items plus .vcf, .vcs, or .ics files attached to an Outlook message or other item, skip ahead to Listing 19.2.

---

**Note:** In previous versions of Outlook, you could use the `CreateItem-FromTemplate` method to make a copy of a saved .msg file, but in the case of a message, it would create a new, unsent message. That technique still works in Outlook 2007, but to import a message intact, with its original sender and recipient information, you should use `OpenSharedItem`.

---

### 15.2.5 Creating a new item from a Word or Excel document

The last method of creating a new item applies only to messages but can be a very powerful shortcut to producing complex HTML messages based on Excel data or Word documents. It is, in essence, the programmatic equivalent of the Send To | Mail Recipient command found on the File menu in previous versions of Word and Excel and available in Office 2007 versions from the Customize Quick Access Toolbar dialog.

---

**Note:** In Chapter 19, we'll see how to post an entire Word or Excel document (or any other type of file) to an Outlook folder.

---

What makes this technique feasible is that the `Word.Document` and `Excel.Worksheet` objects support a `MailEnvelope` property that returns an `Office.MsoEnvelope` object. This object's `Item` property returns a `MailItem` whose `HTMLBody` property will contain an HTML representation

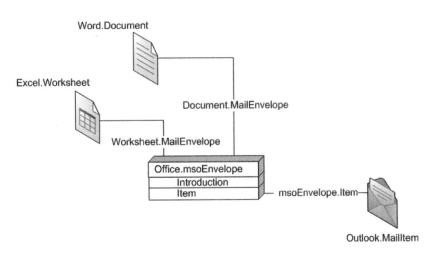

**Figure 15.1**
*Create a mail message from a document or worksheet using the MailEnvelope property.*

of the document or worksheet. It also supports an `Introduction` property that you can use to prefix the document or worksheet content with your own introductory text. Figure 15.1 shows how the `MailEnvelope` property can connect a document or worksheet and a mail message.

You can use `MailEnvelope` from both Outlook code and Word or Excel VBA code. Listing 15.2 is a VBScript version, for use behind an Outlook form; it opens an existing Word document named First_Notice.docx, generates a mail message from that document, then addresses and sends the message. Listing 15.3 is a VBA version that sends the current Excel worksheet as an Outlook message.

**Listing 15.2**   *Send a Word document as an email message (VBScript)*

```
Sub SendDocAsMsg()
    Dim objWord                    ' As Word.Application
    Dim objDoc                     ' As Word.Document
    Dim objItem                    ' As Object
    Dim strID                      ' As String
    Dim blnWeOpenedWord            ' As Boolean
    Const wdDoNotSaveChanges = 0
    On Error Resume Next
    Set objWord = GetObject(, "Word.Application")
    If objWord Is Nothing Then
        Set objWord = CreateObject("Word.Application")
        blnWeOpenedWord = True
    End If
    Set objDoc = objWord.Documents.Open _
                ("C:\First_Notice.docx", , True)
    objDoc.MailEnvelope.Introduction = _
      "Please reply with your thoughts on this matter."
    Set objItem = objDoc.MailEnvelope.Item
    With objItem
        .To = "flaviusl@turtleflock.net"
        .Subject = objDoc.BuiltinDocumentProperties("Title")
        .Save
        strID = .EntryID
    End With
    Set objItem = Nothing
    Set objItem = Application.Session.GetItemFromID(strID)
    objItem.Send
    objDoc.Close wdDoNotSaveChanges
    If blnWeOpenedWord Then
        objWord.Quit
    End If
    Set objDoc = Nothing
    Set objItem = Nothing
    Set objWord = Nothing
End Sub
```

Note: The `SendDocAsMsg` procedure in Listing 15.2 is "well behaved" with regard to Word; it uses the `GetObject` method to check whether an instance of Word is already running. If a new instance has to be created, the procedure shuts down Word when it finishes its work. The Boolean `blnWeOpenedWord` variable tracks whether the procedure started Word or Word was already running.

Both listings try to build the subject for the message from the `Title` property in the document or workbook's `BuiltInDocumentProperties` collection.

To write code for the `MailEnvelope` object in Outlook VBA, use the Tools | References command to add references to the Microsoft Word 12.0

**Listing 15.3**    *Send an Excel worksheet as an email message (Excel VBA)*

```
Sub SendSheetAsMsg()
    Dim objExcel As Excel.Application
    Dim objSheet As Excel.Worksheet
    Dim objWB As Excel.Workbook
    Dim objDocProp As Office.DocumentProperty
    Dim objItem As Object
    Dim strID As String
    Dim strMsg As String
    On Error Resume Next
    Set objExcel = Application
    Set objSheet = objExcel.ActiveSheet
    Set objWB = objExcel.ActiveWorkbook
    objSheet.MailEnvelope.Introduction = _
      "Please reply with your thoughts on this matter."
    Set objItem = objSheet.MailEnvelope.Item
    With objItem
        .To = "flavius1@turtleflock.net"
        If objWB.BuiltinDocumentProperties("Title") <> "" Then
            .Subject = objWB.BuiltinDocumentProperties("Title")
        Else
            .Subject = objSheet.Name
        End If
        .Send
    End With
    If Err <> 0 Then
        objItem.Display
    End If
    Set objExcel = Nothing
    Set objSheet = Nothing
    Set objItem = Nothing
End Sub
```

Object Library and the Microsoft Excel 12.0 Object Library. Once you do that, you can declare Word or Excel object variables and get the same "intellisense" as you do for Outlook objects.

# 15.3  Accessing items

The code samples in previous chapters have shown several methods to access a particular existing item—including an item selected in a folder and a currently displayed item. Outlook also supports code techniques to:

- Return a particular item that you've worked with previously
- Work with all the items in a folder
- Work with items the user has selected in a folder view
- Search for items based on specific criteria

The sections that follow explain many of the different ways available to access Outlook items. Search techniques are covered in the next chapter.

## 15.3.1  Working with selected items

Listing 8.4 introduced the `Selection` object, which represents the items selected by the user in a folder window. A common application of `Selection` within VBA macros is to perform batch operations that you can't do with Outlook's built-in menu and toolbar commands. This VBA code statement sets an `objSel` variable to the items selected in the current folder (the `ActiveExplorer` window's folder):

```
Set objSel = Application.ActiveExplorer.Selection
```

If you want to work with just one selected item, add this statement:

```
Set objItem = objSel.Item(1)
```

---

**Note:** The `Selection` object supports the `Item` and `Count` properties like most other Outlook collections, but not the `Add` and `Remove` methods. You cannot programmatically expand or contract the user's selection to include more or fewer items. The only way to programmatically affect the selection is to execute the Select All menu command using the `CommandBars` methods that we'll see in Chapter 23. It is also impossible to convert a `Selection` object into an `Items` object.

---

The usual procedure with `Selection` is to work with either one selected item, as above, or with the entire `Selection` collection, using a `For Each ... Next` loop. If you plan to delete or move items, a `For ... Next` countdown loop, would be appropriate, instead of a `For Each ... Next` loop. Depending on the operation you plan to perform on the selection, you might want to check the number of items first with the `Selec-`

tion.Count property. Listing 15.4 provides a general VBA code framework you can use to determine the number of items selected and proceed accordingly. Change the value in this statement

```
intMaxItems = 30
```

to reflect the maximum number of selected items that you want the ProcessItem() procedure to handle.

The ProcessItem subroutine included in the listing is just a simple example to show how each object in the Selection can be passed to a separate procedure that does the actual processing. This results in more modular, reusable code. If you set the value for intMaxItems to whatever number you feel is appropriate for your application, the ProcessSelection procedure will warn the user if more than that number of items is selected.

You will see more examples of Selection in the next section. Section 15.3.4 deals with issues related to processing multiple items.

**Listing 15.4**     *Process selected items in a folder*

```
Sub ProcessSelection()
    Dim objOL As Outlook.Application
    Dim objSel As Outlook.Selection
    Dim objItem As Object
    Dim intMaxItems As Integer
    On Error Resume Next
    ' ### USER OPTION ###
    intMaxItems = 30
    Set objOL = Application
    Set objSel = objOL.ActiveExplorer.Selection
    Select Case objSel.Count
        Case 0
            MsgBox "No items were selected!"
        Case 1 To intMaxItems
            For Each objItem In objSel
                Call ProcessItem(objItem)
            Next
        Case Is > intMaxItems
            MsgBox objSel.Count & " items is too big " & _
                    "a selection for this operation."
    End Select
    Set objOL = Nothing
    Set objSel = Nothing
    Set objItem = Nothing
End Sub

Sub ProcessItem(itm As Object)
    Debug.Print itm.Subject
End Sub
```

### 15.3.2    Getting the current item

As discussed earlier in the chapter, where `Explorer` objects represent Outlook folder windows, `Inspector` objects correspond to Outlook item windows. Because you can have more than one Outlook item open, more than one `Inspector` may be available.

To access the item window that the user is currently looking at or most recently viewed, use the `ActiveInspector` method of the `Application` object. To get the actual item that the user sees in that window, use the `CurrentItem` property of the `Inspector`, as in the following example:

```
Dim objItem As Object
Set objItem = Application.ActiveInspector.CurrentItem
```

The current item could be any type of Outlook item—a message, a contact, even a note. Because you can't predict the type of item, you should use a generic `Dim objItem as Object` statement to declare the object variable when you are writing VBA code. In most cases, your code will need to check what kind of item the object represents before working with its properties and methods. If you use a property or method that belongs to the wrong object, your code will raise a runtime error.

To check the type of item, use the `Class` property. Table 15.4 lists the Outlook constants for the `Class` property values for different types of Outlook items, along with their literal values, from the `OlObjectClass` enumeration.

---

**Tip:** Table 15.4 lists just some of the `Class` values that Outlook supports. To learn about other intrinsic constants for the `Class` property, look up the `OlObjectClass` enumeration in the object browser.

---

If you try to access the `Class` property for an object variable that has not been set to an object, Outlook generates an error. Therefore, depending on how you returned that object variable, you may need to use the expression `object Is Nothing` to test whether you have a valid object, before you check the value of the `Class` property, proceeding from the above snippet:

```
If Not objItem Is Nothing Then
    If objItem.Class = olTask ' 48
        MsgBox Item.Subject & " is a task!"
    End If
End If
```

In Listing 8.19, you saw how to use the `ActiveExplorer.Selection` collection to process the items the user has selected in a folder view. In some cases, you will want the flexibility to have a VBA macro operate on either the currently open item or on one or more items selected in a folder window, whichever is the active window. Don't write two complete versions,

**Table 15.4**   *Values of the Class Property for Outlook Items from the OlObjectClass Enumeration*

| Object | Class Constant | Class Value |
|---|---|---|
| Message | `olMail` | 43 |
| Appointment | `olAppointment` | 26 |
| Meeting request | `olMeetingRequest` | 53 |
| Contact | `olContact` | 40 |
| Distribution list | `olDistributionList` | 69 |
| Journal entry | `olJournal` | 42 |
| Note | `olNote` | 44 |
| Post | `olPost` | 45 |
| Task | `olTask` | 48 |
| Task request | `olTaskRequest` | 49 |
| Document | `olDocument` | 41 |

one for `ActiveExplorer.Selection` and one for `ActiveInspector.CurrentItem`. You'll have nightmares trying to keep the code consistent in the two procedures. Instead, use code to determine what type of window is current, and then get the current item or selected items from that window. For example, in Listing 15.5, the `SetFlag` procedure adds one or more messages to the To Do List to remind you to make a decision one week from today. It can operate either on the currently open item or on the items selected in a folder, depending on which window is active.

The `TypeName()` function is the key to the `FlagMessages` subroutine. It returns a string containing the type of variable passed as a parameter to `TypeName()`. Thus, you can use it to determine whether the user is currently looking at an `Explorer` or `Inspector`.

---

**Tip:** You can also use `TypeName()` as an alternative to the `Class` property to check what type of Outlook item your code is working with. For example, if you had an expression `TypeName(mail)` in the `SetFlag` procedure in Listing 15.5, that expression would return the string "MailItem" because `mail` is a `MailItem` object.

---

Listing 15.5 can handle multiple items in a `Selection`, but often you'll want to handle just a single item. For such scenarios, the VBA `GetCurrentItem()` function in Listing 15.6 uses the same `TypeName()` technique

**Listing 15.5**    *Running a procedure against an open item or a folder selection*

```
Sub FlagMessages()
    Dim objOL As Outlook.Application
    Dim objItem As Object
    Dim objMsg As MailItem
    Dim strWindowType As String
    On Error Resume Next
    Set objOL = Application
    strWindowType = TypeName(objOL.ActiveWindow)
    Select Case strWindowType
        Case "Explorer"
            For Each objItem In objOL.ActiveExplorer.Selection
                If objItem.Class = olMail Then
                    Set objMsg = objItem
                    Call SetFlag(objMsg)
                End If
            Next
        Case "Inspector"
            Set objItem = objOL.ActiveInspector.CurrentItem
            If objItem.Class = olMail Then
                Set objMsg = objItem
                Call SetFlag(objMsg)
            End If
    End Select
    Set objOL = Nothing
    Set objItem = Nothing
    Set objMsg = Nothing
End Sub

Sub SetFlag(mail As MailItem)
    If Not mail.IsMarkedAsTask Then
        mail.MarkAsTask olMarkNextWeek
        mail.TaskDueDate = Date + 7
        mail.TaskSubject = "DECIDE: " & mail.Subject
        mail.Save
    End If
End Sub
```

as in Listing 15.5 to return a single item from the current Outlook window, either an `Inspector` or an `Explorer`.

**Note:** You never need a VBScript version of `GetCurrentItem()` for use in an Outlook custom form, because the current item in the context of custom form VBScript code is always the intrinsic `Item` object.

If you wanted to use the `GetCurrentItem()` function from Listing 15.6 to return a single item and then use the `SetFlag` procedure from Listing 15.5 to set its flag, you would want to check the `Class` property of the item first:

Listing 15.6   *Return the currently selected or open Outlook item (VBA)*

```
Function GetCurrentItem() As Object
    Dim objOL As Outlook.Application
    Dim strWindowType As String
    On Error Resume Next
    Set objOL = Application
    strWindowType = TypeName(objOL.ActiveWindow)
    Select Case strWindowType
        Case "Explorer"
            Set GetCurrentItem = _
                objOL.ActiveExplorer.Selection(1)
        Case "Inspector"
            Set GetCurrentItem = _
                objOL.ActiveInspector.CurrentItem
    End Select
    Set objOL = Nothing
End Function
```

```
Set objItem = GetCurrentItem()
If objItem.Class = olMail Then
    Call SetFlag(objItem)
End If
```

Pay attention to the other examples in the book that use the `Class` property. You will see it often.

## 15.3.3   Getting a particular item

As discussed in the previous chapter, if you know the `EntryID` and `Store-ID` values for a folder, you can use the `Namespace.GetFolderFromID` method to return that folder. Similarly, if you know the `EntryID` for an Outlook item and the `StoreID` for its parent folder, you can use the `Namespace.GetItemFromID` method to return the item. If the item is in the user's default information store, you don't even need the `StoreID`; the `EntryID` will be sufficient. Here is an example of the syntax for both Outlook VBA and VBScript:

```
On Error Resume Next
Set objNS = Application.Session
Set objItem = objNS.GetFolderFromID(EntryID, StoreID)
If Not objItem Is Nothing Then
    MsgBox objItem.Subject
End If
```

The `EntryID` property of an item, just like that for a folder, is a long string that uniquely identifies the item within a store. `EntryID` has some important characteristics:

■ An item's `EntryID` property is blank until the item has been saved.

- The EntryID value is not permanent. It may change if you move the item to a different folder, especially to a folder in a different information store.

- When a user receives an update to a meeting request, Outlook deletes the appointment generated from the original request and creates a new appointment from the meeting update. That means that the GetItemFromID method is not a reliable way to retrieve a meeting. A better approach is to use the Find method, which we will see in the next chapter, to return an item based on a value for the GlobalAppointmentID property.

If you want to see an example of Namespace.GetItemFromID, peek ahead to Listing 15.9, which shows how to use it to open an Outlook item from a list box on a form, where the EntryID for the item is contained in the list box in a hidden column.

### 15.3.4  Working with all the items in a folder

The previous chapter demonstrated many techniques that return a specific folder as a Folder object. Once you have a Folder object, three basic techniques are available to work with all the items the folder contains:

- Use a For Each ... Next loop to process each item in the folder's Items collection, as you saw in Listing 8.14.

- If you plan to delete or move items, use a countdown loop instead of a For Each loop.

- Use the new Table object in Outlook 2007 to get faster, read-only access to the items.

We'll concentrate on the Items techniques in this section and then look at the Table object in the next section. We saw a countdown loop in Chapter 8, in the context of deleting attachments from a message. Listing 15.7 shows how to use such a loop to empty all the items in a folder, in this case the Junk E-mail folder.

---

**Tip:** Did you notice how easily you could adapt the techniques in Listing 15.7 to purge the Deleted Items folder? You would only need to replace olFolderJunk with olFolderDeletedItems.

---

Whenever you loop through items in a folder and use any properties or methods specific to a particular type of Outlook item, be sure to check the value of each item's Class property first. For example, when working in a contacts folder, contact and distribution list items may both be present and have very different properties. Only a contact has a FullName property, as shown in this VBA code snippet:

```
Set objNS = Application.Session
Set objFolder = objNS.GetDefaultFolder(olFolderContacts)
For Each objItem in objFolder.Items
    If objItem.Class = olContact Then
        Debug.Print objItem.FullName
    End If
Next
```

If you want to use that snippet to get a sorted list of names, you can use the `Items.Sort` method. Use `Sort` like this:

```
objItems.Sort property, descending
```

The *property* parameter is a string with the name of the property you want to sort by. A user-defined property's name must be enclosed in brackets; brackets are optional for standard properties but make the code more readable. The *descending* parameter is optional. The default is `False`. Set it to `True` if you want to sort in descending order—for example, with the most recent dates first.

To get a sorted list of `FullName` property values from the contacts folder, you'd modify the earlier snippet as follows:

```
Set objFolder = objNS.GetDefaultFolder(olFolderContacts)
Set colItems = objFolder.Items
colItems.Sort "[FullName]"
For Each objItem in colItems
' etc.
```

**Listing 15.7** *Delete all items in the Junk E-mail folder*

```
Sub EmptyJunk()
    Dim objOL As Outlook.Application
    Dim objNS As Outlook.NameSpace
    Dim objFolder As Outlook.Folder
    Set objOL = Application
    Set objNS = objOL.Session
    Set objFolder = objNS.GetDefaultFolder(olFolderJunk)
    Call DeleteFolderItems(objFolder)
    Set objOL = Nothing
    Set objNS = Nothing
    Set objFolder = Nothing
End Sub

Sub DeleteFolderItems(fld As Outlook.Folder)
    Dim colItems As Outlook.Items
    Dim lngCount As Long
    Dim i As Long
    Set colItems = fld.Items
    For i = lngCount To 1 Step -1
        colItems(i).Delete
    Next
    Set colItems = Nothing
End Sub
```

This snippet differs in a key way from the previous snippet to return all items unsorted. It instantiates an explicit object to represent the `Items` collection, the `colItems` object. This is a required step if you plan to use `Sort`. You also need to instantiate an explicit `Items` object before using the the `GetNext` and `GetPrevious` methods and the `IncludeRecurrences` property, which works with `Sort` to return appointments from a specified date range (which the next chapter covers). Therefore, I recommend that you make it a habit to always instantiate an `Items` variable rather than access an `Items` collection through its parent `Folder` object.

Two other important notes on the `Sort` method:

- You cannot use `Sort` on keywords fields, such as `Categories`, on custom formula or combination fields, and on a small number of standard properties that are listed in the Help topic for `Sort`.

- The `Sort` method can sort by a user-defined property only if that property is defined at the folder level and not just in individual items. To find out whether a property is defined at the folder level, you can look in the folder's Field Chooser, under User-Defined Fields in Folder, or use the `Folder.UserDefinedProperties` collection, which is new to Outlook 2007 and will be discussed in Chapter 21.

If your code needs to access only a subset of properties, you may be able to speed up your code by using the `SetColumns` method to cache certain standard properties. (You cannot use it with user-defined properties.) Use `SetColumns` like this, specifying the properties you need in a single string, separated by commas:

```
colItems.SetColumns "FullName, CompanyName"
For Each objItem in objItems
    Debug.Print objItem.FullName, objItem.CompanyName
Next
```

When you use `SetColumns`, Outlook checks only the property values you specify, rather than opening the entire item. As with `Sort`, some properties cannot be cached by `SetColumns`. To discard the cache and return to accessing all properties, use `ResetColumns`:

```
colItems.ResetColumns
```

An alternative to `Items` for potentially much faster access to a limited set of properties is the new `Table` object, discussed in Section 15.3.6, after we look at a practical example of `Items.Sort`.

## 15.3.5  Example: Generate the next number in a sequence

A common Outlook programming task is to apply a sequential ID to new Outlook items. In an application that uses such an ID, you may want each new item in a folder to be marked with the next number in the sequence.

To find the last number used, the `GetLastNumber()` function in Listing 15.8 returns the largest value for a user-defined field in a particular folder (or -1 if there is a problem getting that property's value). It takes two parameters—the name of the numeric field and the folder where the items using that field are stored. You would call it like this:

```
lngLastNumber = GetLastNumber(strFieldName, objFolder)
objProp.Value = lngLastNumber + 1
```

Once you had `lngLastNumber`, you would add 1 to it to set the value for the `Counter` property in a new item being created in that folder.

Call the `GetLastNumber()` function in Listing 15.8 as part of the process of creating a new item in the same folder. The VBScript code would look like this:

```
Const olInteger = 20
strFieldName = "ProjID"
Set objNewItem = objFolder.Items.Add
Set objProp = objNewItem.UserProperties(strFieldName)
If objProp Is Nothing Then
    Set objProp = objNewItem.UserProperties.Add _
                    (strFieldName, olInteger)
End If
objProp.Value = GetLastNumber(strFieldName, objFolder)
objNewItem.Display
```

Listing 15.8 uses the `Items.GetFirst` method to return the first item in the sorted `Items` collection. `Items` also supports `GetNext`, `GetPrevious`, and `GetLast` methods.

**Listing 15.8**    *Return the largest number value for a custom field*

```
Function GetLastNumber(fieldName, theFolder)      ' As Long
    Dim colItems      ' As Outlook.Items
    Dim objItem       ' As Object
    Dim objProp       ' As Outlook.UserProperty
    On Error Resume Next
    Set colItems = theFolder.Items
    colItems.Sort fieldName, True
    Set objItem = colItems.GetFirst
    Set objProp = objItem.UserProperties(fieldName)
    If Not objProp Is Nothing Then
        GetLastNumber = CLng(objProp.Value)
    Else
        GetLastNumber = -1
    End If
    Set colItems = Nothing
    Set objItem = Nothing
    Set objProp = Nothing
End Function
```

## 15.4  **Using the Table object**

New to Outlook 2007 is a `Table` object designed to help you enumerate large numbers of items much faster than with an `Items` collection. It returns a dynamic, forward-only, read-only *rowset* (that is, a structure of rows and columns, as in a database or spreadsheet). Think of each row as an item and the columns as a small subset of the item's properties. Dynamic means that the rowset is updated as changes are made to the underlying data. Read-only means that a `Table` itself provides no way to modify and save Outlook items. Forward-only means that, unlike the `Items` collection, the `Table` object does not support a `GetPrevious` method. Methods like `GetNextRow` and `FindNextRow` move only forward through the table.

Two objects have a `GetTable` method that returns a `Table` object – `Folder`, covered in Chapter 13, and `Search`, which is discussed in the next chapter. Each type of folder returns a different set of columns (that is, property values) by default, but you can also add or remove columns from the table programmatically. Each `Table` object's default columns include five base fields, plus other columns depending on the type of folder. Table 15.5 lists the default columns for `Table` objects returned from different types of folders.

The `Table` object supports several techniques for working with the data in the table, listed in Table 15.6.

The `Table` object provides three ways to return data from its rows:

- As a multidimensional array with `GetArray`
- As a `Row` object with `GetNextRow`, then using `GetValues` to return the data from the row
- To search within a table, with `FindRow` and `FindNextRow`, which also return a `Row` object, then using `GetValues` to return the data from the row

**Table 15.5**  *Default Columns for Table Object*

| Mail/Post Folders Journal Folders Notes Folders | Calendar Folders | Contacts Folders | Tasks Folders |
|---|---|---|---|
| Five base columns: | Base columns, plus: | Base columns, plus: | Base columns, plus: |
| ■ EntryID | ■ Start | ■ FirstName | ■ DueDate |
| ■ Subject | ■ End | ■ LastName | ■ PercentComplete |
| ■ CreationTime | ■ IsRecurring | ■ CompanyName | ■ IsRecurring |
| ■ LastModificationTime | | | |
| ■ MessageClass | | | |

**Table 15.6** *Basic Techniques for Working with Table and Row Objects*

| Table Method | Description |
|---|---|
| MoveToStart | Reposition the row enumerator to just before the first row |
| Sort *SortProperty*, *Descending* | Sort the table by the *SortProperty* standard or custom property name; similar to `Items.Sort` |
| GetRowCount | Return the number of rows in the table |
| GetNextRow | Position the row enumerator on the next row and return that `Row` object |
| GetArray(*MaxRows*) | Returns a multi-dimensional array containing all the columns in the `Table.Columns` collection and *MaxRows* number of rows |
| FindRow(*Filter*) | Returns the first row matching a filter string |
| FindNextRow | Returns the next row matching the filter string specified in an earlier `FindRow` statement. |
| Restrict | Returns a filtered `Table` object |
| **Row Method** | **Description** |
| GetValues | Returns an array of all the values for the row (item); the upper bound of the array is one less than `Table.Columns.Count` |
| Item(*Index*) | Returns the value for the property in the column corresponding to the *Index* number (1-based) or string (name of the property) |

The `Restrict` method provides another way to search, by returning a filtered `Table` object. We will come back to `Table.FindRow` and `.Restrict` in the next chapter, which has a complete discussion of ways to search for and filter Outlook items.

Besides speed, `Table` methods have two additional advantages over other methods of accessing items. Because `Table` methods return only a select set of property values and do not load the entire item, they do not cause the code behind custom forms to run. Therefore, you can use `Table` methods whenever you want to obtain data from custom form items without raising the `Open` event from a custom form. Also, a folder may contain a mix of items, some of which contain a particular MAPI property and some of which don't. If you tried to access that property using `PropertyAccessor` on each item, you'd get an error on items where the property didn't exist. However, no errors occur if you return MAPI property tag values from such a mixed collection of items with a `Table`, as you'll see in the example in the next section.

In the next two sections, you'll see examples of the two basic techniques for working with a `Table`—returning all the data with `GetArray` and returning it a row at a time with `GetNextRow`.

## 15.4.1    Example: Fill a list box from a Table

The `Table.GetArray` method is particularly useful for filling a list or combo box on a VBA form or custom Outlook form by setting the control's `List` property. It takes very little code and works very fast. The VBScript code in Listing 15.9 provides an example, based on a custom form that has a custom page named Contacts that contains a list box named `lstContacts` and a command button named `cmdOpenContact`.

When an item using this custom form opens, the code in the `Item_Open` event handler returns a `Table` object from the user's default Contacts folder. It then deletes the second through fifth default columns (`Subject`, `CreationTime`, `LastModificationTime`, and `MessageClass`) by deleting column number 2 four times:

```
For i = 1 To 4
    objTable.Columns.Remove 2
Next
```

**Note:** Like other collections in Outlook, the `Columns` collection is 1-based. In other words, the first item in the collection has an index value of 1.

It then adds a new column for the `FileAs` property and sorts by that column:

```
objTable.Columns.Add "FileAs"
objTable.Sort "FileAs"
```

The list box on the form is modified to contain five columns; the first (`EntryID`) and last (`FileAs`) are hidden by setting their column widths to 0. Finally, the list box's `List` property is set to the array returned by `GetArray` with all the items with the table:

```
With lstContacts
    .ColumnCount = 5
    .ColumnWidths = "0;75;75;75;0"
    .List = objTable.GetArray(lngCount)
End With
```

The result is a very fast routine to fill the list box with the first, last, and company names of all contacts in the default folder, sorted by the `FileAs` property.

The code for the command button's `Click` event handler uses the `Namespace.GetItemFromID` method discussed earlier in the chapter along with the `EntryID` value that is in the 0th column of the list box, one of the two hidden columns.

**Listing 15.9**     *Use a table to fill a form list box with contacts*

```
Function Item_Open()
    Dim objContacts
    Dim objTable
    Dim lngCount
    Dim objPage
    Dim lstContacts
    Const olFolderContacts = 10
    On Error Resume Next
    Set objOL = Application
    Set objNS = Application.Session
    Set objContacts = _
      objNS.GetDefaultFolder(olFolderContacts)
    Set objTable = objContacts.GetTable
    For i = 1 To 4
        objTable.Columns.Remove 2
    Next
    objTable.Columns.Add "FileAs"
    objTable.Sort "FileAs"
    lngCount = objTable.GetRowCount
    Set objPage = _
      Item.GetInspector.ModifiedFormPages("Contacts")
    Set lstContacts = objPage.Controls("lstContacts")
    With lstContacts
        .ColumnCount = 5
        .ColumnWidths = "0;75;75;75;0"
        .List = objTable.GetArray(lngCount)
    End With
    Set objNS = Nothing
    Set objContacts = Nothing
    Set objPage = Nothing
    Set lstContacts = Nothing
End Function

Sub cmdOpenContact_Click()
    Dim objNS
    Dim objPage
    Dim lstContacts
    Dim lngSelRow
    Dim strEntryID
    Dim objContact
    Set objNS = Application.Session
    Set objPage = _
      Item.GetInspector.ModifiedFormPages("Contacts")
    Set lstContacts = objPage.Controls("lstContacts")
    lngSelRow = lstContacts.ListIndex
    strEntryID = lstContacts.Column(0, lngSelRow)
    Set objContact = objNS.GetItemFromID(strEntryID)
    objContact.Display
    Set objNS = Nothing
    Set objPage = Nothing
    Set lstContacts = Nothing
    Set objContact = Nothing
End Sub
```

A couple of other points regarding the `Table.Columns.Add` method:

- Adding a `Column` to a `Table` repositions the row enumerator to just before the first row—the equivalent of calling `MoveToStart`. (Invoking the `Sort` method also repositions the row enumerator.)

- There is more than one way to add columns for standard properties. You can use their property names from the Outlook object model or use the namespace syntax for schema names, that is, the same property names that you first encountered with the `PropertyAccessor` object in the previous chapter. This statement, for example, adds a `Column` to a `Table` for the property that holds the Internet headers for a message:

```
objTable.Columns.Add _
    "http://schemas.microsoft.com/mapi/proptag/0x007D001E"
```

Such properties are subject to the same limitations when retrieved through a `Table` as through a `PropertyAccessor`, mainly that large binary or string properties may raise an out-of-memory error.

## 15.4.2   Example: Report on message response times

Many organizations want to analyze various aspects of email use, such as how much mail arrives per day or how quickly their employees respond to email from customers. The Outlook object model exposes several date/time fields with information useful to such a reckoning, such as `SentOn`, `ReceivedTime`, and `CreationTime`, but cannot tell you when or if a reply was sent.

Yet, after a user replies to or forwards a message, that item displays information about when the item was sent or forwarded. Outlook shows that information in the "info bar" at the top of the item in the reading pane or an `Inspector` window. So where does it come from? If you look in the Outlook object model, you won't find any `MailItem` properties for this data. The data is in two hidden MAPI properties, one to hold the date, and the other to hold a number corresponding to the type of response:

| | |
|---|---|
| Reply | 102 |
| Reply to all | 103 |
| Forward | 104 |

Once you know what properties hold this hidden information, with the help of the `Table` object, you can produce a report on which messages in a folder have received responses and when. Listing 15.10 creates such a report as a new Excel document. Note that this code sample for Outlook VBA requires that you use Tools | References to add a reference to the Microsoft Office Excel library. You can call the `ReportResponses` subroutine with

**Listing 15.10** *Create a report in Excel on message response times*

```
Sub ReportResponses(fld As Outlook.Folder)
    Dim objTable As Outlook.Table
    Dim objRow As Outlook.Row
    ' requires a reference to the
    ' Microsoft Office Excel library
    Dim objEX As Excel.Application
    Dim objWB As Excel.Workbook
    Dim objWS As Excel.Worksheet
    Dim intR As Integer
    Dim val()
    Const PR_LAST_VERB_EXECUTION_TIME = _
       "http://schemas.microsoft.com/mapi/proptag/0x10820040"
    Const PR_LAST_VERB_EXECUTED = _
       "http://schemas.microsoft.com/mapi/proptag/0x10810003"
    On Error Resume Next
    Set objTable = fld.GetTable
    With objTable
        .Columns.Add "SenderName"
        .Columns.Add "SenderEmailAddress"
        .Columns.Add "SentOn"
        .Columns.Add PR_LAST_VERB_EXECUTION_TIME
        .Columns.Add PR_LAST_VERB_EXECUTED
    End With
    If objTable.GetRowCount > 0 Then
        Set objEX = CreateObject("Excel.Application")
        Set objWB = objEX.Workbooks.Add
        Set objWS = objWB.Worksheets(1)
        intR = 4
        Do Until objTable.EndOfTable
            Set objRow = objTable.GetNextRow
            val = objRow.GetValues
            With objWS
                .Cells(intR, 1).Value = val(7)   ' SentOn
                .Cells(intR, 2).Value = val(2)   ' CreationTime
                ' PR_LAST_VERB_EXECUTION_TIME
                If IsDate(val(8)) Then
                    .Cells(intR, 3).Value = _
                        objRow.UTCToLocalTime(9)
                End If
                ' PR_LAST_VERB_EXECUTED
                .Cells(intR, 4).Value = _
                  LastVerbText(CInt(val(9)))
                .Cells(intR, 5).Value = val(5)   ' SenderName
                ' SenderEmailAddress
                .Cells(intR, 6).Value = val(6)
                .Cells(intR, 7).Value = val(1)   ' Subject
            End With
            intR = intR + 1
        Loop
        With objWS
            .Columns("A:G").EntireColumn.AutoFit
```

**Listing 15.10**    *Create a report in Excel on message response times (continued)*

```
            .Cells(1, 1).Value = _
              "Report on messages in folder: " & _
              fld.FolderPath
            .Cells(3, 1).Value = "Sent"
            .Cells(3, 2).Value = "Received"
            .Cells(3, 3).Value = "Response Date"
            .Cells(3, 4).Value = "Response"
            .Cells(3, 5).Value = "Sender Name"
            .Cells(3, 6).Value = "Sender Address"
            .Cells(3, 7).Value = "Subject"
            .Range("A1:G3").Font.Bold = True
            .Columns("D").EntireColumn.AutoFit
            .Range("A4").AutoFilter
        End With
        objEX.Visible = True
        objWB.Activate
    End If
    Set objTable = Nothing
    Set objRow = Nothing
    Set objEX = Nothing
    Set objWS = Nothing
End Sub

Function LastVerbText(verb As Integer)
    Select Case verb
        Case 102
            LastVerbText = "Reply"
        Case 103
            LastVerbText = "Reply to All"
        Case 104
            LastVerbText = "Forward"
        Case Else
            LastVerbText = ""
    End Select
End Function
```

any `Folder` object. For example, display the folder you want to report on, and then execute this statement in the Immediate window:

```
ReportResponses Application.ActiveExplorer.CurrentFolder
```

After a few seconds, an Excel document will appear containing the data. With AutoFilter turned on, you can immediately start to analyze the data.

These two statements establish constants for the MAPI properties that hold information about when a reply or forward took place and which action was taken:

```
Const PR_LAST_VERB_EXECUTION_TIME = _
    "http://schemas.microsoft.com/mapi/proptag/0x10820040"
Const PR_LAST_VERB_EXECUTED = _
    "http://schemas.microsoft.com/mapi/proptag/0x10810003"
```

By now, you should be able to recognize these as properties from the MAPI proptag namespace, which was discussed in the previous chapter about the `PropertyAccessor` object.

After returning the table and adding the desired columns, the code creates an Excel workbook and sets the value of a variable, `intR`, that represents the row in the worksheet where the code will write data. A `Do` loop does the bulk of the work:

```
Do Until objTable.EndOfTable
    Set objRow = objTable.GetNextRow
    Val = objRow.GetValues
    ' code to process the val array of values
    intR = intR + 1
Loop
```

When processing table rows, you need to know when you have reached the last row. The `EndOfTable` property returns `True` if there are no more rows to return. Once you return a `Row` object with the `Table.GetNextRow` method, you can use the `Row.GetValues` method to return an array of the property values from the table's `Columns` collection.

The basic technique for putting data into an Excel worksheet is to use this syntax:

```
objWS.Cells(r, c).Value = some_value
```

where $r$ and $c$ represent the row and column indexes for a given cell.

---

**Note:** You might be wondering why the code uses `CreationTime`, rather than `ReceivedTime` to fill the second column in the worksheet. `CreationTime` more accurately reflects when the item was first available to the user in Outlook. The `ReceivedTime` property stores the date/time when the user's mail server received the item, which could be somewhat earlier.

---

To help you work with the data returned by `Row.GetValues`, the `Row` object supports the same conversion methods that we saw for the `PropertyAccessor` object in Chapter 13. You can use the `Row.BinaryToString` method to convert binary properties to their string representations, but remember that only small binary property values (those under 4kb) will be returned.

To handle row date values properly, you need to be aware of the type of column. For default columns and standard properties added to the `Table.Columns` collection with their Outlook object model property names, the date/time values returned by `GetValues` will be in local time. However, for properties added using namespace references, such as the property in Listing 15.10 that exposes the time of the last action on the item, the property values will be in UTC time, and therefore, you will need to use Row.UTCToLocalTime to convert them to local time. Take a close look at the way that Listing 15.10 performs the conversion:

```
If IsDate(val(8)) Then
    .Cells(intR, 3).Value = _
        objRow.UTCToLocalTime(9)
End If
```

As mentioned in the previous section, a Table does not generate an error if a property in its Columns collection—in this case, the date/time property whose value is in the array as val(8)—is not present on an individual item. However, Outlook will raise an error if you try to get the date/time with UTCToLocalTime and the value is not a date/time. Therefore, you should use the IsDate() function first to confirm a date is present, before converting it with UTCToLocalTime.

---

**Note:** The time converter methods for both Row and PropertyAccessor round the result to the nearest minute, ignoring any seconds part of the date/time value.

---

Also pay attention to the fact that the array returned by Row.GetValues() is a zero-based array, but the conversion methods like BinaryToString and UTCToLocalTime take as their parameter the column index from Table.Columns, which is a 1-based collection. That explains why the code checks the value of val(8) but performs the conversion with objRow.UTCToLocalTime(9). The date/time property that we are interested in is the ninth element of the zero-based val() array and also the ninth column in the Columns collection.

After the loop, the code uses Excel methods to add column headings to the worksheet, fit each column to the data it contains, turn on the AutoFilter feature, and display the worksheet. We will spend more time working with Excel in Chapter 24, but this sample demonstrates the basics of opening and populating a new worksheet with Outlook data. As with Word, you can learn a lot about Excel methods by turning on the macro recorder.

## 15.5  Using Item methods

Messages, contacts, appointments, and the other different Outlook items have many programming methods in common. Table 15.7 provides a summary. Not all methods apply to each type of item. See the Help topic for an individual method for details. Other methods, specific only to certain types of items, are shown later in Table 15.10.

**Table 15.7**  *Common Item Methods*

| Method | Description |
|---|---|
| ClearTaskFlag | Clears the task flag from a message, contact, or post, removing it from the To Do List |
| Close *SaveMode* | Closes the item, saving changes if desired, using the same *SaveMode* argument values shown in Table 15.1 |
| Copy | Returns an unsaved copy of the item |
| Delete | Deletes the item |
| Display *Modal* | Shows the item in an Inspector window. The default for *Modal* is False; the use of True to show an item modally is not recommended. |
| Forward | Returns a new MailItem object containing the item to be forwarded |
| MarkAsTask *MarkInterval* | Add a message, contact, or post to the To Do List marked for action in the *MarkInterval* time frame |
| Move(*DestFld*) | Moves the item to the *DestFld* destination folder; returns the moved item |
| PrintOut | Prints the item with Outlook's default settings |
| Reply | Returns a new MailItem object addressed to the original sender |
| ReplyAll | Returns a new MailItem addressed to the original sender and any Cc recipients |
| Save | Saves the item in the folder from which it was opened or to which it was added; for a new item, saves to the default folder for the item type |
| SaveAs *Path*, *Type* | Saves the item to a system file using the specified *Path* and one of the *Type* constants listed in Table 15.10 |
| Send | Sends the item (appointment, meeting request, message, task request) |
| ShowCategoriesDialog | Displays the Categories dialog so the user can modify the categories for the item |

**Caution:** Using the item.Close method in VBScript code behind a custom form may cause the initially released version of Outlook to crash. Let's hope that this problem will be eliminated in a hotfix or service pack.

To copy an item to another folder, first use the Copy method to make a copy of the item, and then use the Move method to place the copy in the destination folder, as in the following example, where objItem is an Outlook item and objFolder is the target Folder object:

```
Set newItem = objItem.Copy
Set movedItem = newItem.Move(objFolder)
```

**Table 15.8**   *Behavior of the Delete Method*

| Information Store Holding the Item | Delete Behavior |
| --- | --- |
| User's own Exchange mailbox | Moves item to the mailbox's Deleted Items folder |
| Personal Folders .pst file | Moves item to the .pst file's Deleted Items folder |
| Exchange Public Folders | Permanently deletes the item |
| IMAP account proxy .pst file | Marks the item for deletion during the folder's next purge operation |
| Other user's Exchange mailbox | Moves item to either the current user's Deleted Items folder or other user's Deleted Items folder, depending on the registry value described in Microsoft Knowledge Base Article 202517 |

Note that `Move` returns the new item that was placed in the target folder. If the item you want to copy is in a folder other than the user's own Exchange mailbox or a Personal Folders .pst file, you may be blocked by permissions on the folder from copying or moving the item. To copy an item, you need permission to create new items in the same folder as the original item. To move an item, you need permission to delete items from the item's folder. You always have those permissions for your own mailbox and for any .pst files, but may not have such permission for other Exchange mailbox or Public Folders folders.

The behavior of the `Delete` method depends on what store the item is in. Table 15.8 lists the possibilities.

The process of permanently deleting an item is surprisingly complicated. The VBA code in Listing 15.11 uses this sequence of operations:

1.   Move the item to the Deleted Items folder.

2.   Get the `EntryID` value from the moved item.

3.   Release both the original item and the moved item.

4.   Use the `Namespace.GetItemFromID` method to return the moved item from the the `EntryID` saved in Step 2.

5.   Delete the moved item.

**Caution:** The `DeleteSelectedItem` procedure in Listing 15.11 does not ask the user to confirm the permanent deletion of the selected item. You might want to add such a prompt if you implement this technique in your own applications.

You should recall from the discussion in Chapter 8 that you should use a countdown loop instead of a `For Each ... Next` loop to delete multiple

**Listing 15.11** *Permanently delete an item*

```
Sub DeleteSelectedItem()
    Dim objOL As Outlook.Application
    Dim objNS As Outlook.NameSpace
    Dim objExpl As Outlook.Explorer
    Dim objItem As Object
    Dim objDelItem As Object
    Dim objDelFolder As Outlook.Folder
    Dim strID As String
    On Error Resume Next
    Set objOL = Application
    Set objNS = objOL.Session
    Set objExpl = objOL.ActiveExplorer
    If objExpl.Selection.Count = 1 Then
        Set objItem = objExpl.Selection(1)
        Set objDelFolder = _
          objNS.GetDefaultFolder(olFolderDeletedItems)
        Set objDelItem = objItem.Move(objDelFolder)
        Set objItem = Nothing
        strID = objDelItem.EntryID
        Set objDelItem = Nothing
        Set objDelItem = objNS.GetItemFromID(strID)
        objDelItem.Delete
    End If
    Set objOL = Nothing
    Set objNS = Nothing
    Set objExpl = Nothing
    Set objDelItem = Nothing
    Set objDelFolder = Nothing
End Sub
```

items in a collection. The same applies to moving items, since moving an item involves deleting it. Also remember that, in order to move an item, the user needs delete permission on the source folder and create permission on the target folder.

You saw an example of the new MarkAsTask method in Listing 15.5. Table 15.9 lists the values for the required MarkInterval parameter.

Outlook can save files in system folders in the formats shown in Table 15.10. The formats available for any given item depend on the type of item and, in the case of messages and post items, whether the item body format is HTML, plain text, or rich text. If you do not specify a format with the SaveAs method, the default message (.msg) format is used.

**Note:** The vCard, vCalendar, and iCalendar formats follow accepted specifications for exchanging contact and schedule data over the Internet. These formats are used by many applications besides Outlook.

**Table 15.9**    *OlMarkInterval Constants for Use with the MarkAs Task Method*

| Interval | Constant | Value |
|----------|----------|-------|
| Today | olMarkToday | 0 |
| Tomorrow | olMarkTomorrow | 1 |
| This Week | olMarkThisWeek | 2 |
| Next Week | olMarkNextWeek | 3 |
| No Date | olMarkNoDate | 4 |

**Caution:** The SaveAs method overwrites any existing file with the same name, without any warning.

In addition to the Reply and Forward methods, three other methods—ForwardAsVcal, ForwardAsBusinessCard, ForwardAsVcard—return a new MailItem ready to be completed and sent. Those are among the methods that are specific to individual Outlook items. Table 15.11 summarizes these and other item-specific methods. For more information and usage examples, see the Help topic for each method. We will look at some of these methods in Chapter 20.

**Table 15.10**    *OlSaveAsType Constants for Use with the SaveAs Method*

| Format | Constant | Value |
|--------|----------|-------|
| Message (.msg) | olMSG | 3 |
| Unicode message (.msg)—not compatible with Outlook 2003 or earlier versions | olMSGUnicode | 9 |
| Text only (.txt) | olTXT | 0 |
| Rich text format (.rtf) | olRTF | 1 |
| HTML format (.htm) | olHTML | 5 |
| Outlook form template (.oft) | OlTemplate | 2 |
| vCard (.vcf) | olVCard | 6 |
| vCalendar (.vcs) | olVCal | 7 |
| iCalendar (.ics) | olICal | 8 |
| Word document (.doc) | olDoc | 4 |

**Table 15.11**   *Item-Specific Methods (\* = new in Outlook 2007)*

| Item Type | Method | Description |
|---|---|---|
| AppointmentItem | ClearRecurrencePattern | Changes a recurring appointment to a non-recurring appointment |
| | ForwardAsVcal | Returns a `MailItem` object with an attached vCal .vcs file for the appointment |
| | GetRecurrencePattern | Returns the `RecurrencePattern` object defining a recurring appointment; use only if `IsRecurring = True` for an existing item or if you make the appointment recurring |
| | Respond *Response, fNoUI, fAdditionalTextDialog* | Responds to an `AppointmentItem` contained in a meeting request. *Response* is one of the following `OlMeetingResponse` constants:<br><br>`olMeetingAccepted`   3<br><br>`olMeetingDeclined`   4<br><br>`olMeetingTentative`  2<br><br>*fNoUI* and *fAdditionalTextDialog* are optional Boolean parameters that determine whether the user sees dialog boxes for choosing the response and adding text comments |
| ContactItem | \* AddBusinessCardLogoPicture *Path* | Adds the picture file from *Path* as the new logo for the contact's electronic business card; this picture is stored as a binary property, not in the `Attachments` collection |
| | AddPicture *Path* | Adds the picture file from *Path* as the new picture displayed for the contact. The picture is stored in the `Attachments` collection as ContactPicture.jpg. |
| | \* ForwardAsBusinessCard | Returns a `MailItem` containing the contact's electronic business card both as a .vcf attachment and, if the default message formt is HTML, as a .jpg image in the message body |
| | ForwardAsVcard | Returns a `MailItem` containing the contact's information as a vCard .vcf file |

**Table 15.11**    *Item-Specific Methods (\* = new in Outlook 2007) (continued)*

| Item Type | Method | Description |
|---|---|---|
| ContactItem *(cont'd.)* | RemovePicture | Removes the picture associated with the contact |
| | \* ResetBusinessCard | Resets the electronic business card layout to Outlook's default settings |
| | \* SaveBusinessCardImage *Path* | Saves contact information as a .png file using the electronic business card layout |
| | \* ShowBusinessCardEditor | Displays the Edit Business Card dialog |
| | \* ShowcheckPhoneDialog *Phone-Number* | Displays the Check Phone Number dialog for the *PhoneNumber* represented by the constant from the OlContact-PhoneNumber enumeration, e.g., OlContactPhoneBusiness |
| DistListItem | AddMember *Recipient* | Adds a single *Recipient* to the distribution list |
| | AddMembers *Recipients* | Adds a *Recipients* collection as new members of the distribution list |
| | GetMember(*Index*) | Return a member of the distribution list |
| | RemoveMember *Recipient* | Removes a *Recipient* object from the distribution list membership |
| | RemoveMembers *Recipients* | Removes a *Recipients* collection of members from the distribution list |
| JournalItem | StartTimer | Starts the timer on a Journal entry |
| | StopTimer | Stops the timer on a Journal entry |
| MailItem | \* AddBusinessCard *Contact* | Adds information from the Electronic Business Card for *Contact* to the message as a vCard .vcf attachment and, for HTML-format messages, a .gif image in the message body |
| | ClearConversationIndex | Clears the ConversationIndex property |
| MeetingItem | GetAssociatedAppointment (*AddToCalendar*) | Returns the AppointmentItem associated with the meeting request |
| PostItem | ClearConversationIndex | Clears the ConversationIndex property |
| | Post | Saves the post in the target folder and closes it |

**Table 15.11**  *Item-Specific Methods (\* = new in Outlook 2007) (continued)*

| Item Type | Method | Description |
|---|---|---|
| `TaskItem` | `Assign` | Assigns a task |
| | `CancelResponseState` | Resets the `ResponseState` property to its original value; use to convert a task response to a simple task before responding to a task request |
| `TaskItem` *(cont'd.)* | `ClearRecurrencePattern` | Changes a recurring task to a non-recurring task |
| | `GetRecurrencePattern` | Returns the `RecurrencePattern` defining a recurring task |
| | `MarkComplete` | Updates `PercentComplete` to 100%, `Complete` to `True`, and `DateCompleted` to the current date |
| | `Respond` *Response*, *fNoUI*, *fAdditionalTextDialog* | Responds to an `TaskItem` contained in a task request. *Response* is one of the following `OlTaskResponse` constants: `olTaskAssign` 1 `olTaskAccept` 2 `olTaskDecline` 3 `olTaskSimple` 0 *fNoUI* and *fAdditionalTextDialog* are optional Boolean parameters that determine whether the user sees dialog boxes for choosing the response and adding text comments |
| | `SkipRecurrence` | Clears the current instance of a recurring task and sets the recurrence to the next instance |
| | `StatusReport` | Sends a status report to all recipients listed in the `StatusUpdateRecipients` property |
| `TaskRequestAcceptItem` `TaskRequestDeclineItem` `TaskRequestItem` `TaskRequestUpdateItem` | `GetAssociatedTask` (*AddToTaskList*) | Returns the `TaskItem` object associated with a task request, response, or update |

## 15.6  Summary

In this first of four chapters on working with items, we saw many ways to create new items—including both standard and custom form items—and to access and process existing items. The newest approach is to use the `Table` object that Outlook 2007 introduces for rapid, read-only item iteration.

Any Outlook item can be displayed in an `Inspector` window. In addition to common item methods, such as `Close` and `Save`, each different item type has its own special methods.

Among the practical examples in this chapter are procedures to send a Word document or Excel worksheet as the body of an email message, to process items selected in a folder or get the current item, to delete all the items in a folder or permanently delete an individual item, to generate the next number in a sequence, to fill a custom form list box with the user's contacts, and to report on when a user responded to messages in a folder.

In Chapter 16, we'll explore the many different ways to search for items, and in Chapter 17, we'll examine techniques for working with the bodies of messages and other items. Finally, Chapter 20 demonstrates some of the methods specific to different types of Outlook items.

# 16

# *Searching for Outlook Items*

Finding an item through the Outlook user interface is very easy. When the user types text in an area at the top of the current window, Outlook 2007 begins to search immediately. Performing a search programmatically is not quite as straightforward, because there are six different methods and two different syntaxes for writing search queries. This chapter reviews these different approaches, suggests when it is most appropriate to use each of them, and discusses the implications of the new indexed Instant Search feature in Outlook 2007. On Windows XP and Windows 2003 Server, the Instant Search feature requires Windows Desktop Search (WDS) 3.0. WDS installs automatically on Windows Vista.

Highlights of this chapter include discussions of the following:

- Which search technique to use, depending on what you want to search for, whether you want to search one folder or many, and what you plan to do with the results

- How to write search queries to search inside attachments and/or item bodies

- How to use the `Application.AdvancedSearch` and `Explorer.Search` methods to show search results using Outlook's user interface

- When you should use a DASL query instead of a Jet search string

- How to return all appointments, including recurrences, within a date range

## 16.1 Introduction to Outlook search methods

Outlooks offers programmers multiple search methods to return one or many results; search synchronously or asynchronously; search one folder or many; search on standard, custom, or MAPI properties; and return the search results in an Outlook Explorer interface or with no user interface. With so many options available from six different search methods, it's hard to know which to choose! As a start, let's introduce each of the different methods, and then consider when you might want to use each one.

The `Folder.Items` collection has two search methods, `Find` and `Restrict`, each of which takes a `Filter` parameter containing your *search string*, that is, a string that defines the conditions for the search. The `Find` method returns a single item and can be followed by `FindNext` to return the next item matching the conditions. (You can repeat `FindNext` until it returns `Nothing`—in other words, no result.) The `Restrict` method returns an `Items` collection, which you can iterate using the techniques discussed in the previous chapter. Here is the basic syntax for `Find`, `FindNext`, and `Restrict`:

```
Set objItem = colItems.Find(Filter)
Set objNextItem = colItems.FindNext
Set colFoundItems = colItems.Restrict(Filter)
```

Very similar to the `Find` and `FindNext` methods are the `FindRow` and `FindNextRow` methods of a `Table` object returned from a `Folder` object:

```
Set objRow = objTable.FindRow(Filter)
Set objNextRow = objTable.FindNextRow
```

Similarly, the `Table.Restrict` method returns a new, filtered `Table` object:

```
Set objNewTable = objTable.Restrict(Filter)
```

You should recall from the previous chapter that `Table` is an object new to Outlook 2007 and that the data returned in a `Table` object is read-only.

`Find`, `FindRow`, and `Restrict` only return the data; it is up to the calling application to provide any user interface that the application might need to show the results.

Another new method in Outlook 2007 is `Explorer.Search`, which uses this syntax:

```
objExpl.Search Query, SearchScope
```

where `Query` is the search string and `SearchScope` is either `olSearch-ScopeAllFolders` (literal value `1`) or `olSearchScopeCurrentFolder` (literal value `0`). This is one of two approaches that can return the search results in the Outlook user interface. (The other is to use `AdvancedSearch` to create a search folder.) It is also unlike `Find`, `FindRow`, and `Restrict` in that it can search more than one folder and it does not return an object containing the results for further processing.

**Note:** You can also filter the items displayed in a folder window by updating the value of the `Filter` or `XML` property of a `View` object, using the same DASL query syntax that we'll see in this chapter. We'll discuss views in Chapter 22.

The last method, `Application.AdvancedSearch`, is both the most complex to implement and the most powerful. It can either return individual items for processing or create a permanent *search folder*, a virtual folder that searches in the background to maintain a results set that the user can view at any time. It can search one folder or many folders within the user's Exchange mailbox or any single Personal Folders .pst file. The syntax for Advanced Search looks like this:

```
Set objSearch = Application.AdvancedSearch _
    (Scope, Filter, SearchSubFolders, Tag)
```

All parameters but the first are optional, but as a practical matter, you'll almost always provide a search string for the *Filter* argument as well as a value for *Scope*. (A search wouldn't be much of a search without a search string of some kind, would it?)

Notice that the `AdvancedSearch` method returns a `Search` object. The search results are available either as the `Results` collection of the `Search` object or as a `Table` object returned by `Search.GetTable`. However, in most cases, the complete search results will be unavailable until the search completes. You can perform multiple simultaneous searches with the `AdvancedSearch` method. Outlook 2007 can support up to 100 simultaneous searches launched programmatically or through the UI. As you'll see when we look at `AdvancedSearch` in detail a little later in the chapter, most implementations use the `AdvancedSearchComplete` and `Advanced-SearchStopped` events of the `Application` object to process the results.

Table 16.1 lists recommendations on which methods lend themselves best to particular search scenarios that Outlook programmers often encounter.

After a discussion of how to build search strings, we'll look at each of these search methods in more depth, with examples.

## 16.2  **Building search strings**

Crucial to each search method introduced in the previous section is a search string argument that contains the conditions that define the search. Depending on the method, the search string can use one of four available syntaxes:

- Microsoft Jet syntax, similar to that used by validation formulas on Outlook items
- DASL (Distributed Authoring Search and Location) syntax, using the same namespace schema property names that the `Property-Accessor` object uses
- Content indexer syntax, which adds some additional operators to the DASL syntax

**Table 16.1**     *Recommended Outlook Search Techniques*

| When You Want to . . . | Use this Outlook Search Method . . . |
|---|---|
| Locate a single item in a known folder using a standard or custom property and edit that item | `Items.Find` |
| Locate a single item or multiple items in a known folder using any kind of property and edit the items | `Items.Restrict` |
| Locate all appointments in a date range, including recurrences | `Items.Restrict` |
| Quickly locate a single item in a known folder and read a limited set of properties without editing the item | `Table.FindRow` |
| Locate multiple items in a known folder and rapidly read a limited set of properties without editing the items | `Table.Restrict` |
| Locate multiple hidden items, such as custom forms or views, in a known folder | `Table.Restrict` |
| Search a single folder and show the results in an Explorer window | `Explorer.Search` |
| Search all folders of particular type (all mail folders, all contact folders, and so on) and show the results in an Explorer window | `Explorer.Search` |
| Create a permanent search folder | `Application.AdvancedSearch` |
| Search across specific multiple folders in a .pst file or the user's Exchange mailbox and return results to be processed | `Application.AdvancedSearch` |
| Search for text in any text field (including the item body and attachment contents), and read the results without editing the items | `Table.Restrict` |
| Search for text in any text field (including the item body and attachment contents), and return results to be processed | `Items.Restrict`<br>`Application.AdvancedSearch` |

- Advanced Query Syntax (AQS) for searching the Windows Desktop Search index

The `Find` and `FindRow` methods can use only the Jet syntax, which is not available for the `AdvancedSearch` method. Only the `Explorer.Search` method can use the AQS syntax. Table 16.2 summarizes the syntax options for the different methods. The sections that follow explain how to

—————————▶

**Table 16.2**    *Search String Syntax Support*

| Method | Jet | DASL | DASL with Content Indexer | AQS |
|---|---|---|---|---|
| `Items.Find` | X | | | |
| `Items.Restrict` | X | X (with @SQL=) | X (with @SQL=) | |
| `Table.FindRow` | X | X (with @SQL=) | | |
| `Table.Restrict` | X | X (with @SQL=) | X (with @SQL=) | |
| `Explorer.Search` | | | | X |
| `Application.AdvancedSearch` | | X | X | |

construct Jet and DASL search strings, including those for searching indexed content. The AQS search syntax is covered in Section 16.5, "Using Explorer.Search," since it applies only to that method.

Section 16.2.2 below on "Using the DASL search syntax" explains how to use the prefix `@SQL=` to incorporate a DASL search string into a `Restrict` or `FindRow` search. However, you cannot mix combine Jet and DASL search expressions into a single search string.

## 16.2.1  Using the Jet search syntax

For the simple Jet syntax, a search string should contain at least one field name, a comparison operator, and the value you want to find for that field. Put the field names in brackets. The field can be either a standard field or a custom field (see Section 16.2.6). Surround string values with one set of single quotation marks or two sets of double quotation marks. Express date/time values as strings, without a seconds component. Here are examples of some simple Jet search strings:

```
"[City] = 'Arlington'"
"[Unread] = True"
"[Start] >= ""March 3, 2007 10:00 AM"""
"[Duration] < 1440"
```

If you have multiple criteria, join them with an AND or OR operator, as appropriate, for example:

```
"[City] = 'Arlington' AND [State] = 'VA'"
```

You can use literals, variables, or the results of functions in the search string, as long as they evaluate to a string. When the search expression involves anything other than literal values, you should build the search string as a separate variable, both to make the code more readable and to make debugging easier. Use the `Quote()` function from Listing 7.4 when you need to surround the value from a string or date variable with quotation marks:

```
Function Quote(val)
    Quote = Chr(34) & CStr(val) & Chr(34)
End Function
```

For example, this code snippet builds a search string to locate appointments starting today or at a later date:

```
strFind = "[Start] >= " & Quote(Date)
Set colItems = objFolder.Items.Restrict(strFind)
```

If you use a `Debug.Print` or `MsgBox` statement to display the result of the `strFind` expression, the Immediate window or message box will show text like this (with today's date) to help you confirm that the search string looks good:

```
[Start] >= "4/18/2007"
```

A key limitation of the Jet syntax is that the standard property names from the Outlook object model work only in English. If Outlook is configured for another language, the Jet syntax needs to use localized property names. Unfortunately, no comprehensive list is available. If you need to write code for multiple locales, you should use the DASL syntax for your searches.

Other important Jet limitations are that it supports only three operators (=, >, and <) and wildcards are not allowed. This means that for searches of text properties, you are limited to exact matches and initial string searches. To do a "starts with" search, use the < and > operators. For example, this statement builds the search string to return all contacts whose last name begins with M:

```
strFind = "[LastName] >= 'M' AND [LastName] < 'N'"
```

If you need to search for a *substring match*, in other words, for a string contained within a text property value, use the DASL syntax instead of Jet.

A relatively minor Jet limitation is that it doesn't provide a way to handle apostrophes, such as those you might find in a person's name (O'Brien) or in the subject of an appointment (Sue Mosher's Birthday). In those scenarios, you should use a DASL search instead.

A final limitation is that many standard properties, including `EntryID`, `Body`, `HTMLBody`, and computed properties like `ContactItem.Last-FirstAndSuffix`, are not supported in Jet searches. The Help topics on the `Find` and `Restrict` methods provide a detailed list.

---

**Tip:** You don't need to be able to search for an `EntryID` value, since you can use that value with the `Namespace.GetItemFromID` method to locate an item directly.

---

## 16.2.2 Using the DASL search syntax

The DASL search syntax is supported by all the search methods except `Explorer.Search` and `Items.Find`. It is similar to Jet in that a search string involves a field name, a comparison operator, and the value you want to search for, but there are two big differences. The field names for DASL use the namespace schema names discussed in Chapter 14. This means you can search on many properties that are not exposed in the Outlook object model. Plus, you can perform substring searches using the LIKE operator, which you may be familiar with if you have constructed queries with Microsoft Access or SQL Server.

Table 16.3 should help you compare some the Jet syntax examples from the previous section with their DASL equivalents. Note that, when building a DASL search string, the property name must be enclosed in double quotation marks and, for text and date properties, the search value enclosed in single quotation marks. Omit the seconds element from date property values. Where Jet uses `True` and `False` for Boolean property search values, DASL uses `1` and `0`. Use schema property names that you've looked up in a view's Filter dialog or their equivalents from the MAPI proptag or MAPI ID namespaces.

To use DASL syntax with any method that supports it other than `AdvancedSearch`, you must prefix the search string with `@SQL=`. Compare

**Table 16.3** *Examples of Jet and DASL Search Strings*

| Jet | DASL |
|---|---|
| `"[City] = 'Arlington'"` | `"""urn:schemas:contacts:mailingcity"" = 'Arlington'"` `""" http://schemas.microsoft.com/mapi/id/{00062004-0000-0000-C000-000000000046}/8046001E"" = 'Arlington'"` |
| `"[Unread] = True"` | `"""urn:schemas:httpmail:read"" = 0"` |
| `"[Start] >= ""March 3, 2007"""` | `"""urn:schemas:calendar:dtstart"" >= '3/3/2007 12:00 AM'"` `""" http://schemas.microsoft.com/mapi/id/{00062002-0000-0000-C000-000000000046}/820D0040"" >= '3/3/2007 12:00 AM'"` |
| `"[Duration] < 1440"` | `"""http://schemas.microsoft.com/mapi/id/{00062002-0000-0000-C000-000000000046}/82130003"" < 1440"` |
| `"[MailingAddressCity] = 'Arlington' And [MailingAddressState] = 'VA'"` | `"""urn:schemas:contacts:mailingcity"" = 'Arlington' AND ""urn:schemas:contacts:mailingstate"" = 'VA'"` `""" http://schemas.microsoft.com/mapi/id/{00062004-0000-0000-C000-000000000046}/8046001E"" = 'Arlington' AND ""http://schemas.microsoft.com/mapi/proptag/0x3A28001E"" = 'VA'"` |

the code in the previous section to locate appointments starting on or after a particular date with this DASL equivalent:

```
strFind = Quote("urn:schemas:calendar:dtstart") & _
          " >= '12/18/2006 12:00 AM'"
Set colItems = objFolder.Items.Restrict("@SQL=" & strFind)
```

To perform a DASL substring search, use the `LIKE` operator and `%` as a wildcard. This search string, for example, would find all contacts whose last names begin with "M":

```
"""urn:schemas:contacts:sn"" LIKE 'M%'"
```

Here's a more complicated example that builds a search string, `strFind`, to locate all annual birthday and anniversary events in a calendar folder:

```
Const PR_SUBJECT = _
  "http://schemas.microsoft.com/mapi/proptag/0x0037001E"
strfind = Quote("urn:schemas:calendar:alldayevent") & _
        " = 1 AND " & _
        Quote("http://schemas.microsoft.com/mapi/id/" & _
          "{00062002-0000-0000-C000-000000000046}/" & _
          "82310003") & _
        " = 4 AND (" & _
        Quote(PR_SUBJECT) & " LIKE '%Birthday%' OR " & _
        Quote(PR_SUBJECT) & " LIKE '%Anniversary%')"
```

A `Debug.Print strFind` statement would display this as the search string in the Immediate window:

```
"urn:schemas:calendar:alldayevent" = 1 AND "http://
schemas.microsoft.com/mapi/id/{00062002-0000-0000-C000-
000000000046}/82310003" = 4 AND ("http://
schemas.microsoft.com/mapi/proptag/0x0037001E" LIKE
'%Birthday%' OR " http://schemas.microsoft.com/mapi/
proptag/0x0037001E" LIKE '%Anniversary%')
```

Compare this result with the query built in the Section 16.2.3, "Using the Query Builder," which uses a different namespace to refer to the same `Subject` property.

---

**Tip:** The `PR_SUBJECT` name for the constant for the MAPI proptag schema name for the `Subject` property refers to the property's name in the Extended MAPI programming model, which is well documented on MSDN. Such `PR*` names give you a convenient and familiar shorthand for naming constants to represent various MAPI properties. We'll see them in other examples in this chapter.

---

It may look complex, but the fields in the first, third, and fourth search terms should be recognizable as the `AllDayEvent` and `Subject` properties. The second search term is the MAPI property tag for the recurrence frequency of an appointment; the value 4 corresponds to yearly appointments.

Notice the search term for `AllDayEvent`, a Boolean property in the Outlook object model, takes a value 1 in DASL, corresponding to a value of `True`.

As useful as the `LIKE` operator is, though, if Outlook is configured for indexed search, then you'll probably want to use the content indexer operators discussed in the next section whenever you want to search for words in the text.

### 16.2.3   Using the Query Builder

A good way to learn about the DASL search syntax is to experiment, using the dialog for building filters on folders. To create complex searches with multiple search terms joined by OR as well as AND, you can enhance Outlook's Filter dialog with a Query Builder dialog that allows you to build searches graphically using Outlook field names and see the results in the DASL syntax. Make a backup of your Windows registry, then run Regedit and in the HKCU\Software\Microsoft\Office\12.0\Outlook key, add a new key named QueryBuilder; no value is required. After you add the QueryBuilder key, display the Filter dialog by choosing View | Current View | Customize Current View | Filter. Between the Advanced and SQL tabs, you'll see a new Query Builder tab like that in Figure 16.1.

As an example of how to use the Query Builder to investigate DASL syntax, let's build a query to locate all birthdays and anniversaries. Follow these steps:

1.   Switch to your default Calendar folder.

2.   Choose View | Current View | Customize Current View | Filter, and then switch to the Query Builder tab.

3.   Under Field, choose Subject from the Frequently Used Fields list. For the Condition, choose "contains," and for the Value, type in "Birthday."

**Figure 16.1**
*Add a Query Builder tab to help you work with Outlook's DASL search syntax.*

**Figure 16.2**
*The Query Builder tab adds the ability to construct complex searches with both AND and OR operators.*

4.  Click Add to List to add the Birthday condition to the filter.

5.  Repeat steps 3 and 4, substituting "Anniversary" for "Birthday."

6.  Under Logical Group, choose OR. The Query Builder should look like Figure 16.1.

7.  Under Field, choose All Day Event from the Frequently Used Fields list. For the Condition, choose "equals," and for the Value, select Yes.

8.  Click Add to List to add the All Day Event condition to the filter.

9.  In the list of conditions, select "All Day Event equals Yes."

10. Click Move Up three times to move the All Day Event condition up as far as it will go. The Query Builder should now look like Figure 16.2.

11. Switch to the SQL tab and check the box for Edit These Conditions Directly. You should see the search criteria in Figure 16.3.

**Figure 16.3**
*The DASL syntax supports the LIKE operator for substring searches.*

These expressions

```
"urn:schemas:httpmail:subject" LIKE '%Birthday%'
"urn:schemas:httpmail:subject" LIKE '%Anniversary%'
```

will filter for items whose `Subject` property contains "Birthday" or "Anniversary." Joining those expressions with OR means that any item with "Birthday" or "Anniversary" in the subject will satisfy the search conditions. The expression

```
"urn:schemas:calendar:alldayevent" = 1
```

will filter for items with `AllDayEvent = True`. Joining this expression to the OR'd subject expression produces a search string that will look for all day events with either "Birthday" or "Anniversary" in the subject. You can test how well the filter works by clicking OK to apply it to the Calendar folder.

## 16.2.4 Searching for indexed content

Outlook 2007 includes a new feature, Instant Search, that uses Windows Desktop Search (WDS) 3.0 to perform background content indexing. The WDS content index includes:

- All Outlook standard text and keywords properties, including item bodies
- All custom text properties, including those defined only on individual items
- Certain standard properties whose content can be stored as text, such as `Unread` and `FlagStatus`
- Text from attachments, both files and Outlook items

A search of the content index is potentially much faster than the other types of searches you've seen so far, because it searches the index, not individual items. Furthermore, only with a content index search can you locate items based on text in an attachment.

That indexed content is available to DASL searches using two additional operators:

- `CI_PHRASEMATCH`
- `CI_STARTSWITH`

Neither of the content index operators supports wildcards. The `CI_PHRASEMATCH` operator generates a search for an instance of a whole word or phrase, while the `CI_STARTSWITH` operator generates a search for a whole word or phrase that begins with the specified text. Thus, these are not at all the same as `LIKE '%search text%'` searches, which search for substrings, with no regard for word boundaries.

Five MAPI property tags, listed in Table 16.4, are available for use with content index searches for text in item bodies, attachments, and recipients.

**Table 16.4** *MAPI Property Tags for Body, Attachment, and Recipient Content Searches*

| Mapi Property | Namespace Schema Name |
| --- | --- |
| PR_BODY | urn:schemas:httpmail:textdescription |
| PR_SEARCH_ATTACHMENTS | http://schemas.microsoft.com/mapi/proptag/0x0EA5001E |
| PR_SEARCH_RECIP_EMAIL_TO | http://schemas.microsoft.com/mapi/proptag/0x0EA6001E |
| PR_SEARCH_RECIP_EMAIL_CC | http://schemas.microsoft.com/mapi/proptag/0x0EA7001E |
| PR_SEARCH_RECIP_EMAIL_BCC | http://schemas.microsoft.com/mapi/proptag/0x0EA8001E |

With the exception of urn:schemas:httpmail:textdescription, you cannot use these properties with other DASL search operators, only with CI_PHRASEMATCH and CI_STARTSWITH. Also searches that use the property related to Bcc recipients will return results only for items that the current user has sent; incoming items contain no Bcc information.

Let's look at a few examples. These statements create a search string (strFind) that will find items with attachments that contain the word "error" or "errors":

```
Const PR_SEARCH_ATTACHMENTS = _
    "http://schemas.microsoft.com/mapi/proptag/0x0EA5001E"
strFind = Quote(PR_SEARCH_ATTACHMENTS) & _
        " CI_STARTSWITH 'error'"
```

This next example shows how to construct a search string to locate items sent to someone at microsoft.com:

```
Const PR_SEARCH_RECIP_EMAIL_TO = _
    "http://schemas.microsoft.com/mapi/proptag/0x0EA6001E"
strFind = Quote(PR_SEARCH_RECIP_EMAIL_TO) & _
        " CI_PHRASEMATCH 'microsoft.com'"
```

You can combine CI_PHRASEMATCH and CI_STARTSWITH expressions with DASL search expressions using other operators and other properties, such as this example that creates a search string to locate unread items with the phrase "investment management" in the body of an item:

```
Const PR_BODY = "urn:schemas:httpmail:textdescription"
strFind = Quote(PR_BODY) & " CI_PHRASEMATCH " & _
        "'investment management' AND " & _
        Quote("urn:schemas:httpmail:read") & " = 0"
```

The search string value returned by strFind would be:

```
"urn:schemas:httpmail:textdescription" CI_PHRASEMATCH
'investment management' AND "urn:schemas:httpmail:read" = 0
```

To determine whether the data in a given information store is available for a content index search, check the value of the `Store.IsInstant-SearchEnabled` property. If `IsInstantSearchEnabled` returns `False`, then you cannot use a `CI_PHRASEMATCH` or `CI_STARTSWITH` expression in your DASL search.

You'll see additional examples of content index searches as we review more aspects of searching with Outlook. Also check out this article in Outlook developer Help:

- How to: Filter the Body of a Mail Item (HV10016698)

The number in parentheses is a topic ID you can search for in Help to find the article faster.

## 16.2.5 Searching on item bodies, text, and keyword properties

So far we have seen several different ways to search for content in text properties. Let's recap the most important points:

- Searches with Jet syntax support only the =, >, and < operators, and thus can locate only an exact match for the entire property value or a match for a starting string. They cannot perform substring searches.

- The Jet syntax cannot search for text in Outlook item bodies.

- For substring searches that look for an exact word or phrase (or the beginning of exact word or phrase), use DASL syntax with the `CI_PHRASEMATCH` and `CI_STARTSWITH` operators. This technique is available only in indexed information stores.

- For other substring searches, use DASL syntax with the `LIKE` operator.

The Help topics for the `Items.Find` and `Items.Restrict` methods list other text properties besides `Body` and `HTMLBody` that the Jet filter cannot handle.

The `Categories` property and other keywords properties are a special type of text property. You can locate items with a specific category using both Jet and DASL syntax. This statement builds a Jet search string for items with a category of Important:

```
strFind = "[Categories] = " & Quote("Important")
```

In a Jet query, the search term must be an exact match for the category. The above search would not return any items with the category Important Customer.

If you want to search for items that fit two categories, combine two such `[Categories]` search expressions with the AND operator:

```
strFind = "[Categories] = " & Quote("Important") & _
          " AND [Categories] = " & Quote("Key Customer")
```

Now consider four possible DASL syntax searches in a folder that contains items that have a category of Holiday and also some with the categories of Holiday Card, Vacation Holiday, and HolidayOnIce. This search string for an exact match for Holiday will find only those items that have Holiday and will ignore those with the other three categories:

```
CONST SEARCH_KEYWORDS = _
    "urn:schemas-microsoft-com:office:office#Keywords"
strFind = Quote(SEARCH_KEYWORDS) & " = 'Holiday'"
```

If you use the LIKE operator, as in

```
strFind = Quote(SEARCH_KEYWORDS) & " LIKE '%Holiday%'"
```

Outlook will search each category for the substring "Holiday" and so will find items containing any of the four categories.

If you use the CI_PHRASEMATCH operator, as in

```
strFind = Quote(SEARCH_KEYWORDS) & _
          " CI_PHRASEMATCH 'Holiday'"
```

Outlook will search the words and phrases in each individual category for an exact match for the word "Holiday" and so will find items marked with the Holiday, Holiday Card, or Vacation Holiday category.

If you use the CI_STARTSWITH operator, as in

```
strFind = Quote(SEARCH_KEYWORDS) & _
          " CI_STARTSWITH 'Holiday'"
```

Outlook will look for words and phrases in each individual category that start with "Holiday" and so will find items marked with any of the four categories.

Thus, you should be careful when searching the Categories property—or any other keywords field—to use the operator appropriate to the goal of your search, depending on whether you want to locate an exact match for a category or to locate categories that may be related because they contain the same word or string.

Another common issue related to text properties is how to handle items where a string property may never have received a value. This can create an odd situation where items have more than one kind of "blank." Users see this oddity when they group by a field and see two different groups with the value of (none). One group consists of those items that have never had a value, while the other contains those items that once had a non-blank value for that property but now are blank. This behavior is particularly likely to occur with a user-defined property.

For example, if you have a custom property named Industry in a contacts folder, you might use this Jet search string to try to find contacts that don't have a value for Industry:

```
strFind = "[Industry] = " & Quote("")
```

However, that will not return any items that have never had a value set for `Industry`. It will return only those items that are now blank, but previously had a non-blank value for `Industry`. To locate all blank items, regardless of whether the property has ever had a value, you must use a DASL query with the keywords `Is Null`, for example:

```
strFind = _
    Quote("http://schemas.microsoft.com/mapi/string/" & _
        "{00020329-0000-0000-C000-000000000046}/" & _
        "Industry") & " Is Null"
```

As you'll see in the next section, the `Is Null` keywords are also useful to determine if a date/time property has been set to a value.

### 16.2.6   Searching on date/time fields

As you learned earlier in the section on Jet queries, to search for a value in a date/time property, you must enclose the search value in quotation marks and show time only in hours and minutes, without any seconds. Use those techniques with DASL queries, too. Date/time queries also have some tricky nuances that Outlook developers need to contend with:

- Dealing with "None" date/time values
- Handling time zones and localized date formats
- Searching a date range

Just as with text searches, date/time fields present a challenge when the goal is to return items that do not have a date value assigned. In the user interface, the user will see None both for dates that have never had a value and for those that had a value previously, but the user (or code) removed it. Outlook stores `#1/1/4501#` for the latter "None" values.

In a Jet search, to locate all "None" date/time values, you must look both for items with a blank date/time value and for those with a value of `#1/1/4501#`. This statement builds a Jet search string to locate items that don't have a value for a custom property named `First Met`:

```
strFind = "[First Met] = " & Quote("") & " OR " & _
        "[First Met] = " & Quote("1/1/4501 12:00 AM")
```

The DASL equivalent of that search would use the `Is Null` keywords that you saw in the previous section on string searches:

```
strFind = _
    Quote("http://schemas.microsoft.com/mapi/string/" & _
        "{00020329-0000-0000-C000-000000000046}/" & _
        "First%20Met") & " Is Null OR " & _
    Quote("http://schemas.microsoft.com/mapi/string/" & _
        "{00020329-0000-0000-C000-000000000046}/" & _
        "First%20Met") & " = '1/1/4501 12:00 AM'"
```

**Note:** Since the `First Met` custom property contains a space in its name, to use it in a DASL query, you must replace the space with the escape sequence `%20`.

To ensure that Outlook interprets a date value correctly, according to the locale set in the Regional Settings applet in Control Panel, you should use the `Format()` function in VBA or the `FormatDateTime()` function in VBScript to format the date and time in one of the defined formats for the locale. This Jet search string for VBA could be used to locate items created during the past week:

```
dteDate = DateAdd("d", -7, Now)
strFind = "[CreationTime] >= " & _
          Quote(Format(dteDate, "Short Date") & _
          " " & Format(dteDate, "Short Time"))
```

The `Format()` function is not available in VBScript, so you would need to use `FormatDatetime()` instead:

```
dteDate = DateAdd("d", -7, Now)
strFind = "[CreationTime] >= " & _
   Quote(FormatDateTime(dteDate, vbShortDate) & _
          " " & FormatDateTime(dteDate, vbShortTime))
```

Jet and DASL queries differ significantly in their handling of time zones. A date/time value in a Jet query is compared with the property value expressed in local time, while a DASL query uses Coordinated Universal Time (UTC) time values for its comparisons. Therefore, when building a DASL search string for a date/time property that uses time values, you must convert the search value to UTC using the `LocalToUTC` method of either the `PropertyAccessor` or `Row` object. Here is the DASL equivalent of the above search for recently created items, showing the value returned by the `Now` function converted to UTC by the `PropertyAccessor` for the folder that you want to search:

```
Set objPA = objFolder.PropertyAccessor
dteDate = objPA.LocalTimeToUTC(DateAdd("d", -7, Now))
strFind = Quote("DAV:creationdate") & " >= '" & _
          Format(dteDate, "Short Date") & " " & _
          Format(dteDate, "Short Time") & "'"
```

**Note:** The `CreationDate` property is a good example of a property that has more than one namespace schema property name. In the above example, the DASL query uses `DAV:creationdate`, but these schema property names from other namespaces would also work: `urn:schemas:calendar:created` and `http://schemas.microsoft.com/mapi/proptag/0x30070040`.

**Table 16.5**     *DASL Macros for Date Searches*

| Date Macro | Syntax |
|---|---|
| today | %today("*Property_schema_name*")% |
| tomorrow | %tomorrow("*Property_schema_name*")% |
| yesterday | %yesterday("*Property_schema_name*")% |
| next7days | %next7days("*Property_schema_name*")% |
| last7days | %last7days("*Property_schema_name*")% |
| nextweek | %nextweek("*Property_schema_name*")% |
| thisweek | %thisweek("*Property_schema_name*")% |
| lastweek | %lastweek("*Property_schema_name*")% |
| nextmonth | %nextmonth("*Property_schema_name*")% |
| thismonth | %thismonth("*Property_schema_name*")% |
| lastmonth | %lastmonth("*Property_schema_name*")% |

Oddly enough, for a few standard Outlook properties, you do not need to perform any conversion to UTC for DASL searches. Examples include the `TaskItem.DueDate`, `TaskItem.StartDate`, `MailItem.TaskDue-Date`, and `MailItem.TaskStartDate` properties, all of which truncate their time values to midnight. In fact, when using these properties in queries, you should omit not just the seconds portion of the date/time, but also the hours and minutes. Pass only a date string in the query.

The final date/time search issue that we need to cover is searching a date range. To help with this common programming task, Outlook provides DASL "macros" for the most common date range scenarios. If you use one of the macros in Table 16.5, you do not need to worry about performing any local-to-UTC date/time conversion.

Notice that the namespace schema name for the property needs to be surrounded by quotation marks when you use one of the macros from Table 16.5. For example, this code snippet builds a DASL search string to look for items created in the past seven days:

```
strFind = "%last7days(" & Quote("DAV:creationdate") & ")%"
```

For DASL date ranges that the macros don't cover—and for any Jet query that spans a date range—you must include two expressions in the search string, one for the beginning of the date range, and one for the end. To search for items created last month using Jet, you would use code like this:

```
dteStart = GetMonthStart(Date, -1)
dteEnd = DateAdd("m", 1, dteStart)
```

```
strFind = "[CreationTime] >= " & _
  Quote(FormatDateTime(dteStart, vbShortDate) & " " _
        & FormatDateTime(dteStart, vbShortTime)) & _
  " AND [CreationTime] < " & _
  Quote(FormatDateTime(dteEnd, vbShortDate) & _
        " " & FormatDateTime(dteEnd, vbShortTime))
```

The GetMonthStart() function for VBA is shown in Listing 16.1 and uses the DateAdd() function to step back to the beginning of the month for the dateVal argument and then go forward or backwards a set number of months, depending on whether numMonths is positive or negative. To adjust it for use with VBScript, you would need to remove the As Date clauses.

The above code snippet produces this Jet search string if today's date is in the month of December 2007:

```
[CreationTime] >= "12/1/2007 00:00" AND [CreationTime] <
"1/1/2008 00:00"
```

The code to build an equivalent DASL search string for items created last month uses a similar structure to obtain the start and end dates for the range, only using LocalTimeToUTC method to account for the time zone offset from UTC. This example uses the Format() function and thus is for VBA:

```
Set objPA = objFolder.PropertyAccessor
dteStart = _
  objPA.LocalTimeToUTC(GetMonthStart(Date, -1))
dteEnd = DateAdd("m", 1, dteStart)
strFind = Quote("DAV:creationdate") & " >= '" & _
          Format(dteStart, "Short Date") & " " & _
          Format(dteStart, "Short Time") & "' AND " & _
          Quote("DAV:creationdate") & " < '" & _
          Format(dteEnd, "Short Date") & " " & _
          Format(dteEnd, "Short Time") & "'"
```

Since I live in a time zone that is five hours west of Greenwich, England (during non-Daylight Savings Time hours), my DASL search string would look like this:

```
"DAV:creationdate" >= '12/1/2007 05:00' AND
"DAV:creationdate" < '1/1/2008 05:00'
```

---

**Listing 16.1**    *Get the start date of a month relative to any date*

```
Function GetMonthStart _
  (dateVal As Date, numMonths As Integer) As Date
    Dim dteDate As Date
    dteDate = DateAdd("d", -Day(dateVal) + 1, _
                      dateValue(dateVal))
    GetMonthStart = DateAdd("m", numMonths, dteDate)
End Function
```

---

The final date search scenario of interest is locating appointments that fit a particular date range, including recurring appointments. This is not as simple as the other date range scenarios we've already looked at, because an appointment has both a `Start` and `End` date. Given any date/time range, you may have appointments that lie wholly inside that range, appointments that overlap the range on either end, and appointments that overlap the range completely. For example, if you want to return all the appointments for a particular day, you need to consider not only those that begin and end on that date, but also those that overlap that date and start or end (or both!) on a different date. The trick to capturing all the items in that range may sound counterintuitive, but it works: To search for appointments within a date range, search for items whose `Start` date is earlier than the range end date and whose `End` date occurs after the range start date.

The `GetApptDateSpan()` function in Listing 16.2 takes a folder and two dates as arguments and uses a Jet query with the `Folder.Items.Restrict` method to return all the appointments that fall within the date span. Here is an example of how to call `GetApptDateSpan()` from another VBA procedure to generate a list in the Immediate window of all the appointments for today:

```
Set objFld = _
  Application.Session.GetDefaultFolder(olFolderCalendar)
Set itms = GetApptDateSpan(objFld, Date , Date + 1)
For Each itm In itms
    Debug.Print itm.Subject, itm.Start, itm.End
Next
```

To adapt the code in Listing 16.2 for use in VBScript, simply remove the `As` data type clauses.

The `GetApptDateSpan()` function demonstrates several important aspects of searching for appointments so that individual recurrences that fit the date span are included:

- You must use an explicit `Items` collection, in this example, `colItems`.

- If you want to include recurring appointments in the search results, you must sort the `Items` collection on the `Start` property and set `IncludeRecurrences = True` before running the search:

```
colItems.Sort "[Start]"
colItems.IncludeRecurrences = True
```

- The `IncludeRecurrences` technique works only with Jet queries, not DASL queries.

- You should never use `IncludeRecurrences` without specifying a finite date range. Otherwise, if the resulting `Items` collection contains recurring appointments with no end date, you will have an infinite number of items to process.

**Listing 16.2**    *Return appointments for a given date range*

```
Function GetApptDateSpan(fld As Outlook.folder, _
  startDate As Date, endDate As Date) As Outlook.Items
    Dim colItems As Outlook.Items
    Dim colSpanItems As Outlook.Items
    Dim strFind As String
    On Error Resume Next
    Set colItems = fld.Items
    colItems.Sort "[Start]"
    colItems.IncludeRecurrences = True
    strFind = "[Start] <= " & _
      Quote(FormatDateTime(endDate, vbShortDate) & " " _
            & FormatDateTime(endDate, vbShortTime)) & _
      " AND [End] > " & _
      Quote(FormatDateTime(startDate, vbShortDate) & " " _
            & FormatDateTime(startDate, vbShortTime))
    Set colSpanItems = colItems.Restrict(strFind)
    If Err = 0 Then
        Set GetApptDateSpan = colSpanItems
    End If
    Set colSpanItems = Nothing
End Function
```

■ You cannot process the items in a loop that uses the Items.Count property value. Any time you use IncludeRecurrences = True to retrieve recurring appointments, the Count property will not return an accurate count of the number of appointments retrieved. Therefore, you should process the items in a For Each ... Next loop, as shown above.

### 16.2.7   Searching with custom properties

In general, custom properties can be included in searches just like standard properties. Here are some key points to remember:

■ For Jet search queries, the custom property must be defined in the folder not just in individual items. This architectural issue is covered in Chapter 21. You cannot search on custom formula or combination properties.

■ For DASL search queries, the schema property name for a custom property comes from the MAPI string namespace and always takes this format, where *property_name* is the name you gave to the property when you created it in Outlook:

http://schemas.microsoft.com/mapi/string/{00020329-0000-0000-C000-000000000046}/*property_name*

■ If the property name contains spaces, you must replace them with the %20 escape sequence. For example, a DASL search using a property named Service Contract would use this property schema name:

```
http://schemas.microsoft.com/mapi/string/{00020329-0000-
0000-C000-000000000046}/Service%20Contract
```

- Custom date and text properties are more likely than standard properties to have null values. Use the syntax shown earlier in the chapter to make sure you search both for true nulls and for items whose property has never had a value at all.

- Custom text properties are indexed and thus can be searched with the CI_PHRASEMATCH and CI_STARTSWITH operators in information stores that have been indexed.

## 16.3  Using Items.Find and Items.Restrict

Now that you know how to construct Jet and DASL search strings, let's see some of those searches in action using the different search methods that Outlook 2007 supports. The Folder.Items.Find, .FindNext, and .Restrict methods are the easiest techniques to apply when you need to conduct a search in a single folder. Both Find and Restrict can use Jet queries, and as you'll see, Restrict can also use a DASL query.

The Find method returns the first item (if any) that meets your conditions:

```
Set objItem = objFolder.Items.Find(Filter)
```

If no item meets the conditions, then Find returns Nothing. Which item is the "first" item depends on how the Items collection is sorted. If you want to sort the Items collection or if you plan to use FindNext after calling Find, you must instantiate an explicit Items collection for use with these methods, for example:

```
Set objFolder = _
  Application.Session.GetDefaultFolder(olFolderTasks)
Set colItems = objFolder.Items
colItems.Sort "[CreationTime]", True
strFind = "[Subject] = 'Mail Payment'"
Set objItem = colItems.Find(strFind)
Do While Not objItem Is Nothing
    MsgBox objItem.Subject & " " & objItem.DueDate
    Set objItem = colItems.FindNext
Loop
```

The Restrict method uses the same syntax for Jet queries, but returns an Items collection rather than a single Outlook item object:

```
Set colItems = objFolder.Items.Restrict(Filter)
```

Listing 16.2 provided an example of using a Jet query to return all the appointments within a given date range.

In addition to Jet queries, the Restrict method can also run a DASL query—including a query using the CI_PHRASEMATCH and CI_STARTSWITH content index operators—by prefixing the DASL search string with @SQL=.

It is also possible to take an `Items` collection that has already been filtered with the `Restrict` method and apply `Restrict` again to further narrow the results. To demonstrate both these techniques, the `CelebrationList` procedure in Listing 16.3 (for VBA) uses both a Jet query and a DASL query, in succession, to locate birthdays and anniversaries for next month and create a new Outlook task to remind you that these celebrations are coming up.

Some notes on the `CelebrationList` procedure:

- The `colCal` collection is the result of a Jet query executed by the `GetApptDateSpan()` function to get all the appointments for next month from the Calendar folder.

- The `colBA` collection is the result of a DASL query executed against the `colCal` collection.

- The birthday and anniversary dates are obtained from the contact linked to the event in the calendar folder through the `Appointment-Item.Links` collection. We will discuss this technique in Chapter 20.

**Listing 16.3**　*Create a task to remind you about upcoming celebrations*

```
Sub CelebrationList()
    Dim objOL As Outlook.Application
    Dim objNS As Outlook.NameSpace
    Dim objFld As Outlook.folder
    Dim colCal As Outlook.Items
    Dim colBA As Outlook.Items
    Dim objAppt As Outlook.AppointmentItem
    Dim objTask As Outlook.taskItem
    Dim objContact As Outlook.ContactItem
    Dim dteStart As Date
    Dim dteEnd As Date
    Dim dteEvent As Date
    Dim strFind As String
    Dim strEvents As String
    Dim arrMonthNames() As String
    Dim strYears As String
    On Error Resume Next
    Set objOL = Application
    Set objNS = objOL.Session
    Set objFld = objNS.GetDefaultFolder(olFolderCalendar)
    ' GetMonthStart() from Listing 16.1
    dteStart = GetMonthStart(Date, 1)
    dteEnd = DateAdd("m", 1, dteStart)
    ' GetApptDateSpan() from Listing 16.2
    Set colCal = GetApptDateSpan(objFld, dteStart, dteEnd)
    If objNS.DefaultStore.IsInstantSearchEnabled Then
        strFind = Quote("urn:schemas:httpmail:subject") & _
                " CI_PHRASEMATCH 'Birthday' OR " & _
                Quote("urn:schemas:httpmail:subject") & _
                " CI_PHRASEMATCH 'Anniversary'"
```

**Listing 16.3** *Create a task to remind you about upcoming celebrations (continued)*

```
Else
    strFind = Quote("urn:schemas:httpmail:subject") & _
              " LIKE '%Birthday%' OR " & _
              Quote("urn:schemas:httpmail:subject") & _
              " LIKE '%Anniversary%'"
End If
Set colBA = colCal.Restrict("@SQL=" & strFind)
For Each objAppt In colBA
    dteEvent = #1/1/4501#
    If objAppt.Links.Count > 0 Then
        Set objContact = objAppt.Links.Item(1).Item
        If Not objContact Is Nothing Then
            If InStr(objAppt.Subject, _
                    "Birthday") > 0 Then
                dteEvent = objContact.Birthday
            Else
                dteEvent = objContact.Anniversary
            End If
        End If
    End If
    If dteEvent <> #1/1/4501# Then
        strYears = " (" & _
          CStr(Year(dteStart) - Year(dteEvent)) & _
          " years)"
    Else
        dteEvent = DateValue(objAppt.Start)
        strYears = ""
    End If
    strEvents = strEvents & _
      FormatDateTime(dteEvent, vbShortDate) & vbTab & _
      objAppt.Subject & strYears & vbCrLf
Next
If strEvents <> "" Then
    Set objTask = objOL.CreateItem(olTaskItem)
    With objTask
        .Subject = "Celebration Events for " & _
                    Format(dteStart, "MMMM")
        .DueDate = dteStart
        .StartDate = DateAdd("d", -7, dteStart)
        .ReminderTime = DateAdd("h", 12, dteStart)
        .ReminderSet = True
        .Body = strEvents
        .Display
    End With
Else
    MsgBox "No celebrations in " & Format(dteStart, "MMMM")
End If
Set objOL = Nothing
Set objNS = Nothing
Set colCal = Nothing
Set colBA = Nothing
Set objTask = Nothing
Set objAppt = Nothing
Set objContact = Nothing
End Sub
```

- This expression—`Format(dteStart,  "MMMM")`—returns a string with the full name of the month, in the user's locale language.

- This subroutine is a good example of how you can reuse the basic procedures that you build in VBA to construct new procedures. It uses the `GetMonthStart()` and `GetApptDateSpan()` functions that you saw earlier in Listings 16.1 and 16.2.

- The `MonthName()` function is another handy, reusable function. It returns the text for the name of the month, given the month number.

---

**Tip:** To run the `CelebrationList` procedure once a month, create a monthly recurring task with a reminder and the subject "Run Celebration List" and use the `ReminderFire` event discussed in Chapter 11 to call `CelebrationList` whenever the reminder fires for the Run Celebration List task.

---

Does it make any difference whether you use `Find` or `Restrict`? If you need to return only one particular item from a folder, `Find` is the logical choice. For example, the `Find` method is very commonly used to locate an item that is likely to have a unique property value, such as a contact with a specific name or an appointment based on its `GlobalAppointmentID` property. If your code needs to work with all the items in a folder that meet specific criteria, `Restrict` makes more sense. However, in an Exchange Server environment—especially in public folders—be wary of using `Restrict`. Exchange caches restrictions on its folders. Whenever an item is created or modified, it is matched against existing restrictions on the folder. While this can improve performance if a folder has a few cached restrictions that are used repeatedly, if a folder has many restrictions, that can greatly increase the time required to save an item in the folder.

---

**Note:** When Outlook receives an update to a meeting request that the user has accepted, it creates a new item in the Calendar folder and deletes the old one. Since the update is a completely new item, it will have a different `EntryID` value from the original. Thus, you cannot rely on the `EntryID` to help you track an appointment—even the same appointment in the same folder. The property value that does stay the same, even through multiple updates, is `GlobalAppointmentID`, a new property added to the `AppointmentItem` object in Outlook 2007.

---

For additional examples using `Items.Restrict`, check out these articles in Outlook developer Help:

- How to: Programatically Change the Display Format for All Contacts (HV10178474)

- How to: Enumerate the Contacts Folder and Set Custom Property for only Contact Items (HV10038452)

The numbers in parentheses are topic IDs you can search for in Help to find the articles faster.

## 16.4  Using Table search techniques

As covered in the beginning of this chapter, the `Table` object, new to Outlook 2007, has `FindRow`, `FindNextRow`, and `Restrict` methods that are analogous to the `Find`, `FindNext`, and `Restrict` methods for the `Items` collection. These methods are available only to `Table` objects returned with the `Folder.GetTable` method (not those returned by the `Search.GetTable` method):

```
Set objTable = objFolder.GetTable
Set objRow = objTable.FindRow(Filter)
Set objNextRow = objTable.FindNextRow
Set objNewTable = objTable.Restrict(Filter)
```

The `FindRow` method takes a Jet or DASL query search string as its argument and returns a `Row` object. Use the `Row.GetValues` method to return an array of values from the row's columns or, if you need write access to the item represented by the row, you can use the `Row.Item` method to return the item's `EntryID`, which is one of the default columns in all tables, and then use the `Namespace.GetItemFromID` method to return the actual item.

The `Restrict` method can take a Jet query or a DASL query and returns a new `Table` object whose data you can process using the methods listed in Table 15.6. A key difference between `Items.Restrict` and `Table.Restrict` is that there is no equivalent of `IncludeRecurrences` for a `Table` object. The `Table` object for a calendar folder contains a row for each non-recurring appointment and a single row for the master instance of each recurring appointment.

Another difference is that a DASL query for the item body using the `urn:schemas:httpmail:textdescription` property will operate only on the first 255 characters of the body, because that is the maximum amount of body text that the `Table` can contain.

Another way to return a filtered `Table` object is to specify the filter when `GetTable` is called:

```
Set objTable = objFolder.GetTable(Filter, TableContents)
```

Both parameters are optional. The `Filter` parameter can be either a Jet or a DASL filter. The `TableContents` parameter can be one of these values from the `OlTableContents` enumeration:

```
olHiddenItems     1
olUserItems       0
```

The default value is olUserItems. For example, to return a Table containing all the hidden items in a folder (such as custom forms and views), use this statement:

```
Set objTable = objFolder.GetTable(olHiddenItems)
```

Listing 21.1 in Chapter 21 applies this technique to the task of listing all the forms published to a particular folder or to the Organizational Forms or Personal Forms library.

Use the Table search methods when your primary goal is rapid access to read-only filtered data. For example, you might want to determine whether a particular email address is already represented by a contact. You don't need to edit that contact; you just want to know if it exists at all. To make that determination, the IsInContacts() function in Listing 16.4 performs a FindRow search on the Table for the user's default Contacts folder. If the search returns a row, IsInContacts() returns True; otherwise, it returns False.

In Listing 18.2 in Chapter 18, we'll see the IsInContacts() function at work in a procedure that creates new contacts from the email addresses in outgoing messages. Also, in Listing 20.7 in Chapter 20, we'll use a Table.FindRow search to try to locate contacts that previously were linked

**Listing 16.4**    *Determine if a contact exists with a certain email address*

```
Function IsInContacts(address As String)
    Dim strFind As String
    Dim objNS As Outlook.NameSpace
    Dim objFolder As Outlook.Folder
    Dim objTable As Outlook.Table
    Dim objRow As Outlook.Row
    Dim objItems As Outlook.Items
    Dim blnIsInContacts As Boolean
    blnIsInContacts = False
    Set objNS = Application.Session
    Set objFolder = objNS.GetDefaultFolder(olFolderContacts)
    Set objTable = objFolder.GetTable
    strFind = "[Email1Address] = " & Quote(address) & _
            " OR [Email2Address] = " & Quote(address) & _
            " OR [Email3Address] = " & Quote(address)
    Set objRow = objTable.FindRow(strFind)
    If Not objRow Is Nothing Then
        blnIsInContacts = True
    End If
    IsInContacts = blnIsInContacts
    Set objNS = Nothing
    Set objFolder = Nothing
    Set objItems = Nothing
    Set objRow = Nothing
End Function
```

to an item through the `Links` collection. That example also uses `Row.Item` to get the contact's `EntryID` for use with `Namespace.GetItemFromID`.

For another example of a `Table` filter, check out this article in Outlook developer Help:

- How to: Use the `Table` Object to Performantly Enumerate Filtered Items in a Folder (HV10007264)

The number in parentheses is a topic ID you can search for in Help to find the article faster.

## 16.5 Using Explorer.Search

Use the `Explorer.Search` method when your primary goal is to present the user with the results of a search using an Outlook folder (`Explorer`) window. This method filters the designated `Explorer` window to show the results of a search—either for the current folder or for all folders of the same type as the current folder. The basic syntax for `Explorer.Search` looks like this:

```
objExpl.Search Query, SearchScope
```

where *Query* is the search string and *SearchScope* is either `olSearchScopeAllFolders` (literal value 1) or `olSearchScopeCurrentFolder` (literal value 0).

To remove a temporary search filter from the window, use the `Explorer.ClearSearch` method.

The *Query* search string parameter uses the AQS syntax and thus can be any word or phrase or any search string that the user can build in the Outlook user interface with the dropdown Query Builder that appears in any folder window.

There is no direct method for processing the results of an `Explorer.Search`, which makes it quite different from all the other methods discussed in this chapter. `Explorer.Search` automatically uses the content index, if available, for its searches.

To demonstrate `Explorer.Search`, let's consider a small, but common Outlook frustration: The user can right-click a message and execute a menu command for Find All | Items From Sender to see the results appear in an Advanced Find window. Wouldn't it be nice if you could search not just for all items from the sender but all items sent to the sender and have the results appear in an Explorer window, so that you get more functionality than the Advanced Find window offers? The code in Listing 16.5 gets the sender address (or name, if the sender is an Exchange user) from the current open or selected message using the `GetCurrentItem()` function from Listing 15.5, then creates a new `Explorer` window and calls

**Listing 16.5**    *Search for messages to or from the current message's sender*

```
Sub SearchForCurrentMessageSenderAddress()
    Dim objItem As Object
    Dim objMail As MailItem
    Dim strAddress As String
    Dim objExpl As Outlook.Explorer
    ' GetCurrentItem() from Listing 15.5
    Set objItem = GetCurrentItem()
    If objItem.Class = olMail Then
        Set objMail = objItem
        If objMail.SenderEmailType = "EX" Then
            strAddress = objMail.SenderName
        Else
            strAddress = objMail.SenderEmailAddress
        End If
        Set objExpl = DoSearch(strAddress, olModuleMail, _
                    olSearchScopeAllFolders, True)
        If Not objExpl Is Nothing Then
            objExpl.Activate
        End If
    End If
    Set objItem = Nothing
    Set objMail = Nothing
    Set objExpl = Nothing
End Sub

Function DoSearch(searchText As String, _
  searchModule As Outlook.OlNavigationModuleType, _
  searchScope As Outlook.OlSearchScope, _
  useNewWindow As Boolean) As Outlook.Explorer
    Dim objOL As Outlook.Application
    Dim objNS As Outlook.NameSpace
    Dim objNavPane As Outlook.NavigationPane
    Dim objFld As Outlook.folder
    Dim objExpl As Outlook.Explorer
    On Error Resume Next
    Set objOL = Application
    Set objNS = objOL.Session
    If useNewWindow Then
        If searchModule = olModuleFolderList Then
            Set objFld = objNS.GetDefaultFolder(olFolderInbox)
            Set objExpl = objOL.Explorers.Add(objFld, _
                    olFolderDisplayNormal)
            Set objNavPane = objExpl.NavigationPane
            objNavPane.CurrentModule = _
              objNavPane.Modules.GetNavigationModule _
              (olModuleFolderList)
        ElseIf searchModule <> olModuleShortcuts Then
            Set objFld = _
              GetDefaultFolderForModule(searchModule)
            Set objExpl = objOL.Explorers.Add(objFld, _
                    olFolderDisplayNormal)
        End If
        objExpl.ShowPane olToDoBar, False
```

**Listing 16.5** *Search for messages to or from the current message's sender (continued)*

```
    Else
        Set objExpl = objOL.ActiveExplorer
    End If
    If Not objExpl Is Nothing Then
        objExpl.Search searchText, searchScope
    End If
    Set DoSearch = objExpl
    Set objOL = Nothing
    Set objNS = Nothing
    Set objFld = Nothing
    Set objExpl = Nothing
    Set objNavPane = Nothing
End Function

Function GetDefaultFolderForModule _
  (searchModule As Outlook.OlNavigationModuleType) _
  As Outlook.folder
    Dim objOL As Outlook.Application
    Dim objNS As Outlook.NameSpace
    Dim lngDefaultFolder As Long
    Set objOL = Application
    Set objNS = objOL.Session
    Select Case searchModule
        Case olModuleCalendar
            lngDefaultFolder = olFolderCalendar
        Case olModuleContacts
            lngDefaultFolder = olFolderContacts
        Case olModuleJournal
            lngDefaultFolder = olFolderJournal
        Case olModuleMail
            lngDefaultFolder = olFolderInbox
        Case olModuleNotes
            lngDefaultFolder = olFolderNotes
        Case olModuleTasks
            lngDefaultFolder = olFolderTasks
    End Select
    If lngDefaultFolder <> 0 Then
        Set GetDefaultFolderForModule = _
          objNS.GetDefaultFolder(lngDefaultFolder)
    End If
    Set objNS = Nothing
End Function
```

Explorer.Search to search for that address in all mail folders. This search takes place across all text fields, including the sender and recipient fields and the message body.

The real work of the search is performed by the DoSearch() function, which takes as its parameters the two arguments required by the Explorer.Search method—the search string and the scope—plus two other pieces of information that help configure the Explorer to display correctly—the navigation pane module (always `olModuleMail` in this example) and the option to show the search in a new `Explorer` window. Using the correct navigation pane module is what makes it possible to search all folders of a given type using the `Explorer.Search` method.

The `DoSearch()` function can be reused in any number of ways. For example, these statements search for contacts in a particular city and display them in the current Explorer:

```
Set objExpl = DoSearch("city:Arlington", _
   olModuleContacts, olSearchScopeAllFolders, False)
objExpl.Activate
```

The `"city:Arlington"` search string is an example of the AQS syntax. Use the dropdown search Query Builder in the main Outlook window to experiment with the keywords available for use with the AQS feature and thus also with the `Explorer.Search` method. For more details on the AQS syntax, search the Microsoft Developer Network site at http://msdn.microsoft.com for the article "Advanced Query Syntax."

## 16.6   Using Application.AdvancedSearch

The search techniques discussed so far all operate on a single folder, with the exception of `Explorer.Search`, which can search either one folder or all folders of the same type. To search specific multiple folders, you must use the `Application.AdvancedSearch` method, which always uses the DASL syntax. It can search one or more folders within either a .pst file or the user's own Exchange mailbox. In the Public Folders store or another user's Exchange mailbox, `AdvancedSearch` can search only a single folder.

The other distinguishing feature of the `AdvancedSearch` method is that most of its searches are asynchronous. This means that after the method is invoked, code execution does not wait for the search results to be returned (as they would be with the `Items.Restrict` method). Instead, the search takes place in the background, and your code must determine when the search has ended before it can process the results. It also means that more than one search may be under way at any given moment. Outlook can handle up to 100 simultaneous searches launched either through the Advanced Find dialog in the user interface or programmatically with the `Advanced-Search` method.

The basic syntax to initiate a search with the `AdvancedSearch` method has one required parameter (`Scope`) and three optional parameters (`Filter`, `SearchSubFolders`, and `Tag`):

```
Set objSearch = Application.AdvancedSearch _
                (Scope, Filter, SearchSubFolders, Tag)
```

The `AdvancedSearch` method returns a `Search` object, but because the search is likely to be asynchronous, the `Search.Results` collection of items meeting the search criteria may not be available until some time has passed after AdvancedSearch was called. As you'll see shortly, Outlook provides two Application-level events to help you monitor the status of asynchronous searches.

The *Scope* parameter takes a string that contains the folder paths for the folder(s) to be searched. Enclose each folder's path in single quotation marks, and separate multiple folders with commas. For standard folders in the default information store, you can use the name of the folder instead of the complete path. Since the search scope can be complex, covering multiple folders, it is a good idea to build it using a separate string variable. All these statements are acceptable values for the *Scope* parameter for a user whose mail profile contains an Exchange mailbox as the default store, plus a .pst file with the display name "Personal Folders":

```
strScope = "'Inbox'"
strScope = "'Inbox', 'Sent Items'"
strScope = "'Inbox', 'Sent Items', " & _
           "'Mailbox - Sue Mosher\Current\Betas'"
strScope = "'\\Personal Folders\Old Projects\Web Site'"
strScope = "'\\Personal Folders\Old Projects\Web Site'" & _
           ",'\\Personal Folders\Software\Exchange'"
strScope = "'\\Public Folders\All Public Folders\" & _
           "Sales Department\Sales Contacts'"
```

Remember that you cannot search across information stores with AdvancedSearch, nor can you search across multiple folders in the Public Folders hierarchy or in another user's mailbox.

---

**Tip:** Don't forget that you can use the Folder.FolderPath method to return the full folder path for any folder, ready to use in a Scope expression.

---

The optional *Filter* parameter takes a DASL search string. If the store is indexed, you can use the CI_PHRASEMATCH and CI_STARTSWITH operators.

---

**Tip:** It may seem strange that the *Filter* parameter for the Advanced-Search method is optional, but there are scenarios where it makes sense. For example, you might want to combine the appointments from several calendar folders into one results set. By performing a search with no filter, you could get the complete contents of all those folders in one operation.

---

The optional Boolean parameter *SearchSubFolders* indicates whether the search should traverse the complete subfolders hierarchy for each of the folders in the Folders argument. A value of True is valid only for searches in a .pst file or the user's own Exchange mailbox.

The optional *Tag* string parameter provides an identifier for the search. To understand its importance for managing multiple searches, we will look next at the code necessary to know when a search has completed.

The Application object supports two events related to searches. The AdvancedSearchComplete event fires when a search completes, while the AdvancedSearchStopped event fires if a search stops short of completion for any reason. The code in Listing 16.6 provides a basic framework for

**Listing 16.6**   *Basic framework for handling AdvancedSearch\* events*

```
Public gblnPracticeSearchDone As Boolean
Public gblnPracticeSearchStopped As Boolean

Private Sub Application_AdvancedSearchComplete _
   (ByVal SearchObject As Search)
     If SearchObject.Tag = "PracticeSearch" Then
         Debug.Print "Search completed at " & Time
         gblnPracticeSearchDone = True
     End If
End Sub

Private Sub Application_AdvancedSearchStopped _
   (ByVal SearchObject As Search)
     If SearchObject.Tag = "PracticeSearch" Then
         Debug.Print "Search stopped at " & Time
         gblnPracticeSearchStopped = True
         gblnPracticeSearchDone = True
     End If
End Sub

Sub PracticeSearch()
     Dim objOL As Outlook.Application
     Dim objSearch As Outlook.Search
     Dim strScope As String
     Set objOL = Application
     gblnPracticeSearchDone = False
     gblnPracticeSearchStopped = False
     strScope = "'Inbox', 'Sent Items'"
     Debug.Print "Search started at " & Time
     Set objSearch = objOL.AdvancedSearch _
                   (strScope, , True, "PracticeSearch")
     Do Until gblnPracticeSearchDone
        DoEvents
     Loop
     If gblnPracticeSearchStopped Then
        Debug.Print "Search was stopped"
     Else
        Debug.Print objSearch.Results.count
     End If
     Set objOL = Nothing
     Set objSearch = Nothing
End Sub
```

handling these events. To test it, place all the code in the `ThisOutlook-Session` module in Outlook VBA. (You can also place just the two `Application` event handlers in `ThisOutlookSession` and put the `PracticeSearch` procedure and the declarations for the `gblnPractice-SearchDone` and `gblnPracticeSearchStopped` variables in a regular code module.) When you run the `PracticeSearch` procedure, you should see in the Immediate window a date stamp for the time the search began, followed in a few seconds by a date stamp for the time the search completed and the number of items in the Inbox and Sent Items folders and all their subfolders.

After the `PracticeSearch` procedure launches the search, it uses a `Do Until` loop to wait until the value of the `gblnPracticeSearchDone` variable has been set to `True`. The code depends on the two `Application` events to set the value of `gblnPracticeSearchDone` to `True`. The parameter passed by each event is the `Search` that completed or stopped. From its `Tag` property, you can determine whether the search launched by `PracticeSearch` is the one that completed and set the variable values appropriately, for example:

```
If SearchObject.Tag = "PracticeSearch" Then
    Debug.Print "Search stopped at " & Time
    gblnPracticeSearchStopped = True
    gblnPracticeSearchDone = True
End If
```

**Tip:** You may want to use the `TimeToQuit` function from Listing 11.27 to force the code to exit the `Do` loop if too much time has passed, even if neither of the `AdvancedSearch*` events has fired. You'll see an example of this technique in Listing 16.9 in the next section.

To handle multiple searches in the same code project, you would use a single pair of event handlers, but for each search use a unique `Tag` and a unique pair of Boolean variables to indicate when the search has completed or stopped.

Once the search completes, the `Search.Results` collection provides access to the items matching the *Filter* criteria. You can either iterate that collection as you would an `Items` collection or, for faster, read-only access to the data, use the `Search.GetTable` method to return a `Table` object and use the `Table` methods discussed in the previous chapter.

## 16.6.1   Example: Update all birthday and anniversary events

If you look back at the code for the birthday/anniversary reminder form that you worked with in Chapters 3 and 8, you'll see that it looped through all the items in the Calendar folder. You can speed up the process by applying the `Restrict` method to that folder's `Items` collection, as you saw in Listing 16.3. But what if you have multiple calendar folders? Outlook 2007 is the first version to fire reminders for appointments in calendar folders other than the default. So, won't you want appropriate reminders on birthdays and appointments in those calendar folders, too? That sounds like a job for `AdvancedSearch`, which can search across multiple folders in a single .pst file or primary mailbox store.

Our goal, therefore, is to enhance the birthday/anniversary reminder user form for VBA—the latest version from Section 8.9.3—so that it searches across all calendar folders in the user's default information store to locate any birthday or anniversary item. Once we have those items, the code will update the reminder on each one, just as in the earlier versions of the form.

The first step is to build a `Scope` argument string that includes all calendar folders. The `BuildCalScope()` function in Listing 16.7 takes a `Namespace` parameter and returns a comma-delimited string of folder paths, each surrounded by single quotation marks, for use with `AdvancedSearch`. Notice that the `ProcessFolderPaths` procedure uses folder recursion and a parameter (`scopePaths`) passed `By Ref` to build the string.

**Listing 16.7**    *Build a Scope argument*

```
Function BuildCalScope(ns As Outlook.NameSpace) As String
    Dim objFld As Outlook.Folder
    Dim strScope As String
    Set objFld = ns.DefaultStore.GetRootFolder
    Call ProcessFolderPaths(objFld, strScope)
    BuildCalScope = Mid(strScope, 2)
    Set objFld = Nothing
End Function

Sub ProcessFolderPaths(fld As Outlook.folder, _
  ByRef scopePaths As String)
    Dim objFolder As Outlook.folder
    For Each objFolder In fld.Folders
        If objFolder.DefaultItemType = olAppointmentItem Then
            scopePaths = scopePaths & "," & Chr(39) & _
                        objFolder.FolderPath & Chr(39)
        End If
        Call ProcessFolderPaths(objFolder, scopePaths)
    Next
    Set objFolder = Nothing
End Sub
```

Add the code from Listing 16.7 to the existing code behind the user form, and also add the code in Listing 16.8, which sets up the event handlers. Since a form's code module is a class module, you can handle the AdvancedSearch* events in the module that holds the rest of the form's code. Notice how the parent Application object for these events is instantiated when the form initializes.

The next procedure to add is the subroutine that builds the search filter, which you'll find in Listing 16.9. Notice that it uses the CI_PHRASEMATCH content index keyword if the store is enabled for Instant Search. Otherwise, it uses a normal DASL filter string.

Finally, replace the cmdUpdate_Click and cmdClose_Click procedures for the two buttons on the form with the code in Listing 16.10. When the user clicks Close, the cmdClose_Click procedure stops the search before unloading the form.

Here's how it works: when the user clicks Update in the birthday/anniversary reminder form, the code in Listing 16.9 builds scope and search strings with the BuildCalScope() and BuildFilter() functions from Listing 16.7. It then launches the search, setting the search's Tag to "BAReminders". How does the routine know when the search is finished? The event handlers for AdvancedSearchComplete and AdvancedSearchStopped in Listing 16.8 change the value of the Tag property of the txtProgress control on the form when either of those events fires. A Do loop

---

**Listing 16.8**    *Declarations and event handlers for managing the search*

```
Dim WithEvents mobjOL As Outlook.Application
Dim mobjSearch As Outlook.Search

Private Sub mobjOL_AdvancedSearchComplete _
  (ByVal SearchObject As Search)
    If SearchObject.Tag = "BAReminders" Then
        txtProgress.Tag = "complete"
    End If
End Sub

Private Sub mobjOL_AdvancedSearchStopped(ByVal SearchObject As Search)
    If SearchObject.Tag = "BAReminders" Then
        txtProgress.TabIndex = "stopped"
    End If
End Sub

Private Sub UserForm_Initialize()
    Set mobjOL = Application
End Sub
```

**Listing 16.9**     *Build a filter string to find birthdays and anniversaries*

```
Function BuildFilter(ns As Outlook.NameSpace) As String
    Dim strFilter As String
    Dim objStore As Outlook.Store
    Set objStore = ns.DefaultStore
    If objStore.IsInstantSearchEnabled Then
        strFilter = _
            "(" & Quote("urn:schemas:httpmail:subject") & _
            " CI_PHRASEMATCH 'Birthday' OR " & _
            Quote("urn:schemas:httpmail:subject") & _
            " CI_PHRASEMATCH 'Anniversary')"
    Else
        strFilter = _
            "(" & Quote("urn:schemas:httpmail:subject") & _
            " LIKE '%Birthday%' OR " & _
            Quote("urn:schemas:httpmail:subject") & _
            " LIKE '%Anniversary')"
    End If
    BuildFilter = strFilter
    Set objStore = Nothing
End Function
```

**Listing 16.10**     *New code for the reminder update form's buttons*

```
Private Sub cmdClose_Click()
    mobjSearch.Stop
    Unload Me
End Sub

Private Sub cmdUpdate_Click()
    Dim objOL As Outlook.Application
    Dim objNS As Outlook.NameSpace
    Dim objItem As Outlook.AppointmentItem
    Dim strFind As String
    Dim strScope As String
    Dim sngTimeStart As Single
    Dim strSubject As String
    Dim lngMinutes As Long
    Dim intCount As Integer
    Dim intCountBA As Integer
    On Error Resume Next
    If IsNumeric(txtDays.Value) Then
        Set objOL = Application
        Set objNS = objOL.Session
        ' BuildFilter from Listing 16.9
        strFind = BuildFilter(objNS)
        ' BuildCalScope from Listing 16.7
        strScope = BuildCalScope(objNS)
        txtProgress.Tag = ""
        Set mobjSearch = objOL.AdvancedSearch(strScope, _
                        strFind, False, "BAReminders")
        ' UpdateProgress subroutine from Listing 8.15
```

**Listing 16.10**    *New code for the reminder update form's buttons (continued)*

```
    Call UpdateProgress("Running search with filter: " & _
                        vbCrLf & strFind & vbCrLf & vbTab & _
                        "and scope:" & vbCrLf & strScope)
    sngTimeStart = Timer
    Do While txtProgress.Tag = ""
        DoEvents
        ' TimeToQuit function from Listing 11.27
        If TimeToQuit(sngTimeStart, 120) Then Exit Do
    Loop
    Call UpdateProgress("Search " & txtProgress.Tag)
    If txtProgress.Tag = "complete" Then
        Call UpdateProgress("Processing " & _
        mobjSearch.Results.count & " items")
        lngMinutes = CLng(24 * 60) * txtDays.Value
        intCount = 0
        intCountBA = 0
        For Each objItem In mobjSearch.Results
            strSubject = objItem.Subject
            If InStr(strSubject, "Birthday") > 0 And _
              (optBirthdays.Value Or optBoth.Value) Then
                objItem.ReminderSet = True
                objItem.ReminderMinutesBeforeStart = _
                  lngMinutes
                objItem.Save
                intCountBA = intCountBA + 1
            End If
            If InStr(strSubject, "Anniversary") > 0 And _
              (optAnniversaries.Value Or optBoth.Value) Then
                objItem.ReminderSet = True
                objItem.ReminderMinutesBeforeStart = _
                  lngMinutes
                objItem.Save
                intCountBA = intCountBA + 1
            End If
            intCount = intCount + 1
            If intCount Mod 10 = 0 Then
                Call UpdateProgress _
                    (intCount & " items processed")
            End If
        Next
        Call UpdateProgress _
          ("Finished: " & intCountBA & _
          " items updated out of " & _
          intCount & " items processed")
    Else
        MsgBox "Could not perform update"
    End If
Else
    Call UpdateProgress("Value for days is not numeric.")
End If
Beep
Set objItem = Nothing
Set objNS = Nothing
Set objOL = Nothing
End Sub
```

in the `cmdUpdate_Click` procedure keeps looping until it sees a change in the value of `txtProgress.Tag` or until time runs out, as measured by the `TimeToQuit()` function from Listing 11.27:

```
sngTimeStart = Timer
Do While txtProgress.Tag = ""
    DoEvents
    If TimeToQuit(sngTimeStart, 120) Then Exit Do
Loop
```

After the code execution exits the `Do` loop, if the value of `txt-Progress.Tag` indicates the search completed successfully, the code processes each item in the `mobjSearch.Results` collection. The code to actually do the item processing and show the operation's progress on the form is identical to that in Listing 8.15.

## 16.6.2  Creating a new search folder

The `AdvancedSearch` method has one other unique feature: In addition to returning a results set, it can also be used to create a permanent *search folder*, that is, a virtual folder that continuously performs a background search for items meeting the folder's search criteria. While the Outlook user interface provides a way to create search folders only for mail folders, with `AdvancedSearch` code, you can create a search folder for any type of item.

---

**Note:** Microsoft does not officially support search folders for non-mail folders, even though the `Search.Save` method described in this section does work for folders that hold other types of items besides messages.

---

The syntax for creating a new search folder is very simple; just call the `Save` method of the `Search` object and provide a name, which must be unique. (In any given store, you cannot have two search folders with the same name.) This code starts the search in Listing 16.8 and then saves it as a search folder:

```
Set mobjSearch = objOL.AdvancedSearch(strScope, _
                 strFind, False, "BAReminders")
mobjSearch.Save "Birthdays and Anniversaries"
```

You can save the search folder without waiting for the search to complete. However, if you do wait for the search to complete, then you can display the complete results to the user in a search folder. (This is the second of two built-in techniques for presenting search results to the user, the other being the `Explorer.Search` method.) To see how this works, add the code in Listing 16.11 to the `ThisOutlookSession` module in VBA, and then run the `SenderSearchFolder` procedure. This procedure builds a search for all items in the current store from the sender of the currently selected or open message. It then creates a search folder for the results and, when the

**Listing 16.11** *Create a new search folder from a message's sender address*

```
Private Sub Application_AdvancedSearchComplete _
  (ByVal SearchObject As Search)
    Dim objOL As Outlook.Application
    Dim objNS As Outlook.NameSpace
    Dim objDefStore As Outlook.Store
    Dim objFolder As Outlook.folder
    Dim strTag As String
    On Error Resume Next
    strTag = SearchObject.Tag
    If InStr(strTag, "@") > 0 Then
        Set objOL = Application
        Set objNS = objOL.Session
        Set objDefStore = objNS.DefaultStore
        Set objFolder = _
          objDefStore.GetSearchFolders.item(strTag)
        objFolder.Display
    End If
    Set objOL = Nothing
    Set objNS = Nothing
    Set objDefStore = Nothing
    Set objFolder = Nothing
End Sub

Sub SenderSearchFolder()
    Dim objOL As Outlook.Application
    Dim objNS As Outlook.NameSpace
    Dim objDefStore As Outlook.Store
    Dim objItem As Object
    Dim objMail As Outlook.MailItem
    Dim objSearch As Outlook.Search
    Dim strSender As String
    Dim strFind As String
    Dim strScope As String
    On Error Resume Next
    Set objOL = Application
    ' GetCurrentItem() function from Listing 15.5
    Set objItem = GetCurrentItem()
    If objItem.Class = olMail Then
        Set objMail = objItem
        If objMail.SenderEmailType = "SMTP" Then
            strSender = objMail.SenderEmailAddress
            strFind = BuildSenderSearch(strSender)
            Set objNS = objOL.Session
            Set objDefStore = objNS.DefaultStore
            strScope = "'" & _
            objDefStore.GetRootFolder.FolderPath & "'"
            Set objSearch = objOL.AdvancedSearch _
               (strScope, strFind, True, strSender)
            objSearch.Save strSender
        End If
    End If
    Set objOL = Nothing
```

**Listing 16.11**  *Create a new search folder from a message's sender address (continued)*

```
    Set objNS = Nothing
    Set objDefStore = Nothing
    Set objItem = Nothing
    Set objMail = Nothing
    Set objSearch = Nothing
End Sub

Public Function BuildSenderSearch(sender As String)
    Dim strSearch As String
    Dim objOL As Outlook.Application
    Dim objNS As Outlook.NameSpace
    Const PR_SENDER_NAME = _
        "http://schemas.microsoft.com/mapi/proptag/0x0C1A001E"
    Const PR_SENDER_EMAIL_ADDRESS = _
        "http://schemas.microsoft.com/mapi/proptag/0x0C1F001E"
    Const PR_SENT_REPRESENTING_NAME = _
        "http://schemas.microsoft.com/mapi/proptag/0x0042001E"
    Const PR_SENT_REPRESENTING_EMAIL_ADDRESS = _
        "http://schemas.microsoft.com/mapi/proptag/0x0065001E"
    On Error Resume Next
    Set objOL = Application
    Set objNS = objOL.Session
    strSearch = Quote(PR_SENDER_NAME) & _
                " LIKE '%" & sender & "%' OR " & _
                Quote(PR_SENDER_EMAIL_ADDRESS) & _
                " LIKE '%" & sender & "%' OR " & _
                Quote(PR_SENT_REPRESENTING_NAME) & _
                " LIKE '%" & sender & "%' OR " & _
                Quote(PR_SENT_REPRESENTING_EMAIL_ADDRESS) & _
                " LIKE '%" & sender & "%' "
    BuildSenderSearch = strSearch
End Function
```

search completes, displays the search folder to the user in a new window. The search string produced by the `BuildSenderSearch()` function uses four properties from the MAPI proptag namespace related to the sender address and name. (Remember that since one person can send on behalf of another, a message actually may have two different sets of sender name and address information.)

**Caution:** When constructing a search string to create a search folder, do not use the `CI_PHRASEMATCH` or `CI_STARTSWITH` keywords. They are intended only for use in non-persistent searches; when used for a search folder, they may cause performance issues. Use the `LIKE` operator instead.

This example's code for handling the completion of the search is different from the other examples you've seen, because all the processing of the finished search takes place in the `Application_AdvancedSearchComplete` event handler, rather than in the procedure that launched the search. (Recall that you've also seen the results processed in the procedure that launched the search and that you've seen the `AdvancedSearchComplete` event handler operate in a VBA user form's code module, rather than in the `ThisOutlookSession` module.)

Compared with the `Explorer.Search` method, the advantage of creating a search folder with `Application.AdvancedSearch` and `Search.Save` is that the search folder is a permanent addition to the user's folders. The user can see the current search results at any time, simply by clicking on the search folder in the folder list. The `SenderSearchFolder` macro thus can be a powerful tool for creating search folders to help track messages from the people you correspond with the most.

## 16.7   Summary

Searching for items that meet specific criteria is a fundamental Outlook programming task that can be accomplished faster in Outlook 2007 through the read-only `Table` object and the new content index keywords available to DASL searches on indexed information stores. While this chapter has tried to suggest when each of the six search methods and two syntaxes might be most appropriate, in the end, the only true assessment of their suitability can come from analysis of your own application's performance and the results returned.

Two useful samples in this chapter showed how to generate an Outlook task containing a list of birthdays and anniversaries for next month and how to search for and find all birthdays and anniversaries in the user's default store and update them with reminders. You also learned how to programmatically create a search folder to capture messages from a particular Internet address.

Two new helper functions streamline the process of working with dates. The `GetMonthStart()` function returns the first date of any month, given a date and the number of months forward or backward that you want to move. The `MonthName()` function returns the name of the month in the user's language. You also now have a `GetApptDateSpan()` function to return all appointments, including recurrences, within a specific date range.

# *Working with Item Bodies*

The large text box at the bottom of every standard form exposes what Outlook stores as the `Body` property and, on HTML-format messages and posts, the `HTMLBody` property. Generically, this information can be referred to as the *item body*. In earlier chapters, we learned how to access standard, custom, and hidden MAPI properties of Outlook items, but these two standard properties require a more in-depth treatment. Almost every Outlook programmer will work with item bodies at some point, yet the skills needed to work with them successfully go beyond Outlook programming to include Word text handling techniques and even the ability to read text from a file.

Highlights of this chapter include:

- How to change the format of a message or post
- How to append or prefix text to an item body
- How to insert text at the user's insertion point
- Techniques for creating complex HTML-format messages, including inserting hyperlinks and pictures
- How to create, insert, and remove the user's automatic signature text

## 17.1 Basic item body techniques

Outlook provides three ways to work with the item body, through three different properties:

- Through the plain-text representation provided by the `Body` property
- Through the tagged HTML representation provided for HTML-format messages and posts through the `HTMLBody` property
- Through the `Inspector.WordEditor` property, which returns a `Word.Document` object, even if Word 2007 is not installed, for each item except "sticky notes" and distribution lists.

**Table 17.1**    *Suggested Item Body Techniques*

| When You Want to . . . | Use this Approach |
| --- | --- |
| Parse text from the body of an incoming message | Parse the contents of the `Body` property. |
| Append text to an existing non-message item | If you don't care about formatting, modify the `Body` property. |
| | If you want to preserve formatting, use `Inspector.WordEditor`. |
| Insert text at the location the user has selected | Use `Inspector.WordEditor`. |
| Create a highly formatted email message with no embedded images | Use `HTMLBody`. |
| Create a formatted email message with embedded images | Use `Inspector.WordEditor`. |

**Note:** Earlier versions of Outlook also supported an `Inspector.HTMLEditor` object property, but since Internet Explorer is no longer the rendering engine for HTML messages and posts, `HTMLEditor` is no longer supported.

Table 17.1 suggests when you might want to use which approach.

After a review of some basic item body techniques, we'll look at examples of each of the scenarios in Table 17.1, and also discuss Outlook signatures.

Any new `MailItem` created by the `Application.CreateItem` method uses the default message format set by the user on the Tools | Options | Mail Format dialog. The same is true for any new `PostItem`. To determine what format the message or post is using, check the value of its `BodyFormat` property. Table 17.2 lists the possible values.

Message and post items can be in HTML, rich-text (RTF), or plain text format. "Sticky note" items are always plain text. All other items are always RTF.

You can change the format of a message or post by setting its `BodyFormat` property to a different value. Doing so will lose all formatting if the original message was in HTML or RTF format.

If you set the `HTMLBody` property for a message or post, the message format changes to HTML and the value of `BodyFormat` changes to `olFormatHTML` (2).

If you create and display a message programmatically and automatic signatures are turned on for the user, the displayed message will contain the

**Table 17.2** *OlBodyFormat Constants for the BodyFormat Property*

| Constant | Literal Value |
|---|---|
| olFormatHTML | 2 |
| olFormatPlain | 1 |
| olFormatRichText | 3 |
| olFormatUnspecified | 0 |

user's default signature. If you do not display the message, it will not contain the signature. Later in this chapter, we'll see code for removing the user's signature from a message and adding the default signature to an existing message.

The `Body`, `HTMLBody`, and `WordEditor` properties are all subject to the provisions of Outlook "object model guard" security, as discussed in Chapter 10, because item bodies are a significant source of personal details such as email addresses.

## 17.2  Parsing text from a message body

A common Outlook programming task is to extract information from a message that contains structured text. For example, many Web sites contain forms where site visitors enter information that the Web site, in turn, uses to generate a plain text email message. Such a message likely would have multiple lines, each with a different Label: Data pair, such as:

```
Name: Flavius J. Littlejohn
Email: flaviusj@turtleflock.net
```

The code in Listing 17.1 includes a `ParseTextLinePair()` function you can use to extract the data portion from any such text pair. In this example, the `FwdSelToAddr` procedure calls `ParseTextLinePair()` in order to extract the email address from the body of a selected message; it then forwards the message to that address.

The `ParseTextLinePair()` function uses several built-in functions that we learned about in Chapter 8. It locates the text label (in this example, "Email") in the source string and then extracts it from the line where it was found, by following these steps:

1.  Locate where search text begins (`InStr(strSource, strLabel)`)

2.  Locate the end of the line on which the label text appears (`InStr(intLocLabel, strSource, vbCrLf)`)

3.      Extract the text between the label text and the end of the line (`Mid(strSource, intLocLabel + intLenLabel)`). Alternatively, if this is the last line, extract the text from the end of the label text until the end of the source text (`Mid(strSource, intLocLabel + intLenLabel)`).

**Listing 17.1**     *Extract data from a structured text block*

```
Sub FwdSelToAddr()
    Dim objOL As Outlook.Application
    Dim objItem As Object
    Dim objFwd As Outlook.MailItem
    Dim strAddr As String
    On Error Resume Next
    Set objOL = Application
    Set objItem = objOL.ActiveExplorer.Selection(1)
    If Not objItem Is Nothing Then
        strAddr = ParseTextLinePair(objItem.Body, "Email:")
        If strAddr <> "" Then
            Set objFwd = objItem.Forward
            objFwd.To = strAddr
            objFwd.Display
        Else
            MsgBox "Could not extract address from message."
        End If
    End If
    Set objOL = Nothing
    Set objItem = Nothing
    Set objFwd = Nothing
End Sub

Function ParseTextLinePair _
  (strSource As String, strLabel As String)
    Dim intLocLabel As Integer
    Dim intLocCRLF As Integer
    Dim intLenLabel As Integer
    Dim strText As String
    intLocLabel = InStr(strSource, strLabel)
    intLenLabel = Len(strLabel)
        If intLocLabel > 0 Then
        intLocCRLF = InStr(intLocLabel, strSource, vbCrLf)
        If intLocCRLF > 0 Then
            intLocLabel = intLocLabel + intLenLabel
            strText = Mid(strSource, _
                          intLocLabel, _
                          intLocCRLF - intLocLabel)
        Else
            intLocLabel = _
              Mid(strSource, intLocLabel + intLenLabel)
        End If
    End If
    ParseTextLinePair = Trim(strText)
End Function
```

Three integer variables assist in this operation:

- `intLocLabel` to hold the character position of the label text relative to the entire text body
- `intLocCRLF` to hold the character position of the end of the line where the label text appears
- `intLenLabel` to hold the length of the label text

This basic text parsing technique is worth studying, because it has many applications, both in Outlook programming and in many other environments.

# 17.3   Adding text to an item

Another common Outlook programming task is to append or prefix text to an item. Before you undertake this operation, you should consider whether you need to preserve the formatting of text that may already exist in the item, whether you need to format the text you add, and whether you need to position the cursor in a particular location in the item body after inserting the text. That will help determine which of these three methods to use:

- Modify the `Body` property (does not preserve formatting)
- Modify the `HTMLBody` property (supports formatting)
- Use Word programming methods to add text through `Inspector.WordEditor` (supports formatting and cursor positioning)

If the item in question is an HTML-format message or post and you don't need to position the cursor, whether you use the `HTMLBody` or `WordEditor` technique depends largely on your comfort level with those two very different approaches. In other words, which do you know better, HTML tags or Word objects and methods?

## 17.3.1   Adding text to the Body property

If you don't need to preserve the formatting in an item, you can append or prefix text to the item body by working with the `Body` property. For example, the `StampDate` macro in Listing 17.2 adds the current date/time and user name to the bottom of the currently open item.

If you wanted the date stamp to appear at the top of the item instead of the bottom, you'd use this variation:

```
objItem.Body = Now & " - " & _
    objNS.CurrentUser.Name & vbCrLf & objItem.Body
```

Any formatting in the item will be lost when you run `StampDate`, because the `Body` property provides information only about the plain text representation of the item body.

**Listing 17.2**  *Stamp the date and current user on an Outlook item*

```
Sub StampDate()
    Dim objOL As Outlook.Application
    Dim objNS As Outlook.NameSpace
    Dim objItem As Object
    Dim strStamp As String
    On Error Resume Next
    Set objOL = Application
    Set objItem = objOL.ActiveInspector.CurrentItem
    If Not objItem Is Nothing Then
        Set objNS = objOL.Session
        strStamp = Now & " - " & objNS.CurrentUser.Name
        objItem.Body = objItem.Body & vbCrLf & strStamp
    End If
    Set objOL = Nothing
    Set objNS = Nothing
    Set objItem = Nothing
End Sub
```

## 17.3.2   Adding text to the HTMLBody property

If you do care about the formatting of the original item body, you need to use a different approach. For an HTML-format message or post, you can provide fully tagged HTML content and insert it into the existing HTML body.

Having fully tagged HTML content is critical. You cannot simply concatenate a text string like the date stamp in Listing 17.1 with the existing HTML-Body content. You must format the string you want to add with full HTML tags and insert it into HTMLBody (note: not append or prefix) in such a way that the structure of the existing body is not compromised. An HTML message or post has, at a minimum, two pairs of tags at the beginning—<html><body>—and end—</body></html>—that define the HTML content. Any text you want to add needs to go between those two tags.

To insert text at the very end of a message, you can replace the </body> tag with your fully tagged HTML content plus a new </body> tag. This code snippet inserts a hyperlink at the end of an existing message (objMsg):

```
strLink = "http://www.outlookcode.com"
strLinkText = "Get Outlook code samples here"
strNewText = "<p><a href=" & Chr(34) & strLink & _
             Chr(34) & ">" & strLinkText & "</a></p>"
objMsg.HTMLBody = Replace(objMsg.HTMLBody, "</body>", _
                         strNewText, 1, 1, vbTextCompare)
```

If you took a look at strNewText with a Debug.Print or MsgBox statement, you'd see that it contains a well-formed HTML hyperlink <a> element:

```
<a href="http://www.outlookcode.com">Get Outlook code
samples here</a>
```

Another key concept for adding text to an HTML message or post is that the vbCrLf constant that defines a carriage return/linefeed in VBA and VBScript has no meaning in HTML. In the example above, the code inserts the hyperlink as a new paragraph enclosed inside a pair of <p></p> tags. To insert a single line break, use a <br> tag. This code snippet replaces the vbCrLf instances in a text string with double line breaks:

```
strNewText = Replace(strOldText, vbCrLf, "<br><br>")
```

Listing 17.3 shows another practical application of the </body> replacement technique, stamping the date as a separate paragraph at the end of an HTML-format message or post. Compare with Listing 17.2.

The two main differences between Listing 17.2 and Listing 17.3 are the way the strStamp date stamp string is constructed—one with <p></p> tags and one with vbCrLf—and the use of the Replace() function to insert the new content immediately before the existing </body> tag. Again, the trick is to replace the </body> tag with a new string constructed from the date stamp followed by </body>.

Prefixing the existing content with a date stamp is a little trickier than appending, because the <body> tag may contain attribute settings. In other words, the tag may be something other than just plain <body>. It may be as verbose as <body lang=EN-US link=blue vlink=purple>. To handle that scenario, you need to find the entire tag, using the same kind of text

**Listing 17.3**     *Stamp the date and current user on an HTML-format message or post*

```
Sub StampDateHTML()
    Dim objOL As Outlook.Application
    Dim objNS As Outlook.NameSpace
    Dim objItem As Object
    Dim strStamp As String
    On Error Resume Next
    Set objOL = Application
    Set objItem = objOL.ActiveInspector.CurrentItem
    If Not objItem Is Nothing Then
        If objItem.BodyFormat = olFormatHTML Then
            Set objNS = objOL.Session
            strStamp = "<p>" & Now & " - " & _
                    objNS.CurrentUser.Name & "</p>"
            objItem.HTMLBody = Replace(objItem.HTMLBody, _
                        "</body>", _
                        strStamp & "</body>", _
                        , , vbTextCompare)
        End If
    End If
    Set objOL = Nothing
    Set objNS = Nothing
    Set objItem = Nothing
End Sub
```

parsing with `Instr()` and `Mid()` that you saw in the `ParseTextLine-Pair()` function in Listing 17.1. Once you have the entire tag, you use the same `Replace()` technique as in Listing 17.3. Only this time, you replace the initial `<body>` tag (with all its attributes) with a new string consisting of the full `<body>` tag followed by the date stamp:

```
strHTMLBody = objItem.HTMLBody
intTagStart = InStr(1, strHTMLBody, "<body", _
  vbTextCompare)
intTagEnd = InStr(intTagStart + 5, strHTMLBody, ">")
strBodyTag = _
  Mid(strHTMLBody, _
      intTagStart, intTagEnd - intTagStart + 1)
objItem.HTMLBody = _
  Replace(strHTMLBody, strBodyTag, strBodyTag & strStamp)
```

To insert text into the middle of an HTML-format message or post, you could use the same text-parsing technique to locate the tag or text where you want to place the insertion, then replace that tag or text with a string that consists of the original content concatenated with your new content. Later in this chapter, we'll see a simple application of that technique, as we customize a previously saved message template to tailor it to the current recipient.

If you know a bit about HTML, you can start embellishing such text insertions with formatting. For example, these statements build a date stamp string that will appear in red, bold, Arial text:

```
strStyle = "'font-family:" & Chr(34) & _
           "Arial" & Chr(34) & ";color:red'"
strStamp = "<p><b>" & _
           "<span style=" & strStyle & ">" & _
           Now & " - " & objNS.CurrentUser.Name & _
           "</span></b></p>"
```

The bold formatting is handled by the `<b></b>` tags while the font formatting is handled by the `<span></span>` tag containing a style attribute. We can't cover HTML in detail in this book, but tutorials abound on the Internet. Another good learning tool is to create an email message with some other mail program such as Outlook Express, Windows Mail, or even a Web-based mail service such as Gmail. Send the message to yourself, and then examine its HTML content by clicking in the body of the message and choosing View Source or by looking at the value of its `HTMLBody` property.

The third method for inserting text requires the use of the `Word.Document` object returned by the `Inspector.WordEditor` property. This is the most versatile method, because it allows you not only to preserve formatting in any type of Outlook item, but also to insert text where the user has placed the cursor. We cover it later in this chapter, in the section on `WordEditor`.

# 17.4   Creating a formatted message

The previous sections have been concerned with reading text from a message and inserting text, with some simple formatting options. Sometimes, though, you have a more complicated task—creating a complete message with complex formatting. In almost all cases, this will be an HTML-format message, since RTF messages work only when the recipient has Outlook, and you usually don't know what mail application the recipient uses. We'll look at two techniques in this chapter:

- Reading HTML content from a saved file
- Adding customized text to a boilerplate message created from a saved Outlook template file

You can also build an HTML message on the fly, element by element. Skip ahead to Listings 18.1 and 18.2 in the next chapter to see examples that build an `HTMLBody` that contains a table, one reporting on the user's available address lists, the second example listing colleagues in the same department along with their contact information.

## 17.4.1   Creating an HTML-format message from a file

Chapter 8 explained how to use `FileSystemObject` to work with folders and files. A common application of those techniques is to use the data in a saved HTML file to create a new HTML message. This is a particularly good strategy if you want to use a dedicated HTML editor to create, for example, a newsletter.

---

**Note:** Outlook 2007's support for cascading style sheets and various HTML elements has changed substantially from that in previous versions, now that Word is both the editor and the rendering engine. To learn what is and is not supported in Outlook 2007 HTML-format messages, read the article "Word 2007 HTML and CSS Rendering Capabilities in Outlook 2007" at http://msdn2.microsoft.com/en-us/library/aa338201.aspx.

---

The `CreateHTMLMsg()` procedure in listing 17.4 is a VBA function that reads the text from an existing .htm file and creates and displays a new Outlook message. Recall that you need a reference to the Microsoft Scripting Runtime library to be able to declare `objFSO` as `Scripting.FileSystemObject`. Use code like this to call `CreateHTMLMsg` and display the newly created message:

```
Set objMsg = CreateHTMLMsg("C:\MyNewsletter.htm")
objMsg.Display
```

**Listing 17.4**    *Create a message from an .htm file*

```
Function CreateHTMLMsg(fileHTML As String) _
    As Outlook.MailItem
        Dim objOL As Outlook.Application
        Dim objMsg As Outlook.MailItem
        Dim objFSO As Scripting.FileSystemObject
        Dim objStream As Scripting.TextStream
        Dim strHTMLFile As String
        On Error Resume Next
        Set objFSO = CreateObject("Scripting.FileSystemObject")
        If objFSO.FileExists(fileHTML) Then
            Set objOL = Application
            Set objMsg = objOL.CreateItem(olMailItem)
            Set objStream = objFSO.OpenTextFile(fileHTML, _
                                            ForReading)
            objMsg.HTMLBody = objStream.ReadAll
        End If
        Set CreateHTMLMsg = objMsg
        Set objOL = Nothing
        Set objMsg = Nothing
        Set objFSO = Nothing
        Set objStream = Nothing
End Function
```

---

**When you need to render an HTML message in the browser**

Because Outlook 2007 has shifted the rendering engine for HTML-format messages from Internet Explorer to Word, HTML tags like `<script>` and `<form>` are no longer supported. Earlier versions of Outlook ignored those tags by default. At the same time, though, they supported a View | View in Internet Zone command that would allow users to see the message, but in a less secure fashion. Outlook 2007 doesn't support the concept of different security zones for viewing messages, but it does still have a command that will allow a user to view a message in their default Internet browser—the View in Browser command under Other Actions in the Actions group.

To direct the recipient of a message to use the View in Browser command to see the message content that Outlook 2007 blocks, you can include a special element in your HTML code. To display directions to Outlook 2007 users at the top of the message, put code like this just after the `<body>` tag:

```
<!--[if gte mso 12]><BR>To see the submission button using Outlook
2007, click the <STRONG>Other Actions</STRONG> button, then
<STRONG>View in Browser</STRONG>.<BR><![endif]-->
```

The `<!--[if gte mso 12]>` tag in effect says: Show this tag's content only if the rendering engine is greater than or equal to Office "12"—that is, only if it is Office 2007 or later.

Once you have the message returned by `CreateHTMLMsg()`, you could modify its contents further, using the other methods in this chapter, before displaying it.

## 17.4.2 Creating a message from a boilerplate template

Another common Outlook message scenario is replying to an incoming message with a standard response. For example, you might want to reply to requests for product literature with an attractive, personalized message that includes the literature as one or more attached files. This is not a task that you can accomplish with a published custom form. The solution is to use a saved .oft form template file constructed with text that your code can easily find and replace with personalized information. That text consists of "tokens" in the message body, each beginning and ending with % or some other character that makes them easy to distinguish from the actual message text.

To implement this solution, start by following these steps to create a boilerplate response message:

1. Create a new HTML-format message, and type in the fully formatted message body you want the recipient to see, including your signature, if desired. Don't forget to give the message a subject and attach any desired files.

2. In the message body, type in a "token" wherever you want a customizable text "field," each token starting and ending with %. For example, if you want to address the sender of the original message by name, put "Dear %sender%" in the message body. Add more tokens where you want other fields that can be personalized.

3. Save the message as an .oft file.

Once you have saved the response message, the next step is to write a VBA procedure that creates a new message from the .oft file, using the `Application.CreateItemFromTemplate` method. That code will need to replace each token with specific text, using the `Replace()` function. The `To` address for the new message comes from the `SenderEmailAddress` of the original that you want to reply to.

Figure 17.1 shows an example of such a message, ready for saving as an .oft file. The code to generate a reply using that template is in Listing 17.5. Call the `InquiryReply` procedure by passing it an Outlook message. For example, you could use the `GetCurrentItem()` function from Listing 15.5:

```
Call InquiryReply(GetCurrentItem())
```

**Figure 17.1**
*Use a "tokenized"
boilerplate message
to generate
customized replies.*

**Figure 17.1**
*Use a "tokenized"
boilerplate message
to generate
customized replies.*

As you can see in Figure 17.1, the reply template has two tokens—%sender% and %project_type%. The InquiryReply procedure fills in the %project_type% token from the result of an InputBox() statement and attempts to fill in the %sender% token with the first name of the sender of the original message. Just in case the sender name wasn't available or wasn't parsed correctly, the code uses the Word editor's search capability to highlight the %sender% token (or the text that replaced it) in the displayed reply message. (More on the Word editor is coming up shortly.)

What if you want to include the original sender's message in your reply? That's possible, too, and we'll look at it later in the chapter, after you've learned how to move around in the WordEditor.

## 17.5  Using WordEditor

The Outlook object model itself provides no direct way to determine the position of the cursor in an item body. However, since the editor for every item body (except on "sticky notes" and distribution lists) is a special version of Microsoft Word, you can use Word techniques not only to add text at the insertion point, but also to add formatted text anywhere in the item, or even to add a picture. To use these techniques in Outlook VBA code, use the Tools | References command to add a reference to the Microsoft Word 12.0 Object Library.

Listing 17.5   *Create a reply from a tokenized boilerplate message*

```
Sub InquiryReply(msg)
    Dim objOL As Outlook.Application
    Dim objReply As Outlook.MailItem
    Dim objDoc As Object
    Dim strSender As String
    Dim arr() As String
    Dim strProject As String
    Dim strHTML As String
    On Error Resume Next
    Set objOL = msg.Application
    Set objReply = _
      objOL.CreateItemFromTemplate _
        ("C:\Data\inquiry response.oft")
    objReply.To = msg.SenderEmailAddress
    strSender = msg.SenderName
    strProject = InputBox("Enter project type:", _
                          "Replace %project_type%", _
                          "custom form")
    strHTML = Replace(objReply.HTMLBody, _
                      "%project_type%", strProject)
    If strSender <> msg.SenderEmailAddress Then
        arr = Split(strSender, " ")
        strSender = arr(0)
        strHTML = Replace(strHTML, "%sender%", strSender)
    Else
        strSender = "%sender%"
    End If
    objReply.HTMLBody = strHTML
    objReply.Display
    Set objDoc = objReply.GetInspector.WordEditor
    objDoc.Windows(1).Selection.Find.ClearFormatting
    objDoc.Windows(1).Selection.Find.Execute strSender
    Set objOL = Nothing
    Set objReply = Nothing
    Set objDoc = Nothing
End Sub
```

**Note:** In earlier versions of Outlook, the `WordEditor` was available only for messages and posts and only if the user had configured Word as the email editor. Since Word is the only editor in Outlook 2007 (except for `NoteItem` and `DistListItem` objects), it is available not just for messages and posts, but also for appointments, contacts, tasks, and journal entries. It even works if only Outlook 2007 is installed, and not Word 2007.

As an initial example of how to invoke the Word editor programmatically, using the `Inspector.WordEditor` method, Listing 17.6 builds on the earlier examples in Listings 17.2 and 17.3 and inserts a date stamp at

**Listing 17.6**    *Insert text and reposition the cursor*

```
Sub StampDateDoc()
    Dim objOL As Outlook.Application
    Dim objNS As Outlook.NameSpace
    Dim objDoc As Word.Document
    Dim objSel As Word.Selection
    Dim strStamp As String
    On Error Resume Next
    Set objOL = Application
    If objOL.ActiveInspector.EditorType = olEditorWord Then
        Set objDoc = objOL.ActiveInspector.WordEditor
        Set objNS = objOL.Session
        strStamp = Now & " - " & objNS.CurrentUser.Name
        Set objSel = objDoc.Windows(1).Selection
        objSel.Move wdStory, -1
        objDoc.Characters(1).InsertBefore _
          strStamp & vbCrLf & vbCrLf
        objSel.Move wdParagraph, 1
    End If
    Set objOL = Nothing
    Set objNS = Nothing
End Sub
```

the top of the currently displayed item, with a blank line following it. It also positions the cursor on the blank line, so that if the focus is on the message body control, the user can begin typing right after the date stamp.

Two key objects from the Word object model can be derived from `Document` object that the `Inspector.WordEditor` method returns. If `objDoc` is the object variable representing the `Document`, then the expression `objDoc.Application` returns a Word `Application` object. The other key object is the `Selection` object (not to be confused with `ActiveExplorer.Selection` from the Outlook object model), which represents the text that is currently highlighted in the Outlook item. If no text is highlighted, it represents the cursor position. Use this syntax to return a `Selection` object from an Outlook item's `Document` object:

```
Set objSel = objDoc.Windows(1).Selection
```

The `Selection` object includes a number of methods, including `Move`, to reposition the insertion point. We'll look at `Move` in more detail in the next section.

To insert text at the current insertion point, use the `Selection.InsertBefore` method. (As you might expect, there is also a `Selection.InsertAfter` method.) In this code snippet, `strText` is a variable holding the text you want to insert:

```
Set objOL = Application
Set objDoc = objOL.ActiveInspector.WordEditor
```

```
Set objSel = objDoc.Windows(1).Selection
objSel.InsertBefore strText
```

You can even format the inserted text. The `Selection` expands to include the inserted text whenever you use `Selection.InsertBefore` or `Selection.InsertAfter`. Since the inserted text is selected automatically, it is easy to use the `Selection.Font` object to change the appearance of the new text. This snippet inserts text and then makes it bold, red, Arial:

```
Set objSel = objDoc.Windows(1).Selection
With objSel
    .Collapse wdCollapseStart
    .InsertBefore strText
    .Font.Name = "Arial"
    .Font.Bold = True
    .Font.Color = wdColorRed
End With
```

**Note:** Most of the time, you will want to collapse the selection to the insertion point, using the `Selection.Collapse` method, before inserting the text. If you don't do that, your code will replace any text that the user has selected. The `Selection.Move` method automatically collapses the insertion point.

To learn more about working with formatted text in Word, a good strategy is to open Word 2007, create a new document, and turn on the Word macro recorder. (The Word macro recorder is not available in an Outlook message or other item.) Much of the code it produces uses a `Selection` object. The code you've seen in this section shows how to return the `Selection` object for an Outlook item using `Inspector.WordEditor` and the `Document.Application.Selection` object. You should be able to adapt almost any code that the Word macro recorder produces to a Word `Selection` object derived from an Outlook item.

### 17.5.1 Moving around in the Word editor

The key to moving the cursor position—also known as the *insertion point*—inside the Word editor is found in these statements from Listing 17.6:

```
Set objDoc = objOL.ActiveInspector.WordEditor
Set objSel = objDoc.Windows(1).Selection
objSel.Move wdStory, -1
objSel.Move wdParagraph, 1
```

The `Selection.Move` method collapses the selection and then moves it a specified distance. The first parameter for `Move` is a `wdUnits` constant (from the Word object model) defining how big a step to take during the move. The second parameter is an integer defining how many steps to take. If the number is positive, the insertion point is collapsed to the end of the selection and then moved forward the specified number of units. If the number is negative, the insertion point collapses to the start of the selection and moves backwards the specified number of units. Table 17.3 lists the `wdUnits` constants that are useful in moving through email messages.

Thus, to move the insertion point to the beginning of a message, assuming you already have a `Selection` object (`objSel`), use:

```
objSel.Move wdStory, -1
```

To move the insertion point to the end of the message, use:

```
objSel.Move wdStory, 1
```

To move the insertion point to the cell in the second column of the third row of the first table in a message, use:

```
objSel.Move wdStory, -1
objSel.Move wdTable, 1
objSel.Move wdRow, 2
objSel.Move wdCell, 1
```

**Note:** Word also supports a `Selection.GoTo` method to reposition the insertion point, but it raises an error if Word 2007 is not installed. Since `Move` and related `Selection` methods work even without Word 2007, you should rely on them, not `GoTo`.

In addition, the `Selection` object supports methods like `MoveUp` and `MoveDown` that can be used to extend the selection to cover additional text. You can look them up in the object browser.

**Table 17.3**  *Word wdUnits Constants for Moving the Insertion Point*

| Unit | Constant | Value |
| --- | --- | --- |
| Story (= the entire message) | wdStory | 6 |
| Paragraph | wdParagraph | 4 |
| Line | wdLine | 5 |
| Sentence | wdSentence | 3 |
| Word | wdWord | 2 |
| Character | wdCharacter | 1 |
| Table | wdTable | 15 |
| Row | wdRow | 10 |
| Column | wdColumn | 9 |
| Cell | wdCell | 12 |

The `Move` method can return an integer representing the number of units moved. For example, given this statement

```
intMoved = objSel.Move(wdParagraph, 3)
```

if `intMoved` is less than 3, that means the insertion point is now at the end of the message, because it couldn't move forward three whole paragraphs.

Another useful technique for moving around in the Word editor window is to invoke the Find command programmatically. Earlier in Listing 17.5, you saw these statements that find and highlight the text in a reply message showing the original sender's name, so that the user can confirm and correct it as needed:

```
Set objDoc = objReply.GetInspector.WordEditor
objDoc.Windows(1).Selection.Find.ClearFormatting
objDoc.Windows(1).Selection.Find.Execute strSender
```

Always use the `Selection.Find.ClearFormatting` method to clear any previously used option to search for text with specific formatting. The example above is the simplest implementation of `Find.Execute` to search forward in a document for specific text. The `Find.Execute` method also supports many optional parameters, which you can look up in the object browser, including those that allow you to replace text or control the direction of the search.

## 17.5.2 Example: Boilerplate reply that includes incoming text

Back in the discussion of Listing 17.5, to create a reply message from a saved boilerplate .oft file, we said that it's possible to include the original message text in the reply message, just as a manually created Outlook reply would do. Now that you know how to use the `WordEditor`, we can walk through the steps in that process:

1. Generate a reply to the original message.

2. Create a new message from the boilerplace .oft file

3. Copy the text from the reply body to the end of the new message, using Word methods.

4. The `InquiryReplyWithOrig` procedure in Listing 17.7 builds on the `InquiryReply` procedure Listing 17.5 to add the code to generate a reply and copy its content to the message created from the .oft file.

Listing 17.7 demonstrates several other useful methods in the Word `Selection` object:

- `MoveEnd` to expand the end point of the `Selection` object so that more text is selected; these statements locate the From: text in the reply, select all the text from that point to the end of the reply, then copy that text to the Windows clipboard:

```
With objSel
    .Find.Execute "From:"
    .Collapse wdCollapseStart
    .MoveEnd WdUnits.wdStory, 1, True
    .Copy
End With
```

- InlineShapes to add a shape to the message, in this case, a horizontal line

- PasteAndFormat to paste the text from the clipboard into the new message, preserving its formatting.

The next two sections look at other techniques you're likely to use—inserting hyperlinks and pictures.

---

**Tip:** For another example of the PasteAndFormat method, Listing 20.1 includes a CopyFormattedBody subroutine that copies a complete item body, including formatting, from one Outlook item to another.

---

**Listing 17.7**   *Include the original sender's message with a boilerplate reply*

```
Sub InquiryReplyWithOrig(msg)
    Dim objOL As Outlook.Application
    Dim objReply As Outlook.MailItem
    Dim objOrigReply As Outlook.MailItem
    Dim objDoc As Word.Document
    Dim objDocOrigReply As Word.Document
    Dim objSel As Word.Selection
    Dim strSender As String
    Dim arr() As String
    Dim strProject As String
    Dim strHTML As String
    Dim f As Boolean
    Set objOL = msg.Application
    Set objReply = _
      objOL.CreateItemFromTemplate _
        ("C:\Data\inquiry response.oft")
    objReply.To = msg.SenderEmailAddress
    strSender = msg.SenderName
    strProject = InputBox("Enter project type:", _
                          "Replace %project_type%", _
                          "custom form")
    strHTML = Replace(objReply.HTMLBody, _
                      "%project_type%", strProject)
    If strSender <> msg.SenderEmailAddress Then
        arr = Split(strSender, " ")
        strSender = arr(0)
        strHTML = Replace(strHTML, "%sender%", strSender)
```

➤
**Listing 17.7**    *Include the original sender's message with a boilerplate reply (continued)*

```
Else
      strSender = "%sender%"
End If
objReply.HTMLBody = strHTML
Set objOrigReply = msg.Reply
Set objDoc = objReply.GetInspector.WordEditor
Set objDocOrigReply = objOrigReply.GetInspector.WordEditor
Set objSel = objDocOrigReply.Windows(1).Selection
With objSel
      .Find.Execute "From:"
      .Collapse wdCollapseStart
      .MoveEnd WdUnits.wdStory, 1
      .Copy
End With
Set objSel = objDoc.Windows(1).Selection
With objSel
      .Move wdStory, 1
      .InlineShapes.AddHorizontalLineStandard
      .PasteAndFormat wdFormatOriginalFormatting
      .Move wdStory, -1
      .Find.ClearFormatting
      .Find.Execute strSender
End With
objReply.Display
Set objOL = Nothing
Set objReply = Nothing
Set objDoc = Nothing
End Sub
```

### 17.5.3   Inserting hyperlinks

Earlier in this chapter, we saw how to insert a hyperlink at the end of an HTML-formatted message using the `</body>` tag replacement technique. That technique won't work if you want to insert a hyperlink in an RTF message or an item other than a message or post. It also can't help you insert a hyperlink at the current insertion point. For those scenarios, you need to use `Inspector.WordEditor` and the `Document.Hyperlinks.Add` method from the Word object model. The `Hyperlinks.Add` method uses this syntax:

```
objDoc.Hyperlinks.Add(Anchor, Address, SubAddress, _
                  ScreenTip, TextToDisplay, Target)
```

The *Anchor* parameter is the only required argument. It needs to be an object representing the text or image that you want to mark as a hyperlink; it can also be the `Selection.Range` object representing a collapsed insertion point. The actual URL for the link is passed as the *Address* parameter. Pass the display text for the link with the *TextToDisplay* parameter. The other three parameters do not apply to hyperlinks in email messages.

Compare this code to insert a hyperlink into an existing message (objMsg) with the corresponding code snippet in Section 17.3.2:

```
strLink = "http://www.outlookcode.com"
strLinkText = "Get Outlook code samples here"
Set objInsp = objMsg.GetInspector
Set objDoc = objInsp.WordEditor
Set objSel = objDoc.Windows(1).Selection
If objMsg.BodyFormat <> olFormatPlain Then
    objDoc.Hyperlinks.Add objSel.Range, strLink, _
                          "", "", strLinkText, ""
Else
    objSel.InsertAfter strLink
End If
```

Notice that the syntax for inserting a link into a plain text message is different from that for HTML and RTF messages. For a plain text message, you should insert only the URL.

## 17.5.4  Inserting pictures

If you want a picture to appear in the body of an email message, rather than as an attachment, you should send it as an embedded picture, not as an `<img>` HTML tag with a link to an external URL. Outlook 2003 and Outlook 2007 block external content by default, as do a growing number of other mail programs.

Inserting an embedded picture is very similar to inserting a hyperlink, except that the method is `Selection.InlineShapes.AddPicture`, instead of `Document.Hyperlinks.Add`. The `InlineShapes.AddPicture` method uses this syntax:

```
objSel.AddPicture(FileName, LinkToFile, _
                  SaveWithDocument, Range)
```

where `FileName` is the name of the file that contains the picture. For Outlook items, the `LinkToFile` and `SaveWithDocument` parameters should always be `False` and `True` respectively. Omit the optional `Range` parameter to insert the picture at the current insertion point.

Compare this code snippet for inserting a picture to the one in the previous section for inserting a hyperlink:

```
strFile = "C:\Pictures\logo.gif"
Set objInsp = objMsg.GetInspector
Set objDoc = objInsp.WordEditor
Set objSel = objDoc.Windows(1).Selection
If objMsg.BodyFormat <> olFormatPlain Then
    objSel.InlineShapes.AddPicture strFile, False, True
End If
```

What about combining a picture with a hyperlink? The `Inline-Shapes.AddPicture` method returns an `InlineShape` object. You can use the `InlineShape.Range` object property as the anchor for a hyperlink instead of the `Selection.Range` object used by the hyperlink sample code in the previous section:

```
Set objShape = objSel.InlineShapes.AddPicture _
                    (strFile, False, True)
objDoc.Hyperlinks.Add objShape.Range, strLink, _
                    "", "", strLinkText, ""
```

We don't have room in this book to go into detail on all the functionality available with the Word objects available to you from `WordEditor`, but you can explore them on your own with the object browser and Word's macro recorder (which is available only in Word documents, not in Outlook messages).

## 17.6  Working with Outlook signatures

As in previous versions, Outlook 2007 offers extensive support for personal email signatures, which are stored as .htm, .rtf, and .txt files to support the three different message formats. Users may create one or more signatures and have Outlook apply them automatically or insert signatures manually.

**Note:** One difference between Outlook 2007 and earlier versions is that inserting a signature in Outlook 2007 always replaces any existing signature in the message. Thus, you cannot use signatures in Outlook 2007 as a way of inserting multiple blocks of text into a single message. Instead, you can use the Word insertion methods described earlier in the chapter; the section on inserting the default signature provides another example.

The replacement for the AutoText feature in earlier versions is Quick Parts, found on the ribbon on the Insert tab, in the Text group and stored in the Normalemail.dotm template. To insert a quick part named "Sales Inquiry," use this code:

```
Set objDoc = objOL.ActiveInspector.WordEditor
Set objWord = objDoc.Application
Set objSel = objDoc.Windows(1).Selection
Set objETemp = objWord.Templates(1)
Set colBlocks = objETemp.BuildingBlockEntries
colBlocks("Sales Inquiry").Insert _
   objSel.Range, True
```

The three key signature tasks that we'll cover are creating a signature programmatically, inserting the user's default signature into a message, and removing a signature that has already been inserted.

### 17.6.1  Creating a signature

As part of the task of creating a new signature for the current user, if the user has an Exchange mailbox, we can incorporate company contact information into the signature. For this task, we will make use of the new `ExchangeUser` object that Outlook 2007 introduces. The code in Listing 17.8 is written in VBScript, but it's structured differently from the VBScript for Outlook forms. That's because this script is intended to be run as part of a login or as an independent script stored in a .vbs file. (You saw an example of this technique earlier in Listing 7.8.) The code that actually creates the signature is in the `CreateSignature` subroutine, which takes a `Namespace` object, representing the Outlook session where the user has logged in, as its sole parameter.

**Listing 17.8**     *Script to create and format a new default signature*

```
Dim objOL                         ' As Outlook.Application
Dim objNS                         ' As Outlook.NameSpace
Dim blnWeStartedOutlook           ' As Boolean
Const olFolderInbox = 6
On Error Resume Next
Set objOL = GetObject(, "Outlook.Application")
If objOL Is Nothing Then
    Set objOL = CreateObject("Outlook.Application")
    Set objNS = objOL.GetNamespace("MAPI")
    objNS.Logon "", "", True, True
    ' objNS.Logon "Outlook Settings", "", False, True
    blnWeStartedOutlook = True
Else
    Set objNS = objOL.GetNamespace("MAPI")
    objNS.Logon "", "", False, False
End If
If Not objNS.GetDefaultFolder(olFolderInbox) Is Nothing Then
    Call CreateSignature(objNS)
Else
    MsgBox "Could not start Outlook to set up signature"
End If
If blnWeStartedOutlook Then
    objNS.Logoff
    objOL.Quit
End If
Set objOL = Nothing
Set objNS = Nothing

Sub CreateSignature(objNS)
    Dim objMsg                ' As Outlook.MailItem
    Dim objDoc                ' As Word.Document
    Dim objSel                ' As Word.Selection
    Dim objSig                ' As Word.EmailSignature
    Dim colSig                ' As Word.EmailSignatureEntries
    Dim objExUser             ' As Outlook.ExchangeUser
    Dim objUser               ' As Outlook.AddressEntry
    Dim strSig                ' As String
    Dim objInsp               ' As Outlook.Inspector
    Const olmailitem = 0
```

**Listing 17.8**    *Script to create and format a new default signature (continued)*

```
Const wdCollapseEnd = 0
Const wdStory = 6
Const olDiscard = 1
Const olMinimized = 1
Set objUser = objNS.CurrentUser.AddressEntry
Set objMsg = objNS.Application.CreateItem(olmailitem)
objMsg.Display
Set objInsp = objMsg.GetInspector
objInsp.WindowState = olMinimized
Set objDoc = objInsp.WordEditor
Set objSel = objDoc.Application.Selection
With objSel
    .Move wdStory, -1
    .InsertAfter "--" & vbCrLf & Space(3)
    .Collapse wdCollapseEnd
    .InsertAfter objUser.Name
    .Font.Bold = True
    .InsertAfter "   "
    .Collapse wdCollapseEnd
End With
If objUser.AddressEntryUserType = _
  olExchangeUserAddressEntry Then
    Set objExUser = objUser.GetExchangeUser
    If objExUser.Department <> "" Then
        strSig = vbCrLf & Space(3) & objExUser.Department
    End If
    If objExUser.CompanyName <> "" Then
        strSig = strSig & vbCrLf & Space(3) & _
                objExUser.CompanyName
    End If
        If objExUser.BusinessTelephoneNumber <> "" Then
        strSig = strSig & vbCrLf & Space(3) & _
                objExUser.BusinessTelephoneNumber
    End If
    With objSel
        .InsertAfter objExUser.PrimarySmtpAddress
        .Font.Bold = False
        objDoc.Hyperlinks.Add objSel.Range, _
          "mailto:" & objExUser.PrimarySmtpAddress
        .Collapse wdCollapseEnd
        .InsertAfter strSig
    End With
Else
    With objSel
        .InsertAfter objUser.Address
        .Font.Bold = False
        objDoc.Hyperlinks.Add objSel.Range, _
                            "mailto:" & objUser.Address
        .Collapse wdCollapseEnd
    End With
End If
```

→

**Listing 17.8**   *Script to create and format a new default signature (continued)*

```
objSel.InsertAfter vbCrLf
objSel.MoveStart wdStory, -1
objSel.Font.Color = wdColorBlack
Set objSig = _
  objDoc.Application.EmailOptions.EmailSignature
Set colSig = objSig.EmailSignatureEntries
colSig.Add objUser.Name, objSel.Range
objSig.NewMessageSignature = objUser.Name
objSig.ReplyMessageSignature = objUser.Name
objInsp.Close olDiscard
Set objMsg = Nothing
Set objDoc = Nothing
Set objSel = Nothing
Set objSig = Nothing
Set colSig = Nothing
Set objExUser = Nothing
Set objUser = Nothing
Set objInsp = nothing
End Sub
```

As with the other item body manipulation techniques in this chapter, the `CreateSignature` subroutine uses Word methods to insert and format text. From the `Namespace.CurrentUser.AddressEntry` object, the code can add information about the user to the signature. If the user is an Exchange user, the `GetExchangeUser` method provides access to properties like `Department`, `BusinessTelephoneNumber`, and `PrimarySmtpAddress` as stored in the Global Address List on the server, for example:

```
Set objExUser = objUser.GetExchangeUser
If objExUser.Department <> "" Then
    strSig = vbCrLf & Space(3) & objExUser.Department
End If
```

Surprisingly, the objects used to actually set the default signature for the new messages and replies/forwards are Word objects, not Outlook objects. Thus, the code accesses the signature options through the parent `Application` object of the Word `Document` where the signature text is being built:

```
Set objSig = _
  objDoc.Application.EmailOptions.EmailSignature
Set colSig = objSig.EmailSignatureEntries
colSig.Add objUser.Name, objSel.Range
objSig.NewMessageSignature = objUser.Name
objSig.ReplyMessageSignature = objUser.Name
```

Through the user interface, the user can also set a different automatic signature for each mail account. Those per-account signature settings cannot be programmatically managed through Outlook or Word objects, but are buried in the registry entries for the user's Outlook mail profile.

## 17.6.2 Inserting the default signature

The insertion technique used in Listing 17.7 can also be used to add the user's default automatic signature to an existing message. The technique consists of creating a new message, copying the content, then pasting that content into the existing message. This VBA code snippet creates a new message and then copies the signature:

```
Set objMsg = Application.CreateItem(olMailItem)
Set objSigDoc = objMsg.GetInspector.WordEditor
Set objSel = objSigDoc.Windows(1).Selection
With objSel
    .Collapse wdCollapseStart
    .MoveEnd WdUnits.wdStory, 1
    .Copy
End With
```

You can then use the `Selection.PasteAndFormat` method, as shown in Listing 17.7, to paste the signature into the desired location in another Outlook message.

## 17.6.3 Removing signature text

What if you want to do the opposite—remove a signature that Outlook inserts automatically for the user? The key to that task is knowing that the signature is contained in a hidden Word bookmark named `_MailAutoSig`. The `DeleteSig` procedure in Listing 17.9 locates that bookmark in a message body, selects it, and then deletes the content of the selection.

**Listing 17.9**   *Use a Word bookmark to delete an automatic signature*

```
Sub TestDeleteSig()
    Dim objMsg As Outlook.MailItem
    Set objMsg = Application.CreateItem(olMailItem)
    objMsg.Display
    Call DeleteSig(objMsg)
    Set objMsg = Nothing
End Sub

Sub DeleteSig(msg As Outlook.MailItem)
    Dim objDoc As Word.Document
    Dim objBkm As Word.Bookmark
    On Error Resume Next
    Set objDoc = msg.GetInspector.WordEditor
    Set objBkm = objDoc.Bookmarks("_MailAutoSig")
    If Not objBkm Is Nothing Then
        objBkm.Select
        objDoc.Windows(1).Selection.Delete
    End If
    Set objDoc = Nothing
    Set objBkm = Nothing
End Sub
```

If you wanted to replace an existing signature with another one, you could combine the removal technique in Listing 17.9 with the insertion technique in the previous section.

## 17.7  Summary

As Outlook items are the core of the application's data, the body of each item is the heart of the item. Now that Word is the editor for both mail messages and other Outlook items, you can take advantage of its text manipulation and formatting techniques in most Outlook items. Inserting hyperlinks and pictures also works through the `Document` object returned by the `Inspector.WordEditor` method. Inserting text, hyperlinks, and pictures are all possible through the `WordEditor` object.

Among the things we've learned in this chapter are three different ways to insert a date stamp (or other text) into an item, several methods for creating complex HTML-format messages, and techniques for creating, inserting, and removing a signature. A key reusable routine introduced in this chapter is the `ParseTextLinePair()` function to extract data from a structured text block.

# 18

# *Working with Recipients and Address Lists*

Messages, meeting requests, and task requests are all examples of Outlook items that involve recipients. Recipients are useful not just for sending messages, though. In Chapter 13, we saw that the `Namespace.GetSharedDefaultFolder` method requires a `Recipient` object as one of the parameters necessary to return a folder from another user's Exchange mailbox and that the `Namespace.CreateRecipient` method provides an easy way to create a `Recipient` that is not attached to any message or other Outlook item. The `Recipient` object is also crucial to determining whether a user is available for a meeting at a particular time.

This chapter provides an overview of the key Outlook objects that expose information about recipients and address lists, plus examples of common Outlook programming tasks that use recipients and address lists.

Highlights of this chapter include discussions of the following:

- When to use the `MailItem.To` property versus the `MailItem.Recipients.Add` method to address an email message
- How to use the Select Names dialog to return a name that the user selects
- How to automatically add a Bcc recipient to all outgoing messages
- How to automatically create contacts for the people you send messages to
- What hidden property can help you work with members of a distribution list
- How to find out whether someone is busy at a given time
- What happens when a user clicks the Check Names command

# 18.1   Key recipient and address list objects

Table 18.1 lists the key objects and collections in the Outlook object model that are related to address lists and recipients. All these objects are interrelated, as you can see in Figure 18.1. A `Recipient` object, for example, can be created with the `Namespace.CreateRecipient` method, or it can be derived from the `Recipients` collection available from the `SelectNames-Dialog` object after a user selects one or more recipients from the Select Names dialog, or it can be returned as an item in a `Recipients` collection for a `MailItem` or other Outlook item.

The most basic address-related object is the `AddressEntry`. You have already seen samples that use the `Namespace.CurrentUser` property to return an `AddressEntry` object for the current Outlook user. The `ExchangeUser` and `ExchangeDistributionList` objects, both new to

**Table 18.1**    *Key Objects Related to Addresses and Address Lists (\* = new in Outlook 2007)*

| Object | Description |
|---|---|
| AddressEntries | Collection of `AddressEntry` objects that an `AddressList`  object contains; can also be derived from a `DistListItem` or `ExchangeDistribu-tionList` object |
| AddressEntry | Address details from an item in an `AddressEn-tries` collection or from a `Recipient` object |
| AddressLists | Collection of all the address lists available in the current Outlook mail profile |
| AddressList | Individual list item from the `AddressLists` collection |
| CurrentUser | `AddressEntry` for the current user, as a property of the `Namespace` object |
| \*ExchangeDistributionList | Distribution list from the Global Address List for an Exchange server; read-only, inherits properties and methods from `AddressEntry` |
| \*ExchangeUser | Individual user record from the Global Address List for an Exchange server; read-only, inherits properties and methods from `AddressEntry` |
| Recipient | Individual addressee for a message or other item |
| Recipients | Collection of addressees for a message or other item |
| \*SelectNamesDialog | Dialog where the user can select one or more names from the address lists present in the mail profile |

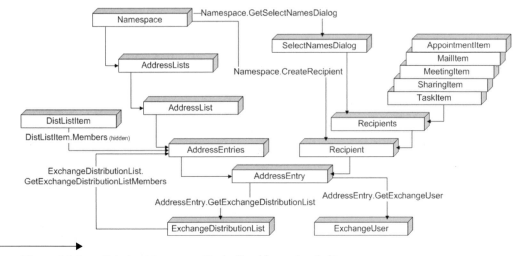

**Figure 18.1**    *Relationships among Outlook's address-related objects.*

Outlook 2007, inherit the properties and methods from the `AddressEntry` object. You'll see an example of their usage later in Listing 18.2.

# 18.2  Understanding address lists

Which address lists are available to the user in the Address Book and Select Names dialogs depend on two factors—the user's email and address book settings in the Tools | Account Settings dialog and what contact folders have been marked to appear in the Outlook Address Book, which is a container to display the user's contact folders in the Address Book. The user's default Contacts folder is always marked as an address list, by default. Other Outlook contacts folders, including those synchronized from a SharePoint contacts list, may also be displayed as address lists.

If a user has an Exchange mailbox, one or more address lists related to the Exchange server will be present. The user may also have LDAP lists and other lists from third-party address book providers. Each `AddressList` has an `AddressEntries` collection that you can use to enumerate the names, addresses, and other information exposed by the address list. The information available will vary with the type of list; the Exchange Global Address List is likely to contain the most information about each entry.

Table 18.2 shows key properties and methods for the `AddressList` object, several of which are new in Outlook 2007. The VBA code in Listing 18.1 iterates the `AddressLists` collection and generates an email message reporting on the properties of the user's address lists. All `AddressList` properties are read-only.

**Table 18.2**    *Key AddressList Properties and Methods (\* = new in Outlook 2007)*

| Property | Description |
|---|---|
| AddressEntries | Collection of entries in the address list |
| *AddressListType | Type of list, from the OlAddressListType enumeration: |
| | olCustomAddressList 4 |
| | olExchangeContainer 1 |
| | olExchangeGlobalAddressList 0 |
| | olOutlookAddressList 2 |
| | olOutlookLdapAddressList 3 |
| *IsInitialAddressList | True if this list is the one the user sees first in the Address Book or Select Names dialog |
| IsReadOnly | In general, True for server-based address lists, and False for Outlook contacts lists |
| Name | Display name for the address list |
| *PropertyAccessor | Object used to return values from hidden MAPI properties |
| *ResolutionOrder | Position of this address list among the lists used to resolve names and addresses to valid recipients; equals -1 if the list is not used for name resolution |

| Method | Description |
|---|---|
| *GetContactsFolder | If AddressListType = olOutlookAddressList, returns the Folder object for the contacts list that the address list exposes |

Notice that the message created in Listing 18.1 is laid out using an HTML <table> element. Each row in the table consists of a set of <tr></tr> tags surrounding several <td> elements, each of which represents a table cell. Formatting in the table is handled with align='center' attributes to center text in some cells and class='header' attributes that point to the header style set up in the <style> element. This example demonstrates some of the relatively complex layouts and formatting you can perform with a little basic knowledge of HTML tables and styles.

## 18.2.1   Displaying a contact folder as an address book

The only technique in the Outlook object model related to showing or hiding an address list is the ability to display any Outlook contacts folder as an address list under the Outlook Address Book. Two properties of the Folder object control this option: ShowAsOutlookAB and AddressBookName.

----------------➤

**Listing 18.1** *Enumerate the user's address lists*

```
Sub EnumAddressLists()
    Dim objOL As Outlook.Application
    Dim objNS As Outlook.NameSpace
    Dim objList As Outlook.AddressList
    Dim objMsg As Outlook.MailItem
    Dim strHTML As String
    Set objOL = Application
    Set objNS = objOL.Session
    Set objMsg = Application.CreateItem(olmailitem)
    ' build HTML style head
    strHTML = "<html><head><style><!-- td.header " & _
            "{font-family: Arial; font-weight: bold; " & _
            "}--></style></head>"
    ' build title and subtitle
    strHTML = strHTML & "<body><p>Address Lists for " & _
            objNS.CurrentUser.Name & "<br>" & _
            "Profile Name: " & objNS.CurrentProfileName & _
            "</p>"
    ' build table header row
    strHTML = strHTML & "<table cellspacing='5' " & _
            "cellpadding='2'><tr><td class='header'>" & _
            "Address List</td>" & _
            "<td class='header'>Type</td>" & _
            "<td class='header' align='center'>" & _
            "Initial<br>List</td>" & _
            "<td class='header' align='center'>" & _
            "Resolution<br>Order</td>" & _
            "<td class='header'>Read-only</td>" & _
            "<td class='header' align='center'>" & _
            "Number<br>of entries" & _
            "</td></tr>"
    ' build table body rows
    For Each objList In objNS.AddressLists
        strHTML = strHTML & AddListRow(objList)
    Next
    ' end table
    strHTML = strHTML & "</table></body></html>"
    objMsg.HTMLBody = strHTML
    objMsg.Subject = "Address Lists for " & _
                    objNS.CurrentUser.Name
    objMsg.Display
    Set objOL = Nothing
    Set objNS = Nothing
    Set objList = Nothing
    Set objMsg = Nothing
End Sub

Function AddListRow(list As Outlook.AddressList) As String
    Dim strRow As String
    Dim lngCount As String
    Dim objFolder As Outlook.Folder
    strRow = "<tr><td>" & list.Name
```

**Listing 18.1**   *Enumerate the user's address lists (continued)*

```
If list.AddressListType = olOutlookAddressList Then
    Set objFolder = list.GetContactsFolder
    strRow = strRow & "<br>" & objFolder.FolderPath
End If
strRow = strRow & "</td>"
Select Case list.AddressListType
    Case olCustomAddressList
        strRow = strRow & "<td>Custom</td>"
    Case olExchangeContainer
        strRow = strRow & "<td>EX Container</td>"
    Case olExchangeGlobalAddressList
        strRow = strRow & "<td>EX GAL</td>"
    Case olOutlookAddressList
        strRow = strRow & "<td>Outlook Contacts</td>"
    Case olOutlookLdapAddressList
        strRow = strRow & "<td>LDAP</td>"
End Select
If list.IsInitialAddressList Then
    strRow = strRow & "<td align='center'>X</td>"
Else
    strRow = strRow & "<td></td>"
End If
If list.ResolutionOrder <> -1 Then
    strRow = strRow & "<td align='center'>" & _
            CStr(list.ResolutionOrder) & "</td>"
Else
    strRow = strRow & "<td align='center'>n/a</td>"
End If
If list.IsReadOnly Then
    strRow = strRow & "<td align='center'>X</td>"
Else
    strRow = strRow & "<td></td>"
End If
If list.AddressListType <> olExchangeContainer Then
    lngCount = list.AddressEntries.Count
    strRow = strRow & "<td align='right'>" & _
        CStr(lngCount) & "</td>"
Else
    strRow = strRow & "<td></td>"
End If
AddListRow = strRow
End Function
```

This code snippet sets the current folder as an address list and builds its display name from the folder name and its parent folder's path:

```
Set objFolder = Application.ActiveExplorer.CurrentFolder
If objFolder.DefaultItemType = olContactItem Then
    objFolder.ShowAsOutlookAB = True
    objFolder.AddressBookName = objFolder.Name & " in " & _
                                objFolder.Parent.FolderPath
End If
```

To stop showing a contacts folder as an address list, set its `ShowAsOut-lookAB` property to `False`.

## 18.2.2    Example: Generate a report on Exchange users

If the user is working in a mail profile that includes an Exchange account, the Exchange Global Address List (or a subset of the GAL, if the administrator so chooses) will be present among the `AddressLists` collection. Use the `Namespace.GetGlobalAddressList` method to return the `AddressList` object for the GAL. The new `ExchangeUser` and `ExchangeDistributionList` objects in Outlook 2007 make it relatively easy to generate a report on the contents of the GAL.

For example, the code in Listing 18.2 creates an Outlook `PostItem` in the user's default Drafts folder and fills it with a table containing names, e-mail addresses, and phone numbers of Exchange users in the GAL, plus information about the number of entries in each Exchange distribution list. Since the GAL may contain tens or even hundreds of thousands of entries in a large organization, the report is limited to the users in the same department as the current user, plus the distribution lists.

**Listing 18.2**    *Report on Exchange user information*

```
Sub CreateGALReport()
    Dim objOL As Outlook.Application
    Dim objNS As Outlook.NameSpace
    Dim objFolder As Outlook.Folder
    Dim objPost As Outlook.PostItem
    Dim objList As Outlook.AddressList
    Dim objEntry As Outlook.AddressEntry
    Dim objEXUser As Outlook.ExchangeUser
    Dim objEXDL As Outlook.ExchangeDistributionList
    Dim strHTML As String
    Dim strDept As String
    Set objOL = Application
    Set objNS = objOL.Session
    Set objList = objNS.GetGlobalAddressList
    Set objEntry = objNS.CurrentUser.AddressEntry
    If objEntry.AddressEntryUserType = _
      olExchangeUserAddressEntry Then
        Set objEXUser = objEntry.GetExchangeUser
        strDept = objEXUser.Department
    End If
    If Not objList Is Nothing And strDept <> "" Then
        Set objFolder = _
          objNS.GetDefaultFolder(olFolderDrafts)
        Set objPost = objFolder.Items.Add("IPM.Post")
        objPost.Subject = "_GAL Report - " & _
                        FormatDateTime(Now, vbGeneralDate)
        strHTML = "<html><body>" & _
                "<table cellspacing='5' cellpadding='2'>"
```

**Listing 18.2**    *Report on Exchange user information (continued)*

```
        For Each objEntry In objList.AddressEntries
            If objEntry.AddressEntryUserType = _
              olExchangeUserAddressEntry Then
                Set objEXUser = objEntry.GetExchangeUser
                If objEXUser.Department = strDept Then
                    strHTML = strHTML & AddUserRow(objEXUser)
                End If
            ElseIf objEntry.AddressEntryUserType = _
              olExchangeDistributionListAddressEntry Then
                Set objEXDL = _
                    objEntry.GetExchangeDistributionList
                strHTML = strHTML & AddDLRow(objEXDL)
            End If
        Next
        strHTML = strHTML & "</table></body></html>"
        objPost.HTMLBody = strHTML
        objPost.Save
        objPost.Display
    End If
    Set objOL = Nothing
    Set objNS = Nothing
    Set objList = Nothing
    Set objFolder = Nothing
    Set objPost = Nothing
    Set objEntry = Nothing
    Set objEXUser = Nothing
    Set objEXDL = Nothing
End Sub

Function AddUserRow(exUser As Outlook.ExchangeUser) As String
    Dim strRow As String
    strRow = "<tr><td>" & exUser.Name & "</td>" & _
             "<td><a href='mailto:" & _
             exUser.PrimarySmtpAddress & "'>" & _
             exUser.PrimarySmtpAddress & "</a></td>" & _
             "<td>" & exUser.BusinessTelephoneNumber & _
             "</td></tr>"
    AddUserRow = strRow
End Function

Function AddDLRow(exDL As Outlook.ExchangeDistributionList) _
  As String
    Dim strRow As String
    Dim lngDLCount As Long
    lngDLCount = _
      exDL.GetExchangeDistributionListMembers.Count
    strRow = "<tr><td>" & exDL.Name & "</td>" & _
             "<td><a href='mailto:" & _
             exDL.PrimarySmtpAddress & "'>" & _
             exDL.PrimarySmtpAddress & "</a></td>" & _
             "<td>" & CStr(lngDLCount) & " members" & _
             "</td></tr>"
    AddDLRow = strRow
End Function
```

As with the report on the user's address lists in Listing 18.1, the report generated by the code in Listing 18.2 uses an HTML table to organize the information, but with an additional twist. This expression builds a cell containing an <a> element, specifically, a mailto: hyperlink to each Exchange user's SMTP address:

```
"<td><a href='mailto:" & _
exUser.PrimarySmtpAddress & "'>" & _
exUser.PrimarySmtpAddress & "</a></td>"
```

The Outlook user can thus look at this report in the Drafts folder and click on any of those mailto: links to create a new email message to that user.

Both the `ExchangeUser` and `ExchangeDistributionList` have many properties and methods useful for creating such reports, including the `PropertyAccessor` object property for returning the values of hidden MAPI properties. For other examples that demonstrate how to work with these new objects, review these articles in Outlook developer Help:

- How to: List the Name and Office Location of Each Manager Belonging to an Exchange Distribution List (HV10046760)
- How to: List the Groups that My Manager Belongs to (HV10034111)

The number in parentheses is the article's topic ID, which you can use to search for the article.

## 18.3 Working with item recipients

Each `Recipient` in a `Recipients` collection supports three methods, listed in Table 18.3.

We will look at the `FreeBusy` and `Resolve` methods in detail later in the chapter.

**Table 18.3**   *Recipient Methods*

| Method | Description |
|---|---|
| Delete | Remove the `Recipient` from its parent `Recipients` collection |
| FreeBusy(*Start, MinPerChar, CompleteFormat*) | Returns free/busy information for a recipient that represents an Exchange user or for an Outlook contact that has a free/busy location listed |
| Resolve | Attempt to resolve name or address to a valid address |

The `Recipient` object includes the basic properties in Table 18.4. If you need to access MAPI properties that are not exposed in the Outlook object model, use the `Recipient.PropertyAccessor` object discussed in Chapter 14.

Notice that the `Address` and `Name` properties of a `Recipient` object are read-only. If you need to set these properties, you can use the `Recipient.AddressEntry` object, whose `Address` and `Name` properties are read/write.

The object browser and Outlook developer Help list some other constants for `Recipient.Type` besides those in Table 18.6, but I've never seen them in "the wild." Notice that for meeting requests, there is no equivalent of a Bcc recipient that you can use to send an informational copy of the

**Table 18.4**   *Key Recipient Properties (\* = new in Outlook 2007)*

| Property | Description |
|---|---|
| Address | Email address; read-only |
| AddressEntry | Address details, available only if `Resolved = True`; use this object to set the name, address, and address type for a `Recipient` |
| AutoResponse | Response received from a recipient in response to a voting button message |
| DisplayType | Type of recipient, using one of the constants from the `OlDisplayType` enumeration in Table 18.5; read-only |
| MeetingResponseStatus | For appointments and meeting items, status of each individual's response to the meeting, using one of the constants from the `OlResponseStatus` enumeration; read-only: |
| | olResponseAccepted         3 |
| | olResponseDeclined         4 |
| | olResponseNone             0 |
| | olResponseNotResponded     5 |
| | olResponseOrganized        1 |
| | olResponseTentative        2 |
| Name | Display name; read-only |
| \*PropertyAccessor | Object used to get and set properties, especially those not exposed in the Outlook object model |
| Resolved | True, if the recipient has been successfully validated as either a valid SMTP address or an Exchange or other non-Internet address listed in one of the address lists for the profile |

**Table 18.4** *Key Recipient Properties (\* = new in Outlook 2007) (continued)*

| Property | Description |
|---|---|
| TrackingStatus | Read and delivery status for the recipient from the OlTrackingStatus enumeration: |
| | olTrackingDelivered      1 |
| | olTrackingNone      0 |
| | olTrackingNotDelivered      2 |
| | olTrackingNotRead      3 |
| | olTrackingRead      6 |
| | olTrackingRecallFailure      4 |
| | olTrackingRecallSuccess      5 |
| | olTrackingReplied      7 |
| | Only the latest tracking status information is stored. |
| TrackingStatusTime | Date/time of the latest tracking status information received |
| Type | Type of entry, such as To, Cc, or Bcc, using the constants in Table 18.6 |

meeting to someone you don't want to actually invite. The `Recipient.Type` value that would designate a Bcc recipient in a mail message is reserved in meeting requests for resource invitees. The best way to send an informational copy of a meeting is, oddly enough, to reply to (not forward!) the item in your own Calendar folder.

**Table 18.5** *OlDisplayType Constants for the Recipient.DisplayType Property*

| OlDisplayType Constant | Value | Description |
|---|---|---|
| olAgent | 3 | An automated agent (generally not seen in Outlook) |
| olDistList | 1 | Exchange GAL distribution list |
| olForum | 2 | Mail-enabled Exchange public folder |
| olOrganization | 4 | Special organization-wide alias (generally not seen in Outlook) |
| olPrivateDistList | 5 | Personal distribution list from Outlook contacts folder |
| olRemoteUser | 6 | External contact from Exchange GAL |
| olUser | 0 | Exchange user or private SMTP recipient |

**Table 18.6**    *Recipient. Type Constants*

| Item Type | Recipient. Type Constant | Value |
|---|---|---|
| `MailItem`<br>`SharingItem` | `olTo` (default) | 1 |
| | `olCC` | 2 |
| | `olBCC` | 3 |
| `AppointmentItem`<br>`MeetingItem` | `olRequired` (default) | 1 |
| | `olOptional` | 2 |
| | `olResource` | 3 |
| `TaskItem` | `olUpdate` | 2 |
| | `olFinalStatus` | 3 |

## 18.3.1    Adding recipients

Outlook provides two ways to add recipients to an outgoing message, meeting request, or task request:

- Set the value of the `To`, `Cc`, and `Bcc` properties, replacing or appending to any previous entries in those properties
- Use the `Recipients.Add` method

It is not possible to copy the members of one `Recipients` collection to another directly.

You can use `To`, `Cc`, and `Bcc` when you have a complete list of people you want to send to, delimited by semicolons. Use `Recipients.Add` when you want to add to an existing set of recipients or when you need to add a single recipient as a Bcc or Cc address. Add a recipient by name or address, and then use the `Resolve` method to check it against the user's address book. Outlook returns `True` if the item can be resolved to a valid address. If the recipient can be resolved, you can set its `Type` property to `olBcc` to make the recipient a Bcc addressee that the people listed as To and Cc recipients won't see in the message. Here is a VBA example:

```
Set objMsg = Application.CreateItem(olMail)
Set objRecip = objMsg.Recipients.Add("Sue Mosher")
If objRecip.Resolve Then
    objRecip.Type = olBcc
End If
```

To perform the same operation in VBScript, add code statements to declare constants for `olMail` and `olBcc`.

In addition to the `Recipients` collection, the `MailItem` object also includes a `ReplyRecipients` collection that defines what address(es) will appear in the To field (instead of the sender) when the user replies to a message. Use the `ReplyRecipients.Add` method to add to that collection.

### 18.3.2 Example: Checking outgoing recipients

Back in Chapter 11, we discussed how to build functions that embody "rules" for outgoing messages and call them from the `ItemSend` event handler. The `CheckCC()` function in Listing 18.3 asks the user to confirm that the message really should go to the people copied in as Cc or Bcc recipients. If the user answers No to the prompt, Outlook aborts the send operation. Compare the `ItemSend` event handler in Listing 18.3 with the one in Listing 11.4 to see how easily the `CheckCC()` function was added as a new "rule."

The `CheckCC()` function uses two properties of the `Recipient` object: `Type` to determine whether it's a Cc or Bcc, and `Name` to get the display name of the recipient.

### 18.3.3 Example: Automatically add a Bcc recipient to an outgoing message

A common request from Outlook users is to add a Bcc recipient automatically to all outgoing messages. Outlook rules provide a Cc action, but not a Bcc action. However, you can accomplish that goal with some simple VBA code that uses the `Application.ItemSend` event. Put the code in Listing 18.4 in the built-in `ThisOutlookSession` module.

Outlook cannot send an email message with unresolved recipients, so you should always make sure that any recipient you add in the `ItemSend` event handler is resolved. The code in Listing 18.4 deletes the Bcc recipient if it cannot resolve to a valid address. Also, it is not possible to set the `Type` property of a `Recipient` until that recipient is resolved to a valid email address. The next section explains this key Outlook concept of address resolution.

### 18.3.4 Understanding address resolution

*Address resolution* matches up the names of recipients with the actual email addresses present in the user's address lists. Before you send any Outlook item (message, sharing item, meeting request, or task request), all recipient names and addresses should be *resolved* to valid addresses. Outlook will attempt to resolve all addresses when the user clicks Send or code executes the Send method, but will raise an error and abort the sending process if any address cannot be resolved.

Resolution occurs in any of these situations:

- The user clicks the Send command.

- The user clicks the Check Names command.
- Background name resolution is enabled, and Outlook finds a match during the background process' execution.

**Listing 18.3**   *Ask the user to confirm Cc and Bcc recipients*

```
Private Sub Application_ItemSend(ByVal Item As Object, _
                                Cancel As Boolean)
    Dim objMail As Outlook.MailItem
    If Item.Class = olMail Then
        Set objMail = Item
        ' CancelBlankOrNoAttachments from Listing 11.3
        If CancelBlankOrNoAttachments(objMail) = True Then
            Cancel = True
        ' CheckSendAccount from Listing 11.4
        ElseIf CheckSendAccount(objMail) = True Then
            Cancel = True
        ElseIf CheckCC(objMail) = True Then
            Cancel = True
        End If
    End If
    Set objMail = Nothing
End Sub

Function CheckCC(mail As Outlook.MailItem)
    Dim strCC As String
    Dim objRecip As Outlook.Recipient
    Dim intRes As Integer
    For Each objRecip In mail.Recipients
        If objRecip.Type = olCC Then
            strCC = strCC & vbCrLf & _
                    "Cc  - " & objRecip.Name
        ElseIf objRecip.Type = olBCC Then
            strCC = strCC & vbCrLf & _
                    "Bcc - " & objRecip.Name
        End If
    Next
    If strCC <> "" Then
        strCC = "Do you really want to copy these " & _
                "recipients?" & vbCrLf & strCC
        intRes = MsgBox(strCC, vbQuestion + vbYesNo, _
                        "Confirm Cc and Bcc Recipients")
        If intRes = vbNo Then
            CheckCC = True
        Else
            CheckCC = False
        End If
    Else
        CheckCC = False
    End If
    Set objRecip = Nothing
End Function
```

- Program code uses the `Recipients.ResolveAll` or `Recipient.Resolve` method.
- Program code executes the `Send` method.

Outlook automatically resolves Internet addresses in the proper `name@domain.dom` format; such addresses do not need to be present in any of the user's address lists. Outlook also automatically resolves any address in this format:

`[TYPE:name@address]`

For example, a fax number: `[FAX:suemosher@17035555678]`. For other names and addresses, Outlook looks for a match in the various address lists in the Address Book. Resolution begins with the list that has a `ResolutionOrder` property value of 1. If Outlook finds a single match, it sets the `Resolved` property of the `Recipient` to `True` and does not search further. If no match is found, Outlook continues the search with the list that has a `ResolutionOrder` property value of 2, and so on until either a single match is found or all address lists have been searched. For performance reasons, Outlook searches address lists one at a time. Once a match has been found, the address resolution process stops, and no further lists are searched. In a displayed Outlook item, resolved recipients are shown underlined.

**Note:** For Internet addresses, resolution does not tell you whether a given SMTP corresponds to an actual mailbox on a real mail server. All it does is tell you that the address is in correct `name@domain.dom` format.

**Listing 18.4** *Set a Bcc recipient for outgoing messages*

```
Private Sub Application_ItemSend _
   (ByVal Item As Object, Cancel As Boolean)
     Dim objMail As Outlook.MailItem
     Dim objRecip As Outlook.Recipient
     If Item.Class = olMail Then
         Set objMail = Item
         Set objRecip = objMail.Recipients.Add _
                          ("flavius1@turtleflock.net")
         If objRecip.Resolve Then
             objRecip.Type = olBCC
         Else
             objRecip.Delete
         End If
     End If
     Set objMail = Nothing
     Set objRecip = Nothing
End Sub
```

In the two resolution scenarios where the user clicks Send or Check Names, if Outlook does not find a match, it displays a dialog where the user can either try to find the recipient or create a new contact with an email address. The Outlook object model's `Resolve` and `ResolveAll` methods do not provide an option for displaying that dialog. If you are creating and sending a message programmatically, several workarounds are available. The simplest is to display the message (`objMsg` in this example) to the user if `ResolveAll` returns `False` to indicate that some recipients could not be resolved:

```
If objMsg.Recipients.ResolveAll Then
    objMsg.Send
Else
    objMsg.Display
End If
```

Another approach would be to use the `CommandBars` techniques that Chapter 23 will cover to execute the Check Names command. You'll need to know the ID for that command: it's 361. A third approach is to use the `SelectNamesDialog` object. We'll cover that technique at the end of the chapter.

In Exchange environments, Outlook will search for a match on an Exchange user's SMTP address, name, or mailbox alias. The alias and SMTP address are guaranteed to be unique. In the case of a large Exchange environment where several people may have similar names, you may want to prefix the name or alias with an equals sign (=) to force Outlook to look for an exact match. Consider for example, a company with a John D. Smith with an alias smithjd and a John Smith with an alias smithj. These statements will ensure that a resolvable match is found for the second John Smith, the one with no middle initial:

```
Set objRecip = objMsg.Recipients.Add("=smithj")
objRecip.Resolve
```

If you used `Recipients.Add("smithj")`, on the other hand, Outlook would not be able to resolve the address.

## 18.4   Reading Recipient and AddressEntry information

Many common Outlook programming tasks involve reading information from recipients. We saw one example in the previous chapter, where the `Create-Signature` subroutine in Listing 17.8 used the `Namespace.Current-User.AddressEntry` property to return an `AddressEntry` object with the details for the current user. That procedure also used the `Address-Entry.GetExchangeUser` property to return an `ExchangeUser` object (an object with properties and methods inherited from `AddressEntry`) so that it could get the user's phone number and other details from the GAL.

Other practical applications of reading recipient information include reporting on meeting request and voting button message responses, creating contacts for outgoing messages, sending a bulk reply to all messages in a folder, creating distribution lists, and reading free/busy information to find out when a person is available for a meeting.

In addition to the very basic address information exposed by the Recipient object (see Table 18.4), the Recipient.AddressEntry object provides more information about each recipient, along with methods to get the Exchange user, Exchange distribution list, or Outlook contact associated with any recipient. Table 18.7 summarizes the key AddressEntry properties and methods.

Notice how the new AddressEntryUserType property added in Outlook 2007 provides information similar to the Recipient.DisplayType and AddressEntry.DisplayType property, but with greater precision. Compare the possible values for AddressEntryUserType in Table 18.8 with those for DisplayType in Table 18.5. Once you know the AddressEntryUserType, you can use one of three new methods—GetContact, GetExchangeDistributionList, and GetExchangeUser—to return the Outlook contact or GAL user or distribution list (DL) associated with the address entry. Both the ExchangeUser and ExchangeDistributionList objects have many properties that expose information about the user or DL.

The next few sections look at common applications related to reading Recipient and AddressEntry information.

**Table 18.7** *Key AddressEntry Properties and Methods (\* = new in Outlook 2007)*

| Property | Description |
| --- | --- |
| Address | Email address |
| *AddressEntryUserType | Type of Exchange or other address using one of the constants from the OlAddressEntryUserType enumeration in Table 18.8 (note similarities to values in Table 18.5); read-only |
| DisplayType | Type of recipient, using one of the constants from the OlDisplayType enumeration in Table 18.5; read-only |
| ID | Unique ID; read-only |
| Name | Display name for address |
| *PropertyAccessor | Object used to get and set properties, especially those not exposed in the Outlook object model |
| Type | String representing the type of address, such as "EX" for an Exchange user or "SMTP" for an Internet address |

**Table 18.7**    *Key AddressEntry Properties and Methods (\* = new in Outlook 2007) (continued)*

| Method | Description |
|---|---|
| Details | Display a modal dialog box with the address entry's name, address, and address type |
| \*GetContact | If AddressEntryUserType = olOutlookContactAddressEntry, returns the ContactItem object associated with the address entry |
| \*GetExchangeDistributionList | If AddressEntryUserType = olExchangeDistributionList-AddressEntry, returns the ExchangeDistributionList object associated with the address entry |
| \*GetExchangeUser | If AddressEntryUserType = olExchangeUserAddressEntry, returns the ExchangeUser associated with the address entry |
| GetFreeBusy(*Start, MinPerChar, CompleteFormat*) | Return 30 days' worth of availability information for the address entry |
| Update | Update the address entry with changes made to the Address, Type, or Name property or to other properties using PropertyAccessor |

**Table 18.8**    *OlAddressEntryUserType Constants for the AddressEntry.AddressEntryUserType Property*

| OlAddressEntryUserType Constant | Value | Description |
|---|---|---|
| olExchangeAgentAddressEntry | 3 | An automated agent (generally not seen in Outlook) |
| olExchangeDistributionListAddressEntry | 1 | Exchange GAL distribution list |
| olExchangeOrganizationAddressEntry | 4 | Special organization-wide alias (generally not seen in Outlook) |
| olExchangePublicFolderAddressEntry | 2 | Mail-enabled Exchange public folder |
| olExchangeRemoteUserAddressEntry | 5 | External contact from Exchange GAL |
| olExchangeUserAddressEntry | 0 | Exchange user or private SMTP recipient |
| olLdapAddressEntry | 20 | Entry from LDAP address list |
| olOtherAddressEntry | 40 | Entry from other type of address list |
| olOutlookContactAddressEntry | 10 | Contact from Outlook contacts folder |
| olOutlookDistributionListAddressEntry | 11 | Personal distribution list from Outlook contacts folder |
| olSmtpAddressEntry | 30 | One-off SMTP address |

## 18.4.1   Example: Create contacts for outgoing message recipients

Some Outlook users want to create a contact for each recipient they send a message to. This is another task you can accomplish with VBA and the `Application.ItemSend` event.

Put the code from Listing 18.5 in the built-in `ThisOutlookSession` module. The `AddRecipToContacts` procedure processes each recipient in the outgoing message, checking to see what kind of recipient it is. For SMTP addresses, it calls the `IsInContacts()` function from Listing 16.4 to determine whether the user's default Contacts folder already contains a contact with the recipient's address. If not, the code creates a new contact in the Contacts folder, populating it with the name and address from the recipient. If you wanted to collect these contacts in a folder other than the default Contacts folder, you would use one of the methods described in Chapter 13 to return the desired folder, then use the `Items.Add` method for that folder to create the new `ContactItem`.

**Listing 18.5**   *Create contacts for outgoing message recipients*

```
Private Sub Application_ItemSend _
  (ByVal Item As Object, Cancel As Boolean)
    Dim objMail As Outlook.MailItem
    If Item.Class = olMail Then
        Set objMail = Item
        Call AddRecipToContacts(objMail)
    End If
    Set objMail = Nothing
End Sub

Sub AddRecipToContacts(msg As Outlook.MailItem)
    Dim objRecip As Outlook.Recipient
    Dim objContact As Outlook.ContactItem
    For Each objRecip In msg.Recipients
        If objRecip.AddressEntry.AddressEntryUserType = _
          olSmtpAddressEntry Then
            ' IsInContacts() function from Listing 16.4
            If Not IsInContacts(objRecip.address) Then
                Set objContact = _
                  Application.CreateItem(olContactItem)
                objContact.EmailAddress = objRecip.address
                objContact.FullName = objRecip.Name
                objContact.Save
            End If
        End If
    Next
    Set objRecip = Nothing
    Set objContact = Nothing
End Sub
```

### 18.4.2   Example: Respond to all the messages in a folder

Instead of collecting contacts, some users collect messages and then want to come back later and send a bulk reply—either a single message with a bunch of Bcc recipients or individual replies all with the same message content. It's better to do bulk mailings as individual messages rather than as one message with a lot of Bcc recipients. For one thing, many mail servers put a limit on the number of recipients per message—possibly even a separate limit on the number of Bcc recipients. Second, a message that arrives addressed to the recipient is more likely to get through the addressee's spam filter than a bulk message that doesn't have the recipient's address in the To field.

The `RespondToFolder` procedure in Listing 18.6, written for Outlook VBA, uses the currently open message (`Application.ActiveInspector.CurrentItem`) as a template and the currently visible folder (`Application.ActiveExplorer.CurrentFolder`) as the source of the messages to which you want to generate a bulk reply.

Instead of relying solely on the sender email address, the procedure also checks the `ReplyRecipients` collection, just in case the original sender wanted replies sent to a different address. Thus, the code relies on two different expressions to get the address to respond to and uses those expressions in two different statements to add addresses to the response message:

```
objResponse.To = objItem.SenderEmailAddress
objResponse.Recipients.Add objRecip.address
```

where `objRecip` is a member of the `ReplyRecipients` collection on a message in the source folder. Since it is not possible to copy the contents of one `Recipients` collection to another, to handle Reply-To recipients, the code must loop through the `ReplyRecipients` collection on the original received message and call `Recipients.Add` as many times as needed to create one recipient in the response message for each member of the `ReplyRecipients` collection on the original message. The task is simpler on items with no Reply-To recipients; the `SenderEmailAddress` property contains the address that the response needs.

## 18.5   Reading free/busy information

When planning a meeting, users often want to know if key personnel or resources are available. On the standard Appointment form, Outlook provides a Scheduling tab that displays this information. However, the data in the Scheduling tab is not exposed programmatically in any direct way. Instead, Outlook provides the `GetFreeBusy` method of the `AddressEntry` and `ExchangeUser` objects to give your code a way of learning about another person's availability. The syntax for `GetFreeBusy` looks like this:

```
strFBInfo = objAddressEntry.FreeBusy _
        (Start, MinPerChar, CompleteFormat)
```

**Listing 18.6**    *Respond to all messages in a folder*

```
Sub RespondToFolder()
    Dim objOL As Outlook.Application
    Dim objFolder As Outlook.Folder
    Dim objInsp As Outlook.Inspector
    Dim objMsg As Outlook.MailItem
    Dim objResponse As Outlook.MailItem
    Dim objItem As Object
    Dim colReply As Outlook.Recipients
    Dim objRecip As Outlook.Recipient
    Dim strMsg As String
    Set objOL = Application
    Set objFolder = objOL.ActiveExplorer.CurrentFolder
    If objFolder.DefaultItemType = olMailItem Then
        Set objInsp = Application.ActiveInspector
        If Not objInsp Is Nothing Then
            If objInsp.CurrentItem.Class = olMail Then
                Set objMsg = objInsp.CurrentItem
                For Each objItem In objFolder.Items
                    If objItem.Class = olMail Then
                        Set objResponse = objMsg.Copy
                        Set colReply = objItem.ReplyRecipients
                        If colReply.Count > 0 Then
                            For Each objRecip In colReply
                                objResponse.Recipients.Add _
                                    objRecip.address
                            Next
                        Else
                            objResponse.To = _
                                objItem.SenderEmailAddress
                        End If
                        objResponse.Send
                    End If
                Next
            Else
                strMsg = "Please display the message " & _
                    "that you want to use to " & _
                    "respond to the items in " & _
                    "this folder."
            End If
        Else
            strMsg = "Please display the message " & _
                "that you want to use to " & _
                "respond to the items in " & _
                "this folder."
        End If
    Else
        strMsg = "Please display the folder that " & _
            "contains the messages you want " & _
            "to reply to."
    End If
    If strMsg <> "" Then
        MsgBox strMsg, vbExclamation, "Cannot Respond to Folder"
    End If
```

**Listing 18.6**    *Respond to all messages in a folder  (continued)*

```
    Set objOL = Nothing
    Set objFolder = Nothing
    Set objInsp = Nothing
    Set objMsg = Nothing
    Set objResponse = Nothing
    Set objItem = Nothing
    Set colReply = Nothing
    Set objRecip = Nothing
End Sub
```

The string returned by `GetFreeBusy` is a long string of numeric characters—one per time period, starting with midnight on the date passed as the *Start* parameter, and covering the next month of data. The length of the time period each character represents is the number of minutes in the *MinPerChar* parameter. Both *Start* and *MinPerChar* are required arguments. The last parameter, *CompleteFormat*, controls whether Outlook returns basic or more detailed availability information. If the parameter value is `False` (the default), Outlook returns `0` for each period the user is free and `1` for each busy period. If the parameter value is `True`, Outlook returns this more detailed information for each time period, corresponding to the `OlBusyStatus` enumeration values for the `AppointmentItem.BusyStatus` property:

| | |
|---|---|
| 0 | Free |
| 1 | Tentative |
| 2 | Busy |
| 3 | Out of office |

Given that the `GetFreeBusy` method returns a string of numeric characters covering 30 days, how can you learn from it whether a user is busy during any particular time period? You must parse the text string to focus on the particular period of time you're interested in. The `IsBusy()` function in Listing 18.7 takes three parameters:

- A name or address that can be resolved to a `Recipient`
- The start date/time for the time period you want to check
- The end date/time for the time period you want to check

**Note:** In the initial released version of Outlook 2007, the `GetFreeBusy` method does not return any information if the user is connecting to a Microsoft Exchange 2007 server that does not have a Public Folders store. Let's hope Microsoft releases an update to fix this problem quickly.

---→

**Listing 18.7** *Get availability information for a person or resource*

```
Function IsBusy(strRecip As String, _
                dteStart As Date, _
                dteEnd As Date) As Integer
    Dim objOL As Outlook.Application
    Dim objNS As Outlook.NameSpace
    Dim objRecip As Outlook.Recipient
    Dim objAEntry As Outlook.AddressEntry
    Dim objContact As Outlook.ContactItem
    Dim blnCanDoFreeBusy As Boolean
    Dim intMinutes As Integer
    Dim intIsBusy As Integer
    Dim intStartChar As Integer
    Dim intDurChars As Integer
    Dim strFB As String
    On Error Resume Next
    Set objOL = Application
    Set objNS = objOL.Session
    Set objRecip = objNS.CreateRecipient(strRecip)
    If objRecip.Resolve Then
        Set objAEntry = objRecip.AddressEntry
        Select Case objAEntry.AddressEntryUserType
            Case olExchangeUserAddressEntry
                blnCanDoFreeBusy = True
            Case olOutlookContactAddressEntry
                Set objContact = objAEntry.GetContact
                If objContact.InternetFreeBusyAddress _
                  <> "" Then
                    blnCanDoFreeBusy = True
                Else
                    intIsBusy = -1
                End If
            Case Else
                intIsBusy = -1
        End Select
    End If
    If blnCanDoFreeBusy Then
        ' adjust dates to 15 minute boundaries
        dteStart = AdjustTimeTo15(dteStart, True)
        dteEnd = AdjustTimeTo15(dteEnd, False)
        ' get starting character
        intMinutes = DateDiff("n", DateValue(dteStart), dteStart)
        intStartChar = (intMinutes / 15) + 1
        ' get number of characters to check
        intMinutes = DateDiff("n", dteStart, dteEnd)
        intDurChars = intMinutes / 15
        strFB = objAEntry.GetFreeBusy(DateValue(dteStart), 15)
        If strFB <> "" Then
            strFB = Mid(strFB, intStartChar, intDurChars)
            If InStr(strFB, "1") > 0 Then
                intIsBusy = 1
            Else
                intIsBusy = 0
            End If
```

**Listing 18.7**    *Get availability information for a person or resource (continued)*

```
        Else
                intIsBusy = -1
        End If
    End If
    IsBusy = intIsBusy
    Set objOL = Nothing
    Set objNS = Nothing
    Set objRecip = Nothing
    Set objAEntry = Nothing
    Set objContact = Nothing
End Function

Function AdjustTimeTo15(dateVal As Date, _
                    adjustDown As Boolean) As Date
    Dim intMin As Integer
    Dim dteAdjusted As Date
    If Minute(dateVal) Mod 15 = 0 Then
        dteAdjusted = dateVal
    ElseIf adjustDown Then
        intMin = (Hour(dateVal) * 60) + _
                ((Minute(dateVal) \ 15) * 15)
        dteAdjusted = DateAdd("n", intMin, _
                            DateValue(dateVal))
    Else
        dateVal = DateAdd("n", 15, dateVal)
        dteAdjusted = AdjustTimeTo15(dateVal, True)
    End If
    AdjustTimeTo15 = dteAdjusted
End Function
```

For example, to check a person's availability between 1 PM and 5 PM on January 26, call the function like this:

```
MsgBox IsBusy("flaviusj", #1/26/2007 01:00PM#, _
                        #1/26/2007 05:00PM#)
```

The `IsBusy()` function returns `-1` if free/busy information is not available—for example, if the name or address does not correspond to an Exchange user or an Outlook contact with a free/busy lookup address. It returns `0` if the person or resource is free, according to the data that `Get-FreeBusy` returns, and `1` if not free.

To check a person's availability for one or more entire days, call the function with the start date and the day after the day(s) you're interested in. Thus to check availability for any time on January 26, you'd use:

```
MsgBox IsBusy("flaviusj", #1/26/2007#, #1/27/2007#)
```

It is necessary to use the day after the actual end date you're interested in because VBA interprets a date without a time element as starting at midnight. The above code snippet is equivalent to:

```
MsgBox IsBusy("flaviusj", #1/26/2007 00:00AM#, _
                          #1/27/2007 00:00AM#)
```

The `IsBusy()` function uses a helper function, `AdjustTimeTo15()`, to adjust the start and end date/time values to 15-minute boundaries, and then returns the free/busy information also in 15-minute segments. These two functions show why it's important to learn the programming basics we covered in Chapter 8. They use many fundamental techniques including date arithmetic, text parsing, and recursion. Let's examine some of the key details of these functions.

Looking up free/busy data is not limited to Exchange users. Outlook can look up free/busy information for an `AddressEntry` based on an Outlook contact if the contact has a valid `InternetFreeBusyAddress` property value. The `IsBusy()` function checks to see whether the name or address belongs to a contact with a free/busy lookup address:

```
Case olOutlookContactAddressEntry
    Set objContact = objAEntry.GetContact
    If objContact.InternetFreeBusyAddress <> "" Then
    ' etc.
```

**Note:** Outlook may not raise an error for the `GetFreeBusy` method if you try to look up availability information for a contact that has no free/busy address or an invalid address or if network problems prevent a connection to the Internet or to the Exchange server's free/busy information. Instead, in those scenarios, you'll get a free/busy availability string with all zeroes. Thus, the `GetFreeBusy` method is not a definitive indicator of a user's availability.

The `AdjustTimeTo15()` function takes a date/time value and returns a date/time value adjusted up or down to the next or previous 15-minute boundary, depending on the value of the `adjustDown` parameter. It first determines whether a time value is already on one of the 15-minute interval boundaries:

```
If Minute(dateVal) Mod 15 = 0 Then
```

`Mod` is an operator that returns the remainder obtained when the first number is divided by the second. Hence, it's 0 if the value for the minutes in the date value is 0, 15, or 45.

The function uses the `Hour()` and `Minute()` functions to return the number of minutes past midnight, rounded down to a 15-minute time:

```
intMin = (Hour(dateVal) * 60) + _
         ((Minute(dateVal) \ 15) * 15)
```

The expression `(Minute(dateVal) \ 15)` uses the integer division operator (`\`) to get the number of whole 15-minute periods in the minutes value for `dateVal`. When `adjustDown` has a value of `False`, the `AdjustTimeTo15()` function uses recursion: It adds 15 minutes to the date/time value and then calls itself to round down to the nearest 15-minute interval:

```
dateVal = DateAdd("n", 15, dateVal)
dteAdjusted = AdjustTimeTo15(dateVal, True)
```

The `GetFreeBusy` method returns a string of "1" and "0" characters, in this case, some 2,800 (30 days * 24 hours * 4 15-minute periods per hour) characters, because the code specifies a 15-minute interval:

```
strFB = objAEntry.GetFreeBusy(DateValue(dteStart), 15)
```

But we're interested only in a small segment of that string—the segment whose characters correspond to the time period from `dteStart` to `dteEnd`:

```
strFB = Mid(strFB, intStartChar, intDurChars)
```

The time period from midnight to 00:15 is represented by the first character. We calculated the position of the character to start with, `intStartChar`, by getting the number of minutes past midnight for the adjusted start date, dividing by 15 and adding 1:

```
intMinutes = _
  DateDiff("n", DateValue(dteStart), dteStart)
intStartChar = (intMinutes / 15) + 1
```

To get the number of characters to check, `intDurChars`, we calculated the duration, based on the adjusted start and end dates, and then divided by 15, because each character in the free/busy string represents a 15-minute period:

```
intMinutes = DateDiff("n", dteStart, dteEnd)
intDurChars = intMinutes / 15
```

Once the code trims the `strFB` string down to the segment covering the time period we're interested in, the code can use the text parsing expression `InStr(strFB, "1") > 0` to determine whether the string contains a "1"—indicating that the user is busy for at least part of that time period.

## 18.6   Showing the Select Names dialog

The last technique to round out this chapter on recipients and address lists involves giving the user the opportunity to select one or more names from the available address lists and return the selection to the calling code. Just as the `Namespace` object has a `PickFolder` method for choosing a folder from the hierarchy, it also supports a `GetSelectNamesDialog` method that returns a `SelectNamesDialog` object. But where `PickFolder` has no options, the `SelectNamesDialog` option has many different options that you can use to customize the display to:

- Show only a particular address list

- Collect just one or up to three types of addresses (corresponding to To, Cc, and Bcc)
- Customize the labels for up to three types of addresses being collected (so the user sees something other than To, Cc, and Bcc)
- Allow only one address to be selected

Accordingly, the process of using the Select Names dialog is more complicated than using the Pick Folder dialog. In a nutshell, it follows these steps:

1. Call `Namespace.GetSelectNamesDialog` to return a `SelectNamesDialog` object.

2. Optionally, call the `SelectNames.SetDefaultDisplayMode` method to set up the dialog to use the localized caption, number of buttons, and localized button labels for eight common Select Names scenarios, such as picking recipients for a message or picking rooms for a meeting request.

3. Set the desired `SelectNamesDialog` properties to handle various options, which are listed in Table 18.9.

4. Call the `SelectNamesDialog.Display` method to show the user the dialog, which is always modal.

5. Check the return value of `SelectNamesDialog.Display`, which will be `True` if the user clicked OK to make a selection.

6. Work with the `SelectNamesDialog.Recipients` collection, which contains the recipients that the user selected from the dialog.

**Table 18.9**    *Key SelectNamesDialog Properties and Methods*

| Property | Description |
|---|---|
| AllowMultipleSelection | `True` (default) to allow the user to select more than one name from the dialog; `False` to allow the user to choose only one name |
| BccLabel | String for the command button used to select Bcc recipients |
| Caption | Title for the dialog, followed by a colon and the name of the initial address list |
| CcLabel | String for the command button used to select Cc recipients |
| ForceResolution | `True` (default) if the user must resolve all addresses or names typed in before clicking OK; otherwise, `False` |
| InitialAddressList | `AddressList` object that the dialog should display initially in the drop-down list of available address lists |

**Table 18.9**   *Key SelectNamesDialog Properties and Methods (continued)*

| Property | Description |
|---|---|
| `NumberOfRecipientSelectors` | Number of address selector buttons to show, using a constant from the `OlRecipientSelectors` enumeration:<br><br>`olShowNone`  0<br><br>`olShowTo`  1<br><br>`olShowToCC`  2<br><br>`olShowToCcBcc`  3 |
| `Recipients` | Collection of recipients entered or selected by the user in the dialog; can also be used to set an initial collection of recipients pre-selected for display in the dialog |
| `ShowOnlyInitialAddressList` | `True` to show only the list in `InitialAddressList`; otherwise, `False` (default) |
| `ToLabel` | String for the command button used to select To recipients |
| **Method** | **Description** |
| `Display` | Display the dialog modally; returns `True` if the user makes a selection and `False` if the user cancels the dialog or closes it without making a selection |
| `SetDisplayDefaultMode` | Set options for the dialog for 8 common scenarios, using constants from the `OlDefaultSelectNamesDisplayMode` enumeration:<br><br>`olDefaultDelegates`  6<br><br>`olDefaultMail`  1<br><br>`olDefaultMeeting`  2<br><br>`olDefaultMembers`  5<br><br>`olDefaultPickRooms`  8<br><br>`olDefaultSharingRequest`  4<br><br>`olDefaultSingleName`  7<br><br>`olDefaultTask`  3 |

To demonstrate the basic procedure, the code in Listing 18.8 presents the user with a dialog where one name can be selected and only from the user's default Contacts folder. You can test the `SelectSingleContact-Name()` function using this syntax from the VBA Immediate window:

```
MsgBox SelectSingleContactName()
```

The `SelectSingleContactName()` demonstrates some of the interesting features of the Select Names dialog. After iterating the `Namespace.Address-Lists` collection to locate the list that exposes data from the user's default Contacts folder, the code sets the dialog to show only that Contacts list:

```
With objSelNames
    .InitialAddressList = objAddrList
    .ShowOnlyInitialAddressList = True
```

A name selected from an address book is the address' display name. For contacts, that often includes both the contact name and the email address. To get the contact name by itself, the code uses two AddressEntry members, which you saw earlier in the chapter, to return the value of the contact's FullName property:

```
If objAddrEntry.AddressEntryUserType = _
   olOutlookContactAddressEntry Then
      Set objContact = objAddrEntry.GetContact
      strName = objContact.FullName
```

The next section uses the Select Names dialog to solve another common Outlook programming challenge—selecting contact links exclusively from a public folder. For another example, see this article in Outlook developer Help:

■  How to: Display a Dialog Box for Selecting Entries from the Contacts Folder (HV10034110)

The number in parentheses is a topic ID you can search for in Help to find the article faster.

**Listing 18.8**    *Select a single item from the default Contacts folder*

```
Function SelectSingleContactName() As String
    Dim objOL As Outlook.Application
    Dim objNS As Outlook.NameSpace
    Dim objContacts As Outlook.Folder
    Dim objAddrList As Outlook.AddressList
    Dim objSelNames As Outlook.SelectNamesDialog
    Dim colRecip As Outlook.Recipients
    Dim objAddrEntry As Outlook.AddressEntry
    Dim objContact As Outlook.ContactItem
    Dim strName As String
    Dim blnAddrListFound As Boolean
    On Error Resume Next
    Set objOL = Application
    Set objNS = objOL.Session
    Set objSelNames = objNS.GetSelectNamesDialog
    Set objContacts = _
      objNS.GetDefaultFolder(olFolderContacts)
    For Each objAddrList In objNS.AddressLists
        If objAddrList.GetContactsFolder = objContacts Then
            blnAddrListFound = True
            Exit For
        End If
    Next
```

**Listing 18.8**    *Select a single item from the default Contacts folder (continued)*

```
If blnAddrListFound Then
    With objSelNames
        .SetDefaultDisplayMode olDefaultSingleName
        .InitialAddressList = objAddrList
        .ShowOnlyInitialAddressList = True
        .Caption = "Select a Name from"
        If .Display = True Then
            If .Recipients.Count > 0 Then
                Set objAddrEntry = _
                    .Recipients(1).AddressEntry
                If objAddrEntry.AddressEntryUserType = _
                    olOutlookContactAddressEntry Then
                    Set objContact = _
                        objAddrEntry.GetContact
                    strName = objContact.FullName
                Else
                    strName = _
                        "User did not select a contact."
                End If
            Else
                strName = "User selected no name."
            End If
        Else
            strName = "User selected no name."
        End If
    End With
Else
    strName = "Contacts folder was not available."
End If
SelectSingleContactName = strName
Set objOL = Nothing
Set objNS = Nothing
Set objSelNames = Nothing
Set colRecip = Nothing
Set objAddrEntry = Nothing
Set objContact = Nothing
Set objContacts = Nothing
Set objAddrList = Nothing
End Function
```

## 18.6.1   Example: Select contact links from a public folder

Our application of the `SelectNamesDialog` is to solve a problem with the `Contacts` controls that appear at the bottom of the standard Outlook forms (except for the message form, where they appear on the Options dialog). In public folder applications, form designers often want to coerce the selection of contact links to a particular public contacts folder or at least display that folder as the default when the user clicks the Contacts button.

Outlook provides no such control over the Select Contacts dialog, but you can solve the problem by using the `SelectNamesDialog` to show only the specific public folder (as we did with the default Contacts folder in Listing 18.8). Ths approach assumes that all the contacts that you want to use as links have email addresses; only contacts with electronic addresses (fax or email) appear in the address book.

To test this solution, create a new custom post form and in design mode, follow these steps to add the necessary controls and code:

1. Shorten the width of the Categories box so that it takes up about half the width of the form.

2. From the Field Chooser, drag the Contacts field to the bottom of the form, to the space you made in Step 1.

3. Delete the Contacts... button.

4. From the control toolbox, drag a command button to the space freed up by deleting the Contacts . . . button. On the Properties dialog for this control, give it the name `cmdContacts` and caption "Contacts . . . ."

5. Widen the Contacts box so it fills out the width of the page.

6. Add the code in Listings 18.9 and 13.7 to the form's code module.

7. In the `AddContacts` procedure, change the value for `strFolderPath` so that it points to any contact folder in your Outlook mail profile.

8. Create a new folder to hold the post form items, and publish the form to that folder. On the Properties dialog for the folder, make the newly published form the default.

**Listing 18.9**   *Add contact links from a public folder*

```
Sub cmdContacts_Click()
    Call AddContacts
End Sub

Sub AddContacts()
    Dim objNS            ' As Outlook.NameSpace
    Dim objFolder        ' As Outlook.Folder
    Dim objAddrList      ' As Outlook.AddressList
    Dim objContact       ' As Outlook.ContactItem
    Dim objRecip         ' As Outlook.Recipient
    Dim objAE            ' As Outlook.AddressEntry
    Dim strFolderPath    ' As String
    Dim objSelNames      ' As SelectNamesDialog
    Dim blnAddrListFound ' As Boolean
```

**Listing 18.9**   *Add contact links from a public folder (continued)*

```
Const olDefaultMembers = 5
Const olOutlookContactAddressEntry = 10
On Error Resume Next
' ### USER OPTION ###
strFolderPath = _
  "\\Public Folders\All Public Folders\Contacts\Sales"
Set objNS = Application.Session
Set objSelNames = objNS.GetSelectNamesDialog
' GetFolder() from Listing 13.7
Set objFolder = GetFolder(strFolderPath)
If Not objFolder Is Nothing Then
    If objFolder.ShowAsOutlookAB = False Then
        objFolder.ShowAsOutlookAB = True
        objFolder.AddressBookName = objFolder.Name & _
          " in " & objFolder.Parent.FolderPath
    End If
End If
For Each objAddrList In objNS.AddressLists
    If objAddrList.GetContactsFolder = objFolder Then
        blnAddrListFound = True
        Exit For
    End If
Next
If blnAddrListFound Then
    With objSelNames
        .SetDefaultDisplayMode olDefaultMembers
        If Not objAddrList Is Nothing Then
            Set .InitialAddressList = objAddrList
            .ShowOnlyInitialAddressList = True
            .NumberOfRecipientSelectors = 1
            .Caption = "Select Contacts"
            .ToLabel = "Contacts"
            If .Display = True Then
                For Each objRecip In .Recipients
                    Set objContact = Nothing
                    Set objAE = objRecip.AddressEntry
                    If objAE.AddressEntryUserType = _
                      olOutlookContactAddressEntry Then
                        Set objContact = _
                          objAE.GetContact
                        Item.Links.Add objContact
                    End If
                Next
            End If
        End If
    End With
End If
Set objNS = Nothing
Set objFolder = Nothing
Set objAddrList = Nothing
Set objContact = Nothing
Set objAE = Nothing
Set objRecip = Nothing
Set objSelNames = Nothing
End Sub
```

To use this custom contact linking mechanism, create a new item in the folder and click the Contacts . . . button at the bottom of the item. You should see the address book dialog display your chosen folder from the path in `strFolder`. After you select a few contacts, the code behind the form will add them to the post as links in the `Links` collection, which Outlook displays in the Contacts box. We spend more time with `Links` in Chapter 10.

If you compare the code in Listing 18.9 with that in Listing 18.8, you will see one oddity in this statement:

```
Set .InitialAddressList = objAddrList
```

The corresponding statement in Listing 18.8, which was designed as VBA code, has no `Set` keyword, but the VBScript code in Listing 18.9 requires `Set`.

## 18.7  Summary

The various objects that expose information about address lists and recipients in Outlook are all interrelated. Outlook 2007 includes new objects that can return information about Exchange users and distribution lists and Outlook contacts without using `PropertyAccessor` or assorted hacks that previous versions required.

As practical applications, you've learned how to report on the Global Address Lists and other address lists, enhance outgoing messages with a Bcc recipient and a saved contact for each outgoing message recipient, send a response to all the messages in a folder, look up any person's availability for scheduling purposes, and present the user with a dialog for selecting names from the address book. The address book display has particular application for some common custom form challenges, such as selecting contacts from a particular public contacts folder.

As a bonus, you saw two examples of building an HTML-format message or post item with a table that organizes out a report in a highly readable layout.

# 19

# *Working with Attachments*

Many email messages exist solely for the purpose of transmitting a file. Appointments, tasks, journal entries, and contacts also can contain attachments, links to files on the network, and even other Outlook items. Inserting attachments and extracting attachments and their content are key Outlook programming tasks that can help you create highly functional Outlook items and process incoming data.

Highlights of this chapter include discussions of the following:

- What different types of attachments an Outlook item may contain
- Why you need to save an attachment as a file before you can access its content
- How to add a file or Outlook item as an embedded attachment or a link
- How to import any kind of embedded Outlook item
- How to reply to a message, attaching the files contained in the original item
- How to distinguish hidden from "real" attachments

We already learned one key attachment technique in Chapter 16: how to search the content inside attachments using the new content index keywords in Outlook 2007.

## 19.1   Understanding Outlook attachments

Outlook differs from many mail applications in that it stores attachments not as separate files on the user's hard drive but as part of each Outlook item. In other words, the attachments that you see in Outlook are stored, like the items themselves, in your Personal Folders.pst file, Exchange mailbox, or other store. To work with the attachments, your code will need to go through an individual item's `Attachments` collection.

Outlook items can contain many different types of attachments:

- Word documents, Excel worksheets, HTML files, pictures you send to friends and family, and other "normal" file attachments
- Hidden file attachments, such as the picture associated with an Outlook contact or the images embedded in an HTML-format mail message
- Links to files on the hard drive or on a network drive
- Files that are hidden from the user because they are blocked by Outlook's attachment security
- Embedded Outlook items
- Links to Outlook items (available only in items using rich-text format for the item body)
- Objects embedded using Object Linking and Embedding (OLE) technology

Each Outlook item, except for "sticky notes," supports an `Attachments` collection containing the item's attachments, each as an `Attachment` object. Table 19.1 lists the key properties and methods for the `Attachment` object.

If you study Table 19.1, you might notice a glaring omission: There is no property that provides access to the content of the attachment itself. For "normal" file attachments (`Type = olByValue`) and attachments that are embedded Outlook items (`Type = olEmbeddedItem`), the only way to work with the attachment's content is to save it as a file first, using the `SaveAsFile` method, which we'll examine later in the chapter. Once you save the attachment, your code can use methods appropriate to the saved file to work with its content.

Attachments that are shortcuts to files—say, a file on a network drive—have `Type = olByReference` and a `PathName` property value pointing to the actual location of the file. In that case, you already know the location of the saved file and can use methods appropriate for that type of file to open it.

Files attached by reference are the only type of attachment for which `PathName` has a meaningful value. Outlook does not "remember" the path of the original file when a file is attached `olByValue`. (If you think about it, this makes some sense: The original file could be moved or even deleted and Outlook wouldn't care, because it has a complete copy of the original file stored as an attachment.)

Attachments that are shortcuts to Outlook items have `Type = olOLE` and will not have meaningful values for `DisplayName`, `FileName`, or `PathName`, nor is there any way to save or open such a linked item programmatically.

→

**Table 19.1**   *Key Attachment Properties and Methods (\* = new in Outlook 2007)*

| Property | Description |
|---|---|
| \*BlockLevel | Indicates whether or not an item has a security block which prevents it from being opened; read-only, using a constant from the OlAttachmentBlockLevel enumeration: <br><br> olAttachmentBlockLevelNone       0 <br><br> olAttachmentBlockLevelOpen       1 |
| DisplayName | Display name for the attachment; useful only for Type = olEmbeddedItem; Outlook displays only the first 30 characters as labels for attachment icons in rich-text format items |
| FileName | File name for the attachment; read-only |
| PathName | Path to a linked file, present only if Type = olByReference; read-only |
| Position | For rich-text format items, long integer for the position of the attachment icon on the item body; largely non-functional in the original release of Outlook 2007 |
| \*PropertyAccessor | Object used to access hidden properties |
| \*Size | Size of the attachment, in bytes; read-only |
| Type | Type of attachment, using a constant from the OlAttachmentType enumeration shown in Table 19.2 |

| Method | Description |
|---|---|
| Delete | Remove the attachment from the Attachments collection |
| SaveAsFile Path | Save the attachment to the designated Path, which should be a complete path and file name, not just a path |

→

**Table 19.2**   *Constants from the OlAttachmentType Enumeration for Use with Attachment.Type*

| Constant | Value | Description |
|---|---|---|
| olByReference | 4 | Link to a file stored in the file system |
| olByValue | 1 | File embedded in the Outlook item |
| olEmbeddedItem | 5 | Outlook item embedded in the Outlook item |
| olOLE | 6 | Content embedded using Object Linking and Embedding (OLE) technology |

## 19.2   Adding attachments to Outlook items

To add an attachment to an Outlook item, use the `Attachments.Add` method with this syntax:

```
objItem.Attachments.Add Source, Type, Position, DisplayName
```

The *Source* parameter is the only required parameter and can be either a file or an Outlook item. The *Type* parameter uses one of the first three values in Table 19.2; the default is `olByValue`. The *Position* parameter applies only to items in rich-text format (RTF) and, according to the Outlook object model documentation, determines where in the body of the item the attachment icon will appear. However, this parameter apparently does not work in the original release of Outlook 2007, except that you can set it to 0 to hide the attachment. If you set *Position* to a non-zero value, Outlook ignores the value and displays the attachment icon at the end of the item body, rather than at the specified position. The *DisplayName* parameter is meaningful only for an Outlook item attached with `Type = olEmbeddedItem`.

All of the following are examples of attaching different types of items in different ways; assume that `objAppt` is an `AppointmentItem` object and that `objInbox` is a `Folder` object representing the Inbox:

- Insert a file into the item:

  ```
  objAppt.Attachments.Add "C:\data\agenda.doc", olByValue
  ```
- Add a shortcut to a file:

  ```
  objAppt.Attachments.Add _
      "\\nas-01\suedata\OL2007 Book\promo.doc", olByReference
  ```
- Insert an Outlook item:

  ```
  Set objItem = objInbox.Items(1)
  objAppt.Attachments.Add objItem, olEmbeddedItem, , _
      objItem.Subject & " from " & objItem.Parent.Name
  ```
- Add a shortcut to an Outlook item:

  ```
  objAppt.Attachments.Add objInbox.Items(2), olByReference
  ```

Note that the last approach—inserting a shortcut to an Outlook item—works only on items that are in rich-text format (RTF). Outlook will not raise any error if you add a shortcut to an Outlook item to a plain text or HTML-format message or post, but the shortcut simply won't work.

### 19.2.1   Viewing attachments in the user interface

To be able to add attachments to an item, the message body control must be present. If you have customized a form to remove the message body, neither users nor your code will be able to add any attachments to items that use that form. Existing attachments will be available, but only through programming code, not through the user interface.

Plain text and HTML-format messages and posts display attachments in a small separate pane above the message body control. RTF-format messages and posts and all other Outlook items display attachments as icons in the item body control. In the initial release of Outlook 2007, all attachments added programmatically to RTF items appear at the end of the item.

## 19.2.2 Creating a "freedoc" in an Outlook folder

Outlook allows users to drag files from the file system into an Outlook folder. Such an independent file, not attached to an Outlook message, appointment, etc. is called a *freedoc* and appears in Outlook with an icon related to the original file type. However, it is actually a `DocumentItem` object with a single attached file. You can create such freedocs programmatically using the `PostFile()` procedure in Listing 19.1, which takes a file path string and an `Outlook.Folder` object as its parameters. The code sample is for VBA, but can be adapted to VBScript simply by removing the `As` clauses in the procedure and variable declarations.

As a usage example, this VBA code snippet would copy a file named agenda.pdf into the Drafts folder:

```
Set objFolder = _
   Application.Session.GetDefaultFolder(olFolderDrafts)
Call PostFile("C:\data\agenda.pdf", objFolder)
```

Changing the value of the `MessageClass` property from the original class, IPM.Document, to a new file-specific class will change the icon to one appropriate for the type of file. To discover more message classes for different types of files, drag a file into a folder and check the value of the `MessageClass` property on the item that Outlook creates.

**Listing 19.1**    *Create a "freedoc" DocumentItem in an Outlook folder*

```
Sub PostFile(strFilePath As String, objFolder As Folder)
    Dim objDocItem As Outlook.DocumentItem
    Dim strFileType As String
    Dim intLoc As Integer
    Dim objAtt As Outlook.Attachment
    On Error Resume Next
    Set objDocItem = objFolder.Items.Add("IPM.Document")
    Set objAtt = objDocItem.Attachments.Add(strFilePath)
    objDocItem.Subject = objAtt.FileName
    intLoc = InStrRev(strFilePath, ".")
    strFileType = LCase(Mid(strFilePath, intLoc + 1))
    Select Case strFileType
        Case "doc", "docx"
            objDocItem.MessageClass = _
                            "IPM.Document.Word.Document"
        Case "xls", "xlsx"
            objDocItem.MessageClass = "IPM.Document.Excel.Sheet"
```

**Listing 19.1** *Create a "freedoc" DocumentItem in an Outlook folder (continued)*

```
    Case "pps", "pptx"
        objDocItem.MessageClass = _
                        "IPM.Document.PowerPoint.Show"
    Case "pub", "pubx"
        objDocItem.MessageClass = _
                        "IPM.Document.Publisher.Document"
    Case "jpg"
        objDocItem.MessageClass = "IPM.Document.jpegfile"
    Case "pdf"
        objDocItem.MessageClass = _
                        "IPM.Document.AcroExch.Document"
    Case Else
        objDocItem.MessageClass = "IPM.Document." & _
                            strFileType & "file"
    End Select
    If Err = 0 Then
        objDocItem.Save
    End If
    Set objDocItem = Nothing
End Sub
```

## 19.3 Working with attachments on existing items

As noted earlier, file and Outlook item attachments are stored in individual Outlook items and are not accessible directly as Outlook files or items. This means that to work with the data in an attachment, you must first save the item or file to the file system.

Outlook does this automatically when users work with files in the user interface. When a user opens an attachment from the reading pane, Outlook copies the file to a folder to hold temporary files, and opens the file as read-only. No changes the user makes are saved back into the file.

In contrast, when the user opens an attachment from an open item, Outlook copies the file to the file system and opens it for editing. If the user makes changes and closes and saves the file, those changes are saved back to the open Outlook item. The user must then save the changes to the Outlook item in order to persist the changes to the attachment. If the user doesn't save the file or doesn't save the item, the changes do not get stored in the original Outlook item.

**Note:** It bears repeating that if a file is attached (`Type = olByValue`), not linked (`Type = olByReference`), Outlook maintains no connection to the original file and neither knows nor cares where the original file is located.

Code that makes changes to an attached file must follow a similar process. To update an attachment already present in an item's `Attachments` collection, you must:

1. Save that attachment as a file using the `Attachment.SaveAsFile` method

2. Make any changes you want to the file using the application appropriate for that file

3. Save the updated file

4. Remove the old file from the Outlook item using the `Attachments.Remove` or `Attachment.Delete` method

5. Attach the updated file to the Outlook item using `Attachments.Add`

In the following sections, we will learn how to save attachments to the file system, how to detect files that are not visible in the user interface, and how to open saved files in their appropriate application. We will also see some practical applications of these techniques, such as replying to a message and including the original attachments and saving an HTML-format message without saving its embedded images twice.

## 19.3.1  Saving attachments to the file system

To save an attachment to the file system, the `Attachment.SaveAsFile` method requires one parameter, a string containing the path and name for the file. Usually, you will want to use the file's original name. Therefore, most code routines using `SaveAsFile` build a path string, for example:

```
Set objAtt = objItem.Attachments(1)
strPath = "C:\Data\" & objAtt.FileName
objAtt.SaveAsFile strPath
```

Three important things to remember about the `SaveAsFile` method:

- It is available only if the value of `Attachment.Type` is `olByValue` or `olEmbeddedItem`.

- The `Attachment.PathName` property is irrelevant to the `SaveAsFile` method; it is relevant only if `Attachment.Type` is `olByReference`. Your code must always supply the path, not just the file name.

- The `SaveAsFile` method overwrites any existing file with the same name, without warning. Therefore, if you are planning to save a file permanently (rather than just use it temporarily), it is a good practice to use the `FileSystemObject` techniques that we saw in Chapter 8 to determine if a file with the same name already exists. If it does, you can ask the user whether to overwrite that file. Listing 19.5 provides an example of this technique.

A review of the `FileSystemObject` material might be worthwhile in any case, since even saving files temporarily—as in our first two examples— uses `FileSystemObject` techniques such as returning the user's Temp folder and deleting a file. In this chapter, we'll also see an example of creating a new system folder to hold saved attachment files. Notice that the VBA samples require that you use the Tools | References command to add a reference to the Microsoft Scripting Runtime Library.

## 19.3.2   Example: Import embedded Outlook items

The first `SaveAsFile` example demonstrates how to import Outlook items that may be embedded in an email message and save and display them. To make this VBA sample as useful as possible, it handles not just Outlook items embedded with `Attachment.Type = olEmbedded`, but also vCard .vcf and iCalendar .ics and .vcs files that are attached as `Attachment.Type = olByValue` or as links with `Attachment.Type = olByReference`.

To test the `ImportOutlookItems` procedure in Listing 19.2, call it by passing an Outlook item as a parameter, for example:

```
Call ImportOutlookItems(GetCurrentItem())
```

where `GetCurrentItem()` is the procedure from Listing 15.5 that returns the currently open or selected item.

**Listing 19.2**   *Import Outlook item attachments*

```
Sub ImportOutlookItems(item As Outlook.MailItem)
    Dim objAtt As Outlook.Attachment
    Dim objNS As Outlook.NameSpace
    Dim objItem As Object
    Dim objFolder As Outlook.Folder
    ' requires reference to Microsoft Scripting Runtime
    Dim objFSO As Scripting.FileSystemObject
    Dim objFldTemp  As Scripting.Folder
    Dim strPath As String
    Dim strFile As String
    Dim strFileExt As String
    Dim intPos As Integer
    Dim blnUseTempFile As Boolean
    On Error Resume Next
    Set objNS = item.Session
    Set objFSO = CreateObject("Scripting.FileSystemObject")
    Set objFldTemp = objFSO.GetSpecialFolder(TemporaryFolder)
    strPath = objFldTemp.Path & "\"
    For Each objAtt In item.Attachments
        intPos = InStrRev(objAtt.fileName, ".")
        If intPos > 0 Then
            strFileExt = Mid(objAtt.fileName, intPos)
            Select Case objAtt.Type
                Case olByReference
```

**Listing 19.2** *Import Outlook item attachments (continued)*

```
                If InStr(".vcf.ics.vcs", strFileExt) > 0 Then
                    strFile = objAtt.PathName
                    strFileExt = Mid(strFileExt, 2)
                    blnUseTempFile = False
                Else
                    strFileExt = ""
                End If
            Case olByValue
                If InStr(".vcf.ics.vcs", strFileExt) > 0 Then
                    strFile = strPath & objAtt.fileName
                    objAtt.SaveAsFile strFile
                    strFileExt = Mid(strFileExt, 2)
                    blnUseTempFile = True
                Else
                    strFileExt = ""
                End If
            Case olEmbeddeditem
                strFile = Left(objAtt.fileName, intPos - 1)
                strFile = CleanFileName(strFile)
                strFile = strPath & strFile & ".msg"
                objAtt.SaveAsFile strFile
                strFileExt = "msg"
                blnUseTempFile = True
            End Select
        End If
        If strFileExt <> "" Then
            Select Case strFileExt
                Case "msg", "vcf", "vcs"
                    Set objItem = objNS.OpenSharedItem(strFile)
                    objItem.Save
                    objItem.Display
                Case "ics"
                    Set objItem = objNS.OpenSharedItem(strFile)
                    If Err.Number <> 0 Then
                        Set objFolder = _
                            objNS.OpenSharedFolder(strFile)
                        objFolder.GetExplorer.Activate
                    Else
                        objItem.Display
                    End If
            End Select
            If blnUseTempFile Then
                objFSO.DeleteFile strFile, True
            End If
        End If
    Next
    Set objAtt = Nothing
    Set objItem = Nothing
    Set objFolder = Nothing
    Set objNS = Nothing
    Set objFldTemp = Nothing
    Set objFSO = Nothing
End Sub
```

**Listing 19.2**    *Import Outlook item attachments (continued)*

```
Function CleanFileName(fileName As String) As String
    Dim strBadChars As String
    Dim strChar As String
    Dim i As Integer
    strBadChars = "*|\:<>?/" & Chr(34)
    For i = 1 To Len(strBadChars)
        fileName = Replace(fileName, Mid(strBadChars, i, 1), "_")
    Next
    CleanFileName = fileName
End Function
```

After the procedure runs, you should see each attached Outlook item open in its own window, and also an open window showing any calendar folder that was attached as an .ics calendar file. Notice how the procedure deals with the possibility that an .ics file can hold either a single appointment or an entire calendar's worth of appointments:

```
Set objItem = objNS.OpenSharedItem(strFile)
If Err.Number <> 0 Then
    Set objFolder = _
       objNS.OpenSharedFolder(strFile)
    objFolder.GetExplorer.Activate
Else
    objItem.Display
End If
```

It tries first to open the .ics file as an appointment, but if that fails (`Err.Number <> 0`), it tries again, this time opening the file as a shared calendar folder.

The `CleanFileName()` helper function is useful any time you need to make sure that your file name does not contain any characters that Windows does not allow in file names. We'll use it again later in Listing 19.6.

### 19.3.3    Example: Reply with attachments

For our second example, let's look at a more general Outlook programming challenge and a specific application of the solution to that challenge. The challenge is to copy an attachment from one item to another. Recall that you cannot copy a `Recipient` object from one message to another but need to use `Recipients.Add` method instead. Attachments work the same way: You cannot copy an `Attachment` object from one item to another directly, but must add the attachment through the `Attachments.Add` method. The `Attachments.Add` method requires a saved file. Therefore, to copy an attached file from one item to another, you must save the file first. As with the code in Listing 19.2, the `CopyAtts()` procedure in Listing 19.3 uses a temporary folder to save the files and deletes them afterwards. This time, the code is for VBScript; you can use it in VBA by commenting out the three Outlook constant declarations.

**Listing 19.3**  *Copy attachments between Outlook items*

```
Sub CopyAtts(source, target)
    Dim objFSO, fldTemp, strPath, strFile
    Dim objAtt, blnUseTempFile
    Const olByReference = 4
    Const olByValue = 1
    Const olEmbeddeditem = 5
    Const TemporaryFolder = 2
    Set objFSO = CreateObject("Scripting.FileSystemObject")
    Set fldTemp = objFSO.GetSpecialFolder(TemporaryFolder)
    strPath = fldTemp.Path & "\"
    For Each objAtt In source.Attachments
        Select Case objAtt.Type
            Case olByReference
                strFile = objAtt.PathName
                blnUseTempFile = False
            Case olByValue, olEmbeddeditem
                strFile = strPath & objAtt.fileName
                objAtt.SaveAsFile strFile
                blnUseTempFile = True
        End Select
        If blnUseTempFile Then
            target.Attachments.Add strFile, olByValue
            objFSO.DeleteFile strFile
        Else
            target.Attachments.Add strFile, olByReference
        End If
    Next
    Set fldTemp = Nothing
    Set objFSO = Nothing
End Sub
```

**Listing 19.4**  *Reply with attachments from the original message*

```
Sub ReplyWithAtts()
    Dim objItem    ' As Object
    Dim objReply  ' As Outlook.MailItem
    ' GetCurrentItem() from Listing 15.6
    Set objItem = GetCurrentItem()
    Set objReply = objItem.Reply
    ' CopyAtts from Listing 19.3
    Call CopyAtts(objItem, objReply)
    objReply.Display
    Set objReply = Nothing
    Set objItem = Nothing
End Sub
```

As an application of the `CopyAtts()` procedure, consider this common Outlook scenario: You want to reply to someone who sent you an attachment, but you want to include the latest version of the attachment with your own edits. Outlook does not include attachments in replies, only in forwards. The `ReplyWithAtts()` procedure in Listing 19.4 provides a solution, replying to the original message and copying the attachments from the original message to the reply.

The code in Listing 19.4 is for VBScript, but would also work in VBA without modification.

## 19.3.4    Opening attachments

The right technique to open an attachment depends on the type of attachment. For an embedded Outlook item, the `ImportOutlookItems` procedure in Listing 19.2 shows how to open it with the `Namespace.OpenSharedFolder` method. That method can also handle .ics, .vcs, or .vcf files.

Another common scenario is opening an attached file so that you can process the data in it. Chapter 8 showed how to display a file using the Windows Script Host technique. However, if you want to work with the file's data, you need to know the programming methods appropriate to that particular type of file. For text files, use the `FileSystemObject` methods discussed in Chapter 8. We can't cover all types of files in this book, but to give you an example of how to approach this scenario, Listing 19.5 is a VBA procedure to open an Excel worksheet attachment and display a message box with the contents of the first cell. You can test the `OpenExcelWB` procedure with this statement, which uses the `GetCurrentItem()` function from Listing 15.5 to return the currently selected or open item:

```
Call OpenExcelWB(GetCurrentItem())
```

A typical application using this technique might be to process new incoming messages using the `NewMailEx` event or one of the other techniques from Chapter 11, extracting data from an attached Excel workbook for use in another VBA procedure or to create a report.

There are two key differences between this sample and the previous two. The `OpenExcelWB` procedure uses a fixed folder (C:\Data) not the user's Temp folder, and it asks the user to overwrite if a workbook file with the same name as the attachment already exists in that folder.

**Note:** We'll see more code for working with Excel in upcoming chapters. Listing 21.3 in Chapter 21 demonstrates how to import data from an Excel worksheet into Outlook. Listing 24.6 in Chapter 24 works in the other direction, filling a worksheet with details from items in the Inbox.

**Listing 19.5**    *Open an Excel workbook*

```
Sub OpenExcelWB(msg As Outlook.MailItem)
    Dim objAtt As Outlook.Attachment
    ' requires reference to Microsoft Excel library
    Dim objExcel As Excel.Application
    Dim objWB As Excel.Workbook
    ' requires reference to Scripting Runtime
    Dim objFSO As Scripting.FileSystemObject
    Dim intPos As Integer
    Dim strFile As String
    Dim strFileExt As String
    Dim strMsg As String
    Dim intRes As Integer
    For Each objAtt In msg.Attachments
        If objAtt.Type = olByValue Then
            strFile = objAtt.fileName
            intPos = InStrRev(strFile, ".")
            strFileExt = LCase(Mid(strFile, intPos + 1))
            If Left(strFileExt, 3) = "xls" Then
                strFile = "C:\Data\" & strFile
                Set objFSO = _
                  CreateObject("Scripting.FileSystemObject")
                If Not objFSO.FileExists(strFile) Then
                    objAtt.SaveAsFile strFile
                Else
                    strMsg = "File exists in temp folder. " & _
                            "Overwrite?"
                    intRes = MsgBox(strMsg, _
                                vbYesNo + vbQuestion, _
                                "Open attachment " & _
                                objAtt.fileName)
                    If intRes = vbYes Then
                        objFSO.DeleteFile strFile, True
                        objAtt.SaveAsFile strFile
                    Else
                        strMsg = "Could not save file"
                        MsgBox strMsg, vbExclamation, _
                                "Open attachment " & objAtt.fileName
                    End If
                    Exit For
                End If
                Set objExcel = CreateObject("Excel.Application")
                Set objWB = objExcel.Workbooks.Open(strFile)
                If Not objWB Is Nothing Then
                    strMsg = objWB.Sheets(1).Cells(1, 1)
                    MsgBox strMsg, , "Data in " & objAtt.fileName
                    objExcel.Visible = True
                    objWB.Activate
                End If
            End If
        End If
    Next
```

**Listing 19.5**   *Open an Excel workbook (continued)*

```
    Set objAtt = Nothing
    Set objExcel = Nothing
    Set objWB = Nothing
    Set objFSO = Nothing
End Sub
```

### 19.3.5  **Working with hidden attachments**

Just as Outlook items and the `AddressEntry` and `Folders` object support a `PropertyAccessor` property for access to hidden MAPI properties, so can you use `PropertyAccessor` to assist with some special attachment scenarios—especially working with hidden attachments. Such attachments, which the user does not see as attached files, play a role in at least two types of Outlook items:

■   Outlook contacts, which may contain a contact picture as a hidden attachment named ContactPicture.jpg

■   HTML-format messages and posts, which may contain hidden image files shown to the user as inline images through `<img>` tags

To help us explore the concept of hidden attachments, the VBA sample code in Listing 19.6 saves an HTML-format message to the file system as an HTML file, along with all its attachments. Outlook automatically creates a folder to hold embedded images and other content files that help format the item. Therefore, the code doesn't need to save those hidden attachment files a second time. It should save only the non-hidden files—the ones the user actually sees in the user interface. You can test the `Save-HTMLMessage` procedure with this statement, using the `GetCurrent-Item()` function from Listing 15.5:

```
    Call SaveHTMLMessage(GetCurrentItem())
```

These code statements are the key to determining if an attachment is a hidden component of the message and saving only the "real" attachments:

```
Set objPA = objAtt.PropertyAccessor
strContentID = objPA.GetProperty(PR_ATTACH_CONTENT_ID)
If Err = 0 Then
  If InStr(1, strHTML, strContentID, vbTextCompare) > 0 Then
      objAtt.SaveAsFile strAttFolderPath & objAtt.fileName
  End If
Else
  objAtt.SaveAsFile strAttFolderPath & objAtt.fileName
End If
```

If the `PR_ATTACH_CONTENT_ID` property is present—that is, if `Get-Property(PR_ATTACH_CONTENT_ID)` does not return an error—then you

Listing 19.6   *Save an HTML-format message with all attachments*

```
Sub SaveHTMLMessage(msg As Outlook.MailItem)
    Dim objPA As Outlook.PropertyAccessor
    Dim objAtt As Outlook.Attachment
    ' requires reference to Scripting Runtime library
    Dim objFSO As Scripting.FileSystemObject
    Dim objFolder As Scripting.Folder
    Dim strPath As String
    Dim strCleanSubject As String
    Dim strAttFolderPath As String
    Dim strAttFilePath As String
    Dim strContentID As String
    Dim strHTML As String
    Const PR_ATTACH_CONTENT_ID = _
      "http://schemas.microsoft.com/mapi/proptag/0x3712001E"
    If msg.BodyFormat <> olFormatHTML Then
        Exit Sub
    End If
    strPath = "C:\Data\"
    ' CleanFileName from Listing 19.2
    strCleanSubject = CleanFileName(Trim(msg.Subject))
    strHTML = msg.HTMLBody
    msg.SaveAs strPath & strCleanSubject & ".htm", olHTML
    strAttFolderPath = strPath & strCleanSubject & "_files"
    Set objFSO = CreateObject("Scripting.FileSystemObject")
    If objFSO.FolderExists(strAttFolderPath) Then
        Set objFolder = objFSO.GetFolder(strAttFolderPath)
    Else
        Set objFolder = objFSO.CreateFolder(strAttFolderPath)
    End If
    strAttFolderPath = strAttFolderPath & "\"
    For Each objAtt In msg.Attachments
        Set objPA = objAtt.PropertyAccessor
        strContentID = _
          objPA.GetProperty(PR_ATTACH_CONTENT_ID)
        If Err = 0 Then
            If InStr(1, strHTML, _
                    strContentID, vbTextCompare) > 0 Then
                objAtt.SaveAsFile _
                  strAttFolderPath & objAtt.fileName
            End If
        Else
            objAtt.SaveAsFile _
              strAttFolderPath & objAtt.fileName
        End If
    Next
    MsgBox "Message saved!", , "Save HTML Message"
    Set objAtt = Nothing
    Set objPA = Nothing
    Set objFolder = Nothing
    Set objFSO = Nothing
End Sub
```

know you have a probable hidden attachment. The confirmation that it's an attachment associated with the message content comes from the result of the `Instr()` function, which searches the HTML content of the message to see if the content ID is present there. If it is, you know the attachment is hidden and does not need to be saved a second time, because Outlook already saved it when you called `SaveAs` on the message itself.

## 19.4  Summary

This chapter demonstrated how to insert files and Outlook items into Outlook items as embedded or linked attachments and how to extract those attachments so your applications can use them and the data they contain. Of particular interest is the fact that HTML-format messages may include hidden attachments that the user doesn't see with a paperclip icon but that are essential to the layout and formatting of the message.

To work with Outlook attachments, you often need to look beyond Outlook to other object models, such as the Scripting Runtime library and its `FileSystemObject`, which provides key methods for working with the Windows file system, or object models for Excel, Word, and other Office applications. For example, copying an attachment from one item to another involves saving the item first to the file system and later deleting it after the copy operation is complete.

For more on attachments, see Chapter 23, where we'll discuss how to program the context menu that appears when the user right-clicks on an attachment in the reading pane or an open item.

# Common Item Techniques

Earlier chapters in this section have covered many basic techniques for working with Outlook items—creating them, finding them, manipulating text in item bodies, dealing with attachments, adding and removing recipients, and so on. This chapter rounds out your Outlook item skills with some techniques that are common to all Outlook items and some that are specific to messages, contacts, and other individual item types.

Most of the examples in this chapter combine several of the techniques covered earlier and involve multiple steps. For example, to create a meeting request, you need to set a property, and then add recipients. To create a task request, you need to execute a method, and then add recipients. To add a contact's phone number to a task, you need to look up the contact, read a property value to get the phone number, set a property on the task, then save the task. As you look at these examples, think about how you might combine the basic Outlook item techniques they illustrate to construct your own Outlook applications.

Highlights of this chapter include discussions of the following:

- Why Outlook message forms usually are a poor choice for surveys and other data-gathering operations

- How to use voting buttons to create a vacation request form that generates an appointment for approved requests

- How to determine the user's default email account and use that account to send all messages

- How to create a meeting request and assign a task

- What different methods are available to build links between Outlook items

- How to automatically add a contact's phone number to a task

- How to create appointments related to a custom date field on a contact form

# 20.1  Using custom message forms

Two key Outlook security features discussed in Chapter 10 limit the practical applications of Outlook custom message forms:

- Code runs only on published forms.

- Unpublished forms that include custom properties will not display their custom layouts if launched from an .oft file.

A third factor hindering custom message form usage is the mysterious Winmail.dat file. For messages created with a published form, Outlook transmits information about the form and any custom fields by attaching a file named Winmail.dat to the outgoing message. The Winmail.dat file also encapsulates any attachments added to the custom form message. Only Outlook recipients can make sense of the data in this file. If you use a published custom form to send a message to a non-Outlook recipient, at best the recipient will be puzzled by the Winmail.dat attachment. But worse, the recipient will not see any normal attachments that you included in the message.

**Note:** Voting button messages, which are covered later in the chapter, also carry a Winmail.dat attachment, so you'll want to be careful to use them only with known Outlook recipients.

These limitations restrict the practical use of Outlook message forms to this narrow list of applications:

- Message templates with no custom fields or code, saved as .oft files

- Published message forms that use code to generate new messages based on the standard message form

- Message forms that are internal to an organization and are published to the Organizational Forms library on an Exchange server or to each user's Personal Forms library

The first application, message templates saved as .oft files, covers the boilerplate messages that you send frequently, including voting button messages. As long as the message "form" consists only of your custom message body, subject, recipients, custom actions, and other standard properties, it will work fine when saved and launched from an .oft file. What will cause problems is including custom fields in such a saved message template. The chief practical implication of this limitation is that you cannot conduct a survey by sending a message form .oft file to other users or to customers to fill out and return to you.

**Tip:** The Microsoft Office applications that can conduct surveys by email are InfoPath 2007 and Access 2007. Access can generate HTML-format messages that collect data to populate a database table. Included with Office 2007 is an add-in for Outlook that automatically updates the records in the database with the email responses received. InfoPath is a relatively new application with robust form design capability that is much easier to use than Outlook's designer.

For an example of the second application—published message forms that generate a message based on the standard form—consider this scenario: Much of the mail you send involves the same subjects or the same recipients. You want to streamline the process by providing dropdown lists for the Subject, To, or Cc fields. Such a form might help you work more efficiently, but any recipients who don't use Outlook will encounter the Winmail.dat problem described above. The solution is to write code behind your published form that creates a new standard message using the information that you've gathered with the custom form. The code in Listing 20.1 shows how to use the `Item_Send` event handler on the published form to create a new message that uses the body, recipients, attachments, and other properties of the original item (the one created from the published form).

The procedure uses three different techniques to copy the item body from the original message to the outgoing message, depending on the message format of the original. For a plain text message, it copies the `Body` property. For an HTML message, it copies `HTMLBody`. For an rich-text message, it uses Word objects in the `CopyFormattedBody` helper procedure to copy and paste the content from one item to another. It also changes the `BodyFormat` property so that the outgoing message is in HTML format.

The original custom form message stays open on the screen after the `Item_Send` event handler creates and sends the new standard message. Using the `Close` method in a form's VBScript code can cause the original release of Outlook 2007 to crash.

The third type of custom message form—that used internally in an organization—can serve many purposes. It can conduct a survey of staff members or facilitate a workflow, for example. It can even distribute custom Outlook settings, as we'll see in Chapter 22. What distinguishes this type of message form is that, because it is a published form, it can run code both for the sender and for the recipient.

**Listing 20.1**    *Create a new standard message from the content of a custom form message*

```
Function Item_Send()
    Dim objMsg       ' As Outlook.MailItem
    Dim objRecip     ' As Outlook.Recipient
    Dim objNewRecip  ' As Outlook.Recipient
    Const olMailItem = 0
    Const olFormatPlain = 1
    Const olFormatHTML = 2
    Const olFormatRichText = 3
    On Error Resume Next
    Item_Send = False
    Set objMsg = Application.CreateItem(olMailItem)
    For Each objRecip In Item.Recipients
        Set objNewRecip = _
          objMsg.Recipients.Add(objRecip.address)
        If objNewRecip.Resolve Then
            objNewRecip.Type = objRecip.Type
        End If
    Next
    If Item.Attachments.Count > 0 Then
        Call CopyAtts(Item, objMsg)      'CopyAtts procedure from Listing 19.3
    End If
    With objMsg
        Select Case Item.BodyFormat
            Case olFormatPlain
                .BodyFormat = olFormatPlain
                .Body = Item.Body
            Case olFormatHTML
                .BodyFormat = olFormatHTML
                .HTMLBody = Item.HTMLBody
            Case olFormatRichText
                .BodyFormat = olFormatHTML
                Call CopyFormattedBody(Item, objMsg)
        End Select
        .Categories = Item.Categories
        .DeferredDeliveryTime = Item.DeferredDeliveryTime
        .DeleteAfterSubmit = Item.DeleteAfterSubmit
        .ExpiryTime = Item.ExpiryTime
        .Importance = Item.Importance
        .OriginatorDeliveryReportRequested = _
          Item.OriginatorDeliveryReportRequested
        .ReadReceiptRequested = _
          Item.ReadReceiptRequested
        .ReminderSet = Item.ReminderSet
        .ReminderTime = Item.ReminderTime
        .Subject = Item.Subject
        If .Recipients.count > 0 _
          And .Recipients.ResolveAll Then
            .Send
            MsgBox "Message sent successfully. " & _
                   "You can close the original now."
        Else
            .Display
        End If
```

**Listing 20.1**  *Create a new standard message from the content of a custom form message (continued)*

```
    End With
    Set objMsg = Nothing
    Set objRecip = Nothing
    Set objNewRecip = Nothing
End Function

Sub CopyFormattedBody(oldItem, newItem)
    Dim objOldDoc    ' As Word.Document
    Dim objNewDoc    ' As Word.Document
    Dim objRange     ' As Word.Range
    Const wdPasteDefault = 0
    Set objOldDoc = oldItem.GetInspector.WordEditor
    Set objNewDoc = newItem.GetInspector.WordEditor
    Set objRange = objOldDoc.Content
    objRange.Select
    objRange.Copy
    Set objRange = objNewDoc.Content
    objRange.Select
    objRange.PasteAndFormat wdPasteDefault
    Set objOldDoc = Nothing
    Set objNewDoc = Nothing
    Set objRange = Nothing
End Sub
```

> **Tip:** In Chapter 22, we'll build a message form that installs a custom form for a user and another message form that transmits a report on the user's Outlook rules. Both of these work only if published to the Organizational Forms library.

However, before you start designing a custom message form for internal use, be aware that many organizations cannot meet the minimum prerequisites for forms that run code. Some that have Exchange as their mail server do not permit users to publish forms to the Organizational Forms library, which is the central forms registry. Others don't have Exchange and are not inclined to go to the effort to publish a custom form to each user's Personal Forms library. (The next chapter includes a script to publish a custom form programmatically.) Before you put a lot of effort into writing code for a custom message form, find out whether you will be able to publish that form so others can use it.

The next few sections discuss the Reply, Forward, and CustomAction actions and associated events, which are crucial to the operation of many custom message forms.

### 20.1.1   Controlling the settings for replies and forwards

The options on the (Actions) page of a custom form govern the behavior of the standard Reply, Reply to All, and Forward commands. You can disable any of these commands by setting the Enabled option to `False` on the (Actions) page.

If you are creating a custom message form, you should always visit the (Actions) page and update the Forward action's Message Class option so that it points to the same published custom form. This form must be in the Personal Forms library or Organizational Forms library. For example, if you have a custom message form published with the class IPM.Note.MyForm, use the (Actions) page to set the Message Class option for the Forward action also to IPM.Note.MyForm. If you leave the Message Class option on its default setting (IPM.Note), when the user forwards an item that uses your custom form, the form definition will one-off, becoming embedded in the item, where it will no longer run code and may not even be able to display your custom page layout.

You can also set the Reply action to use a custom form. However, replies do not automatically copy property values from the original item to the reply, unless you write code to perform that task.

### 20.1.2   Adding code to the Reply and Forward events

The `Reply`, `ReplyAll`, and `Forward` events fire when the user replies to or forwards a message through the user interface or when code calls the `Reply`, `ReplyAll`, or `Forward` method. Each of these events creates a new message. Whether the new message uses a custom form depends on the settings on the (Actions) tab of the form, as described in the previous section.

However, replying to a message does not copy data from the original message to the reply, except for the subject and message body. Forwarding a message copies attachments, as well as the subject and message body, but neither reply nor forward messages copy the categories set on the original message. This has substantial implications for a scenario that would seem to be a natural fit for an Outlook custom message form solution: gathering information from users. Because replies and forwards won't copy data fields automatically, to perform information gathering with custom message forms, you must write code to propagate property values from one message to another. That also means that custom message forms can't be used to gather data from customers, even if they use Outlook, because such forms outside your organization won't run code.

Let's assume, though, that you can publish forms to the Organizational Forms library or each user's Personal Forms library. The event handlers for the `Reply`, `ReplyAll`, and `Forward` events all follow a similar structure:

Outlook passes the new item created by the event as a parameter to the event handler. For example, this code behind a custom form would pop up a message box with the subject of each newly created reply or forward message before displaying it:

```
Function Item_Reply(ByVal Response)
    MsgBox Response.Subject, , "Reply"
    Response.Display
End Function

Function Item_ReplyAll(ByVal Response)
    MsgBox Response.Subject, , "Reply to All"
    Response.Display
End Function

Function Item_Forward(ByVal ForwardItem)
    MsgBox ForwardItem.Subject, , "Forward"
    ForwardItem.Display
End Function
```

Just because the event creates a new message doesn't mean that you have to use that message. To cancel any of these events so that the new item is not created, set the return value of the function to `False`. This statement, for example, cancels the `Item_Reply` event:

```
Item_Reply = False
```

As an example, let's say that your organization always use a certain custom form to send particular documents and wants the users to send back those attached files when they reply. A reply message doesn't transmit the original message's attachments, but a forward message does include the attachments. On the other hand, forwarding the item doesn't address the new message to the original sender. To get the best of both events, the `Item_Reply` event handler in Listing 20.2 uses the `Forward` method to create a new message and populates the message's `To` property from the sender information on the original item. The user clicks Reply as usual, without any need for a special command.

The `Reply` event handler in Listing 20.2 replies either to all the recipients in the `ReplyRecipients` collection or, if that collection is empty, to the original sender. When using this technique, you may want to use the (Actions) page to disable the Reply to All command. Alternatively, you could expand the code in Listing 20.2 to iterate all the original `Item.Recipients` and `ReplyRecipients` collections and add each of those recipient addresses to the `Recipients` collection on the new forward item. Go back to Listing 18.5 if you want to see an example of working with the `ReplyRecipients` collection.

To copy property values other than the subject, item body, and attachments, you need code behind the form. This code snippet expands the `With objForward` block in Listing 20.2 to copy the `Categories` property

**Listing 20.2**      *Discard a reply and send a forward instead*

```
Function Item_Reply(ByVal Response)
    Dim objForward  ' As Outlook.MailItem
    On Error Resume Next
    Item_Reply = False
    For Each objRecip In Item.ReplyRecipients
        If objRecip.Type = True Then
            strAddress = strAddress & ";" & _
                         objRecip.Name & " [" & _
                         objRecip.AddressEntry.Type & _
                         ":" & objRecip.address & "]"
        End If
    Next
    If strAddress = "" Then
        strAddress = Item.SenderName & " [" & _
                     Item.SenderEmailType & _
                     ":" & Item.SenderEmailAddress & "]"
    End If
    Set objForward = Item.Forward
    With objForward
        .To = strAddress
        .Subject = Response.Subject
        .Display
    End With
    Set objForward = Nothing
End Function
```

value and the values of all custom properties from the original item to the forward message:

```
With objForward
    .To = strAddress
    .Subject = Response.Subject
    .Categories = Item.Categories
    For Each objProp in Item.UserProperties
        Set objFwdProp = .UserProperties(objProp.Name)
        objFwdProp.Value = objProp.Value
    Next
    .Display
End With
```

You could expand this technique further to copy other property values such as Importance.

## 20.2  Working with voting buttons and other custom actions

Each Outlook item has an Actions collection that contains various Action objects that represent key "verbs" for the item; Reply, Reply to All, and Forward are all represented in the Actions collection, along with any custom actions created for the item. Custom actions are a unique Outlook tech-

**Figure 20.1**
*Outlook clearly marks voting button messages in the reading pane.*

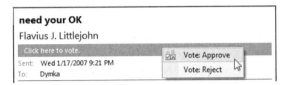

nique that can create a new item from an existing item and run code related to the new item.

Voting buttons are the most familiar application of custom actions. To add voting buttons to an open message, switch to the Options tab in the ribbon, and then click Use Voting Buttons. You can choose from one of three standard sets of buttons or click Custom and type in your own names for the buttons, separated by semicolons.

Only one set of voting buttons appears per item. When a user receives a voting button message and clicks on one of the voting buttons (see Figure 20.1), Outlook generates a response back to the sender. The sender's copy of Outlook tallies those responses and stores them in the original voting button message (as long as that original message remains in the Sent Items folder). Each person's `Recipient` object stores that person's "vote" in the `AutoResponse` property.

As with other custom action applications, a voting button message works only if both the sender and all the recipients are using Outlook as their mail program. Each voting button corresponds to a custom action in the outgoing message's `Actions` collection and uses default property values that determine what kind of response will come back from recipients. Figure 20.2 shows two voting buttons, Approve and Disapprove, and the Form Action Properties dialog for the Approve button.

Voting buttons create custom actions with properties that return the "votes" to the original sender. As you'll see in the next section, Outlook provides many options for customizing voting buttons and creating actions other than voting buttons.

### 20.2.1 Custom Action Properties

The `Actions` collection supports `Add`, `Item`, and `Remove` methods like most other Outlook collections. To create a new voting button or other custom action for an Outlook item, call the `Actions.Add` method to create the action and then set properties for the new `Action`. Here's a code snippet from Listing 10.3, which creates a message (`objMsg`) and then adds voting buttons, getting the names for the actions from a comma-delimited string:

```
arrActions = Split(strActions, ",")
Set objAction = objMsg.Actions.Add
```

```
With objAction
    .CopyLike = olRespond
    .Enabled = True
    .Name = Trim(arrActions(i))
    .Prefix = ""
    .ReplyStyle = olOmitOriginalText
    .ResponseStyle = olPrompt
    .ShowOn = olMenuAndToolbar
End With
```

Use Table 20.1 to help understand which option in the Form Action Properties dialog box (refer to Figure 20.2) corresponds to a particular property of the `Action` object.

How does a user know that an item has custom actions? Messages with voting button actions have a clear indicator in the reading pane—the "Click here to vote" area, shown in Figure 20.1. For an open voting button message, Outlook shows a Vote command on the ribbon. Vote options are also listed on the right-click context menu for the item in the folder view.

Users will see custom action command buttons only on sent or saved items. The indicators are similar to those for voting button messages. If the `ShowOn` property of the action is set to `olMenu` or `olMenuAndToolbar`, the custom action command will appear on the right-click context menu for

**Figure 20.2**
*Voting buttons create custom Response actions.*

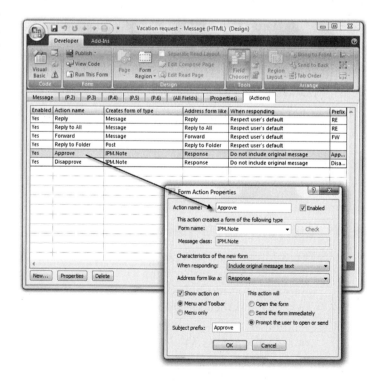

**Table 20.1** *Outlook Form Action Properties*

| Form Action Property Settings | Object Property | Possible Values | Outlook Constant (Value) |
|---|---|---|---|
| Address Form Like | CopyLike | Reply | olReply (0) |
| | | Reply to all | olReplyAll (1) |
| | | Forward | olForward (2) |
| | | Reply to folder | olReplyFolder (3) |
| | | Response | olRespond (4) |
| Enabled | Enabled | True or false | |
| Message Class | MessageClass | (Any published form) | |
| Action Name | Name | (Any name) | |
| Subject Prefix | Prefix | (Any prefix) | |
| When Responding | ReplyStyle | Do not include original message text | olOmitOriginalText (0) |
| | | Attach original message | olEmbedOriginalItem (1) |
| | | Include original message text | olIncludeOriginalText (2) |
| | | Include and indent original message text | olIndentOriginalText (3) |
| | | Prefix each line of the original message | olReplyTickOriginalText (1000) |
| | | Attach link to the original message | olLinkOriginalItem (4) |
| | | Respect user's default | olUserPreference (5) |
| This Action Will | ResponseStyle | Open the form | olOpen (0) |
| | | Send the form immediately | olSend (1) |
| | | Prompt the user to open or send | olPrompt (2) |
| Show Action On | ShowOn | Don't show | olDontShow (0) |
| | | Menu and toolbar | olMenu (1) |
| | | Menu only | olMenuAndToolbar (2) |

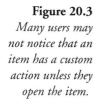

**Figure 20.3**
*Many users may
not notice that an
item has a custom
action unless they
open the item.*

the item. The clearest indicator that the item has a custom action comes
from an open item (Figure 20.3), which displays the Custom Action button
on the ribbon to indicate that it has one or more custom actions. Later in
this chapter, we'll see how to use a command button on a custom form to
make a custom action more visible.

---

**Note:** For the Show Action On option, the "Menu and Toolbar" and
"Menu Only" settings are essentially equivalent, since Outlook 2007 does
not have the Response toolbar that previous versions did.

---

**Caution:** Do not add a custom action programmatically to an item created
from a published form. Doing so will cause the form to one-off, embedding
it in the item, where it will no longer run code. Put all your custom actions
into the published form.

---

One of the key functions of a custom action is to create a new item. For
example, each action on a voting button message generates an email message containing the recipient's response. Custom actions also have a special
feature that can copy property values from the original item to the new
item. The CopyLike property (labeled on the (Actions) tab as Address
Form Like) governs how Outlook copies properties from the original item
to the new item that the custom action creates. Table 20.2 offers suggestions on when to use which option.

Notice that in Table 20.2, there's no Address Form Like option to copy
data from one message to another message. Instead, you'd need to write
code to copy data from one item to another, as shown in the example for
the Reply event in Listing 20.2.

## 20.2.2  Writing code for custom actions

A custom action can create other types of items besides messages. For example, a custom action on a custom contact form could generate a new task.

**Table 20.2**   *Suggested Uses for the Address Form Like Options*

| If You Want to . . . | Address Form Like . . . |
| --- | --- |
| Send a reply to the sender of the original item | Reply |
| Send a reply to the sender of the original item and any Cc recipients | Reply to all |
| Copy data from fields on one post item to fields of the same name on a different post item | Reply to folder (reply post form must be published in the same folder) |
| Copy data from fields on one task, contact, or appointment item to another item of the same type | Forward |
| Present the user with voting buttons, whose responses will be tracked on the Tracking tab of the original message in the sender's Sent Items folder | Response |
| Create a task, appointment, journal entry, or contact | Reply to Folder |

In fact, as a project that will help you learn about custom actions, let's add some actions to a custom contact form to restore functionality that Outlook 2003 has but Outlook 2007 doesn't. Outlook 2007 lacks the earlier version's menu command to create a new appointment related to a contact without creating a meeting request. It's not hard to add that functionality with a little code to go with a custom action.

The first thing you need to know in order to write that code is that, when the user clicks a voting button or other custom action button, the item's CustomAction event fires. In most cases an item will have more than one custom action. Therefore, the Item_CustomAction event handler has an extra parameter, compared with the event signatures for Item_Reply and Item_Forward. The two parameters for the Item_CustomAction event handler are:

Action          The custom action executed by the user

NewItem         The new Outlook item that the custom action creates

This event handler would pop up a message box for each Action whose button is clicked, displaying the Subject of the new item that the action creates and the display name of the Action:

```
Function Item_CustomAction(ByVal Action, ByVal NewItem)
    MsgBox NewItem.Subject, , Action.Name
End Function
```

For a more practical application, we can create a custom actions to replace a command that Outlook 2007 left out: the New Appointment with Contact command to create a linked appointment that isn't a meeting request. Open a new contact form in design mode and on the (Actions) page, create a custom action, using New Appointment with Contact  for the action name and entering IPM.Appointment for the corresponding form name:

For the "Address form like a" setting, choose Reply to Folder. You can accept the defaults for all the other action settings.

Next, add this code to the form:

```
Function Item_CustomAction(ByVal Action, ByVal NewItem)
    If Action.Name = "New Appointment with Contact" Then
        NewItem.Links.Add Item
    End If
End Function
```

Publish the form to your Contacts folder with the form name IPM.Contact.Actions. Use the Actions | New Actions command to create a contact with the new form, and then save and close the contact. (Remember that custom actions don't appear until you save an item.) Right-click the contact in the folder view; to see the New Appointment with Contact custom action you just created, refer to Figure 20.4. Open the item to see the custom action on the ribbon, as shown in Figure 20.3. Click the action to see Outlook create a new item that is linked to the current contact through the Links collection, which we'll discuss later in the chapter.

---

**Tip:** The New Journal Entry for Contact is also missing from the ribbon, but you can add it by customizing the Quick Access Toolbar. Look for the command on the All Commands list.

---

This is a very simple example of code for the CustomAction event, because there is only action on the form. More often, though, you'll want to

**Figure 20.4**
*Custom actions create commands on an item's right-click context menu.*

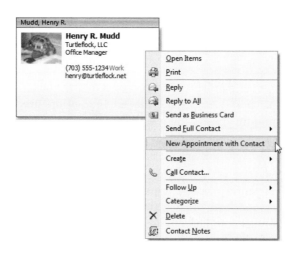

run code for several different actions. The best way to handle that scenario is with a `Select Case` block. Use a different `Case` for each action, or more precisely for each `Action.Name`, since it is the `Name` string property that distinguishes the actions.

For example, if you had a custom form with two voting buttons, Approve and Disapprove, the code to handle each action would fit into a structure such as this:

```
Function Item_CustomAction(ByVal Action, ByVal NewItem)
    Select Case Action.Name
        Case "Approve"
            ' approval code goes here
        Case "Disapprove"
            ' disapproval code goes here
        Case Else
            ' no need to do anything
    End Select
End Function
```

If you added a third action, you'd add another `Case` block after `Case "Disapprove"`.

The `NewItem` parameter for the `CustomAction` event is analogous to the `Response` parameter for the `Reply` event or the `ForwardItem` parameter for the `Forward` event and represents the new item that the action creates. As with those other events, you can prevent the item from being created by setting the return value of the `Item_CustomAction` event handler to `False`. This example sets the `Importance` property to `High` on the new item created by the `Approve` action, but cancels the creation of a new item for the `Disapprove` action

```
Function Item_CustomAction(ByVal Action, ByVal NewItem)
    Const olImportanceHigh = 2
    Select Case Action.Name
        Case "Approve"
            NewItem.Importance = olImportanceHigh
        Case "Disapprove"
            Item_CustomAction = False
    End Select
End Function
```

To put this technique to work, in the next section we'll build a simple vacation request form that sends an approved appointment back to the person making the request.

### 20.2.3  Example: A vacation approval form

Everyone likes to take vacations, right? However, unless you're the boss, someone must approve your time off. Instead of having every staffer submit their vacation request in their own fashion, an organization can standardize an Outlook message form with Approve and Disapprove buttons that a supervisor can use to act on a vacation request. To create the form, follow these steps:

1. Open a new message.

2. Enter "Vacation request" as the text for the subject.

3. Switch to the Options tab of the ribbon, click Use Voting Buttons, and then choose Custom.

4. On the Message Options dialog box, in the "Use voting buttons" box, replace the default button text ("Approve; Reject") with ("Approve; Disapprove"), and then click Close.

5. Switch to the Developer tab, and click Design This Form to put the message into design mode.

6. Set the Subject text box to read-only.

7. Select the large message body text box at the bottom of the form and drag the top of it down to make some room above the body of the message.

8. In the Field Chooser, create two new fields, VacationStart and VacationEnd, both as date/time fields. Drag them to the blank space above the message body to create two text boxes. Give the text box controls the names txtVacationStart and txtVacationEnd. Edit their labels so that the form looks like Figure 20.5. On the Value tab of each text box's Properties dialog, change the

**Figure 20.5**
*This custom message form will make it easy to request time off.*

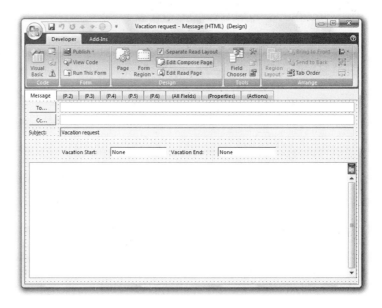

Format option so that it shows only the day of the week and the date, not the hours and minutes.

9. Select the `txtVacationStart` and `txtVacationEnd` text boxes and their labels, right-click, and choose Copy to copy them to the Clipboard.

10. Click Edit Read Page to switch to the form's read layout. Adjust the height of the large-message text box as you did in step 2.

11. Paste the copied text boxes and labels from step 4 into the blank area.

12. Set the `txtVacationStart` and `txtVacationEnd` text boxes on the read layout to be read-only.

---

**Tip:** Did you notice that we're using a message form, not an appointment form? This is a good example of how you can put Outlook forms to unexpected uses, based on the different features that each supports. Because the goal of the vacation approval form is simply to generate a response, not to schedule a meeting, a message form is more appropriate than an appointment form.

---

To see the properties of the voting buttons, switch to the (Actions) page of the form. You should see that two custom actions, Approve and Disapprove, were added.

The next step is to add code to the form that will automatically create an appointment item and send it back with the approval. The user who made the vacation request then can open the appointment and save it to the Calendar folder.

In the code window for the Vacation Request form, add the code shown in Listing 20.3. To test the form, you can publish it to your own Personal Forms library and send a vacation request to yourself. If other people are going to use it, though, you will need to publish it to the Organizational Forms library on the Exchange server or have each person publish it to their own Personal Forms library.

The `Item_CustomAction` event handler in Listing 20.3 handles both the Approve and Disapprove actions and puts appropriate text in the response message for each action. It enhances the Approve action by creating a new appointment from the data in the request message and attaching that appointment to the approval message. Once the saved appointment is attached, it is no longer needed, and so the code deletes it from the approver's mailbox.

---

**Note:** Why does Listing 20.3 use a vCalendar attachment created with the `objAppt.ForwardAsVCal` method instead of simply attaching `objAppt` itself? When a user receives and opens a vCal or iCal attachment, the open item's Save command will save the appointment in the Calendar folder. If the attachment were an Outlook appointment item, the user would need to drag the attached appointment to the Calendar folder—not as intuitive or easy a process as simply opening the vCal attachment and clicking Save.

---

**Listing 20.3**   *Enhance custom actions with code to build a more functional vacation request form*

```
Const olOutOfOffice = 3
Const olAppointmentItem = 1

Function Item_CustomAction(ByVal Action, ByVal NewItem)
    Dim objAppt      ' As Outlook.AppointmentItem
    Dim objMsg       ' As Outlook.MailItem
    Dim dteStart     ' As Date
    Dim dteEnd       ' As Date
    On Error Resume Next
    Select Case Action.Name
        Case "Approve"
            Item_CustomAction = False
            dteStart = _
                Item.UserProperties.Find("VacationStart")
            dteEnd = _
                Item.UserProperties.Find("VacationEnd")
            Set objAppt = _
                Application.CreateItem(olAppointmentItem)
            With objAppt
                .Start = dteStart
                .End = dteEnd
                .ReminderSet = False
                .Subject = "Vacation"
                .AllDayEvent = True
                .BusyStatus = olOutOfOffice
            End With
            objAppt.Save
            Set objMsg = objAppt.ForwardAsVcal
            ' CopyAtts from Listing 19.3
            Call CopyAtts(objMsg, NewItem)
            NewItem.Body = "Your vacation has been " & _
                        "approved. Open the attached " & _
                        "Appointment and save it " & _
                        " to your Calendar folder."
            NewItem.Send
```

Listing 20.3   *Enhance custom actions with code to build a more functional vacation request form (continued)*

```
            Case "Disapprove"
                NewItem.Body = "Your vacation has not been " & _
                               "approved. Please feel free " & _
                               "to submit other proposed dates."
                NewItem.Send
        End Select
        Set objAppt = Nothing
        Set objMsg = Nothing
End Function
```

### 20.2.4   **Using command buttons with custom actions**

To make the commands associated with your custom actions more noticeable, you may want to use command buttons on a custom form page to run them. You can enhance the Vacation Request form by adding two command buttons to the custom Message page's read layout. Give them the names `cmdApprove` and `cmdDisapprove`, with matching captions, and then add this code to the code that is already in the form:

```
Sub cmdApprove_Click()
    Item.Actions("Approve").Execute
End Sub

Sub cmdDisapprove_Click()
    Item.Actions("Disapprove").Execute
End Sub
```

Each `Click` event handler runs a different action using the `Execute` method of the `Action` object.

## 20.3   **Sending a message with a specific account**

One new Outlook 2007 programming feature is the ability to specify which account Outlook will use to send a message, thanks to the new `MailItem.SendUsingAccount` property. That means you now have two ways to specify the sender, one appropriate within Exchange environments and one for more general uses.

To send a message in the name of another Exchange user, set the value of the `SentOnBehalfOfName` property of the message to the alias or SMTP address of the other user. If you use the alias, prefix it with an equals sign to force Outlook to look for an exact match:

```
objMsg.SentOnBehalfOfName = "=flaviusj"
```

Whether the recipient sees the actual sender's name or the name of the user in whose name you sent the message is not something the sender can control. It depends on the permissions set on the other user's mailbox. If User A has Send On Behalf permission over User B's mailbox, recipients will see in the From field, "From User A on behalf of User B." If User A has Send As permission, recipients will see "From User A." Only an administrator can grant Send As permission over a mailbox to another user.

The new `SendUsingAccount` property returns an `Account` object representing an account from the `Namespace.Accounts` collection (also new in Outlook 2007). This is the account that Outlook will use to send the

**Listing 20.4**   *Set all outgoing messages to use the default account*

```
Private m_objDefAcct As Outlook.Account
Private WithEvents m_colInsp As Outlook.Inspectors
Private WithEvents m_objInsp As Outlook.Inspector

Private Sub Application_MAPILogonComplete()
    Dim objMail As Outlook.MailItem
    Set objMail = Application.CreateItem(olMailItem)
    With objMail
        .Subject = "GETACCOUNT"
        .To = Application.Session.CurrentUser.Address
        .Send
    End With
    Set m_colInsp = Application.Inspectors
End Sub

Private Sub Application_ItemSend(ByVal Item As Object, _
                                 Cancel As Boolean)
    If Item.Subject = "GETACCOUNT" Then
        Set m_objDefAcct = Item.SendUsingAccount
        Cancel = True
        Item.Delete
    End If
End Sub

Private Sub m_colInsp_NewInspector _
  (ByVal Inspector As Inspector)
    Set m_objInsp = Inspector
End Sub

Private Sub m_objInsp_Activate()
    Dim objItem As Object
    Set objItem = m_objInsp.CurrentItem
    If objItem.Class = olMail Then
        If objItem.Size = 0 Then
            objItem.SendUsingAccount = m_objDefAcct
        End If
    End If
End Sub
```

message. This property has one significant limitation, though: On a new message (not a reply or forward), it returns a value of `Nothing`. Furthermore, there is no property in Outlook to tell you which `Account` corresponds to the user's default email account, nor does an unsent message give you any information in `SendUsingAccount` unless the user has explicitly set an account for that message. Getting the user's default account is not impossible, though: To determine the default account, send a message and check the `SendUsingAccount` property of the `Item` passed as a parameter by the `ItemSend` event handler.

A practical application of this technique is to force Outlook to always use the user's default account to send messages. Normally, Outlook will send a reply or forward using the account that the original message arrived on. But some users want to receive on multiple accounts, but send only with their default account. There are two parts to this solution—determining the default account and using that account to set the sending account for all messages. Place all the code in Listing 20.4 in the built-in `ThisOutlookSession` module and run the `Application_MAPILogonComplete` procedure or restart Outlook, which will cause the `MAPILogonComplete` event handler to run automatically.

A new message always uses the default account for sending. The code in the `MAPILogonComplete` event handler creates and sends such a new message, and then the `ItemSend` event handler processes it to set a module-level variable, `m_objDefAcct`, to the `Account` that represents the user's default account. That operation takes place only once—and therein lies the limitation of this solution: If the user changes the default account during the Outlook session, the value of `m_objDefAcct` does not change. The `MAPILogonComplete` event handler also instantiates a module-level `Inspectors` collection, `m_colInsp`.

For later messages that the user creates, the `Inspectors.NewInspector` and `Inspector.Activate` events fire. Code in the `m_colInsp_NewInspector` event handler instantiates a module-level `Inspector` object, `m_objInsp`. In the `m_objInsp_Activate` event handler, Outlook sets the `SendUsingAccount` property for any new outgoing message to the user's default `Account`, stored in `m_objDefAcct`.

For another example that uses the `SendUsingAccount` property, go back to Listing 11.4 in Chapter 11.

## 20.4 Creating a meeting request

The secret to creating a meeting request, as opposed to a simple appointment, is the `AppointmentItem.MeetingStatus` property, which takes the values from the `OlMeetingStatus` enumeration shown in Table 20.3.

**Table 20.3**    *OlMeetingStatus enumeration constants for use with AppointmentItem.MeetingStatus*

| Constant | Value |
| --- | --- |
| olMeeting | 1 |
| olMeetingCanceled | 5 |
| olMeetingReceived | 3 |
| olMeetingReceivedAndCanceled | 7 |
| olNonMeeting | 0 |

This VBA code snippet creates a new one-hour appointment for tomorrow at 2 PM, turns it into a meeting request by setting the MeetingStatus property, and then sends it:

```
Set objAppt = Application.CreateItem(olAppointmentItem)
With objAppt
    .Subject = "Project Meeting"
    .Start = DateAdd("h", Date, 38)
    .End = DateAdd("h", Date, 39)
    .MeetingStatus = olMeeting
    .Location = " "
    .RequiredAttendees = "flaviusj@turfleflock.net"
    .Send
End With
```

It is necessary to give the Location property some value—even if it's just a space—in order to avoid the prompt that Outlook displays when the user attempts to send a meeting request with no Location information. Also, remember that instead of setting the values for OptionalAttendees and Resources, you can use the Recipients.Add method to add each invitee and then set the Recipient.Type property appropriately to olOptional or olResource, as we saw in the previous chapter.

To update a meeting that you have already created in your Calendar folder, make whatever changes you need to make, and then call the Send method again to generate a meeting update, for example:

```
objAppt.Location = "Conference Room B"
objAppt.Send
```

To cancel a meeting, change the MeetingStatus property value to olMeetingCanceled and send again:

```
objAppt.MeetingStatus = olMeetingCanceled
objAppt.Send
```

To delete a meeting without sending a cancellation—for example, if you were creating the meeting for someone else and don't need it on your own calendar—use the Delete method without sending a cancellation.

Listing 20.5    *Convert a meeting to a plain appointment*

```
'VBA version
Sub ConvertMeetingToAppt(myMeeting As
Outlook.AppointmentItem)
    With myMeeting
        ' remove all recipients
        Do Until .Recipients.count = 0
            .Recipients.Remove 1
        Loop
        ' reset meeting status
        .MeetingStatus = olNonMeeting
        .Save
    End With
End Sub

'VBScript version
Sub ConvertMeetingToAppt(myMeeting)
    Const olNonMeeting = 0
    With myMeeting
        ' remove all recipients
        Do Until .Recipients.count = 0
            .Recipients.Remove 1
        Loop
        ' reset meeting status
        .MeetingStatus = olNonMeeting
        .Save
    End With
End Sub
```

To convert an appointment that was originally a meeting into a simple non-meeting appointment, remove all the recipients and then set the value of the `MeetingStatus` property to `olNonMeeting`. The `ConvertMeetingToAppt` procedure in Listing 20.5 takes an `AppointmentItem` as its sole parameter. Notice that the recipients are removed in a `Do` loop. An alternative would be to use a down-counting `For ... Next` loop.

## 20.5  Assigning a task

To assign a task to someone else, call the `TaskItem.Assign` method and then add recipients. Tasks have three different recipient properties for different purposes:

| | |
|---|---|
| `Recipients` | Contains the person to whom the task is assigned |
| `StatusOnCompletionRecipients` | Semi-colon delimited string of people who should be notified when the task is completed |

StatusUpdateRecipients          Semi-colon delimited string of people who should get a message when the task is updated

If you don't set `StatusOnCompletionRecipients` or `StatusUpdate-Recipients`, Outlook automatically sets them to the original task creator. This code snippet assigns an existing task (`objTask`) and sends the task request:

```
Set objRecip = _
   objTask.Recipients.Add("flaviusj@turtleflock.net")
If objRecip.Resolved Then
    objTask.Send
End If
```

You can assign a task to only one person. If you need to assign it to multiple people, make as many copies of the task as you need and assign each to a different person. To maintain some connection among these "subtasks," assign the same category to each one.

# 20.6   Linking Outlook items

Once you get a taste for Outlook items, especially for custom forms and custom properties, you will probably encounter situations where you want to link different Outlook items together. For example, you might want to keep a master record for a company and be able to find the individual contacts at that company easily. Or, you might have a project going and want to collect all the items related to that project—messages, contacts, meetings, tasks, and so on.

Different types of Outlook items offer various methods for linking with other items. In this section, we look at both built-in methods and those links that you can create with programming code.

The simplest way to create a connection among different items is to assign the same category to them. Users can then search for the items by category, or programming code can perform a search using the techniques discussed in Chapter 16. You could, for example, use a different category for all items related to each distinct project that you're working on.

Two other approaches are common in Outlook applications:

- In each item, use a standard or custom property to hold a unique ID that your code can employ to look up a related item
- Maintain a relationship between various items and a related contact using the `Links` collection

The next few sections cover these techniques.

### 20.6.1 Linking with a unique identifier

One linking technique that is familiar to database programmers is the idea of using a unique ID or *key* to look up an item. Because the key value is unique, once you know that value, you can use the techniques discussed in Chapter 16 to locate the one item that meets the condition `key_field = "key value"`.

To implement this kind of linking in an Outlook application, you need to make two decisions:

- What field should hold the key information
- How to generate the key values

Each Outlook item has two standard text properties—`BillingInformation` and `Mileage`—that have no established function and thus can be used to hold a key value. The `ContactItem` object has four additional text properties, `User1` through `User4`. If you are building an application for your personal use, you can use any of these properties as a key. If you are building an application for someone else, you can't guarantee that they won't already be using these properties for some other purpose. In that case, you should use a custom property, text or numeric depending on the type of ID you plan to use.

How should you generate the key values? If your application needs a unique identifier that will never appear in the user interface, you can use a value from the `EntryID` property, which Outlook populates when an item is saved for the first time. Take an item's initial `EntryID` and copy it into the field that you want to use to hold the key value for that item, for example:

```
objItem.Save
objItem.Mileage = objItem.EntryID
objItem.Save
```

The value of the item's actual `EntryID` property may change if you move the item (depending on the information store), but the value in the key field won't.

---

**Tip:** If the item is never moved, then you can use the `EntryID` property itself as the key field and use the `Namespace.GetItemFromID` method to return the item with a particular `EntryID` value.

---

If you prefer a human-readable ID, you can use the code in Listing 20.6, which will work in VBA or VBScript. The `DateID()` function builds an ID from the current date and time by mapping the month, hour, and the last two digits of the year to alphabetic characters, leaving the day, minute, and

**Listing 20.6**    *Build an ID from the current date/time*

```
Function DateID()
    DateID = Chr(64 + Month(Now)) & _
             AddLeadingZeroUnderTen(Day(Now)) & _
             Chr(64 + Right(Year(Now), 2)) & _
             "-" & Chr(64 + Hour(Now)) & _
             AddLeadingZeroUnderTen(Minute(Now)) & _
             AddLeadingZeroUnderTen(Second(Now))
End Function

Function AddLeadingZeroUnderTen(strNum)
    If CInt(strNum) < 10 Then
        strNum = "0" & strNum
    End If
    AddLeadingZeroUnderTen = strNum
End Function
```

second as numeric. For example, running the `DateID()` function on January 5, 2007, at 10:56:30 AM returns the string `A05G-J5630`. Running it again five minutes later will return the string `A05G-K0130`.

The `DateID()` function will not reliably generate a guaranteed unique ID if used in a high-volume situation, but it's quite suitable for an Outlook form where the user creates a new item at most every few minutes, but not several items per second. If you want to use it in a multi-user environment, you could use the `Namespace.CurrentUser.Name` property to return the user's name and append the initials or a few characters from the user's name to the string returned by `DateID()`.

If you need a sequential number, not just a unique number, you can use the `GetLastNumber()` function from Listing 15.7 to find the item with the largest value for a particular field and then increment it.

To retrieve a linked item, use the `Items.Find` or `Items.Restrict` method or one of the other search methods shown in Chapter 16 to search the property that holds the key for the unique key value.

## 20.6.2   Understanding the Activities page

As explained in Chapter 4, the contact form has a special page called Activities that can display items related to the current contact. The different activities groups shown on the page are defined in the Properties dialog for the parent contacts folder. An activities group cannot show multiple Exchange public folders, nor can it show folders from different information stores. It also cannot show multiple folders from another user's Exchange mailbox. That somewhat limits the Activities page's usefulness, especially in Exchange public and shared folder applications.

Outlook uses a variety of properties to build the lists that show in the Activities page—including the sender and recipients on mail messages, invitees on appointments, and people assigned to perform different tasks. It also uses a special collection called Links that allows the user to make a connection manually between an Outlook item and any contact. That's the subject of the next section.

### 20.6.3    Using the Links collection

The contact-linking feature is turned off by default in Outlook 2007 (unlike previous versions). To enable it, the user can choose Tools | Options | Contact Options and check the box for "Show Contact Linking on all Forms." Administrators can enable this feature with a Group Policy Object.

If the user has turned on contact linking, a Contacts button and text box (see Figure 20.6) will appear at the bottom of each task, appointment, contact, and journal entry and on the Options dialog for a mail message. For "sticky notes," the Contacts command appears on the menu for the top-left icon. Click the Contacts button to display the default Contacts folder in a dialog box, where you can select one or more contacts related to the item. The user can also navigate to other contact folders to pick a contact to link to.

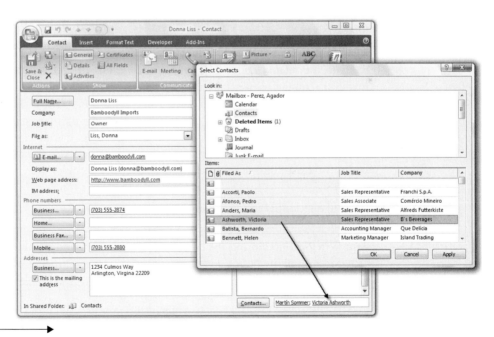

**Figure 20.6**    *Choose one or more contacts to link to the current item.*

**Note:** Clicking the Contacts button always displays the user's default Contacts folder. Outlook provides no way to display a different folder programmatically. It's up to the user to navigate to some other contacts folder. However, as we saw in Listing 18.8, the address book dialog can be used as a substitute for selecting contact links, especially if it is essential to your custom form application that the links be chosen from a particular folder.

When the user adds a contact link, Outlook stores that link in the current item's `Links` collection. If you modify a contact to add a link to another contact, the linking is reciprocal; Outlook automatically adds a link from the linked contact back to the current item.

While you can create a link on any type of Outlook item, the target of a link can only be a contact. You cannot, for example, link a task to an appointment with the `Links` collection.

If you don't want to select a contact from the Select Contacts dialog, you can also type a name into the box next to the Contacts button. When you save the item, Outlook will resolve the link to the actual contact, just as it resolves a name in an email message's To box. You cannot link to an entry in the Global Address List from an Exchange server, though, only to an Outlook contact.

If a name is underlined in the Contacts box, the user can double-click it to open the related contact. (Names that are not underlined do not have matching contact entries.) As a programmer, you can gain access to the target contact for a link through the `Links` collection. This collection supports the standard `Add`, `Item`, and `Remove` methods that you have seen for other Outlook collections. An individual `Link` object has an `Item` property that returns the actual `ContactItem` object that the `Link` points to. Thus, you can return a linked contact from a task, for example, with a statement like this:

```
Set objContact = objTask.Links(1).Item
```

**Tip:** When programming the `Links.Add` method to add a link on a newly created Outlook item, you must save the item first.

One limitation of the `Links` collection is that all the links will be broken if the user exports the data, then imports it onto another machine. Even if a contact name is still underlined, double-clicking it will not pop up the related contact. You can, however, use the `ReconnectLinks` subroutine in Listing 20.7, for Outlook VBA, to try to reconnect the links to the right contacts. To test the procedure, display the folder you want to

**Listing 20.7** *Restore connection using the Links collection*

```
Sub ReconnectLinks(fld As Outlook.Folder)
    Dim objOL As Outlook.Application
    Dim objNS As Outlook.NameSpace
    Dim objContTable As Outlook.Table
    Dim objItem As Object
    Dim colItems As Outlook.Items
    Dim objContact As Outlook.ContactItem
    Dim objRow As Outlook.Row
    Dim colLinks As Outlook.Links
    Dim objLink As Outlook.Link
    Dim objMsg As Outlook.MailItem
    Dim objRecip As Outlook.Recipient
    Dim objAE As Outlook.AddressEntry
    Dim strFind As String
    Dim strFindContact As String
    Dim intCount As Integer
    Dim i As Integer
    Dim SEARCH_CONTACTS As String
    Const PR_MESSAGE_CLASS = _
      "http://schemas.microsoft.com/mapi/proptag/0x001A001E"
    On Error Resume Next
    Set objOL = fld.Application
    Set objNS = objOL.Session
    Set objContTable = _
      objNS.GetDefaultFolder(olFolderContacts).GetTable
    SEARCH_CONTACTS = "http://schemas.microsoft.com/" & _
      "mapi/id/{00062008-0000-0000-C000-000000000046}/" & _
      "8586001E"
    strFind = "NOT (" & Quote(SEARCH_CONTACTS) & " IS NULL)"
    Set colItems = fld.Items.Restrict("@SQL=" & strFind)
    For Each objItem In colItems
        Set colLinks = objItem.Links
        intCount = colLinks.Count
        If intCount > 0 Then
            For i = intCount To 1 Step -1
                Set objLink = colLinks.item(i)
                If objLink.item Is Nothing Then
                    strFindContact = _
                      Quote("urn:schemas:contacts:cn") & _
                      " = '" & objLink.Name & _
                      "' AND " & _
                      Quote(PR_MESSAGE_CLASS) & _
                      " LIKE 'IPM.Contact%'"
                    Set objRow = objContTable.FindRow _
                            ("@SQL=" & strFindContact)
                    If Not objRow Is Nothing Then
                        colLinks.Remove i
                        Set objContact = objNS.GetItemFromID _
                          (objRow.item("EntryID"))
                        colLinks.Add objContact
```

**Listing 20.7**     *Restore connection using the Links collection (continued)*

```
                    Else
                        Set objMsg = objOL.CreateItem(olMailItem)
                        Set objRecip = _
                          objMsg.Recipients.Add(objLink.Name)
                        If objRecip.Resolve Then
                            Set objAE = objRecip.AddressEntry
                            If objAE.AddressEntryUserType = _
                              olOutlookContactAddressEntry Then
                                colLinks.Remove i
                                colLinks.Add objAE.GetContact
                            End If
                        End If
                    End If
                End If
                objItem.Save
            Next
        End If
    Next
    MsgBox "Done!", vbInformation, "Reconnect Links"
    Set objOL = Nothing
    Set objNS = Nothing
    Set objContTable = Nothing
    Set colItems = Nothing
    Set objItem = Nothing
    Set objContact = Nothing
    Set objRecip = Nothing
    Set objAE = Nothing
    Set colLinks = Nothing
    Set objLink = Nothing
End Sub

Private Function Quote(val) As String
    Quote = Chr(34) & CStr(val) & Chr(34)
End Function
```

process, and then call `ReconnectLinks` with this statement in the VBA Immediate window:

```
ReconnectLinks Application.ActiveExplorer.CurrentFolder
```

The `ReconnectLinks` procedure uses two of the different search procedures we learned about in Chapter 16. First, it uses an `Items.Restrict` statement to return an `Items` collection of all items in the folder that have a non-empty `Links` collection. Then it uses the `FindRow` method on a `Table` object for the default Contacts folder to try to locate a contact matching the link. (The `Link.Name` property stores the value of the `FullName` property of the original linked contact.) If it finds a match, it gets the `EntryID` value of the item using the `Row.Item` method, returns a contact using `Namespace.GetItemFromID` and that `EntryID` value, and finally, creates a link using that contact.

If there is no matching contact in the Contacts folder, the Recon-nectLinks procedure makes one more attempt to find a matching contact in the contacts folders. It creates a new mail message, adds the name as a recipient, and if the name can be resolved to a contact's address, it uses that contact (returned by Outlook 2007's new AddressEntry.GetContact method) to create a new link.

### 20.6.4   Example: Add a contact phone number to a task

Any Outlook folder view shows only the data in that folder, although Outlook does not prevent you from adding fields appropriate for other folders to the view. For example, you can drag the Business Phone field to a Tasks folder view, expecting that it will show the phone numbers of linked contacts, but that field will stay empty because the Tasks folder itself contains no data in that field.

To populate tasks with phone or other information from linked contacts, you can use a VBA event handler to watch for new items in your Tasks folder, look up any linked contact, and add the phone information. Put the code in Listing 20.8 in the ThisOutlookSession module in Outlook VBA and then either run the Application_Startup procedure or restart Outlook to initialize the event-enabled m_colTasks object.

The code in Listing 20.8 is like the other ItemAdd examples we saw in Chapter 11. It instantiates an Items collection for the Tasks folder and then watches for new tasks. If a new task's Subject property contains the word "call" or "phone," the ItemAdd event handler looks for a contact linked to the task. If it finds one, it appends the contact's business, home, or mobile number to the task subject.

## 20.7   Creating an annual event from a custom date field

If you add an additional date field to a custom contact form, Outlook does not give such date fields the same functionality as the standard Birthday and Anniversary properties. It does not automatically create an annual event in the Calendar folder when the user sets a value for a custom date field.

You can build your own solution to create related annual events using either VBScript code behind a custom contact form or VBA code that monitors the Contacts folder for new and changed items. The VBA technique is similar to that shown in Listing 20.8. As you'll see, the VBA approach has a couple of advantages over the VBScript method.

**Listing 20.8**    *Add phone numbers for task calls*

```
Private WithEvents m_colTasks As Outlook.Items

Private Sub Application_Startup()
    Dim objNS As Outlook.NameSpace
    Set objNS = Application.Session
    Set m_colTasks = _
       objNS.GetDefaultFolder(olFolderTasks).Items
    Set objNS = Nothing
End Sub

Private Sub m_colTasks_ItemAdd(ByVal Item As Object)
    Dim objTask As Outlook.TaskItem
    Dim objContact As Outlook.ContactItem
    Dim strPhone As String
    On Error Resume Next
    If Item.Class = olTask Then
        Set objTask = Item
        If InStr(1, objTask.Subject, "Phone", _
                vbTextCompare) > 0 Or _
           InStr(1, objTask.Subject, "Call", _
               vbTextCompare) > 0 Then
            If objTask.Links.Count > 0 Then
                Set objContact = objTask.Links(1).Item
                strPhone = objContact.BusinessTelephoneNumber
                If strPhone = "" Then
                    strPhone = objContact.HomeTelephoneNumber
                End If
                If strPhone = "" Then
                    strPhone = _
                        objContact.MobileTelephoneNumber
                End If
            End If
        End If
        If strPhone <> "" Then
            objTask.Subject = objTask.Subject & " - " & strPhone
            objTask.Save
        End If
    End If
    Set objTask = Nothing
    Set objContact = Nothing
End Sub
```

We'll build both solutions, using a custom date field named Employee-
StartDate, so you can see that they have a lot in common. Both handle
four different scenarios:

- Creating a related appointment after the user fills in the Employee-
  StartDate for the first time

- Updating the related appointment when the user changes the
  EmployeeStartDate

- Deleting the related appointment if the user changes the Employee-StartDate to "None"
- Deleting the related appointment if the user deletes the contact

For the VBScript solution, open a contact form in design mode. In the Field Chooser, add an EmployeeStartDate date property. Drag that property to any custom page. Add the code in Listing 20.9 to the form. Finally, publish the form to the Contacts folder with the display name "Date Form."

To test the custom form, click the Actions menu, and choose New Date Form. Enter a value for the person's name and EmployeeStartDate, and then save the item. You should see a link appear in the item body. Double-click it and Outlook should display the related appointment with the correct date. Close the contact, and then delete it. If you look in the Calendar folder, the related appointment should still be there.

Now, repeat the test without closing the item. Delete the contact using the Delete command in the open item. Check the Calendar: The related appointment should be gone, too.

What you're seeing is the significant limitation of the BeforeDelete event for individual items. This event fires only when an item is open in an Inspector window. If the user deletes the item from a folder view, BeforeDelete does not fire.

The other limitation of the VBScript approach is that we can't create a link in the appointment's Links collection to point back to the original contact. The obstacle is that we need a saved contact in order to create a link, but we're creating the appointment in the contact's Item_Write event handler, where the contact is not yet saved.

**Listing 20.9**  *Create an appointment related to a custom date property (VBScript)*

```
Dim m_dteEmployeeStart   ' As Date

Function Item_Open()
    If Item.Size = 0 Then
        Item.UserProperties("EmployeeStartDate") = #1/1/4501#
    End If
    m_dteEmployeeStart = _
      Item.UserProperties("EmployeeStartDate")
End Function

Function Item_Write()
    Dim objAppt      ' As Outlook.AppointmentItem
    Dim objAtt       ' As Outlook.Attachment
    Const olByReference = 4
    On Error Resume Next
```

---------→

**Listing 20.9**     *Create an appointment related to a custom date property (VBScript) (continued)*

```
' contact never had a start date before
'   create the related appointment
If m_dteEmployeeStart = #1/1/4501# Then
    If Item.UserProperties("EmployeeStartDate") _
        <> #1/1/4501# Then
        Set objAppt = CreateAllDayAppt( _
          Item.UserProperties("EmployeeStartDate"), 1)
        objAppt.Subject = Item.FullName & "'s Start Date"
        objAppt.Save
        Item.Attachments.Add objAppt, olByReference
        m_dteEmployeeStart = _
          Item.UserProperties("EmployeeStartDate")
    End If
' contact had a start date earlier but now has none
'   delete the related appointment
ElseIf Item.UserProperties("EmployeeStartDate") _
        = #1/1/4501# Then
    Set objAppt = GetContactStartAppt()
    objAppt.Delete
    For Each objAtt In Item.Attachments
        If objAtt.Type = olByReference Then
            If objAtt.DisplayName = _
              Item.FullName & "'s Start Date" Then
                objAtt.Delete
                Exit For
            End If
        End If
    Next
' contact's start date has changed
'   update the related appointment
ElseIf Item.UserProperties("EmployeeStartDate") _
        <> m_dteEmployeeStart Then
    Set objAppt = GetContactStartAppt()
    If Not objAppt Is Nothing Then
        objAppt.Start = CDate(FormatDateTime _
          (Item.UserProperties("EmployeeStartDate"), _
          vbShortDate))
        objAppt.Save
    End If
    m_dteEmployeeStart = _
      Item.UserProperties("EmployeeStartDate")
End If
Set objAppt = Nothing
Set objAtt = Nothing
End Function

Function Item_BeforeDelete(ByVal Item)
    Dim objAppt     ' As Outlook.AppointmentItem
    On Error Resume Next
    If Item.UserProperties("EmployeeStartDate") _
        <> #1/1/4501# Then
        Set objAppt = GetContactStartAppt()
```

──────────➤

**Listing 20.9** *Create an appointment related to a custom date property (VBScript) (continued)*

```vbscript
        If Not objAppt Is Nothing Then
            objAppt.Delete
        End If
    End If
End Function

Function CreateAllDayAppt(startDate, numDays)
    Dim objAppt      ' As Outlook.AppointmentItem
    Dim objRP        ' As Outlook.RecurrencePattern
    Const olAppointmentItem = 1
    Const olRecursYearly = 5
    Set objAppt = Application.CreateItem(olAppointmentItem)
    Set objRP = objAppt.GetRecurrencePattern
    With objRP
        .RecurrenceType = olRecursYearly
        .DayOfMonth = Day(startDate)
        .MonthOfYear = Month(startDate)
        .PatternStartDate = objAppt.Start
        .StartTime = #12:00:00 AM#
        .NoEndDate = True
        .Interval = 1
        .Duration = numDays * 24 * 60
    End With
    With objAppt
        .AllDayEvent = True
        .ReminderSet = False
    End With
    Set CreateAllDayAppt = objAppt
    Set objAppt = Nothing
End Function

Function GetContactStartAppt()
    Dim objNS        ' As Outlook.NameSpace
    Dim objCal       ' As Outlook.Folder
    Dim strFind      ' As String
    Dim colItems     ' As Outlook.Items
    Const olFolderCalendar = 9
    On Error Resume Next
    Set objNS = Application.Session
    Set objCal = objNS.GetDefaultFolder(olFolderCalendar)
    strFind = Quote("urn:schemas:httpmail:subject") & _
            " = '" & Item.FullName & "'s Start Date'"
    Set colItems = objCal.Items.Restrict("@SQL=" & strFind)
    If colItems.Count > 0 Then
        Set GetContactStartAppt = colItems.GetFirst
    End If
    Set objNS = Nothing
    Set objCal = Nothing
End Function

Function Quote(val)
    Quote = Chr(34) & CStr(val) & Chr(34)
End Function
```

The VBA approach to this scenario gets around both those problems. Again, you need a custom form, but the form won't run any code. Create a custom contact form containing two custom fields—EmployeeStartDate and OldEmployeeStartDate, making sure that both fields are visible on the "User-defined fields in this item" list on the All Fields page of the form in design mode. If you display the OldEmployeeStartDate property on a custom page, set its control to read-only. Publish the form to your Contacts folder with the display name "Date Form VBA" and message class "IPM.Contact.Date Form VBA." Add the code in Listing 20.10 to the ThisOutlookSession module in Outlook VBA, then either restart Outlook or run the Application_MAPILogonComplete procedure to initialize the objects declared WithEvents.

To test this approach, display the Contacts folder, and use the Actions | New Date Form VBA command to launch a new contact using the custom form. As before, set a value for the EmployeeStartDate property and save the contact. Experiment with deleting contacts from both the folder view and the open Inspector window. With the VBA approach, you should see links in the appointment items' Contacts box and also see the appointment items disappear when the related contacts are deleted, even if you delete a contact from its Inspector window.

---

**Note:** The VBA approach uses the new Folder.BeforeItemMove event in Outlook 2007. This cancelable event fires whenever the user moves or deletes an item from the folder. It passes the item that will be deleted or moved as a parameter.

---

Both solutions require a way to track the original value of EmployeeStartDate, in order to respond to a change in value. The VBScript version uses a module-level variable (m_dteEmployeeStart), while the VBA version uses a second custom property (OldEmployeeStartDate). Using the CustomPropertyChange event in the VBScript version would be overkill, because we're only interested in whether the property has changed values since the last time it was saved.

Also worth noting is the way that the code looks up the related appointment, with a DASL query:

```
strFind = Quote("urn:schemas:httpmail:subject") & _
          " = '" & cont.FullName & "''s Start Date'"
Set colItems = objCal.Items.Restrict("@SQL=" & strFind)
```

The code creates appointments whose Subject property uses the format "*Full Name*'s Start Date." A DASL search string for Items.Restrict can handle the apostrophe in the subject while a Jet search string for Items.Find can't.

**Listing 20.10**   *Create an appointment related to a custom date property (VBA)*

```
Private WithEvents colContacts As Outlook.Items
Private WithEvents objContacts As Outlook.Folder

Private Sub Application_MAPILogonComplete()
    Dim objNS As Outlook.NameSpace
    Set objNS = Application.Session
    Set objContacts = _
      objNS.GetDefaultFolder(olFolderContacts)
    Set colContacts = objContacts.Items
    Set objNS = Nothing
End Sub

Private Sub colContacts_ItemAdd(ByVal Item As Object)
    Dim objAppt As Outlook.AppointmentItem
    On Error Resume Next
    If Item.MessageClass = "IPM.Contact.Date Form VBA" Then
        If Item.UserProperties("EmployeeStartDate") _
            <> #1/1/4501# Then
            Set objAppt = CreateAllDayAppt( _
              Item.UserProperties("EmployeeStartDate"), 1)
            objAppt.Subject = Item.FullName & "'s Start Date"
            objAppt.Links.Add Item
            objAppt.Save
            Item.Attachments.Add objAppt, olByReference
            Item.UserProperties("OldEmployeeStartDate") = _
                Item.UserProperties("EmployeeStartDate")
            Item.Save
        End If
    End If
    Set objAppt = Nothing
End Sub

Private Sub colContacts_ItemChange(ByVal Item As Object)
    Dim objAppt As Outlook.AppointmentItem
    On Error Resume Next
    If Item.MessageClass = "IPM.Contact.Date Form VBA" Then
        If Item.UserProperties("OldEmployeeStartDate") <> _
                Item.UserProperties("EmployeeStartDate") Then
            Set objAppt = GetContactStartAppt(Item)
            If Not objAppt Is Nothing Then
                objAppt.Start = CDate(FormatDateTime _
                  (Item.UserProperties("EmployeeStartDate"), _
                  vbShortDate))
                objAppt.Save
            End If
            Item.UserProperties("OldEmployeeStartDate") = _
              Item.UserProperties("EmployeeStartDate")
            Item.Save
        End If
    End If
    Set objAppt = Nothing
End Sub
```

**Listing 20.10**   *Create an appointment related to a custom date property (VBA) (continued)*

```
Private Sub objContacts_BeforeItemMove(ByVal Item As Object, _
   ByVal MoveTo As MAPIFolder, Cancel As Boolean)
    Dim objNS As Outlook.NameSpace
    Dim objDelItms As Outlook.Folder
    Dim objAppt As Outlook.AppointmentItem
    Dim blnDelAppt As Boolean
    If Item.MessageClass = "IPM.Contact.Date Form VBA" Then
        If MoveTo Is Nothing Then
            blnDelAppt = True
        Else
            Set objNS = Application.Session
            Set objDelItms = _
              objNS.GetDefaultFolder(olFolderDeletedItems)
            If MoveTo.EntryID = objDelItms.EntryID Then
                blnDelAppt = True
            End If
        End If
    End If
    If blnDelAppt Then
        Set objAppt = GetContactStartAppt(Item)
        If Not objAppt Is Nothing Then
            objAppt.Delete
        End If
    End If
    Set objNS = Nothing
    Set objDelItms = Nothing
    Set objAppt = Nothing
End Sub

Function CreateAllDayAppt _
   (startDate As Date, numDays As Integer) _
   As Outlook.AppointmentItem
    Dim objAppt As Outlook.AppointmentItem
    Dim objRP As Outlook.RecurrencePattern
    Set objAppt = Application.CreateItem(olAppointmentItem)
    Set objRP = objAppt.GetRecurrencePattern
    With objRP
        .RecurrenceType = olRecursYearly
        .DayOfMonth = Day(startDate)
        .MonthOfYear = Month(startDate)
        .PatternStartDate = objAppt.Start
        .StartTime = #12:00:00 AM#
        .NoEndDate = True
        .Interval = 1
        .Duration = numDays * 24 * 60
    End With
    With objAppt
        .AllDayEvent = True
        .ReminderSet = False
    End With
    Set CreateAllDayAppt = objAppt
    Set objAppt = Nothing
End Function
```

Listing 20.10    *Create an appointment related to a custom date property (VBA) (continued)*

```
Private Function GetContactStartAppt _
  (cont As Outlook.ContactItem) As Outlook.AppointmentItem
    Dim objNS As Outlook.NameSpace
    Dim objCal As Outlook.Folder
    Dim strFind As String
    Dim colItems As Outlook.Items
    On Error Resume Next
    Set objNS = Application.Session
    Set objCal = objNS.GetDefaultFolder(olFolderCalendar)
    strFind = Quote("urn:schemas:httpmail:subject") & _
            " = '" & cont.FullName & "''s Start Date'"
    Set colItems = objCal.Items.Restrict("@SQL=" & strFind)
    If colItems.Count > 0 Then
        Set GetContactStartAppt = colItems.GetFirst
    End If
    Set objNS = Nothing
    Set objCal = Nothing
End Function

Private Function Quote(val) As String
    Quote = Chr(34) & CStr(val) & Chr(34)
End Function
```

Another key technique that this sample demonstrates is creating a recurring appointment. Outlook stores recurrence details in a `RecurrencePattern` object—in this example, `objRP`:

```
Set objRP = objAppt.GetRecurrencePattern
With objRP
    .RecurrenceType = olRecursYearly
    .DayOfMonth = Day(startDate)
    .MonthOfYear = Month(startDate)
    .PatternStartDate = objAppt.Start
    .StartTime = #12:00:00 AM#
    .NoEndDate = True
    .Interval = 1
    .Duration = numDays * 24 * 60
End With
With objAppt
    .AllDayEvent = True
    .ReminderSet = False
End With
```

When creating a recurring appointment, set the `RecurrenceType` property first, and then set the properties that define the details of the recurrence, such as the month and day in which a yearly appointment occurs.

If you plan to implement the VBA solution permanently, you might want to make the custom form the default for your Contacts folder and convert existing items to use it, as discussed in the next chapter. If you use a different message class, be sure to change the value in the `Item.Message-Class` = expressions to match.

## 20.8  Summary

Individual Outlook items support a great deal of built-in functionality, such as task assignments, meeting requests, recurrence patterns for appointments and tasks, custom actions to add new commands, and links between items and contacts. The key to putting that functionality to work is using the methods and properties that each item supports.

Event handlers, either behind custom forms or in VBA, can enhance Outlook's functionality, especially by creating or updating items related to existing items. Specific examples in this chapter have included custom actions to restore a contact command that Outlook 2007 omits, a vacation request form that generates an approved appointment ready to save in the requestor's Calendar, tasks that look up phone numbers for contacts, and appointments related to a custom date field on a contact.

Pay special attention to the limitations on the use of custom message forms. Unless you can publish a message to the Organizational Forms library on an in-house Exchange server or in each user's Personal Forms library, you're not going to be able to use that form for data gathering or any other task that requires code behind the form.

# *Deploying and Managing Outlook Forms*

By now, you may have quite a few Outlook forms that you're eager to put into action, and perhaps even share them with other people. But before you start depending on those forms in your daily work, it's important to understand the architecture behind Outlook custom forms, so that you can anticipate and (hopefully) avoid potential problems.

Four specific architectural issues deserve special attention. We need to consider how Outlook decides which form to display for a certain message class, given that there are three different types of form libraries, plus the new form regions in Outlook 2007. Second, unexpected and unwanted effects occur in situations where the form becomes part of the data item, a situation known to Outlook developers as one-off forms. Third, for best results, the fields in a form and a folder should match. Finally, for better performance, Outlook caches custom forms locally. Recovering from forms cache corruption is an important technique.

We'll also cover key maintenance issues, such as publishing and removing forms programmatically, importing data with a custom form, and converting existing items to use a custom form.

Highlights of this chapter include discussions of the following:

- What key architectural issues can cause problems for Outlook forms developers
- Where Outlook looks for custom form definitions
- How to publish an Outlook form programmatically
- How to create custom form items using imported data
- How to convert existing items to use a custom form
- How to use the Forms Manager to move and delete forms

# 21.1   Understanding Outlook forms architecture

You can build legacy Outlook forms without understanding the underlying architecture, but it helps to know how forms interact with Outlook data items. An Outlook form is a template that provides a custom view of the data that an individual Outlook item contains. It may also contain code that modifies the behavior of an individual item to add new functionality or suppress existing functionality for that type of item. The form's designer decides what information should be displayed to the user, what it should look like, and what interactivity the form should offer.

One of the most confusing things about legacy custom form design in Outlook is that the form designer presents three different commands that can save the form. The three methods available are:

- Click the Office button, and then click Save. This saves the form design and the item (that is, the data record) in the default Outlook folder for that type of item. The form design is embedded in the item. This embedded form is called a *one-off form*. Such a form cannot run any VBScript code behind the form and causes the item to be much larger than an item without an embedded form. Therefore, using Save to save a form and data item together is not recommended.

- Click the Office button, and then click Save As to save the form as an Outlook template .oft file. Use this technique to make backup copies of your custom forms. To use a saved .oft file form, use the Tools | Forms | Choose Form or Design Form command. Such a form will not run code.

- In the Form group in design mode, click Publish. This publishes the form in the forms library you choose. Only a published form can run VBScript code. This is the preferred method for putting forms into production.

Of these three commands, you should be using only the last one to put your forms into production.

**Note:** If you alter an Outlook item—say, by typing some text into a blank message—and save it as an .oft file, that file technically is also a custom form. However, if it doesn't have custom fields, a custom layout, or code behind it, it can be opened by double-clicking it. You don't have to use the Choose Form command. Throughout the rest of this chapter, we'll be talking about published forms, not these "templates" that don't have custom page layouts or code.

**Table 21.1**    *Three Types of Outlook Form Libraries*

| Form Library | Purpose | Location |
|---|---|---|
| Organizational Forms | Forms for enterprise-wide use in an organization using Microsoft Exchange as its mail server | Hidden system folder on the Exchange server |
| Personal Forms | Forms for the user's personal use | Hidden folder in the root of the user's default information store |
| Folder libraries | Forms for use with a particular folder, often a folder in an Exchange server's Public Folders hierarchy | In the particular folder |

Publishing a form stores the form definition as a hidden Outlook item in the target location. This hidden item has a `MessageClass` property value of IPM.Microsoft.FolderDesign.FormsDescription. Table 21.1 lists the three locations where you can publish a form.

**Note:** In the Tools | Forms | Choose Form dialog, you will also see a Standard Forms library. This is the library of standard Outlook forms. You cannot publish custom forms to it or modify any of the forms it contains.

As discussed in the previous chapter, to be fully functional, message forms with code behind them must be published to the Organizational Forms or Personal Forms library, not to a folder library. Non-message forms for use with items in a folder are usually published to that folder. If you want to replace one of the standard non-message forms with your own custom form, as described later in the chapter, the custom form must be published to the Personal Forms or Organizational Forms library.

**Tip:** Understanding how custom forms are stored helps explain why performing an export with Outlook's File | Import and Export command does not transfer any custom forms; only the data items are exported, not the hidden form items. Also not exported are custom views and field definitions for a folder, which also are stored as hidden items.

To see a list of the forms stored in a particular folder, use the `EnumCustomForms()` VBA procedure in Listing 21.1, which lists the display name and message class in the Immediate window. Call it like this to generate a list of the forms in your Personal Forms library:

```
Call EnumCustomForms(olPersonalRegistry)
```

**Listing 21.1**     *List the custom forms in a folder*

```
Sub EnumCustomForms(reg As Outlook.OlFormRegistry, _
                    Optional fld As Outlook.Folder)
    Dim objTable As Outlook.Table
    Dim objRow As Outlook.Row
    Dim objFld As Outlook.Folder
    Dim strFind As String
    Const SEARCH_FORM_MESSAGECLASS = _
       "http://schemas.microsoft.com/mapi/proptag/0x6800001E"
    Const PR_DISPLAY_NAME = _
       "http://schemas.microsoft.com/mapi/proptag/0x3001001E"
    On Error Resume Next
    Select Case reg
        Case olPersonalRegistry
            Set objFld = GetCommonViews()
            If Not objFld Is Nothing Then
                Debug.Print "Forms in Personal Forms Library"
            Else
                Debug.Print "Could not get Personal Forms"
            End If
        Case olFolderRegistry
            If fld Is Nothing Then
                Debug.Print "Must supply folder argument"
            Else
                Set objFld = fld
            End If
        Case olOrganizationRegistry
            Set objFld = GetOrgForms()
            If Not objFld Is Nothing Then
                Debug.Print "Forms in Organizational Forms: "
            Else
                Debug.Print "Could not get Org Forms"
            End If
    End Select
    If Not objFld Is Nothing Then
        strFind = "[MessageClass] = " & _
          Quote("IPM.Microsoft.FolderDesign.FormsDescription")
        Set objTable = objFld.GetTable(strFind, olHiddenItems)
        objTable.Columns.Add PR_DISPLAY_NAME
        objTable.Columns.Add SEARCH_FORM_MESSAGECLASS
        objTable.Restrict strFind
        Do Until objTable.EndOfTable
            Set objRow = objTable.GetNextRow
            Debug.Print , objRow(PR_DISPLAY_NAME), _
              objRow(SEARCH_FORM_MESSAGECLASS)
        Loop
    End If
    Set objFld = Nothing
    Set objTable = Nothing
    Set objRow = Nothing
End Sub
```

**Listing 21.1**   *List the custom forms in a folder (continued)*

```
Function GetCommonViews() As Outlook.Folder
    Dim objOL As Outlook.Application
    Dim objNS As Outlook.NameSpace
    Dim objStore As Outlook.Store
    Dim objPA As Outlook.PropertyAccessor
    Dim strEntryID As String
    Const PR_COMMON_VIEWS_ENTRYID = _
      "http://schemas.microsoft.com/mapi/proptag/0x35E60102"
    Set objOL = Application
    Set objNS = objOL.Session
    Set objStore = objNS.DefaultStore
    Set objPA = objStore.PropertyAccessor
    strEntryID = objPA.BinaryToString _
      (objPA.GetProperty(PR_COMMON_VIEWS_ENTRYID))
    If strEntryID <> "" Then
        Set GetCommonViews = objNS.GetFolderFromID(strEntryID)
    End If
    Set objOL = Nothing
    Set objNS = Nothing
    Set objStore = Nothing
    Set objPA = Nothing
End Function

Function GetOrgForms() As Outlook.Folder
    Dim objOL As Outlook.Application
    Dim objNS As Outlook.NameSpace
    Dim objStore As Outlook.Store
    Dim objPA As Outlook.PropertyAccessor
    Dim strEntryID As String
    Dim blnPFFound As Boolean
    Dim objFolder As Outlook.Folder
    Const PR_EFORMS_REGISTRY_ENTRYID = _
      "http://schemas.microsoft.com/mapi/proptag/0x66210102"
    Set objOL = Application
    Set objNS = objOL.Session
    For Each objStore In objNS.Stores
        If objStore.ExchangeStoreType = _
          olExchangePublicFolder Then
            blnPFFound = True
            Exit For
        End If
    Next
    If blnPFFound Then
        Set objPA = objStore.PropertyAccessor
        strEntryID = objPA.BinaryToString _
          (objPA.GetProperty(PR_EFORMS_REGISTRY_ENTRYID))
        If strEntryID <> "" Then
            Set objFolder = objNS.GetFolderFromID(strEntryID)
            If Not objFolder Is Nothing Then
                Set objFolder = objFolder.folders.GetFirst
            End If
        End If
```

⟶

**Listing 21.1**     *List the custom forms in a folder (continued)*

```
    End If
    Set GetOrgForms = objFolder
    Set objOL = Nothing
    Set objNS = Nothing
    Set objStore = Nothing
    Set objPA = Nothing
    Set objFolder = Nothing
End Function

Private Function Quote(val) As String
    Quote = Chr(34) & CStr(val) & Chr(34)
End Function
```

Call it like this to generate a list of the forms in the currently displayed folder:

```
Call EnumCustomForms(olFolderRegistry, _
  Application.ActiveExplorer.CurrentFolder)
```

Notice that because the forms are hidden items, the code calls the `Folder.GetTable` method in a way that returns only such hidden items:

```
Set objTable = objFld.GetTable(strFind, olHiddenItems)
```

The `GetCommonViews()` function returns a hidden folder at the root of the default information store that holds forms for the Personal Forms library, cached copies of folder views, information about search folders, and other storage items that Outlook uses internally. Similarly, the `GetOrgForms()` function returns the hidden folder that holds forms published to the Organizational Forms library. Both these functions depend on the fact that the default store and the Public Folders store each have hidden properties that store the `EntryID` values for other key Outlook folders.

### 21.1.1   **Understanding the forms cache**

To improve performance, Outlook uses a folder on the local hard drive to cache a copy of each published form that the user invokes. This folder is not normally visible to the user in Windows Explorer. On Windows XP and Windows Server 2003, the location of that folder is %userprofile%\Local Settings\Application Data\Microsoft\FORMS. Windows Vista machines (see Figure 21.1) use %userprofile%\appdata\local\Microsoft\FORMS. The location of the forms cache folder cannot be changed.

The forms cache contains a folder for each form, plus a FRM-CACHE.DAT file that holds information about what's in the cache. If a form is used in multiple folders, the cache will keep folder-specific copies of the form. In other words, if you use a form named IPM.Task.MyForm in three different folders, the forms cache may contain three separate

**Figure 21.1**
*The Outlook forms
cache is a folder
on the user's
hard drive,
normally hidden
from the user.*

folders for that form with folder names like IPM.Task.MyForm, IPM.Task.MyForm000, and IPM.Task.MyForm001.

By default, Outlook maintains the size of the forms cache at 2MB, removing the oldest unused forms as necessary to keep the size under the limit. The user can change the size of the forms cache with the Manage Forms dialog discussed later in the chapter. The size of the forms cache cannot be changed programmatically; it is stored in the FRMCACHE.DAT file in an undocumented binary format.

Most of the time, "forms cache" refers to this cache of forms in the FORMS folder. However, there is one other forms cache you should be aware of. To facilitate the use of forms from the Organizational Forms library while a user is working offline, Outlook 2007 can synchronize forms during a send/receive session. Configure this setting in the properties of the main send/receive group, as shown in Figure 21.2.

## 21.1.2  Launching a custom form

The link between a data item and the form used to display it depends on the value of the `MessageClass` property of the data item. When you publish a form, you set properties on the form definition that control its display name and message class. When you create a new item or open an existing item, Outlook uses the `MessageClass` value to determine what form to display.

**Figure 21.2**
*Outlook 2007 can
synchronize forms
with the Exchange
server for offline
use.*

A user can create a new item using a published custom form using any of these techniques:

- Choose Tools | Forms | Choose Form (or File | New | Choose Form), and select a form from any of the form libraries. If you have any replacement and replace-all form regions, you'll see them in the Form Regions library.

- If the form is the default for a non-message folder, display that folder, and then click New.

- On the Actions menu for a folder, click the New *name_of_form* menu command to create an item using a form published to the folder.

When the user creates a new item using any of those techniques, Outlook sets the value of the MessageClass property of the new item to the class stored in the published form definition. Thus, the MessageClass value for an item created with a published contact form would be IPM.Contact.*formname*, where *formname* is the name you gave to the form when you published it. When the user creates an item or opens an existing item, Outlook decides what form to use to display the item by looking at the item's MessageClass property value.

**Note:** There is one other, less widely used technique for launching a custom form, which we cover a little later in the chapter. A custom form can be set as a default form replacing the standard appointment, contact, task, or journal form.

As a practical matter, this means there are two requirements for an item to display a particular custom form:

- The item's `MessageClass` needs to point to that form.
- The form needs to be published in one of the locations where Outlook looks to find published forms and form regions.

It's important to consider form regions, as well as legacy published forms, since form regions can not only stack on an existing standard or published form, but can also replace a non-default form.

So, where does Outlook look for form definitions when the user opens an item with a particular message class? It first looks to see there is a form region registered for the message class. If there is a form region, Outlook doesn't look for legacy custom forms unless the region's `<loadLegacy-Form>` option is set to `false`. Otherwise, Outlook looks to see if an instance of the legacy custom form is already open. If so, Outlook loads the form from memory. If the form is not in memory, Outlook looks to see if the form is in the local forms cache because you've used it before. If the form isn't in the cache, Outlook looks in the libraries for published forms, in this order:

1. Currently displayed folder's forms library
2. Personal Forms library
3. Organizational Forms library

This load order helps explain why custom message forms are often impossible to use in an organization: Unless the form is published to the Organizational Forms library or to each user's Personal Forms library, Outlook probably will not be able to locate a published form definition it can use to display the form. The only time it will look in a folder in the Public Folders hierarchy is when the user is currently viewing a public folder.

If Outlook loads a form from the local cache, it also checks the published form locations to see if a later version of the form is available. If so, it loads the later version and refreshes the copy in the cache.

Actually, the above description of how form regions load was oversimplified. While an item can display the layout of only a single legacy form, form regions are additive. A given message class could even have different types of regions registered for it—an adjoining region and a separate region, for example.

Also, by default, regions are inherited by derived message classes. For example, a region registered for IPM.Contact will also display on items from the message class IPM.Contact.Customer. A region registered for IPM.Contact.Customer will also display on items using the message class IPM.Contact.Customer.International.

---

**Note:** The region developer can specify in the region's manifest that the region should be used only for items with the exact message class that the region is registered to. The Help topic "How to: Specify a Form Region to be Used Only for the Exact Message Class" (HV10205415) explains how to use the `<exactMessageClass>` element in the manifest.

---

If Outlook finds a replacement region for the item's message class, it will replace the main page with the replacement region. If it finds one or more replace-all regions, Outlook will hide all the pages of the standard or legacy custom form for that message class and show only the replace-all region(s).

## 21.2  Managing Outlook forms

To manage legacy custom forms, choose Tools | Options | Other | Advanced Options | Custom Forms to display the Custom Forms dialog box shown in Figure 21.3. This is the dialog where you can set the size of the forms cache discussed above. The check box for "Allow forms that bypass Outlook" controls whether older MAPI forms built with C++, rather than the Outlook form designer, are allowed to run.

---

**Note:** Oddly, the Password button on the Custom Forms dialog box is not related to Outlook forms at all. It performs a reset of the user's Windows password.

---

To manage individual forms, click the Manage Forms button to display the Forms Manager shown in Figure 21.4. You can also open the Forms Manager for a particular folder: Right-click the folder, choose Properties, switch to the Forms tab, and then click Manage.

In the Forms Manager dialog box, use the Set buttons to select a folder or one of the two general forms libraries. Use the Copy, Update, and Delete buttons to manage forms, or the Properties button to find out more about a form. The dialog also includes a Clear Cache button to empty the forms cache if it shows signs of corruption.

**Figure 21.3**
*Manage the forms cache size and allow or disable older forms.*

The Save As button on the Forms Manager allows you to save a form as an .fdm file. This is a good alternative to .oft files for custom form backups. The Install button imports an .fdm file into a forms library.

Here's a typical Forms Manager task. Let's say you have successfully tested a form in your Personal Forms library. You can use the Forms Manager to make a backup as an .fdm file, copy it to the Organizational Forms library, and then delete it from your Personal Forms library. Remember that you must have appropriate permissions from the Exchange administrator to put a form in the Organizational Forms library and must be a folder owner to add to a folder forms library.

**Note:** The Forms Manager handles only published legacy custom forms. To manage saved .oft form templates, use Windows Explorer; those forms are stored in the file system. There is no equivalent of the Forms Manager for form regions. Regions are managed completely by the settings in their manifests and their entries in the Windows Registry.

**Figure 21.4**
*Copy, move, install, and delete forms in the Forms Manager.*

**Figure 21.5**
*To set the default form for a folder, use the General tab of the folder's Properties dialog, not the Forms page.*

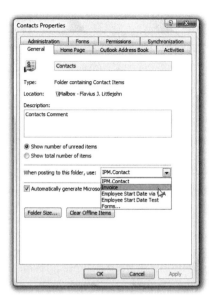

To set a custom form as the default form for a folder, use not the Forms Manager but the folder's Properties dialog as shown in Figure 21.5. Remember that you cannot make a message form the default for any folder. If your application needs to set the default form for a folder programmatically, turn back to Listing 14.3 for a code sample that shows how to accomplish that task with the new `PropertyAccessor` object in Outlook 2007.

Later in this chapter, we'll address the issue of publishing forms programmatically.

## 21.2.1  Making a custom form the new global default

Even though you cannot edit the standard Outlook forms directly, you can replace any standard form with a custom form that has been published to the Organizational Forms or Personal Forms library. For example, you might want to make a custom task form the default so that Outlook will use it even when the user creates a new task by typing in the To Do List.

---

**Caution:** Using registry substitution to force Outlook to use a custom form for all outgoing messages is not recommended. See the discussion in the previous chapter of the problems involved in using a custom message form over the Internet.

---

Substituting a custom form for a standard form requires a change to the Windows registry. Before attempting this, you should make a backup of the registry. Depending on your access level on your computer, you may not be able to make the necessary changes to the Windows registry. If that's the case, you will not be able to use this technique.

To facilitate the substitution process, Microsoft provides a Forms Administrator tool. This tool was designed to work with Outlook 2000, but can assist with the process for later versions. Follow these steps to download and install the Forms Administrator tool:

1. From the Web page at http://www.microsoft.com/office/orkar-chive/2000ddl.htm#outladm, download the Formsadmin.exe file.

2. Run the downloaded Formsadmin.exe file.

3. When prompted for "the location where you want to place the extracted files," choose a folder on your local hard drive. This will extract the actual tool, FormSwap.exe, to the folder you indicate.

To use the Forms Administrator to make a published task form (for example, IPM.Task.All Fields) the default form replacing IPM.Task, follow these steps:

1. Run the FormSwap.exe tool.

2. In the Outlook Forms Administrator dialog (Figure 21.6), choose the basic Outlook form to override, in this case the task form, IPM.Task.

3. Under "For composing use," enter the published form's class, IPM.Task.All Fields.

4. Also enter the published form's class under "For reading use."

5. Click Save, then Export Saved Settings and choose a file name and location for the .reg file that the tool exports.

6. Click Close to close the tool.

**Figure 21.6**
*Use the free Forms Administrator tool to help modify the registry so that a custom form can replace a standard form as the global default.*

7.   Browse to the folder where you saved the .reg file, right-click it, and choose Edit to open the file in Notepad.

8.   Change the references to Office\9.0\Outlook to Office\12.0\ Outlook, as shown in Figure 21.7.

9.   Save and close the .reg file.

10.  Right-click the file again, choose Merge, and answer any prompts that ask if you want to merge this data with the registry.

What this process does is update the HKCU\Software\Microsoft\Office\ 12.0\Outlook\Custom Forms key with entries that tell Outlook how to substitute custom forms for the standard forms. Figure 21.8 shows one of the two registry values added in the above steps.

---

**Caution:** Replacing any default form is not a trivial matter. You should ensure that your replacement form includes all the functionality of the default form in addition to any special operations you have designed into the custom form. Also make sure that you enter the correct message class for a form published to the Personal Forms or Organizational Forms library. The Outlook Forms Administrator tool does not check to make sure that the form name you enter is a valid, published form of the correct type.

---

The registry entries have two separate effects on new and existing items. Existing items that used the default form will open in the form whose message class you substituted, but the value of the MessageClass property on

**Figure 21.7**
*The Forms Administrator tool was designed for use with Outlook 2000, but you can modify its output to work with Outlook 2007.*

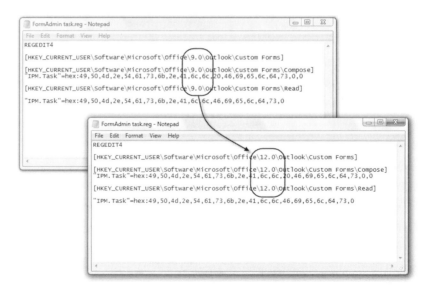

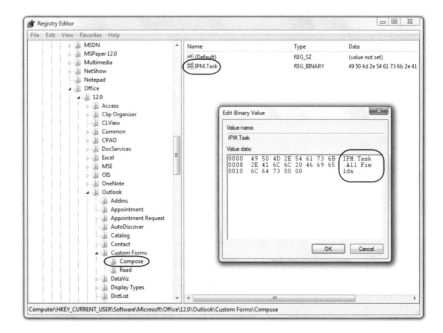

**Figure 21.8**
*Substituting a
custom form for a
default form
requires a new
Windows registry
value.*

the existing items will remain that of the standard form. For new items, however, the `MessageClass` property value will be that of the custom form that was substituted. If you later remove the substitution registry entry, the message class of those items does not change; Outlook will continue to look for the custom form, even if it is no longer available. In that scenario, if you want the items to revert to the built-in default form, you will need to change the value of the `MessageClass` property on the items using the technique covered in the next section.

A better solution is to use code in the published custom form to reset the `MessageClass` value on new items to the default form. For example, this code ensures that tasks will always be associated with the IPM.Task form, even if they're created with a substitute custom task form (IPM.Task.All Fields):

```
Function Item_Write()
    Item.MessageClass = "IPM.Task"
End Function
```

To completely remove a substitution, just delete the registry entries in the Outlook\Custom Forms key.

## 21.2.2 Converting existing items to use a custom form

Many times, you'll want to make existing items use a newly published custom form. For example, you may have a contacts folder with hundreds of items that you want to display in a new, customized contact form. Converting data from one form to another is a simple operation of changing one property value on each individual item—the `MessageClass` property—so that it points to the new published form.

You can run the `RunUpdateMessageClass` VBA macro in Listing 21.2 to update items in a folder to use a custom form instead of one of Outlook's default forms. The user selects the folder from the Select Folder dialog and supplies the name of the custom form via an input box.

The `RunUpdateMessageClass` procedure gets the default message class for a folder, and then calls the `UpdateMessageClass` procedure, which does the actual updating and has a lot of flexibility built in with its three parameters, which include the folder whose items are to change, the old message class, and the new message class. For example, the calling statement in the `RunUpdateMessageClass` procedure changes only the items that match the default message class for the folder, for example, only items with a message class of IPM.Task:

```
Call UpdateMessageClass(objFolder, _
                    strFolderClass, strNewClass)
```

You can also call `UpdateMessageClass` from other procedures. For example, this statement would update all the contacts in the currently displayed folder, whether they use the standard form or a custom form:

```
Call UpdateMessageClass( _
   Application.ActiveExplorer.CurrentFolder, _
   "IPM.Contact.Customer", True)
```

After the `UpdateMessageClass` procedure performs some validation to confirm that the new message class is appropriate for the items in the target folder, it filters the target folder with an `Items.Restrict` statement, and then processes the filtered items. This is the heart of the procedure, the part that actually updates the message class:

```
For Each objItem In colItems
    objItem.MessageClass = class
    objItem.Save
Next
```

If you have hundreds of items in the folder, the procedure may take a while to complete the update.

## 21.2.3  Importing to a custom form

Outlook does not allow you to export directly to custom forms or custom fields using its File, Import and Export command. The same limitation applies to importing data. If you want to import to a custom form or to an item that contains custom fields, you must write code to copy the data into each field.

**Listing 21.2**   *Update the MessageClass for existing items to point to a new form*

```
Sub RunUpdateMessageClass()
    Dim objOL As Outlook.Application
    Dim objNS As Outlook.NameSpace
    Dim objFolder As Outlook.Folder
    Dim strMsg As String
    Dim strFolderClass As String
    Dim strNewClass As String
    On Error Resume Next
    Set objOL = Application
    Set objNS = objOL.Session
    Set objFolder = objNS.PickFolder
    If Not objFolder Is Nothing Then
        strMsg = "Change all items in folder to what class?"
        strFolderClass = objFolder.DefaultMessageClass
        strNewClass = InputBox(strMsg, "Update Message Class", _
                        strFolderClass)
        If strNewClass <> "" Then
            Call UpdateMessageClass(objFolder, strFolderClass, strNewClass)
        End If
    End If
    Set objOL = Nothing
    Set objNS = Nothing
    Set objFolder = Nothing
End Sub

Sub UpdateMessageClass(fld As Outlook.Folder, _
                    oldClass As String, newClass As String)
    Dim colItems As Outlook.Items
    Dim objItem As Object
    Dim strFolderClass As String
    Dim strBaseClass As String
    Dim strMsg As String
    Dim strTitle As String
    Dim strFind As String
    Dim lngCount As Long
    Const PR_MESSAGE_CLASS = _
      "http://schemas.microsoft.com/mapi/proptag/0x001A001E"
    On Error Resume Next
    strFolderClass = fld.DefaultMessageClass
    If UCase(Left(newClass, 8)) <> "IPM.POST" Then
        If InStr(1, newClass, strFolderClass, _
                vbTextCompare) = 0 Then
            strMsg = "The class you specified is not " & _
                    "the normal type for this folder. " & _
                    "Conversion will not proceed."
            strTitle = "Convert Items in " & fld.Name & _
                    " to " & newClass
            MsgBox strMsg, , strTitle
            Exit Sub
        End If
```

**Listing 21.2**    *Update the MessageClass for existing items to point to a new form (continued)*

```
End If
strFind = Quote(PR_MESSAGE_CLASS) & _
        " LIKE '" & oldClass & "'"
Set colItems = fld.Items.Restrict("@SQL=" & strFind)
For Each objItem In colItems
    objItem.MessageClass = newClass
    objItem.Save
    lngCount = lngCount + 1
Next
strMsg = CStr(lngCount) & " items updated to " & newClass
MsgBox strMsg, vbInformation, "Update Message Class"
Set colItems = Nothing
Set objItem = Nothing
End Sub

Private Function Quote(val) as String
    Quote = Chr(34) & CStr(val) & Chr(34)
End Function
```

**Note:** It is also not possible to program Outlook's built-in Import and Export feature to automate importing or exporting even when custom fields or forms are not involved. Chapter 24 provides a number of code and non-code techniques for extracting data from Outlook items.

The exact code, of course, will depend on the data source. You must use the appropriate syntax for any particular source to get the source records and fields. If the data is in a delimited text file, an Excel worksheet, or a database you can access with ADO, the VBA code to write the code should follow this basic sequence:

1.  Open the source file or database.

2.  Create a new Outlook item using the custom form.

3.  Get the first record from the source file or database.

4.  Copy the data from the data source fields to the corresponding properties in the Outlook item.

5.  Save the Outlook item.

6.  Repeat steps 2 to 7 until you run out of source data.

7.  Close the data source and perform any other cleanup.

Let's consider a relatively simple example—an Excel workbook with one active worksheet that contains data in two columns. Column A contains a list of contact names, while Column B contains their email addresses. The data rows in these two columns are marked with a range named Customers.

The goal is to import these rows into Outlook contact items that use a custom form named IPM.Contact.Customer. The code in Listing 21.3 includes a ### USER OPTIONS ### section where the workbook file name, range name, and custom form class are hard-coded. Adjust the names to fit your own scenario.

**Tip:** To insert a named range in Excel 2007, select the data you want to include in the range. Type the name of the range in the Name Box control at the top left of the worksheet, and press Enter.

Breaking down the `ExcelToContacts` procedure in terms of the seven basic import steps, Step 1 is opening the data source:

```
Set objExcel = GetObject(, "Excel.Application")
If objExcel Is Nothing Then
    Set objExcel = CreateObject("Excel.Application")
    blnWeOpenedExcel = True
End If
Set objWB = objExcel.Workbooks.Add(strWB)
Set objWS = objWB.Worksheets(1)
Set objRange = objWS.Range(strRange)
```

**Listing 21.3**  *Import from an Excel worksheet to a custom contact form*

```
Sub ExcelToContacts()
    Dim objExcel As Excel.Application
    Dim objWB As Excel.Workbook
    Dim objWS As Excel.Worksheet
    Dim objRange As Excel.Range
    Dim strWB As String
    Dim strRange As String
    Dim strForm As String
    Dim objOL As Outlook.Application
    Dim objNS As Outlook.NameSpace
    Dim objFolder As Outlook.Folder
    Dim objContact As Outlook.contactItem
    Dim intRowCount As Integer
    Dim i As Integer
    Dim blnWeOpenedExcel As Boolean
    Dim strMsg as String
    Dim i as Integer
    On Error Resume Next
    ' ### USER OPTIONS ###
    strWB = "C:\Data\Customers.xlsx"
    strRange = "Customers"
    strForm = "IPM.Contact.Customer"
    ' ### END USER OPTIONS ###
    blnWeOpenedExcel = False
    Set objExcel = GetObject(, "Excel.Application")
```

**Listing 21.3**   *Import from an Excel worksheet to a custom contact form  (continued)*

```
If objExcel Is Nothing Then
    Set objExcel = CreateObject("Excel.Application")
    blnWeOpenedExcel = True
End If
Set objWB = objExcel.Workbooks.Add(strWB)
Set objWS = objWB.Worksheets(1)
Set objRange = objWS.Range(strRange)
intRowCount = objRange.Rows.Count
intCount = 0
If intRowCount > 0 Then
    Set objOL = Application
    Set objNS = objOL.Session
    Set objFolder = objNS.GetDefaultFolder(olFolderContacts)
    For i = 1 To intRowCount
        Set objContact = objFolder.Items.Add(strForm)
        With objContact
            .FullName = objRange.Cells(i, 1)
            .EmailAddress = objRange.Cells(i, 2)
            .Save
            If Err.Number = 0 Then
                intCount = intCount + 1
            Else
                Err.Clear
            End If
        End With
    Next
End If
objWB.Close False
If blnWeOpenedExcel Then
    objExcel.Quit
End If
strMsg = "Items imported:" & CStr(intCount)
MsgBox strMsg, vbInformation, "Import from Excel to Contacts"
Set objExcel = Nothing
Set objWB = Nothing
Set objWS = Nothing
Set objRange = Nothing
Set objOL = Nothing
Set objNS = Nothing
Set objContact = Nothing
End Sub
```

The code checks to see if Excel is already running and, if it is not, starts an instance. The `blnWeOpenedExcel` variable helps track Excel's initial state, so we can invoke an `objExcel.Quit` statement to shut down Excel if it wasn't already running. The `objRange` variable contains the rows and columns that we want to import.

Step 2 is to create a new Outlook item from the desired custom form. As we discussed in Chapter 15, that operation involves using the `Add` method on the target folder's `Items` collection and passing the message class as the argument. In this case, the target folder is the default Contacts folder:

```
Set objFolder = objNS.GetDefaultFolder(olFolderContacts)
Set objContact = objFolder.Items.Add(strForm)
```

To get a record (in this case, a row) from the named range (Steps 3 and 6), the code uses a loop:

```
intRowCount = objRange.Rows.Count
For i = 1 To intRowCount
    ' process the data
Next
```

During each pass through the loop, Steps 4 and 5 read a record from the data source, set the Outlook property values, and save the item:

```
With objContact
    .FullName = objRange.Cells(i, 1)
    .EmailAddress = objRange.Cells(i, 2)
    .Save
End With
```

where `i` is the number of the current row in the Customers range. The syntax for returning the value of an Excel cell is very simple: `objRange.Cells(row_number, column_number)`.

In Step 6, the loop continues processing until it has read all the rows from the named range and created a new contact for each one. The final step is to close the data source and leave Excel as we found it:

```
objWB.Close False
If blnWeOpenedExcel Then
    objExcel.Quit
End If
```

The process of importing from a delimited text file would follow the same structure. Instead of Excel objects, you could use the `FileSystemObject` methods discussed in Chapter 8.

---

**Note:** Importing from Microsoft Access or another database would follow exactly the same sequence of steps using a Microsoft programming interface called ADO. One of the trickier aspects of database import is that there are many different kinds of databases, each with its own syntax for connecting to the database. Once you get a database connection, though, the process of reading the records and fields with ADO is the same for every database.

---

## 21.3 Managing custom fields

Outlook is sometimes referred to as a "semi-structured" database. This means that while there is a default data structure for items stored in a particular folder, any individual item may contain a custom property that is not defined as part of the folder. It might not even be defined on any other items in that folder!

Publishing or copying a form to a folder only saves the form definition in the folder. It does not automatically create custom fields in the folder that match the custom fields in the form definition. Why does this matter? There are three main reasons:

- A custom view can display only fields defined in the folder.

- Searches that use the Jet and basic DASL query syntaxes can only search fields that are defined in the folder.

- If the field is not defined in the folder, the user could create a new custom field in the folder with a different data type from the field with the same name in the individual items.

**Note:** Searches using content index keywords can handle custom text properties that are in the items, but not defined in the folder. The content indexer indexes all custom text properties in each item.

Problems can also arise in the opposite scenario, where the folder contains field definitions that are not carried over into the forms used in the folder. For example, consider a tasks folder with a custom `ProjectStatus` field added to the folder. A table view can show that property, and with in-cell editing turned on, users can set the value for individual items by typing values into the view. However, if an item is using a custom form that doesn't include the `ProjectStatus` property, setting a value for that property will one-off the item, with the negative consequences discussed later in the chapter.

The ideal situation, therefore, is a three-way match between:

- custom properties in the folder
- custom properties in each custom form used in the folder
- custom properties in the items stored in the folder

The biggest challenge is achieving that congruence when you decide to use an existing form in a different folder. For example, if you make a form available to another user, either by publishing it in the Organizational Forms library or using the deployment methods discussed later in the chapter, the other user probably will not have the required fields in his or her folders. The same is true if you decide to use an existing form to create items in a newly added folder.

Unfortunately, Outlook provides no straightforward way to copy a set of custom properties from one folder to another: Publishing a custom form to a folder's forms library does not propagate custom properties to the folder. While Exchange users have available a File | Folder | Copy Folder Design command that can copy forms and views, that command does not copy folder-level field definitions.

## 21.3.1  Deploying custom fields

Three methods are available to deploy custom field definitions to a new folder:

1.  Copy an entire folder

2.  Create new fields manually using the Field Chooser

3.  Create new fields programmatically

If you already have a folder that contains not just the published form you want to use, but also the custom properties, views, and other folder design elements, you can copy that folder to another location elsewhere in the folder hierarchy to create a new folder with exactly the same characteristics. This is a very good method to use when one department in an organization wants to start using a folder-based application that was developed for a different department.

You can, of course, also create new fields manually with the Field Chooser, but this approach not only is tedious, but also holds the potential for inaccuracies, since the data type and field name must exactly match those used by the forms and items in the folder.

The best practice is to take care to build the custom forms for use in the folder in such a way that each field added to the form is also present as a folder-level field definition. The next section reviews the recommend technique for adding custom fields to custom forms.

If you have a folder that already contains the fields you want to use in another folder, Outlook 2007 makes it possible to write code to copy the folder-level field definitions, through a new `Folder.UserDefined-Properties` collection, analogous to the `UserProperties` collection on an individual Outlook item. The code in Listing 21.4 iterates all the fields in a source folder and creates new fields of the same type in a destination folder. Use a statement like this to call the `CopyFields` procedure:

```
Call CopyFields(objSourceFolder, objTargetFolder)
```

After running the `CopyFields` procedure, the target folder should contain all the fields that were in the source folder, except for any fields of the same name that already existed in the target folder.

**Caution:** Do not attempt to use the fields in the `UserProperties` collection of an Outlook item as a model for creating fields in the `UserDefined-Properties` collection of a folder. The item-level property definitions will not have all the detail needed to create the correct properties at the folder level.

**Listing 21.4**    *Use a custom form as a template for defining fields at the folder level*

```
Sub CopyFields(source As Folder, target As Folder)
    Dim colProps As Outlook.UserDefinedProperties
    Dim objOldProp As Outlook.UserDefinedProperty
    Dim objProp As Outlook.UserDefinedProperty
    On Error Resume Next
    Set colProps = target.UserDefinedProperties
    For Each objOldProp In source.UserDefinedProperties
        With objOldProp
            If .Type = olCombination Or .Type = olFormula Then
                Set objProp = colProps.Add( _
                    .Name, .Type, , .Formula)
            Else
                Set objProp = colProps.Add( _
                    .Name, .Type, .DisplayFormat, .Formula)
            End If
        End With
    Next
    Set objProp = Nothing
    Set objOldProp = Nothing
    Set colProps = Nothing
End Sub
```

## 21.3.2   Best practices for adding fields to custom forms

Having considered how to transfer field definitions from one folder to another, let's return to the issue of how best to ensure that a folder, its forms, and the items created from those forms all have the same field definitions. The key is to use a very specific method to add fields to any non-message form designed for use in a specific folder. If you add fields correctly to the form, they'll be defined correctly at the folder level, at the form level, and in the individual items created from the form.

**Note:** If you are designing a message form or a form that will be used in multiple folders, use these techniques to design the initial form. Then use the `CopyFields` procedure in Listing 21.4 to propagate the fields from the original folder to the additional folder(s) that will hold items created from the custom form. If you're creating a message form, the "source" folder containing the field definitions will be the Inbox.

First, if you are designing a form for use in a non-default folder, create a new item in the folder where you plan to use your form. Open the item and on the Developer tab, click Design This Form. If you are designing a form for use in a default folder, such as Contacts, you can use the New button or the Tools | Forms | Design a Form command to create the item used as the basis for the form.

On the form's Field Chooser, create each yes/no field that your form needs. This adds the field to the folder's field definitions. Drag each field to the desired custom page. This adds a check box control to the form, bound to the yes/no field, and adds the field to the form's field definitions.

Follow the same procedure for any text fields that you plan to display on the form in text boxes: Create the field in the Field Chooser, then drag it to the form.

For other types of fields besides yes/no and text fields, and for text and yes/no fields that you plan to display with combo boxes, list boxes, or option buttons, you will need to follow a different procedure. Create the control first, instead of the field, by dragging the desired control from the control toolbox. Then, right-click the control, choose Properties, switch to the Value tab, and click New to create the new field. This will place the field definition in the form and also in the folder.

After you finish adding fields to the form, check the All Fields page, and look under both "User-defined fields in this item" and "User-defined fields in folder." Each field that you added should appear in both lists.

---

**Tip:** Another approach is to simply drag all custom fields from the Field Chooser to a custom form page. This ensures that the fields are defined in the custom form. You don't need to show that page to the user. You don't even need to keep the controls on the page. Feel free to delete them and hide the page. Continue with your form design, adding controls only for those fields you want the user to see or interact with.

---

To remove a field definition from both the folder and a form used in that folder, you must delete each field twice. It's easiest to do this on the custom form, in design mode. On the All Fields page, delete the field from the "User-defined fields in this item" and also from the "User-defined fields in folder" list. Remember that folders and forms have completely separate field definitions. If you want to get rid of a field, you must delete the definition from both folder and form. Deleting a field definition from the folder or a custom form does not delete the data that any existing items may already be storing in that field, however.

## 21.4   Deploying Outlook forms

From the very beginning of our discussion of custom forms in Chapter 4, we've emphasized the need to publish forms in order to get full functionality from them. Forms that you design for your personal use should be published to your Personal Forms library or perhaps to individual folders' form libraries. In an organization where Microsoft Exchange is the mail server, you may have an Organizational Forms library available to hold forms for enterprise-wide use, along with a Public Folders hierarchy for folder-based applications that depend on published custom forms.

In some organizations, though, there is no central forms repository. Putting custom forms into the hands of users requires either that you provide detailed instructions or that you give users a file and some code to install the form from that file. The next section provides examples of both form installation instructions and such code.

## 21.4.1  Distributing forms to remote users

One way to distribute a form to remote users is to save it as an .oft template file or export it from the Forms Manager as an .fdm file and email it to the users, along with instructions on how to publish it to the Personal Forms library or import it into Forms Manager. Below are sample instructions you can provide to users if you send them an .oft file; note that they include details on how to display the Developer tab, which contains the Publish Form command.

---

To install the attached .oft file in your Personal Forms library, follow these steps:

1.  From Outlook's main menu, choose Tools | Options | Other | Advanced Options.

2.  In the Advanced Options dialog, under "In all Microsoft Office programs," check the box for "Show Developer tab in the Ribbon." Click OK twice to save the change.

3.  Right-click the .oft file attachment, choose Save As, and save it to your hard drive.

4.  From Outlook's main menu, choose Tools | Forms | Choose Form.

5.  In the Choose Form dialog, in the Look In list, select "User Templates in File System."

6.  Click the Browse button to browse to the location where you saved the .oft file in Step 3.

7.  Select the .oft file, and click Open.

8.  On the open form, switch to the Developer tab in the ribbon.

9.  In the Form group, click Publish | Publish Form.

10. The Publish Form As dialog should display your Personal Forms library. If it doesn't, use the Look In list to switch to that library.

11. For the display name, enter **My Form**. For the form name, enter **MyForm**.

12. Click Publish to complete the process.

---

In Step 11, replace **My Form** and **MyForm** with the names that you want the user to use for the published form.

Below are sample instructions you can provide to users if you send them an .fdm file.

---

To install the attached .fdm file in your Personal Forms library, follow these steps:

1. Right-click the .fdm file attachment, choose Save As, and save it to your hard drive

2. From Outlook's main menu, choose Tools | Options | Other | Advanced Options | Custom Forms | Manage Forms.

3. The right side of the Forms Manager dialog should show the Personal Forms library. If it does not, click the right-hand Set button, and set the library to the Personal Forms library.

4. On the Forms Manager dialog, click Install.

5. In the Open dialog, from the dropdown list of file types, select Form Message (*.fdm), and browse to the location where you saved the .fdm file in Step 1.

6. Select the saved .fdm file, and click Open.

7. On the Form Properties dialog, click OK.

8. Click Close, then click OK three times to return to the main Outlook window.

---

An alternative is to skip the instructions and provide code that publishes the form from an .oft file. The next section provides an example of such code.

### 21.4.2 Publishing a custom form programmatically

What makes it possible to install a custom form programmatically is that each Outlook item includes a `FormDescription` object that defines the properties of the form associated with the item. Once you retrieve this object from the item, you can use its `PublishForm` method to publish the form to the user's Personal Forms Library or any folder's forms library. Setting the `Name` property of the `FormDescription` object controls the display name and message class of the published form.

Listing 21.5 demonstrates this technique with a VBA sample that you could use to deploy multiple forms to one or more public folders. To publish a form to a particular folder, call the `PublishForm()` function with the path to an .oft form template file, the target forms library, and for a folder's forms library, the folder, for example:

```
    MsgBox PublishForm("C:\data\allfields2.oft", _
        olFolderRegistry, _
        Application.ActiveExplorer.CurrentFolder)
```

To publish a form to the Personal Forms library, call `PublishForm()` like this:

```
    MsgBox PublishForm("C:\data\allfields2.oft", _
                    olPersonalRegistry
```

The `PublishForm()` function gets the form name from the name of the .oft file. It returns a string that gives you the result of the operation, whether the form was published successfully or whether an error occurred.

The `PublishForm()` function is useful largely in situations where an administrator needs to publish a form to multiple folders—say to several public folders. It's less useful for installing a form for another user, because, as discussed in Chapter 2, Outlook doesn't provide a good way to distribute VBA code to others. A possible workaround would be to incorporate the function into a macro contained in a Word document; in that scenario, refer back to the material in Chapter 7 on writing code to automate Outlook from other applications.

**Listing 21.5**    *Publish a form using an item's FormDescription (VBA)*

```
Function PublishForm(oftPath As String, _
  reg As Outlook.OlFormRegistry, _
  Optional fld As Outlook.Folder) As String
    Dim objOL As Outlook.Application
    Dim objItem As Object
    Dim objFormDesc As Outlook.FormDescription
    Dim intLoc As Integer
    Dim intLoc2 As Integer
    Dim strName As String
    Dim strTarget As String
    Dim strRes As String
    On Error Resume Next
    Err.Clear
    Set objOL = Application
    Set objItem = objOL.CreateItemFromTemplate(oftPath)
    If Err.Number = 0 Then
        Set objFormDesc = objItem.FormDescription
        intLoc = InStrRev(oftPath, ".oft")
        intLoc2 = InStrRev(oftPath, "\")
        strName = Left(oftPath, intLoc - 1)
        strName = Mid(strName, intLoc2 + 1)
        objFormDesc.Name = strName
        Select Case reg
            Case olPersonalRegistry
                objFormDesc.PublishForm reg
                strTarget = "Personal Forms"
```

Listing 21.5 *Publish a form using an item's FormDescription (VBA) (continued)*

```
            Case olFolderRegistry
                If Not fld Is Nothing Then
                    objFormDesc.PublishForm reg, fld
                    strTarget = fld.Name
                Else
                    strRes = "Error: No folder specified."
                End If
            Case Else
                strRes = "Error: This procedure can " & _
                    "publish only to Personal Forms or " & _
                    "a folder's forms library."
        End Select
        If Err.Number = 0 Then
            strRes = objFormDesc.Name & _
                " was published to " & strTarget
        Else
            strRes = "Error " & Err.Number & _
                ": " & Err.Description
        End If
    Else
        strRes = "Error " & Err.Number & _
            ": " & Err.Description
    End If
    PublishForm = strRes
    Set objOL = Nothing
    Set objItem = Nothing
    Set objFormDesc = Nothing
End Function
```

**Note:** The `PublishForm()` function does not check to see whether a published form with the same name already exists in the target library. If you want to add that functionality to the procedure, use the techniques demonstrated in the `EnumCustomForms` procedure in Listing 21.1 to access the hidden folder that contains the published form definitions.

Another approach for deploying a form to users programmatically would be to use VBScript in a login script, a Web page, or even a published custom form in a special .pst file or in Organizational Forms if you're using Exchange. Listings 21.6 and 21.7 provide VBScript versions of the `PublishForm()` function, one for publishing to the Personal Forms library and one for publishing to a folder's forms library.

**Tip:** Chapter 22 demonstrates how to get Outlook to run an automation script at startup.

**Listing 21.6**   *Publish a form to Personal Forms (VBScript)*

```
Function PublishFormToPersonal(oftPath)
    Dim objOL                    ' As Outlook.Application
    Dim objNS                    ' As Outlook.NameSpace
    Dim objItem                  ' As Object
    Dim objFormDesc              ' As Outlook.FormDescription
    Dim intLoc                   ' As Integer
    Dim intLoc2                  ' As Integer
    Dim strName                  ' As String
    Dim strRes                   ' As String
    Dim blnWeStartedOutlook      ' As Boolean
    Const olPersonalRegistry = 2
    On Error Resume Next
    Err.Clear
    blnWeStartedOutlook = False
    Set objOL = GetObject(, "Outlook.Application")
    If objOL Is Nothing Then
        Set objOL = CreateObject("Outlook.Application")
        If Not objOL Is Nothing Then
            Set objNS = objOL.GetNamespace("MAPI")
            objNS.Logon
            blnWeStartedOutlook = True
        End If
    End If
    If objOL Is Nothing Then
        strRes = "Error: Could not start Outlook"
    Else
        Set objItem = objOL.CreateItemFromTemplate(oftPath)
        If Err.Number = 0 Then
            Set objFormDesc = objItem.FormDescription
            intLoc = InStrRev(oftPath, ".oft")
            intLoc2 = InStrRev(oftPath, "\")
            strName = Left(oftPath, intLoc - 1)
            strName = Mid(strName, intLoc2 + 1)
            objFormDesc.Name = strName
            objFormDesc.PublishForm olPersonalRegistry
            If Err.Number = 0 Then
                strRes = objFormDesc.Name & _
                    " was published to Personal Forms"
            Else
                strRes = "Error " & _
                    Err.Number & ": " & Err.Description
            End If
        Else
            strRes = "Error " & Err.Number & _
                ": " & Err.Description
        End If
    End If
    If blnWeStartedOutlook Then
        objNS.Logoff
        objOL.Quit
    End If
```

**Listing 21.6**   *Publish a form to Personal Forms (VBScript) (continued)*

```
PublishFormToPersonal = strRes
Set objOL = Nothing
Set objNS = Nothing
Set objItem = Nothing
Set objFormDesc = Nothing
End Function
```

Call these VBScript publishing routines like this:

```
MsgBox PublishFormToPersonal("C:\data\allfields2.oft")
MsgBox PublishFormToFolder("C:\data\allfields2.oft", _
        anyfolder)
```

where the *anyfolder* parameter is the Folder object where you want to publish the form.

If you use a script to deploy programmatically a form that has custom fields, you may want to enhance the script to use the Folder.UserDefinedProperties.Add method, as shown in Listing 21.4, add field definitions to the folder(s) where the items created from the form will be stored.

**Listing 21.7**   *Publish a form to a folder's forms library (VBScript)*

```
Dim objOL                     ' As Outlook.Application
Dim objNS                     ' As Outlook.NameSpace
Dim objItem                   ' As Object
Dim objFormDesc               ' As Outlook.FormDescription
Dim intLoc                    ' As Integer
Dim intLoc2                   ' As Integer
Dim strName                   ' As String
Dim strRes                    ' As String
Dim blnWeStartedOutlook       ' As Boolean
Const olFolderRegistry = 3
On Error Resume Next
Err.Clear
blnWeStartedOutlook = False
Set objOL = GetObject(, "Outlook.Application")
Function PublishFormToFolder(oftPath, fld)
If objOL Is Nothing Then
    Set objOL = CreateObject("Outlook.Application")
    If Not objOL Is Nothing Then
        Set objNS = objOL.GetNamespace("MAPI")
        objNS.Logon
        blnWeStartedOutlook = True
    End If
End If
If objOL Is Nothing Then
    strRes = "Error: Could not start Outlook"
```

**Listing 21.7**    *Publish a form to a folder's forms library (VBScript) (continued)*

```
Else
    Set objItem = objOL.CreateItemFromTemplate(oftPath)
    If Err.Number = 0 Then
        Set objFormDesc = objItem.FormDescription
        intLoc = InStrRev(oftPath, ".oft")
        intLoc2 = InStrRev(oftPath, "\")
        strName = Left(oftPath, intLoc - 1)
        strName = Mid(strName, intLoc2 + 1)
        objFormDesc.Name = strName
        objFormDesc.PublishForm olFolderRegistry, fld
        If Err.Number = 0 Then
            strRes = objFormDesc.Name & _
                " was published to " & fld.Name
        Else
            strRes = "Error " & _
                Err.Number & ": " & Err.Description
        End If
    Else
        strRes = "Error " & Err.Number & _
            ": " & Err.Description
    End If
End If
If blnWeStartedOutlook Then
    objNS.Logoff
    objOL.Quit
End If
PublishFormToFolder = strRes
Set objOL = Nothing
Set objNS = Nothing
Set objItem = Nothing
Set objFormDesc = Nothing
End Function
```

# 21.5  Troubleshooting Outlook forms

In general, custom forms created in earlier versions should work in Outlook 2007. They are, however, subject to a number of security issues covered in Chapter 10. Also, forms can't grow beyond a certain size or complexity. If you add too many fields to a form, it will stop saving values for some properties or may no longer calculate formula fields. If your form contains 150 or more custom fields, keep very good backups; you're probably getting close to the limit.

The two main problems plaguing developers of legacy Outlook forms are those related to one-off forms and the forms cache.

### 21.5.1  **Understanding one-off forms**

*One-off forms* are items where the form definition has become embedded in the item. Such items are nothing but trouble. They won't run code. They usually will not show the custom form layout. The embedded form design adds considerably to the size of the saved item. Avoid the most common causes of one-off forms with these tips:

- Always create items with published custom forms, rather than saved .oft form templates files. Use .oft files only for backups and for simple template-like solutions, such as sending messages with standard text, that do not include custom page layouts or custom forms.

- On the (Properties) page in the form designer, never check the "Send form definition with item" box.

- Make sure that all the custom properties your form needs are visible on the All Fields page under "User-defined fields in this item" before you publish the form, as discussed earlier in the chapter.

- Never use the `ItemProperties.Add` or `UserProperties.Add` method to add a custom property to an item that uses a published custom form. Instead, include the property as part of the published form design.

- Never use the `Actions.Add` method to add a voting button or other custom action to an item that uses a custom form. Instead, build the action into the published form design.

- Never use the `PossibleValues` property to populate the rows of a list or combo box. Instead, use the `AddItem` or `List` techniques discussed in Chapter 6, "Extending Form Design with Fields and Controls."

- On a custom message form, on the (Actions) tab, set the custom form for the Forward action to the same message class as the original form. In other words, publish the form, then go to the (Actions) tab, set the Forward action's form to the message class you just published, and publish the form a second time. (Remember, too, that published message forms generally are useful only if they're published to the Organizational Forms library on your company's Exchange server.)

To determine whether you have a one-off form situation, check the value of the `Size` and `MessageClass` properties for the item. If the `Size` value is larger than that for a normal item of that type and the `Message-Class` no longer shows your custom form's class but has reverted to the standard form's class, you have a one-off. Another telltale sign is that the icon for the item will revert from your custom form's icon to the standard icon for that type of item.

**Listing 21.8**    *Maintain the correct MessageClass value for a published custom form*

```
Dim m_strMessageClass

Function Item_Open()
        m_strMessageClass = Item.FormDescription.MessageClass
End Function

Function Item_Write()
        Item.MessageClass = m_strMessageClass
End Function
```

If you already have one-off items, resetting the `MessageClass` property to the custom form's class, as shown in Listing 21.2, provides a partial cure. The form remains embedded in the item, so the size is still large, but the item should recover its connection to the published form so that the code will run again.

---

**Tip:** The free MFCMAPI.exe tool mentioned in Chapter 14 includes a Remove One-Off Properties command to purge the embedded form definition from a one-off item.

---

To prevent one-offing, you can incorporate the code in Listing 21.8 into a custom form's VBScript code. The `Item_Open` event handler gets the item's published form class from its `FormDescription` object property, and then the `Item_Write` event handler sets the item's `MessageClass` value to the published class.

### 21.5.2    Dealing with forms cache problems

Even though the forms cache improves performance for legacy custom forms, it can also experience problems, usually problems that seem quite random. If the Frmcache.dat file or an individual cached form becomes corrupted, the user may see an error message that says, "The form you selected could not be displayed. Contact your administrator." Other times, the user might see the item open in the standard form instead of the custom form.

If the user is having what looks like a cache problem with only one form, you can try deleting from the cache just the folder that contains the cached copy of that form.

The brute force solution to forms cache corruption is to clear the cache completely, using the Clear Cache button on the Forms Manager dialog, shown in Figure 21.4. This wipes out the entire contents of the forms cache folder and also generates a fresh Frmcache.dat file. Outlook then will load a new copy of each form into the cache as the user opens it.

To minimize the impact from severe forms cache problems, Outlook supports this registry value:

Key: `HKEY_LOCAL_MACHINE\SOFTWARE\Microsoft\Office\12.0\Outlook`
Value name: `ForceFormReload`
Value type: `REG_DWORD`
Value: `1` (enabled)

Adding the `ForceFormReload` value and setting it to `1` causes Outlook to suppress the user prompt that normally appears when a form load problem occurs. Instead, Outlook clears the cache for that form and reloads it from the original source. The result is that the user should be unaware that a forms cache problem occurred, but may see poorer performance from custom forms.

### 21.5.3  Recovering a form from the forms cache

Another benefit of the forms cache is that it often can be used to recover a form if the user accidentally deletes the original published version. Locate the folder in the cache (in other words, the subfolder in the Microsoft\FORMS folder) that has a display name similar to the form name. Inside the folder, you will find a single file with a .tmp file extension. Copy that file to another folder, and rename it to .oft. Open the .oft file with the Tools | Forms | Choose Form or Tools | Forms | Design a Form command, and republish it to the original location with the same message class.

## 21.6  Summary

In this chapter, we've moved from the details of creating individual Outlook forms to the "big picture" of how to find, manage, deploy, and troubleshoot Outlook forms. Knowing where Outlook forms are stored as hidden items and cached files can help you understand why some form scenarios that may seem attractive—such as interoffice message forms—simply may not work in some environments.

Best practices for creating good Outlook forms include creating custom fields so that the field definition in the form matches those in the related folder and avoiding common causes of one-off forms. In the worst case scenario, when a form becomes corrupted, you can try to recover it either from a backup .oft or .fdm file or from the copy stored in the forms cache.

Several of the concepts in this chapter touch on the work that an administrator may need to do to make custom forms and folder-based applications available to users. In the next chapter, we'll look at some other administrative tasks that Outlook code can help, such as creating custom rules and views.

# 22

# *Rules, Views, and Administrator Scripting Tasks*

Outlook programming can not only help individual users become more productive, but can also help network administrators meet some of the challenges that they face in gathering information from users and deploying Outlook options. Custom message forms and folder home pages are two ways administrators can use to get script to run inside a user's Outlook session.

However, this chapter isn't just for administrators. Outlook 2007 adds two new sets of objects that should interest all users who write Outlook VBA code—an expanded set of objects for managing folder views and completely new objects creating and managing Rules Wizard rules.

Highlights of this chapter include discussions of the following:

- Why writing scripts to configure Outlook is a challenge
- How to create and modify a view programmatically
- How to create a new rule
- How to run rules programmatically against any folder
- Where a custom message form can be useful in gathering information or deploying options
- Why a folder home page with an Outlook View Control can help you deploy Outlook settings

Most of the settings that the user sees in the Tools | Options dialog are not exposed in the Outlook object model, but are configurable through Group Policy Objects or the Office Configuration Tool. If you're interested in managing those settings or controlling the settings for individual email accounts, I suggest that you visit Microsoft's Web site and read the articles in the Office Resource Kit about those configuration tools. We won't be covering those settings in this chapter, since they are not exposed in the Outlook object model.

## 22.1   Why Outlook scripting is a challenge

Several factors make scripting Outlook settings a challenge. First, Outlook must be running before any code can invoke its objects, but many desktop anti-virus applications block access to the `Outlook.Application` object. Even if an external script can successfully start Outlook with a `Create-Object("Outlook.Application")` call, it still must make sure that Outlook is running with the right mail profile. Unless you're working in an environment where the desktop is locked down, the user might have more than one mail profile, and sneaky users might not even have their main profile set as the default.

Given those issues, I'm not going to recommend any specific external scripting approaches. That said, if your network environment makes it possible to start Outlook with a particular profile, then you should be able to incorporate the procedures in this book into your external scripts.

What I propose instead are two "internal scripting" approaches: published custom forms (only for Exchange environments) and folder home pages. Both of these can run the right code, at the right time, in the right place to update Outlook with new settings.

---

**Note:** I'm using "settings" loosely here and throughout the rest of the chapter to denote any change that you might want to make to Outlook, aside from the data in Outlook items themselves.

---

Before we look at those solutions in detail, there is one other factor that makes Outlook scripting a challenge: Outlook's non-registry settings are stored all over the place—in external files, in hidden folders, in hidden items, and in hidden properties. Only a thorough knowledge of the Outlook object model and hours spent with tools like Outlook Spy, MFCMAPI.exe, and various registry analysis utilities can unlock all the secrets of Outlook's settings. Even after working with Outlook for more than ten years, I'm still learning new things about how it works "under the hood."

Because of the many mysteries involved in Outlook settings, I hesitate to say that some particular operation is impossible. But to save you the trouble of digging, I can confidently say that these tasks cannot be done, at least not with the Outlook object model in the initial Office 2007 release:

- Add an address or domain to any of the Junk E-mail lists (Use the Office Customization Tool from the Office 2007 Resource Kit for this task)

- Delete a custom form from the Organizational Forms library or from an Exchange public folder's forms library

- Add, modify, or remove an email account or send/receive group
- Modify the lists used for address resolution
- Change the name display order for the Outlook Address Book
- Set permissions on Exchange mailbox folders
- Set the default view on an Exchange public folder

The good news is that Outlook 2007 makes more Outlook configuration settings accessible to programming than ever before. It exposes some—like the master category list, views, and rules—directly in the object model, while you can get at many others through the new `PropertyAccessor` and `StorageItem` objects.

With that background, we'll look first at how custom message forms can contribute to configuration and reporting challenges, then at the end of the chapter, we'll examine the potential role of folder home pages. In between, we'll dive into the new Outlook 2007 objects that expose rule and view features.

## 22.2   Internal scripting with custom message forms

If your mail server is not Microsoft Exchange, or if you have Exchange but no one is allowed to publish to the Organizational Forms library, you can skip this section. Why? Because only through the Organizational Forms library on an Exchange server can you get the functionality needed to run scripts behind custom Outlook message forms.

If you do have the ability to place forms in the Organizational Forms library, you can build custom forms to help deploy settings to users and to collect data from users. Anything that can be done with a VBA macro can be scripted in a custom form.

### 22.2.1   Deploying settings with a custom form

To see how a custom form can help propagate Outlook settings, let's incorporate the form publishing technique discussed in the previous chapter into a published custom form. In other words, we're going to make one form publish another!

To design the form that will do the publishing, open a custom message form and click the Edit Read Page button. (You do not need to customize the compose layout, although you are certainly free to do so if you like.) On the Message page, remove the message body control. Add a command button control, name it `cmdInstall`, and give it a caption such as "Install Form." Add a label control, and name it `lblInstructions`. You can leave the label's caption as is, because the form's code will change it. The label should be tall enough to display several lines of text.

**Listing 22.1**     *Use one custom form to install another*

```
Dim m_objOFT            ' As Outlook.Attachment

Sub cmdInstall_Click()
    Dim objAtt          ' As Outlook.Attachment
    Dim objFSO          ' As Scripting.FileSystemObject
    Dim fldTemp         ' As Scripting.Folder
    Dim strPath         ' As String
    Dim strMsg          ' As String
    Const TemporaryFolder = 2
    If Not m_objOFT Is Nothing Then
        Set objFSO = _
          CreateObject("Scripting.FileSystemObject")
        Set fldTemp = _
          objFSO.GetSpecialFolder(TemporaryFolder)
        strPath = fldTemp.Path & "\" & m_objOFT.fileName
        m_objOFT.SaveAsFile strPath
        ' PublishFormToPersonal from Listing 21.6
        strMsg = PublishFormToPersonal(strPath)
        MsgBox strMsg, , "Form Installer"
        objFSO.DeleteFile strPath
    End If
End Sub

Function Item_Open()
    Dim objInsp         ' As Outlook.Inspector
    Dim objPage
    Dim lblInstructions
    If Item.Size <> 0 Then
        Call SetOFT
        If Not m_objOFT Is Nothing Then
            Set objInsp = Item.GetInspector
            Set objPage = _
              objInsp.ModifiedFormPages("Message")
            Set lblInstructions = _
              objPage.Controls("lblInstructions")
            lblInstructions.Caption = _
              "To install this form" & vbCrLf & vbCrLf & _
              vbTab & m_objOFT.fileName & vbCrLf & vbCrLf & _
              "Please click the Install button."
        End If
    End If
    Set objInsp = Nothing
    Set objPage = Nothing
    Set lblInstructions = Nothing
End Function

Function Item_Send()
    Dim strMsg          ' As String
    Call SetOFT
    If m_objOFT Is Nothing Then
        strMsg = "Can't send without an .oft file attached."
        MsgBox strMsg, vbExclamation, "Form Installer"
    End If
End Function
```

**Listing 22.1** *Use one custom form to install another (continued)*

```
Function Item_BeforeAttachmentAdd(ByVal NewAttachment)
    Dim strMsg     ' As String
    If StrComp(Right(NewAttachment.fileName, 4), _
               ".oft", vbTextCompare) <> 0 Then
        NewAttachment.Delete
        strMsg = "This form supports only .oft attachments."
        MsgBox strMsg, vbExclamation, "Form Installer"
        BeforeAttachmentAdd = False
    Else
        Item.Subject = "Open this message to install a form"
    End If
End Function

Sub SetOFT()
    Dim objAtt        ' As Outlook.Attachment
    For Each objAtt In Item.Attachments
        If StrComp(Right(objAtt.fileName, 4), _
                   ".oft", vbTextCompare) = 0 Then
            Set m_objOFT = objAtt
            Exit For
        End If
    Next
    Set objAtt = Nothing
End Sub
```

Add the code in Listing 22.1 to the form, and also add the `Publish-FormToPersonal()` function from Listing 21.6. To test the form, publish it to your Personal Forms library, perhaps with a message class of IPM.Note.InstallForm. Create a new message from the published form, attach an .oft form template file, and send the message to yourself. When it arrives, open it, and click the Install Form button to install the attached .oft file to your Personal Forms library.

If you like the way it works, you can copy the form with the publishing script to the Organizational Forms library for everyone to access.

The only technique in this form's script that should be new to you is the use of the `BeforeAttachmentAdd` event to prevent the user from adding files other than .oft files to the form. This event is new to Outlook 2007, but the Script | Event Handler command in the custom form code window does not list it. It uses the same `FileSystemObject` techniques that we saw in Chapter 19 to save the attached .oft file to the local hard drive and later delete it.

This approach to distributing Outlook settings—running code from a command button on a custom form—can be applied to many other scenarios. You could, for example, write a script that creates a rule for the user or adds an Exchange public folder to the Outlook address book.

## 22.2.2   **Using custom forms to generate reports**

We've used Outlook VBA code in several scenarios to generate reports—outputting the results to the VBA Immediate window, to a new message, or even to an Excel worksheet. Code behind a custom form can also generate reports, using similar Outlook object model techniques, only in VBScript code. As an example that's relevant to one of the other key topics of this chapter, let's build a form that enables the user to send back a report about the Outlook rules in the current session.

The form design process is almost identical to that for the form installer. To design the form, open a custom message form and click the Edit Read Page button. (You do not need to customize the compose layout, although you are certainly welcome to do so.) On the Message page, remove the message body control. Add a command button control, name it `cmdReport` and give it a caption such as "Send Report." Add a label control, and name it `lblInstructions`. The label should be tall enough to display several lines of text. Set its caption to "Click the Send Report button to send back a report of your Outlook rules." On the All Fields page, set the Subject to "Open message to run a rules report."

Add the code in Listing 22.2 to the form. To test the form, publish it to your Personal Forms library. Create a new message from the published form, and send the message to yourself. When it arrives, open it, and click the Send Report button to display a message containing a report on your rules (see Figure 22.1). If you like the way it works, you can copy it to the Organizational Forms library so that your Help Desk can send requests for a rules report to individual users.

The R/S column shows whether a rule operates on received or sent messages. The other columns in the report are self-explanatory. Rules that invoke a VBA macro using the "run a script" rule action are listed in the report as "Unknown or Script." That action should report an `ActionType` of `olRuleActionRunScript` (20), but in the initial release of Outlook 2007, it returns `olRuleActionUnknown` (0) instead.

Each `Rule` object has `Conditions`, `Actions`, and `Exceptions` collections that work a bit differently from the other Outlook collections that you are familiar with. Each collection holds a fixed number of items—one item for each type of condition, action, and exception that Outlook supports. Whether a condition applies to the current rule depends on the value of each `RuleCondition` object's `Enabled` property (`True` or `False`). Actions and exceptions work the same way. The `Exceptions` collection, in fact, contains `Condition` objects, which is why we can use one function—`GetConditions()`—to build both the condition and exception lists in the report.

────────────────▶

**Listing 22.2**   *Generate a report on Outlook rules*

```
Dim m_strHTML    ' As String

Sub cmdReport_Click()
    Dim msg       ' As MailItem
    Set msg = Item.Reply
    msg.Subject = "Rules report for " & _
                 Application.Session.CurrentUser
    msg.HTMLBody = BuildRulesReport
    msg.Display
End Sub

Function BuildRulesReport()
    Dim objNS       ' As Outlook.NameSpace
    Dim objStore    ' As Outlook.Store
    Dim colRules    ' As Outlook.Rules
    On Error Resume Next
    Set objNS = Application.Session
    m_strHTML = BuildHTMLHead & "<body>" & _
      "<p>Rules Report For " & objNS.CurrentUser & _
      " <br>Profile Name: " & _
       objNS.CurrentProfileName & "</p>"
    For Each objStore In objNS.Stores
        Set colRules = objStore.GetRules
        m_strHTML = m_strHTML & "<p>Number of rules in " & _
                   objStore.DisplayName & ": "
        If Err.Number = 0 Then
            m_strHTML = m_strHTML & _
                       CStr(colRules.Count) & "</p>"
            m_strHTML = m_strHTML & BuildRulesTable(colRules)
        Else
            m_strHTML = m_strHTML & Err.Description
            Err.Clear
        End If
    Next
    BuildRulesReport = m_strHTML & "</body></html>"
End Function

Function BuildRulesTable(allRules)
    Dim objRule    ' As Outlook.Rule
    Dim strHTML    ' As String
    strHTML = "<table cellspacing='5' cellpadding='2'>" & _
             "<tr>" & AddColHead("Order") & _
             AddColHead("Name") & AddColHead("Active") & _
             AddColHead("R/S") & _
             AddColHead("Conditions") & _
             AddColHead("Actions") & _
             AddColHead("Exceptions")
    For Each objRule In allRules
        With objRule
            strHTML = strHTML & "<tr>" & _
             AddCell(.ExecutionOrder) & AddCell(.Name)
```

**Listing 22.2**      *Generate a report on Outlook rules (continued)*

```
            If .Enabled Then
                strHTML = strHTML & AddCell("X")
            Else
                strHTML = strHTML & AddCell("")
            End If
            If .RuleType = olRuleReceive Then
                strHTML = strHTML & AddCell("R")
            Else
                strHTML = strHTML & AddCell("S")
            End If
        End With
        strHTML = strHTML & _
          AddCell(GetConditions(objRule, False)) & _
          AddCell(GetActions(objRule)) & _
          AddCell(GetConditions(objRule, True)) & "</tr>"
    Next
    BuildRulesTable = strHTML & "</table>"
End Function

Function AddColHead(headText)
    AddColHead = "<td class='header'>" & headText & "</td>"
End Function
Function AddCell(newText)
    AddCell = "<td>" & newText & "</td>"
End Function

Function GetConditions(myRule, getExceptions)
    Dim objCond      ' As Outlook.RuleCondition
    Dim colCond      ' As Outlook.RuleConditions
    Dim strCond      ' As String
    If getExceptions Then
        Set colCond = myRule.Exceptions
    Else
        Set colCond = myRule.Conditions
    End If
    For Each objCond In colCond
        If objCond.Enabled Then
            Select Case objCond.ConditionType
                Case 0      ' olConditionUnknown
                    strCond = strCond & "Unknown"
                Case 1      ' olConditionFrom
                    strCond = strCond & "From"
                Case 2      ' olConditionSubject
                    strCond = strCond & "Subject"
                Case 3      ' olConditionAccount
                    strCond = strCond & "Account"
                Case 4      ' olConditionOnlyToMe
                    strCond = strCond & "OnlyToMe"
                Case 5      ' olConditionTo
                    strCond = strCond & "To"
                Case 6      ' olConditionImportance
                    strCond = strCond & "Importance"
```

```
        Case 7        ' olConditionSensitivity
            strCond = strCond & "Sensitivity"
        Case 8        ' olConditionFlaggedForAction
            strCond = strCond & "FlaggedForAction"
        Case 9        ' olConditionCc
            strCond = strCond & "Cc"
        Case 10       ' olConditionToOrCc
            strCond = strCond & "ToOrCc"
        Case 11       ' olConditionNotTo
            strCond = strCond & "NotTo"
        Case 12       ' olConditionSentTo
            strCond = strCond & "SentTo"
        Case 13       ' olConditionBody
            strCond = strCond & "Body"
        Case 14       ' olConditionBodyOrSubject
            strCond = strCond & "BodyOrSubject"
        Case 15       ' olConditionMessageHeader
            strCond = strCond & "MessageHeader"
        Case 16       ' olConditionRecipientAddress
            strCond = strCond & "RecipientAddress"
        Case 17       ' olConditionSenderAddress
            strCond = strCond & "SenderAddress"
        Case 18       ' olConditionCategory
            strCond = strCond & "Category"
        Case 19       ' olConditionOOF
            strCond = strCond & "OOF"
        Case 20       ' olConditionHasAttachment
            strCond = strCond & "HasAttachment"
        Case 21       ' olConditionSizeRange
            strCond = strCond & "SizeRange"
        Case 22       ' olConditionDateRange
            strCond = strCond & "DateRange"
        Case 23       ' olConditionFormName
            strCond = strCond & "FormName"
        Case 24       ' olConditionProperty
            strCond = strCond & "Property"
        Case 25       ' olConditionSenderInAddressBook
            strCond = strCond & "SenderInAddressBook"
        Case 26       ' olConditionMeetingInviteOrUpdate
            strCond = strCond & "MeetingInviteOrUpdate"
        Case 27       ' olConditionLocalMachineOnly
            strCond = strCond & "LocalMachineOnly"
        Case 28       ' olConditionOtherMachine
            strCond = strCond & "OtherMachine"
        Case 29       ' olConditionAnyCategory
            strCond = strCond & "AnyCategory"
        Case 30       ' olConditionFromRssFeed
            strCond = strCond & "FromRssFeed"
        Case 31       ' olConditionFromAnyRssFeed
            strCond = strCond & "FromAnyRssFeed"
    End Select
    strCond = strCond & "<br>"
```

→

**Listing 22.2**      *Generate a report on Outlook rules (continued)*

```
        End If
    Next
    GetConditions = strCond
End Function

Function GetActions(myRule)
    Dim objAct  ' As Outlook.RuleAction
    Dim strAct  ' As String
    For Each objAct In myRule.Actions
        If objAct.Enabled Then
            Select Case objAct.ActionType
                Case 0  ' olRuleActionUnknown
                    strAct = strAct & "Unknown or Script"
                Case 1    ' olRuleActionMoveToFolder
                    strAct = strAct & "MoveToFolder"
                Case 2    ' olRuleActionAssignToCategory
                    strAct = strAct & "AssignToCategory"
                Case 3    ' olRuleActionDelete
                    strAct = strAct & "Delete"
                Case 4    ' olRuleActionDeletePermanently
                    strAct = strAct & "DeletePermanently"
                Case 5    ' olRuleActionCopyToFolder
                    strAct = strAct & "CopyToFolder"
                Case 6    ' olRuleActionForward
                    strAct = strAct & "Forward"
                Case 7    ' olRuleActionForwardAsAttachment
                    strAct = strAct & "ForwardAsAttachment"
                Case 8    ' olRuleActionRedirect
                    strAct = strAct & "Redirect"
                Case 9    ' olRuleActionServerReply
                    strAct = strAct & "ServerReply"
                Case 10    ' olRuleActionTemplate
                    strAct = strAct & "Template"
                Case 11    ' olRuleActionFlagForActionInDays
                    strAct = strAct & "FlagForActionInDays"
                Case 12    ' olRuleActionFlagColor
                    strAct = strAct & "FlagColor"
                Case 13    ' olRuleActionFlagClear
                    strAct = strAct & "FlagClear"
                Case 14    ' olRuleActionImportance
                    strAct = strAct & "Importance"
                Case 15    ' olRuleActionSensitivity
                    strAct = strAct & "Sensitivity"
                Case 16    ' olRuleActionPrint
                    strAct = strAct & "Print"
                Case 17    ' olRuleActionPlaySound
                    strAct = strAct & "PlaySound"
                Case 18    ' olRuleActionStartApplication
                    strAct = strAct & "StartApplication"
                Case 19    ' olRuleActionMarkRead
                    strAct = strAct & "MarkRead"
```

**Listing 22.2** *Generate a report on Outlook rules (continued)*

```
            Case 20      ' olRuleActionRunScript
                strAct = strAct & "RunScript"
            Case 21      ' olRuleActionStop
                strAct = strAct & "Stop"
            Case 22      ' olRuleActionCustomAction
                strAct = strAct & "CustomAction"
            Case 23      ' olRuleActionNewItemAlert
                strAct = strAct & "NewItemAlert"
            Case 24      ' olRuleActionDesktopAlert
                strAct = strAct & "DesktopAlert"
            Case 25      ' olRuleActionNotifyRead
                strAct = strAct & "NotifyRead"
            Case 26      ' olRuleActionNotifyDelivery
                strAct = strAct & "NotifyDelivery"
            Case 27      ' olRuleActionCcMessage
                strAct = strAct & "CcMessage"
            Case 28      ' olRuleActionDefer
                strAct = strAct & "Defer"
            Case 30      ' olRuleActionClearCategories
                strAct = strAct & "ClearCategories"
            Case 41      ' olRuleActionMarkAsTask
                strAct = strAct & "MarkAsTask"
        End Select
        strAct = strAct & "<br>"
      End If
    Next
    GetActions = strAct
End Function

Function BuildHTMLHead()
    BuildHTMLHead = "<html><head><style>" & _
      "<!-- td.header {font-family: Arial; " & _
                "font-weight: bold;} " & _
      "td {vertical-align: top;" & _
        "font-family: Arial, Helvetica, sans-serif;" & _
        "font-size: x-small;}--></style></head>"
End Function
```

The rest of the report is similar to other reports that generate HTML messages, such as Listings 18.1 and 18.2—an exercise in building HTML code, mainly a table, with a couple of styles to format the information. We've kept this report relatively simple by omitting the details, such as what specific folder a rule is moving items to, but it should give you an idea of how such reporting forms can assist the Help Desk in gathering information from both in-house and remote users who connect to your Exchange server.

**Figure 22.1**
*A custom message
form can generate
reports like this to
send back to the
Help desk.*

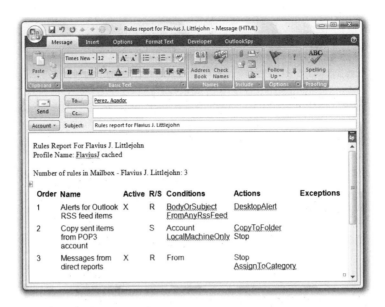

**Tip:** To test your own understanding of this technique and your ability to
convert VBA code to VBScript, try your hand at adapting the code in Listing 13.10 or Listing 18.1 to build a message form that reports back a list of
all the user's folders or address lists.

## 22.3 **Working with Outlook rules**

As you saw in the previous section, Outlook 2007 introduces a `Rules` collection containing `Rule` objects that represent all of the user's rules. Not
only can code report on those rules, as in Listing 22.2, but you can also create new rules programmatically and write code to run them, modify them,
delete them, or disable them.

Rules are store-specific. Each information store has its own set of rules,
although not all stores support rules. For example, stores for non-default
.pst files or SharePoint proxy folders do not support rules. Table 22.1 lists
the important property and methods of the `Rules` collection, all of which
are new in Outlook 2007.

What should stand out from the list of `Rules` collection methods in
Table 22.1 is that there is no `Add` method like other Outlook collections
have. Instead, the `Create` and `Save` methods are the beginning and end of
the process of creating a rule. As you'll see, this process is very different
from creating a folder, a message, or any of the other Outlook objects you've
encountered so far.

**Table 22.1** *Key Rules Collection Property and Methods*

| Property | Description |
|---|---|
| IsRssRulesProcessingEnabled | True or False; corresponds to the value of the "Enable rules on all RSS Feeds" on the Tools \| Rules and Alerts dialog box |

| Method | Description |
|---|---|
| Create(*Name, RuleType*) | Returns a new rule with the given name and a *RuleType* from the OlRuleType enumeration:<br>olRuleReceive    0<br>olRuleSend    1 |
| Item(*Index*) | Returns the rule represented by the given *Index* number or Name of the rule |
| Remove *Index* | Removes the rule represented by the given *Index* number or Name of the rule |
| Save *ShowProgress* | Save changes to individual rules in the collection, with an option to show a progress dialog; raises an error for rules with improperly defined conditions, actions, or exceptions or rules incompatible with the store |

Table 22.2 shows the key properties and methods for the individual Rule object, which is also completely new in Outlook 2007.

The Conditions, Actions, and Exceptions collections of the Rule object correspond to the three screens in the Rules Wizard where the user can set the conditions, actions, and exceptions for the rule. Unlike most other collections in the Outlook object model, these collections have no Add or Remove method. The only method they support is the Item method to return a member of the collection. These are so-called *fixed collections*, because each one already contains all the items it needs—one item for each supported condition, action, or exception—twenty-four available conditions or exceptions and seventeen actions.

**Tip:** The Select Case blocks in the GetConditions() and GetActions() functions in Listing 22.2 list the conditions and actions available to new rules created programmatically, plus quite a few additional conditions and actions that can only be enumerated.

To incorporate any condition, action, or exception into a rule, the code to create or modify that rule first gets the appropriate RuleCondition or RuleAction object from the collection, and then sets that object's Enabled property to True. (Exceptions being the same as conditions, only negated, they use the same RuleCondition object.)

**Table 22.2** *Key Rule Object Properties and Methods*

| Properties | Description |
|---|---|
| Actions | Fixed collection exposing all available actions |
| Conditions | Fixed collection exposing all available conditions |
| Enabled | True if the rule is active; False if it is not |
| Exceptions | Fixed collection exposing all available exceptions |
| ExecutionOrder | Integer that indicates the relative position of the rule in the execution order |
| IsLocalRule | True if the rule can run only when Outlook is running; False if the information store is an Exchange mailbox and the rule can run on the server; read-only |
| Name | Display name for the rule |
| RuleType | Read-only value that indicates whether the rule acts on received messages and RSS feeds or outgoing messages, from the OlRuleType enumeration:<br><br>olRuleReceive  0<br><br>olRuleSend    1 |

| Method | Description |
|---|---|
| Execute(*ShowProgress, Folder, IncludeSubfolders, RuleExecuteOption*) | Execute the rule immediately against the specified *Folder* and optionally its subfolders, with an optional progress dialog; if no *Folder* is specified, the rule runs against the Inbox. The fourth parameter, also optional, determines whether the rule runs against all, read, or unread items, according to the OlRuleExecuteOption enumeration:<br><br>olRuleExecuteAllMessages (default)  0<br><br>olRuleExecuteReadMessages        1<br><br>olRuleExecuteUnreadMessages      2 |

Before we walk through the process of creating a new rule, here are a few other basics you should know:

- Some rule conditions and actions cannot be added to a rule created programmatically. For example, you cannot create an out-of-office rule with the Rules collection.

- All send rules (RuleType = olRuleSend) are client-side rules.

- Some actions are appropriate only for receive or only for send rules.

- Whether a receive rule is a server-side (IsLocalRule = False) or client-side rule depends on the conditions, actions, and exceptions defined for that rule. It is not possible to directly designate a particular rule as a server-side or client-side rule.

- The "redirect" and "have server reply" actions are server-only and cannot be mixed with client-only actions such as "mark it as read."
- Saving a set of newly created rules may be a time-consuming process, especially if the store is an Exchange mailbox. You can use the optional `ShowProgress` parameter of the `Rules.Save` method to give the user an opportunity to cancel the operation.

### 22.3.1 Creating new rules

Any code to create and turn on a new, permanent rule needs to follow this sequence of steps:

1. Call the `Rules.Create` method, giving the rule a name and specifying whether the rule will act on received items (messages and/or RSS feeds) or on sent messages.

2. Enable each desired condition, and set any necessary property value.

3. Enable each desired action, and set any necessary property value.

4. Enable each desired exception, and set any necessary property value.

5. Set the `Enabled` property of the rule to `True`.

6. Call the `Save` method on the `Rules` collection.

If you are creating multiple rules, you can defer Step 6 and call `Save` after you have added all rules.

To create a rule but not activate it, skip Step 5.

To create a rule and execute it immediately but not save it permanently, skip both Steps 5 and 6 and call the `Rule.Execute` method.

Enabling and configuring a condition, action, or exception (as in Steps 2–4 above) is itself a multi-step process:

A. Return the rule condition object for the given condition or exception or, for an action, the rule action object.

B. If applicable, set the required property associated with the condition or action object.

C. Set the `Enabled` property of the condition or action object to `True`.

To manage the behavior of the twenty-four available rule conditions and exceptions, the Outlook object model contains ten different rule condition objects, listed in Table 22.3. Each rule condition object is based on the `RuleCondition` object and inherits from it the `Enabled` property used in

Step C above and the read-only `ConditionType` property that Listing 22.2 uses to build its rules report.

---

**Note:** Tables 22.3 and 22.4 list only the conditions and actions that can be used to create or modify rules programmatically. Other conditions and actions are possible, but the Outlook object model only allows them to be enumerated, as in Listing 22.2.

---

Each rule condition object derived from the `RuleCondition` object also contains a property that must be set before the rule can be saved or executed. The nature of that property varies. For example, the `TextRuleCondition` object is used to create rules to search in the body, subject, message header, and so on; it requires a value for its `Text` property—an array of the string or strings to search for. The `ToOrFromRuleCondition` object requires at least one recipient in its `Recipients` property. Table 22.3 lists the available conditions, along with the corresponding rule condition object for each one and the required property for each condition that has one. It also indicates which conditions can be used in send rules for outgoing messages.

For example, the following code handles Steps 1 and 2 of the six-step rule-creation sequence, adding a receive rule to a store's `Rules` collection and enabling the condition that looks for specific sender addresses:

```
' Step 1: Create the rule
   Set objRule = colRules.Create("From Customers", _
                              olRuleReceive)
' Step 2: Enable condition and set mandatory property
   ' Step A: Get the rule condition
   Set objSenderRule = objRule.Conditions.SenderAddress
   ' Step B: Set the required property
   arrSenders = Array("flaviusj@turtleflock.net", _
                   "dymka@turtleflock.net")
   objSenderRule.Address = arrSenders
   ' Step C: Enable the condition
   objSenderRule.Enabled = True
```

**Table 22.3**   *Rule Conditions Available to Outlook Code*

| Condition | Rule Condition Object | Required Rule Condition Property | Property Takes this Data Type or Object | OK for Send Rule |
|---|---|---|---|---|
| Account | AccountRuleCondition | Account | Outlook.Account | X |
| AnyCategory | RuleCondition | None | None | X |
| Body | TextRuleCondition | Text | String array | X |

**Table 22.3** *Rule Conditions Available to Outlook Code (continued)*

| Condition | Rule Condition Object | Required Rule Condition Property | Property Takes this Data Type or Object | OK for Send Rule |
|---|---|---|---|---|
| BodyOrSubject | TextRuleCondition | Text | String array | X |
| Category | CategoryRuleCondition | Categories | String array | X |
| Cc | RuleCondition | None | None | X |
| FormName | FormNameRuleCondition | FormName | String array of form message classes | X |
| From | ToOrFromRuleCondition | Recipients | Outlook.Recipients | |
| FromAnyRssFeed | RuleCondition | None | None | |
| FromRssFeed | FromRssFeedRuleCondition | FromRssFeed | String array of one or more RSS subscription names from the Outlook.Sharing.xml.obi file on the client machine | |
| HasAttachment | RuleCondition | None | None | X |
| Importance | ImportanceRuleCondition | Importance | Constant from the OlImportance enumeration | X |
| MeetingInviteOrUpdate | RuleCondition | None | None | X |
| MessageHeader | TextRuleCondition | Text | String array | |
| NotTo | RuleCondition | None | None | |
| OnLocalMachine | RuleCondition | None | None | X |
| OnlyToMe | RuleCondition | None | None | |
| RecipientAddress | AddressRuleCondition | Address | String array | X |
| SenderAddress | AddressRuleCondition | Address | String array | |
| SenderInAddressList | SenderInAddressListRule Condition | AddressList | Outlook.AddressList | |
| SentTo | ToOrFromRuleCondition | Recipients | Outlook.Recipients | X |
| Subject | TextRuleCondition | Text | String array | X |
| ToMe | RuleCondition | None | None | |
| ToOrCc | RuleCondition | None | None | |

**Table 22.4**    *Rule Actions Available to Outlook Code*

| Action | Rule Action Object | Required Rule Action Property | Property Takes This Data Type or Object | OK for Receive Rules | OK for Send Rules |
|---|---|---|---|---|---|
| AssignToCategory | AssignToCategoryRuleAction | Categories | String array | X | X |
| Cc | SendRuleAction | Recipients | Outlook.Recipients | | X |
| ClearCategories | RuleAction | None | None | X | X |
| CopyToFolder | MoveOrCopyRuleAction | Folder | Folder | X | X |
| Delete | RuleAction | None | None | X | |
| DeletePermanently | RuleAction | None | None | X | |
| DesktopAlert | RuleAction | None | None | X | |
| Forward | SendRuleAction | Recipients | Outlook.Recipients | X | |
| ForwardAsAttachment | SendRuleAction | Recipients | Outlook.Recipients | X | |
| MarkAsTask | MarkAsTaskRuleAction | None | None | X | |
| MoveToFolder | MoveOrCopyRuleAction | Folder | Folder | X | |
| NewItemAlert | NewItemAlertRuleAction | Text | String | X | |
| NotifyDelivery | RuleAction | None | None | | X |
| NotifyRead | RuleAction | None | None | | X |
| PlaySound | PlaySoundRuleAction | FilePath | String with full file path to a .wav file | X | |
| Redirect | SendRuleAction | Recipients | Outlook.Recipients | X | |
| Stop | RuleAction | None | None | X | X |

As there are ten kinds of condition objects, there are seven types of action objects to manage the behavior of the seventeen possible actions listed in Table 22.4. Each action object is based on the `RuleAction` object and inherits its `Enabled` and `ActionType` properties. Each action object derived from `RuleAction` has a required property you must set before saving or executing the rule. Table 22.4 shows the rule actions that you can add programmatically, along with the corresponding rule action objects and the action objects' required properties. It also indicates whether each action is available for receive and send rules.

To complete the "sender address" rule in the above snippet with a "move to folder" action, the code needs to return a `Folder` object:

```
' Step 3: Enable action and set mandatory property
  ' Step A: Get the rule action
    Set objMoveAction = objRule.Actions.MoveToFolder
  ' Step B: Set the required property
    Set objInbox = objNS.GetDefaultFolder(olFolderInbox)
    Set objFolder = objInbox.folders("Customers")
    objMoveAction.Folder = objCustomers
  ' Step C: Enable the action
    objMoveAction.Enabled = True
' Step 5: Enable the rule
    objRule.Enabled = True
' Step 6: Save the rule
    colRules.Save
```

We skipped Step 4, because this rule has no exceptions. Step 4 is identical to Step 2 except that you work with the Exceptions collection of the Rule object instead of the Conditions collection. The entire procedure, with object declarations, appears in Listing 22.3.

As you probably noticed from the omissions from Table 22.4, it is not possible to create programmatically certain types of rules—those to run a VBA macro, custom action, or external application; clear or set a message flag; mark a message as read or with a specific importance or sensitivity; print a message; have the server reply or reply with a template; or defer delivery.

For another example of a custom rule, check out "How to: Create a Rule to Move Specific E-mails to a Folder" (HV10038598) in Outlook developer Help.

The number in parentheses is a topic ID you can search for in Help to find the articles faster.

**Listing 22.3**   *Create a rule to move items to a folder*

```
Sub CreateFromCustomersRule()
    Dim objOL As Outlook.Application
    Dim objNS As Outlook.NameSpace
    Dim objStore As Outlook.Store
    Dim colRules As Outlook.Rules
    Dim objRule As Outlook.Rule
    Dim objInbox As Outlook.Folder
    Dim objCustomers As Outlook.Folder
    Dim objSenderRule As Outlook.AddressRuleCondition
    Dim objMoveAction As Outlook.MoveOrCopyRuleAction
    Dim arrSenders()
    Set objOL = Application
    Set objNS = objOL.Session
' Step 1: Create the rule
    Set objStore = objNS.DefaultStore
    Set colRules = objStore.GetRules
    Set objRule = colRules.Create( _
                "From Customers", olRuleReceive)
```

→

**Listing 22.3**   *Create a rule to move items to a folder (continued)*

```
' Step 2: Enable condition and set mandatory property
    Set objSenderRule = objRule.Conditions.SenderAddress
    arrSenders = Array("flaviusj@turtleflock.net", _
                        "dymka@turtleflock.net")
    objSenderRule.address = arrSenders
    objSenderRule.Enabled = True
' Step 3: Enable action and set mandatory property
    Set objMoveAction = objRule.Actions.MoveToFolder
    Set objInbox = objNS.GetDefaultFolder(olFolderInbox)
    Set objCustomers = objInbox.folders("Customers")
    objMoveAction.Folder = objCustomers
    objMoveAction.Enabled = True
' Step 5: Enable the rule
    objRule.Enabled = True
' Step 6: Save the rule
    colRules.Save
    Set objOL = Nothing
    Set objNS = Nothing
    Set objStore = Nothing
End Sub
```

### 22.3.2   **Running rules programmatically**

One of the most useful features of the `Rule` object is its `Execute` method, which allows code to run any rule on demand—either a saved rule or an ad hoc rule that is created, run, and then discarded. As shown in Table 22.2, the `Execute` method has options to show a progress dialog, run rules against any folder (the default being the Inbox), include subfolders in the execution, and run rules against only unread items, only read items, or all items. The `RunAllInboxRules` in Listing 22.4 executes all available receive rules against the Inbox, regardless of whether each rule is currently set to run automatically (in other words, regardless of whether its `Enabled` property is `True` or `False`).

To silently run a rule against only read items in a specific folder and its subfolders, you could use this statement:

```
objRule.Execute False, objFolder, True, _
            olRuleExecuteReadMessages
```

Outlook does not fire an event to indicate when a rule has finished its execution.

## 22.4   **Managing folder views**

Outlook 2007 improves on earlier versions by making it easier to create and modify views programmatically. In addition to a basic `View` object, the

**Listing 22.4**    *Run all receive rules against the Inbox*

```
Sub RunAllInboxRules()
    Dim objStore As Outlook.Store
    Dim colRules As Outlook.Rules
    Dim objRule As Outlook.Rule
    Dim intCount As Integer
    Dim strRuleList As String
    On Error Resume Next
    Set objStore = Application.Session.DefaultStore
    Set colRules = objStore.GetRules
    For Each objRule In colRules
        If objRule.RuleType = olRuleReceive Then
            objRule.Execute ShowProgress:=True
            intCount = intCount + 1
            strRuleList = strRuleList & vbCrLf & objRule.Name
        End If
    Next
    strRuleList = "These rules were executed " & _
      "against the Inbox: " & vbCrLf & strRuleList
    MsgBox strRuleList, vbInformation, _
            "Macro: RunAllInboxRules"
    Set objRule = Nothing
    Set objStore = Nothing
    Set colRules = Nothing
End Sub
```

object model now also supports view classes for specific view types, each of which exposes properties that are particular to that type of view:

- `BusinessCardView`
- `CalendarView`
- `CardView`
- `IconView`
- `TableView`
- `TimelineView`

Modifying views in earlier versions required an understanding of XML (Extensible Markup Language) and the XML schema that defines a view's configuration. In Outlook 2007, most view settings—including fields, sort order, and group order—are exposed through properties on the different view objects.

A view name is unique in any `Folder.Views` collection, so you can return a view from a folder knowing just its name:

```
Set objView = objFolder.Views(view_name)
```

To create a new view, return a `Views` collection from the `Folder`, and then use the `Add` method. You must specify the name of the view and the

**Table 22.5**   *Possible ViewType Values from the OlViewType Enumeration*

| ViewType Constant | Value |
|---|---|
| olBusinessCardView | 5 |
| olCalendarView | 2 |
| olCardView | 1 |
| olIconView | 3 |
| olTableView | 0 |
| olTimelineView | 4 |

type of view using one of the constants in Table 22.5. To save the new view and apply it, use the `Save` and `Apply` methods:

```
Set colViews = objFolder.Views
Set objView = colViews.Add(Name, ViewType, SaveOption)
objView.Save
objView.Apply
```

The third parameter in the `Views.Add` method, `SaveOption`, is optional and defines the scope of the view, using one of the constants in Table 22.6. The scope—where the view can be used and by whom—depends on where Outlook saves the view. As Table 22.6 shows, views visible to everyone are stored in the folder itself. General-use views and folder-specific views available only to the user are kept in a hidden folder in the user's default store. Since search folders are virtual folders and do not contain any actual items, they also cannot contain any view definitions. Therefore, you cannot create a view on a search folder using the scope, "This folder, visible to everyone." If you do not specify a `SaveOption` argument for a `Views.Add` statement, Outlook defaults to `OlViewSaveOptionThisFolderOnlyMe` for search folders and `OlViewSaveOptionThisFolderEveryone` for other folders.

**Table 22.6**   *Possible SaveOption Values from the OlViewSaveOption Enumeration*

| View Scope | SaveOption Constant | Value | Creates View Stored In . . . |
|---|---|---|---|
| All folders of a specific type | OlViewSaveOptionAllFoldersOfTYpe | 2 | Store (hidden folder) |
| This folder, visible to everyone | OlViewSaveOptionThisFolderEveryone | 0 | Folder |
| This folder, visible only to me | OlViewSaveOptionThisFolderOnlyMe | 1 | Store (hidden folder) |

The `OlViewType` enumeration also exposes an `olDailyTaskListView` (value = 6), but you cannot create a new view of this type.

You must have owner permission on the folder to create, modify, or delete a view that has a `SaveOption` property value of `OlViewSave-OptionThisFolderEveryone`.

To delete a custom view, return the `View` object from the `Views` collection and use its `Delete` method. As with other Outlook collections, you can also use the `Views.Remove` method.

If you use `objFolder.Views(view_name)` to return a standard view, such as the Messages view for a mail folder, modifying the view will cause Outlook to create a copy of the view definition for that one folder. It is not possible to modify the master copy of a standard view, such as Messages, programmatically. It is also not possible to clean up such folder-level cached view copies with the `View.Delete` or `Views.Remove` method. However, Listing 14.5 in Chapter 14 showed how to return such cached standard views as `StorageItem` objects and delete them.

Table 22.7 lists the important properties and methods of the `View` object.

You cannot change the `SaveOption` or `Type` of a view after the view is created. You can only set those properties as arguments in a `Views.Add` statement.

**Table 22.7**    *Key View Properties and Methods (\* = new in Outlook 2007)*

| Property | Description |
| --- | --- |
| Filter | String that generates a restriction on the view, using DASL syntax |
| Language | String for an ISO language tag (for example, `"EN-US"` for the United States); if present, the view will appear only on menus for that language |
| LockUserChanges | If `True`, changes that the user makes to the view are not stored permanently; default is `False` |
| Name | Name for the view |
| SaveOption | Scope constant from Table 22.6; read-only |
| Standard | `True` for built-in views; `False` for custom views; read-only |
| ViewType | Type constant from Table 22.5; read-only |
| XML | XML representation of a view's layout and options |
| **Method** | **Description** |
| Apply | Make the view the currently displayed view for the folder |

**Table 22.7**     *Key View Properties and Methods (\* = new in Outlook 2007) (continued)*

| Method | Description |
|---|---|
| `Copy(Name, SaveOption)` | Make a copy of the view, giving the new copy a `Name` and optional `SaveOption` using one of the constants from Table 22.6 |
| `Delete` | Delete the view |
| `*GoToDate(Date)` | In a calendar or timeline view, change the display so that the focus is on the specified date |
| `Reset` | On built-in views (`Standard = True`), reset the view to its original settings; does not apply to custom views |
| `Save` | Save |

### 22.4.1   Setting view properties

The Customize View dialog box invoked by users with the View | Current View | Customize Current View command gives users many different options for customizing views:

- Fields
- Group By
- Sort
- Filter
- Other Settings (fonts and other settings specific to the type of view)
- Automatic Formatting (user-defined font rules)
- Format Columns (display formats for each field)

Outlook 2007's expanded view programmability support makes it possible to configure most of these options with code. The necessary properties are exposed not in the general View object, but in the objects specific to the different types of views listed at the beginning of the previous section. Table 22.8 lists the key properties that the individual view types support in common, while Table 22.9 lists other properties that work only with one particular view type.

**Note:** While automatic formatting settings can be configured with the `Auto-FormatRules` collection and the individual `AutoFormatRule` objects it contains, those rules don't persist to the next Outlook session. Therefore, you might want to run any code that sets view automating rules either when Outlook starts, using the `Application.MAPILogonComplete` event, or when the user switches views, using the `Explorer.BeforeViewSwitch` event.

**Table 22.8** *Properties Common to Multiple View Types*

| Property | BusinessCardView | CalendarView | CardView | IconView | TableView | TimelineView |
|---|---|---|---|---|---|---|
| AllowInCellEditing | | | X | | X | |
| AutoFormatRules | | X | X | | X | |
| DefaultExpand CollapseSetting | | | | | X | X |
| GroupByFields | | | | | X | X |
| HeadingsFont | X | X | X | | | |
| EndField | | X | | | | X |
| SortFields | X | | X | X | X | |
| StartField | | X | | | | X |
| ViewFields | | | X | | X | |

**Table 22.9** *Properties Specific to Individual View Types*

| View Type | Properties |
|---|---|
| BusinessCardView | CardSize |
| CalendarView | BoldDatesWithinItems<br>BoldSubjects<br>CalendarViewMode<br>DaysInMultiDayMode<br>DayWeekFont<br>DayWeekTimeFont<br>DayWeekTimeScale<br>DisplayedDates<br>MonthFont<br>MonthShowEndTime |
| CardView | BodyFont<br>ShowEmptyFields<br>MultiLineFieldHeight<br>Width |
| IconView | IconPlacement<br>IconViewType |

**Table 22.9**    *Properties Specific to Individual View Types (continued)*

| View Type | Properties |
|---|---|
| TableView | AutomaticColumnSizing |
|  | AutomaticGrouping |
|  | AutoPreview |
|  | AutoPreviewFont |
|  | ColumnFont |
|  | GridLineStyle |
|  | HideReadingPaneHeaderInfo |
|  | MaxLinesInMultiLineView |
|  | MultiLine |
|  | MultiLineWidth |
|  | RowFont |
|  | ShowItemsInGroups |
|  | ShowNewItemRow |
|  | ShowReadingPane |
|  | ShowUnreadAndFlaggedMessages |
| TimelineView | ItemFont |
|  | LowerScaleFont |
|  | MaxLabelWidth |
|  | ShowLabelWhenViewingByMonth |
|  | ShowWeekNumbers |
|  | TimelineViewMode |
|  | UpperScaleFont |

Five other objects are important to setting view options:

- The `OrderFields` object returned by the `GroupByFields` and `SortFields` properties of all but the `CalendarView` object
- The individual `OrderField` objects in the `OrderFields` collection
- The `ViewField` objects in the `ViewFields` collection
- The `ColumnFormat` object returned by the `ViewField.ColumnFormat` property

To demonstrate how to use these objects and how to modify an existing view, let's update the standard Active Tasks view in the default Tasks folder to make three changes:

1. Define two new custom properties in the folder—`Project` and `Next Milestone Date`—and display them in the view

2. Sort the view by `Next Milestone Date`, which we will display in a format other than the default date format

3. Turn on in-cell editing and the new item row

As with rules, views are sufficiently complex that it's helpful to break down the operation into steps:

1. Get the Tasks folder.

2. Define the custom properties in the folder.

3. Get the existing table view.

4. Insert the properties into the view's field list.

5. Format the new columns as needed.

6. Set the view's sort order.

7. Turn on in-cell editing and the new item row.

8. Save the view.

9. Apply the view.

Listing 22.5 shows the complete operation, with all the steps marked.

To create a new property and add it to the view, first add it to the folder's `UserDefinedFields` collection, as discussed in the previous chapter. Then use the MAPI schema property name for the custom property to insert it into the `ViewFields` collection at the desired position:

```
With objTasks.UserDefinedProperties
    .Add "Project", olText
    .Add "Next Milestone Date", olDateTime
End With
strProjectProp = _
  "http://schemas.microsoft.com/mapi/string/" & _
  "{00020329-0000-0000-C000-000000000046}/Project"
Set objTextViewField = _
  objTableView.ViewFields.Insert(strProjectProp, 6)
```

**Tip:** If you're doing code experiments that involve adding fields to the folder, so that you can use them in a view, you may want to start with an empty `Folder.UserDefinedProperties` collection each time. This little procedure will remove all existing custom property definitions from the folder. It won't affect data stored in existing items.

```
Sub DeleteAllFolderCustomProps()
    Dim objFolder As Outlook.Folder
    Set objFolder = _
      Application.ActiveExplorer.CurrentFolder
    Do While objFolder.UserDefinedProperties.count > 0
        objFolder.UserDefinedProperties.Remove 1
    Loop
    Set objFolder = Nothing
End Sub
```

**Listing 22.5**   *Modify the standard Active Tasks view*

```
Sub UpdateActiveTasksView()
    Dim objOL As Outlook.Application
    Dim objNS As Outlook.NameSpace
    Dim objTasks As Outlook.Folder
    Dim colViews As Outlook.Views
    Dim objView As Outlook.View
    Dim objTableView As Outlook.TableView
    Dim objTextViewField As Outlook.ViewField
    Dim objDateViewField As Outlook.ViewField
    Dim objColFormat As Outlook.ColumnFormat
    Dim colOrderFields As Outlook.OrderFields
    On Error Resume Next
    Dim strProjectProp As String
    Dim strMilestoneProp As String
'Step 1.  Get the Tasks folder.
    Set objOL = Application
    Set objNS = objOL.Session
    Set objTasks = objNS.GetDefaultFolder(olFolderTasks)
'Step 2.  Define the properties in the folder.
    With objTasks.UserDefinedProperties
        .Add "Project", olText
        .Add "Next Milestone Date", olDateTime
    End With
'Step 3.  Get the existing table view.
    Set colViews = objTasks.Views
    Set objView = colViews.Item("Active Tasks")
    If objView.viewType = olTableView Then
        Set objTableView = objView
'Step 4.  Insert the properties into the view's field list
        strProjectProp = _
            "http://schemas.microsoft.com/mapi/string/" & _
            "{00020329-0000-0000-C000-000000000046}/Project"
        Set objTextViewField = _
          objTableView.ViewFields.Insert(strProjectProp, 6)
        strMilestoneProp = _
            "http://schemas.microsoft.com/mapi/string/" & _
            "{00020329-0000-0000-C000-000000000046}/" & _
            "Next%20Milestone%20Date"
        Set objDateViewField = _
          objTableView.ViewFields.Insert(strMilestoneProp, 7)
'Step 5.  Format the new columns as needed
        Set objColFormat = objTextViewField.ColumnFormat
        objColFormat.Width = 30
        Set objColFormat = objDateViewField.ColumnFormat
        objColFormat.FieldFormat = _
          olFormatDateTimeShortDayMonth
        objColFormat.Width = 30
'Step 6.  Set the view's sort order.
        Set colOrderFields = objTableView.SortFields
        colOrderFields.RemoveAll
        colOrderFields.Add strMilestoneProp, True
```

➤

**Listing 22.5**  *Modify the standard Active Tasks view (continued)*

```
'Step 7.  Turn on in-cell editing and new item row.
        objTableView.AllowInCellEditing = True
        objTableView.ShowNewItemRow = True
'Step 8.  Save the view.
        objTableView.Save
'Step 9.  Apply the view.
        objTableView.Apply
    End If
    Set objOL = Nothing
    Set objNS = Nothing
    Set objTasks = Nothing
    Set colViews = Nothing
    Set objView = Nothing
    Set objTableView = Nothing
End Sub
```

If a view is already sorted, adding a new field to the `SortFields` collection adds a new level of sorting to the levels that already exist. To start with a fresh sort order, remove all the existing sort fields before you add a new one:

```
Set colOrderFields = objTableView.SortFields
colOrderFields.RemoveAll
colOrderFields.Add strMilestoneProp, True
```

The sample in the next section shows how to create multiple new views in a batch operation.

### 22.4.2  **Example: Create category-filtered views**

Not only can you add fields to views, but you can also filter them to show only certain items, similar to the way you use `Items.Restrict` to return a filtered `Items` collection. In fact, the syntax for a view filter uses the same DASL syntax for a `Restrict` filter, the same syntax we learned in Chapter 16.

For each unique category represented in a folder, the `CreateCategoryViews` procedure in Listing 22.6 creates a new view that displays only the items in that category. The category list comes from a helper function, `GetFolderCatArray`, which uses the rapid, read-only access provided by an Outlook `Table` object to read all the items in a folder and build a list of unique categories, using a `Scripting.Dictionary` object, in just seconds.

The `CreateCategoryViews` procedure requires two arguments, the folder where you want to create the new views and one of the `OlViewType` values from Table 22.5. Optionally, if the view type is a table view (`olTableView`), you can specify an option to group by category to make it

**Listing 22.6**  *Create category-filtered views on any folder*

```
Sub CreateCategoryViews(fld As Folder, _
   viewType As OlViewType, Optional groupByCat As Boolean)
    Dim varCats As Variant
    Dim i As Integer
    Dim objView As Outlook.View
    Dim objTableView As Outlook.TableView
    Dim strCat As String
    Dim strMsg As String
    Dim strViewName As String
    Dim strFind As String
    Dim intScope As Outlook.OlViewSaveOption
    Const SEARCH_KEYWORDS = _
      "urn:schemas-microsoft-com:office:office#Keywords"
    varCats = GetFolderCatArray(fld)
    If Not IsEmpty(varCats) Then
        For i = 0 To UBound(varCats)
            strCat = varCats(i)
            strViewName = "Category: " & strCat
            Set objView = fld.Views(strViewName)
            If objView Is Nothing Then
                Set objView = fld.Views.Add(strViewName, _
                                    viewType)
                strFind = Quote(SEARCH_KEYWORDS) & _
                  " = '" & Replace(strCat, "'", "''") & "'"
                objView.Filter = strFind
                If viewType = olTableView Then
                    If groupByCat = True Then
                        Set objTableView = objView
                        objTableView.GroupByFields.Add _
                          SEARCH_KEYWORDS
                        objTableView.Save
                    End If
                End If
                objView.Save
                If Err.Number <> 0 Then
                    strMsg = strMsg & vbCrLf & _
                      strViewName & " - error occurred"
                    Err.Clear
                End If
            Else
                strMsg = strMsg & vbCrLf & _
                  strViewName & " - already exists"
            End If
        Next
        strMsg = CStr(UBound(varCats) + 1) & _
          " unique categories in " & fld.Name & vbCrLf & strMsg
    Else
        strMsg = "No categories for items in " & fld.Name
    End If
    MsgBox strMsg, vbInformation, "Create Category Views"
    Set objView = Nothing
    Set objTableView = Nothing
End Sub
```

**Listing 22.6** *Create category-filtered views on any folder (continued)*

```
Function GetFolderCatArray(fld As Folder) As Variant
    ' requires reference to Scripting.Runtime library
    Dim objCats As Scripting.Dictionary
    Dim objTable As Outlook.Table
    Dim objCol As Outlook.Column
    Dim objRow As Outlook.Row
    Dim varCats As Variant
    Dim strFind As String
    Dim strCat As String
    Dim i As Integer
    Const SEARCH_KEYWORDS = _
      "urn:schemas-microsoft-com:office:office#Keywords"
    Set objCats = CreateObject("Scripting.Dictionary")
    objCats.CompareMode = TextCompare
    strFind = "NOT (" & Quote(SEARCH_KEYWORDS) & " IS NULL)"
    Set objTable = fld.GetTable("@SQL=" & strFind)
    objTable.Columns.Add SEARCH_KEYWORDS
    Do Until objTable.EndOfTable
        Set objRow = objTable.GetNextRow
        varCats = objRow(SEARCH_KEYWORDS)
        If Not IsEmpty(varCats) Then
            For i = 0 To UBound(varCats)
                strCat = varCats(i)
                If Not objCats.Exists(strCat) Then
                    objCats.Add strCat, 0
                End If
            Next
        End If
    Loop
    GetFolderCatArray = objCats.Keys
    Set objCats = Nothing
    Set objTable = Nothing
    Set objCol = Nothing
    Set objRow = Nothing
End Function

Private Function Quote(val) as String
    Quote = Chr(34) & CStr(val) & Chr(34)
End Function
```

easier to see what other categories are applied to the items in the current filter. For example, to create category-based table views, with items grouped by category, call the CreateCategoryViews procedure like this:

```
Set objFolder = Application.ActiveExplorer.CurrentFolder
Call CreateCategoryViews(objFolder, olTableView, True)
```

The first step in building the views is to use the GetFolderCatArray() function to return the list of unique categories in the folder as an array. To build the list, the function checks the value of the Categories property for each item in the folder, using a `Table` object to which a new `Column` has been added to expose the `Categories` property:

```
Const SEARCH_KEYWORDS = _
  "urn:schemas-microsoft-com:office:office#Keywords"
objTable.Columns.Add SEARCH_KEYWORDS
```

Because the `Column` was added with the MAPI schema property name, not the Outlook object model property name, it returns the data for the `Categories` property, which is a keywords field, as a string array instead of a comma-delimited string. For each row of the table, the code reads the item in that string array and compares them to the keys of a `Scripting.Dictionary` object (`objCat`):

```
Set objRow = objTable.GetNextRow
varCats = objRow(SEARCH_KEYWORDS)
If Not IsEmpty(varCats) Then
    For i = 0 To UBound(varCats)
        strCat = varCats(i)
        If Not objCats.Exists(strCat) Then
            objCats.Add strCat, 0
        End If
    Next
End If
```

Whenever the code finds a category that doesn't already exist in the `objCats` dictionary, it adds that category to the dictionary:

```
objCats.Add strCat, 0
```

In this procedure, we care only about the key, but the `Dictionary.Add` method requires a value for the second parameter, so `0` is a good choice. When the code has processed the entire table, it can return the array of lookup values from the dictionary with just one code statement:

```
GetFolderCatArray = objCats.Keys
```

For each item in the array, the `CreateCategoryViews` procedure constructs the view name from the current entry in the array:

```
strCat = varCats(i)
strViewName = "Category: " & strCat
```

and adds a view with that name, if one doesn't already exist:

```
Set objView = fld.Views.Add(strViewName, viewType)
```

using the `viewType` value passed to the procedure as an argument. To construct the filter query string, the code needs to replace any apostrophe characters with two apostrophes to meet a requirement of the DASL syntax:

```
strFind = Quote(SEARCH_KEYWORDS) & _
                " = '" & Replace(strCat, "'", "''") & "'"
```

All it takes to apply the filter to the view is to set the value of the `Filter` property to the filter query string:

```
objView.Filter = strFind
```

**Note:** We've seen so many uses of DASL search strings with the `Restrict` method that it's worth noting that the view filter usage does not take the `"@SQL="` prefix that `Restrict` requires.

If the view is a table view and if the optional third parameter is set to `True`, the code gets a `TableView` object and groups the view by the same property used to filter the view:

```
Set objTableView = objView
objTableView.GroupByFields.Add SEARCH_KEYWORDS
```

All the views that Listing 22.6 creates have similar names: "Category: *name of the category*." If you run the `CreateCategoryViews` procedure and find that you want to keep just a few of the filtered views, use the View | Current View | Define Views dialog to rename the views you want to keep to "Category = *name of the category*" or something similar. Then, call the `DeleteAllCategoryViews` procedure in Listing 22.7, passing the folder as an argument, to remove all the remaining views with "Category:" names.

You may be surprised at how many categories are being used in a folder! These procedures can help you start cleaning them up and organizing them better. They can also make it easier to print out a quick phone list of all your contacts marked with a favorite category.

**Listing 22.7** *Clean up unwanted Category: views*

```
Sub DeleteAllCategoryViews(fld As Outlook.Folder)
    Dim objView As Outlook.View
    Dim strMsg As String
    Dim intCount As Integer
    Dim i As Integer
    Dim j As Integer
    intCount = fld.Views.count
    j = 0
    If intCount > 0 Then
        For i = intCount To 1 Step -1
            Set objView = fld.Views(i)
            If objView.Standard = False Then
                If Left(objView, 10) = "Category: " Then
                    objView.Delete
                    j = j + 1
                End If
            End If
        Next
        strMsg = "Processed " & CStr(j) & " views"
    End If
    MsgBox strMsg, vbInformation, "Delete All Category Views"
    Set objView = Nothing
End Sub
```

### 22.4.3   **Managing public folder views**

A frequent request in Exchange environments is to control the behavior of custom folder views to:

- Show a particular view when the user first displays the folder
- Show only views created specifically for that folder
- Prevent the user from making changes to the view created for the folder

The first two settings can be controlled through the user interface, the first one on the Properties dialog for the folder and the second on the View | Current View | Define Views dialog. However, the third can be set only in code. Therefore, it's useful to have a VBA macro that can be run against any folder to lock down all views.

---

**Note:** Remember that a user has full access to all the views in the primary Exchange mailbox and any .pst file, so this technique is relevant only to folders in the Public Folders hierarchy and shared folders in other users' mailboxes.

---

The `LockViews` procedure in Listing 22.8 sets the `CustomViewsOnly` property of the folder to `True`, so that the folder can display only views created for that folder. To prevent users from caching their own copy of any folder view, the `LockUserChanges` property for each view is set to `True`. You can lock the views on the currently displayed folder by executing this statement from the VBA Immediate window:

```
Call LockViews(Application.ActiveExplorer.CurrentFolder)
```

It is not possible to set the default view for a public folder programmatically with the Outlook 2007 object model, because the `StorageItem` object does not work for public folders.

## 22.5   **Internal scripting with folder home pages**

Any configuration changes that you can make in Outlook VBA—including creating rules and views—can also be scripted in a custom form, using the techniques from the first part of the chapter. And, anything that can be scripted in a custom form can also be scripted in a folder home page that uses the Outlook View Control. A folder home page, as we learned in Chapter 1, is a Web page that Outlook displays instead of the contents of a folder.

When a user first connects to a newly created Exchange mailbox, Outlook 2007 opens to the Inbox folder. Here's how a folder home page on the Inbox can help deploy the kinds of settings we've been talking about in this chapter, the kind that can't be set unless Outlook is running:

1. Using your organization's preferred method to deploy registry changes, an administrator sets a registry value for a user or machine that tells Outlook to load a Web page instead of the Inbox and another value that tells Outlook to display the Inbox when it starts.

2. When the user starts Outlook, the folder home page displays instead of the usual Inbox view. An Outlook View Control (OVC) on the page displays the Inbox items (so the user doesn't panic and think all the mail is missing).

3. Code in the Web page's `onload` event handler gets a reference to an `Outlook.Application` object from the OVC's `Outlook-Application` property and runs code to configure rules, views, search folders, and so on.

4. After completing the configuration tasks, the code turns off the folder home page by setting a couple of properties on the Inbox folder.

**Listing 22.8** *Lock down views for an Exchange public or shared folder*

```
Sub LockViews(fld As Outlook.Folder)
    Dim objView As Outlook.View
    Dim strMsg As String
    On Error Resume Next
    For Each objView In fld.Views
        If objView.Standard = False Then
            If objView.SaveOption = _
              olViewSaveOptionThisFolderEveryone Then
                objView.LockUserChanges = True
                objView.Save
                strMsg = strMsg & vbCrLf & objView.Name
                If Err.Number = 0 Then
                    strMsg = strMsg & " - Locked"
                Else
                    strMsg = strMsg & " - Error"
                End If
            End If
        End If
    Next
    If strMsg = "" Then
        strMsg = vbCrLf & "No custom views available to lock"
    Else
        strMsg = _
          "These views were processed:" & vbCrLf & strMsg
    End If
    MsgBox strMsg, vbInformation, "Lock Views"
    fld.CustomViewsOnly = True
    Set objView = Nothing
End Sub
```

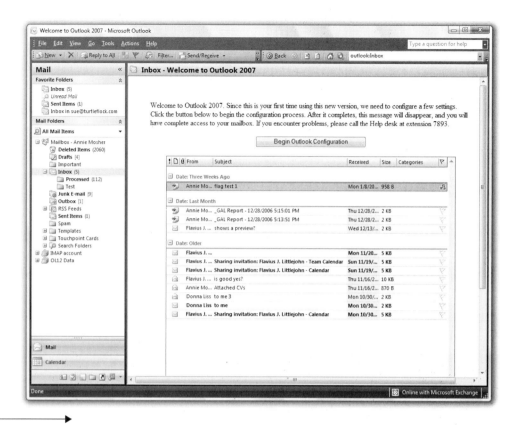

**Figure 22.2**   *A folder home page can show Outlook data and run code to configure Outlook options.*

Ideally, the Web page would be a page on your Intranet, but it could also be an .htm file that a login script copies to the local hard drive. Figure 22.2 shows a simple folder home page set up to configure a first-time user's machine.

---

**Note:** One way in which Outlook 2007 has improved security is that it will no longer load a folder home page for a folder that is in a .pst file other than the user's default information store. A setting is available in the administrative template for Outlook 2007 to override this default behavior.

---

Set these two registry values to make Outlook show the folder home page for a user's Inbox:

Show the associated Web page

Key: `HKEY_CURRENT_USER\Software\Microsoft\Office\12.0\Outlook\WebView\Inbox`
Value name: `Show`

Value type: REG_SZ (string)
Value data: Yes

URL address of associated Web page

Key: HKEY_CURRENT_USER\Software\Microsoft\Office\12.0\
Outlook\WebView\Inbox
Value name: Url
Value type: REG_SZ (string)
Value data: The URL that you want to display as a folder home page

Similar keys are available for other default folders and are documented in the administrative template for Outlook 2007.

As Figure 22.2 shows, a folder home page can offer solutions to a couple of other Outlook challenges. This page shows a customizable welcome message to provide new Outlook users with the information you want them to know; the text is simply part of the HTML content of the Web page. It also automatically switches the user to the Folder List navigation module. This is helpful to users who need to be able to access folders in the Public Folders hierarchy, which appears only in the Folder List navigation module.

The code in Listing 22.9 is the complete code used to create the folder home page shown in Figure 22.2. The visible portion of the page is that within the `<body>` and `</body>` tags at the end of the listing. This portion was created in an HTML editor by inserting a table, adding text, a button, and an instance of the Outlook View Control, which is an ActiveX control that we first encountered in Chapter 6.

The really interesting portion of Listing 22.9 lies in the three procedures contained between the `<script>` and `</script>` tags. The first procedure, `window_onload`, runs when the page loads, in other words, when Outlook displays the Web page. This statement is the key to its operation:

```
Set objOL = ViewCtl1.OutlookApplication
```

The fact that the Web page is running as a folder home page in Outlook and that it contains an Outlook View Control allows the code to return an `Outlook.Application` object from the OVC's `OutlookApplication` property. If the page were running in an external Web browser, this statement would raise an error, because the `OutlookApplication` property is blocked in that environment.

Where does the `ViewCtl1` object come from? It is defined by the tag in the HTML layout code that adds the OVC control:

```
<object classid="clsid:0006F063-0000-0000-C000-
000000000046" id="ViewCtl1" data="DATA:application/x-
oleobject;BASE64,Y/
AGAAAAAADAAAAAAAAARhAHAACqZwAA6EAAAAgAEgAAAE0AZQBzAHMAYQ
BnAGUAcwAAAgAAAAAAAgACgAAAAE0AQQBQAEkAAAAJAAAAAAAAAAAAAAA
AAAAAAAAJAAAAAAAAAAAAAAAAAAAAAAAIAAAAAAALAAAA"
width="100%" height="100%">
```

**Listing 22.9**   *Use a folder home page script to create a rule*

```
<html>
<head>
<meta http-equiv="Content-Language" content="en-us">
<meta http-equiv="Content-Type" content="text/html; charset=windows-1252">
<title>Welcome to Outlook 2007</title>
<script id=clientEventHandlersVBS language=vbscript>
<!--

Sub window_onload()
    Dim objOL    ' As Outlook.Application
    Const olPreview = 3
    Const olToDoBar = 5
    Const olFolderList = 2
    Set objOL = ViewCtl1.OutlookApplication
    objOL.ActiveExplorer.ShowPane olPreview, False
    objOL.ActiveExplorer.ShowPane olToDoBar, False
    objOL.ActiveExplorer.ShowPane olFolderList, True
    Set objOL = Nothing
End Sub

Sub btnBegin_onclick()
    Dim objOL    ' As Outlook.Application
    Dim objFld   ' As Outlook.Folder
    Const olFolderSentMail = 5
    Const olPreview = 3
    Const olToDoBar = 5
    ' perform all Outlook configuration tasks
    Set objOL = ViewCtl1.OutlookApplication
    Call MakeSpamMoveRule
    ' turn off folder home page
    Set objFld = objOL.ActiveExplorer.CurrentFolder
    objFld.WebViewOn = False
    objFld.WebViewURL = ""
    Set sentMail = _
      objOL.Session.GetDefaultFolder(olFolderSentMail)
    Set objOL.ActiveExplorer.CurrentFolder = sentMail
    Set objOL.ActiveExplorer.CurrentFolder = objFld
    objOL.ActiveExplorer.ShowPane olPreview, True
    objOL.ActiveExplorer.ShowPane olToDoBar, True
    Set objOL = Nothing
    Set objFld = Nothing
End Sub

Sub MakeSpamMoveRule()
    Dim objOL               'As Outlook.Application
    Dim objStore            'As Outlook.Store
    Dim colRules            'As Outlook.Rules
    Dim objRule             'As Outlook.Rule
    Dim objCondSubject      'As Outlook.TextRuleCondition
    Dim objActionMove       'As Outlook.MoveOrCopyRuleAction
    Dim objStopMove         'As Outlook.RuleAction
    Dim objFldJunk          'As Outlook.Folder
    Dim arr
    Const olFolderJunk = 23
    Const olRuleReceive = 0
    On Error Resume Next
```

→

**Listing 22.9**   *Use a folder home page script to create a rule (continued)*

```
Set objOL = ViewCtl1.OutlookApplication
Set objStore = objOL.Session.DefaultStore
Set colRules = objStore.GetRules
Set objRule = colRules.Create _
  ("Move marked spam to Junk E-mail", olRuleReceive)
Set objCondSubject = objRule.Conditions.Subject
With objCondSubject
    arr = Array("[spam]")
    objCondSubject.Text = arr
    objCondSubject.Enabled = True
End With
Set objActionMove = objRule.Actions.MoveToFolder
With objActionMove
    Set objFldJunk = _
      objOL.Session.GetDefaultFolder(olFolderJunk)
    Set .Folder = objFldJunk
    .Enabled = True
End With
Set objStopMove = objRule.Actions.Stop
objStopMove.Enabled = True
colRules.Save
Set objStopMove = Nothing
Set objActionMove = Nothing
Set objCondSubject = Nothing
Set objFldJunk = Nothing
Set objRule = Nothing
Set colRules = Nothing
Set objStore = Nothing
Set objOL = Nothing
End Sub

-->
</script>
</head>
<body>
<table border="0" cellpadding="0" cellspacing="0" width="800" height="825">
    <tr>
        <td valign="top" colspan="3" height="112">
        <blockquote>
            <p>Welcome to Outlook 2007. Since this is your first
            time using this new version, we need to configure a
            few settings. Click the button below to begin the
            configuration process. After it completes, this
            message will disappear, and you will have complete
            access to your mailbox. If you encounter problems,
            please call the Help desk at extension 7893.
            </p>
            <p align="center"><input type="button" value="Begin Outlook
Configuration" name="btnBegin"></p>
        </blockquote>
        </td>
    </tr>
    <tr>
        <td> </td>
        <td valign="top">
```

→

**Listing 22.9**    *Use a folder home page script to create a rule (continued)*

```
        <object classid="clsid:0006F063-0000-0000-C000-000000000046"
id="ViewCtl1" data="DATA:application/x-oleobject;BASE64,Y/
AGAAAAAADAAAAAAAAARhAHAACqZwAA6EAAAAgAEgAAAE0AZQBzAHMAYQBnAGUAcwAAAAgAAAAAA
AgACgAAAE0AQQBQBQAEkAAAAJAAAAAAAAAAAAAAAAAAAAJAAAAAAAAAAAAAAAAAAAAAAAIAAAA
AAALAAAA" width="100%" height="100%">
        </object>
        </td>
        <td height="638"> </td>
    </tr>
    <tr>
        <td width="81"> </td>
        <td width="700"> </td>
        <td height="75" width="81"> </td>
    </tr>
</table>
</body>
</html>
```

**Tip:** Don't worry about typing in the long `<object>` tag for the OVC. If you build your Web page in a tool such as Expression Web Designer or even FrontPage 2003, the Web designer will add those tag details for you automatically.

After the `window_onload` procedure gets the `Application` object, it turns off the reading pane and To Do Bar and switches the navigation pane to the Folder List module. The next chapter includes a section on working with the navigation pane and its modules.

The second procedure, `btnBegin_onclick`, contains the code that runs when the user clicks the button on the page. The button is defined in this element from the HTML layout:

```
<input type="button" value="Begin Outlook Configuration"
name="btnBegin">
```

The `btnBegin_onclick` procedure also returns an `Outlook.Application` object from the OVC and then calls the third procedure, `MakeSpamMoveRule`, which silently creates a new rule to move messages with "[spam]" in the subject to the user's Junk E-mail folder, using the rule techniques discussed earlier in the chapter. After creating the rule, the `btnBegin_onclick` procedure turns off the folder home page by setting two properties on the currently displayed folder:

```
Set objFld = objOL.ActiveExplorer.CurrentFolder
objFld.WebViewOn = False
objFld.WebViewURL = ""
```

Because Outlook doesn't refresh the display cleanly when the folder home page is turned off programmatically, the code switches the display to the Sent Items folder and back again:

```
Set sentMail = _
    objOL.Session.GetDefaultFolder(olFolderSentMail)
Set objOL.ActiveExplorer.CurrentFolder = sentMail
Set objOL.ActiveExplorer.CurrentFolder = objFld
```

As its last task, the `btnBegin_onclick` procedure turns on the reading pane and To Do Bar that the `window_onload` procedure turned off:

```
objOL.ActiveExplorer.ShowPane olPreview, True
objOL.ActiveExplorer.ShowPane olToDoBar, True
```

While this folder home page performs only one configuration task—creating the spam move rule—there is no limit to what you could do from inside the page's code. The `btnBegin_onclick` procedure could, for example, also call a subroutine to mark a public folder for display in the Outlook Address Book using the `Folder.ShowAsOutlookAB` property. Another subroutine could create a new view or modify an existing view. Think of a folder home page as a potential platform to run almost any of the script code you've seen in this book; the main difference is that it derives its `Outlook.Application` object from an Outlook View Control on the page instead of from the intrinsic `Application` object exposed in Outlook VBA and custom forms' VBScript.

## 22.6  Summary

Expanded support for views and totally new support for programming rules are two of the most exciting features in the Outlook 2007 object model. They provide powerful mechanisms for running rules on demand, reporting on rules, and creating rules to manage incoming and outgoing messages. Views, too, become far easier to create, modify, and delete than in previous versions.

Administrators eager to script some of these and other Outlook options quickly discover that many can be changed only when Outlook already is running with the correct user mail profile. Such configuration challenges lend themselves to an "internal" scripting solution, such as custom message forms in an Exchange environment and, in almost any environment, a folder home page hosting the Outlook View Control.

As bonuses, this chapter includes a `GetFolderCatArray()` function that returns an array containing the names of all the categories used by items in a particular folder and a `LockFolderViews()` procedure to prevent users from creating their own views for an Exchange public or shared mailbox folder.

# *Menus, Toolbars, and the Navigation Pane*

For VBA programmers, the most exciting improvement in programmability for the Outlook 2007 user interface is support for six right-click context menus. Other than the new access to context menus, though, Outlook offers limited options for VBA programmers to customize and manipulate the Outlook user interface, fewer than those available to developers of Outlook add-ins. It is possible to use VBA to add and remove toolbars, menus, and commands from the main Outlook window, but not to modify the "ribbon" user interface in an individual item window. The navigation pane falls somewhere in between, with a certain amount of programmability, though less than many Outlook programmers would want to have.

One good reason to learn how to work with toolbars and menus is that some Outlook features simply don't have programmatic equivalents. A workaround in many cases is to execute the corresponding Outlook toolbar or menu command.

Highlights of this chapter include discussions of the following:

- Why menus and toolbars are actually the same thing
- How to add a new custom toolbar and populate it with controls
- How to run a macro from a right-click context menu
- What code can run any menu or toolbar command programmatically
- How to show and hide the navigation pane and control what module is displayed
- How to display any Web page in Outlook's built-in browser
- How to work with the folder links in the navigation pane

## 23.1 Programming Outlook menus and toolbars

The first thing you need to know about Outlook menus and toolbars is that `Explorer` windows are different from `Inspector` windows. `Inspector` windows, those that display individual items, use the new "ribbon" interface, which cannot be manipulated from VBA.

In an `Explorer` window, however, you can not only execute commands, but also remove, add, and modify menus, toolbars, and commands. The `Explorer` window has four standard `CommandBar` objects you can access programmatically—the Menu Bar and the Standard, Advanced, and Web toolbars. Also available for the first time in Outlook 2007 is the ability to customize the most heavily used right-click context menus.

The basic building blocks of menus and toolbars are the `CommandBars` collection and the individual `CommandBar` objects that collection contains. The `Explorer` object exposes a child `CommandBars` collection consisting of all the menus and toolbars. Each `CommandBar` in the collection contains a `CommandBarControls` collection, which holds items representing buttons, combo boxes, submenus, and other menu and toolbar controls.

---

**Tip:** To use the Object Browser to locate information on the `CommandBar` object, don't look in the Outlook library. The `CommandBar` object is common to all Office programs, so you will find it in the Office library. Where Outlook differs from the other Office programs is that for those programs, the `CommandBar` collection is a member of the `Application` object, but in Outlook it is a member of the `Explorer` and `Inspector` objects.

---

To see what `CommandBar` objects are intrinsic to Outlook, run the VBA code in Listing 23.1 to create a post in your Drafts folder that lists the built-in menus and toolbars for the current `Explorer` window, along with the commands on them and the ID for each built-in command. Run the `Enum-CommandBars` procedure once for each type of Outlook folder; different types of folders have different commands visible on the `Explorer` window, particularly on the View and Actions menus.

The `EnumOneBar` procedure, which generates the list of controls on a menu or toolbar, is recursive, so it can handle any number of submenus. The post items stored in Drafts will list toolbars and menus that are currently visible, as well as those that are not currently activated. The first few lines of the post item created by the `EnumCommandBars` procedure for an `Explorer` window should look like this:

```
CommandBar: Menu Bar
&File (Submenu) - 30002
CommandBar: File
Ne&w (Submenu) - 30037
CommandBar: New Item
    &Mail Message - 1757
    &Post in This Folder - 2687
```

The listing starts with the Menu Bar, which contains all the menus and controls for Outlook's menus. The File and New controls are submenus. The New Item command bar corresponds to the New submenu and contains commands to create a new mail message and a new post in the current folder, along with other commands. The listing shows the ID for each standard control that can be executed programmatically or added to a menu or toolbar using code. A little later in the chapter, we'll cover how to use those control IDs to disable or execute any built-in command.

**Listing 23.1**   *Generate a list of menus and toolbars for the current Outlook window*

```
Sub EnumCommandBars()
    Dim objOL As Outlook.Application
    Dim objNS As Outlook.NameSpace
    Dim objDrafts As Outlook.Folder
    Dim objPost As Outlook.PostItem
    Dim colCB As Office.CommandBars
    Dim objCB As Office.CommandBar
    Dim strWindow As String
    Dim strExplBars As String
    Dim strText As String
    Dim arrBars() As String
    Dim i As Integer
    On Error Resume Next
    Set objOL = Application
    Set objNS = objOL.Session
    Set objDrafts = objNS.GetDefaultFolder(olFolderDrafts)
    strExplBars = "Menu Bar,Standard,Advanced,Web"
    Set colCB = objOL.ActiveExplorer.CommandBars
    arrBars = Split(strExplBars, ",")
    If Not colCB Is Nothing Then
        Set objPost = objDrafts.Items.Add("IPM.Post")
        objPost.Subject = "CommandBars for Explorer: " & _
                          colCB.Parent.Caption
        objPost.BodyFormat = olFormatPlain
        For i = 0 To UBound(arrBars)
            Set objCB = colCB.Item(arrBars(i))
            Call EnumOneBar(objCB, strText)
            strText = strText & vbCrLf & "==========" & vbCrLf
        Next
        objPost.Body = Mid(strText, 5)
        objPost.Save
        objPost.Display
    End If
    Set objOL = Nothing
    Set objNS = Nothing
    Set objDrafts = Nothing
    Set objPost = Nothing
    Set colCB = Nothing
    Set objCB = Nothing
End Sub
```

**Listing 23.1**   *Generate a list of menus and toolbars for the current Outlook window (continued)*

```
Sub EnumOneBar(cb As Office.CommandBar, ByRef postText)
    Dim objControl As Office.CommandBarControl
    Dim objPopupControl As Office.CommandBarPopup
    postText = postText & vbCrLf & vbCrLf & _
            "CommandBar: " & cb.Name
    For Each objControl In cb.Controls
        If objControl.BuiltIn = True Then
            Select Case objControl.Type
                Case msoControlPopup, _
                    msoControlButtonPopup, _
                    msoControlGraphicPopup, _
                    msoControlSplitButtonPopup
                    Set objPopupControl = objControl
                    Call EnumOneBar( _
                      objPopupControl.CommandBar, postText)
                    postText = postText & vbCrLf & vbCrLf & _
                      objControl.Caption & _
                      " (Submenu) - " & objControl.ID
                Case Else
                    postText = postText & vbCrLf & vbTab & _
                      objControl.Caption & " - " & objControl.ID
            End Select
        End If
    Next
    Set objControl = Nothing
    Set objPopupControl = Nothing
End Sub
```

**Listing 23.2**   *Show and hide the Web toolbar*

```
Sub ToggleExplorerWeb()
    Dim objOL As Outlook.Application
    Dim objExpl As Outlook.Explorer
    Dim colCB As Office.CommandBars
    On Error Resume Next
    Set objOL = Application
    Set objExpl = objOL.ActiveExplorer
    If Not objExpl Is Nothing Then
        Set colCB = objExpl.CommandBars
        colCB.Item("Web").Visible = _
            Not colCB.Item("Web").Visible
    End If
    Set objOL = Nothing
    Set objExpl = Nothing
    Set colCB = Nothing
End Sub
```

To work with a specific CommandBar object menu or toolbar, use its name or index number to retrieve it from the CommandBars collection as you would with any other collection. The code in Listing 23.2, for example, toggles the Visible property of the Web toolbar on the current Explorer window. Visible is one of the key CommandBar properties listed in Table 23.1.

**Table 23.1**    *Key CommandBar Properties and Methods*

| Property | Description |
|---|---|
| AdaptiveMenu | True if the CommandBar should adapt to usage and size by removing and adding controls |
| BuiltIn | True if the CommandBar is a built-in menu or toolbar (read-only) |
| Controls | Returns a CommandBarControls object that represents all the controls on the toolbar or menu |
| Enabled | True if the CommandBar is enabled |
| Left | The distance in pixels from the left edge of the window to the left edge of the CommandBar |
| Name | The display name; read-only and in English for built-in command bars |
| NameLocal | The display name in the current language version of Outlook |
| Parent | The parent object of the CommandBar, either an Explorer window, an Inspector window, or for a submenu or pop-up menu, another CommandBar |
| Position | The screen location, using one of these constants from the Office.MsoBarPosition enumeration: |
| | msoBarLeft 0 |
| | msoBarTop 1 |
| | msoBarRight 2 |
| | msoBarBottom 3 |
| | msoBarFloating 4 |
| Protection | Whether the toolbar or menu is protected from customization, using one of these constants from the Office.MsoBarProtection constants: |
| | msoBarNoProtection 0 |
| | msoBarNoCustomize 1 |
| | msoBarNoResize 2 |
| | msoBarNoMove 4 |
| | msoBarNoChangeVisible 8 |
| | msoBarNoChangeDock 16 |
| | msoBarNoVerticalDock 32 |
| | msoBarNoHorizontalDock 4 |

**Table 23.1**     *Key CommandBar Properties and Methods (continued)*

| Property | Description |
|---|---|
| RowIndex | Sets the relative position of the CommandBar within the docking area specified in the Position property; can be an integer number or one of these constants from the Office.MsoBarRow enumeration:<br><br>msoBarRowFirst    0<br><br>msoBarRowLast    -1 |
| Top | The distance in pixels from the top of the screen or, for docked menus or toolbars, from the top of the docking area to the top of the CommandBar |
| Type | The type of toolbar or menu, using one of these constants from the Office.MsoBarType enumeration:<br><br>msoBarTypeNormal  0<br><br>msoBarTypeMenuBar  1<br><br>msoBarTypePopup   2 |
| Visible | True if the toolbar is visible; the Enabled property must be True before Visible can be set to True |
| Width | The width in pixels |
| **Method** | **Description** |
| Delete | Deletes the CommandBar |
| FindControl(*Type*, *Id*, *Tag*, *Visible*, *Recursive*) | Returns the first CommandBarControl matching the given Type, Id, and/or *Tag*; optionally searches only visible or hidden controls; if Recursive = True, searches all child submenus |
| Reset | Resets a built-in toolbar or menu to its original appearance |

## 23.1.1   Working with submenus and other controls

As you can see in the EnumOneBar procedure in Listing 23.1, each CommandBar has a CommandBarControls collection that contains its submenus and other controls. Each CommandBarControl object in the CommandBarControls collection for a menu or toolbar has a Type property that tells you what kind of control it is. A Select Case block in the EnumOneBar procedure distinguishes submenus and pop-up menus from other controls:

```
Select Case objControl.Type
    Case msoControlPopup, _
         msoControlButtonPopup, _
         msoControlGraphicPopup, _
         msoControlSplitButtonPopup
        Set objPopupControl = objControl
        Call EnumOneBar( _
          objPopupControl.CommandBar, postText)
```

Each pop-up menu control has its own `CommandBar` property. The `EnumOneBar` procedure calls itself to get the controls from that submenu:

```
Call EnumOneBar(objPopupControl.CommandBar, postText)
```

Why is it so useful to gather this information about toolbar and menu commands? First of all, administrators can use the `ID` values with Group Policy Objects to disable any control. But more important to Outlook programmers is that the `ID` value is usually all you need to return the control and thus gain access to its properties and methods, including the ability to execute the command programmatically. You do not need to know what menu or toolbar the control is on. If you know the `ID` value for a control, you can use the `CommandBars.FindControl` method to return the control with this syntax:

```
Set objControl = objExpl.CommandBars.FindControl(, ID)
```

Once you return a control, you can use its properties to hide or show it, enable or disable it, change its style or tooltip text, and so on. Table 23.2 lists the key properties and methods common to the different toolbar and menu control classes, which are all based on the `CommandBarControl` object. Since three types of controls can be added to Outlook menus and toolbars programmatically—the `CommandBarButton`, `CommandBarComboBox` and `CommandBarPopup` (submenu) classes—Table 23.2 notes which properties and methods apply to each of these types.

We'll put some of these properties to use later in the chapter in several examples that add custom commands to toolbars and menus.

**Table 23.2** *Key Properties and Methods for Menu and Toolbar Controls*

| Property | Description | Button | Combo | Pop-Up |
|---|---|---|---|---|
| BeginGroup | True if the control displays a separator bar to its left in a toolbar and above it in a menu | X | X | X |
| BuiltIn | True if the control is built into Outlook; read-only | X | X | X |
| BuiltInFace | True if the control displays the original image built in for that control | X | | |
| Caption | Text that the user sees on the control | X | X | X |
| CommandBar | Object containing the controls for a submenu or pop-up menu | | | X |
| DropDownLines | Number of lines to show when the combo list is dropped | | X | |
| DropDownWidth | Width of the dropped combo list, in pixels | | X | |
| Enabled | True if the control can be clicked | X | X | X |
| FaceID | ID number for the image on a control | X | | |

**Table 23.2**    *Key Properties and Methods for Menu and Toolbar Controls (continued)*

| Property | Description | Button | Combo | Pop-Up |
|---|---|---|---|---|
| Height | Height of the control, in pixels | X | X | X |
| HyperlinkType | Constant from the `Office.MsoCommandBarButton-HyperlinkType` enumeration:<br><br>msoCommandBarButtonHyperlinkNone      0<br><br>msoCommandBarButtonHyperlinkOpen      1<br><br>msoCommandBarButtonHyperlinkInsertPicture   2 | | | |
| Id | ID value for the control; unique for built-in controls, meaningless for custom controls | X | X | X |
| IsPriorityDropped | `True` if the control is currently hidden from the menu because of lack of use | X | X | X |
| Left | Horizontal position from the left side of the parent `CommandBar`'s docking area; read-only | X | X | X |
| ListCount | Number of items in the dropdown list | | X | |
| ListHeaderCount | Number of items from the list that should appear above the separator line | | X | |
| ListIndex | Row number of the item selected in the list; 0 if no row is selected | | X | |
| Mask | Object used to determine what parts of the button's picture are transparent | X | | |
| OnAction | Name of a VBA macro to execute when the control is clicked | X | X | X |
| Parameter | String value associated with the control | X | X | X |
| Picture | Object used to place a picture on a button | X | | |
| Priority | Number between 0 and 7 that determines whether a toolbar control will be hidden if all the controls on a toolbar don't fit into a single row; use 1 to prevent a control from ever being dropped | X | X | X |
| ShortcutText | Set the shortcut key text (e.g., Ctrl+P) when the button appears on a menu; does not actually assign a command to a shortcut key | X | | |
| State | Value of the button state from the `Office.MsoButton-State` enumeration:<br><br>msoButtonDown       1<br><br>msoButtonMixed      2<br><br>msoButtonUp         0 | X | | |

---→

**Table 23.2** *Key Properties and Methods for Menu and Toolbar Controls (continued)*

| Property | Description | Button | Combo | Pop-Up |
|---|---|---|---|---|
| Style | Value of the button style from the Office.MsoButton- Style enumeration listed in Table 23.3 or, for combo boxes, a style from the Office.MsoComboStyle enumeration:<br><br>msoComboLabel 1<br>msoComboNormal 0 | X | X | |
| Tag | String value associated with a control; used in Outlook add-ins to help uniquely identify controls | X | X | X |
| ToolTipText | String for the control's screen tip | X | X | X |
| Top | Distance from the top of the control to the top of the screen; read-only | X | X | X |
| Type | Type of control from the Office.MsoControlType enumeration; these are the types of controls found on standard Outlook toolbars and menus:<br><br>msoControlButton 1<br>msoControlComboBox 4<br>msoControlGraphicCombo 20<br>msoControlGrid 18<br>msoControlLabel 15<br>msoControlPopup 10 | X | X | X |
| Visible | True if the control is visible | X | X | X |
| Width | Width of the control, in pixels | X | X | X |
| **Method** | **Description** | | | |
| AddItem *Text, Index* | Insert the *Text* argument at the optional *Index* position; if *Index* is omitted, adds the item at the bottom of the list; applies only to custom controls | | X | |
| Clear | Removes all items from the list; applies only to custom controls | | X | |
| Copy(*Bar, Before*) | Copies the control to the CommandBar represented by the *Bar* parameter or to the current CommandBar; *Before* represents the position for the copied control; both parameters are optional; returns the copied CommandBarControl | X | X | X |
| CopyFace | Copies the face image from a button to the clipboard | X | | |
| Delete *Temporary* | Deletes the control, with the option of making the deletion temporary, just for the current session | X | X | X |
| Execute | Executes the built-in procedure associated with the control or the VBA macro set in its OnAction property | X | X | X |

**Table 23.2**    *Key Properties and Methods for Menu and Toolbar Controls (continued)*

| Method | Description | | | |
|--------|-------------|---|---|---|
| Move *Bar*, *Before* | Moves the control to the CommandBar represent by the *Bar* parameter or to the end of the current CommandBar; *Before* represents the position for the copied control; both parameters are optional | X | X | X |
| PasteFace | Pastes the image face on the clipboard to the button | X | | |
| RemoveItem *Index* | Removes the item in the *Index* position from the list | | X | |
| Reset | Resets a control to its original function and face image | X | X | X |
| SetFocus | Moves the focus to the control | X | X | X |

**Table 23.3**    *Styles for CommandBarButton Controls from the MsoButtonStyle Enumeration*

| Constant | Value | Description |
|----------|-------|-------------|
| msoButtonAutomatic | 0 | Uses the default behavior for a built-in button; for a custom button, text only |
| msoButtonCaption | 2 | Displays text only; default for custom buttons |
| msoButtonIcon | 1 | Displays image only |
| msoButtonIconAndCaption | 3 | Displays image with text to the right |
| msoButtonIconAndCaptionBelow | 11 | Displays image with text below |
| msoButtonIconAndWrapCaption | 7 | Displays image with text wrapped to the right |
| msoButtonIconAndWrapCaptionBelow | 15 | Displays image with text wrapped below |
| msoButtonWrapCaption | 14 | Displays text only, with text centered and wrapped |

## 23.1.2    Executing a toolbar command

Perhaps the most useful CommandBarControl method for an Outlook VBA or custom forms programmer is the Execute method, which runs whatever command is associated with the control. You can use Execute from both VBA procedures and scripts behind Outlook custom forms.

For example, the ShowWebPage procedure in Listing 23.3 displays a Web page in Outlook's built-in browser. You could use it in a VBA macro or call it from the Click event on a command button or label control on a

**Listing 23.3** *Show a Web page in Outlook's browser*

```
Sub ShowWebPage(url)
    Dim objExpl, objWeb
    Set objExpl = Application.ActiveExplorer
    Set objWeb = objExpl.CommandBars.FindControl(, 1740)
    objWeb.Text = url
    objWeb.Execute
End Sub
```

custom form. In this VBScript example, the URL comes from the Caption property of a control located on a custom form page named "My Page."

```
Sub lblWebURL_Click()
    Set objPage = Item.GetInspector("My Page")
    Set lblWebURL = objPage.Controls("lblWebURL")
    Call ShowWebPage(lblWebURL.Caption)
End Sub
```

The above example uses a label control (lblWebURL) to illustrate the flexibility of repurposing form controls for unexpected applications—like making a label clickable.

## 23.1.3 Adding a new Explorer toolbar and controls

In Outlook VBA, there are several scenarios where building your own toolbar with custom controls can be useful:

- To keep visible some built-in controls that the standard toolbars and menus don't normally show

- To add buttons that open other applications or Web pages

- To add buttons to run Outlook macros

  To create a new toolbar on an Explorer window, use this syntax:

  ```
  Set objCB = objExpl.CommandBars.Add( _
          Name, Position, MenuBar, Temporary)
  ```

  The CommandBars.Add method returns a CommandBar object, ready for you to add controls to. All the parameters are optional, although you'll normally specify the *Name*, rather than have Outlook assign a default name. The *Position* parameter uses one of the Office.MsoBarPosition constants listed in Table 23.1. If the value of the *MenuBar* parameter is True, the new CommandBar replaces the active menu bar. If the value of the *Temporary* parameter is True, the new CommandBar is discarded when the current Outlook session ends.

To add a control to a toolbar, use the `Add` method on the `Controls` collection of the newly created `CommandBar`:

```
Set objCBB = objCB.Controls.Add( _
          Type, ID, Parameter, Before, Temporary)
```

All the parameters are optional. If you omit them all, the `Add` method creates a new, permanent `CommandBarButton` object at the end of the toolbar or menu.

The *Type* parameter supports only these three values from the `Office.MsoControlType` enumeration:

| | |
|---|---|
| `msoControlButton` | 1 |
| `msoControlComboBox` | 4 |
| `msoControlPopup` | 10 |

Other types of toolbar and menu commands cannot be created programmatically in Outlook.

Omit the *Type* and specify an *Id* value if you want to add a control to run a built-in command.

Use the *Parameter* value to store information related to the control, especially a parameter value that you might want the control to process in a macro.

To position the control at a particular place on the toolbar, provide a number for the *Before* parameter.

To tell Outlook to discard the control when you quit Outlook, use `True` for the *Temporary* argument.

Did you notice that the `CommandBar.Controls.Add` method does not include any parameter to uniquely identify a custom control? As soon as you add any custom control, you should set its `Tag` property to some unique value, so that you will be able to return the control later with `CommandBars.FindControl`.

Looking back to the three custom control scenarios listed at the beginning of the section, we now have enough information to show how to implement each one in a custom toolbar. You don't want to create duplicate toolbars, so it's always a good idea to check first if a toolbar with the same name exists. Since we want to create a new one, the code looks for an existing toolbar named "My First Toolbar" and, if it's found, deletes it:

```
Set objOL = Application
Set objExpl = objOL.ActiveExplorer
Set objCB = objExpl.CommandBars("My First Toolbar")
If Not objCB Is Nothing Then
    objCB.Delete
End If
```

These two statements create the toolbar as a temporary toolbar, position it so that it floats over the Explorer window, and make it visible:

```
Set objCB = objExpl.CommandBars.Add( _
  "My First Toolbar", msoBarFloating, False, True)
objCB.Visible = True
```

These two statements add the built-in Back command and change the style of the button from its default style to show the caption below the icon:

```
Set objCBB = objCB.Controls.Add(ID:=6881)
objCBB.Style = msoButtonIconAndCaptionBelow
```

To add a button that displays a Web site in the user's default browser, add another button and set its HyperlinkType and TooltipText properties:

```
Set objCBB = objCB.Controls.Add(Type:=msoControlButton)
With objCBB
    .BeginGroup = True
    .Caption = "Go to OutlookCode.com"
    .Tag = "OutlookCode.com link"
    .HyperlinkType = msoCommandBarButtonHyperlinkOpen
    .Style = msoButtonWrapCaption
    .TooltipText = "http://www.outlookcode.com"
End With
```

To add a pop-up menu to the toolbar, add a pop-up control and return another CommandBar object from the new control:

```
Set objCBPop = objCB.Controls.Add(Type:=msoControlPopup)
With objCBPop
    .BeginGroup = True
    .Caption = "My Favorite Macros"
    .Tag = "Macro submenu"
    Set objCBSub = objCBPop.CommandBar
End With
```

**Note:** It is not possible to add a pop-up menu control that displays an icon or picture.

To add a button that runs a macro, add a button to the submenu control and set the button's OnAction property:

```
Set objCBB = _
  objCBSub.Controls.Add(Type:=msoControlButton)
With objCBB
    .BeginGroup = True
    .Caption = "Enumerate CommandBars"
    .Tag = "Run EnumCommandBars"
    .OnAction = "EnumCommandBars"
    .Style = msoButtonIconAndWrapCaption
    .TooltipText = "Run the EnumCommandBars macro"
End With
```

**Figure 23.1**  *A custom toolbar can mix built-in and custom commands and use different display styles for each.*

As the last step in creating the toolbar, locate the Visual Basic Editor command using `CommandBars.FindControl` and copy and paste its icon to the macro button:

```
Set objCBBTemp =
objExpl.CommandBars.FindControl(ID:=1695)
If Not objCBBTemp Is Nothing Then
    objCBBTemp.CopyFace
    objCBB.PasteFace
End If
```

Figure 23.1 shows the newly created toolbar, with six buttons (we added the built-in Forward and Up One Level buttons to go with Back, plus another macro). The buttons are in three groups, using three different display styles, with two of the buttons on a submenu. The complete annotated code procedure, with variable declarations, is in Listing 23.4. Experiment with different values for the `Position` parameter for `CommandBars.Add` and for the button's `Style` property to get a feel for the different display options that are available.

## 23.2  Working with context menus

With a good grounding in how to add controls to toolbars or menus and run code when users click them, we're ready to tackle one of the most exciting new features in Outlook 2007—the ability to work with the context menus that appear when the user right-clicks on an item in a folder, a folder in the navigation pane, an attachment, and so on.

Context menus are dynamic and, by definition, contextual. The code that adds controls to the menu runs just before the menu displays. Those controls should be relevant to the object that received the right-click. To expose that context, the event handler includes an appropriate object. For example, here is the signature for the `AttachmentContextMenuDisplay` event:

```
Private Sub Application_AttachmentContextMenuDisplay( _
    ByVal CommandBar As Office.CommandBar, _
    ByVal Attachments As AttachmentSelection)
```

It has two arguments—a `CommandBar`, which represents the context menu itself, and an `Attachments` object representing the attachment(s) the user

**Listing 23.4**    *Create a custom toolbar with buttons*

```
Sub BuildMyFirstToolbar()
    Dim objOL As Outlook.Application
    Dim objExpl As Outlook.Explorer
    Dim objCB As Office.CommandBar
    Dim objCBB As Office.CommandBarButton
    Dim objCBPop As Office.CommandBarPopup
    Dim objCBSub As Office.CommandBar
    Dim objCBBTemp As Office.CommandBarButton
    On Error Resume Next
    Set objOL = Application
    Set objExpl = objOL.ActiveExplorer
' Step 1: Delete existing toolbar
    Set objCB = objExpl.CommandBars("My First Toolbar")
    If Not objCB Is Nothing Then
        objCB.Delete
    End If
' Step 2: Create the new toolbar
    Set objCB = objExpl.CommandBars.Add( _
      "My First Toolbar", msoBarFloating, False, True)
    objCB.Visible = True
    With objCB.Controls
' Step 3: Add built-in commands to the toolbar
        Set objCBB = .Add(ID:=6881)
        objCBB.Style = msoButtonIconAndCaptionBelow
        Set objCBB = .Add(ID:=6882)
        objCBB.Style = msoButtonIconAndCaptionBelow
        Set objCBB = .Add(ID:=1762)
        objCBB.Style = msoButtonIconAndCaptionBelow
' Step 4: Add a hyperlink button to the toolbar
        Set objCBB = .Add(Type:=msoControlButton)
        With objCBB
            .BeginGroup = True
            .Caption = "Go to OutlookCode.com"
            .Tag = "OutlookCode.com link"
            .HyperlinkType = msoCommandBarButtonHyperlinkOpen
            .Style = msoButtonWrapCaption
            .TooltipText = "http://www.outlookcode.com"
        End With
' Step 5: Add a submenu to the toolbar
        Set objCBPop = .Add(Type:=msoControlPopup)
        With objCBPop
            .BeginGroup = True
            .Caption = "My Favorite Macros"
            .Tag = "Macro submenu"
            Set objCBSub = objCBPop.CommandBar
        End With
    End With
    With objCBSub.Controls
' Step 6: Add a button to run a macro, putting it on the submenu
        Set objCBB = .Add(Type:=msoControlButton)
        With objCBB
            .BeginGroup = True
```

**Listing 23.4**     *Create a custom toolbar with buttons (continued)*

```
              .Caption = "Enumerate CommandBars"
              .Tag = "Run EnumCommandBars"
              .OnAction = "EnumCommandBars"
              .Style = msoButtonIconAndWrapCaption
              .TooltipText = "Run the EnumCommandBars macro"
          End With
' Step 6: Copy the icon from the Visual Basic Editor command to
'         the button that runs the macro
          Set objCBBTemp = _
            objExpl.CommandBars.FindControl(ID:=1695)
          If Not objCBBTemp Is Nothing Then
              objCBBTemp.CopyFace
              objCBB.PasteFace
          End If
          Set objCBB = .Add(Type:=msoControlButton)
          With objCBB
              .BeginGroup = True
              .Caption = "Toggle Web Toolbar"
              .Tag = "Run ToggleExplorerWeb"
              .OnAction = "ToggleExplorerWeb"
              .Style = MsoButtonStyle.msoButtonCaption
              .TooltipText = "Run the ToggleExplorerWeb macro"
          End With
      End With
      Set objOL = Nothing
      Set objExpl = Nothing
      Set objCB = Nothing
      Set objCBB = Nothing
      Set objCBBTemp = Nothing
      Set objCBSub = Nothing
End Sub
```

---

## Where's the Click Event Code?

If you've written programs for Outlook or other Office applications in Visual Basic 6.0, you may be wondering why we're not showing code for the `Click` event for `CommandBarButton` and the `Change` event for `CommandBarComboBox`. While those events work just fine in VB and even VBA code for Outlook 2007, they are not the preferred way to handle events in .NET languages. In VB.NET, the better approach is to use the `AddHandler` method to connect a control's `Click` event with a specific procedure. This allows a more dynamic approach to command bar control event handling, without the need to declare every single control object `WithEvents`.

The use of the `OnAction` property to "wire" controls to procedures is the closest thing in VBA to VB.NET's `AddHandler`, especially when the VBA code uses the `CommandBars.ActionControl` property to determine which control was clicked, as in the example in Listing 23.9. The context menus discussed in the next section also work well with such a dynamic approach.

**Table 23.4**   *Application-Level Events for Right-Click Context Menus*

| Context Menu Event | Fires for | Context Object Passed as Argument |
|---|---|---|
| AttachmentContextMenuDisplay | Attachment(s) | AttachmentSelection |
| FolderContextMenuDisplay | Folder | Folder or, for search folders, Nothing |
| ItemContextMenuDisplay | Item(s) in folder view | Selection |
| ShortcutContextMenuDisplay | Shortcut in Shortcuts pane | OutlookBarShortcut |
| StoreContextMenuDisplay | Store root folder | Store |
| ViewContextMenuDisplay | New line row or blank view area | View |

selected, either in the reading pane or in an open item. AttachmentSelection is a new object in Outlook 2007 and, like the Selection object that holds the items selected in a folder view, it has a Count property. Therefore, the code in the AttachmentContextMenuDisplay event handler might check the value of the Count property and then take different actions depending on whether the user selected one attachment or more than one.

Table 23.4 lists the names of the context menu display events, the context in which they display, and the key object that each passes as an argument. In addition, a ContextMenuClose event fires when the context menu is no longer displayed, offering an opportunity to release objects and perform any other necessary cleanup.

Handling a context menu event in VBA requires several components:

- An event handler in the ThisOutlookSession module (or another class module)
- Code to add a control to the context menu
- Optionally, a global variable to hold the key object for the current context
- A macro that runs when the user clicks the menu control
- Code in the ContextMenuClose event to release the global variable

You can, of course, add multiple controls to the context menu, each linked to a different macro through its OnAction property.

**Note:** One right-click context menu that will be sorely missed in Outlook 2007 is the one that appears when the user right-clicks in the message body. In previous versions of Office, it was possible to write code to work with that menu, provided that Word was the user's choice as Outlook email editor. In Outlook 2007, however, even with Word being the only email editor, the right-click context menu for the message body is not accessible to developers.

To see all six context menus in action, add the code in Listing 23.5 to the built-in `ThisOutlookSession` module. Choose Insert | Module to insert a new code module, and place the code from Listng 23.6 there. To test the menus, right-click on any of the locations listed in the "Fires for" column in Table 23.4. You should see a new command at the top of the context menu. Click it to see a pop-up message with information about the object you right-clicked.

**Listing 23.5**    *Basic event handlers for Context Menu*

```
Private Sub Application_AttachmentContextMenuDisplay( _
  ByVal CommandBar As Office.CommandBar, _
  ByVal Attachments As AttachmentSelection)
    Set g_colAttSel = Attachments
    Call AddDemoButton(CommandBar, "Attachment")
End Sub

Private Sub Application_FolderContextMenuDisplay( _
  ByVal CommandBar As Office.CommandBar, _
  ByVal Folder As Folder)
    Set g_objFolder = Folder
    Call AddDemoButton(CommandBar, "Folder")
End Sub

Private Sub Application_ItemContextMenuDisplay( _
  ByVal CommandBar As Office.CommandBar, _
  ByVal Selection As Selection)
    Set g_colSel = Selection
    Call AddDemoButton(CommandBar, "Item")
End Sub

Private Sub Application_ShortcutContextMenuDisplay( _
  ByVal CommandBar As Office.CommandBar, _
  ByVal Shortcut As OutlookBarShortcut)
    Set g_objShortcut = Shortcut
    Call AddDemoButton(CommandBar, "Shortcut")
End Sub

Private Sub Application_StoreContextMenuDisplay( _
  ByVal CommandBar As Office.CommandBar, _
  ByVal Store As Store)
    Set g_objStore = Store
    Call AddDemoButton(CommandBar, "Store")
End Sub

Private Sub Application_ViewContextMenuDisplay( _
  ByVal CommandBar As Office.CommandBar, ByVal View As View)
    Set g_objView = View
    Call AddDemoButton(CommandBar, "View")
End Sub
```

**Listing 23.5** *Basic event handlers for Context Menu (continued)*

```
Private Sub Application_ContextMenuClose( _
  ByVal ContextMenu As OlContextMenu)
    Select Case ContextMenu
        Case olAttachmentContextMenu
            Set g_colAttSel = Nothing
        Case olFolderContextMenu
            Set g_objFolder = Nothing
        Case olItemContextMenu
            Set g_colSel = Nothing
        Case olShortcutContextMenu
            Set g_objShortcut = Nothing
        Case olStoreContextMenu
            Set g_objStore = Nothing
        Case olViewContextMenu
            Set g_objView = Nothing
    End Select
End Sub
```

The code in Listings 23.5 and 23.6 provides a basic framework for working with all of the context menu events. Of course, your code probably won't need to work with all six events. To understand how just one event handler works, let's look at the context menu that appears when the user right-clicks on an attachment. The `AttachmentContextMenuDisplay` event handler performs two operations:

```
Private Sub Application_AttachmentContextMenuDisplay( _
  ByVal CommandBar As Office.CommandBar, _
  ByVal Attachments As AttachmentSelection)
    Set g_colAttSel = Attachments
    Call AddDemoButton(CommandBar, "Attachment")
End Sub
```

It sets the value of a global variable, `g_colAttSel`, which is declared in the regular code module (see Listing 23.6) and it calls the `AddDemoButton` procedure in the regular code module. The `AddDemoButton` procedure uses the techniques you've seen earlier in the chapter to add a new, temporary `CommandBarButton` to the context menu and link it to a macro through the control's `OnAction` property:

```
Set objCBB = cb.Controls.Add( _
  msoControlButton, , , 1, True)
With objCBB
    .Caption = "Run " & context & "MenuDemo macro"
    .OnAction = context & "MenuDemo"
End With
```

The `context` argument is passed to the `AddDemoButton` procedure with the value `"Attachment"` so the `Caption` becomes `"Run Attach-mentMenuDemo macro"` and the `OnAction` property links the control to the

**Listing 23.6**   *Global variables and macros for Context Menu controls*

```
Public g_colAttSel As Outlook.AttachmentSelection
Public g_objFolder As Outlook.Folder
Public g_colSel As Outlook.Selection
Public g_objShortcut As Outlook.OutlookBarShortcut
Public g_objStore As Outlook.Store
Public g_objView As Outlook.View
Dim strMsg As String

Sub AddDemoButton(cb As Office.CommandBar, context As String)
    Dim objCBB As Office.CommandBarButton
    Dim objCBBFirst As Office.CommandBarButton
    Set objCBB = cb.Controls.Add( _
                 msoControlButton, , , 1, True)
    With objCBB
        .Caption = "Run " & context & "MenuDemo macro"
        .OnAction = context & "MenuDemo"
    End With
    Set objCBBFirst = cb.Controls.Item(2)
    objCBBFirst.BeginGroup = True
    Set objCBB = Nothing
    Set objCBBFirst = Nothing
End Sub

Sub AttachmentMenuDemo()
    strMsg = "Number of attachments selected: " & g_colAttSel.count
    MsgBox strMsg, vbInformation, "Attachment Menu"
End Sub

Sub FolderMenuDemo()
    strMsg = "Folder selected: " & g_objFolder.FolderPath
    MsgBox strMsg, vbInformation, "Folder Menu"
End Sub

Sub ItemMenuDemo()
    strMsg = "Number of items selected: " & g_colSel.count
    MsgBox strMsg, vbInformation, "Item Menu"
End Sub

Sub ShortcutMenuDemo()
    strMsg = "Shortcut target: " & g_objShortcut.target
    MsgBox strMsg, vbInformation, "Shortcut Menu"
End Sub

Sub StoreMenuDemo()
    strMsg = "Store name: " & g_objStore.DisplayName
    MsgBox strMsg, vbInformation, "Store Menu"
End Sub

Sub ViewMenuDemo()
    strMsg = "View name: " & g_objView.Name
    MsgBox strMsg, vbInformation, "View Menu"
End Sub
```

`AttachmentMenuDemo` macro. That's all it takes to add a functional button to the context menu!

However, the `AddDemoButton` code did a little bit more. To make the new command more visible, it locates the command that was originally at the top of the list and puts a group separator above it:

```
Set objCBBFirst = cb.Controls.Item(2)
objCBBFirst.BeginGroup = True
```

The "Run AttachmentMenuDemo macro" button should appear at the top of the context menu. When the user clicks it, that macro uses the global variable, `g_colAttSel`, to determine the number of attachments clicked and display that information to the user:

```
strMsg = "Number of attachments selected: " & _
          g_colAttSel.count
MsgBox strMsg, vbInformation, "Attachment Menu"
```

Finally, the context menu closes automatically, and the `ContextMenu-Close` procedure determines the type of menu that closed and releases the corresponding global variable:

```
Private Sub Application_ContextMenuClose( _
   ByVal ContextMenu As OlContextMenu)
     Select Case OlContextMenu
        Case olAttachmentContextMenu
           Set g_colAttSel = Nothing
```

The `ContextMenu` argument for the `ContextMenuClose` event handler exposes which menu closed, so the code can determine which global object variable to release.

The next two sections provide additional examples for the store and items context menus. You should also check out the code samples in these articles in Help:

- How to: Add or Remove a Menu Item on a Context Menu (HV10038565)
- How to: Hide or Disable a Menu Item on a Context Menu (HV10038566)
- How to: Customize an Item Context Menu (HV10045272)
- How to: Customize a Context Menu to Support Moving Items between Calendars (HV10046161)
- How to: Share Contact Information Including the Business Card (HV10038576)

The numbers in parentheses are article IDs you can search for in Help to find the articles faster.

## 23.2.1   **Example: Display a store's data location**

This example is a little bit different from the ones in the previous section, because it doesn't involve running any code when the user clicks a button on the context menu. The buttons—two in this example—are there simply to display information about what file holds the store's data and whether it contains any rules. Since there is no macro to run from the button click, all the code can go into the event handler in the `ThisOutlookSession` module. Alternatively, you can put the three helper functions—`GetStore-Path()`, `Hex4ToString()`, and `Hex2ToString()`—in a regular code module. These three functions help extract the file path for certain types of stores by examining the `Store` object's `StoreID` value. Listing 23.7 shows the code.

The other different feature of this store menu event handler is that it looks for another control on the context menu to help determine whether the store is the .pst file for an IMAP mail account:

```
Set objIMAP = CommandBar.FindControl(, 5595)
If Not objIMAP Is Nothing Then
    objCBB.Caption = "Store for IMAP account: " & _
                    Store.DisplayName
```

The control whose `ID` is 5595 is the IMAP Folders command. Since it appears only on the context menu for IMAP account stores, it's a reliable indicator that the `Store` object is indeed associated with an IMAP account.

**Listing 23.7**   *Show the data file location and rules count for any information store*

```
Private Sub Application_StoreContextMenuDisplay( _
  ByVal CommandBar As Office.CommandBar, _
  ByVal Store As Store)
    Dim objCBB As Office.CommandBarButton
    Dim objIMAP As Office.CommandBarButton
    Dim objFolder As Outlook.Folder
    Dim colRules As Outlook.Rules
    Dim intCount As Integer
    On Error Resume Next
    Set objCBB = CommandBar.Controls.Item(1)
    objCBB.BeginGroup = True
    Set objCBB = CommandBar.Controls.Add( _
      Type:=msoControlButton, Before:=1, Temporary:=True)
    objCBB.Style = msoButtonWrapCaption
    Select Case Store.ExchangeStoreType
        Case olPrimaryExchangeMailbox
            If Store.IsCachedExchange Then
                objCBB.Caption = _
                  "Exchange .ost location: " & Store.FilePath
            Else
                objCBB.Caption = "Exchange mailbox: Primary"
            End If
```

**Listing 23.7**     *Show the data file location and rules count for any information store (continued)*

```
        Case olExchangeMailbox
            objCBB.Caption = "Exchange mailbox: Secondary"
        Case olExchangePublicFolder
            objCBB.Caption = "Exchange Public Folder Store"
        Case Else
            If Store.IsDataFileStore Then
                Set objFolder = Store.GetRootFolder
                intCount = objFolder.folders.count
                Set objFolder = objFolder.folders(intCount)
                If objFolder.IsSharePointFolder = True Then
                    objCBB.Caption = "Sharepoint store: " & _
                                      GetStorePath(Store)
                Else
                    objCBB.Caption = _
                        "Store location: " & Store.FilePath
                End If
            Else
                Set objIMAP = CommandBar.FindControl(, 5595)
                If Not objIMAP Is Nothing Then
                    objCBB.Caption = _
                    "Store for IMAP account: " & _
                    GetStorePath(Store)
                Else
                    objCBB.Caption = "Store for account: " & _
                                      GetStorePath(Store)
                End If
            End If
    End Select
    Set objCBB = CommandBar.Controls.Add( _
      Type:=msoControlButton, Before:=2, Temporary:=True)
    Set colRules = Store.GetRules
    If Err.Number = 0 Then
        objCBB.Caption = "Number of rules in store: " & colRules.count
    Else
        objCBB.Caption = "This store does not support rules."
    End If
    Set objCBB = Nothing
    Set objIMAP = Nothing
End Sub

Function GetStorePath(str As Outlook.Store)
    Dim intStart As Integer
    Dim intEnd As Integer
    Dim strProvider As String
    Dim strPathRaw As String
    Dim strStoreID As String
    strStoreID = str.StoreID
    intStart = InStr(9, strStoreID, "0000") + 4
    intEnd = InStr(intStart, strStoreID, "00")
    strProvider = Mid(strStoreID, intStart, intEnd - intStart)
    strProvider = Hex2ToString(strProvider)
```

Listing 23.7    *Show the data file location and rules count for any information store (continued)*

```
Select Case LCase(strProvider)
    Case "mspst.dll", "pstprx.dll"
        intStart = InStrRev(strStoreID, "00000000") + 8
        strPathRaw = Mid(strStoreID, intStart)
        GetStorePath = Trim(Hex4ToString(strPathRaw))
    Case "msncon.dll"
        intStart = InStrRev(strStoreID, _
                            "00", Len(strStoreID) - 2) + 2
        strPathRaw = Mid(strStoreID, intStart)
        GetStorePath = Trim(Hex2ToString(strPathRaw))
    Case Else
        GetStorePath = "Unknown store path"
End Select
End Function

Public Function Hex4ToString(Data As String) As String
    Dim strTemp As String
    Dim strAll As String
    Dim i As Integer
    For i = 1 To Len(Data) Step 4
        strTemp = Mid(Data, i, 4)
        strTemp = "&H" & Right(strTemp, 2) & Left(strTemp, 2)
        strAll = strAll & ChrW(CDec(strTemp))
    Next
    Hex4ToString = strAll
End Function

Public Function Hex2ToString(Data As String) As String
    Dim strTemp As String
    Dim strAll As String
    Dim i As Integer
    For i = 1 To Len(Data) Step 2
        strTemp = "&H" & Mid(Data, i, 2)
        strAll = strAll & ChrW(CDec(strTemp))
    Next
    Hex2ToString = strAll
End Function
```

## 23.2.2   Example: Find related items

When the user right-clicks on a single item, the resulting context menu shows a Find All | Messages from Sender command, but there's no comparable "Messages to Sender" command. For senders with Internet (SMTP) addresses, we're going to add a third command to the bottom of the Find All submenu to search for all messages to the given sender and display them in a separate Explorer window. This process uses the DoSearch() function and GetDefaultFolderModule() functions from Listing 16.5.

Put the event handler code in Listing 23.8 in the `ThisOutlookSession` module. Put the macro in Listing 23.9 in a regular code module, along with the above-mentioned functions from Listing 16.5, if they're not already present in your VBA project.

Here's how the `ItemContextMenuDisplay` event handler locates the Find All submenu and adds a button there to run the `FindRelatedItems` macro in Listing 23.9:

```
Set objCBPopup = CommandBar.Controls("Find All")
Set objCB = objCBPopup.CommandBar
Set objCBB = objCB.Controls.Add( _
            Type:=msoControlButton, Temporary:=True)
objCBB.OnAction = "FindRelatedItems"
```

Since the search needs only one piece of information—the sender's e-mail address—the event handler stores that data in the `Parameter` property of the `CommandBarButton`:

```
Set objMsg = Selection(1)
strSender = objMsg.SenderEmailAddress
objCBB.Parameter = strSender
```

**Listing 23.8**  *Event handler for the item's Context Menu*

```
Private Sub Application_ItemContextMenuDisplay( _
  ByVal CommandBar As Office.CommandBar, _
  ByVal Selection As Selection)
    Dim objCBB As Office.CommandBarButton
    Dim objCBPopup As Office.CommandBarPopup
    Dim objCB As Office.CommandBar
    Dim objMsg As Outlook.MailItem
    Dim strSender As String
    If Selection.count = 1 Then
        If TypeOf Selection(1) Is Outlook.MailItem Then
            Set objMsg = Selection(1)
            If objMsg.SenderEmailType = "SMTP" Then
                Set objCBPopup = CommandBar.Controls("Find All")
                Set objCB = objCBPopup.CommandBar
                Set objCBB = objCB.Controls.Add( _
                        Type:=msoControlButton, _
                        Temporary:=True)
                strSender = objMsg.SenderEmailAddress
                objCBB.Caption = _
                  "Messages to " & strSender
                objCBB.Parameter = strSender
                objCBB.OnAction = "FindRelatedItems"
            End If
        End If
    End If
    Set objCBB = Nothing
    Set objMsg = Nothing
End Sub
```

**Listing 23.9**    *Search for messages to or from the right-clicked message's sender*

```
Sub FindRelatedItems()
    Dim objOL As Outlook.Application
    Dim objExpl As Outlook.Explorer
    Dim colCB As Office.CommandBars
    Dim objCBB As Office.CommandBarButton
    Dim strFind As String
    On Error Resume Next
    Set objOL = Application
    Set objExpl = objOL.ActiveExplorer
    Set colCB = objExpl.CommandBars
    Set objCBB = colCB.ActionControl
    strFind = "to:" & objCBB.Parameter
    ' uses DoSearch from Listing 16.5
    Set objExpl = DoSearch(searchText:=strFind, _
                searchModule:=olModuleMail, _
                searchScope:=olSearchScopeAllFolders, _
                useNewWindow:=True)
    objExpl.Activate
    Set objOL = Nothing
    Set objExpl = Nothing
    Set colCB = Nothing
    Set objCBB = Nothing
End Sub
```

The sender name is also used to set the caption for the button:

```
objCBB.Caption = "Messages to " & strSender
```

When the user clicks the "Messages to" button, the `FindRelatedItems` macro uses the the `CommandBars.ActionControl` property to locate the control that the user clicked:

```
Set colCB = objExpl.CommandBars
Set objCBB = colCB.ActionControl
```

The control's `Parameter` property contains the address needed to search for the address using the `DoSearch()` procedure from Listing 16.5. This procedure relies on the `Explorer.Search` method, so we use the correct syntax for that method, adding `"to"` before the address, just as you'd see in Outlook's search box in the user interface:

```
strFind = "to:" & objCBB.Parameter
```

`DoSearch()` returns its results in a separate `Explorer` window, which the code displays:

```
Set objExpl = DoSearch(searchText:=strFind, _
  searchModule:=olModuleMail, _
  searchScope:=olSearchScopeAllFolders, useNewWindow:=True)
objExpl.Activate
```

In this example, you've seen how to work with a submenu on the context menu. The other new technique covered is how to pass information to a macro associated with a menu command by using a parameter on a menu control, instead of the global variables used earlier in Listings 23.5 and 23.6.

## 23.3  Working with the navigation pane and other Explorer panes

Along with menus and toolbars, the navigation pane and the other panes of the `Explorer` window help give the Outlook user context—to know what can be done at any given moment. You can show different panes and add new groups and folder links on the navigation modules, but you cannot create a totally new navigation module, nor can you remove folder links in many cases.

Figure 23.2 shows the hierarchy of objects, starting with the parent `Explorer`. The `Panes` collection on the right side of the diagram is somewhat strange, because the only pane that can be accessed through it is the `OutlookBarPane`. This pane, known as the Outlook Bar in early versions of Outlook, appears in Outlook 2007 as the Shortcuts module of the navigation pane. As it is largely overshadowed by the other modules in the navigation pane, we are not going to cover it in this chapter.

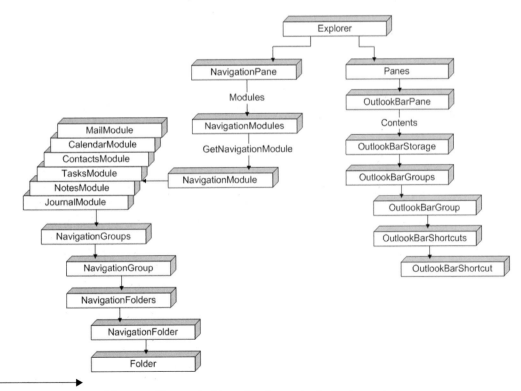

**Figure 23.2**  *Objects making up the hierarchy of panes in the Explorer window .*

### 23.3.1   **Showing and hiding panes**

Two `Explorer` methods are useful for working with the panes—`ShowPane` and `IsPaneVisible`.

To show or hide a pane, use the `ShowPane` method on an `Explorer` object, with this syntax:

```
objExplorer.ShowPane(Pane, Visible)
```

where *Pane* is one of the constants from the `OlPane` enumeration shown in Table 23.5. Use `True` for the value of *Visible* when you want to show a pane and `False` to hide a pane.

To find out whether a pane is visible, call the `IsPaneVisible` method with this syntax:

```
blnICanSeeIt = objExplorer.IsPaneVisible(Pane)
```

where *Pane* again is a value from Table 23.5. `IsPaneVisible` returns `True` or `False`.

The `olNavigationPane` constant in Table 23.5 refers to the navigation pane on the left side of the screen that has item-specific modules—Mail, Calendar, Contacts, Tasks, Notes, and Journal. Also capable of occupying the same space on the left side of the screen are the Folder List and Outlook Bar. Only one of those three panes can be visible at a time.

The To Do Bar occupies the right side of the screen, while the reading (preview) pane appears in the middle, along with the list of items in the folder.

To collapse the navigation pane, set its `IsCollapsed` property to `True`:

```
Set objOL = Application
objOL.ActiveExplorer.NavigationPane.IsCollapsed = True
```

The Outlook object model has no methods to control the position of the reading pane or to minimize the To Do Bar. However, those options are available indirectly, through the corresponding commands on the main Outlook menu using the `CommandBars` techniques from earlier in

**Table 23.5**   *OlPane Enumeration Constants for Use with ShowPane*

| Constant | Value |
|---|---|
| olFolderList | 2 |
| olNavigationPane | 4 |
| olOutlookBar | 1 |
| olPreview | 3 |
| olToDoBar | 5 |

the chapter. For example, this code snippet switches the position of the reading pane to the bottom of the screen through the parent Reading Pane submenu, using that submenu's `Controls` collection, rather than directly by using `CommandBars.FindControl`.

```
Set objOL = Application
Set objCB = objOL.ActiveExplorer.CommandBars
Set objCBPopup = objCB.FindControl(, 31134)
If Not objCBPopup Is Nothing Then
    Set objCBB = objCBPopup.CommandBar.Controls("Bottom")
    objCBB.Execute
End If
```

Unexpectedly, it is necessary to access the Bottom and Right commands for the reading pane through the parent Reading Pane submenu, using that submenu's `Controls` collection, rather than directly by using `Command-Bars.FindControl`.

For other commands, such as the one to minimize the To Do bar, the `FindControl` method returns the right command directly, using the same parent `CommandBars` object (`objCB`) as in the above snippet:

```
Set objCBB = objCB.FindControl(, 14859)
objCBB.Execute
```

You'll probably want to experiment with executing other commands from the lists generated with the `EnumCommandBars` procedure in Listing 23.1 to control the way the user interface looks in different scenarios.

### 23.3.2  Working with navigation pane modules

As Figure 23.2 shows, the `NavigationPane` object has a `Modules` property that returns a `NavigationModules` collection. Use the `GetNavigation-Module` method to return any individual module—that is, the individual Mail, Calendar, Contacts, Tasks, Notes, and Journal modules that display in the navigation pane, as well as the Folder List and Shortcuts modules.

To show more or fewer module buttons at the bottom of the navigation pane, change the value of the `DisplayedModuleCount` property. This code snippet sets the navigation pane to display just the first two modules in the module list as buttons:

```
Set objOL = Application
Set objNavPane = objOL.ActiveExplorer.NavigationPane
objNavPane.DisplayedModuleCount = 2
```

The order in which the module buttons stack depends on the value of the `Position` property for each module.

The basic item in the `NavigationModules` collection is the `Naviga-tionModule` object. To return the current module or switch to a different module, use the `NavigationPane.CurrentModule` property. To return any other module, use the `GetNavigationModule` method, passing as an

**Table 23.6**   *OlNavigationModuleType Enumeration Constants for Use with GetNavigationModule*

| Constant | Value |
|---|---|
| olModuleCalendar | 1 |
| olModuleContacts | 2 |
| olModuleFolderList | 6 |
| olModuleJournal | 4 |
| olModuleMail | 0 |
| olModuleNotes | 5 |
| olModuleShortcuts | 7 |
| olModuleTasks | 3 |

argument one of the constants from the OlNavigationModuleType enumeration, shown in Table 23.6.

**Tip:** The DoSearch() function in Listing 16.5 uses the CurrentModule property to switch modules in order to be able to conduct a search of all folders of a given type.

To get information about the folder links in any of the six item-specific modules, your code must find out what kind of module it is and instantiate an object of the correct class. For example, this code snippet gets the Calendar module:

```
Set objOL = Application
Set objNavPane = objOL.ActiveExplorer.NavigationPane
Set colNavMods = objNavPane.Modules
Set objNavMod = _
  colNavMod.GetNavigationModule(olModuleCalendar)
Set objCalPane = objNavMod
```

Once you have the specific module object, you can drill down into its NavigationGroups collection, which contains NavigationGroup objects. To get a particular navigation group, use the GetDefaultNavigation-Group method, passing as an argument one of the constants from the OlGroupType enumeration, shown in Table 23.7.

Each NavigationGroup contains a NavigationFolders collection, containing NavigationFolder items. Continuing with the objCalPane calendar pane module from the above snippet, this code drills down to the

**Table 23.7** *OlGroupType Enumeration Constants for Use with GetDefaultNavigationGroup*

| Constant | Value | Description |
|---|---|---|
| olCustomFoldersGroup | 0 | Custom group created either in the user interface or by code |
| olFavoriteFoldersGroup | 4 | Favorite Folders navigation group in the Mail module |
| olMyFoldersGroup | 1 | My Folders group containing items from the default store and .pst files |
| olPeopleFoldersGroup | 2 | Shared folders from other people |
| olOtherFoldersGroup | 3 | Other shared folders |

navigation folders in the My Folders group and switches all selected calendars to overlay mode:

```
Set colNavGroups = objCalPane.NavigationGroups
Set objNavGroup = _
  colNavGroups.GetDefaultNavigationGroup _
  (olMyFoldersGroup)
Set colNavFold = objNavGroup.NavigationFolders
For Each objNavFold In colNavFold
    If objNavFold.IsSelected Then
        objNavFold.IsSideBySide = False
    End If
Next
```

The `IsSelected` and `IsSideBySide` properties apply only to navigation folders in the Calendar module.

The `NavigationGroups` and `NavigationFolders` collections support the same `Add`, `Item`, and `Remove` methods as most other Outlook collections. For an example of `NavigationFolders.Add`, go back to Listing 11.15, where the `AddToMailFavs` adds a mail folder to the Favorite Folders group in the Mail module. It is not possible, however, to remove built-in navigation groups. It is also not possible to remove from the `NavigationFolders` collection any folder other than a shared folder, such as a Web calendar or a folder from another Exchange user's mailbox. The `NavigationFolder.IsRemovable` property tells you which folders can be removed.

Outlook Help has many useful code samples on using these new navigation objects. Be sure to check out these articles:

- How to: Show or Hide the Navigation Pane (HV10038583)
- How to: Display Specific Modules in the Navigation Pane (HV10038587)

- How to: Set a Module as the Currently Selected Module in the Navigation Pane (HV10038585)

- How to: Enumerate, Show, Hide, and Position Modules in the Navigation Pane (HV10038584)

- How to: Add a Folder to the Favorite Folders Group (HV10045312)

- How to: Add a Custom Folder to a Group and Display It in Overlay Mode by Default (HV10038592)

- How to: Enumerate Active Folders in the Calendar View (HV10045329)

- How to: Add a New Navigation Group and Move a Folder into That Group (HV10045291)

The numbers in parentheses are topic IDs you can search for in Help to find the articles faster.

As a final sample in this chapter, the next section shows how to set your own default folder for the Contacts module, so that Outlook shows that folder first, instead of the default Contacts folder.

### 23.3.3    Example: Show a favorite Contacts folder first

Some users don't like the way that Outlook always shows the default Contacts folder when a user switches to the Contacts navigation module for the first time during an Outlook session. They'd rather see a different default folder, and they'd like some way to tell Outlook which folder to show first. The code sample in Listing 23.10 makes that happen: The first time the user shows the Contacts module, the code displays the contacts folder that is at the top of the My Contacts group.

To try out this technique, follow these steps:

1.    Put all the code from Listing 23.10 in the `ThisOutlookSession` module.

2.    Display the Contacts module, showing your default Contacts folder, and drag the folder you want to use as the default to the top of the My Contacts list.

3.    Display a different navigation pane module.

4.    Go back to VBA and run the `Application_Startup` procedure.

5.    Now, display the Contacts module again.

You should see your default folder from Step 3.

The code relies on the `ModuleSwitch` event of the `NavigationPane` object to detect when the user has switched to the Contacts navigation pane. With the `CurrentModule` object passed by the event handler as an argument, the `m_objNavPane_ModuleSwitch` procedure instantiates a

**Listing 23.10**    *Display a user-defined default folder in the contacts module*

```
Dim WithEvents m_objNavPane As Outlook.NavigationPane

Private Sub Application_Startup()
    Set m_objNavPane = _
      Application.ActiveExplorer.NavigationPane
End Sub

Private Sub m_objNavPane_ModuleSwitch _
  (ByVal CurrentModule As NavigationModule)
    Dim objContMod As Outlook.ContactsModule
    Dim colNavGroups As Outlook.NavigationGroups
    Dim objNavGroup As Outlook.NavigationGroup
    Dim colNavFolders As Outlook.NavigationFolders
    Dim objNavFolder As Outlook.NavigationFolder
    Dim objFolder As Outlook.Folder
    If CurrentModule.NavigationModuleType = _
      olModuleContacts Then
        Set objContMod = CurrentModule
        Set colNavGroups = objContMod.NavigationGroups
        Set objNavGroup = _
          colNavGroups.GetDefaultNavigationGroup( _
          olMyFoldersGroup)
        Set colNavFolders = objNavGroup.NavigationFolders
        Set objNavFolder = colNavFolders(1)
        Set objFolder = objNavFolder.Folder
        Set Application.ActiveExplorer.CurrentFolder = objFolder
        Set m_objNavPane = Nothing
    End If
    Set objContMod = Nothing
    Set colNavGroups = Nothing
    Set objNavGroup = Nothing
    Set colNavFolders = Nothing
    Set objNavFolder = Nothing
    Set objFolder = Nothing
End Sub
```

`ContactsModule` object, then drills down to its My Contacts group to locate the first `NavigationFolder` in the group. From that `objNavFolder` object, the code obtains a `Folder` object and displays it in the current `Explorer`.

Since the intent of this application is to show the "default" contacts folder only the first time the user accesses the Contacts module, the `m_objNavPane` object is released, so the `ModuleSwitch` event will no longer fire.

You can, of course, apply this technique to any navigation pane module. If you expand the `ModuleSwitch` event handler to apply defaults to more modules, replace this statement:

```
If CurrentModule.NavigationModuleType = _
    olModuleContacts Then
```

with this statement:

```
Select Case CurrentModule.NavigationModuleType
```

and build Case statement blocks to handle each desired module. You'll also want to eliminate the statement that releases the m_objNavPane object, since you need to keep it active to fire the ModuleSwitch event for modules the user has not yet seen during the current session. If you still want to show the "default" folder for each module only on the initial visit to that module, use a module-level Boolean variable for each module type to track whether it has been seen yet.

## 23.4 Summary

Custom toolbars, menu bars, and the navigation pane make it easy for users to run VBA macros and navigate to their favorite Outlook folders. You can also set toolbar buttons to jump to specific Web pages. Key new features in Outlook 2007 related to the user interface include programmable context menus and a hierarchy of objects to provide access to the modules, groups, and folder links in the navigation pane.

Practical applications of these techniques have included examples that show a Web page in Outlook's built-in browser, view the data file location for any information store, search for messages sent to the sender of a message, and show a "default" contacts folder in the Contacts module.

# 24

# *Generating Reports on Outlook Data*

If any single area of Outlook falls short, it's printing and reporting. Outlook's built-in ability to regurgitate its data—either as printed reports or as files in other formats—is very limited. For example, when you use Outlook's File, Import and Export command, you cannot export user-defined fields, and some useful standard fields don't export at all! Furthermore, there is no method for printing a legacy custom form or form region in a format that resembles the on-screen form. An individual item always prints in Outlook's memo style, which produces a simple list of fields. Any custom fields print in alphabetical order.

Because of these major limitations, being able to extract Outlook data into some other format—either a file or a printed report—is an essential skill for Outlook programmers. This chapter discusses how you can export and print from Outlook without programming, using techniques such as Outlook views. You will also see how to push Outlook data into Excel or Word. These reporting techniques can be adapted not just for printed output, but also to produce files of exported data.

Highlights of this chapter include discussions of the following:

- Why folder views are the key to simple tabular reports
- How to use a Word mail merge to build a contact report
- How to build tabular reports with Excel
- How to print invoices and other reports that combine data from two different folders

## 24.1 Built-in report techniques

Users can print individual items or lists from Outlook folders by using the File | Print command. On a custom form's VBScript code, you can print an item by calling `Item.PrintOut`. For an individual item, Outlook prints first its standard fields in a preset order (which neither user nor developer

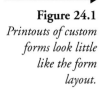

**Figure 24.1**
*Printouts of custom forms look little like the form layout.*

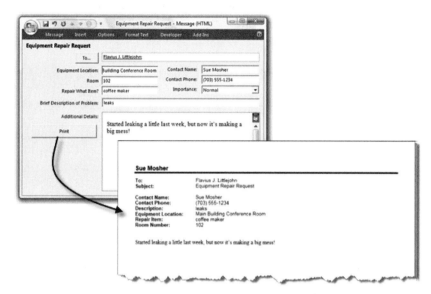

can control), then any custom fields in alphabetical order, and finally the contents of the item body. For example, Figure 24.1 shows a custom equipment repair request form and the standard printout you'd get from the Print command on the ribbon or the PrintOut method. The printout doesn't follow the order of the form layout at all.

Printing from a folder view can be a good way to generate a report on multiple items because the user gets pretty much what is displayed on the screen. You have other built-in reporting options, both programmatic and those involving no code at all, if you have Microsoft Word and Excel.

Another technique is to use Outlook's File | Import and Export command. However, as noted above, this command cannot export custom fields or even all standard fields. Also, the export feature is not programmable in any way. If you want to export data to another file format, you will need to write code to create the file and push Outlook data into it.

### 24.1.1   Printing from customized folder views

Why are folder views important to Outlook reports? Because almost anything you can show in a view can be printed out. Table views (such as the default view of your Inbox folder) are particularly useful for quick tabular reports on all kinds of Outlook data, including custom properties. Other types of views include timeline (which cannot be printed), card, icon, and day/week/month.

To create a new view from scratch, choose View | Current View | Define Views. In the Define Views dialog box, click New or Copy. It is often easier

**Table 24.1**   *Table View Customization Techniques*

| To Make This Change . . . | Do This . . . |
|---|---|
| Add columns to show other fields | Right-click on any column heading in the view, choose Field Chooser, and then drag fields from the Field Chooser to the view |
| Remove a field from a table view | Drag the column heading for the field out of view |
| Display fields in a different order | Drag a column heading to a new position |
| Change the width of a column | Drag the right border of a column heading to the left to make it narrower or to the right to make it wider |
| Adjust the width of a column to the best fit for the data | Double-click on the right border of the column heading |
| Organize related items by values in a particular field | Right-click the field's column heading, and then choose Group By This Field |
| Sort by particular field(s) | Click the column heading for the field you want to sort by; to sort up to three additional fields, hold down the Ctrl key as you click the column heading |
| Show only items that meet particular criteria | Choose View, Current View, Customize Current View, click Filter, and set criteria in the Filter dialog box |
| Display data that meets particular criteria in a different font | Choose View, Current View, Customize Current View, and click Automatic Formatting |

to make a copy of an existing table view and modify it to suit your needs than create a totally new view.

Table 24.1 lists many different ways to customize a table view. These techniques can also be accessed by choosing View | Current View | Customize Current View and using the buttons on the Customize View dialog box, shown in Figure 24.2. Also use the commands in the Customize View dialog to customize non-table views.

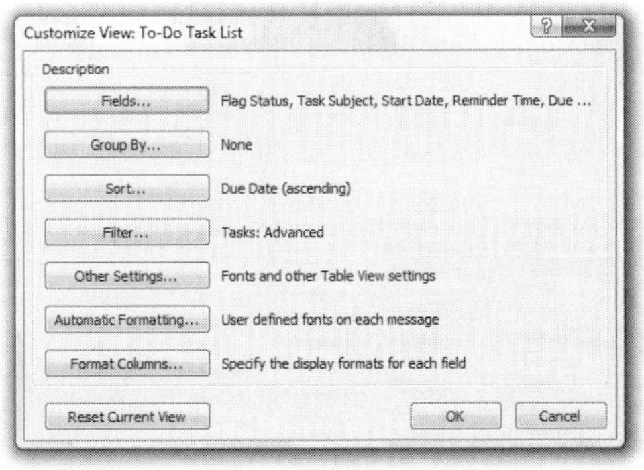

**Figure 24.2**
*Modify a view with any of these commands.*

As we saw in Chapter 22, it is also possible to create and modify views programmatically. The manual and programmatic approaches run up against the same limitations, though. For example, Outlook provides no way to display the entire item body in a view. In a table or timeline view with AutoPreview turned on, users can see only the first 255 characters. The same limitation applies to card views showing the `Note` field (in other words, the `Body` property).

**Note:** The Group By feature functions in a table view to group related items, such as those with the same category, and displays the number of items in each group. However, it cannot perform any subtotals or other calculations. If you need subtotals, a good strategy is to use the Excel method in the next section, then add formulas to do the calculations.

If a column in a table view is too narrow to show the full data in the field, the print output will also be truncated. To adjust columns accurately so that they print at the width you want, you may need to turn off automatic column sizing by following these steps:

1.  Right-click on a column heading and then choose Customize Current View.

2.  In the Customize View dialog box (see Figure 24.2), click Other Settings.

3.  In the Other Settings dialog box (see Figure 24.3), clear the box for "Automatic column sizing" and then click OK twice to return to the view.

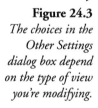

**Figure 24.3**

*The choices in the Other Settings dialog box depend on the type of view you're modifying.*

Turning off automatic column sizing also turns off the two-line or "compact" layout, allowing you to adjust the column widths for all fields in a single line.

Printing from an Outlook view is definitely a what-you-see-is-what-you-get operation. Be sure to use the Preview command on the File | Print dialog box to check whether all your columns fit on the page before you print, especially if you turn off automatic column sizing. To change the margins for printing, choose File | Page Setup | Table Style, and then switch to the Paper tab.

## 24.1.2  Copying data to Excel

One benefit of table views is that you can copy their data to Microsoft Excel with just a few keystrokes and then use Excel for additional formatting or data manipulation. Even custom properties can be exported in this fashion. Follow these steps in any Outlook table view:

1.  Add and remove fields from a table view until it shows only the fields you want to copy. (You don't need to worry about column width.)

2.  Choose Edit, Select All, then Edit, Copy.

3.  Switch to a blank Excel worksheet, and then choose Edit, Paste.

Once you have the data in Excel, you can use Excel's formatting, formula, pivot table, and other features to get a good-looking printout with the summary and analysis that you need. For example, you might want to analyze the messages from an Exchange public discussion folder to find out how many messages are being posted by each person every month.

---

**Tip:** If you try to copy and paste a field that contains carriage returns, the data will get split into different cells in Excel. One solution is to use an Outlook formula field to strip the carriage returns. For example, you could use this formula to extract the first line from the Business Address Street field:

```
IIf(Left([Business Address Street], InStr([Business
Address Street], Chr(10)))="", [Business Address Street],
Left([Business Address Street], InStr([Business Address
Street], Chr(10)) - 1))
```

and this one to generate any text on a second line:

```
IIf(InStr([Business Address Street], Chr(10)) > 0,
Mid([Business Address Street], InStr([Business Address
Street], Chr(10)) + 1, Len([Business Address Street]) -
InStr([Business Address Street], Chr(10))),"")
```

Use such formula fields instead of Outlook's built-in fields to "clean up" the data before you copy and paste to Excel.

---

The copy-and-paste technique works, of course, only with standard and hidden properties that are visible in folder views. For hidden properties, you can write code to push data into Excel, a technique we'll cover in detail a little later in the chapter. We've already seen a good example of this, though, in Listing 15.9, which creates an Excel report on message response times using two hidden MAPI properties.

## 24.1.3   **Performing a Word mail merge**

One of the most powerful ways to report on Outlook contact data is to perform a Word mail merge, starting the merge directly from any Outlook contacts folder. You will need Word 2007 installed. You can even include custom fields in the merge document, as long as they are defined in the folder (as discussed in Chapter 21).

Start in the Outlook contacts folder that contains the data you want to print and follow these steps:

1.   Select one or more contacts in the folder.

2.   Choose Tools | Mail Merge.

3.   Make your choices on the Mail Merge Contacts dialog box (Figure 24.4), then click OK.

4.   After Word displays the merge document, add merge fields, other text, and formatting as needed. Save the merge document if you think you might use it again.

5.   Click the merge button in Word.

**Tip:** Mail merge to Word is particularly helpful if you need to export data from a contacts folder in the Public Folders hierarchy. The built-in File | Import and Export command doesn't work with public folders.

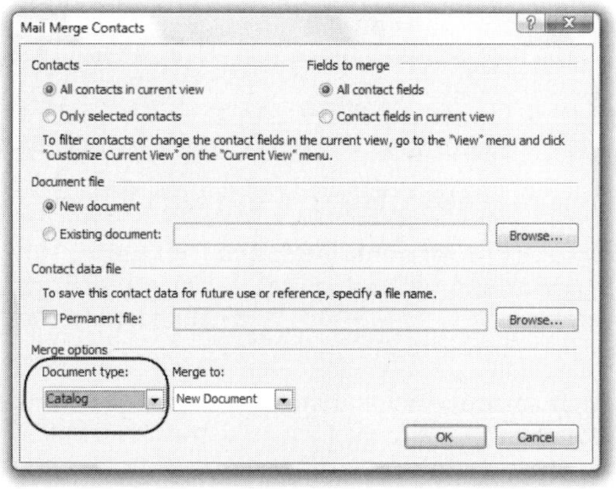

**Figure 24.4**
*Perform a mail merge to Microsoft Word from any Outlook contacts folder.*

**Figure 24.5** *Outlook fields are available in mail merges from the Insert Merge Field command.*

In Step 3, if you want to build a list or table of items, select Catalog under "Document type," as Figure 24.4 shows. If you want to see custom fields in the Word merge field list, make sure you choose "All contact fields" under "Fields to merge." Any custom fields must be defined in the User-Defined Fields in Folder list in the Field Chooser.

After the Word document opens, to insert any Outlook contact field into the merge document, use the Insert Merge Fields command from the Write & Insert Fields group (see Figure 24.5). To insert the contact body into the merge document, select the Notes field.

## 24.2 Coding reports with the Outlook object model

Once you know how to loop through all the items in a folder, as discussed in Chapter 15, you are halfway toward the goal of building reports using the Outlook object model. The other half of the project is to lay out the data in an informative format. These are all potential "documents" that can store a report to be printed or saved:

- Outlook email messages—especially good if you need to transmit the report to someone else
- Outlook post items—if you want to keep the report in an Outlook folder
- Text files
- Word documents
- Excel workbooks

Chapter 8 showed us how to create a text file and write data to it using `FileScriptingObject` techniques. Here are other code samples from earlier chapters that demonstrate different techniques related to report-building:

- Listing 13.10—Create a message listing all folders, with item count, in the current Outlook session
- Listing 14.2—Create a message listing a spam message's Internet headers
- Listing 15.9—Create a report in Microsoft Excel on message response times

- Listing 17.5—Create a reply from a tokenized boilerplate message, inserting property values from another message into the reply
- Listing 18.1—Create a message enumerating the user's address lists
- Listing 18.2—Create a post filled with the names, email addresses, and phone numbers of Exchange users in the Global Address List (GAL)
- Listing 22.1—Create a message reporting on a user's rules

Listings 18.1, 18.2, and 22.1 are particularly valuable as examples of how to use an HTML `<table>` element and related tags to organize information in a tabular format inside an Outlook message or post. Word and Excel can hold tables, too, and we'll spend the rest of the chapter examining how to get data from Outlook into documents in those two applications.

If you code a report in the form of an Outlook message or post, you can use the `PrintOut` method of the `MailItem` or `PostItem` object to print the report to the default printer. Outlook exposes no objects, however, to control printing. Therefore, if you need to change printers, print multiple copies, or otherwise customize the printing operation, consider generating the printable output in Word or Excel and using those applications' objects related to printing.

## 24.3  Sending output to Microsoft Excel

For reports that require more formatting than Outlook views can provide or in which you want to perform complex data manipulation, Microsoft Excel is a good tool. The row and column layout of an Excel worksheet is very similar to a table view in Outlook and is easy to handle in code.

The feature that makes it possible to write code in Outlook to produce reports in Excel is called Office automation. You can start an instance of any other Microsoft Office program (or use an existing copy if it's already running), create a new document, and add data to it. Conversely, you can design an Excel workbook with VBA code that instantiates an `Outlook.Application` object and uses Outlook objects and properties to fill the worksheet cells. If you want to take that approach, Chapter 7 has information on how to start an Outlook session programmatically from external code.

To create an Excel report using Outlook VBA code, you first need to learn the basics of opening a worksheet in Excel and adding data to it. Then, we'll look at a specific example that extracts the names and addresses from an Outlook distribution list.

### 24.3.1  Understanding Excel report basics

To work with Excel objects in VBA, choose Tools, References, and then check the box for Microsoft Excel 12.0 Object Library. In Outlook VBA, use the Insert | Module command to insert a new code module for your report samples and add the code in Listing 24.1.

The `GetExcelWS()` function in Listing 24.1 not only returns an `Excel.Worksheet` object that you can later fill with Outlook data, but it also sets the module-level variable `m_blnWeOpenedExcel` to `True` or `False` depending on whether Excel was already open. Knowing the state of Excel before your Outlook code runs is crucial to being able to return Excel to the same state when your Outlook code finishes. The `Set objExcel = GetObject(, "Excel.Application")` statement checks whether Excel is already running. If Excel is not running, the code creates a new instance of Excel with the `Set objExcel = CreateObject("Excel.Application")` statement.

The `RestoreExcel` subroutine uses the value of `m_blnWeOpenedExcel` to put Excel back in its original state after your code runs. A standard framework for populating and printing an Excel worksheet, therefore, looks like this:

```
Sub PrintGenericExcelReport()
    Dim objWB As Excel.Workbook
    Dim objWS As Excel.Worksheet
    Set objWB = GetExcelWB()
    If Not objWB Is Nothing Then
        Set objWS = objWB.Sheets(1)
        ' code to fill a worksheet with data
        objWS.Cells(1, 1) = "My First Excel Report"
        objWS.Application.Visible = True
        objWS.Activate
        objWS.PrintOut
        objWB.Close SaveChanges:=False
        Call RestoreExcel
    End If
    Set objWS = Nothing
    Set objWB = Nothing
End Sub
```

If you want to print the worksheet without showing it to the user, omit the `Application.Visible` and `Activate` statements. If you want to display the worksheet but not print it, omit the `Printout`, `Close`, and `Call-RestoreExcel` statements. You don't need to restore Excel to its former state if you're displaying a worksheet.

---

**Tip:** You can make Excel or Word print to a specific printer by changing the value of the `ActivePrinter` property of the `Word.Application` or `Excel.Application` object to the name of the printer you want to use. For example, for a worksheet object `objWS`:

```
objWS.Application.ActivePrinter = "OKI C5500"
```

That's something you can't do with Outlook.

---

**Listing 24.1**   *Create a new workbook and set a variable to track the status of Excel*

```
Private m_blnWeOpenedExcel As Boolean

Function GetExcelWB() As Excel.Workbook
    Dim objExcel As Excel.Application
    On Error Resume Next
    m_blnWeOpenedExcel = False
    Set objExcel = GetObject(, "Excel.Application")
    If objExcel Is Nothing Then
        Set objExcel = CreateObject("Excel.Application")
        m_blnWeOpenedExcel = True
    End If
    Set GetExcelWB = objExcel.Workbooks.Add
    Set objExcel = Nothing
End Function

Sub RestoreExcel()
    Dim objExcel As Excel.Application
    On Error Resume Next
    Set objExcel = GetObject(, "Excel.Application")
    If Not objExcel Is Nothing Then
        If m_blnWeOpenedExcel Then
            objExcel.Quit
        End If
    End If
    m_blnWeOpenedExcel = False
    Set objExcel = Nothing
End Sub
```

The next step is to put data into the worksheet. Within a worksheet, use the `Cells` object to specify a particular cell and put data into it. The `Cells` object takes row and column numbers as parameters using the syntax `Cells(row, col)`. This code fragment puts the text "My First Excel Report" into cell A1 (or row 1, column 1) and the text "End of Report" into cell E4 (or row 4, column 5) of a `Worksheet` object (`objWS`):

```
objWS.Cells(1, 1) = "My First Excel Report"
objWS.Cells(4, 5) = "End of Report"
```

**Tip:** Unlike Outlook, Excel includes a macro recorder that turns your keystrokes into VBA code. To start the Excel macro recorder, click the macro recorder button on the status bar at the bottom of the Excel window. Perform various operations in Excel and click the macro recorder button again. Press Alt+F11 to enter Excel's VBA environment, where you will find the recorded macro in one of the modules under Modules. You can copy code from Excel's VBA window into your Outlook project, editing it as necessary to change the variable names. This can be a useful technique for discovering formatting properties and other methods in the Excel object model.

→

**Listing 24.2** *Apply formatting to Excel worksheets with range objects*

```
Sub MyFirstExcelReport()
    Dim objWB As Excel.Workbook
    Dim objWS As Excel.Worksheet
    Dim objRange As Excel.Range
    ' GetExcelWB from Listing 24.1
    Set objWB = GetExcelWB()
    If Not objWB Is Nothing Then
        Set objWS = objWB.Sheets(1)
        objWS.Cells(1, 1) = "My First Excel Report"
        objWS.Cells(4, 5) = "End of Report"
        Set objRange = objWS.Range _
            (objWS.Cells(1, 1), objWS.Cells(4, 5))
        objRange.Font.Bold = True
        objWS.Application.Visible = True
        objWS.Activate
    End If
    Set objRange = Nothing
    Set objWS = Nothing
    Set objWB = Nothing
End Sub
```

Another useful Excel object is the `Range` object, which can cover an area that includes more than one cell, even nonadjacent areas. For simple rectangular ranges, you can use the `Cells` object to define a `Range` by its upperleft and lower-right corners. The `MyFirstExcelReport` procedure in Listing 24.2 adds the text from the code snippet above, then gives it bold formatting and displays it to the user. It uses the `GetExcelWS()` function from Listing 24.1.

To find out more about Excel objects, properties, and methods, you can use the object browser in either Outlook or Excel VBA.

## 24.3.2 Building a distribution list report

Back in Chapter 8, Listing 8.21 demonstrated how to create a distribution list by reading data from a text file. Let's go the other way and export an existing Outlook personal distribution list to an Excel workbook. The `DLToExcel()` subroutine retrieves each member of the distribution list and puts its display name and email address into an Excel worksheet. It takes a `DistListItem` object as its parameter. To test it, open any personal distribution list from a contacts folder and run this statement in the Outlook VBA Immediate window:

```
Call DLToExcel(Application.ActiveInspector.CurrentItem)
```

Here are a few notes on the code in Listing 24.3:

■ The `DLToExcel` procedure uses the `GetExcelWB()` function from Listing 24.1.

**Listing 24.3**     *Extract the members of a distribution list to an Excel worksheet*

```
Sub DLToExcel(dl As Outlook.DistListItem)
    Dim objOL As Outlook.Application
    Dim objNS As Outlook.NameSpace
    Dim objWB As Excel.Workbook
    Dim objWS As Excel.Worksheet
    Dim objRecip As Outlook.Recipient
    Dim objTempRecip As Outlook.Recipient
    Dim objAddrEntry As Outlook.AddressEntry
    Dim objRange As Excel.Range
    Dim strAddress As String
    Dim strExType As String
    Dim strType As String
    Dim i As Integer
    Dim intRow As Integer
    Dim intCol As Integer
    On Error Resume Next
    Set objOL = Application
    Set objNS = objOL.Session
    ' GetExcelWB from Listing 24.1
    Set objWB = GetExcelWB()
    Set objWS = objWB.Sheets(1)
    objWS.Cells(1, 1) = dl.Subject
    intRow = 3
    For i = 1 To dl.MemberCount
        strExType = ""
        Set objRecip = dl.GetMember(i)
        If objRecip.AddressEntry.Type = "MAPIPDL" Then
            strExType = "Personal DL"
        Else
            Set objTempRecip = objNS.CreateRecipient _
                              (objRecip.Address)
            If objTempRecip.Resolve Then
                Set objAddrEntry = objTempRecip.AddressEntry
                Select Case objAddrEntry.AddressEntryUserType
                    Case olExchangeUserAddressEntry
                        strExType = "Exchange User"
                    Case olExchangeDistributionListAddressEntry
                        strExType = "Exchange DL"
                    Case olExchangePublicFolderAddressEntry
                        strExType = "Exchange Public Folder"
                    Case olExchangeRemoteUserAddressEntry
                        strExType = "Exchange Contact"
                End Select
            End If
        End If
        objWS.Cells(intRow, 1) = objRecip.Name
        objWS.Cells(intRow, 2) = objRecip.Address
        objWS.Cells(intRow, 3) = objRecip.AddressEntry.Type
        objWS.Cells(intRow, 4) = strExType
        intRow = intRow + 1
    Next
```

**Listing 24.3**    *Extract the members of a distribution list to an Excel worksheet (continued)*

```
intRow = intRow - 1
Set objRange = objWS.Range _
    (objWS.Cells(3, 1), objWS.Cells(intRow, 4))
For i = 1 To 4
    objRange.Columns(i).EntireColumn.AutoFit
Next
objWB.Names.Add _
    Name:=Replace(dl.Subject, " ", ""), _
    RefersTo:="=" & objWS.Name & _
    "!" & objRange.Address & ""
objWS.Application.Visible = True
objWS.Activate
Set objOL = Nothing
Set objNS = Nothing
Set objRecip = Nothing
Set objTempRecip = Nothing
Set objAddrEntry = Nothing
Set objWS = Nothing
Set objWB = Nothing
Set objRange = Nothing
End Sub
```

- The address for each entry in the personal distribution list (DL) is in SMTP format, except for nested DLs, which have no address.

- Even though the `DistListItem.GetMember` method returns a `Recipient` object, the `AddressEntry` from that recipient doesn't have as much information as it would if the `Recipient` were coming from a message. To determine the type of entry, the code must create a new `Recipient` using the `Namespace.CreateRecipient` method and use the `AddressEntry` details from that new `Recipient` object. The code in the `Select Case` block uses the new `Address-Entry.AddressEntryUserType` property to find out what kind of recipient we're dealing with.

- The `Autofit` method adjusts the width of each column in the `Range` object for the DL member list to make sure that the user can see the complete name and address.

- The procedure also assigns a name to the range that contains the data. Named ranges are an important Excel feature that make it easy to use a particular set of cells for mail merge, import into Outlook, and other functions.

The `For ... Next` block is the heart of the `DLToExcel` subroutine. You can use this type of block to put any kind of Outlook data into Excel cells. For example, if you wanted to copy data from all items in an Outlook `Folder` object (`objFolder`) into an Excel worksheet (`objWS`), you would set the value for the starting row and use a `For Each ... Next` loop to pick up properties from all items in the folder:

```
intRow = 1
For Each objItem in objFolder.Items
    objWS.Cells(intRow, 1) = objItem.property1
    objWS.Cells(intRow, 2) = objItem.property2
    objWS.Cells(intRow, 3) = _
            objItem.UserProperties("property3")
        intRow = intRow + 1
Next
```

The last line in the `For Each ... Next` loop increments `intRow` so that data input for the next item takes place on a blank new row. After the loop finishes with the last item, the worksheet will contain a block of `intRow - 1` rows, containing data from `intRow - 1` items from the folder.

This type of loop is a valuable technique for exporting information from both standard and custom fields for use in Excel or in another program that can read Excel data files (or a comma-delimited file saved from an Excel worksheet). However, some data values from Outlook need a bit of formatting to work properly in Excel.

### 24.3.3  Formatting Outlook data for Excel

Because Outlook and Excel display data in different ways, you may need some small helper functions to make Outlook data look good in Excel. The functions in this section will help you format date/time, Boolean, and text property values properly.

Use the `DateToExcel()` function in Listing 24.4 to handle the `#1/1/4501#` date that Outlook displays as "None" when the user has not selected a date.

**Listing 24.4**  *Convert "None" date values to null*

```
Function DateToExcel(propVal)
    Dim dteDate       ' As Date
    If IsDate(propVal) Then
        dteDate = CDate(propVal)
        If dteDate = #1/1/4501# Then
            DateToExcel = Null
        Else
            DateToExcel = dteDate
        End If
    Else
        DateToExcel = propVal
    End If
End Function
```

**Listing 24.5** *Convert true and false values to strings*

```
Function YesNoToString(propVal)
    Select Case propVal
        Case True
            YesNoToString = "Yes"
        Case False
            YesNoToString = "No"
        Case Else
            YesNoToString = CStr(propVal)
    End Select
End Function
```

Use the `YesNoToString()` function in Listing 24.5 to convert data in yes/no properties to the strings `"Yes"` and `"No"`. Otherwise, Excel will use the values `-1` and `0` for values that Outlook stores as `True` and `False`.

Use the `TextToExcel()` function in Listing 24.6 to remove carriage returns and tabs from text and truncate the last string to the maximum number of characters an Excel cell can hold. (Excel displays these control characters with an ugly little rectangle.)

The functions in this section do not use data types for the arguments and function declarations for two reasons. First, omitting the data typing makes them suitable for use with VBScript behind Outlook forms, as well as in VBA. Second, all the functions are designed so that you can pass through data of any type. If the data does not need to be changed to work well in a worksheet, the function returns the data unchanged.

To put those functions to work, let's build a rather generic procedure for exporting Outlook messages to Excel.

The `InboxToExcel` procedure in Listing 24.7 uses a `Table` object to read the data from different properties. But instead of writing code for each property, just one code statement does all the work of telling the procedure which properties to export:

```
strProps = _
    "SenderName,To,Subject,SentOn,ReadReceiptRequested"
```

**Listing 24.6** *Clean up text to fit into Excel cells*

```
Function TextToExcel(propVal)
    If VarType(propVal) = vbString Then
        propVal = Replace(propVal, vbCr, " ")
        propVal = Replace(propVal, vbTab, " ")
        propVal = Left(propVal, 32767)
    End If
    TextToExcel = propVal
End Function
```

**Listing 24.7**    *Export message properties from the Inbox to Excel*

```
Sub InboxToExcel()
    Dim objOL As Outlook.Application
    Dim objNS As Outlook.NameSpace
    Dim objInbox As Outlook.Folder
    Dim objTable As Outlook.Table
    Dim objRow As Outlook.Row
    Dim objMsg As Outlook.MailItem
    Dim objWB As Excel.Workbook
    Dim objWS As Excel.Worksheet
    Dim objRange As Excel.Range
    Dim strFind As String
    Dim strProps As String
    Dim arr() As String
    Dim val As Variant
    Dim i As Integer
    Dim intRow As Integer
    Const PR_MESSAGE_CLASS = _
        "http://schemas.microsoft.com/mapi/proptag/0x001a001e"
    On Error Resume Next
    ' ### USER OPTION ###
    strProps = _
        "SenderName,To,Subject,SentOn,ReadReceiptRequested"
    Set objOL = Application
    Set objNS = objOL.Session
    Set objInbox = objNS.GetDefaultFolder(olFolderInbox)
    strFind = Quote(PR_MESSAGE_CLASS) & " LIKE 'IPM.Note%'"
    Set objTable = objInbox.GetTable("@SQL=" & strFind)
    ' GetExcelWB function from Listing 24.1
    Set objWB = GetExcelWB()
    Set objWS = objWB.Sheets(1)
    objWS.Name = "Inbox"
    arr = Split(strProps, ",")
    intRow = 1
    For i = 0 To UBound(arr)
        objWS.Cells(intRow, i + 1) = arr(i)
        objTable.Columns.Add arr(i)
    Next
    Set objRange = objWS.Range _
                (objWS.Cells(1, 1), objWS.Cells(1, i + 1))
    objRange.Font.Bold = True
    Do Until objTable.EndOfTable
        intRow = intRow + 1
        Set objRow = objTable.GetNextRow
        For i = 0 To UBound(arr)
            val = objRow(arr(i))
            Select Case VarType(val)
                Case vbDate
                    ' DateToExcel from Listing 24.3
                    val = DateToExcel(val)
                Case vbBoolean
                    ' YesNoToString from Listing 24.4
                    val = YesNoToString(val)
```

Listing 24.7    *Export message properties from the Inbox to Excel (continued)*

```
                    Case vbString
                        ' TextToExcel from Listing 24.5
                            val = TextToExcel(val)
                End Select
                objWS.Cells(intRow, i + 1) = val
            Next
        Loop
        For i = 1 To (UBound(arr) + 1)
            objWS.Columns(i).EntireColumn.AutoFit
        Next
        objWS.Application.Visible = True
        objWS.Activate
        Set objOL = Nothing
        Set objNS = Nothing
        Set objRow = Nothing
        Set objWB = Nothing
        Set objWS = Nothing
        Set objRange = Nothing
End Sub

Private Function Quote(val) As String
    Quote = Chr(34) & val & Chr(34)
End Function
```

From this one statement, the code creates an array that controls the column headings for the worksheet and columns added to the `Table.Columns` collection to expose the data. Not all properties can be handled this way, but most standard properties can. The Help topic on the `Table` object provides details on those that can't, such as `Body` and `HTMLBody`. You can also add custom and hidden properties to the list of processed properties by adding their MAPI schema property names to the `strProps` list.

A few notes on the code in Listing 24.6:

- The `Table` object (`objTable`) is filtered to show only messages by searching for items whose `MessageClass` property begins with `"IPM.Note"`. This statement constructs the filter string:

  ```
  strFind = Quote(PR_MESSAGE_CLASS) & " LIKE 'IPM.Note%'"
  ```

- The `Select Case VarType(val)` block adds a little efficiency by checking the type of value before running it through one of the converters. `VarType()` is a built-in function that returns a constant value that indicates the type of value—such as `vbBoolean` for a Boolean value.

- The code uses the same techniques as in Listings 24.2 and 24.3 to define ranges to give bold formatting to the column headings and autofit the columns.

- Some cells will probably be blank if no value has ever been set for that property on the item.

To change the list of properties exported from the Inbox, all you need to do is change the `strProps` = assignment statement to include more or fewer properties.

## 24.4  Sending output to Microsoft Word

Microsoft Word is an even more flexible reporting tool than Excel. Not only can it handle data in rows and columns like Excel, but it can also reproduce the look of a custom Outlook form, complete with checkboxes. Word reports are also ideal for combining information from different types of Outlook items. For example, you might need an invoice that totals the time you spent working on a particular contact's projects.

Two of the basic techniques involved are parallel to those in Excel:

- Create a new Word document, tracking whether Word was already open
- Convert data in Outlook to text that looks good in Word

In most cases, your Word report will start with a document template—an existing .dot file that contains text, formatting, and other components you want to include in the report. The Outlook code creates a new document based on that template, and then populates it with the Outlook data. One of the advantages of that approach is that the report "consumer"—someone from the department that will generate or use it—can design the report template file using Word, without any need to know Outlook code.

### 24.4.1  Understanding Word report basics

The basics of building reports with Word are very similar to the Excel techniques discussed earlier in the chapter. For VBA code, you must first use Tools, References to add a reference to the Microsoft Word 12.0 Library that is installed on your system.

Compare the basic `GetWordDoc()` and `RestoreWord` procedures for VBA in Listing 24.8 with the corresponding Excel procedures in Listing 24.1. Since Word is often used to print the details of a single Outlook custom form item, the procedures for VBScript code behind an Outlook form are in Listing 24.9.

One difference from the Excel code is the addition of a parameter—optional in the VBA version—to create a Word document using a specific template. As you will see, this is the key to making Word printouts that duplicate the look of Outlook form pages.

**Listing 24.8** *Create a new document and set a variable to track the status of Word (VBA)*

```
Private m_blnWeOpenedWord As Boolean

Function GetWordDoc(Optional templatePath As String) _
  As Word.Document
    Dim objWord As Word.Application
    On Error Resume Next
    m_blnWeOpenedWord = False
    Set objWord = GetObject(, "Word.Application")
    If objWord Is Nothing Then
        Set objWord = CreateObject("Word.Application")
        m_blnWeOpenedWord = True
    End If
    If templatePath = "" Then
        templatePath = "Normal.dotm"
    End If
    Set GetWordDoc = objWord.Documents.Add(templatePath)
    Set objWord = Nothing
End Function

Sub RestoreWord()
    Dim objWord As Word.Application
    On Error Resume Next
    Set objWord = GetObject(, "Word.Application")
    If Not objWord Is Nothing Then
        If m_blnWeOpenedWord Then
            objWord.Quit
        End If
    End If
    m_blnWeOpenedWord = False
    Set objWord = Nothing
End Sub
```

A Word template can contain boilerplate text, plus marked areas that you can use to place Outlook data in the text. To create a template from a new or existing Word document, click the Office button, and then choose Save As | Word Template. If you specify only a file name and no path for the template argument for the `GetWordDoc()` function, Word looks in the user's default templates folder.

A standard framework for populating and displaying or printing a Word document in VBA looks like the code in Listing 24.10, which adds one sentence at the top of the document, using the `objDoc.Content.Insert-Before` method. Compare with the Excel report in Listing 24.2.

To print the document without showing it to the user, omit the `Application.Visible` and `Activate` statements. To display the document without printing it, omit the `Printout`, `Close`, and `Call RestoreWord` statements. There is no need to restore Word to its former state if you're displaying a document, because you will leave Word open.

**Listing 24.9**    *Create a new document and set a variable to track the status of Word (VBScript)*

```
Private m_blnWeOpenedWord    ' As Boolean

Function GetWordDoc(templatePath)    ' As Word.Document
    Dim objWord      ' As Word.Application
    On Error Resume Next
    m_blnWeOpenedWord = False
    Set objWord = GetObject(, "Word.Application")
    If objWord Is Nothing Then
        Set objWord = CreateObject("Word.Application")
        m_blnWeOpenedWord = True
    End If
    If templatePath = "" Then
        templatePath = "Normal.dotm"
    End If
    GetWordDoc = objWord.Documents.Add(templatePath)
    Set objWord = Nothing
End Function

Sub RestoreWord()
    Dim objWord        ' As Word.Application
    On Error Resume Next
    Set objWord = GetObject(, "Word.Application")
    If Not objWord Is Nothing Then
        If m_blnWeOpenedWord Then
            objWord.Quit
        End If
    End If
    m_blnWeOpenedWord = False
    Set objWord = Nothing
End Sub
```

To use the code in VBScript, remove the apostrophe to uncomment the Const statement and remove the data typing from the Dim statements.

This statement is important to code-driven printouts:

```
objDoc.PrintOut False
```

The False argument tells Word not to print the document in the background. Instead, code execution waits for the document to print. Don't use background printing if your code closes the document immediately after printing. That will avoid the user seeing a prompt about the document trying to close while it's still printing.

As with Excel, you can use the macro recorder to investigate Word's methods and properties, then adapt at least some of the resulting VBA code to your Outlook projects. Many Word macros use the Selection object, which represents the currently selected text in a document, and Chapter 17 has other examples of moving around in and adding text to a Word Document object using the Selection object.

**Listing 24.10** *Create and print a simple Word document with VBA*

```
Sub GenericWordReport()
    Dim objDoc As Word.Document
    Dim objSel As Word.Selection
    ' Const wdDoNotSaveChanges = 0
    Set objDoc = GetWordDoc("Normal.dotm")
    If Not objDoc Is Nothing Then
        'fill the document with data
        objDoc.Content.InsertBefore "Today is " & _
            FormatDateTime(Date, vbLongDate)
        objDoc.Application.Visible = True
        objDoc.Activate
        objDoc.PrintOut False
        objDoc.Close wdDoNotSaveChanges
        Call RestoreWord
    End If
    Set objDoc = Nothing
    Set objSel = Nothing
End Sub
```

However, you will gain flexibility if you use the Range object instead, as it allows you to manipulate the document independently of the user's selection. The Content property of a Word document, which Listing 24.10 uses, is a Range object that represents the entire content of the document. The Range.InsertBefore method inserts text before the Range. Other examples in this chapter use the Range.InsertAfter method, which adds text after the area of the document that the Range object represents.

## 24.4.2 Formatting Outlook data for Word

It would be tedious to write code to insert text into a Word document, write more code to add data from an Outlook field, then write code to add more text, and then another field, and so on. In addition, it would be very difficult to revise such a report if you wanted to change some of the standard text in the report. And it would be a nightmare to create versions in different languages.

A better approach is to lay out the report as a Word document template with content controls acting as placeholders for the Outlook data. If you include all the boilerplate text in the template itself, the only code you need to write is that to place the data into the content controls. As an added benefit, this approach makes it easy to divide up the work. For example, a user who is going to use the printouts could design the template, while you write the code.

You probably will want to perform the same kind of data conversion for Outlook date/time and yes/no properties that we did earlier for Excel. The YesNoToString() function in Listing 24.4 would work just as well in

**Listing 24.11**    *Convert date values to a string*

```
Function DateToString(propVal)   ' As String
    Dim dteDate      ' As Date
    If IsDate(propVal) Then
        dteDate = CDate(propVal)
        If dteDate = #1/1/4501# Then
            DateToString = "None"
        Else
            DateToString = _
                FormatDateTime(dteDate, vbLongDate)
        End If
    Else
        DateToString = CStr(propVal)
    End If
End Function
```

Word automation code as in Excel code. Listing 24.11 is a `DateTo-String()` function to convert Outlook dates to strings. For dates that Outlook shows as "None" and stores as `#1/1/4501#`, it returns the string `"None"`.

So that the `DateToString()` function can be used in VBScript, it uses `FormatDateTime()` instead of `Format()` to format the returned date string. Also, it returns just the date. If you want time values as well as date values, you might want to build a similar function of your own to return a date string with both date and time values. Other useful functions for formatting that work in both VBScript and VBA are `FormatCurrency()` and `FormatNumber()`. You'll see both of those in the sample project in the next section.

## 24.5   Using Word to build an invoice report

To complete your Outlook report skills, you need to be able to put data from a single Outlook item into a Word document and also generate a report on multiple items. This final example combines those two operations by reporting on an Outlook item—and on its related items contained in a different folder.

This application depends on the `Links` collection covered in Chapter 20 to build an invoice with a contact's details and a table listing the hours spent working for that contact, as recorded by the linked journal entries in the Journal folder. It introduces techniques for working with Word tables and with the new content controls in Word 2007. You'll see how to write data into content controls and then lock them, as well as how to insert data into cells and create new table rows.

**Figure 24.6**
*Use Word 2007's
new content
controls to design
reports on Outlook
data.*

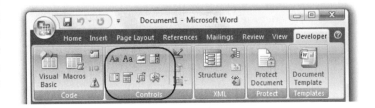

**Note:** To build this template, you'll need to display the Developer tab in the ribbon. If you haven't done that already for Outlook custom forms design, in Outlook, choose Tools | Options, switch to the Mail Format tab, click Editor Options, check the box for "Show Developer tab in the Ribbon," and then click OK.

*Content controls* are a new feature in Word 2007, providing an improved alternative to the form fields that you might have used in earlier Word versions. They provide a more modern look that gives better visual feedback to the user. In a document using content controls, you don't need to activate any kind of document protection. Only the controls are available for input. The user can press the Tab key to jump from one control to the next. Any control can be locked.

Look for the content controls in the left half of the Developer tab's Controls group, as shown in Figure 24.6. Besides a plain text input box and a combo box, there are content controls that support rich-text input, images, insertion of building blocks (another new Word 2007 feature), and a date picker. There is, however, no check box content control.

The invoice sample application consists of a Word template and Outlook code—in this case, VBA code to work with the currently selected contact. No custom form is involved, although it would certainly be possible to write the code that generates the invoice as VBScript code for a custom form, rather than as VBA. After presenting the complete example, we'll go over what would be necessary to convert it to VBScript.

## 24.5.1 Building the invoice template

The steps involved in designing the invoice template are as follows:

1. Lay out a table at the top of the document with a content control for each Outlook contact property the invoice should display and for the invoice details like the date, invoice number, and comments.

2.    Lay out the first two rows of a table at the bottom of the document with column headings for the data that will be pulled from the Journal folder. Leave the second row blank.

3.    In design mode, set the Tag and other properties for each content control.

4.    Add three rich-text content controls to encompass the contact information at the top of the form, the invoice detail in the table at the bottom, and the entire template content. These help lock the content.

5.    Save the template file in the default templates folder (%appdata%\Microsoft\Templates) or in any other folder.

To design the Word template, you can start from a blank Word document or from an existing document that already has a layout you want to use for your invoice. The area at the top of the template will hold the contact details. A table at the bottom will contain a list of the related journal entries. Let's walk through the five steps in detail.

**Step 1:** At the top of the page, type in and format the static text that you want to appear on every invoice. Add a company logo if you like. I recommend that you use a table to help align the different pieces of information you want to list. Figure 24.7 shows the invoice with a company logo, some static text, and a table with no borders that is ready to receive the first content controls. To turn off the table borders, we used the Borders command in the Table Styles group on the Design tab. To turn on the table gridlines to make it easier to adjust column widths, switch to the Layout tab, and click View Gridlines.

To insert content controls, display the Developer tab in the ribbon.

Where the contact name and address should appear—in the blank table cell to the right of the "Invoice submitted to:" text, click the Text button in the Controls group (second from left in top row) to add a text content control for each Outlook property. This invoice needs text controls for the user's name, street address, city, state, and postal code—five controls in all—with the usual punctuation for the address elements.

---

**Tip:** To move the insertion point to the right of a content control so that you can type text on the same line, press End after you insert the control.

---

For the date, insert a date picker content control (second from left in bottom row).

**Figure 24.7** *Start a Word template with static text and perhaps a table to help create a tidy layout.*

Add a blank table row and then another table row in the top section so that you can insert static text and additional content controls for the invoice number and hourly rate. Adjust the table cell widths as needed.

To complete the top section, in the paragraph below the table, click Rich Text in the controls group to insert a control to hold the comments that the user will type in after your code generates the invoice. At this stage in the design process, with step 1 of 5 completed, the template should look similar to Figure 24.8.

**Step 2:** For the bottom section that will hold the invoice information, insert a second table with two rows and four columns. Type column headers (Date, Activity, Hours, Total) into the cells in the first row. Leave the second row empty. You may want to experiment with the different table styles found on the Design tab.

Make sure there is at least one paragraph below the second table.

**Step 3:** Once you're happy with the basic layout of the invoice, click the Design Mode button in the Controls group on the Developer tab so that you can modify the controls' properties. Click on each content control to

**Figure 24.8**    *Content controls act as placeholders for data to be entered either manually or through code.*

select it. Then, display its Properties dialog box (see Figure 24.9) by clicking the Properties button in the Controls group.

You must enter a value for the Tag property, which the code will use to identify each control. Use the values in Table 24.2, which also lists the `ContactItem` property that the code will use to fill in the content control, where applicable. Some controls may have more options in the Properties dialog than others. For example, as Figure 24.9 shows, you can choose a date format for the date picker.

**Tip:** The Title property for a content control is optional, but may be helpful if you want the user to see an identifying name above the control when it has the focus.

After you have entered a value for the Tag property for each control, the template should look like Figure 24.10. See how the Tag values from Table 24.2 bracket each control. The Comments control has a Title as well as a Tag.

**Figure 24.9**
*Set a value for the
Tag property of
each content
control you use in
an Outlook report
template.*

**Table 24.2** *Tag Values for Invoice Content Controls*

| Control Description | Tag | Will Hold Outlook Property |
|---|---|---|
| Customer name | Name | `FullName` |
| Company name | Company | `CompanyName` |
| Street address | Address | `BusinessAddressStreet` |
| City | City | `BusinessAddressCity` |
| State | State | `BusinessAddressState` |
| Postal code | Postal Code | `BusinessAddressPostalCode` |
| Invoice number | Invoice Number | n/a—generated by code |
| Invoice date | Invoice Date | n/a—generated by code |
| Comments | Comments | n/a—user types in |
| Hourly rate | Hourly Rate | `BillingInformation` |
| Top portion of template, including upper table | Contact Info | n/a—container for other controls |
| Bottom portion of template, including lower table | Invoice Info | n/a—container for other controls |
| Entire document | Invoice | n/a—container for other controls |

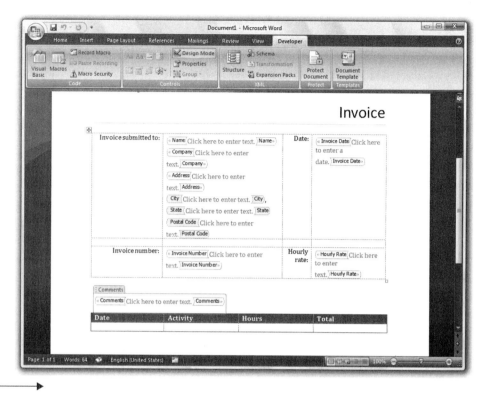

**Figure 24.10**   *Tags on content controls provide the information that code needs to access them programmatically.*

**Step 4:** Select the document content from the top of the page down through the table in the first section, leaving out the Comments control. Click the Rich Text button (top, left of the Controls group) to put the entire selection inside a new control. Select this control, click Properties, and give this new control a Tag named "Contact Info."

Select the document content from the bottom of the page, up through the second table, again leaving out the Comments control. Click Rich Text to create a new control containing the table, select the new control, click Properties, and give this control a Tag named "Invoice Info."

Now press Ctrl+A to select the entire document, and click Rich Text again to insert another rich-text control around all the template content. Set the Tag property to "Invoice" and check the boxes for "Content control cannot be deleted" and "Contents cannot be edited." By grouping the content controls, you can give the template behavior like that in a protected form. The outermost (or parent) control can be locked to prevent the user from changing the text, allowing input only in the content controls. A "container control" can also be used to identify a range in a similar manner as a bookmark, but can be protected against deletion. The code will use both the locking and identification features of these controls.

---

**Caution:** Make sure that the rich-text controls that enclose the tables at the top and the bottom of the document, plus the third control that encloses all the content, have their anchors completely outside the tables. If an anchor is in a table cell, the code will not be able to put a value into that cell.

---

**Step 5:** You've completed the template design and can now save and close the template. Click the Office button, click the arrow next to Save As, and then choose Word Template. To store it in your default templates folder, give the file the path and name %appdata%\Microsoft\Templates\ Invoice.dotx. If you use a different path or file name, make a note of it, as you'll need it in the code.

## 24.5.2  Coding the invoice report

Now that you have prepared the template, it's time to start looking at the code to enter data into the content controls and fill in the invoice details table. Listing 24.12 at the end of this section contains the entire code for the invoice application. You may want to put all the code in a separate Outlook VBA module to make it easier to manage. Don't forget to add references to the Microsoft Word 12.0 Library and Microsoft Scripting Runtime libraries, if you have not done so already.

The invoice report code makes several assumptions:

- The hourly billing rate for the contact item is stored in the `Billing-Information` property. You can use the All Fields page of the contact to enter this rate.

- The Journal folder contains only items that have not yet been invoiced.

- Several procedures are available either as private procedures in the same module or as public procedures in other Outlook VBA modules: `GetCurrentItem()` from Listing 15.5, and `DateID()` and `AddLeadingZeroUnderTen()` from Listing 20.6. These are not repeated in Listing 24.12, but the code will fail if they are not available in your VBA project.

Which procedure actually runs the invoice application? It's the `GenerateWordInvoice` routine, the only procedure not declared `Private`. The `GenerateWordInvoice` routine calls four other routines in turn:

1. `GetCurrentItem()` from Listing 15.5 to get the currently selected or open contact and assign it to the `objItem` variable.

2.    `GetNewDocument()` to create a new document from the Invoice.dotx template and assign it to the `objDocument` variable. Note that this procedure will only be called if `GetCurrent-Item()` returns a contact item type.

3.    `FillContactInfo()` to fill the Word content controls in the new document with corresponding data from the selected contact.

4.    `FillInvoiceInfo()` to filter the Journal folder for entries matching the contact, post entries linked to the contact to the Word table, calculate the charge for each entry, and keep a running total of the charges to post in the last row of the table.

If you store the invoice template using a file name other than Invoice.dotx or in a location other than the user's default Templates folder, change the `GetNewDocument` statement in the `GenerateWordInvoice` procedure to match your file name and path. For example, if you store the template as MyInvoice.dotx in a folder named C:\Samples, use this statement:

```
Set objDoc = GetNewDocument("C:\Samples\MyInvoice.dotx")
```

Figure 24.11 shows the finished product: an invoice produced entirely from Outlook items, but laid out with a Word template. The Comments content control is the only one where the user can type any text. The rest of the document's content is locked.

Let's review the Word techniques involved and then examine the Outlook techniques.

The challenge of writing code for Word content controls is that they can't be addressed by name like many other objects in Outlook and Word collections can. For example, even though the template should have a control whose `Tag` property has the string value `"Company"`, you can't return that control with an expression like this:

```
objDoc.ContentControls("Company")
```

Instead, to return a specific control, you need to know either a control's position in the document or the value of its `ID` property. Word assigns the `ID` property value when the control is generated; a typical value is 72569880. Since obtaining and noting `ID` values then using them in your code would involve a lot of work and is not intuitive, we'll use a helper procedure named `GetContentControls()` to create our own index of the controls, using the `Tag` property value for each one. This procedure loops through the entire document and adds each content control to a global `Scripting.Dictionary` variable (`m_ContentControls`) with the `Tag` property value as the key (index) value. (Go back to Chapter 8 if you don't recall how the `Dictionary` object works.) Subsequent procedures use this

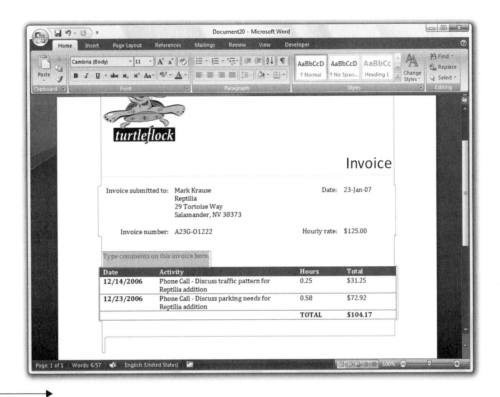

**Figure 24.11** *This invoice demonstrates how well Word works as a reporting tool that can combine data from items in different Outlook folders.*

collection to access the content controls, looking up each with the value assigned to the Tag property. The following code snippet, for example, returns the content control that has a Tag property with the value "Invoice Info", in other words, the control containing the table that will hold the Journal folder information:

```
Set objInvoiceControl = objDoc.ContentControls( _
  m_ContentControls("Invoice Info"))
```

To add text to a plain text content control, which is the type this report uses most, assign a string value to its Range.Text property, as in this example from the FillContentControl procedure:

```
objContentControl.Range.Text = strContent
```

That technique works for the date picker content control as well, assuming that strContent is a string representing a date.

Content controls can be locked so that the user cannot edit the content. A locked control also blocks programmatic data entry. So that the code can enter data programmatically, each content control is locked not at design time, but at run time, only after its value has been filled in. To lock a content control, set its `LockContents` property to `True`:

```
objContentControl.LockContents = True
```

The steps of obtaining a content control object from the `m_Content-Controls` collection, assigning the contact information to each control, then locking the content control, are consolidated in the procedure `Fill-ContentControl`. This procedure is used by the `FillContactInfo` procedure, which fills in all the content in the top half of the report, calling `FillContentControl` once for each control that needs to be filled.

Word tables do not support any property that allows them to be assigned a name with which to easily identify them. The only way to pick up a Word table is by its index number within a specified range of text. The range can be the entire document, or you can narrow it down by various means, such as assigning a bookmark to the table. Since content controls can be nested, and a content control has a `Range` property, we used a content control ("Invoice Info") to act as a container for the table that will hold the journal entry data. Since it is the only table inside that control, we can access it like this:

```
Set objInvoiceControl = objDoc.ContentControls( _
  m_ContentControls("Invoice Info"))
Set objTable = objInvoiceControl.Range.Tables(1)
```

The cells in a Word table can be addressed in a similar manner as cells in Excel by their row and column positions using the syntax `objTable.Cell(row, col)`, or by using `objRow.Cells(index)` within a specified range. Since the data for the invoice is filled row by row, this sample code works through each row's cells in turn, inserting the text at the end of the cell's current content. For example, to insert the Activity information for the second column of the first data row, the row you left blank at design time:

```
Set objRow = objTable.Rows.Last
objRow.Cells(2).Range.InsertAfter expr
```

where *expr* is an expression returning the text to insert. As you'll see below, the code generates that expression from an Outlook `Table` object.

Appending a new row to an existing Word table is quite straightforward:

```
Set objRow = objTable.Rows.Add
```

To apply formatting to text in a Word document, first identify the range, and then specify the format. In this sample, the current table row is formatted as bold:

```
objRow.Range.Font.Bold = True
```

The most interesting Outlook technique used in the invoice report is a filtered `Table` object. The filter matches the `FullName` of the contact that we're invoicing against the names in the Contacts box on the journal entry form (which, as you should recall from Chapter 20, exposes the contents of the `Links` collection).

**Note:** In taking this approach—searching for a name rather than confirming a `Link`—we're making a significant assumption: that the name of the contact has not changed since the journal entries were created. If the contact name has changed, then the search won't return all the linked items, because the field we're searching will still have the old names. The performance tradeoff, though, is considerable. By searching just on the name, we can get back a filtered, read-only `Table` very quickly. If the code had to depend on confirming an actual `Link` in the `Links` collection, it would be necessary to examine the `Links` collection of each item in the Journal folder.

These code statements in the `FillInvoiceInfo` procedure filter the Journal folder to return a `Table` with journal entries related to the contact being invoiced:

```
SEARCH_LINKS = "http://schemas.microsoft.com/" & _
    "mapi/id/{00062008-0000-0000-C000-000000000046}/" & _
    "853A101E"
Set objOL = objContact.Application
Set objNS = objOL.Session
Set objJournal = objNS.GetDefaultFolder(olFolderJournal)
strFind = Quote(SEARCH_LINKS) & " = '" & _
        objContact.FullName & "'"
Set objOLTable = objJournal.GetTable("@SQL=" & strFind)
```

Since the default `Columns` collection for a journal folder does not contain all the properties that the invoice needs, the code adds a few properties and sorts the `Table`:

```
With objOLTable
    intItemsCount = objOLTable.GetRowCount
    .Columns.Add "Start"
    .Columns.Add "Duration"
    .Columns.Add "Type"
    .Sort "Start"
```

To complete the `With objOLTable` section, a `Do` loop processes each row in the `Outlook.Table` object, adding a new `Word.Table` row on each pass:

```
        Do Until .EndOfTable
            Set objOLRow = .GetNextRow
            ' code to fill in the Word table
            If objRow.Index <= intItemsCount Then
                Set objRow = objTable.Rows.Add
            End If
        Loop
End With
```

Inside the `Do` loop, the code to fill in the Word table combines the `Cells(index).Range.InsertAfter` method discussed above with the very simple `objOLRow("property")` syntax to return a property value from an Outlook table `Row` object. For example, this statement combines the `Type` and `Subject` property values from the journal entry and inserts them into the second column of the current row in the Word table:

```
objRow.Cells(2).Range.InsertAfter _
    objOLRow("Type") & " - " & objOLRow("Subject")
```

### 24.5.3   Possible enhancements for the invoice report

Even though Listing 24.12 contains a lot of code, converting it to VBScript so that it could be incorporated into an Outlook custom form is not as hard as it looks. You'd need to make these five changes:

- Remove or comment all `As` clauses from `Dim` statements and procedure declarations.

- Remove the `GetCurrentItem()` function.

- Replace this statement in the `GenerateWordInvoice` procedure

  ```
  Set objItem = GetCurrentItem()
  ```

  with this statement:

  ```
  Set objItem = Item
  ```

- In the declarations section, after the `Option Explicit` statement, add this Outlook constant declaration:

  ```
  Const olFolderJournal = 11
  ```

- Add a command button to the contact form and a `Click` event handler to run the `GenerateWordInvoice` procedure when the user clicks the button:

  ```
  Sub CommandButton1_Click()
      Call GenerateWordInvoice
  End Sub
  ```

Porting the invoice report code to VBScript behind an Outlook form is certainly one way to extend its usefulness. What other ways to enhance the report can you think of? Here are a couple of ideas:

The filter in the `FillInvoiceInfo` procedure assumes that the Journal folder contains only uninvoiced entries. If you want to keep all entries, even after they're invoiced, you'll need some way to tell them apart. The `Billing-Information` property is a good candidate to hold this information. You could update each journal entry with the date of the invoice or the invoice number and save it. You'd also need to modify the filter string so that it looks for items with an empty or null `BillingInformation` property.

Another possible enhancement would be to save the invoice and create a new link to it in the journal folder. Surely you can think of other ways

---------------------▶

**Listing 24.12**  *Collate data from two folders into one Word document*

```
Option Explicit

' requires reference to Microsoft Scripting Runtime
Private m_objContentControls As Scripting.Dictionary

Sub GenerateWordInvoice()
    ' requires reference to Microsoft Word 12.0 library
    Dim objDoc As Word.Document
    Dim objContentControl As Word.ContentControl
    Dim objItem As Object
    On Error Resume Next
    ' GetCurrentItem() from Listing 15.5
    Set objItem = GetCurrentItem()
    If objItem.Class = olContact Then
        Set objDoc = GetNewDocument("Invoice.dotx")
        Call FillContactInfo(objDoc, objItem)
        Call FillInvoiceInfo(objDoc, objItem)
        objDoc.Application.Visible = True
        objDoc.Activate
        Set objContentControl = _
          objDoc.ContentControls( _
          m_objContentControls.Item("Comments"))
        objContentControl.SetPlaceholderText , , _
          "Type comments on this invoice here."
        objContentControl.Range.Select
        objDoc.ActiveWindow.View.TableGridlines = False
    End If
    Set objDoc = Nothing
    Set objContentControl = Nothing
    Set objItem = Nothing
    Set m_objContentControls = Nothing
End Sub

Private Function GetNewDocument(strTemplate As String) _
  As Word.Document
    ' requires reference to Microsoft Word 12.0 library
    Dim objWord As Word.Application
    Dim objDoc As Word.Document
    On Error Resume Next
    Set objWord = GetObject(, "Word.Application")
    If objWord Is Nothing Then
        Set objWord = CreateObject("Word.Application")
    End If
    Set objDoc = objWord.Documents.Add(strTemplate)
    Call GetContentControls(objDoc)
    Set GetNewDocument = objDoc
    Set objWord = Nothing
    Set objDoc = Nothing
End Function

Private Sub GetContentControls(objDoc As Word.Document)
    Dim objContentControl As Word.ContentControl
```

**Listing 24.12**        *Collate data from two folders into one Word document (continued)*

```
      ' requires reference to Microsoft Scripting Runtime
      Set m_objContentControls = _
        CreateObject("Scripting.Dictionary")
      For Each objContentControl In objDoc.ContentControls
          m_objContentControls.Add objContentControl.Tag, _
                                   objContentControl.ID
      Next
      Set objContentControl = Nothing
End Sub

Private Sub FillContactInfo(objDoc As Word.Document, _
                            objItem As Object)
      Dim objContentControl As Word.ContentControl
      Call FillContentControl("Name", objItem.FullName, objDoc)
      Call FillContentControl( _
        "Company", objItem.CompanyName, objDoc)
      Call FillContentControl( _
        "Address", objItem.BusinessAddressStreet, objDoc)
      Call FillContentControl( _
        "City", objItem.BusinessAddressCity, objDoc)
      Call FillContentControl( _
        "State", objItem.BusinessAddressState, objDoc)
      Call FillContentControl("Postal Code", _
        objItem.BusinessAddressPostalCode, objDoc)
      ' DateID() from Listing 20.6
      Call FillContentControl( _
        "Invoice Number", DateID(), objDoc)
      Call FillContentControl("Hourly Rate", _
        FormatCurrency(objItem.BillingInformation), objDoc)
      Call FillContentControl("Invoice Date", _
        FormatDateTime(Date, vbLongDate), objDoc)
      Set objContentControl = _
         objDoc.ContentControls( _
         m_objContentControls.Item("Contact Info"))
      objContentControl.LockContents = True
      Set objContentControl = Nothing
End Sub

Private Sub FillContentControl(strControl As String, _
      strContent As String, objDoc As Word.Document)
      Dim objContentControl As Word.ContentControl
      Dim strControlID As String
      strControlID = m_objContentControls.Item(strControl)
      Set objContentControl = _
         objDoc.ContentControls(strControlID)
      If Len(strContent) > 0 Then
         objContentControl.Range.Text = strContent
         objContentControl.LockContents = True
      Else
         objContentControl.Delete
      End If
      Set objContentControl = Nothing
End Sub
```

**Listing 24.12**     *Collate data from two folders into one Word document (continued)*

```
Private Sub FillInvoiceInfo(objDoc As Word.Document, _
    objContact As Object)
    Dim objOL As Outlook.Application
    Dim objNS As Outlook.NameSpace
    Dim objJournal As Outlook.Folder
    Dim objOLTable As Outlook.Table
    Dim objOLRow As Outlook.Row
    Dim objTable As Word.Table
    Dim objRow As Word.Row
    Dim objInvoiceControl As Word.ContentControl
    Dim curHourly As Currency
    Dim curItem As Currency
    Dim curTotal As Currency
    Dim intItemsCount As Integer
    Dim strFind As String
    Dim SEARCH_LINKS As String
    On Error Resume Next
    Set objInvoiceControl = objDoc.ContentControls( _
    m_objContentControls("Invoice Info"))
    Set objTable = objInvoiceControl.Range.Tables(1)
    Set objRow = objTable.Rows.Last
    curHourly = CCur(objContact.BillingInformation)
    Set objOL = objContact.Application
    Set objNS = objOL.Session
    Set objJournal = objNS.GetDefaultFolder(olFolderJournal)
    SEARCH_LINKS = "http://schemas.microsoft.com/" & _
      "mapi/id/{00062008-0000-0000-C000-000000000046}/" & _
      "853A101E"
    strFind = Quote(SEARCH_LINKS) & _
              " = '" & objContact.FullName & "'"
    Set objOLTable = objJournal.GetTable("@SQL=" & strFind)
    With objOLTable
        intItemsCount = objOLTable.GetRowCount
        .Columns.Add "Start"
        .Columns.Add "Duration"
        .Columns.Add "Type"
        .Sort "Start"
        Do Until .EndOfTable
            Set objOLRow = .GetNextRow
            objRow.Cells(1).Range.InsertAfter _
              FormatDateTime(objOLRow("Start"), vbShortDate)
            objRow.Cells(2).Range.InsertAfter _
              objOLRow("Type") & " - " & objOLRow("Subject")
            objRow.Cells(3).Range.InsertAfter _
              FormatNumber(objOLRow("Duration") / 60, 2)
            curItem = objOLRow("Duration") / 60 * curHourly
            objRow.Cells(4).Range.InsertAfter _
              FormatCurrency(curItem)
            curTotal = curTotal + curItem
            If objRow.Index <= intItemsCount Then
                Set objRow = objTable.Rows.Add
            End If
```

**Listing 24.12**    *Collate data from two folders into one Word document (continued)*

```
      Loop
   End With
   Set objRow = objTable.Rows.Add
   objRow.Range.Font.Bold = True
   objRow.Cells(3).Range.InsertAfter "TOTAL"
   objRow.Cells(4).Range.InsertAfter _
      FormatCurrency(curTotal)
   objInvoiceControl.LockContents = True
   Set objInvoiceControl = Nothing
   Set objTable = Nothing
   Set objRow = Nothing
   Set objOL = Nothing
   Set objNS = Nothing
   Set objJournal = Nothing
   Set objOLTable = Nothing
   Set objOLRow = Nothing
End Sub

Private Function Quote(val)
   Quote = Chr(34) & CStr(val) & Chr(34)
End Function
```

to apply the Word and Outlook techniques in this chapter, which comprise a fitting end to your initial excursion into the world of Outlook 2007 programming.

## 24.6  Summary

Making Outlook data available through reports is an important programming technique, because not everyone who needs to see your data will have Outlook. Outlook supports several techniques for generating reports—printing from customized folder views, mail merge to Word, even copy and paste to Excel. However, no single built-in technique has the flexibility to handle all Outlook data, including custom fields and "large" properties like item bodies.

By writing code to automate Outlook, Excel, and Word, developers can produce custom reports with every imaginable feature. Reports can be generated as email messages, printed output, or files where the user can fill in additional information, such as comments on an invoice. Word is a particularly fine reporting tool, especially if you need to print from a custom form or combine information from two types of folders. The search techniques covered in Chapter 16 can help you speed up report generation, particularly if you use the read-only `Table` object that is new to Outlook 2007.

# *Index*